# Renaissance

*of*

# American Coinage
# 1905 – 1908

Roger W. Burdette

ISBN: 0-9768986-1-6

Seneca Mill Press LLC

**P. O. Box 1423**
**Great Falls, Virginia 22066-1423**

Printed by Signature Book Printing, Inc.
www.sbpbooks.com

No warranty or representation of any kind is made concerning the accuracy or completeness of the information presented herein, or its usefulness in numismatic sales or purchases, or its suitability for any purpose. The opinions of others may differ from those of the author and/or publisher.

# Renaissance of American Coinage
# 1905 – 1908

# CONTENTS

# Author's Preface

The reader may wonder why anyone would attempt to "rewrite" numismatic history. After all, the broad outline of early twentieth century coinage redesign has been known for decades, or at least was thought to be known. Since beginning the renaissance of American coinage design over one hundred years ago, people and events of the era seem to have been pressed into narrowly defined pigeonholes whose information was brought forth in undeviating conformity. The thought that reporting of tradition-bound events might be incorrect, or incomplete, has been almost heretical to catalogers, researchers and authors. Yet, investigation shows that what was once thought of as "known," is often as much speculation as reality. Numismatists of long standing will find much herein that is new, unexpected or contrary to conventional accounts of the Saint-Gaudens and Pratt gold coins. The numismatic events described herein are, as best the author can make them, accurate and faithful to events a century ago.

The idea for this book and its companions goes back to the author's neophyte collector days when coin collecting involved blue cardstock folders and rolls of "pennies" and nickels bought from the local bank with proceeds from mowing the neighbor's lawn. The occasional Indian head nickel, "V" nickel or Indian penny brought quick reference to a spine-broken Red Book® to see if it was a keeper. For a beginner, all knowledge was between those red covers, and if the Red Book® said a nickel was worth eight cents, the coin went into a folder, or a cigar box of duplicates – even if the preferred use was to buy an ice cream cone! By the time the author saw his first gold coin – an Indian head quarter eagle owned by a cousin – there was a certain curiosity about who designed the coins and how the designs got there. Over the years books were purchased and auction catalogs read and reread. Most of these catalogs were filled with coins far beyond the author's means, and with information that further piqued his curiosity.

Several years ago, the author pulled out some of the old books on coins and read them in the context of greater experience. After purchasing more up-to-date versions and some new titles, a pervasive similarity began to infuse the information. There was an emphasis on collecting dates, mintmarks, rarity, cost and deep analysis of luster and strike for each year's issues. Scant attention was paid to the artistry exhibited on these little lumps of stamped metal, how they originated, or if traditional assumptions about their creation were true. In trying to understand who created the designs on our historical coinage, and how it was done, the writer kept being pulled into the same circle bounded by Taxay, Breen and a handful of others. Much of their research was a half century old, and examination of additional works led to increasingly conflicting assertions. Claims and counterclaims were made with little factual support, and articles in popular hobby magazines only made the situation more confusing.

From this thicket, the only way out seemed to be a journey back in time: to the people, places and events that shaped contemporary views a hundred years ago. This book and its companion volumes are the result of that long, enjoyable journey. It is hoped the reader will find the results both informative and provocative, and that the next generation of researchers will expand this research and correct the inevitable errors.

## Research Approach

Research for this book and its siblings represents many thousands of hours of work in government, institutional, art, trade association and private archives. This has been performed by the writer, and by numerous associates, archivists, curators and academic specialists who generously provided assistance in locating the often-obscure materials on which this work is based. Locating useful material for this type of research is often frustrating. Old publications may say nothing about the location of documents, or may simply state "National Archives" with no indication of where a relevant letter might be filed. In many instances, archives thought to be rich in pertinent documents produced little or nothing of relevance. Other, seldom-used archives produced letters which completely revised our understanding of events. Although considerable information is available on Augustus Saint-Gaudens and much has been written about his coin designs, most modern numismatic writers have been content to rewrite material from previous authors. This recycling combined with frequent embellishment of material has occasionally obscured the full meaning of original texts. Further, most early numismatic authors either reproduced only selected portions of correspondence or, having only an edited, printed extract, assumed this small portion was the only relevant part of a document. The present writer has chosen the opposite approach: most original documents are reproduced in their entirety thereby better establishing the document writer's intent than when relying on extracts. In addition, no modern account has been accepted unless it is fully referenced to original documents or events. In a few instances much-used quotes, such as those attributed to President Roosevelt about producing high relief double eagles if it took all day to strike one coin, are omitted from this book. This is because the original document cannot be located (or perhaps never existed) or the earliest known reference is unattributed.

The quality of available information has a critical impact on potential accuracy of the finished product. The most reliable data come from ordinary, day-to-day reports and correspondence between various parts of governmental bureaucracy. These contemporary operational documents chronicle the results of mint activities, sometimes including problems encountered and how they were resolved. Daily reports of coins struck or dies made, shipping receipts and bills of lading, production account books, transfer warrants and similar materials fall into this category. Nearly equal to these in research value are letters and memoranda between the mint director's office in Washington, DC and officials at the Philadelphia Mint. These consist of orders and instructions for actions to be taken, or an exchange of information between the director, superintendent, engraver and others. For the Saint-Gaudens designs there are also many letters between the President and the sculptor. These often indicate opinions and instructions from the President, or comment on the progress of work and issues not directly part of official correspondence. Significant, previously untapped sources of information are the correspondence of director Leach and Charles Brewster, Augusta Saint-Gaudens' attorney. These letters resolve many points of confusion in the months following the artist's death, particularly matters involving the low relief double eagles, payment to the widow and her acquisition of an extremely high relief (EHR) double eagle. Well-documented secondary sources, such as those on mint procedures or previous attempts to alter designs are also valuable. It is the combination of these sources, which forms the flesh and bone of the present volume.

To this must be added reports and commentary in numismatic publications of the time, and contemporary letters by coin collectors. The factual value of these sources is substantially lower than bureaucratic documents because the writers were not participants in events under discussion. Coin dealers and collectors were also predisposed to opinion since this best suited and supported their hobby or business interests. This does not diminish the deep interest in numismatics held by these writers, only that what many writers of the time claim to be facts are not well supported by more reliable sources.

Last, and very much at the bottom of any quality scale, are articles and editorial comments in contemporary newspapers. Reporters whose job was to fill space with stories designed to sell newspapers usually wrote these articles. Most had no understanding of numismatics or art, and could be relied upon to confuse as much as inform their readers. The daily papers were prohibited by law from printing photos of new coin designs, and had to resort to contorted, occasionally colorful, and consistently incorrect descriptions of new coins. Newspapers were responsible for distortions, wild speculations and factual errors that brought considerable inconvenience to artists such as Bela Pratt, Victor Brenner, Adolph Weinman and Anthony de Francisci.[1]

Into this mix a word must be added about changes in technology. Before the widespread use of long distance telephone, all communication between government offices in distant cities was either written or verbal during face-to-face consultations (at which written minutes were usually taken). As mint officials explained their work to one another, their internal memoranda and letters often included detailed explanations of designs or mint processes. With increasing use of the telephone, particularly after about 1905, the quantity of significant detail in written documents decreases. Gradually, officials abbreviated explanations of events and presented only the results of their actions. By 1916 it is common to find U. S. Mint documents which are nothing more than instructions confirming a much longer and more detailed telephone conversation. After 1925, most detail has been lost. All that remains are the bureaucratic justifications for decisions; the real reasons for certain decisions remain forever obscured.

Thus, the present work is based on official reports and documents, letters to and from the artists and other participants, and a very few secondary sources that contain cop-

---

[1] Pratt seldom received full credit for his Indian design for the half and quarter eagles during his lifetime; Brenner's initials were removed from the cent. Weinman came close to having his initials removed from the dime, and de Francisci had to alter the original reverse design of the Peace dollar – all due largely to newspaper reporting.

ies of evidently genuine documents that no longer appear to exist. To this is added a certain measure of reasonable assumption, sufficient to plausibly connect events without contradicting the original sources. Articles by contemporary numismatic writers and popular newspapers are used to supplement and expand on the original sources, but have been given little emphasis in developing conclusions. The writer admits to climbing onto a speculative limb occasionally, and has made every attempt to state this in the text and footnotes.

References to experimental, pattern and trial pieces are from Andrew Pollock's book *United States Pattern and Related Issues*, and *United States Pattern Coins, Experimental and Trial Pieces*, 8th Edition by J. Hewitt Judd, MD, edited by Q. David Bowers.

Illustrations of coins are enlarged to better present detail of the designs; coin models and drawings are illustrated at reduced size.

## About the Series

There are three books in the *Renaissance of American Coinage* series: the present volume covering gold coins from 1905 to 1908, a second volume covering from 1909 to 1915 including minor coins and Panama-Pacific Exposition commemoratives, and the final issue investigating subsidiary silver coins and the Peace dollar from 1916 to 1921. The date range for each book is somewhat fluid: text reaches backward and forward in time to help place events within their historical context, and to improve continuity between the books. The first and last books of the series stick closely to explanations of how relevant coin designs originated. The middle volume, covering 1909–1915, goes well beyond the Lincoln cent and Buffalo nickel and explores previously unknown events at the Mint Bureau, including the destruction of hundreds of pattern coin master dies and hubs.

The principal characters in this and the other volumes change with time; however, certain individuals have prominent roles in more than one book. Notable among these are mint directors George Roberts and Frank Leach, sculptors Adolph Weinman and James Fraser, businessman Clarence W. Hobbs, Sr., and Charles Moore chairman of the Commission of Fine Arts. Four other men play important roles in defining the overall concepts for the 1905–1921 period. Augustus Saint-Gaudens and Charles Barber, whose artistic animosity blossomed as early as 1891, and which continued to some extent beyond Saint-Gaudens' death to his former assistants who later designed coins. These men established the creative battleground for all of the new coin designs. President Theodore Roosevelt provided political momentum that outlived both him and his direct artistic collaborator. Last, the little-recognized mineralogist/numismatist George F. Kunz, Ph.D., who seemed to know all that occurred in and around the mint and who used his connections to enhance the American Numismatic Society's collections. It was Kunz who publicized, promoted, advised and may have occasionally "brokered" coinage designs from 1906 to 1917.

## Acknowledgements

No research of this nature can be performed without the selfless assistance of archivists, research associates, curators, collection managers and the many others who are guardians of our history. Without their dedication, patience and understanding of the collections entrusted to their care, meaningful research would be impossible. To these the author extends a sincere "Thank you!"

Special appreciation is extended to the following individuals and organizations who have aided this project: David Akers, David Alexander, Harry W. Bass, Jr., Q. David Bowers, Ken Bressett, David J. Camire, Mark Coen, Jane Colvard, David J. Corrigan, Richard Doty, PhD, Henry Duffy, PhD, Bill Fivaz, Kay Freeman, Ann Benson Green, Jim Halpern, Eleanor Harvey, PhD, Petra Hays, Robert W. Julian, David Lange, Julian Leidman, Joseph Levine, Douglas Mudd, Dean E. Nelson, Eric P. Newman, James R. Reckner, PhD, Russ Rowlett, PhD, Cynthia Kennedy Sam, William B. Smith, Joan Stahl, Saul Teichman, Thayer Tolles, Judith Trom, Heidi Wastweet, Fred Weinberg, Vicken Yegparian, Albany University – Thomas E. Dewey Graduate Library, American Numismatic Association, American Numismatic Rarities, American Numismatic Society, Museum of Fine Arts – Boston, Bowers & Merena Galleries, Cairo Museum, California Historical Society, Commission of Fine Arts, Connecticut State Library, Cornell University, Court Street Baptist Church, Dartmouth College, Delaware County Historical Society, George Washington University, Georgetown University, Goldberg Coins and Collectibles, Harry W. Bass, Jr. Research Foundation, Harvard University, Harry W. Bass, Jr. Research Foundation, Heritage Coin, Johns Hopkins University, Library of Congress, Page Belting Company, Presidential Coin & Antique Co., Monnaie de Paris, Museum of American History (NYC), National Archives and Records Administration, New Hampshire Historical Society, Numismatic Conservation Service LLC, Oklahoma State Historical Society, Saint-Gaudens National Historic Site – National Park Service, Smithsonian Institution, Stack's Rare Coins, Inc., U. S. Naval Historical Center, United States Mint, University of Chicago, University of North Carolina, University of Richmond, University of Virginia.

Numismatist David Tripp provided important insights into the extremely high relief double eagles, in addition to pointing out errors and omissions in the text. This volume is much the better for his thoughtful suggestions.

The author is also indebted to numismatic writers and researchers of the past. They have created a foundation of knowledge upon which the present work is built, and upon which future researchers will continue to expand our understanding of America's numismatic heritage.

Arlene Prunkl of Vancouver, BC, Canada was particularly diligent in copy editing the manuscript, offering productive suggestions in a careful and thoroughly professional manner.

Artist Jane Berte Waldron used items relevant to the book's time period to produce an excellent cover illustration featuring President Theodore Roosevelt calmly steering the Ship of State. Udo Keppler (aka Joseph Keppler, Jr.) drew the central figure of Roosevelt for the January 1, 1902 issue of the humor magazine "Puck." The Smithsonian National Numismatic Collection, David J. Camire and NGC, Saint-Gaudens National Historic Site and the author provided coin images.

# Foreword

by David Enders Tripp
Author of *Illegal Tender: Gold, Greed, and the Mystery of the 1933 Double Eagle.*

Giorgio Vasari's *Italian Renaissance* lasted some two hundred and fifty years. Roger W. Burdette's *Renaissance of American Coinage*, sadly, lasted less than a score of years (with a decade more of minor ripples). But what an extraordinary nexus of political will and artistic incandescence it was.

This volume of Burdette's trilogy addresses the birth of the renaissance from 1905 through 1908 and encompasses three important chapters of the period's evolution.

The first, the heroic story of Augustus Saint-Gaudens and his "partner in crime" Theodore Roosevelt to create a new direction in modern coinage, has been told before and, rightly, it will be told again and again, for it is a wonderful saga of inspiration, imagination, tragedy and tenacity. Its outcome was an iconic imagery, and proof of just what brilliance our nation's mint was capable if pushed to the limit.

The second, Roosevelt's lonely battle with Congress to keep the motto IN GOD WE TRUST off his newly designed coins, and his rationale, strikes a fascinating and most contemporary chord.

Finally, and undoubtedly the least told episode, is that of William Sturgis Bigelow, Bela Lyon Pratt and Theodore Roosevelt. Boston Brahman Bigelow had an idea to utilize the ancient Egyptian sculptural technique of sunk relief. He privately commissioned the art work, and the result, the Indian head quarter and half eagles, were no less revolutionary in concept and technical bravura than Saint-Gaudens high relief issues nor were they any less controversial.

Future authors of articles and books concerning these episodes will owe an incalculable debt to Roger Burdette's book, for his work will become the handbook to which future researchers will look first before heading off on their own journeys of discovery.

For decades, the tale of Gus and Teddy has been told a hundred times in books, articles and auction catalogues but, with rare exceptions, these recitations have slavishly repeated previously published information and misinformation.

One of my favorite examples of the latter is the famous correspondence between the President and Saint-Gaudens when they share a private, if rueful, joke about mint engraver Charles Barber. In a letter to the artist on January 6, 1906 President Roosevelt commented that their efforts to create the new coinage may "increase the mortality of the employees of the Mint." Saint-Gaudens replied in the same humorous vein three days later by noting that "one gentleman [Barber]... may have nervous prostration...but killed no."

In his transcription of this amusing letter, Don Taxay in his *U.S. Mint and Coinage* misquoted a portion of the sentence, which became "nervous prostitution." (The original letter in the Library of Congress from Saint-Gaudens is typed, and so the artist's notoriously scratchy scrawl cannot be blamed). It is this mis-reading which has been repeated (perhaps because of its quasi-salacious tone) *ad nauseam* since Taxay's book appeared forty years ago, and is unfortunately indicative of a substantial sector of modern American numismatic research.

Roger Burdette has not only relied on primary source material first and foremost (he has, naturally, also backstopped gaps in the record with less direct sources), but has generously provided the next researcher with the benefit of his substantial labors by citing the precise source. In this Mr. Burdette has done us all an enormous favor. While other numismatic researchers have indeed utilized the wonderful resources of the National Archives and Library of Congress which are open to us all, regrettably most have not referenced their find spots.

The lack of documentary evidence relating to the development of our nation's coinage has, for years, been bemoaned by American numismatic researchers. And while, yes, there was some frightfully distressing destruction of United States Mint Records in the 1970s, there is still a treasure trove of vital, essential material that is readily available, and there is more yet to be discovered. It is not held only in governmental repositories. The story of America's numismatic metamorphosis, most particularly at this period, was also a personal and private undertaking, and much exists in diaries, personal correspondence and private institutional archives. Burdette has utilized these invaluable resources as well.

But *Renaissance of American Coinage 1905-1908* is not merely a bibliographical source book. Burdette has also endeavored to examine the physical evidence the coins themselves provide, and link it to the archival road map. Sometimes it has led to discovery (Burdette's recent identification of two pattern 1907 eagles in the National Numismatic Collection), sometimes it has helped to dispel certain claims (the so-called pattern 1907 plain edge high relief double eagle), and occasionally, and most tantalizingly, he has pointed the way for more discoveries to be made (the 1907 pattern very high relief double eagles and pattern 1908 quarter and half eagles for example).

I have never met Roger Burdette. Rather, I was electronically introduced to him by Dave Bowers via e-mail. Over the years I have been fortunate enough to have had the privilege of examining numerous examples of the output described in this volume, and the story of the president and the artist has always appealed to me enormously. I was at the time in the process of writing my own book, *Illegal Tender: Gold, Greed, and the Mystery of the 1933 Double Eagle,* and found that Roger and I had trod similar paths of research. His first inquiries to me were stimulating and made me not only double-check my own information but examine certain issues more critically, and I hope that my responses may have sent him off on new paths as well.

What Roger Burdette has provided us with is a much needed book on a pivotal chapter of American numismatic history. He has also provided us with a marvelous primer on how future American numismatic references may be approached. While there is still more archival information yet to be discovered, and future researchers may challenge some of his interpretations, Burdette has admirably thrown down the gauntlet, and he is to be congratulated.

David Enders Tripp
Stuyvesant, New York
February 20, 2006

*David Enders Tripp is a numismatic and fine art consultant and writer. He has degrees in classical archeology and was formerly the director of Sotheby's coin, tapestry and musical instruments departments. He discovered the Saint-Gaudens extremely high relief, sans serif edge double eagle, and was first to propose its connection to the 1906 double eagle pattern by Barber and Morgan. Mr. Tripp is a former member of the United States Citizens Coinage Advisory Committee; and is a Fellow of the American Numismatic Society, a Fellow of the Royal Numismatic Society, a member of the American Numismatic Association and the Swiss Numismatic Society; a life member of The Player's Club in New York, and a member of the National Cartoonist Society. His biography also appears in Who's Who in America.*

# A Golden Promise – The Renaissance Begins

# 1905 – 1908

# Cameos, Courage and Coins

Our *Renaissance of American Coinage* begins with the "gilded age"[2] of American art and with the personal courage of two men: one the son of a shoemaker and apprenticed as a cameo cutter, the other a weak, asthmatic boy expected to die from his respiratory illness. Each found his personal path to overcome hardships and eventually command a place at the center of world events: the artist, to declare American creative equality; the politician, to symbolize the nation's vigor, confidence and political maturity to its European cousins. Both men lived full, rewarding lives; both men died before they should have: Augustus Saint-Gaudens of cancer, Theodore Roosevelt of a coronary embolism. "The Saint" was 59; "Theodore Rex," 60; they were missed by a world that still valued ideals and heroes, yet seemed ever shorter of both.

Augustus, or "Gus," as his family called him, was born in Dublin, Ireland on March 1, 1848, the third child[3] of a French shoemaker, Bernard Saint-Gaudens, and his Irish wife, Mary McGuiness. The country was in the midst of widespread famine caused by failure of the potato crop, and Bernard's business had few customers. In August that year, the little family took ship for Boston, landing six weeks later. Bernard immediately decided business would be better in New York, and left his wife and son with friends in Boston while he set up shop offering "French Ladies' Boots and Shoes." The shoe business succeeded and little Gus was to call New York City his hometown.

New York was also home to one Theodore Roosevelt, born October 27, 1858. His family was from "old Knickerbocker" Dutch stock and its members were among the city's elite citizens. Father was Theodore Roosevelt, Sr., known by his nickname "Thee;" mother

---

[2] The phrase "The Gilded Age" comes from a novel of the same name published in 1873 by Charles Dudley Warner and Samuel Clemens (Mark Twain). It examines politics, corruption, and ostentatious display of wealth in the United States during the latter half of the nineteenth century. The term is often extended to cover the ornate neo-classic style of sculpture and decorative arts popular from the 1870s through about 1915.

[3] There were two previous children: George, who died at age six, and Louis, who died in infancy. Augustus' middle name was Louis. There was also a younger brother, also named Louis, who later worked in the sculptor's studio. Bernard was from the village of Saint-Gaudens in southern France and had emigrated to Ireland.

was Martha Bullock, "Mittie," daughter of a Georgian patrician family with ties to pre-Revolutionary America. In a family where everyone had a nickname little Theodore was called "Teedie." It was later that his first wife, Alice, changed the title to the more affectionate "Teddykins" or "Teddy."[4]

Events of the city were to influence both men as they grew to adulthood. Gus attended school and ran the rough streets of the Bowery with the other boys. At age thirteen he was apprenticed to a cameo cutter, and as a teenager watched the draft riots of July 1863 from his workbench at the front of the shop. Poor men, many of Irish stock, resented being drafted while wealthy men, such as Thee Roosevelt, could buy a draft exemption for $300. Augustus saw canon pulled into the street at 21st Street and Gramercy Park to prevent the mob from attacking the neighborhood where young Theodore lived. Teedie, not old enough to understand what was happening, must have felt the anxiety of his parents as sniper's bullets sang through his streets. Gus, who admitted to being nearly oblivious to political events, walked home through empty streets on the first night of riots and remained there at his mother's command until the threat was over. Only when Union troops left the battlefield of Gettysburg to restore order in New York, could families return to their normal routine.

Young Theodore's first goal in life was to overcome asthma. The attacks were severe and frequent, and the family often wondered if the illness would soon kill the boy. With Thee's encouragement, Theodore began a program of strenuous activity including boxing and hiking that he hoped would build his strength and cure the asthma. In an era when the causes of asthma were unknown, and effective treatment nonexistent, Thee's advice was as good as any doctor's. He built a complete home gymnasium, comparable to the

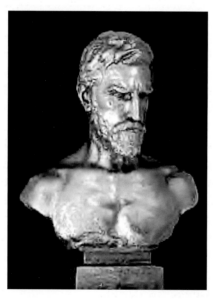 

*Figure 1. Augustus Saint-Gaudens and Theodore Roosevelt as portrayed by contemporary artists. Left, Saint-Gaudens by James E. Fraser (1905); right, Roosevelt by Victor D. Brenner (1908).* (Courtesy Smithsonian Peter A. Juley & Son collection.)

one he had donated to the YMCA founded by Thee and other wealthy New Yorkers.

Augustus' goal was to become an artist. Years of work as a cameo cutter plus evening classes at the Cooper Institute and the National Academy of Design had prepared him

---

[4] Privately, Roosevelt did not appreciate use of the nickname "Teddy" by those other than his family and friends.

for the next step – Paris. Bernard paid for the young man's passage to Europe, also giving him $100 he had secretly saved from his son's meager wages.

Each young man – artist and politician – went his way unaware of the other until sometime around 1889. By then Augustus was an established sculptor, trained in Paris, with a rising reputation for expressiveness and power in his work. Theodore sat in the New York State Assembly, and was active among the "regulars" of the Republican party along with his close friend Henry Cabot Lodge of Boston. Both occasionally attended informal gatherings at the home of author Henry Adams in New York, where discussion ranged from politics to literature, art, history, hunting, "conservation" and social science. We have no correspondence between the two, yet they must have occasionally spoken, and it is probable that Roosevelt more than once expressed admiration for Saint-Gaudens' art. The sculptor, for his part, likely had little opinion about Teddy's political ambitions.

*Figure 2. Senator Henry Cabot Lodge, long-time friend of Theodore Roosevelt.* (Courtesy Library of Congress.)

Through the next decade politician and artist came to share acquaintance with some of the same creative people. These included Adams, politician John Hay, architect Charles McKim, stained-glass artist John LaFarge, and author Henry James. When Roosevelt became vice-president, one of his greatest pleasures was attending weekly evenings of conversation hosted by Hay and Adams in the large house they shared in Washington. Saint-Gaudens attended whenever he was in Washington, and Roosevelt began to turn to the sculptor for advice on artistic matters.

## Gobrecht-Longacre Designs

The introduction of steam-powered presses and rolling mills at the Philadelphia Mint in 1836 had lead to the complete redesign of all coin denominations by 1840. For the gold pieces this effort resulted in monotonous consistency: all gold had a similar basic design (Figure 3, below), all silver shared its design, and the copper cent and half-cent also had their own design. Occasional variety was introduced as Congress mandated new denominations, yet the overall appearance of America's circulating coins was of uniformity. The coinage system had been simplified by the Act of 1873, and again in 1890,[5] which eliminated duplicative and under utilized denominations, but the designs for the remaining coins were left intact. During the fourteen-year period between 1907 and 1921, the United States Treasury Department performed the most radical redesign of the nation's coinage ever attempted. Every denomination was redesigned, and with the exception of the $2-½ and $5 gold coins, each denomination had its own unique design.

Christian Gobrecht had created the portrait of Liberty used on the primary gold denominations in 1838 when he was engraver at the U. S. Mint. When the $20 or double eagle denomination was introduced in 1850 the mint's engraver, James Barton Longacre, provided the design. These coins remained little changed until 1907 and 1908 when

---

[5] 51st Congress, Session I, Chapter 945 – *An act to discontinue the coinage of the three-dollar and one-dollar gold pieces and three-cent nickel pieces.* Passed September 26, 1890.

Augustus Saint-Gaudens and Bela Pratt, supported by President Roosevelt, created new designs for the $2.50, $5, $10, and $20 coins.

| Quarter Eagle | Half Eagle | Eagle | Double Eagle |
| --- | --- | --- | --- |

*Figure 3. Liberty head design used for the principal gold denominations from 1838 to 1907–08. Note omission of the motto "In God We Trust" on the quarter eagle.* (Images courtesy Ira & Larry Goldberg Rare Coin Gallery, Benson Collection Part I, Lots 2165, 2215 and 2286.)

When Theodore Roosevelt took office after President McKinley's assassination in September 1901, a new, more vibrant attitude came to the executive departments of the government. With McKinley's passing also went a tumultuous, conservative, narrow time in America. The 1890s had seen the tentative opening of America as a world power and challenger to Great Britain for mastery of the oceans. Adventures in the Philippines, Cuba and China broadened national outlook while complicating diplomacy. Expansionists, like Roosevelt, had pushed McKinley and the isolationists onto the world stage. It was clearly evident from political, military, economic and social impetus that the new President was not going to tolerate a "second-rate America" – in anything. Roosevelt brought an eclectic view of the world to the presidency. He was a student of all things around him, a world expert on some, and had an opinion on practically everything. He spoke good French, passable German, college Latin and Greek, and bits of other languages. He was supremely the American nationalist, using every opportunity to modernize the national psyche, pulling and prodding his countrymen to open the door to a new century. His bombastic speaking style, filled with broad gestures, pounding fists and a wagging index finger, helped communicate his ardor to audiences large and small.

Although the great issues of the day did not include the nation's coinage, Roosevelt devoted an unusual amount of time to its improvement. His grand plan was for a complete redesign of the nation's coins, but after talking with the country's most prominent sculptor, Augustus Saint-Gaudens, and reviewing the coinage laws with Secretary of the Treasury Leslie M. Shaw, Roosevelt settled for beginning with the four gold coins and cent.

For numismatists of today, Roosevelt's political energy and his ability to harness Saint-Gaudens' artistic ego began a "renaissance" of creativity and symbolism on American coins. Some of the world's finest artists, homegrown and adopted from Europe, tackled the problems of making tiny pieces of stamped metal into inspirational carriers of national pride. Lasting less than a generation as semi-official policy, the coins lingered on in the worn pocket change of soldiers and civilians. By the time most of America's circulating coinage boasted portraits of dead politicians, the gold had become nickel-clad copper and artists' works, monumental and prosaic, no longer inspired.

Much has been written in art and numismatic history about Augustus Saint-Gaudens, and his designs for the gold eagle and double eagle of 1907. The conventional story of President Theodore Roosevelt and Saint-Gaudens fighting against an entrenched U. S. Mint bureaucracy is plausible and overall believable. However, to accept this without further inquiry is to ignore the complex relationship between the two men, their friends and the interactions of the Roosevelt administration with its own political appointees in the treasury department. It also marginalizes the most important artistic-political collaboration for American coinage since the first pattern and circulation issues of 1792–1795. The legacy outlived them. As late as 1922 James E. Fraser, one of Saint-Gaudens' former assistants, called forth their spirits as he commented on the new Peace dollar:[6]

> The new design follows the ideals urged by Saint-Gaudens and others concerning richness and suggestiveness for our coins. President Roosevelt gave much attention to this subject when the new twenty-dollar coin was struck in his Administration. I recall that after the design for that piece was accepted, the reduction of it and in the coinage the bas-relief was unsatisfactory and had to be changed so as to get away from the ordinary standards and raise it in its suggestiveness and richness. The design of the peace dollar conforms to this ideal.

As with much of the old social order, America's gilded age largely vanished amid the gore and hatred of World War I. The neo-classic and *beaux arts* style, favored by Paris-trained Saint-Gaudens and his assistants, in concert with the popular *art nouveau*, gradually disintegrated under the weight of excessive ornamentation. The best of this age retain their beauty and strength; the least adorn online auctions, flea markets and "jumbles" tables at "best offer" prices.

---

[6] *Commission of Fine Arts*, NARA-DC, record group 66, Peace dollar file. Newspaper clipping from the *New York Tribune* January 5, 1922. The interview was given on January 4.

# Chapter 1 – The Rare Shamelessness of Such Offense

Interest in changing the timeworn circulating coin designs had been around since Henry Linderman's tenure as mint director in the 1870s, and a competition was planned for 1887. The mint director, James P. Kimball, stated "...our coin is widely held in disesteem...even in derision...[they] are far behind the art of the day."[7] Plans had also been made to have artists John LaFarge or Augustus Saint-Gaudens prepare "a critique on the artistic execution of individual coins...[where] nobody's feelings would be injured, as the existing designs have been handed down from a period when artistic excellence was little considered."[8] Unfortunately, at that time the attorney general of the United States decided only Congress could change existing coin designs and the idea of a competition was deferred.[9]

By September 1890, with changes in the coinage laws about to be approved by Congress, Philadelphia mint engraver Charles Barber offered his suggestions for "...a circular [to be] issued among artists:"[10]

1st – That designs must be models not drawings;
2nd – The models to be from 4 to 8 inches diameter;
3rd – Models must be in low relief, though they need not be in what is understood as coin relief, but of course suitable for that very low relief;
4th – I would suggest that the design be submitted complete with denomination of the coin and all inscriptions that are required by law, together with the date of year.

---

[7] *US Mint*, NARA-CP, record group 104, entry 229, box 3. Letter dated April 2, 1887 to treasury secretary Fairchild from Kimball.

[8] *US Mint*, NARA-CP, op. cit., entry 41, "Misc. Correspondence of James P. Kimball." Letter dated May 10, 1887 to R. W. Gilder from Kimball.

[9] *US Mint*, NARA-CP, op. cit., entry 229, box 3. Letter dated May 9, 1887 to Fairchild from attorney general.

[10] *US Mint*, NARA-CP, op. cit., entry 229, box 4. Letter dated September 23, 1890 to superintendent Bosbyshell from Barber.

As a partial design without the above would not give a first idea of the appearance of the coin.

Concepts for a silver coin design competition matured over the next months. Andrew Mason, superintendent of the New York assay office, was given the task of preparing a list of possible competitors and sent out an employee, Thomas O. Conant, to interview Saint-Gaudens and J. Q. A. Ward for their recommendations for suitable artists,[11]

> I called first on Mr. St. Gaudens, who was interested at once, and spent some time talking the matter over. He gave me the names of several of those included [on the final list]. But he said that he himself would not be willing to enter a <u>competition</u>, though he would be proud to be invited by the Government to prepare designs....He also suggested that the competition should be limited to artists who were especially qualified for doing fine and noble work, and...they should be compensated for the large amount of time and thought required to make the designs. Mr. Ward...said the same thing...and said it should not be allowed to go to incompetent hands.

By April 3 Mason had prepared a final list of ten artists. It included: Saint-Gaudens, Ward, Daniel C. French, Olin Warner, Herbert Adams, Charles Niehaus, Frederick William MacMonnies, Kenyon Cox, Will H. Low and H. Siddons Mowbray.[12] Saint-Gaudens was recommended, along with several other artists, by mint engraver Charles Barber.[13] Invitations to compete were sent based on the 1887 terms, but the artists felt there was insufficient time and compensation to ensure "any good result." Saint-Gaudens and several others signed a letter asking for changes to the competition terms. These included three months to make the designs, $100 for each design sketch, $500 for each design accepted, an additional $1,000 for each design actually used, and each artist was to design both sides of a coin. Saint-Gaudens made sure that director Edward Leech understood that although he had signed the letter, "...I could under no condition compete."[14]

On receipt of these demands, the secretary of the treasury abruptly cancelled the invitations and announced a public competition. Although there were more than three hundred entries, a jury of three artists – seal engraver Henry Mitchell from Boston, Engraver of the United States Mint at Philadelphia, Charles E. Barber and Saint-Gaudens – decided that none of the entries were suitable for coinage:[15]

> ....We are of the opinion that none of the designs or models submitted are such a decided improvement upon the present designs of the silver coins of the United States as to be worthy of adoption by the Government.
> We would respectfully recommend that the services of one or more artists distinguished for work in designing and relief, be engaged at a suitable compensation to prepare, for consideration of the Department, new designs for the coins of the United States.

---

[11] *US Mint*, NARA-CP, op. cit., entry 229, box 4. Memorandum dated April 3, 1891 to mint director Leech from Conant.

[12] *US Mint*, NARA-CP, op. cit., entry 229, box 4. Letter dated April 3, 1891 to Leech from Mason.

[13] *US Mint*, NARA-CP, op. cit., entry 229, box 4. Letter dated April 2, 1891 to Bosbyshell from Barber. The others were J. Q. A. Ward, Martini, Ellicott, Hearns, deKosebko and Gorham Co.

[14] *US Mint*, NARA-CP, op. cit., entry 229, box 4. Letter dated May 19, 1891 to Leech from Saint-Gaudens.

[15] *US Mint*, NARA-CP, op. cit., entry 229, box 4. Letter dated June 3, 1891 to secretary Charles Foster from adjudicators Mitchell, Saint-Gaudens, and Barber. Countersigned by director Leech.

Henry Mitchell wrote on June 11 suggesting he could prepare suitable designs,[16] and unsuccessful competitor John R. Conway complained that insufficient time had been allowed for good designs to be made.[17]

But appeals were to no avail. Mint director Leech dashed all hope of a successful competition by declaring in a letter "…he found it doubtful that any '…high-class artist…any distinguished sculptor, or designer can prepare a practical model for a coin.'"[18] The work was promptly turned over to mint engraver Charles Barber, who prepared models and patterns for the new subsidiary silver coins. His designs were typically mediocre imitations of the current French-style – hardly better than the arcane Seated Liberty type they replaced.

Barber and Saint-Gaudens evidently disagreed on many points of art during the jury's discussions, and had little in common. It is likely they were so far apart in their artistic understanding that neither listened to what the other had to say. Barber and Saint-Gaudens came from different artistic backgrounds. Barber was from the English trades-apprentice approach where engraving and die sinking were crafts closely aligned to other metal workers such as machine tool makers. His father and grandfather were both engravers. Saint-Gaudens was a classically trained sculptor who began his career as an apprentice cameo cutter in New York, later moving to Paris and Rome for extensive training while perfecting his artistry. Barber generally worked in small, circular formats – a three-inch medal was a large size for his sculptures. Saint-Gaudens was uncomfortable with small medals and typically designed life-size or larger figures, and relatively large bas-reliefs. Additionally, his major sculptures utilized multiple visual planes to add scale and vitality to the works. The 1891 competition turned the two against one another for the rest of their lives.

Barber's animosity was so deeply felt that fourteen years after the incident, he seemed to view Saint-Gaudens with fresh ire: "The Director of the Mint, Mr. Leech, advertised for designs [in 1891] and many were sent in, but Mr. St. Gaudens, who was appointed one of the committee to pass upon designs, objected to everything submitted. Therefore Mr. Leech called upon the Engraving Department…to prepare designs and have the dies ready for…1892."[19]

## Columbian Exposition Award Medal

The failed 1891 competition was a very minor event and might have faded from both men's memories, except for the approach of the World's Columbian Exposition planned for Chicago.

The Chicago World's Colombian Exposition was one of the signal achievements of the artistic world for American artists.[20] It was also a federally supported project and along with the government money came conditions, one of which was use of the U. S. Mint to

---

[16] *US Mint*, NARA-CP, op. cit., entry 229, box 4. Letter dated June 11, 1891 to Leech from Mitchell.

[17] *US Mint*, NARA-CP, op. cit., entry 229, box 4. Letter dated June 12, 1891 to Leech from Conway. Similar letters were received from other entrants, primarily those mentioned in newspaper articles.

[18] Tolles, Thayer, *A Bit of Artistic Idealism: Augustus-Saint Gaudens's World Columbian Exposition Commemorative Presentation Medal*, p.142. Coinage of the Americas Conference, November 8-9, 1997. American Numismatic Society.

[19] *US Mint*, NARA-CP, op. cit., entry 229, box 234. Letter dated August 24, 1905 to director Roberts from Barber via Albert Norris. Balance of letter refers to changes in size of stars on 1892 quarter.

[20] The subject of the Columbian Exposition medal is dealt with in additional detail in Thayer Tolles' article previously cited.

12

prepare and produce medals and commemorative coins. Daniel H. Burnham, chief architect for the fair, arranged for Saint-Gaudens to become a general advisor, and he suggested the use of Daniel Chester French's statue *Republic* at one end of the central lagoon.

*Figure 4.* **Republic *by Daniel Chseter French in place at one end of the great lagoon.*** (Courtesy Library of Congress.)

At the other end was a monumental *Ship of State* fountain that Burnham wished Saint-Gaudens to design. The Chicago Fair Committee offered to pay Saint-Gaudens $15,000 to "supervise the creation of sculptural projects." This included French's seventy-five foot statue and the *Ship of State* fountain. This was agreed to only if Frederick MacMonnies would assist him in the work, but MacMonnies decided he would rather not do this. Saint-Gaudens then recommended the entire fountain be done by MacMonnies, which it was. Saint-Gaudens commented in his memoirs: [21]

> I was invited by Daniel H. Burnham to journey to Chicago together with Robert M. Hunt, Charles F. McKim and others to view the layout of buildings on the fair site. Mr. Burnham was anxious for me to supervise the entire development of sculpture for the Exposition, but I was unable to do this due to many other commitments. My only direct relation to the sculpture was the figure of Columbus in front of the Administration Building created by Miss Mary Lawrence (later Mrs. M. L. Tonetti), who was a student of mine. [22]

Saint-Gaudens was overwhelmed by work in his studio and agreed to indicate "a general scheme" for $3,000, then to let the artists work free of other supervision. [23] John Boyd Thacher, chairman of the Executive Committee on Awards, approached Saint-Gaudens in the fall of 1892 with a proposal to design an award medal for the fair. However, the commission was controlled by the Quadro-Centennial Committee of the U. S.

[21] *Reminiscences*, vol. 2, p.73 *et supra.*
[22] *Reminiscences*, vol. 2, p.73.
[23] Tharp, *Saint-Gaudens and the Gilded Era*, pp.253–254.

Senate, and this apparently made Saint-Gaudens uneasy. Thacher wrote to treasury secretary Charles Foster:[24]

> We respectfully suggest that you might invite Augustus Saint-Gaudens to make the model in plaster for the medal and Will H. Low the design for the diploma. While there are other artists of eminent ability in both sculpture and in flat drawing, we feel sure that the selection of these artists would be commended by the art world.

After considerable persuasion and appeals to the artist's nationalism and support for other artists at the fair, Saint-Gaudens reluctantly accepted $5,000 to design the medal.[25]

The sculptor was also working on the Shaw memorial for Boston Common and the local committee was concerned about the slow progress. On November 10, 1892 Saint-Gaudens wrote to Edward Atkinson, treasurer of the Shaw committee, explaining part of his reason for wanting to design the medal:[26]

> I only wish to do it to keep it out of the hands of the man at the mint[27] who I am positively assured…will certainly do it if I don't. If I thought that it were at all possible that one of two or three other artists could obtain the work, I should certainly refuse to have anything to do with the matter.

Other reasons may have been bandied about, but it was clear that Saint-Gaudens accepted the medal commission "to keep it out of the hands of [U. S. Mint engraver Charles Barber]…." The sculptor may have felt he had to support the maturity of American art even though he expressed doubts about his own capacity to design a satisfactory medal. According to his son, Homer, initially "…he refused to accept the task, saying neither he nor anyone else in the country could model a decent medal, and that it was necessary to go to Europe for it."[28]

Apparently, Saint-Gaudens, and treasury officials disagreed on where the hubs and dies were to be made. The artist wanted them prepared in France and treasury secretary John G. Carlisle insisted on having the work done at the Philadelphia Mint, as stipulated in the enabling legislation. Saint-Gaudens expressed his displeasure in a letter to Thacher:[29]

> …My last letter from Secretary Carlisle says that they still wish the dies made at the Mint. I am disgusted with the whole matter. In order to do this medal, after much solicitation, I dropped important lucrative work for this Senate commission so that if possible something we need not be ashamed of should be awarded by the United States.
>
> Now, as what I wish seems to be an impossibility in the making of the dies, I cannot be held responsible for them and if any liberties are taken with my work at the Mint, such as have been taken with others, I shall surely publish it….

Thatcher appealed to secretary Carlisle on June 5,[30]

---

[24] *US Mint*, NARA-CP, op. cit., entry 229, box 4. Letter dated October 7, 1892 to Foster from Thacher.

[25] Tolles, op. cit., p.142.

[26] Tolles, op. cit., p.143. *Lee Family Papers*. Letter dated November 10, 1892 to Atkinson from Saint-Gaudens.

[27] This was engraver Charles Barber.

[28] *Reminiscences*, vol. 2, pp.66–72.

[29] *US Mint*, NARA-CP, op. cit., entry 229, box 5. Letter dated June 2, 1893 to Thacher from Saint-Gaudens.

[30] *US Mint*, NARA-CP, op. cit., entry 229, box 5. Letter dated June 5, 1893 to Carlisle from Thacher.

14

...I would much prefer to have the medal made in this country and at the Mint, but my experience with artists is that the Lord has not made them as other men and therefore if you can yield to Mr. Saint-Gaudens and have the medals made in Kamtschatka if he desires it, I hope you will. The important thing is to get them out at once.

Mr. Saint-Gaudens fears that the cutting will not be satisfactorily done. Could you not yield so far as to let him select someone to cut them but really under the directions of the Mint?

The secretary refused to have dies made anyplace except the Philadelphia Mint and the dispute likely increased enmity between the mint and artist.

By the end of October 1893 Saint-Gaudens had completed obverse and reverse designs for the medal, although the exhebition had closed. The models were sent to the U. S. Mint in Philadelphia for reduction and die making. According to previous agreement with treasury secretary Carlisle, the designs were to be kept secret until the medals were actually issued to recipients.

*Figure 5. Columbian Exposition Award Medal (1893) as originally designed by Saint-Gaudens. The obverse has* **Augustus Saint-Gaudens Fecit** *in small, incuse letters at the lower rim.* (Courtesy U. S. Department of Interior National Park Service, Saint-Gaudens National Historic Site, Cornish, NH. #1220)

Saint-Gaudens' description provides insight into his design:[31]

The obverse of the medal is devoted to that which the exhibition commemorates and represents Columbus stepping to the shore with a gesture of thanks to God for the final accomplishment of his great labors. He is followed by a standard bearer and others who are seen coming up from the boat he is just leaving. The inscription on that side is "Christopher Columbus Oct. XII, 1492 [in Roman numerals]. The device on this side is, the Pillars – of Hercules, representing the Rocks of Gibraltar with the three Caravels sailing out and the inscription "Plus Ultra..."

The reverse is devoted to the inscription stating what the Medal is struck for, and to the representation of the Spirit of America by a young man in the full vigor of young life, holding a torch in one hand and resting the other on a shield bearing the emblems of the United States, eagle, etc. He stands on an eminence and a young oak is next the shield.

---

[31] *Saint-Gaudens, Augustus; papers*, Dartmouth College, Rauner Special Collections. Microfilm reel 5, frames 41-42. Letter dated November 27, 1893 to President of Exposition from Saint-Gaudens.

The reverse inscription reads: "The Columbia Exhibition in commemoration of the four hundredth anniversary of the landing of Columbus to..." followed by a blank space for the recipient's name. Below the youth's feet are the dates "MDCCCXCII – MDCCCXCIII" (1892–1893).

In the midst of the mint's work Senator William E. Chandler of New Hampshire made an unusual request.[32] He wrote a letter to the superintendent of the Mint introducing an employee of the Page Belting Company, Concord, New Hampshire, asking that he be given a tour of the mint. The man, who claimed to be interested in art, was shown the model for the medal and permitted to make drawings of it.[33]

Unlike most other fairs and international expositions, the Columbian Exposition did not issue competitive awards. *The Book of the Fair*, a post-exhibition souvenir book, explains:[34]

> In bestowing its awards the Columbian Exposition differed in some respects from most of its predecessors. First of all they were non-competitive; for as the executive committee remarked, in an exposition designed to illustrate the development of the resources of the United States and the progress of civilization in the New World, as compared with all participating nations, the results should be placed on a higher plane than merely to indicate the relative merits of competing exhibits. Rather should be indicated some independent and essential excellence in the article displayed, denoting improvement in the condition of the art which it represents. Thus the awards would constitute an enduring record of progress as represented by the exhibits in question, the certificate serving for identification and the medal as a memento of success. Of the latter there would be but a single class; nor would there be granted either money or graded awards of any description. All the medals were to be made of bronze and all must be alike, except that on each would inscribed the name of the exhibitor. Under such a system there was, as might be expected, less friction than at former expositions, only 259 complaints being entered among more than 65,000 exhibitors, while of these but 43 were carried to appeal.
>
> ...Both medals and diplomas were prepared under the direction of the secretary of the treasury, and with these the executive committee had nothing to do, except for the correction of clerical errors. For the diplomas the design was intrusted [sic] to William Low, by whom was executed much of the fresco work of the Fair, and for the medal to Augustus St. Gaudens, of whom mention is made in connection with its decorative statuary. Both are of excellent workmanship and have been pronounced by competent critics superior to any before provided for similar purposes.

Competition between fair exhibitors for publicity was keen and each company wanted to get as much value from their exhibit and awards as possible. The earlier a company could publicize its award medal and diploma, the greater the publicity value. The Page Belting Company of Concord, New Hampshire had an excellent reputation for making high-quality leather belts used to connect equipment to steam and electric engines used

[32] William Eaton Chandler was a native of Concord and likely knew Charles Page. He served as Secretary of the Navy under President Chester A. Arthur. He objected to the practice of repairing wooden vessels, which were worthless in the new era of post-Civil War ordinance. He fought to reduce the extravagant Philadelphia Navy Yard establishment. He resigned his position after three years (March 7, 1885). On June 14, 1887 Chandler was chosen by New Hampshire to fill the unexpired term of (Republican) U. S. Senator Austin F. Pike. Chandler was subsequently elected to two full terms as United States senator (1889–1895, 1895–1901).
[33] Tharp, *Saint-Gaudens and the Gilded Era*, pp.253-254.
[34] Hubert Howe Bancroft, *The Book of the Fair*. The Bancroft Company, Chicago, San Francisco: 1893. pp. 964-965.

in factories. Their belts were used to transfer power for the huge Allis-Corliss steam engine featured in the fair's technology exhibit.

***Figure 6. Watercolor illustration of the Allis-Corliss engine at the Columbian Exposition. The Page Belting Company made the wide power transfer belts.***

Company president Charles F. Page took every opportunity to promote his company and apparently arranged for drawings of the "secret" medal to be made. These were printed on an advertising circular and mailed to businesses throughout the country.[35] An editorial comment in the respected trade publication *The Manufacturer and Builder* for January 1894 explains what occurred in contemporary terms:[36]

### St. Gaudens' Columbian Medal.

Just after the advent of the new year, one of New Hampshire's well-known manufacturing firms, located at the capital of the Granite State startled the entire business community of the country, and more especially those who were exhibitors at the Columbian Exposition, by mailing broadcast from their office thousands of what they made bold to designate as "Facsimiles (full size) of the two medals awarded to the Page Belting Company, made from the St. Gaudens design, adopted by the Bureau of Awards." The sheet upon which they were printed also contained this further announcement: "We have at this time the exclusive publication of the Columbian Medal as we are the only exhibitor possessed of either the medal or a facsimile of its design, as adopted by the Bureau of Awards. We are the only leather belting manufacturer to whom were awarded two medals and two diplomas at the World's Fair."

It appears Page's intent was to be the first to promote their award of the medals. It does not appear they cared anything about the design or who did the work, except to mention Saint-Gaudens did it. Company documents do not state how they got to see the de-

---

[35] *US Mint*, NARA-CP, op. cit., entry 229, box 5. Letter dated January 7, 1895 to mint director Preston from Scoville Manufacturing Company. This appears to be the first time Preston was made aware of unauthorized use of the design.
[36] Library of Congress, *The Manufacturer and Builder*, vol. 26, No.1, January 1894. p.23.

signs or who was responsible for obtaining access to the original models. One could reasonably suspect the engraver's office had a hand in events.

> That this "facsimile" might be received by the public as the genuine article, more convincing proof was offered by an accompanying document purporting to contain the full text and exact language of the reports and awards as made by judges R. C. Carpenter and Louis E. Reber, including a facsimile of their autographs appended thereto. This sheet was quite artistic in its design, having at the top a cut of the Allis engine, which was used at the fair for driving two 72-inch Page belts for the running of dynamos. At each side of the picture were miniature cuts of the medals; at the bottom of the sheet a golden embossed seal, inscribed, "Columbian Exposition 1893. The highest award." The seal held in place a bit of blue ribbon upon which were the words "compliments of the season. New Year's, 1894." The whole was surrounded by a border representing a wide endless belt passing over pulleys at each of the four corners. On the reverse were cuts of their first 40 feet square [*sic*: 400] location at Manchester, and their present mammoth establishment at Concord.

As noted above, Page Belting also appears to have concocted an imitation certificate complete with medal images and a blue ribbon. All the better to convince readers that his company was given the "upper hand" in promoting their awards.

> The medals displayed as "facsimiles" of the St. Gaudens' design, were three inches in diameter, printed in bronze. When it was decided to give 27,000 medals to those exhibitors at the World's Fair whose exhibits were of surpassing excellence, Secretary Carlisle had it in his power to offer a reward of $5,000 for the best design for such a medal. Augustus St. Gaudens of 148 West Thirty-sixth street, this city [New York], one of the leading sculptors in this country, was one of the competitors, and his design was accepted. …The historical side of this medal represents Columbus just stepping upon the shores of America, with his hand raised on high, giving thanks to the Almighty. On the reverse is a shield bearing the words "E Pluribus Unum," and on the right of it is a tall, stalwart young man, nude and typifying America.
>
> It is now alleged that someone skilled in drawing was employed by the worthy president of the Page Belting Company to surreptitiously obtain a view of the accepted design and then to reproduce it from memory. As might naturally be supposed, Mr. St. Gaudens was full of indignation when he learned of this attempt to palm off upon an unsuspecting public this fraudulent and imperfect rendering of his beautiful conception. The representatives of the press in this city [New York] sought an interview with Mr. St. Gaudens and drew his attention to the rumor that leading members of Congress were condemning in severe terms his design of the Columbian Medal, and that it was reported that Secretary Carlisle had decided to suppress it.
>
> In answer Mr. St. Gaudens made this reply:
>
> *"I have as yet received no communication from Secretary Carlisle or any one else in authority about the medals, with the exception of the fact that they have been accepted. All the news I have received of shocked Senators and anticipated modifications has been through the newspapers. So far as I know my design has been accepted, and until I hear differently I shall continue to believe that it is to be used. I have not been informed of any sudden action on the part of the Secretary; in fact the only action that I know of at all relative to this case is the action I shall have against that ass, that consummate ass, who said that the chromos he puts at the top of a business house's letter paper were exact reproductions of my design for the medal. I doubt if this wide world contains a bigger ass than that man. But my lawyer will attend to his case, you may rest assured of that. No one was to see the design of the medal before it was issued, and if the artist of the business house in question did see the medal and did attempt to make a copy he violated the law and is liable to severe punishment. I know nothing about it save what I have read in the papers. I have turned in*

*my design, it has been accepted, and it is my design and nothing else that will come out on the medals. As I said before, I have received no notification of any change in my design, and until I do I will not believe that any such change as mentioned is contemplated. If anything was to be done with the design you may be sure that I would be the first person to be notified."*

Obviously Saint-Gaudens was furious with Page Belting Company, but he was also upset with the mint for "leaking" the design. The article noted that Saint-Gaudens had his attorney contact Charles Page threatening legal action. His wife, Augusta, "… stated the pirating was 'all a monstrous, infamous lie.' Worse, the drawing was crude and ugly. Newspapers got hold of it and called the design immoral. One newspaper made 'a pretty bad man out of the sculptor.'"[37] Whoever did the drawing must have had considerable time to make his sketches, since the pirated drawings included much detail from the originals, although they were crudely drawn.

Augusta also wrote to her brother Tom Homer, who was a lawyer, about the situation. "Saint-Gaudens asked advice on suing the paper for libel, but his brother-in-law talked him out of it by reminding him the jury would be local residents who probably would not understand the artistic subtleties of the case."[38] Although legal action against the newspaper was averted, *Page Belting Company* was forced to destroy the remaining offending brochures. These were later reprinted without images of the medals and the offending text.[39]

**Figure 7. Imitations of the Columbian Award Medal as printed on an advertising brochure by Page Belting Company, Concord, NH.** (Courtesy Page Belting Company.)

But the matter did not end there. The press had hold of a "sensational" story and tossed it from page to page of the daily editions for weeks. When facts were not available, reporters invented them.

Details of how Senator Chandler learned of the medal design and events in the Senate were included in a letter to Charles C. Beaman, member of a law firm in New York City, from Senator Edward Wolcott:[40]

My Dear Mr. Beaman:
Your telegram was received this morning. I at once saw Senator Vilas about the St. Gaudens medal. It seems that Senator Chandler of New Hampshire, who is al-

---

[37] Tharp, *Saint-Gaudens and the Gilded Era*, pp.253–254.
[38] Ibid., p.254.
[39] Communication from Mr. Mark Coen, president of Page Belting Co., Concord, NH. E-mail message December 7, 2002. Amazingly, the company is still in business after 135 years in the same community, and doing very well under the leadership of Mr. Coen. Only a handful of the original brochures are known.
[40] *SG*, Dartmouth, op. cit. Microfilm reel 5, frames 29–30. Letter dated January 29, 1894 to Charles Coatsworth Beaman from Sen. Edward Wolcott.

ways a busy man, found an advertisement of a New Hampshire Belting Company which re-produced (I understand incorrectly) the proposed medal. It shocked his sensitive nature and he took it to Senator Vilas and called his attention to what he deemed an objectionable feature on the medal. Mr. Vilas informs me that he at once agreed with Senator Chandler and called for a copy of the cast which he had brought down to the Senate. He then invited the members of the Quadro-Centennial Committee and a few other Senators to view this awful figure in the committee room. He says he heard but one voice on the subject and that was in condemnation of the medal. He thereupon urged Secretary Carlisle to suppress it and to insist upon it being changed. There the matter stands…

I cannot imagine a smaller or more belittling piece of business. The very suggestion of any impropriety in the medal is degrading. I wish I knew what I could do. I am promised an inspection of the medal within a day or two, and if the matter comes up in the Senate I shall of course do anything in my power, but I fear it will not come there. Mr. Vilas did not show me St. Gaudens' letter. [This is the letter dated January 25 to Carlisle – RWB.] I will again ask him for it. If there is any further literature which you have on the subject, I should be glad to have it.

This generation owes a debt to St. Gaudens that it can never pay. I feel a personal sense of shame, that instead of availing itself of a fair opportunity to express its appreciation of his artistic qualities and his genius, this government is inclined to an exhibition of a false modesty that would be ludicrous if it were not humiliating.

Finally, Senator Chandler complained to the Quadro-Centennial Committee who voted to reconsider Saint-Gaudens' accepted design. Secretary of the Treasury John Griffin Carlisle formally rescinded the acceptance in a letter to Saint-Gaudens, January 23, 1894:[41]

The Senate Committee on the Quadro-Centennial object to the reverse of the design of the medal of award for the Columbian Exposition, on account of the nude figure. The design is a work of art, and while there might be no objection to it in the form of statuary in a gallery, I am frank to say that inasmuch as there are to be 20,000 of these medals struck, I am satisfied that it would be severely criticized by a large majority of the people in its present form. In view of these facts, I have to request that as designer of the model, you will be kind enough to submit some design covering the objectionable part of the figure.

Saint-Gaudens replied two days later asking Carlisle to reconsider but also emphatically stating his prerogative as an artist:[42]

I feel that if it is changed I shall in self defense be bound to see that in all proper ways "the people" know what my original design was, and trust the design as made by me and as accepted by your department several months ago, was not one to which they would have objected could they have seen it first…

I of course shall feel at liberty at all times to publish the correspondence between us.

By early March 1894 Saint-Gaudens had altered his design to hide the offending portions behind either a fig leaf or a narrow ribbon (depending on which of two versions was considered). According to Charles Barber, Saint-Gaudens provided the mint with eight-inch plaster models reduced from much larger originals,[43]

[41] *SG*, Dartmouth, op. cit. Microfilm reel 5, frame 25. Letter dated January 23, 1894 to Saint-Gaudens from Carlisle.
[42] *SG*, Dartmouth, op. cit. Microfilm reel 5, frame 25. Letter (excerpt) dated January 25, 1894 to Carlisle from Saint-Gaudens.
[43] *US Mint*, NARA-CP, op. cit., entry 229, box 290. Letter dated May 11, 1910 to John Landis, Superintendent of the Philadelphia Mint from Charles Barber, engraver.

...Saint-Gaudens also had reductions and castings made in Paris, one about three inches in diameter, and another about two inches in diameter....These cast medals were from the rejected design and were very good. One of the Commissioners to the Columbian Exposition, a Mr. Woodside of Philadelphia, had one of the three inch cast medals, rejected design, and had castings made, how many, I do not know, at the time Mr. Woodside had these made he showed me some half dozen and they were very poor castings...

The reductions that Saint-Gaudens had made were made by M. Tasset of Paris....

Secretary Carlisle again rejected these revisions claiming, "...that Saint-Gaudens had really accentuated the objections already made."[44]

*Figure 8. One attempt by Saint-Gaudens to "fix" offending portions of the original medal reverse by adding a narrow ribbon. Another version added a fig leaf. Neither was effective artistically and the secretary of the treasury rejected the version with the ribbon as exaggerating the problem.* (Courtesy U. S. Department of Interior National Park Service, Saint-Gaudens National Historic Site, Cornish, NH. #1120)

The sculptor was ready to drop the whole matter when the mint director, Robert Preston, asked him to furnish yet another model.[45] Saint-Gaudens wrote to his friend, journalist Richard Watson Gilder:[46]

I am doing a reverse, but am eliminating the figure entirely, confining it only to an inscription.... The figure that I had composed was composed to be nude, and I find it impossible to drape it without entirely destroying the composition.

The design, omitting any offensive figures, was sent to treasury secretary Carlisle on June 23 with anticipation of prompt acceptance.

---

[44] *US Mint*, NARA-CP, op. cit., entry 229, box 290. Letter dated May 2, 1910 to Landis from Barber.
[45] Preston took office in November, 1893. He was reminded of the Columbian medal incident by Charles Barber in 1906 (see note below).
[46] Tolles, op. cit., p.147. Gilder papers. Letter dated May 22, 1894 to Gilder from Saint-Gaudens.

*Figure 9. Final reverse designs for the Columbian Award Medal. Left, design by Saint-Gaudens and rejected by secretary Carlisle; right, Charles Barber's rendition as eventually muled with Saint-Gaudens' obverse. Barber's name is in small, incuse letters at the lower reverse rim.* (Courtesy U. S. Department of Interior National Park Service, Saint-Gaudens National Historic Site, Cornish, NH.)

Instead, yet another rejection appeared, and not long afterward Saint-Gaudens learned that a reverse design prepared by mint engraver Charles Barber had been accepted.[47]

> I have received and examined the new design for the reverse of the World's Columbian Exposition Medal submitted by you and I regret to say that it is not satisfactory and I have, therefore, decided to reject it.
>
> In my letter of the 21st of February, last, asking you to submit a new design for the reverse of the medal, it was expressly stated that it should be done without any additional expense to the Government.
>
> No allowance will be made by the Government for the design submitted which will be returned to you.

This combination with the original obverse created an artistic "mule." Making good on his 1893 threat, the angry sculptor fired off a letter to the New York *Tribune* summarizing the situation:[48]

> **To the Editor of the New York *Tribune*:**
> Sir:
> It occurs to me that the following resume of my relations with the Washington authorities in charge of the commission for the Columbian Exposition medal, may not be without a pleasant moral to others moved to entertain government proposals. I therefore send it, for insertion, to your influential journal.
>
> On the twenty-seventh of June, I received official notification of the rejection of my third design for the Reverse of the Columbian medal. At the same time it was publicly announced that a design by Mr. Barber, of the United States Mint, had been adopted in its stead.
>
> I had myself undertaken the execution of this medal only after earnest solicitation by those then in authority, to the detriment of other and important interests.
>
> My first design, although it had been formally accepted by Hon. J. G. Carlisle, was immediately afterwards rejected because its composition included a nude figure, to which impertinent attention was drawn by an incorrect and offensive copy, made and published by private parties.

---

[47] *SG*, Dartmouth, op. cit. Microfilm reel 5, frame 31. Letter dated June 27, 1894 to Saint-Gaudens from Carlisle.
[48] *Reminiscences*, vol. 2, pp.72–73.

I regret to admit that, subsequently, at the urgent request of Mr. Carlisle, and upon his representations, I foolishly altered my design, to flatter the sensitivities of the rampant "pure."

This second design, in which neither my feelings nor my draperies were spared, was again refused, and I was formally requested, through Mr. Preston, Director of the Mint, to furnish an entirely new model "at an early date." Unpardonable as it now appears, I complied, producing once more the required model, which was again in due course of time to be set aside.

The rejection of this third and last model is the more curious to explain, in that, with excessive care for the sensitive acuteness of the Hon. Secretary of the Treasury, I had this time in my composition – scrupulously turning from classic thought of humanity, draped or undraped – surely avoided all erotic insinuation by the substitution, for the offending figure, of "The Bird," whose fair fame is beyond suggestive possibilities.

I have reserved, in this mortifying confession of criminal naivete, the final letter of vast persuasion that undid me. Let me print it, that others may judge of the frank tone and incredible bonhomie that may be dangerously imported into government communications, and also that I may find in their opinion "extenuating circumstances."

*To: Augustus Saint-Gaudens, New York City*
*May 18, 1894*

*Dear Sir:*
*I am very much gratified by the receipt of your letter of yesterday, stating that you would prepare and submit another design for the Reverse of the World's Columbian Exposition Medal. As soon as the Reverse is received, preparation will be made to have it engraved immediately, and to make a faithful reproduction of the same. I feel sure that the Mint has made a success in the engraving of the Obverse, and will be equally successful in the engraving of the Reverse.*
*Very truly yours,*
*Robert Preston, Director of the Mint*

On receipt of this guarantee to accept my further work, accompanied as it was by expressions of interest in its completeness and an assurance that every care should be bestowed upon its reproduction, it was, for me, impossible to hesitate.

Never was [a] commission clearer or more kindly thoughtful in detail. In the face of this promise, that "as soon as the Reverse is received, preparations will be made to have it engraved immediately and to make a faithful reproduction of the same," to harbor further uncertainty would have implied unmannerly doubt of the word of the gentleman who had written it. I may be excused if, in my simplicity, the idea even of such possibility never occurred to me.

And I am now willing to confess that the condition of good faith common among gentlemen, which could contemplate an engagement with another man to produce this same Reverse at the very moment of holding out to me as an encouragement in my work that the "Mint has made a success in the engraving of the Obverse," does suggest a complication of Bureaucratic Conscience and Machiavellian Subtlety with which I have shown myself utterly unable to cope.

I shall, in all humility, await from these official gentlemen their own explanation.
And I have, sir, the honor to be,
Very truly yours,

P.S. Mr. Carlisle's may be the legal right to combine my work with that of another on the same medal, but the rare shamelessness of such offense will be appreciated by all my confreres at home and abroad, and it is as much in their interest as in my own unbridled astonishment that I make this protest public.

A similar letter was also sent to secretary Carlisle on July 3. An earlier draft dated June 30 shows that Saint-Gaudens toned down his public comments considerably. Included in the draft was this concluding paragraph:[49]

> The proposition to place my work in combination with that of any one else on a medal, and particularly with that of the designer of our present coinage, is absurd [preposterous; incompetent, inept...]...

A newspaper article in the *New York World* offered this comment on the situation:[50]

> It is announced that the controversy over the World's Fair medal has been "settled" by the adoption by Secretary Carlisle of a "composite design" for the obverse being allowed to remain, while the much offending nude figure on the reverse is to be replaced by a very "composite" design indeed, created by Mr. Barber, the designer of our present silver coinage. Whether such a preposterous "settlement" as this will be allowed to stay settled remains to be seen. It does not seem to have occurred to the settlers that Mr. St Gaudens might object, with some show of reason, in our humble opinion, to being bracketed in this way with a vastly inferior designer, and might insist on the government's taking all of his design or none. The whole chapter of our government's dealings with this distinguished artist is a disgraceful one, but this last action is of a coolness that takes one's breath away.... The joy of our artists...is likely to be somewhat dashed by this revelation that the days of barbarism are not yet over.

The editorial writer was able to resist the obvious pun of trading "barbarism" for "Barberism" in the last line.

Charles Barber's synopsis of the creation of his reverse design states:[51]

> ...The [Saint-Gaudens] designs were delivered and paid for as the Secretary had become impatient at the delay that had already taken place, and at this stage of the case I was appealed to for a design to take the place of the rejected one of St. Gaudens' and though very reluctant to enter into this unpleasant situation furnished one that was accepted and used....

The same day Carlisle wrote to Saint-Gaudens rejecting his last design, the secretary wrote to Charles Barber accepting one of his:[52]

> I have decided to accept Model No. 1, of the design for the reverse of the World's Columbian Exposition Medal submitted by you, which I am pleased to say, to my mind, exhibits considerable artistic taste.
> Very respectfully,
> J. G. Carlisle, Secretary

Nothing is known about why Carlisle rejected Saint-Gaudens' last and most innocuous design. There is nothing offensive about any part of the design other than its obvious inferiority to previous submissions. Barber's characteristically dull reverse design was officially described thus:[53]

[49] *SG*, Dartmouth, op. cit. Microfilm reel 5, frames 38–40. Draft letter dated June 30, 1894 to Carlisle from Saint-Gaudens.
[50] *SG*, Dartmouth, op. cit. Microfilm reel 5, frame 24. Clipping, *New York World*, June 26, 1894.
[51] *US Mint*, NARA-CP, op. cit., entry 229, box 290. Letter dated May 2, 1910 to Landis from Barber.
[52] *US Mint*, NARA-CP, op. cit., entry 229, box 290. Letter dated June 27, 1894 to Barber from John G. Carlisle.
[53] *US Mint*, NARA-CP, op. cit., entry 229, box 32. Letter dated June 19, 1896 to Preston from Hermon Kretz, superintendent of the Philadelphia Mint. The description was intended for use by George Kunz during an exhibit by members of the

This design contains a shield with the following inscription: "Worlds Columbian Exposition In Commemoration of the Four Hundredth Anniversary of the Landing of Columbus, MDCCCXCII, MDCCCXCIII." And place for insert to receive name of recipient of medal. The shield is surmounted by the globe, at either side of which are female figures representing Fame.

The figure at the right of globe has trumpet in one hand and is proclaiming the award, and in the other hand she holds wreaths [of victory] ready to present; on the left of globe, she has tablet in left hand while in the right she holds a stylus ready to inscribe the award as proclaimed. On either side of shield are flaming torches representing light or knowledge.

Beneath the shield and partially hidden by the shield, is the Caravel, which is used to make a unity or completeness of idea, and allegory between the two sides of the medal, the one side having the landing of Columbus, the other the above described design, the whole to commemorate the four hundredth anniversary of the landing of Columbus and the Worlds Exposition held 1892-1893.

The dies for the medals were engraved at the Mint of the United States, Philadelphia.

The medal finally made it into the hands of exhibitors beginning in April 1896. It was struck by Scoville Manufacturing Company in Waterbury, Connecticut from dies made at the mint.[54] Barber personally inspected at least 23,597 of the finished medals from approximately 27,000 bronze copies distributed to exhibitors.[55] Some exhibitors offered to pay for gold or silver copies of the medal but the Department of Justice issued an opinion that these could not be struck and none were officially issued.[56]

This protracted episode of poor communication, bad faith and outright deception undoubtedly hardened Saint-Gaudens to any further work for the federal government. He had plenty of commissions and was soon on his way to Paris, where he would remain until July 1900. After his return from Europe, he was to have many conversations with the new President, Theodore Roosevelt, but it was not until 1905 that Roosevelt's diplomatic skills finally broke through Saint-Gaudens' defenses when it came to coin designs.

## Cancer Strikes

By 1897 Saint-Gaudens' fame was such that there was a constant stream of visitors to his New York studios. Regardless of which of the four locations he happened to be working in, the interruptions were frequent. Some wanted to commission a bas-relief or memorial tablet, others seemed to have the artist on their sightseeing list as a souvenir of their New York visit. Under these conditions, work on the *Sherman Memorial*, already four years late, proceeded erratically. The Saint was exhausted from the interruptions, teaching at the Art Student's League and general overwork. Although funds were short, he made plans to go to Paris where he could work in relative calm. Fortunately, a large commission for a statue of Lincoln came from a bequest by John Crerar in Chicago.[57] The sub-

---

National Sculpture Society. This exhibition included proposed designs for the standard silver dollar produced for a NSS-sponsored contest.

[54] Tolles, op. cit., pp.149–151.

[55] *US Mint*, NARA-CP, op. cit., entry 229, box 24 Letter dated January 11, 1896 to Preston from Barber

[56] *US Mint*, NARA-CP, op. cit., entry 229, box 24. Letter dated November 11, 1895 to Secretary of the Treasury from Holmes Conrad, solicitor general.

[57] This seated Lincoln became the prototype for Daniel Chester French's version in the *Lincoln Memorial*, Washington, DC.

stantial advance payment was sufficient to cover the considerable cost of travel and a Paris studio. For the next three years, Saint-Gaudens explored France, Spain and Italy from his Paris base while working on the *Sherman* and other large commissions.

Early in June 1900, while in his Paris studio, Saint-Gaudens began experiencing intestinal pain and in July was examined by three Parisian physicians. Within days he was on a ship back to New York to see an internal medicine specialist. Augusta wrote to their son, Homer, on July 25, just after Saint-Gaudens arrived:[58]

> Dear Homer,
> Your father has arrived and is very nervous as you may imagine. Still, he wasn't seasick and looks very well. Dr. Polk might not arrive until tomorrow morning so until then I suppose he will continue in this state of mind thinking he has something dreadful the matter with him, the result of 3 French doctors' examinations.... I can tell nothing until I have seen Dr. Polk.
> Lovingly,
> Mother

The Parisian doctors' diagnosis of intestinal cancer was confirmed and surgery was performed at Corey Hill Hospital in Brookline, Massachusetts to remove the tumor. Augusta wrote to Homer three days after the surgery:[59]

> ...Your father is better today altho suffering a great deal from gas in the stomach, which is always the case after operations on any one, Dr. Harrington is very much pleased with his progress & today seemed to waver in the opinion he expressed on Friday that the tumor would return much sooner than Dr. Richardson had thought viz. 5 or 6 years — so I am taking up my courage anew...I believe...as we all do the necessity of keeping it all from your father. He has good natural color & is beginning to eat a little.

By August 5, Saint-Gaudens had been discharged and was back at Aspet to recuperate and coordinate the return of models and casts from Paris.[60] The initial prognosis was better than it might have been: he could expect five to seven years before another operation would be necessary. But after follow-up surgery in November, Augusta seemed to feel the treatment was not as successful as the doctors thought. Augustus was often tired and had to take occasional doses of opium for the persistent pain.

During the next years, he tried everything: fad diets, electroshock, and radiation believing they would relieve pain or cure the cancer. His letter of April 15, 1903 to Dr. Edward Hooker Dewey is typical:[61]

> ...This is the eleventh day of the no breakfast whatever until 12:30, and I do not seem to get used to it; I am so faint that I almost stagger round the streets.
> The plan I adopted in Windsor of delaying my breakfast an hour beyond what was my custom and making it much lighter than had been my habit, seemed to produce better results in every way. By the time the breakfast hour has arrived now I am so faint I can hardly eat. Perhaps I delay taking the breakfast too long? I

---

[58] *SG*, Dartmouth, op. cit. Microfilm reel 22, frame 565–566. Letter dated July 25, [1900] to Homer from Augusta.

[59] *SG*, Dartmouth, op. cit. Microfilm reel 22, frame 261–263. Letter [last Sunday in July, 1900] to Homer from Augusta.

[60] Aspet was the name given to Saint-Gaudens' home and studio located near the village of Cornish, New Hampshire. Mail, shopping and railway connections were through the nearby town of Windsor, Vermont.

[61] Thomas B. Brumbaugh, *A Saint-Gaudens Correspondence.* Emory University Quarterly, Vol. XIII (December 1957), No.4, pp.239–244. Dr. Dewey was the author of several books dealing with diet and health that circulated in the early twentieth century.

get up at 7 o'clock. Do you think a glass of milk at breakfast is objectionable? You speak against the use of milk for sick people; do you think it is good for the strong?

Only radiation was partially successful in reducing the tumor's size. Exploratory surgery was performed in March 1906, but it gave no relief and did not arrest the spread of cancer.

## Senate Park Commission

In 1901 the Committee on the District of Columbia of the United States Senate appointed a commission known as the Senate Park Commission (or the McMillan Commission after Senator James McMillan, who was the committee chairman). The commission grew from ideas presented by the American Institute of Architects inspired by the centennial of Washington, DC in 1900. Its purpose was to examine ways to improve the appearance and public utility of the central portion of the capital city.

Initial appointees were Daniel H. Burnham, a Chicago architect, and Frederick Law Olmested, Jr., a Massachusetts landscape architect. Immediately upon appointment, the two invited architect Charles F. McKim to join the little committee. This triumvirate then decided they needed the advice of a "pure" artist, and the three convinced Augustus Saint-Gaudens to join them on the commission. All four were recognized experts in their professions, and made it their duty to make a study of the Washington area architecture, open spaces and parks. To gain a better understanding of open space and park design and their relationship to building designs, all except Saint-Gaudens made a short trip to Europe to study examples of the types of designs they envisioned for Washington.

By the time the commission disbanded at the end of 1901, it had recommended the adoption of the L'Enfant/LaTrobe plan of 1791, extensive parks in the city, and placement of a monument to Abraham Lincoln at the western end of the Mall, where it now stands. Their suggestions were collectively known as the *Plan of 1901 for Washington.*

Saint-Gaudens entered into some of the discussions and contributed to the overall concepts, but he was too busy with commissions and recuperation from his operations to play a leading role. It was a good opportunity for him to experience the new McKinley administration and renew acquaintance with Theodore Roosevelt, now vice-president of the United States and thoroughly bored with the job. The sculptor also met the commission's secretary, Charles Moore, who would later become chairman of the Commission of Fine Arts, which would oversee many government commissions awarded to Saint-Gaudens' former assistants.

# Chapter 2 – A Source of National Pride

More than a decade passed after the 1894 fiasco before Saint-Gaudens agreed to consider designing anything that involved the United States Bureau of the Mint.[62] During this interval his stature as sculptor and the leading American artist of the era increased. His memorial to Civil War hero Colonel Robert Gould Shaw found its home on The Common in central Boston, Massachusetts. Praise for the work was immediate and universal. Enthusiasts made special excursions to the city to view the memorial, some even spending the day watching as changing light exposed first one visual plane then another on the complex assembly of forms and faces.

*Figure 10. Memorial to Colonel Robert Gould Shaw, Boston, Massachusetts.* (Courtesy U. S. Department of Interior National Park Service, Saint-Gaudens National Historic Site, Cornish, NH.)

---

[62] His first twentieth-century commission involving the mint was for a government medal (designed by his brother, Louis) honoring Benjamin Franklin. The medals were produced by Tiffany & Co.

28

Equally lauded was the statue of General William Tecumseh Sherman installed at the entrance to Central Park in New York City. Models and preliminary castings of portions had been displayed at various art exhibitions for several years to critical acclaim. In 1903 the final version was complete and officially dedicated. Again, the praise was unanimous and international, reinforcing Saint-Gaudens' reputation and further increasing the demands on his time and talent. At a time when a respectable wage was $800 a year, Saint-Gaudens' studio and home, Aspet, cost $1,000 a week to sustain. Commissions for large-scale (and fee) heroic monuments were necessary to maintain the studios and workshops. Regardless of the talents of his assistants, the ultimate artistic vision was the Saint's.

*Figure 11. Monument to General William Tecumseh Sherman, New York.*

Location and the exact position relative to the sun of the Sherman statue were very important to Saint-Gaudens, and he fought for a site near the Grant Tomb as both artistically and historically optimum. After a chance meeting on a train returning from the Buffalo Exhibition in May 1901, he sought the intervention of vice-president Theodore Roosevelt in an attempt to secure his preferred location for the statue.[63]

> My dear Mr. Saint Gaudens:
> It was a great pleasure to catch a glimpse of you the other day in the cars. We certainly hope that Mrs. St. Gaudens and yourself can come out here for a night when next you are in New York. Probably you will never realize what a real comfort and source of pride you have been to me. I am very proud of America and very jealous of American achievement. It has been to me a source of real regret and concern to see how our writers have passed away and left no one to take their place and so no amount of more material achievement seems to me worth while, if taken purely by itself – I mean mere increase in wealth and in industrial facilities – it is always a relief to be able to think that there is one American in the prime of his powers who is leaving us the Lincoln, the Farragut, the Sherman, the monument to Shaw and so much else that represents a real addition to the national sum of permanent achievement.

*Theodore Roosevelt papers*, Library of Congress, Manuscript Division. Vol. 29, p.045, microfilm reel 326. Letter dated May 31, 1901 to Saint-Gaudens from Roosevelt.

With regards to Mrs. St. Gaudens, believe me,
Very sincerely yours,

PS: I have just received your letter and shall write to Root at once, urging the adoption of your view.

As promised, the vice-president wrote to Secretary of War Elihu Root:[64]

Dear Elihu:
Your pain at receiving a letter from me will be mitigated when I explain that it has nothing in the world to do with the Rough Riders, or with a commission for a gallant volunteer in the Philippines, nor with the application of a worthy comrade who served beside me at Santiago.
Will you look at the enclosed letter from Saint Gaudens? It explains itself. I think I have rarely seen a nobler monument than his Sherman. New York is thrice fortunate to have it, and it seems to me that it would be peculiarly appropriate to have it where saint Gaudens desires; that is, not far from Grant's tomb. The relationship between the two men was so close that this also would make it appropriate. Owing to the nature of the two monuments if either suffered it would be the Sherman, and Saint Gaudens' confidence that this will not be the case seems to me to be sufficient guaranty of the appropriateness from the artistic standpoint.
I am concerned over the Cuban situation. If it is proper for me to know anything about what is going on, I would be very much obliged.
Always yours,

Root contacted the Sherman Memorial Committee and used his most persuasive technique in support of Saint-Gaudens' preference. Unfortunately, both Sherman and Grant families refused to cooperate. "…General Dodge on behalf of the Sherman people and General Porter on behalf of the Grant Memorial Association both object."[65] Saint-Gaudens continued the location fight, giving up only after the 1903 dedication.

Between 1901 and early 1905 President Roosevelt and Saint-Gaudens exchanged occasional letters concerning artistic matters. These were generally limited to the President asking the sculptor for his opinion about a particular artist, or if someone were the best choice for a small government commission.[66] Saint-Gaudens' typical reply was to praise an artist if he felt him deserving – often one of his former assistants – and condemn anyone he felt was unworthy. Neither Roosevelt nor Saint-Gaudens was reticent about expressing his opinions although the artistic deference was toward Saint-Gaudens. Throughout the letters Roosevelt takes every opportunity to praise Saint-Gaudens' work and elevate his stature as an American artist. In an August 1903 letter, Roosevelt says "…your Sherman is the greatest statue of a commander in existence…I know of no man – of course of no one living – who could have done it. To take grim, homely, old Sherman, the type and ideal of a democratic general, and put with him an allegorical figure…[resulted in] striking the highest note of the sculptor's art."[67] Saint-Gaudens seemed touched by the President's comment

[64] *Roosevelt*, LoC, op. cit., vol. 29, p.070, microfilm reel 326. Letter dated June 1, 1901 to Elihu Root, Secretary of War from Roosevelt. (The "Cuban situation" refers to a proposal of the Cuban constitutional convention to limit American rights to lease naval bases and be involved in internal matters of Cuba.)
[65] *Roosevelt*, LoC, op. cit., vol. 29, p.129, microfilm reel 326. Letter dated June 6, 1901 to Saint-Gaudens from Roosevelt.
[66] John Gutzon de la Mothe Borglum, later designer of the Stone Mountain commemorative half dollar and initial design for the Stone Mountain, Georgia memorial, came in for special condemnation by Saint-Gaudens, although his brother Solon was highly praised for his animal sculptures.
[67] *SG*, Dartmouth, op. cit. Box 16, folder 35. Letter dated August 3, 1903 to Saint-Gaudens from Roosevelt.

and replied, "...when I realize that you have taken the time to say this to me, amid the multitude of other things on your mind, it...touches me deeply...."[68]

## Nobility of the President's Head: The Inaugural Medal

Roosevelt became President when President McKinley died in September 1901. But it was not until after he was elected President in his own right on November 5, 1904, that he seemed to become more aggressive with respect to matters relating to art and the coinage. This was consistent with Roosevelt's behavior in other arenas, and may have been a direct expression of greater confidence and his own increasingly "progressive" opinions about government policy. Through suggestions from painter Frank Millet and Roosevelt's wife, Edith, by late 1904 the President had concluded that the coins American workers carried in their pockets and received in pay envelopes were in need of artistic improvement. He wrote to Secretary of the Treasury Leslie Mortier Shaw on December 27, 1904:[69]

> My dear Secretary Shaw:
> I think our coinage is artistically of atrocious hideousness. Would it be possible, without asking permission of Congress, to employ a man like Saint-Gaudens to give us a coinage that would have some beauty?
> Sincerely yours,

Obviously, Roosevelt had developed an opinion and now wanted to do something about it. We don't know how this opinion was created, or if there was any defining moment when the President decided to act. However, Edith Roosevelt had spoken with Frank Millet on several occasions and the idea may have been prompted by Millet's comments. Based on other circumstances, Roosevelt usually came to a decision and sought action on it very quickly – he was not one to study the situation at length. Less than three weeks after the letter to Shaw, Roosevelt had "button-holed" Saint-Gaudens and flattered, cajoled and possibly bullied the artist into accepting the task of redesigning the coinage.

Roosevelt had consistently praised the artist in previous letters and public comments, but intense ego-stroking began with Saint-Gaudens attending the American Institute of Architects' (AIA) lavish dinner on January 11, 1905, followed by the annual Diplomatic Reception at the White House on January 12. The AIA dinner was a formal affair attended by over 250 guests including the President, several cabinet members, Supreme Court justices, a Catholic cardinal and an Episcopal bishop, architects from McKim, Meade and White, other notables and one sculptor – Saint-Gaudens. In a letter to his wife, Augusta, he described the event:[70]

> January 12, 1905
> I am here *faisant antechambre* to the Office of Secretary of War Taft, where I have come to talk about the Von Steuben monument. It's unpleasant, the waiting when you have no ax to grind, but all the more so when you are trying to do the decent thing by others.

---

[68] *SG*, Dartmouth, op. cit. Box 16, folder 35. Letter dated August 15, 1903 to Roosevelt from Saint-Gaudens.

[69] *Roosevelt Letters*, Harvard, op. cit., vol. 4, p.1088. Letter dated December 27, 1904 to Leslie Mortier Shaw from Roosevelt.

[70] *SG*, Dartmouth, op. cit. Box 21, folder 13. Letter (excerpt) dated January 12, 1905 to Augusta from Saint-Gaudens. This is the original text copied from the manuscript. Portions of this letter are quoted in Tharp's biography, and in the *Reminiscences (SG Reminiscences*, op. cit., vol. 2, pp.281–283), but the texts differ. The *Reminiscences* version omits the toastmaster being drunk and rewords many sentences. Homer Saint-Gaudens "edited" his father's letters for publication and it is likely he rewrote portions to present a more flattering portrait of his father.

Well Gussie, the dinner is over at 1:30 this morning. Henry James, LaFarge and his Jap valet Awoki (or some name like that), and I got into a cab built for two, and came home to bed. The dinner was a monumental success from the President of the A.I.A. who presided was toast master and who was quite drunk!, down to my speech which was decidedly the best because it was much the briefest.

You can get an impression of the dinner by the remarks made by Justice Harlan who said he "...could not refuse to come to a dinner at which would be the President of the United States, the Ambassador from the French Nation, the Cardinal of the Roman Catholic church, Gibbon, the great Secretary of State, Hay, the great ex-Secretary of War, Root, the Attorney General of the United States, [the Speaker of the House of Representatives], and last, but not least, *Saint-Gaudens.*

I read my speech after evidently one of the biggest storms of applause on rising. It was followed by still another as I sat down. Cassatt, President of the Pennsylvania Railroad, and Pierpont Morgan were there, the latter having given one hundred thousand dollars to the Academy of Rome, following the gift of a like amount the day before by Mr. Walters of Baltimore. It's an enormous triumph for McKim.

I enclose a copy of my speech which if memorized and delivered with the proper intonations of voice and vanity of smile, and quality of visage, would have been the sum of all that I said.

Here is the speech:

*"Charles the Charmer, in other words Charles F. McKim, has assured me that it is essential that I should speak tonight. This is as flattering as it is fallacious for although I have doubts about many things in life, on one subject I have absolutely none, and that is the hopeless and helpless limitations on my oratory. It is much more calculated to reduce listeners to tears than to contribute to their enlightenment or entertainment. You will therefore understand why I refrain from expressing anything more than my great pleasure at being included in a company assembled to honor that which makes for the nobility and elevation of life, the love of Beauty, Character, and Dignity in our surroundings as much in the halls of Government and Law as in our homes and wherever we live, move and have our being."*

Luncheon on the 12th was taken with Edith Roosevelt and several of her friends. After the diplomatic reception that evening, Saint-Gaudens was "swept upstairs for 'supper' amid a sea of velvet-and-gold lace uniforms." Writer Henry James found himself there also, sitting "one dowager away from Roosevelt…elsewhere, at a point hardly less privileged, next to Mrs. Roosevelt, sat sculptor Augustus Saint-Gaudens." Both creative men were seated well above many representatives of other nations as if to say, "art mattered here as much as politics."[71] During or just after dinner, Roosevelt evidently outlined his grand plan to remake the coinage. Like any good sportsman, the President set fresh bait for his quarry. Here the bait was to work directly with the President and to have a completely free hand in the inaugural medal and coin designs.[72] A convivial setting, plenty of food and spirits, and Roosevelt's ebullient personality conspired to bring the sculptor to Roosevelt's point of view, even if he didn't have time to complete the commissions he already had. His report to Augusta was simply, "I had an interesting time with Roosevelt."[73]

Unknown to Saint-Gaudens, painter and medal designer Francis (Frank) D. Millet, a creative favorite of Mrs. Roosevelt, had been commissioned by Secretary of War William Howard Taft to prepare nine military award medals for the Civil War, Spanish-

---

[71] Morris, *Theodore Rex.* op. cit., p.369–370.

[72] This is the same technique Roosevelt used later in the year to get the Russians and Japanese to end their war and agree on a peace settlement. He received the Nobel Peace Prize for his efforts.

[73] Tharp, *Saint-Gaudens and the Gilded Era*, op. cit., p.345.

American War, and Peking Relief Expedition.[74] Taft liked the new designs (which were accepted on January 11, 1905), and Millet had been approached in mid-December, 1904 by Edith about designing an inaugural medal for Roosevelt and also questioned about who could redesign the coins.[75] This may have been the stimulus for Roosevelt's letter to Shaw. Millet took a month to consider the situation and decided he didn't have the requisite skill to do justice to "the nobility of the president's head." It must have been a difficult situation for Millet since the opportunity to design a presidential medal free of interference from the mint engravers had never occurred before.

Millet wrote to Edith Roosevelt on January 13, with obvious emotion and concern:[76]

> Dear Mrs. Roosevelt:
> I must begin by begging pardon for inflicting a long letter upon you – because I fear this will be rather more extended than I could wish, and possibly I will try your patience. But the subject will, I am confident, excuse in some measure, the number of words.
> Briefly it is this.
> For a month or more I have had constantly in my mind the subject of the presidential medal and at last I have (with the encouragement of Mrs. Robinson) hardened my heart and made up my mind to make a clean breast of it to you.
> I cut from one of the New York Sunday papers the enclosed clip which is the fons et vrigo of my mental trouble. [An illustration of the U. S. Mint's inaugural medal by Charles Barber.]
> This medal will be dug up from the earth when Washington will be in ruins, when all other forms of art will have disappeared. That is no exaggeration.
> Then, all other arguments apart, this is a cogent reason why the medal should represent the nobility of the President's head.
> This medal to which I refer in the newspaper cutting has no nobility about it; it does not satisfy any of the cannons of the medallists' art; it is commonplace (even worse); it is a libel.
> You are too familiar with the President's profile to need to have your attention called to its character. You must have observed the nobility of the lines, the individual strength of the forms, the suggestive proportions. You know the ears, small, close to the head, refined but indicative of great strength, both physical and mental. The chin, the neck – in fact every point is his and his alone. To express this character, these characteristics, in a noble way, is the task of the medallist; it is his duty.
> Cannot you bring it about that the President shall have a medal which will at least hold its own? Why can't he have as good a medal as Millard Fillmore, for example?
> Until within a very few years this matter was considered of importance. Recently, however, it has fallen into such a place in the estimation of the authorities that at least one medal voted by Congress has never been struck at all, and out of the 86 official medals struck, the Mint has failed to preserve a goodly number of the dies.

---

[74] *Francis Millet Rogers papers*, Smithsonian Archives of American Art. Microfilm reel 1095, pp.1208–1213. The medals were: Civil War Campaign; Indian Campaign; Spanish Campaign; Spanish War Service; Army of Cuban Occupation; Army of Puerto Rican Occupation; Philippine Campaign; Philippine Congressional, and China Campaign.

[75] *Millet*, AAA, op. cit. Microfilm reel 1095. Letter dated December 14, 1904 to Millet from Edith Roosevelt.

[76] *Roosevelt*, LoC, op. cit. Microfilm reel 52. Letter dated January 13, 1905 to Edith Roosevelt from Millet.

Here, Millet inserted an 1846 quotation from General Winfield Scott calling medals monuments to history and to individual distinction. Three days later the quote appeared in one of Roosevelt's letters. Millet continued his letter to Edith:

> "As medals are among the surest monuments of history as well as monuments of individual distinction, there should be given to them, besides intrinsic value and durability of material, the utmost grace of design with the highest finish in mechanical execution. * * * * What the state of this art (The medallists' art) may be now in the United States, I know not. But I beg leave again to suggest that the honor of the country requires that medals voted by Congress should always exhibit the arts involved, in their highest state of perfection wherever found, for letters, science and the fine arts constitute but one republic, embracing the world. So thought our early government and Mr. Jefferson – a distinguished member of that general republic."
>
> In order to point my moral, I am sending with this the set of eight medals struck by the French mint in honor of patriots of Revolutionary Times. They were, with the exception of the Lafayette, ordered by Congress through Mr. Jefferson. If you care to keep the set it would give me great pleasure to have you do so. At all event, you will enjoy seeing them and you will see by these examples what I mean by nobility in a medal.
>
> And, to repeat, why cannot we have of President Roosevelt a medal which will be at least as good as the average of these presidential medals or the Indian medals?
>
> I was very glad to hear the President say that Art is not the most important thing. I never thought it was myself and that is why I have had to take occasional flutters into more active fields. But it has sufficient degree of importance in any community to demand the thoughtful attention of the authorities and we cannot afford to be at the end of the procession in this regard. I refrain, with difficulty, from any critical allusion to our coinage, and our postage stamps.
>
> > "The medal faithful to its charge of fame,
> > "Tho' chimes and ages bears each form and name,
> > "In one short view subjected to our eye,
> > "Gods, emp'rors, heroes, sages, beauties lie."
> > *Pope's epistle to Addison.*
>
> I shall be disappointed if this matter does not enlist your interest and I promise you to say nothing more about it. And I shall also hope that you will accept the medals I send in the spirit in which I offer them. They have slight, very slight intrinsic value but they are worth looking at because they give one an exalted idea of the personages whom they honor.
>
> May I add my thanks for your presence at the dinner the other night?
>
> Yours faithfully,

Underneath the florid prose, Millet was declining the medal commission based on a personal assessment of his skills. He also refused to comment on the coinage, which suggests that the subject, possibly including Saint-Gaudens' involvement, may have been discussed in December at the same time as the medal.

34

*Figure 12. Official presidential inaugural medal (top) designed in 1901 by Charles E. Barber, engraver of the U. S. Mint, as copied by Joseph K. Davison's Sons, Inc. in 1905. One thousand five hundred bronze specimens were struck (44.4mm diameter). Below is the mint's revised version from the presidential medal series with a reverse design by George Morgan.* (Top photos courtesy Presidential Coin & Antique Co., Inc.)

When the President read Edith's letter from Millet, he must have realized that Frank Millet had given him the perfect bait to dangle in front of the cautious Saint-Gaudens: a private, presidential commission for the inaugural medal. Although the coins were on Roosevelt's agenda, he first wanted to deal with design of a small medal to commemorate his inauguration. Naturally, Saint-Gaudens had some reservations about anything to do with the U. S. Mint even if the President was personally pushing the bureaucrats. He had likely expressed these impediments to Roosevelt during the dinner conversation.

Roosevelt had a short conversation with secretary Shaw, who provided a copy of the relevant U. S. Code, the President then followed up with a letter on January 16:[77]

> The Secretary of the Treasury:
> In accordance with our conversation and the agreement we came to in connection with the coinage, I would like you to submit this letter to the Director of the Mint. I suppose it comes under his immediate supervision.
> In the first place, about the coinage. How soon will it be possible to have Saint-Gaudens employed for at least one set of coins? Of course he is to be given an absolutely free hand. This is not a reflection upon the Director of the Mint or any of his subordinates. It is out of the question that great artists should be put in the po-

---

[77] *Roosevelt Letters*, Harvard, op. cit., vol. 4, pp.1103–1104. Letter dated January 16, 1905 to Shaw from Roosevelt.

sition of Director of the Mint or of his subordinates, if only for the reason that they would probably be wholly incompetent to do the work; but it is of the utmost importance that the artist should be left absolutely unhampered in working out the design and execution of the coin or medal. I do not wish there to be the slightest interference with Saint-Gaudens in connection with the coinage from its artistic side. Please have the matter taken up at the earliest moment, and advise me about it. In the next place, please have the Director of the Mint write at once to Saint-Gaudens, and to F. D. Millet, whose address is 6 West 23rd Street, New York City, as to the medal to be struck for the inauguration. General Winfield Scott, in July 1846, wrote to the Secretary of War in regard to the medal for the Mexican War veterans as follows:

"As medals are among the surest monuments of history as well as monuments of individual distinction, there should be given to them, besides intrinsic value and durability of material, the utmost grace of design with the highest finish in mechanical execution. * * * * What the state of this art (The medallists' art) may be now in the United States, I know not. But I beg leave again to suggest that the honor of the country requires that medals voted by Congress should always exhibit the arts involved, in their highest state of perfection wherever found, for letters, science and the fine arts constitute but one republic, embracing the world. So thought our early government and Mr. Jefferson – a distinguished member of that general republic."

We find that all artists are one in feeling that our recent medals are markedly inferior to the medals struck for foreign nations, notably the French. I desire that this medal represent fine artistic work, and that either Saint-Gaudens or someone chosen by Millet and Saint-Gaudens be given an absolutely free hand in making it. Please have an immediate report made to me on this matter also.

Very truly yours,

Roosevelt devotes approximately equal space to the coinage redesign and the inaugural medal. Interestingly, however, he inserted the quotation from General Scott that Millet had used in the letter to Edith to bolster his argument. The coinage terms are reasonably clear: Saint-Gaudens will design at least one "set" of coins; and, he is to have a completely free hand in artistic aspects of the design.[78] The medal work is more ambiguous: Millet and Saint-Gaudens are to select a sculptor, who will have complete freedom in the design work. The next day Roosevelt expanded on these concepts in a letter to Saint-Gaudens:[79]

My dear St. Gaudens:

It appears that under the law the silver coinage can not be changed until 1917, and the five cent nickel piece can not be changed until 1908. The gold coins and the one cent piece are the only ones that can be changed now without act of Congress. But I suppose that gold coins are really the most important. Could you make designs for these; and what would be the expense?

Unfortunately, there is no authority to employ an artist to make designs for the inaugural medal. The medals made at the mint can be designed by the regular force of engravers, or a design paid for from some other source than the regular appropriation. It is possible, however, that I could get some outside appropriation by which I could pay for a design for the medal, and then direct the mint people to execute it. The mint people would be entirely competent to work out the design,

---

[78] This is similar to the approach that was used in France, where outside artists made the designs and engravers at the *Monnaie de Paris* cut suitable dies. The differences in results were due partially to the inexperience of the American engravers with modern reducing lathes.

[79] *Roosevelt*, LoC, op. cit., vol. 53, pp.300–301. Microfilm reel 337. Letter dated January 17, 1905 to Saint-Gaudens from Roosevelt.

would they not? What about this? Now, can you tell me about what the cost of a design for the medal would be? Then I will see whether I can get means to pay for it. Would you mind consulting with Frank Millet on this matter? It was delightful to get a glimpse of you at supper the other evening.

Sincerely yours,

The additional details probably came from the same meeting with secretary Shaw, but were not important to repeat in the President's letter to Shaw. The commission for Saint-Gaudens included four gold coins and possibly the cent. Roosevelt wanted to know if the sculptor could make designs for these coins and if so, what the cost would be. Secretary Shaw sent Saint-Gaudens a short letter confirming the conversation during the president's diplomatic reception, also asking, "I write to ascertain whether, in your opinion, the gold coins can be improved on. If so, what will be your charge for the designs?"[80]

Terms for the inaugural medal are also more clearly stated. There was no authority to hire a medallist for the inaugural medal, but the President said he might be able to find funding from private sources. Roosevelt asked if the mint staff would be competent to make the medals from an outside design, and what the cost of design would be. Lastly, he wanted Saint-Gaudens to contact Frank Millet and discuss the medal with him. Saint-Gaudens replied on January 20:[81]

Dear Mr. President:

If the inauguration medal is to be ready for March the first, there is not a moment to lose. I cannot do it, but have arranged with the man best fitted to execute it in this country [Adolph A. Weinman]. He has a most artistic nature, extremely diffident. He would do an admirable thing. He is also supple and takes suggestion intelligently. He has made one of the great Indian groups at St. Louis that would have interested you if brought to your attention. He is so interested that he begged me to fix a[ny] price. I named two hundred and fifty dollars…

…That is a low sum for such work although he considers it would be fair remuneration. I assume the cutting of the die and the striking of the medals will be done at the mint, if not, that part will cost $. [The cutting of the die can be done perfectly at the mint, the question is whether they can do it within the time. Of course nothing elaborate can be done in the period, it must be simple, but that simplicity can be well done and impressive.]

…In the matter of the coinage I will write you tomorrow or Monday after and in the meantime will see Millet.

The basic terms of the two commissions were now established. Saint-Gaudens was to redesign the United States' gold coins and possibly the cent. He was to have complete artistic freedom within the limits of coinage law, with the cost and schedule yet to be determined. The inauguration medal was supposed to be ready in March, so it took precedence. It also suited Roosevelt and Saint-Gaudens to have a small project together and completed before the coinage was addressed. The coins were put aside until the medal was finished.[82] Interestingly, the sculptor says the die cutting "can be done perfectly at the mint" – presumably including Charles Barber's work.

---

[80] *US Mint*; NARA-CP, op. cit., entry 330, box 45. Letter dated January 18, 1905 to Saint-Gaudens from Shaw.

[81] *Reminiscences*, op. cit., vol. 2, p.253. Letter (excerpt) dated January 20, 1905 to Roosevelt from Saint-Gaudens; top paragraph. *SG*, Dartmouth, op. cit. Box 16, folder 36 contains the original manuscript draft including the last two paragraphs of the quotation, and the bracketed text in the first paragraph.

[82] The complete story of the 1905 inaugural medal would occupy more space than is available in this volume, so only a summary has been presented here.

General John M. Wilson, chairman of the Inaugural Committee, provided Saint-Gaudens with a photo of the mint's Roosevelt inaugural medal by Charles Barber that elicited the following comment from the sculptor:[83]

Dear Mr. President:
General Wilson showed me the inauguration medal, which is so deadly that I had Weinman go down to Philadelphia. The man there who has charge of the bulk of the ordinary medals already contracted for cannot possibly do an artistic work. He is a commercial medallist with neither the means nor the power to rise above such an average. Mr. Weinman writes to General Wilson tonight that our reliefs must be put into other hands and this is to beg you to insist that the work be entrusted to Messrs. Tiffany or Gorham. Otherwise I would not answer for its not being botched.

...I made studies on the train on my way up from Washington and I have struck a composition which I hope will come out well. Mr. Weinman is enthusiastic about it and I am certain would execute it admirably. You know that the disposition of the design on the medal is nine-tenths of the battle.

In other matters my composition calls for the simplest form of inscription and here also I wish your support, of course provided you think well of the idea. On the side of your portrait I propose placing nothing more than the words, "Theodore Roosevelt, President of the United States" and on the reverse, under the emblematic design, the words. "Washington, D. C., March 4, 1905."

The simplicity of inscription greatly aids the dignity of the arrangement; but if you believe that more is needed, I will add it with pleasure.

Roosevelt responded by supporting everything Saint-Gaudens wanted to do:[84]

My dear Mr. Saint Gaudens:
I have your letter and shall at once take the matter up with General Wilson. I think I can arrange everything as you desire, including the lettering. I should think "President of the United States" would do; although the full title is, I believe, "President of the United States of America."

Let me know when you get to the coin matter, which I suppose will be some months hence.

With hearty thanks,
Sincerely yours,

The President sent a copy of Saint-Gaudens' letter to General Wilson asking that he do everything possible to comply with the artist's wishes.[85] Adolph Weinman worked diligently to convert the Saint's rough design sketches into plaster models. Because of the press of other commissions and failing health, Saint-Gaudens appears to have done little of the actual work on the models. Weinman remodeled the eagle from the Shaw monument and Saint-Gaudens added several small adjustments. The size of lettering was changed several times, as were other details. The portrait of Roosevelt was completed largely from photographs, although Weinman did get one afternoon sitting with the President.

A blustery March 4 Presidential Inauguration came and went without the Saint-Gaudens medal. As late as the end of February, Tiffany's was promising Weinman delivery of part of the order by March 3, but the committee's indecision about size of the med-

[83] *Reminiscences*, op. cit., vol. 2, p.254. Letter dated January 2?, 1905 to Roosevelt from Saint-Gaudens.
[84] *Roosevelt*, LoC, op. cit., vol. 53, p.417A, microfilm reel 337. Letter dated January 28, 1905 to Saint-Gaudens from Roosevelt.
[85] *Roosevelt*, LoC, op. cit., vol. 53, p.419, microfilm reel 337. Letter dated January 28, 1905 to Gen. John M. Wilson, Chairman, Inaugural Committee from Roosevelt.

38

als prevented timely production. Additionally, Saint-Gaudens made small changes to the designs even as Weinman was pushing Tiffany's to make casts from one set of designs or another. Reductions and master casts were made by Henri Weil (who would later figure prominently in producing the first 1907 experimental double eagles) and there were frequent problems with quality of the work. Since the cost of medals was being paid by the committee, every change in specification resulted in a new cost estimate which had to be reviewed and approved. By the time the committee settled on seventy-four millimeter (about 2 7/8-inches) diameter medals – two in fourteen-karat gold for the President and vice-president,[86] and 120 in bronze – the inaugural was over and General Wilson was tying up loose ends.[87] The President left on April 2 for a two month-long tour of the western states, and it is unlikely the medal was much in his thoughts.

The first completed medals were not delivered until July 6, when an obviously pleased Saint-Gaudens wrote:[88]

Dear Mr. President:
The medal is completed and was to be sent to General Wilson yesterday by Messrs. Tiffany & Co. who did the metal casting.
As far as the actual casting in gold is concerned, I wish it were better, but it is impossible to have it executed in this country as it should be and as is done by workmen in their little shops in France. This is the best that can be produced in the United States.
As to the designs, I am responsible for the composition and interpretation and supervised closely its execution by Mr. Weinman. He has done his work admirably, following my desires with great conscience. He deserves high credit and it is a pleasure for me to have our initials together on the work.
I send you by this mail a bronze replica, which although precisely similar to the gold, has more vigor and character because of the better treatment of the metal.
Allow me to thank you for this opportunity to help in the execution of a medalic production connected with the United States Government. It has been a great pleasure as well as a duty to be so associated with your administration.
I have waited for the experience I would have in this work before taking steps about the coinage. I will now write to the Secretary of the Treasury in reference to that.
Not withstanding my great desire to accede to your wish that I execute the statue of President McKinley, the project will fall through I fear, because the sum at the disposal of the committee is far below what I receive for work of that character and importance.
Faithfully yours,

[86] *SG*, Dartmouth, op. cit. Box 20, folder 27. Letter dated March 13, 1905 to Saint-Gaudens from Weinman. Vice-president Charles Warren Fairbanks from Indiana was not mentioned on either the U. S. Mint or the private inaugural medals. His gold medal was given as a courtesy, nothing more. Roosevelt thought Fairbanks was useless and didn't mention him in his autobiography.
[87] The limited number produced was intentional. Roosevelt wanted one medal for each member of the committee, plus 35 for personal distribution to cabinet members and friends. Saint-Gaudens received one from George Kunz of Tiffany's only after the President specifically approved the transaction.
[88] *Roosevelt*, LoC, op. cit. Microfilm reel 56. Letter dated July 6, 1905 to Roosevelt from Saint-Gaudens.

*Figure 13. 1905 inaugural medal authorized by the Inaugural Committee. Designed by Saint-Gaudens and modeled by Adolph A. Weinman. Notice the extensive (some might say excessive) use of periods, or "text stops," before and after words and each of the Roman numerals. (Medal is 73.6 millimeters in diameter.)*

The President wrote back on the 8th indicating his pleasure with the medal, particularly with the bronze example.[89]

> My dear Saint Gaudens:
> Really I do not know whether to thank most Frank Millet, who first put it in my rather dense head that we ought to have a great artist to design these medals, or to thank you for consenting to undertake the work. My dear fellow, I am very grateful to you, and I am very proud to have been able to associate you in some way with my administration. I like the medals immensely but that goes without saying for the work is entirely characteristic of you. I thank heaven we have at last some artistic work of permanent worth done for the Government.
> Will you present my compliments and thanks to Mr. Weinman? Perhaps you know that we got him to undertake the life-saving medal, also.
> I was rather exasperated with the McKinley Memorial Committee at their failure to understand what securing your services of course meant.
> With hearty thanks,
> Faithfully yours,
>
> *(Handwritten note below signature)*
> I don't want to flop over, but I feel just as if we had suddenly implanted a little of Greece of the 5th or 4th centuries B. C. into America; and am very proud and very grateful that I personally happen to be the beneficiary.
> I like the special bronze medal particularly.

The medal was not actually "…done for the government…" but was a private commission by the Inaugural Committee: the governmental insinuation served Roosevelt's purpose. As soon as more examples became available, Roosevelt sent bronze copies to members of the cabinet, committee and several friends. Public perception was carefully maintained that the President was exceptionally pleased with the entire medal. However, in

[89] *Roosevelt*, LoC, op. cit., vol. 56 pp.299–300. Microfilm reel 338. Letter dated July 8, 1905 to Saint-Gaudens from Roosevelt.

a private letter to Secretary of State John Hay, Roosevelt suggested the obverse portrait was less than fully satisfactory:[90]

> .....Will you tell Nannie that I have sent her at Nahant one of the Saint-Gaudens inauguration medals. I am very glad we got Saint-Gaudens to do this work. Edith makes me believe that she thinks it is a good likeness of me, which I regard as most wifely on her part. [emphasis added] But of the eagle on the reverse I do approve and also of the Latin rendering for "a square deal." [aequum cuique]

Artistic opinion of the time was kept in check, but later critics complained about the scrawny-necked image of Roosevelt.[91] Saint-Gaudens wrote back to the President on July 14:[92]

> Dear Mr. President:
> Your very kind letter of July 8th is at hand.
> It is a positive delight to do for so appreciative a man.
> If you will send a short note to Mr. Weinman you will please a deserving man immensely and if there are other medals you can [direct ?] the execution of, [you] may consider Mr. John Flanagan, 107 East 27th Street, N.Y. City and Mr. Earl Fraser, 3 MacDougal Alley, N. Y. City, they are both talented and would do excellent work.
> Faithfully yours,

The President did as asked, then wrapped up his letters of appreciation with one to Frank Millet stating: "I am very, very proud at having Saint-Gaudens connected in any way with my administration – and you too, my dear fellow, for the thought was yours."[93]

With successful completion of the Roosevelt inaugural medal Saint-Gaudens had gained confidence in the President's determination to follow through on his promises. It also gave him a somewhat misleading impression of what it would be like to design the gold coins and cent.

## Defining The Coinage Commission – 1905

We don't know precisely when the idea to redesign the coinage occurred to the President. Circumstantial evidence indicates the suggestion was made by painter Frank Millet during a December dinner with President and Mrs. Roosevelt. Millet was a friend of Edith Roosevelt and perfectly capable of originating the unusual phrase "...artistically of atrocious hideousness..." the President used when he wrote to secretary Shaw. The earliest letter mentioning this possibility is the one to Shaw of December 27, 1904, six weeks after Roosevelt won a landslide victory at the polls. "I think our coinage is artistically of atrocious hideousness. Would it be possible to employ a man like Saint-Gaudens to give us a coinage that would have some beauty?"[94]

This letter (quoted in full earlier) suggests one or more previous conversations with Frank Millet, Edith, and possibly others about the coinage, and indicates the President had

---

[90] *Roosevelt Letters*, Harvard, op. cit., vol. 4, pp.1270–1272. Letter dated July 11, 1905 to John Hay from Roosevelt. (Excerpt from last paragraph; balance of letter is not relevant.)

[91] See also, Cornelius Vermeule's caustic opinion of the medal, including a comment about the portrait looking like "...some relative of the German Kaiser," in *Numismatic Art In America,* pp.109–110.

[92] *Roosevelt*, LoC, op. cit. Microfilm reel 56. Letter dated July 14, 1905 to Roosevelt from Saint-Gaudens. The letter of appreciation was sent to Adolph Weinman July 17.

[93] *Millet*, AAA, op. cit. Microfilm reel 1097, frame 1017. Letter dated July 15, 1905 to Millet from Roosevelt.

[94] *Roosevelt Letters*, Harvard, op. cit., vol. 4, p.1088. Letter dated December 28, 1904 to Shaw from Roosevelt.

already decided to sidestep the mint engravers. By the time of the AIA dinner Roosevelt had a better concept of what he wanted done with the coinage, and probably outlined the plan to Saint-Gaudens during the evening. (The confluence of Millet's letter, AIA dinner, Diplomatic Reception and treasury department letters imply that several undocumented conversations occurred during the first weeks of January.)

In early 1905, Director of the Mint George E. Roberts wrote to Saint-Gaudens indicating the treasury department was interested in making changes to the current coin designs, and asking for his suggestions.[95] Saint-Gaudens and the President had possibly agreed on a plan during the American Institute of Architects' dinner on January 12, so the letter was a formality. A letter from the President on January 17 narrowed the coinage redesign somewhat:[96]

> My dear St. Gaudens:
> It appears that under the law the silver coinage can not be changed until 1917, and the five cent nickel piece cannot be changed until 1908. The gold coins and the one cent piece are the only ones that can be changed now without act of Congress. But I suppose the gold coins are really the most important. Could you make designs for these; what would be the expense?

Saint-Gaudens replied to director Roberts on January 20 telling him it would be a pleasure to help, but "…I shall need some time for thought and consultation with others…"[97] The next months were occupied with the inaugural medal and nothing more was said of the coinage until Saint-Gaudens' letter to the President on July 6, 1905 announcing the completion of the medal. "I have waited for the experience I would have in this work before taking steps about the coinage. I will now write to the Secretary of the Treasury in reference to that."[98]

The sculptor sent director Roberts a much-delayed reply to his January inquiry:[99]

> Dear Sir:
> I have postponed giving a definite reply with regard to the design of the coinage till after my experience with the Inaugural medal, which I knew would help me in forming conclusions as to the cost.
> I shall state $5,000 (five thousand dollars) as my price for making the designs for both side of the gold pieces and the penny. In fixing this amount I name a sum considerably below what I receive for work of like character.
> I have this so much at heart, however, that should the sum I have named prove greater than the funds at your disposal, I should be glad to consider the execution of the models for whatever amount there may be at your command for the purpose.
> I assume the same design may be adopted for both the gold and copper coinage. Should some part of the latter require different treatment, that would necessitate some further remuneration. This however, can be decided later.
> I think it will be necessary that I supply the die [hub] also, as (unless I am mistaken) the machine at the mint requires retouching of the dies by hand. The modern one obviates that.
> Yours very truly,

---

[95] *SG*, Dartmouth, op. cit. Box 19, folder 34. Letter dated January 13, 1905 to Saint-Gaudens from Roberts.

[96] *Roosevelt*, LoC, op. cit., vol. 53, pp.300–301, microfilm reel 337. Letter dated January 17, 1905 to Saint-Gaudens from Roosevelt.

[97] *SG*, Dartmouth, op. cit. Box 16, folder 28. Letter dated January 20, 1905 to Roberts from Saint-Gaudens.

[98] *Roosevelt*, LoC, op. cit. Microfilm reel 56; two pages. Letter dated July 6, 1905 to Roosevelt from Saint-Gaudens.

[99] *SG*, Dartmouth, op. cit. Box 16, folder 28. Letter dated July 10, 1905 to Roberts from Saint-Gaudens.

The basic terms of the commission were now set forth:

1. Saint-Gaudens would make obverse and reverse coin designs;
2. These would be used on the gold coins and the cent;
3. Saint-Gaudens would provide hubs (steel reductions);
4. If additional designs were needed the compensation could be adjusted;
5. The fee was to be $5,000, but negotiable based on available funds.

On this basis Saint-Gaudens began work designing the gold coins and cent. More than money was on the artist's mind, as evidenced by his notation on a draft press release about the inaugural medal:[100]

> I think that this is all very good – must be, to be grateful to the President for that we do not have to hide our faces when at least one of the American coins or medals is seen.

Evidently he decided to use the same process for the coins as for the inaugural medal. He would make the designs, and another sculptor would make the models based on the designs and his personal "advisement."[101] This had been reasonably successful for the medal in part because of the skill and personal interest of Adolph Weinman. Also, during inaugural medal work Saint-Gaudens was in better health than in 1906–07. For the coin project, Henry Hering, Saint-Gaudens' principal assistant, and an artist of lesser talent than Weinman, would be doing the models. Hering probably had greater difficulty realizing the Saint's creativity in plaster than did Weinman. It is possible that had Weinman or Jim Fraser been working with Saint-Gaudens, some of the difficulties might have been avoided, or at least minimized. Weinman, in particular, was already known to the President through the inaugural medal. Later, both Fraser and Weinman were to tangle with Charles Barber and the mint bureaucracy, with results that were somewhat closer to their artistic vision.

## Factory in Philadelphia

The Philadelphia Mint was, and still is, a factory for the manufacture of coins. During the era of the coinage renaissance from 1905 to 1921, it was a complete, self-contained production facility. Raw materials came in, were fabricated into components, products were made, and customers ordered the finished goods. The mint's raw materials were gold, silver, copper and nickel for coins, and tool steel for hubs, dies and machinery repair, as well as coal, gas and electricity. The components were dies, planchets, logo punches; and the finished products were coins and medals. The customers were the United States Treasury, foreign governments, and small numbers of commissions and official organizations for whom medals and commemorative coins were produced.

Most of the time the mint was demand-driven – the Treasurer of the United States requested certain quantities of each denomination of coin, and the mint was expected to

---

[100] *SG*, Dartmouth, op. cit. Microfilm reel 23, #717. Draft press release undated (partial) by Homer Saint-Gaudens with Augustus' annotations.

[101] This is the term Saint-Gaudens used in a draft press release about the inaugural medal. Homer had written the draft and the sculptor made a few editorial changes including crossing out the word "supervisement" and replacing it with "advisement." It suggests advice rather than daily supervision of the person making the model.

supply them quickly. To support demand, the various mints usually had coins stored in their vaults ready for shipment to sub-treasuries or major banks. The Bureau of the Mint in Washington coordinated production for the four operating facilities (mints in Philadelphia, Denver, New Orleans and San Francisco) and bullion handling at the assay offices. Due to the cost and delay involved in transporting coin large distances, production was often driven by local/regional economics. For example, the 1907 Knickerbocker Trust financial panic, which boosted demand for gold coin, was limited to New York and northeast United States – Chicago, Denver, St. Louis and San Francisco were almost completely unaffected. Coin was occasionally transferred from one mint or assay office to another, but every effort was made to keep this to a minimum.

Like any well-run factory, the Philadelphia Mint attempted to operate on a consistent production schedule, balancing input of materials with demand for coins. The reality was often different, with demand and production fluctuating from week to week. The cost of production was largely dependent on the number of people required to complete all steps necessary to make the coins. One of the ways the mint dealt with this variability was to reduce staff whenever there was a lessening of demand for coins. The mint had a small number of professional supervisory personnel, another group of skilled mechanics, a group of experienced adjusters (nearly always women), press operators, several clerical and auditing staff, and a large number of semi-skilled and unskilled laborers. During peak-demand periods, the mint hired men for this last group as temporary laborers. When demand fell, temporary workers were fired, often to be rehired a few days later when the treasury sent an order for more coinage.

The mint superintendent tried to keep all departments running at an even pace. Enough ingots of gold, silver, copper and copper-nickel had to be cast and rolled to supply stock to the cutting mills, which made the blanks, without having too many or too few metal strips on hand. Planchets, blanks that had been through the upsetting mill, needed to be available but could not pile up waiting to be coined – the blanks could easily tarnish if not struck soon after annealing and cleaning. Enough gold adjusters had to be available to provide correct-weight planchets for the coining department. Weighers had to be available to check the pieces after they were struck and group them into "lights" and "heavies" for bagging. Dies had to be available to the chief coiner, but making too many dies would be a waste of time and tool steel if demand slackened. Dies also had to be made for the branch mints and each branch had different demands from their local sub-treasuries than the Philadelphia Mint.[102] It was not uncommon for the eastern states to have low demand for gold while western state banks were clamoring for more gold coin. Late in each calendar year the director attempted to predict how much coinage was needed and where it should be struck. He was as often right as he was wrong. If special work were added to the normal ebb and flow of production operations, it could severely impact the ability to respond to the Treasurer's requests – and that was not acceptable.

Engraver Barber was sent to Europe in early May 1905 to investigate the equipment and methods used by the largest European mints.[103] This was possibly in response to

---

[102] Working dies were often made in advance, then stamped with a mintmark if one of the branch mints needed dies. Working dies for the next calendar year were made as early as October, but routinely in November and December in anticipation of the next production year. Occasionally, coins were produced in large quantities before a new design was formally designated. This was the case in July 1909, when the Philadelphia Mint produced 20 million new Lincoln cents before the secretary of the treasury had issued official production orders.

[103] *US Mint*; NARA-CP, op. cit., entry 229, box 232. Report dated July 31, 1905 to Roberts from Barber.

44

Roosevelt's coinage redesign ideas of which director Roberts was aware. The journey was semi-official in the sense that Barber was an employee of the United States whose task was to officially report on European mint operations. However, so far as the United States government was concerned, he was traveling as a private citizen and no assistance was provided by the local American embassies. Visits were made to national mints in Italy, Austria, Switzerland, Belgium, France and England, where the engraver examined planchet preparation, coinage operations and medal finishing among other topics of his investigation. He returned in late July 1905 only a few weeks after Saint-Gaudens had officially accepted the commission to redesign the nation's gold coins.[104]

Within the carefully managed "golden dance" at the Philadelphia Mint, any disruption was unappreciated. During 1907, when a new design model came in from Saint-Gaudens, hubs and dies were created as quickly as possible and samples prepared. However, once that was done the mint staff had to wait for a response from the artist's studio. This created disruption in the orderly flow of work and was likely viewed by staff as intrusive and unnecessary.

---

[104] *US Mint*, NARA-CP, op. cit., entry 229, box 232. Memorandum dated July 27, 1905 to Roberts from Barber.

# Chapter 3 – Simply Immense

While coinage ideas took shape in Saint-Gaudens' thoughts, Roosevelt was engaged in international diplomacy. Japan and Russia had been at war for some time, with Japan quickly gaining the upper hand. The Russian city of Port Arthur in Siberia, under siege for months, was captured on January 1, 1905. European sentiment heavily favored Russia with its large store of weapons and huge navy: the Siberian setbacks were thought to be temporary. Roosevelt left subtle hints and suggestions that the United States was prepared to help negotiate a peace treaty. America's ambassador to Russia, George von Lengerke Meyer, did the same with Tsar Nicholas II, but both efforts fell on deaf ears. By May 27, the Russian Baltic Fleet, having come halfway around the world, finally sailed into battle against the Japanese at Tsu Shima. The result was a rout of Russia's fleet. Twenty-two ships including four new battleships were sunk, and Russia's Commander, Admiral Rozhdestvenski, was captured. Japan lost three torpedo boats.[105]

Despite a resounding Japanese victory, Roosevelt sensed Japan's resources were strained and took the opportunity to push both countries to the negotiating table. After months of careful personal diplomacy by the young American President (and some fruitful ground work by William H. Taft, who was in Japan at the time and visited with Japanese Prime Minister Katsura), the *Treaty of Portsmouth* was signed September 5, ending the Russo-Japanese War.[106] Praise for Roosevelt came from throughout the world, and in December 1906 he became the first American to be awarded the Nobel Peace Prize.[107] Off of

---

[105] Morris, *Theodore Rex.* pp.367–395.

[106] Russia was to experience mutiny aboard the battleship *Potemkin* and revolution resulting in the formation of an elected Duma (or parliament). Tsar Nicholas II continued his befuddled reign under the thumb of Tsarina Alexandra until 1917. The humiliation of Russia put Japan on the world scene as a major power in Asia and of considerable influence elsewhere. The analogy with the little island nation of Great Britain was lost on no one, especially Roosevelt, who again warned against naval complacency, as he had done a decade earlier as assistant secretary of the navy.

[107] Theodore Roosevelt tried to use the Nobel Prize money to establish a foundation to promote industrial peace in the United States through a committee of Congress. The idea failed, and during the World War Roosevelt asked Congress to authorize return of the money. Congress passed legislation to do this and Roosevelt then donated the fund to charities and war relief work.

his diplomatic triumph and looking toward future battles with the Senate, Roosevelt used the new coin designs as a personal diversion and "secret" jibe at Congress.

The tactic of having Saint-Gaudens complete the inaugural medal before beginning work on the coin was successful. It gave the artist an opportunity to see how much time it took to work with government officials and also tested the resolve of President Roosevelt to give him a free hand in creating a design. Roosevelt got a clearer idea of how artists worked and of the possible delays that could be expected. It is obvious that without the prodding of General Wilson and his control of the Inaugural Committee, the work would have taken much longer and could have been a fiasco.

Saint-Gaudens worked on pencil sketches of possible designs for the double eagle and cent during the late summer and early autumn. These are found on scraps of paper, note sheets from the *Players Club* in New York – whatever was handy when an idea struck. There are few documents mentioning the coins, possibly because everyone at Aspet was concentrating on the large-scale works filling the studios.

The President had been browsing the Smithsonian Museum's collection of artifacts, and was taken by the strength and beauty of some of the ancient Greek coins, particularly those of Alexander the Great of Macedonia and his father, Phillip II.

*Figure 14. Examples of ancient Greek coins possibly seen by President Roosevelt during a visit to the Smithsonian Museum in November 1905. (L to R) Alexander the Great – silver tetradrachm, gold stater; gold stater of Phillip II.*

By November 1905, President Roosevelt was wondering how things were progressing with the coin designs and wrote to Saint-Gaudens:[108]

> My dear St. Gaudens:
> How is that gold coinage design getting along? I want to make a suggestion. It seems to me worth while to try for a really good coinage, though I suppose there will be a revolt about it! I was looking at some gold coins of Alexander the Great today, and I was struck by their high relief. Would not it be well to have our coins on high relief, and also to have the rims raised? The point of having the rim raised would be, of course, to protect the figure on the coin; and if we have the figures in high relief, like the figures on the old Greek coins, they will surely last longer. What do you think of this?
> With warm regards.
> Faithfully yours,

The original prize was $36,734.79. By 1918, the fund, including interest, totaled $45,482.83. On August 22, 1918, Roosevelt wrote to Representative James Ambrose Gallivan, Democrat from Massachusetts, giving a full accounting of the distribution of the fund.
[108] *SG*, Dartmouth, op. cit. Box 16, folder 36. Letter dated November 6, 1905 to Saint-Gaudens from Roosevelt. Confirmed by the President's appointment calendar.

Roosevelt reasoned that by having a high rim surrounding the central design, modern coins could be made in high relief; this might also better protect the design from wear. This was Roosevelt's first explicit statement of the design concepts he had in mind, and it was to influence the remainder of the process. It was this event which forced the design from the artist's original idea of coinlike relief to emulation of ancient Greek coins. Saint-Gaudens, prepared to accept whatever ideas the President might have for the coinage, replied on November 11:[109]

> Dear Mr. President:
> Your note of the 6th is at hand. You have hit the nail on the head with regard to the coinage. Of course the great coins (and you might say the only coins) are the Greek ones you speak of, just as the great medals are those of the fifteenth century by Pisani and Sperandie. Nothing would please me more than to make the attempt in the direction of the heads of Alexander, but the authorities on modern monetary requirements would I fear "throw fits" to speak emphatically if the thing were done now. It would be great if it could be accomplished and I do not see what the objection would be if the edges were high enough to prevent the rubbing. Perhaps an inquiry from you would not receive the antagonistic reply from those who have the say in such matters that would certainly be made to me.
> Up to the present I have done no work on the actual models for the coins, but have made sketches, and the matter is constantly in my mind. I have about determined on the composition of one side, which would contain an eagle very much like the one I placed on your medal with a modification that would be advantageous; on the other side some kind of a (possibly winged) figure of Liberty striding forward as if on a mountain top, holding aloft on one arm a shield bearing the stars and stripes with the word Liberty marked across the field; in the other hand perhaps a flaming torch, the drapery would be flowing in the breeze. My idea is to make it a living thing and typical of progress.
> Tell me frankly what you think of this and what your ideas may be. I remember you spoke of the head of an Indian; of course that is always a superb thing to do, but would it be a sufficiently clear emblem of Liberty as required by the law?
> I send you an old book on coins, which I am certain you will find of interest, while waiting for a copy that I have ordered from Europe.
> Faithfully yours,

After speculating about the mint authorities' reaction to a high relief design, the sculptor asked Roosevelt to inquire in hopes of getting a useful response. Here, Saint-Gaudens first described his concept for the double eagle coin: on the reverse an eagle similar to that on the inaugural medal; on the obverse a full-length figure of Liberty striding forward with shield bearing stars and stripes on one arm, and a flaming torch in the other hand. Graphically, these are similar to the some of the pencil sketches apparently made between July and November 1905. He also questioned the President's idea of using a portrait of an American Indian, wondering if it would satisfy the law.[110]

---

[109] *Roosevelt*, LoC, op. cit. Microfilm reel 160. Letter dated November 11, 1905 to Roosevelt from Saint-Gaudens.
[110] The American Indian portrait idea came up again when Bela Pratt designed the half eagle obverse. This time it was crafted as a literal portrait of a Native American, not "Liberty" wearing a feathered war bonnet as eventually used on the $10.

48

*Figure 15. Sample sketches of Striding Liberty obverse with a torch in one hand and a federal shield inscribed "Liberty" in the other; an eagle rests on the top of the shield. Standing eagle reverse, concept sketch (center) and a more developed sketch (right).* (Courtesy Dartmouth College Library Special Collections; Saint-Gaudens papers.)

Roosevelt wasted little time in talking to secretary Shaw about the high relief coins, and told Saint-Gaudens he had arranged for a conference with the mint authorities, "…and I am going to see if I cannot persuade them that coins of the Grecian type but with raised rims will meet the commercial needs of the day." He continued by suggesting a relief between the ancient Greek and modern low relief:[111]

> Of course, I want to avoid too heavy an outbreak of the mercantile classes, because after all it is they who do use the gold. If we can have an eagle like that on the inauguration medal, only raised, I should feel that we would be awfully fortunate. Don't you think that we might accomplish something by raising the figures more than at present but not so much as the Greek coins were? Probably the Greek coins would be so thick that modern banking houses, where they have to pile up gold, would simply be unable to do so. How would it do to have a design struck off in tentative fashion – that is, to have a model made? I think your Liberty idea is all right. Is it possible to make Liberty with that Indian feather head-dress? The figure of Liberty as you suggest it would be beautiful. If we get down to bedrock facts, would the feather head-dress be any more out of keeping with the rest of Liberty than the canonical Phrygian cap which never is worn and never has been worn by any free people in the world?
> Faithfully yours,

The President suggested using an Indian headdress on the figure of Liberty, justifying his request by claiming that it is just as appropriate as the Phrygian cap worn by Liberty on some other American coins. No one mentioned the befuddled design of the current one cent coin by James B. Longacre, with its Indian headdress-clad bust of Liberty. Neither was anything said about the cultural *faux pas* of putting a male warrior's headdress on a female portrait.

He also suggested having a model made but it is unclear whether "…to have a design struck off..." refers to full production or a few samples. A week later, November 22, Saint-Gaudens wrote that he could use the headdress on the figure of Liberty:[112]

Dear Mr. President:
Thank you for your letter of the 14th and the return of the book on coins.

[111] *SG*, Dartmouth, op. cit. Box 16, folder 36. Letter dated November 14, 1905 to Saint-Gaudens from Roosevelt.
[112] *Roosevelt*, LoC, op. cit. Microfilm reel 61. Letter dated November 22, 1905 to Roosevelt from Saint-Gaudens.

I can perfectly well use the Indian head dress on the figure of Liberty. It should be very handsome. I have been at work for the last two days on the coins and feel quite enthusiastic about it.

Enclose copy of a letter to Secretary Shaw which explains itself. If you are of my opinion and will help, I shall be greatly obliged.

Faithfully yours,

*(manuscript note below)*

I think something between the high relief of the Greek coins and the extremely low relief of the modern is possible and as you suggest I will make a model with that in view.

***Figure 16. Obverse of the "Indian" cent designed by James B. Longacre (left), and an early sketch of Liberty with an Indian headdress as suggested by Roosevelt.*** (Courtesy Dartmouth College Library Special Collections; Saint-Gaudens papers.)

Further, Roosevelt endorsed the idea of a coin with intermediate relief, and enclosed a letter to secretary Shaw with questions about the required inscriptions:[113]

Dear Sir:

I am now engaged on the models for the coinage. The law calls for, viz., "On one side there shall be an impression emblematic of liberty, with an inscription of the word 'Liberty' and the year of the coinage." It occurs to me that the addition on this side of the coins of the word "Justice" (or "Law", preferably the former) would add force as well as elevation to the meaning of the composition. At one time the words "In God We Trust" were placed on the coins; I am not aware there was authorization for that, but I may be mistaken. Will you kindly inform me whether what I suggest is permissible.

Roosevelt replied to Saint-Gaudens two days later supporting the idea of adding the word "Justice" and stating the intermediate relief coins would be "…not only beautiful…yet worthy of a civilized people – which is not true of our present coins."[114]

My dear Mr. Saint-Gaudens:

That is first class. I have no doubt we can get permission to put on the word "Justice," and I firmly believe that you can evolve something that will not only be beautiful from the artistic standpoint, but that, between the very high relief of the Greek and the very low relief of the modern coins, will be adapted both to the mechanical necessities of our mint production and the needs of modern commerce, and yet will be worthy of a civilized people – which is not true of our present coins.

Faithfully yours,

---

[113] *Roosevelt*, LoC, op. cit. Microfilm reel 61. Letter dated November 22, 1905 to Shaw from Saint-Gaudens.

[114] *SG*, Dartmouth, op. cit. Box 16, folder 36. Letter dated November 24, 1905 to Saint-Gaudens from Roosevelt.

50

*Figure 17. Double eagle obverse sketch showing addition of the word "Law" to the Federal shield; note also the suggestion of wings.* (Courtesy Dartmouth College Library Special Collections; Saint-Gaudens papers.)

One of Saint-Gaudens' sketches clearly shows the word *Law* incorporated onto the shield as suggested in his letter, above. The artist also experimented with placing the shield on the ground, altering the angle of the torch arm, and adding wings to the figure. Secretary Shaw checked Section 18 of the Coinage Laws, and advised the President that certain inscriptions were required, but that did not preclude others. He wrote to Saint-Gaudens on December 12:[115]

> Referring to your letter of the 22nd ultimo, suggesting that in addition to the word "Liberty" the word "Justice" be placed on the coins of the United States, you are respectfully informed that the President has approved of the suggestion.
> You are authorized in preparing the designs you are now making for the coins, to place the word "Justice" on the models.
> Respectfully,
> L. M. Shaw, Secretary

The motto IN GOD WE TRUST was not mentioned.[116]

By the end of 1905 Saint-Gaudens was nearly finished with his preliminary sketches of the Liberty figure and told Roosevelt "…[I] will probably in a month send you a sketch of the side with the figure of Liberty put up in a large model…"[117] The clay sketch, below, appears to be as close to a large plaster model as the artist got with the shield version. Dated 1906, it was likely made after Shaw approved adding the word "Justice" and before the artist entered the hospital.

---

[115] *US Mint*, NARA-CP, op. cit., entry A1 328I, folder "Coins, Lincoln cent." Letter dated December 12, 1905 to Saint-Gaudens from Shaw. This is an example of a misfiled document.

[116] *US Mint*, NARA-CP, op. cit., entry 330, box 45. Letter dated November 28, 1905 to Shaw from Loeb (secretary to the President).

[117] *SG*, Dartmouth, op. cit. Box 16, folder 36. Letter dated December 24, 1905 to Roosevelt from Saint-Gaudens.

*Figure 18. Clay sketch based on the winged Liberty with shield concept. Note the date MCMVI (1906) above the figure and the shield inscribed "Liberty" and "Justice."* (Courtesy U. S. Department of Interior National Park Service, Saint-Gaudens National Historic Site, Cornish, NH. #0947)

## Inflexible Modern Requirements – 1906

"I think it would be best to know at once if there are not some inflexible modern requirements that necessitate extreme flatness." With this comment to secretary Shaw, Saint-Gaudens asked directly if there was an impediment to using high relief on the coins he was designing. He asked Shaw to let him know what the situation was so he could work accordingly.[118]

> Dear Sir:
> In my correspondence with Mr. Roosevelt on the matter of the coins, we concluded it would be well to try and make a coin with the design in higher relief than those now in use. Perhaps, as he suggested, a trial between the extreme high relief of the Greek coins and the very low relief of the modern ones might show that a higher relief is permissible in our currency than now prevails. I am working at this now and on reflection, I think it would be best to know at once if there are not some inflexible modern requirements that necessitate extreme flatness. If that is the case, it is useless to lose time on trials, also, to a certain degree, the relief determined on may modify the composition. If you will kindly give me a reply to this at your earliest convenience, I should be much obliged.
> Yours truly
> Augustus Saint-Gaudens
>
> P.S. Of course in what I propose doing, the rim will be as high as the highest relief, so that the piling of the coins will not be interfered with.

---

[118] *US Mint*, NARA-CP, op. cit. Box 71, folder "Gold coin designs." Letter dated January 2, 1906 to Shaw from Saint-Gaudens.

52

Like Charles Barber, Saint-Gaudens understood there were practical limits to the relief of circulating coins. He seemed willing to forgo high relief if it were not possible to strike the pieces. By January 6, Roosevelt had talked with Shaw and apparently rejected doing anything about the relief except what he had suggested to Saint-Gaudens:[119]

> My dear Saint-Gaudens:
> I have seen Shaw about that coinage and told him that it was my pet baby. We will try it anyway, so you go ahead. Shaw was really very nice about it. Of course he thinks I am a mere crack-brained lunatic on the subject, but he said with great kindness that there was always a certain number of gold coins that had to be stored up in vaults, and that there was no earthly objection to having those coins as artistic as the Greeks could desire. (I am paraphrasing his words, of course.) I think it will seriously increase the mortality among the employees of the mint at seeing such a desecration, but they will perish in a good cause!
> Always yours,

Roosevelt's letter indicates secretary Shaw pointed out the problems with attempting to use a high relief design on a circulating coin. He also suggested the new coins could be struck and kept as part of the government's gold reserve rather than as actual circulating coins. Having not heard from Shaw or mint director Roberts, Saint-Gaudens optimistically replied to the President on January 9:[120]

> Dear Mr. President:
> Your letter of the 6th is at hand. All right, I shall proceed on the lines we have agreed on. The models are both well in hand, but I assure you I feel mighty cheeky, so to speak, in attempting to line up with the Greek things. Well! Whatever I produce cannot be worse than the inanities now displayed on our coins and we will at least have made an attempt in the right direction, and serve the country by increasing the mortality at the mint. There is one gentleman there however, who, when he sees what is coming, may have "the nervous prostration" as termed by a native here, but killed, no. He has been in that institution since the foundation of the Government and will be found standing in its ruins.
> Yours faithfully,

The gentleman referred to is engraver Charles Barber, who was aware of the redesign commission. Thus, it was Roosevelt who insisted on high relief coins, even when the artist was willing to accept a more modest contour. Saint-Gaudens was trained in France and deeply influenced by French sculptors and medallists. The example of Jules-Clemet Chaplain and the Monnais de Paris may have been in his thoughts.

Saint-Gaudens' January 2 letter was passed to mint director George Roberts, who provided his thoughts to Shaw on January 13.[121] Secretary Shaw's official reply, which was nothing more than a copy of Roberts' comments, came on the 18th and, given its tone and content, should have alerted Saint-Gaudens to the potential for severe problems ahead in producing coins with relief significantly higher than the current double eagle.[122]

[119] *SG*, Dartmouth, op. cit. Box 16, folder 37. Letter dated January 6, 1906 to Saint-Gaudens from Roosevelt.
[120] *Roosevelt*, LoC, op. cit. Microfilm reel 62. Letter dated January 9, 1906 to Roosevelt from Saint-Gaudens.
[121] *US Mint*, NARA-CP, op. cit., entry 330, box 45. Letter dated January 13, 1906 to Shaw from Roberts.
[122] *US Mint*, NARA-CP, op. cit. Letter dated January 16, 1906 to Saint-Gaudens from Shaw.

Replying to your letter of January 2, relative to a design for gold coin with high relief, I beg to quote a letter on the subject this day received from George E. Roberts, Director of the Mint:

*"Referring to the letter of Mr. Saint-Gaudens, dated January 2, 1906, as to the practicality of giving greater relief to our gold coins, I beg to say that the judgement of the authorities of all countries is that modern coins must be of low relief. The government of France is one of the most responsive in the world to artistic sentiment, and ignores no opportunity to cultivate the artistic taste of its people; the French Mint leads the world in artistic medal work; but the French coins are as low in relief as our own.*

*"There are several practical reasons which dictate this policy. The most important of these is that with the magnitude of modern business transactions it is of the highest importance that the standard coins shall not deviate in the slightest possible degree from their prescribed contents. To accomplish this a coin must be made at a single stroke of the press and must not, by high relief or sharp lines, be exposed to a high rate of abrasion.*

*"In doing a medal the piece of metal passes through the press a number of times in order to bring up the relief, the Saint Louis award medal, for example, thirteen times. The piece is started with much more metal than it is to contain when completed, and after each stroke, as the metal spreads, is taken out of the press and trimmed.*

*"The double eagle of the United States weighs 516 grains and a variation of only one-half (1/2) grain is allowed. The experts at the mint tell me that the design must be such that every part will come up perfectly at one stroke, in order to keep within this exceedingly narrow margin. To take a piece out after a stroke and remove part of the metal, as is done with a medal, and adjust the weight to the nicety required, is impractical when pieces must be made by the million.*

*"I respectfully urge that Mr. Saint-Gaudens be urged to visit the Philadelphia Mint and carefully examine the practical details of coinage operations before proceeding with his design."*

I heartily concur in the views expressed by the Director, and have taken occasion to submit the same to the President. The President, however, agrees with the position taken by you, and by his direction you are authorized to proceed, notwithstanding this adverse report, and prepare a design as outlined in your letter of the 2^nd^ instant.

I hope you will take occasion to visit the Mint at Philadelphia under the appointment as a member of the visiting committee, and there study the practical operations incident to the production of the coins of the character you suggest.

Very truly yours,

Director Roberts' comments completely ignored what could be done to solve the relief problem without resorting to the ordinary "flat" designs presently in use. He lists why it cannot be done instead of how it might be accomplished. With this negative approach reinforced by the director, the Philadelphia Mint became more of an obstruction than a positive agent for success. The opportunity was thus presented for Saint-Gaudens to design the coin in any relief he desired, rather than one that could actually be coined, with the full support of the President. This is also one of those times when the compelling egos of artist and President might have paid greater attention to director Roberts' comments. By continuing with the design in a relief that was not coinable, Saint-Gaudens lost his best chance to explore the limits of artistry on circulation coinage. By the close of 1907 the result was Charles Barber's re-engraving of the Saint's design, rather than Saint-Gaudens producing the highest art within the practical limits of commerce. The President was en-

54

joying the battle and it was a good diversion for him during the normal course of politics; details of the work may have eluded him.

Saint-Gaudens wrote Weinman on January 7, 1906 requesting the loan of "…an Indian head dress such as you used in your group…."[123] The headdress actually belonged to Solon Borglum, who was pleased to loan it to Saint-Gaudens. Weinman also sent several photos of standing and flying eagles.[124] About a month later he wrote to Weinman again, asking to borrow models of goose or eagle wings that he remembered Weinman or Fraser had.[125] These would be used to help model the version of the Striding Liberty with wings and small Indian headdress.

*Figure 19. Example of Adolph Weinman's treatment of feathers. 1907 American Institute of Architects gold medal (reverse).* (Courtesy Commission of Fine Arts)

## Refining the Designs

Through the first half of 1906 Saint-Gaudens was in almost constant pain. There were good days – sometimes several in a row – to give hope that the latest X-ray or electric shock treatment or "miracle" diet had been successful. But the bad days of stabbing pain came more frequently, subsiding only on taking an ampoule of opium, then two ampoules, then opium and morphine. He spent most of March 1906 in Corey Hill Hospital, Brookline, Massachusetts for tests and another operation. Augusta wrote letters to Homer telling him the truth but wishing to hide "the Saint's" condition from others:[126]

> …Dr. Harrington [and Dr. Richardson]…were enabled to look in through the cut they made and found <u>not a tumor</u>, this you must say emphatically to everyone – but, for you and me, we must know that they did find swollen diseased glands which probably…will result in a tumor…and on which they cannot operate.

Productive time was increasingly limited with each passing day; Saint-Gaudens depended on Hering to do the modeling and complete his designs for Roosevelt. Available hours had to be spent on the large, high-fee commissions that sat about the studio craving attention.

The artist Saint-Gaudens was not the only one in pain. Roosevelt himself, the public image of a vigorous life, continued to suffer from asthma. When an attack occurred, he quickly vanished from public view and hearing, to cough and wheeze accompanied only by his personal secretary, William Loeb, or military advisor Col. Archibald Butts. He had persistent hypertension, for which there was no effective treatment, and was taking drugs to suppress the "Cuban fever" contracted in Santiago during his Rough Rider days. His joints were arthritic, often stiff and sore, and unknown to all but Edith and his personal physician, he had lost most of the sight in his left eye – the result of a blow struck by his Navy aide Lt. Dan Moore during an White House boxing match the previous December.[127]

[123] *Weinman*, AAA, op. cit. Microfilm reel 283. Letter dated January 7, 1906 to Weinman from Saint-Gaudens.
[124] *SG*, Dartmouth, op. cit. Box 20, folder 27. Letter dated January 11, 1906 to Saint-Gaudens from Weinman.
[125] *SG*, Dartmouth, op. cit. Box 21, folder 13. Letters dated January 8, and February 15, 1906 to Adolph A. Weinman from Saint-Gaudens.
[126] *SG*, Dartmouth, op. cit. Microfilm reel 22, frames 264–267. Letter dated March [18?], 1906 to Homer from Augusta.
[127] Morris, *Theodore Rex*, op. cit., p.376 and end note p.696.

In early May, Augustus wrote to Homer including a brief report on the coin designs:[128]

I am working on the coin and I expect in a day or two to be finished with as much as I will do on my side of things; Hering will then take it up and finish it.

By May 10 work had progressed enough that Saint-Gaudens was ready for more information on the coining process. He wrote to superintendent Landis:[129]

Dear Sir:
Mr. Henry Hering, my friend and principal assistant, and the bearer of this note goes to Philadelphia in order to obtain all the information that can possibly assist in the execution of the coins I am doing, and every facility you can afford him, I shall greatly appreciate. I have asked him to make inquiries about every possible point that may be necessary to cover in this matter. Mr. Hering is helping me on the coins, so he understands the matter very thoroughly and has had a good deal of experience with me in the making of medals.
Believe me,
Very truly yours,

*Figure 20. Henry Hering (1935), Saint-Gaudens' principal assistant for the coin designs.* (Courtesy James Murphy Collection, box 6, folder 27. Georgetown University Library, Special Collections Division, Washington, DC.)

Hering was more than helping – he was doing all the relief modeling based on Saint-Gaudens' sketch models and verbal instructions. Two weeks later, the sculptor wrote to secretary Shaw:[130]

The reverse of the twenty dollar gold piece is almost finished. The obverse is very far along.
I should like to make the date in Roman numerals; is there any objection to doing it? The law specifies nothing and unless you advise to the contrary, I shall do them in that way.
It is necessary in making the models that I have a plaster cast made of the present twenty dollar gold piece. According to law, I am not allowed to do this without your authorization. I shall be thankful if you will give me such permission at your earliest convenience.

Shaw's reply two days later was unreceptive, but he agreed to put the issue to the President:[131]

My dear Mr. Saint-Gaudens:
While we are making coins for the people of the United States I think we should confine ourselves to the English language. I have reminded our architects that I will dismiss the first one who puts a V on a public building where a U is intended.
So much for my ideas. I will submit your letter with a copy of my reply to the President, however, for his direction.
Very truly yours,

---

[128] *SG*, Dartmouth, op. cit. Microfilm reel 22, frame 798. Letter (excerpt) dated May 4, 1906 to Homer from Saint-Gaudens.
[129] *US Mint*, NARA-CP, op. cit. Letter dated May 10, 1906 to Landis from Saint-Gaudens.
[130] *US Mint*, NARA-CP, op. cit., entry 330, box 45. Letter dated May 23, 1906 to Shaw from Saint-Gaudens.
[131] *US Mint*, NARA-CP, op. cit., entry 330, box 45. Letter dated May 25, 1906 to Saint-Gaudens from Shaw.

The same day, Saint-Gaudens also asked about the motto that had been used on the 1905 inaugural medal:[132]

> Dear Sir:
> I have written you to-day about putting the date on the coin in numerals. There is another question which is more delicate and I am embarrassed as to what to do. The words "Aequum Cuique" that I have placed on the Roosevelt medal would come in very well on this twenty dollar coin, but I fear that possibly it might be criticized. What is your feeling about it, do you agree with me that it might be a mistake?
> Yours very sincerely,
>
> P.S. As you no doubt are aware, the "Aequum Cuique" is a very dignified translation of "A square deal for every man."

The President's reply to Shaw was very clear about the date: it was to be exactly as Saint-Gaudens wished it and that meant Roman numerals. Roosevelt took a few lines to "educate" his treasury secretary, and to make sure nothing of the inaugural medal motto was used in the coin design:[133]

> Referring to the Saint Gaudens Correspondence, there does not seem to be any reason for not putting the date on the coin in numerals. Those numerals are Latin and our figures are Arabic. If Mr. Saint Gaudens is clear that the effect would be better if numerals should be used, I should give him his head about it. In such a case a V would have to be used and not a U because of the simple reason that it would actually be a V and not a U that he was trying to put on. V means 5; U is not a numeral at all.
> But under no circumstances should Mr. Saint Gaudens use the words "Aequum Cuique", which were used on the inauguration medal. The coin must have no reference either direct or indirect to the President.
> I suppose you have sent Mr. Saint Gaudens the permission to make a plaster cast of the present twenty-dollar gold piece.

Obtaining a plaster cast of the current double eagle, possibly needed in an attempt by Hering to determine the correct relief by enlarging the scale of the cast, took multiple internal mint telegrams and nearly two weeks to provide.[134] Saint-Gaudens believed that making a cast of a coin was in violation of the counterfeiting laws, and he needed permission from the secretary of the treasury to have one made. Hering's visit to the mint and receipt of the cast on June 8 appears to have satisfied Saint-Gaudens about what was necessary to make a good coin model,[135] but within a few weeks Hering was off to New York for the summer. This left the sculptor without his principal assistant through four critical months of the design process, of which Saint-Gaudens spent almost half in the hospital.

Nearly a year after Saint-Gaudens began working on the coin design, President Roosevelt and the sculptor were still making changes in the concept. The artist's prefer-

---

[132] Ira Goldberg, "A Letter from Saint-Gaudens," *The Numismatist*, August, 1994. pp.1119–1121. Letter dated May 23, 1906 to Shaw from Saint-Gaudens.

[133] *SG*, Dartmouth, op. cit. Box 16, folder 37. Letter dated May 26, 1906 to Saint-Gaudens from Roosevelt.

[134] *US Mint*, NARA-CP, op. cit. Letter dated June 2, 1906 to Landis from Roberts. Hering made a similar suggestion to Barber in December 1907 in relation to the half eagle design.

[135] *US Mint*, NARA-CP, op. cit. Letter dated June 8, 1906 to A. A. Norris from Saint-Gaudens.

ence was to use Roman numerals in dating the coins rather than the customary European decimal figures commonly used and had stated this to secretary Shaw.[136]

One of the characteristics of the *beaux arts* style was the affectation of ancient Greek or Roman forms. Thus, the letter *U* was rendered as *V* within inscriptions (even if the text was not in Latin), and dates were in Roman numerals. These were a constant source of confusion for less artistically inclined citizens.

Roosevelt thought the work was nearing its end, and was anxious to see results from the collaboration:[137]

> My dear Saint Gaudens:
> I enclose a copy of a letter I have just sent to Secretary Shaw. I am delighted that you are getting along so well with the coin. It is one of the things in which I have taken the most genuine interest. I am so pleased that it is nearly concluded.
> Sincerely yours,
>
> *(Handwritten note below.)*
> Use latin or arabic numerals as you think best & could you show me the design when you get it ready?

The artist was still working out the one cent coin design and wrote to director Roberts for advice:[138]

> Dear Sir:
> Will you be kind enough to let me know if there is any objection to the use of something of the character of the flying eagle made in 1857 in the new cent that I am designing. I am considering the making of something which will recall that.
> Very truly yours,

Roberts responded a few days later, also including his own opinion:[139]

> My dear Sir:
> Replying to your inquiry of the 16th instant I would say that there is no legal or mechanical objection to the flying eagle design. I have myself a predisposition in

[136] According to Professor Russ Rowlett of the University of North Carolina at Chapel Hill, "...the modern system of numeration is based on place value, with the same symbol, such as 4, taking on different meaning (4, 40, 400, etc.) depending on its location within the representation of the number. Place value numeration was invented by Hindu mathematicians in India, probably by the sixth century and perhaps even earlier. The modern numerals 1, 2, 3, ..., are sometimes called "Arabic" numerals in the West because they were introduced to Europeans by Arab scholars. The key figure was the great Arab mathematician Mohammed ibn-Musa al-Khowarizmi, who taught at Baghdad sometime between 800 and 850. He wrote a book on the Hindu number system known today only in a later Latin translation as *De numero indorum*, 'On the Hindu Numbers.' Subsequently he wrote a longer and very influential work, *Al-jabr w'al muqabalah*, known in Europe as *Algebra*, which included all the techniques of arithmetic still taught in schools today. The author's name, Latinized as *Algorismus*, is the root of the English word *algorithm*.

"The Hindu-Arabic numeration system was known in Europe by 1000, but at first it didn't make much of a dent in the use of Roman numerals. During the 1100s the 'Arabic' numerals were a topic of great interest among European scholars, and several translations of the *Algebra* appeared. In 1202, Leonardo of Pisa (ca. 1180–1250) published a famous book, *Liber abaci*, explaining and popularizing the Hindu-Arabic system, the use of the zero, the horizontal fraction bar, and the various algorithms of the *Algebra*. (Leonardo is better known today by his patronymic Fibonacci, 'son of Bonaccio.') Thereafter modern numerals and the standard operations of arithmetic were commonly used by scholars, but Roman numerals continued to be used for many purposes, including finance and bookkeeping, for many centuries to come.

"Incidentally, the numerals 0123456789 are properly known as European digits. The numerals actually used in Arabic script, the true Arabic numerals, are of different forms." (Source: Russ Rowlett, *Dictionary of Units of Measurement*, University of North Carolina, Chapel Hill, NC. Used by permission.)
[137] *SG*, Dartmouth, op. cit. Box 16, folder 17. Letter dated May 26, 1906 to Saint-Gaudens from Roosevelt.
[138] *US Mint*, NARA-CP, op. cit., entry 330, box 45. Letter dated June 16, 1906 to Roberts from Saint-Gaudens.
[139] *US Mint*, NARA-CP, op. cit., entry 330, box 45. Letter dated June 20, 1906 to Saint-Gaudens from Roberts.

58

favor of the retention of an Indian Head for the one cent piece, although I have no doubt you could improve upon the head we now have. We have few memorials to this race we have displaced and I think the design has a character of its own. I do not know, however, what the President's view would be.

Very truly yours,

The President must have enjoyed "instructing" Shaw, and again expressed his interest in fighting the mint bureaucracy, "Don't forget to tell me when you want me to take up our brethren of the mint and grapple with them on the subject of the coins."[140] Saint-Gaudens, now fully engaged in both the design and the "adventure" of fighting the mint wrote back from his hospital bed in New York:[141]

> Dear Mr. President:
> I thank you for your letter of June 22nd. I will certainly inform you when your help will be needed with our friends in Philadelphia.
> I am here on the sick list, where I have to remain in the hands of the doctors until the first week of August, but my mind is on the coins! which are in good hands at Windsor.
> The making of these designs is a great pleasure, but the job is even more serious than I anticipated. You may not recall that I told you I was "scared blue" at the thought of doing them; now that I have the opportunity, the responsibility looms up like a specter.
> The eagle side of the gold piece is finished, and is undergoing the interminable experiments with reductions before I send it to you. The other side is well advanced.
> Now I am attacking the cent. It may interest you to know that on the "Liberty" side of the cent I am using a flying eagle, a modification of the device which was used on the cent of 1857. I had not seen that coin for many years, and was so impressed by it, that I thought if carried out with some modifications, nothing better could be done. It is by all odds the best design on any American coin.
> Yours sincerely,

The proposed design for the double eagle consisted of a forward-striding figure of Liberty similar to that finally used on circulation coins, but with wings, a small feather headdress, and the date in Roman numerals. The reverse used a standing eagle similar to the inaugural medal. Experimental reductions of the standing eagle were being made in Paris by Janvier et Duval, something Saint-Gaudens had not told the President.[142]

Saint-Gaudens had experimented with several concepts for the obverse and reverse of the cent, including a left-facing portrait resembling Jules-Clemet Chaplain's 20-franc coin, and a rendition of the Capitol building set against a rising sun.

---

[140] *SG*, Dartmouth, op. cit. Box 16, folder 37. Letter dated June 22, 1906 to Saint-Gaudens from Roosevelt.
[141] *Roosevelt*, LoC, op. cit. Microfilm reel 65. Letter dated June 28, 1906 to Roosevelt from Saint-Gaudens. This second hospital stay followed an operation in March at Corey Hill Hospital in Brookline, Massachusetts near Boston. The doctors thought the pain was caused by scar tissue from the incision of the original operation in 1900.
[142] *SG*, Dartmouth, op. cit. Microfilm reel 8, pp.811–812. Letter dated June 29, 1906 to Saint-Gaudens from Janvier et Duval, Paris.

*Figure 21. Sketches for the obverse ("Liberty side") and reverse of the cent.* (Courtesy Dartmouth College Library Special Collections; Saint-Gaudens papers.)

As finally decided, the cent obverse ("Liberty" side, as Saint-Gaudens called it) was going to show a flying eagle similar that on the cent of 1857-58, but more refined.[143]

*Figure 22. L-R Reverse of silver dollar, 1836–39 (designed by Christian Gobrecht), flying eagle cent (1857–58) obverse based on Gobrecht's design, and Saint-Gaudens' flying eagle also intended for the cent obverse.* (Model photo courtesy U. S. Department of Interior National Park Service, Saint-Gaudens National Historic Site, Cornish, NH. #1098.)

Saint-Gaudens was still hospitalized when the President wrote on July 30:[144]

> My dear Saint Gaudens:
> I do not want to bother you, but how is that coinage business getting on? This summer is the best time to settle it, because I would like to do it free from all supervision by the co-ordinate branch!
> Faithfully yours,

---

[143] Presumably, the artist had not seen Christian Gobrecht's original flying eagle drawings, or the reverse of the 1836–39 silver dollars.

[144] *SG*, Dartmouth, op. cit. Box 16, folder 37. Letter dated July 30, 1906 to Saint-Gaudens from Roosevelt.

The sculptor's son, Homer, replied on August 2 explaining that his father remained in the hospital but that Hering had finished the studio work and experimental reductions were being made in Paris.[145]

> Dear Mr. President:
> Your note of the 30th is at hand. As my father is at present ill with sciatica, I am writing you in accordance with his wishes. He fears that the model will not be ready for use in the Mint this summer. The work in the studio is finished, but experimental reductions are now being carried out in Paris which is the only place where they can give the reductions their proper relief. They will be shipped to America by the end of this month when they will be decided upon by you and Mr. Saint-Gaudens. Then, if it is considered advisable, the models now in the studio will be sent abroad to Paris where the die can be properly made, unless there will be any difficulty in the way of striking American coins with the French die.
> If you desire to see the large models, I can go down to Oyster Bay with them at once, but as another journey will be needed on the arrival of the reductions, it would seem, perhaps, a trifle useless at present.
> Faithfully yours,

Homer refers to a standing eagle version of the reverse model as being in Paris. It was intended that the obverse model would remain at Aspet until the reverse reduction had been received. This appears to be the first time the President was told about models being shipped to Europe, and Saint-Gaudens' plan to have reductions and hubs made in Paris. Any proposal to bypass the mint would probably have been opposed by many in the administration. Also, one might expect Roosevelt to have mixed feelings about having his uniquely American coins struck from French hubs prepared in Paris, but his reply of August 6 offered only acceptance of the delay. "That is all right. What I shall probably do is to defer action until after the 4th of March next."[146]

Saint-Gaudens had sent plaster models to Janvier et Duval in Paris on several previous occasions, and preferred their work to that of American companies such as Gorham, or Tiffany & Co. His brother Louis' recent difficulties with getting satisfactory reductions of his Franklin commemorative medal by American companies, further encouraged the artist to call on his French contacts for the work. The standing eagle model was received by Janvier et Duval on June 29. Saint-Gaudens ordered three reductions in bronze of 136 millimeters diameter (5-3/8 inches), this being four times the size of the double eagle coin. Each reduction was to have a different relief so they ranged from shallow to the full relief of the model.[147]

By September the President had been incorrectly informed that the mint could not cut dies with the relief that he and Saint-Gaudens desired. What the mint director had actually said was that they could not cut high relief hubs directly from the *large diameter* models. The mint had cut high relief dies for medals on a routine basis for many years. The key point for the mint was diameter of the models, not relief. It appears this fundamental issue was not well understood by either Roosevelt or Saint-Gaudens, and no one seems to have explained the situation. With this misunderstanding firmly implanted in the President's thoughts, the argument became one of the mint's competence.

[145] *SG*, Dartmouth, op. cit. Box 16, folder 37. Letter dated August 2, 1906 to Roosevelt from Homer Saint-Gaudens.
[146] *SG*, Dartmouth, op. cit. Box 16, folder 37. Letter dated August 6, 1906 to Saint-Gaudens from Roosevelt.
[147] *SG*, Dartmouth, op. cit. Microfilm reel 8, frames 811–812. Letter dated June 29, 1906 to Saint-Gaudens from V. Janvier and L. Duval.

In a personal letter to treasury secretary Shaw dealing primarily with tariff reform, Roosevelt digressed onto the subject of the coins. His blast at the mint, and specifically engraver Barber, did little except further confuse and alienate the people who were expected to produce the new coins:[148]

> My dear Shaw:
> …Now, a word as to my pet iniquity, the coinage, which I am getting Saint-Gaudens to start. I am afraid I shall have some difficulty with the Mint people, who are insisting that they cannot cut the coins [i.e., dies] as deep as they should be made. I enclose [for] you a specimen, and I direct that Mr. Barber have the dies made as Saint-Gaudens, with my authority, presents them. Mr. Barber is quoted as saying that they could not cut them as deep as this. We then applied to Tiffany and Gorham, the two great silversmiths and jewelers of New York. Mr. Kunz of Tiffany, and Mr. Buck of Gorham's, at once stated that their houses could without difficulty at a single stroke make a cut as deep as this. Mr. Barber must at once get into communication with Tiffany and Gorham, unless he is prepared to make such a deep impression without such consultation. Will you find out from him how long it will take, when the full casts of the coins are furnished you by Saint-Gaudens, to get out the first of the new coins – that is, the twenty-dollar gold piece, which is the one I have most at heart? All I want to know from Mr. Barber is how long it will take to make them, and the cost; and if there is likely to be a long delay and seemingly too much expense I shall want him to communicate with Messrs. Buck and Kunz. But if he has to communicate with them I should regard it as a rather black eye for the Mint and a confession of the inferiority on their part to Tiffany and Gorham. Will you communicate all this to the Mint people?
> Sincerely yours,

Shaw sent the section quoted above to his private secretary in Washington, Charles H. Keep, with a note: "Please communicate this to Mr. Barber and have him proceed at once. As soon as you get a report as to the length of time necessary to produce the first coins, wire me and I will wire the president. The specimen I am sending by the same mail."[149]

Director Roberts responded to Shaw on September 25:[150]

> About six weeks will be required to make the hubs and first two dies for the new Saint Gaudens coin. The cost will [be] unimportant as they will be made by the regular salaried men. Work will begin as soon as the model for one side is received and there will be no delay.
> The making of these dies presents no difficulties. The only uncertainty about the proposed coinage is as to the adaptability of the high relief to the modern coinage press and all the conditions of practical coinage operations. The best way to determine this is to make the practical test, and everybody at the mint will cooperate cordially in making the experiment. The coinage presses used in our mints are similar to those in use in all the important mints of the world and I would add that in all processes and equipment used in coinage operations the United States mints are fully abreast of similar establishments in other countries. Twice within the last six years we have sent men to inspect the principal mints of Europe and many devices originating here have been adopted abroad. Within the last month an em-

[148] *Roosevelt Letters*, Harvard, op. cit., vol. 5, pp.405–406. Letter dated September 11, 1906 to Shaw from Roosevelt. George F. Kunz appears as a "behind the scenes" player throughout the period of coinage redesign. His association with Tiffany & Company as mineralogist and supervisor of the company's lucrative medal stamping business, and active membership in the American Numismatic Society, kept him in touch with mint officials.
[149] *US Mint*, NARA-CP, op. cit., entry 330, box 45. Letter dated September 18, 1906 to C. H. Keep from Shaw.
[150] *US Mint*, NARA-CP, op. cit., entry 330, box 45. Letter dated September 25, 1906 to Shaw from Roberts.

ployee of Tiffany & Co. has visited the mint at Philadelphia to gain information concerning a process which originated in the latter institution and which is being adopted all over the world.[151] It is, however, quite possible that such concerns as Tiffany's and Gorham's, in their extensive operations in stamping the metals, may have developed presses better adapted to high relief work than any known to the coinage institutions of the world. If they have, our mint people should know it and there will be no hesitation about seeking the information.

Charles Keep sent Shaw a telegram at his Ft. Smith, Arkansas vacation home advising, "…Think it would be well to send complete copy of director of mint's letter to Oyster Bay. Shall I do this?"[152]

Experimental reductions of the standing eagle arrived from Paris on schedule, and Homer showed Roosevelt a 5-3/8-inch bronze reduction sometime around the first of September. It is unlikely that anyone made a hub from any of the three reductions at this point. The specimen sent to secretary Shaw on September 11 could have been one of the reductions made by Janvier. Barber and the mint were clearly sitting within the President's gun sights, and lists of excuses were not what the commander-in-chief wanted to hear.

**Figure 23 Two of the three standing eagle design reductions (#1091, #1092) made in Paris by Janvier et Duval. They differ only in height of the relief. Reduction on the left has lower relief than the one on the right. The remaining reduction was probably sent to the Philadelphia Mint, where Barber made a hub and die from it.** (Courtesy U. S. Department of Interior National Park Service, Saint-Gaudens National Historic Site, Cornish, NH. #1091, #1092.)

Toward the end of September Roosevelt met Homer Saint-Gaudens to again examine a sample reduction and discuss the required inscriptions. Later, he read Roberts' letters and reviewed the law inscriptions. As a result Roosevelt accepted that the coins had to include the mottoes and legends required by law. Adding "Justice" or "Law" would take congressional action and Roosevelt wanted as little to do with the House and Senate as possible.

A mature version of the Striding Liberty design dated MCMVII (1907) with Indian headdress, below, apparently dates from the June period. It has the same basic design elements as the MCMVI-dated clay sketch model (except shield), and now conforms to director Roberts' comments about inscriptions.

---

[151] Charles Barber had been taught a process for bronzing medals used by the Paris Mint during his visit to Europe in 1905. Tiffany & Co. wanted to know how it was done but Barber refused to disclose the method because he felt it had been shown to him in confidence.

[152] *US Mint*, NARA-CP, op. cit., entry 330, box 45. Telegram dated September 26, 1906 (1:35 p. m.) to Shaw from C. H. Keep.

*Figure 24. Plaster model of the Striding Liberty figure holding a torch. The shield incorporated in earlier sketches has been replaced with an olive branch. Saint-Gaudens retained the figure's expansive wings and Indian headdress, included at the suggestion of President Roosevelt. It was probably completed by June 1906.* (Courtesy U. S. Department of Interior National Park Service, Saint-Gaudens National Historic Site, Cornish, NH. #1050.)

The President wrote to Saint-Gaudens saying,[153]

> The Mint people have come down, as you can see from the enclosed letter [i.e., September 25 from Roberts] which is in answer to a rather dictatorial one I sent to the Secretary of the Treasury [ i.e., September 11 to Shaw]. When can we get that design for the twenty-dollar piece? I hate to have to put on the lettering, but under the law I have no alternative; yet, in spite of the lettering I think, my dear sir, that you have given us a coin as wonderful as any of the old Greek coins. I do not want to bother you, but do let me have it as quickly as possible. I would like to have the coin well on the way to completion by the time Congress meets.
>
> It was a pleasure seeing your son the other day.
>
> Please return Director Roberts' letter to me when you have noted it.
>
> Sincerely yours,

The President had been pushing the mint to do its work, and further delay by Saint-Gaudens made it difficult to keep on the pressure. A copy of Roberts' letter was sent to engraver Barber, who was asked if he had heard anything further.[154] Barber responded on October 5:[155]

> Your letter of the 4th inst with enclosed copy of your letter to Hon. Secretary of the Treasury, just received.
>
> I beg to state that I have had no communication from Mr. St. Gaudens relative to the designs for the new gold coins. Should there be any correspondence upon this subject I will at once inform you as to the nature of the same, or should Mr. St. Gaudens send any one for consultation upon this matter, I will notify you, that you may be in possession of all that is being done.

---

[153] *SG*, Dartmouth, op. cit. Box 16, folder 37. Letter dated October 1, 1906 to Saint-Gaudens from Roosevelt.
[154] *US Mint*, NARA-CP, op. cit., entry 330, box 45. Letter dated October 4, 1906 to Barber from Roberts.
[155] *US Mint*, NARA-CP, op. cit., entry 229, box 248. Letter dated October 5, 1906 to Roberts from Barber.

> Your letter to the Hon. Secretary contains all that could be said and explains our position exactly, the only criticism that could be made, would be that you are too modest in allowing the possibility that Tiffany or Gorham Manufacturers might be in possession of any appliance or knowledge upon the subject of coinage that might make it possible for them to succeed when we might fail. I do not know but you are right in taking this position, leaving the demonstration, when the dies are finished, to settle the question without argument.
> Respectfully,

It is thought the sculptor had planned to use his Striding Liberty with wings for the obverse and the standing eagle reverse for the coin. However, an exchange of letters and his own reexamination of the compositions may have caused him to later submit different designs as the final ones for the $20 gold coin.

Saint-Gaudens entered the discussion on October 6 with two letters; the first, dictated to Homer, went to director Roberts. The second, evidently written by Homer alone, went to the President:[156]

> Referring to your letter to the Secretary of the Treasury which has been forwarded to me by the President, I must tell you that one of my models for the Twenty Dollar gold piece which has been reduced in Paris to the 5-3/8 inch size or thereabouts, for which I understand, you have the proper reduction machine for making that practical test, is not the model selected by the President for the final coin, although in relief it is practically the same as the model he had chosen.
> The models chosen are from eleven to fourteen inches in diameter and if while I am completing these to my satisfaction in this size, you will provide yourself with the proper machine for making the five and three-eighths or thereabouts reduction from them, as you suggest in your letter, there will be little time lost.
> If, however, after I am ready with my eleven to fourteen inch model, they have to be sent to Paris for reduction to five and three-eighth inch size, there will be a delay of six months or more.
> If you wish, I can send you at once the five and three-eighths inch model I have for an experimental test.
> Faithfully yours,

As noted in the letter to secretary Shaw, discussion occurred about why reductions could not be done at the mint, and Roberts suggested the mint might not have the proper reducing machine to make the high relief hubs. The President heard from Saint-Gaudens on October 6 confirming the director's comment. Both Tiffany's and Gorham used the Janvier reducing lathe in their businesses and regularly made reductions from large, high relief plaster models such as Saint-Gaudens'.[157] Since Janvier et Duval in Paris, and the Paris Mint, used the Janvier reducing machine, it was reasoned that the problem of getting high quality reductions could be solved by purchasing the correct reducing equipment for the Philadelphia Mint. Homer Saint-Gaudens tried to explain to the President why the first standing eagle model was sent to Paris:[158]

> Sometime since when my father sent … Mr. Hering to the Mint to inquire into the practical reducing of the coin from his models, he was met with objections by Mr. Barber as to reducing it from the size models he has made. To overcome this

[156] *US Mint*, NARA-CP, op. cit., entry 330, box 45. Letter dated October 6, 1906 to Roberts from Saint-Gaudens.
[157] The first models were between twelve and fourteen inches in diameter and too large for the mint's 40-year-old reducing lathe. This diameter would have been appropriate for a 2.5- to three-inch medal, but was too large for a coin design.
[158] *SG*, Dartmouth, op. cit. Box 16, folder 37. Letter dated October 6, 1906 to Roosevelt from Homer Saint-Gaudens.

he sent the model to Paris and received the five and three-eighths reduction of the <u>standing eagle you have seen</u>.

Now that you have been kind enough to interest yourself in the matter, the situation is quite different and if my father is met with any refusal by the Mint to adopt such a machine as is to be had in Paris, he will again refer the matter to you.

Hering's visit had occurred in May, but within a few weeks he left for New York for the summer. It wasn't until he returned to Aspet in the fall that the problem of making reductions at the mint was approached. The mint's Hill Engraving Machine had been purchased on May 2, 1867 from H. W. Field, in London. It was suitable for making hubs from models up to ten inches in diameter. However, if the reduction ratio exceeded approximately 5:1 it was nearly impossible to retain fine details of the design. The machine also could not perform extremely fine cuts at any reduction ratio, so the mint engravers had to punch in peripheral details and retouch each new hub by hand. Saint-Gaudens had suggested the mint buy the "proper machine," meaning the latest Janvier reducing lathe, which could produce much higher-quality cuts than the old Hill equipment. It was felt this would eliminate the need to send models to Paris for reductions.[159]

Before Roberts could forward the letter to the President, Roosevelt wrote the director that he did not like the idea of a six-month delay (based on Homer's letter) in getting the reductions made:[160]

My dear Sir:
I enclose a letter from Mr. Saint-Gaudens, which explains itself. I do not want that six months' delay; so will you please have arrangements made to reduce the eleven and fourteen inch diameter models as suggested.

This pushed the mint to proceed with the purchase of a new reducing lathe. An earlier solicitation to purchase a custom-made machine from Keller Mechanical Engraving Company in May 1904 for $3,850 had been abandoned because the vendor had failed to provide the equipment.[161] This time there would be no delay:[162]

Mr. William Loeb, Jr.
Secretary to the President
Referring to the President's note of this morning, will you please advise him that the purchase for the Mint of a machine which will make a reduction from a sixteen-inch model has been in contemplation, and will be closed immediately to expedite the Saint Gaudens' coin. Mr. Saint Gaudens will be asked to forward the five and three-eighths model at once.
Respectfully,

Roberts sent a short note to Saint-Gaudens stating, with slight exaggeration, that the mint had been "…considering for some time the purchase of a Janvier machine…" and

---

[159] The term "reduction" is used by Saint-Gaudens in several different meanings. Technically, it is an exact copy of the original large model only in a smaller diameter. Thus the original eleven-inch plaster model was mechanically reduced to create a 5-3/8-inch diameter version. This could be in plaster, hard wax, steel or other material, but most commonly done in wax with a bronze cast made from the wax reduction. The cast then became a new original from which a steel hub the diameter of the coin was cut on the reducing lathe. The same term is used by Saint-Gaudens and sometimes the mint staff to refer to the hub which is the final product of the reducing lathe. The hub is used to make dies for striking coins.

[160] *Roosevelt*, LoC, op. cit., vol. 167, p.240, microfilm reel 343. Letter dated October 8, 1906 to Roberts from Roosevelt.

[161] *US Mint*, NARA-CP, op. cit., entry 330, box 45. Letter dated June 25, 1906 to Landis from Roberts. The letter cancels the order to Keller Co. because they were to have delivered the equipment in nine months and had done nothing acceptable to Barber in over three years.

[162] *US Mint*, NARA-CP, op. cit., entry 330, box 45. Letter dated October 9, 1906 to Loeb from Roberts.

also that the five-and-three-eighths-inch reduction made in Paris should be sent directly to the Philadelphia Mint. Barber and Roberts went to New York on October 12 and 13 to examine a Janvier reducing lathe at Dietsch Brothers facilities. Barber took with him a high relief model of his own work and asked the company to make a sample reduction. He reported the results of his visits to superintendent Landis on October 30:[163]

> The reduction made by the Messrs Dietsch Brothers of New York at my solicitation from a model furnished by me and intended as a sample of the work of reducing from models for medals or coin, by the machine known as the Janvier Machine of Paris, France, is completed, and is entirely satisfactory.
>
> It was perhaps unnecessary to ask for this specimen as the machine is so well known, being in use in the following Mints: Vienna, London, Rome and Switzerland. I therefore feel no hesitancy in saying that this machine will prove entirely satisfactory and add to the efficiency of the department.
>
> I have the honor to recommend the purchase of the machine at the price stated by Messrs Dietsch and also suggest, that it might be well to insert a clause guaranteeing the machine for a stated period and providing for the renewal of any parts that may fail during that time.
>
> Respectfully,

The next day Landis recommended that Roberts accept the proposal from Dietsch Brothers Company to provide "...one large size, electrically driven, automatic Janvier Reducing Machine, equipped with a direct connected motor, suitable for 220 volt direct current, together with other accessories required to make a complete, satisfactory working machine for the purposes intended."[164] The New York company submitted a bid of $2,500 including installation and one day of training, and the bid was accepted by Charles Barber on behalf of the U. S. Mint on November 3, 1906. The new reducing lathe was installed next to the old Hill machine by November 20, and Barber and Morgan received a day of training on the new equipment from Henri Weil.[165]

## Delivering Miss Liberty

During the fall and winter of 1906 Saint-Gaudens' health grew worse. Radiation treatments that had earlier produced limited relief from the intestinal cancer were now ineffective. Assistant Henry Hering wrote:[166]

> ...I saw him every day and grew used to his gaunt face...and his look of being hunted by death... When they could carry him out to the studios and place him in front of his work, the dejection, the grim unhappy will, the constant looking over his shoulder... as if death were there, would vanish in an illumination of beauty; his eyes would burn again in the moment's victory..."

Although in considerable pain and unable to work for more than short periods, he continued both his regular commissions and the coinage redesign. Director Roberts asked to have

---

[163] *US Mint*, NARA-CP, op. cit., entry 229, box 248. Letter dated October 30, 1906 to Landis from Barber.

[164] *US Mint*, NARA-CP, op. cit., entry 229, box 248. Letter dated October 31, 1906 to Roberts from Landis.

[165] *US Mint*, NARA-CP, op. cit., entry 4A, Box 2, "Supply Requisitions – Engraving Department, 1900–1906." Triplicate copy of a mint purchase requisition dated November 3, 1906 signed by Charles Barber. This document was originally kept in "Mint file 349 – Jan. Reduc. Mach.," but later [1960s ?] moved to the above storage box where it languished with purchase requisitions for abrasives and die steel. It was located only after many hours of searching through hundreds of intermixed requisitions and "Work Authorization" forms at NARA. The original topical filing may have been easier for researchers to use.

[166] Tharp, op. cit., p.363. Letter (date not given – fall, 1906) to Barry Faulkner from Hermon Hering.

an experimental reduction of the standing eagle sent to Philadelphia, and Saint-Gaudens shipped it on October 20. Barber used the old reducing machine to cut a reverse hub from this French-made reduction, completing the work on November 6.[167]

By early November, with promises of new models piling up, and the President expecting to see coins very soon, Barber asked Roberts about the models:[168]

> As you were about to start for the West you sent me a letter stating that I would receive the models for the new designs for gold coinage, made by Mr. St. Gaudens, and also urged me to "push these coin designs along without delay."
>
> I beg to state that I have received but one design, namely, the reverse with the [standing] eagle and that I started the work immediately and now have finished same, but I hear nothing of the other side and unless we receive the other model quite soon there will be but little accomplished by the time you return.
>
> I wish to be on record that we are waiting anxiously to go on with the dies.
>
> One other question, this week I will have ready to send to San Francisco ten pairs of fifty centavo dies for Mexican Coinage, date 1906. As it will be impossible to coin many of these pieces this year, I will thank you to advise me regarding the number of these dies that will be wanted this year and whether the date is to be changed for the calendar year of 1907.
>
> Respectfully,

The engraver indicated he had made a working die of the standing eagle $20 reverse based on the reduction made in Paris by Janvier et Duvall, and was ready to proceed with the obverse.

Roberts sent a soothing reply the next day:[169]

> …Of course you can do nothing further in the matter until the other side of the model has been received by you. I would suggest that you advise Mr. St. Gaudens that you have finished the design of the reverse and that you are now awaiting the design of the obverse, and ready to proceed as soon as it is received….

It was still unclear to Barber and some mint officials that President Roosevelt intended this new design to replace all four of the current gold coin designs. No official order had been issued for replacement of the old designs, and without a properly executed document the mint staff felt resentful of the time and expense devoted to experiments.

Homer Saint-Gaudens asked that it be sent to Aspet so his father could compare it with the final plaster model and make any necessary adjustments.[170]

> Dear Sir:
>
> The models for the coins have been delayed somewhat through my father's illness, but they should be ready before long. You state in your letter of November tenth that you have received word from the Engraver of the United States Mint that he has finished the [hub for the] design for the reverse of the new gold coinage.
>
> I am enclosing copies of two letters…which show you that… we sent [the standing eagle reduction] only as an experimental model on which they might test their machinery, and not as the final model of the new coin.

---

[167] *US Mint*, NARA-CP, op. cit., entry 235, vol. 356, "Letters Signed by the Secretary," p.98. Letter dated November 10, 1906 to Saint-Gaudens from Shaw.

[168] *US Mint*, NARA-CP, op. cit., entry 229, box 248. Letter dated November 6, 1906 to Roberts from Barber.

[169] *US Mint*, NARA-CP, op. cit., entry 330, box 45. Letter dated November 7, 1906 to Barber from Roberts.

[170] *US Mint*, NARA-P, op. cit. Letters dated November 14 and 21, 1906 to Shaw from Homer Saint-Gaudens.

68

Apparently, Barber thought this was the new coin's final reverse design and indicated this to other mint officials. In his letter of November 14, Homer Saint-Gaudens reminded secretary Shaw that the standing eagle reduction sent to the mint was not intended for coinage, but he does not mention anything about using the flying eagle. The situation is further confused by Homer's statement on August 2 that the studio work was finished and the models could be seen anytime the President wished. While Homer wanted to examine the sample hub, mint engraver Charles Barber was fuming about what he saw as the futility of the experiment:[171]

> Sir:
> I am prepared to take the models chosen by the President for the twenty-dollar gold coin, which Mr. Saint Gaudens states are from eleven to fourteen inches in diameter, and make the required reductions.
> As the whole proposition is only an experiment, I fail to see the object of sending a design that is not intended to be used and only one side of that.
> The only experiment that can be made that will be worthy the name, and of any utility, will have to be made with the design that is intended for use, anything else would be futile.
> Respectfully,

Everyone at the mint had been on edge for nearly two months anticipating arrival of the new designs, and their opportunity to prove the President wrong in his impression of the mint's capabilities. Homer Saint-Gaudens' comments about having used an experimental reduction to make a die only made the situation worse: time had been wasted on a design not intended for production. On the 21st Homer asked for the standing eagle die, "…my father desires to see the result in order that he may model his final copy so that it will meet the demands of the machine."[172] This innocent-seeming request was, according to superintendent John Landis, contrary to mint regulations and he made his objection known to director Roberts on November 26:[173]

> In reply to your letter of the 24th instant, enclosing a copy of a letter from Homer Saint-Gaudens to the Honorable Secretary of the Treasury, asking that the result of the reproduction of the eagle for the twenty dollar gold piece be sent to Mr. Saint-Gaudens, I beg to send you herewith, by the hands of the Chief Clerk, an impression in lead taken from the die made by the Engraver.
> I am not satisfied that I have the right to forward impressions from any dies made for coinage, or experimental purposes, to any one outside the mint, with the exception of yourself. It seems to me that this matter is covered by Art. 15, Sec. 16 (4), of the Regulations, which reads:
>
> > Experimental pieces of proposed designs or of new coins for the official use of the Director of the Mint under section 3510, Revised Statutes, and on his written requisition, shall be struck in such metal or alloy only and of such weight and fineness as prescribed by law for coins of the same denomination. Such experimental pieces will be receipted for by the Director, and if not adopted for regular coinage during the same year will be defaced by him as soon as the use is subserved for which that were struck, and forthwith returned to the superintendent, who shall cause them to be melted in his presence and that of the melter and refiner, when both of these officers shall join in a written statement to that effect, which statement, to be sent to the Director of the Mint, shall be a voucher to the Director of the Mint, and so put upon

---

[171] *US Mint*, NARA-P, op. cit. Letter dated November 20, 1906 to Landis from Barber.
[172] *US Mint*, NARA-CP, op. cit., entry 330, box 45. Letter dated November 21, 1906 to Shaw from Homer Saint-Gaudens.
[173] *US Mint*, NARA-CP, op. cit., entry 229, box 249. Letter dated November 26, 1906 to Roberts from Landis.

> record in the regular archives of the Bureau of the Mint. Such pieces, if adopted for
> coinage, will be returned by the Director and receipted for by the superintendent.

And the second sentence of Sec. 6, of the same Article:

> All dated dies shall be defaced at the end of each year, and such impressions as the
> engraver may find necessary to take while preparing the dies shall be destroyed in
> the presence of the superintendent when the dies are finished.

Respectfully,

Landis felt he did not have authority to release the lead impression to anyone outside the Philadelphia Mint except the director. A generation earlier, the Philadelphia Mint had earned a reputation for "leaking" patterns, experimental pieces and other items to coin collectors and well-connected dealers. Directors Leech and Preston, who instituted tight controls on all experimental work, had largely cleaned up the mess. The result was that few patterns and die trials had left the mint during the previous twenty years, and Landis was very protective of his facility's reputation for security.

Engraver Barber had been shown Homer's letter and wrote a personal note to acting director Preston. Here, the engraver expressed his disdain for Saint-Gaudens, much as the sculptor had expressed for Barber. The two had not met since 1891, yet animosity lay close to the surface:[174]

> Dr. Norris will write you officially and I wish to say a word unofficially, but first to put you in possession of all the facts of the case.
>
> I cannot for the life of me see what Mr. Saint Gaudens wants with the "result of the reduction" he now asks for, it in no way aids him in making his model, as we have told him, that if he will send us the models which he informs the department are from eleven to thirteen inch diameter, that we will take charge of the rest, and get dies made, he need not trouble his soul about our reducing machine, we will take all responsibility regarding the reductions, and know far better than he how to get the best effects.
>
> He talks so much about experiments, it may be to him; but to us it is no experiment, as we are just as certain that the relief of his eagle will never coin, as we are certain that the Sun will rise each morning, and the only object in all this trouble and waste of money is to convince those who will be convinced in no other way, that to comply with the restrictions of the law, and requirements of the civilized commercial world, you cannot depart from the experience of all nations namely, that to make coins of a given weight and fineness the operation of stamping the design on the piece of metal or planchet must be but one, and therefore the relief must be made to suit that operation, any repetition of the operation involves a number of others, and then both weight and fineness become an unknown quantity.
>
> I think our friend is playing a game as he did when you [i.e., Robert Preston] and John G. [Carlisle] had to call him down, and that he is not anxious to show his hand, he possibly thought we would say we cannot coin your work and that would end the matter, but our willingness, nay more, our desire to let the work tell its own story has rather called his hand, and he is not prepared to show it, and therefore is sparing for wind, or time.
>
> To repeat that which we have said before, give him to understand that if he will let us have the models we are prepared to do all the rest, namely produce the dies.

[174] *US Mint*, NARA-CP, op. cit., entry 330, box 45. Letter dated November 26, 1906 to Preston from Barber. This is one of the few times Barber lets his guard down and states his personal opinion about Saint-Gaudens. The sculptor is more open in his letters to President Roosevelt, although we do not know if he realized that many of them were forwarded to the director or secretary. John G. Carlisle was treasury secretary and Robert Preston was director of the mint in 1894 when Saint-Gaudens' reverse design for the Columbian Exposition Special Award Medal was rejected. See Chapter 1.

I send the reduction of the reverse, or eagle sent us, and wish to remind you that the regulation is very clear regarding impressions for experimental dies, and plainly states, "that all such are to be destroyed," to this case we appear to be quite lax as Mr. Saint Gaudens has had reductions made in Paris and no doubt has many impressions on hand of this proposed coin, at some future date these impressions will appear in the collection of some collector, or at some sale and then the old questions will arise how did they get away from the Mint? And perhaps the old insinuation that they were made by the officers of this Mint when something rare or unique is desired.

Excuse my interference but I do want to stand in the right position and I am just as desirous that you should know why nothing's doing, so that when the patience of all folks in Washington is exhausted, the wrath shall not descend upon us.

Yours sincerely,

Charles E. Barber, Engraver

The lead impression was sent to Saint-Gaudens on November 28 along with a cautioning comment about the "sanctity" of experimental pieces:[175]

Responding to your request, addressed to the Secretary of the Treasury, I am sending you herewith by registered mail, an impression in lead of the die made from the design you have submitted. The Mint is waiting for the other side. It is prepared to receive models eleven to fourteen inches in diameter, as yours are understood to be, and to make the required reductions. No test that will have any significance can be made upon coinage metal until both dies are ready for use. The relief upon both sides must be brought up at the same time, and the amount of relief upon one side affects the impression upon the other side.

As the law requires that all experimental pieces struck in the development of the new coinage designs, whether the same are adopted or not, shall be destroyed in the presence of the Mint officials, I must ask you to return this piece to me when you are through with it. I am personally responsible to the Superintendent of the Mint for its return. In this connection permit me to say a word of caution about allowing any experimental pieces or models to pass out of your hands. The law contemplates the most stringent surveillance of all designs, models and dies which have any relation to our coinage.

While Barber and Landis fumed, director Roberts was looking for ways to make a high relief design coinable. George Kunz from Tiffany's had been one of those called on to assist the President and director in September in the search for information on making high relief coins. Tiffany's process, like the mint's medal production, involved repeated blows from the press, and trimming and finishing of the high relief specimen between strikes. Although Roberts had not learned how to strike high relief coins, he did sense the respect President Roosevelt had for Dr. Kunz, whose profession was mineralogy – a favorite pastime of Roosevelt's. When Kunz wrote to the director on November 25, Roberts saw a chance to have a respected "objective" party waiting in the wings to help:[176]

Dear Mr. Kunz:

Your pleasant note of the 25th ultimo came while I was on a trip to the Pacific Coast. I shall improve the first opportunity afforded by a trip to New York to look in on you and see the new Alexander of which you speak and to talk with you further about our own coinage. I feel greatly obliged to you for the opportunity to go

[175] *US Mint*, NARA-CP, op. cit., entry 235, vol. 357, pp.1899–1900. Letter dated November 28, 1906 to Saint-Gaudens from Roberts.

[176] *US Mint*, NARA-CP, op. cit., entry 330, box 45. Letter dated November 28, 1906 to Kunz from Roberts.

through the Tiffany work shop and for the further privilege of conferring with you about our proposed new coinage.

We have completed the die for the design which you saw but now learn that this is not the design determined upon, only an experiment to see how high relief will work. We are now waiting for the other side. Our people at the mint do not believe it possible to strike a coin in such high relief at a single blow and it is certain that it has never been done. In your works I saw that the high relief was obtained by repeated processes. We shall see what can be done with the use of a forming die before giving the final impression. I agree with you that the slight additional cost of an extra impression could well be borne by the country for the sake of a beautiful coinage. The only question is whether the designs to be submitted are possible of perfect execution with a large coinage and whether the coins will be subject to too great a loss by abrasion. I want to talk to you about all these matters.

By the way, have you ever served upon the Annual Assay Commission which meets at the Philadelphia Mint in February of each year to review the pyx coins? The Commission is appointed by the President and I will take pleasure in submitting your name for appointment the next time.

Very truly yours,

Roberts was lining up outside expertise in case the mint failed: "…unless the people at the mint succeed promptly I shall draw on every available resource. The mint officials understand this…"[177] A copy of the letter to George Kunz was shown to Barber, who had a few comments of his own for the director:[178]

.....I assure you that nothing will be neglected on my part to demonstrate the possibility or the contrary of coining anything that may be sent us….

You ask if I have given consideration to the forming die theory, I certainly have, although I must confess that it holds out no hope to me of ever accomplishing any good results, nevertheless as soon as the models that are intended for use arrive, I will go over the question in a careful serious manner.

At every step I find some objection and insurmountable difficulty that is not understood by Mr. Kunz or Mr. Hannweber, in fact [this] is only appreciated by some of us who are engaged in the actual production of coin and know from experience the limitations. At present nothing has been said about the edge of the coins, whether it is to be reeded, plain or lettered, I must know this before making any dies, as the collar governs the diameter of the piece and the dies must fit the collar.

Homer returned the lead trial on December 1 along with a letter (now unlocated) apparently discussing the designs and asking about striking the coins without a collar.[179] On December 8, the sculptor sent a note to Roberts, advising, "The models for both sides of the new $20.00 gold piece are now ready to be sent to the mint for reduction…."[180] Robert's reply to Homer indicated a measure of confusion:[181]

Your letter of the 1st instant was received when I was so occupied with my annual report that I did not read it carefully. It contained only the lead impression of the standing eagle, and I judged upon casual reading that you were forwarding an-

[177] *US Mint*, NARA-CP, op. cit. op. cit., entry 330, box 45. Letter dated December 27, 1906 to Roosevelt from Roberts.
[178] *US Mint*, NARA-CP, op. cit., entry 229, box 250. Letter dated November 30, 1906 to Roberts from Barber. Louis Hannweber was production manager of the Tiffany's medal plant in New Jersey until his retirement in 1915.
[179] *US Mint*, NARA-P, op. cit. Letter dated December 1, 1906 to Landis from Roberts.
[180] *US Mint*, NARA-P, op. cit. Letter (manuscript) dated December 8, 1906 to Roberts from Saint-Gaudens.
[181] *US Mint*, NARA-CP, op. cit., entry 330, box 45. Letter dated December 11, 1906 to Homer Saint-Gaudens from Roberts.

72

other design under a separate enclosure, and so laid the letter aside until it came. Having received nothing more, and re-reading your letter, I judge you intended to enclose the new design but omitted to do so. There is nothing here but the standing eagle. Did you send it to Philadelphia?

Now in regard to the experiments with high relief, I do not anticipate conclusive results on the first trial. The judgement of our experienced people is that the standing eagle cannot be brought up with our presses. We have been coining gold pieces for Mexico during the past year which bear a much lower relief than this eagle, and have had trouble bringing up all the lines. The Philippine coins have also given us some trouble; so we know about where our limitations under present methods are.

I have been in the works of the Gorham Company at Providence and in the works of the Tiffany Company and am familiar with the method by which they get high relief. They use a drop press, and do not confine the metal in a collar. The old Greek coins were not confined in a collar. The absence of a collar allows the metal to spread or spew out on every side and gives the die a chance to sink more deeply and the metal fills the intaglio. But with a collar confining the metal the die does not sink so readily, and when greater pressure is applied the die and collar will break before the metal is forced into all the interstices.

We cannot make coin without a collar. The silverware manufacturers finish their pieces by hand with a file. This is impracticable with coins, made by the million. Furthermore the law provides that the double eagle piece shall weigh 516 grains and allows a tolerance of but one-half a grain for variations, while silverware people sell their wares by the ounce and variations are not important to them.

In conclusion, then, there are no presses anywhere, in mints or in use among silversmiths, which can bring up your proposed relief at a single stroke. But I think it may be possible to first give the piece a stroke under a "forming die", which will give it part of the form which it must take, or, in other words, bunch up the metal where this relief is wanted and thus prepare it so the final stroke will be successful. This is an experiment. It involves double press work, but I do not consider the additional cost prohibitive, if we can get a beautiful coin.

We must, however, have time to work on the problem after receiving both dies. I have no idea that we can give you an immediate result. Success depends upon accomplishing something that has not been done up to this time.

Director Roberts, alone among senior mint officials, appeared ready to try something different, even if Barber and others insisted it wouldn't work. Using a forming die would produce its own set of problems, but at least the director was willing to make the attempt. Meanwhile, the President was getting anxious to have final models and wrote to the artist on December 11:[182]

I hate to trouble you, but it is very important that I should have the models for those coins at once. How soon may I have them?
With all good wishes, believe me,

Saint-Gaudens responded by sending models to the White House on December 14. However, they were not the ones President Roosevelt had expected. The only obverse and reverse designs anyone with the administration had seen were the Striding Liberty with wings and standing eagle derived from the inaugural medal. The new models were simpler, stronger and the reverse now featured a flying eagle. During October and November, while correspondence focused on the standing eagle, Saint-Gaudens had apparently been experimenting with his Striding Liberty without the wings and Indian headdress. He also re-

[182] *SG*, Dartmouth, op. cit. Box 16, folder 37. Letter dated December 11, 1906 to Saint-Gaudens from Roosevelt.

placed the original reverse with the now-familiar flying eagle. In a follow-up letter the artist apologized for markings that suggested these initial models were not finished:[183]

> I am afraid from the letter sent you on the fourteenth with the models for the Twenty Dollar Gold piece that you will think the coin I sent you was unfinished. This is not the case. It is the final and completed model, but I hold myself in readiness to make any such modifications as may be required in the reproduction of the coin.
>
> This will explain the words "test model" on the back of each model.

The Saint may have described the models as "final and complete," but examination of models and coins made from them suggests the designation "test model" and Hering's

*Figure 25. First obverse model delivered to the U. S. Mint in December 1906. The model is somewhat rough and has less detail than the second model delivered in March 1907. This was used to make dies for the extremely high relief experimental coins of February 1907. Note text on the back of the model.* (Courtesy U. S. Department of Interior National Park Service, Saint-Gaudens National Historic Site, Cornish, NH. #1056)

comment that relief was intentionally made too great were correct. In addition to the relief, little had been done about the edge of the coin. The sculptor had tried placing E PLURIBUS UNUM on the rock below Liberty's foot, but evidently did not like the new arrangement. Possibly, the image of Liberty stepping on "unity" was too clear to ignore. This left only the edge for the legally required motto.

Charles Barber commented about the edge motto and stars:[184]

> ...Regarding the lettering upon the edge, if Mr. Saint Gaudens will send a sketch of the character of the letter he desires and also a sketch of the star to be used I will attend to the rest, which you know is made in the collar.
>
> I cannot give the thickness of the piece as I do not know whether the design has a border or is made the same as the standing eagle, but Mr. Saint Gaudens need not go further than to furnish the sketches asked for with any instructions he wishes regarding the position of the letters and stars, whether they are to entirely encircle the coin or only partly, any of the directions given will be strictly adhered to.

---

[183] *US Mint*, NARA-CP, op. cit., entry 330, box 45. Letter dated December 19, 1906 to Roosevelt from Saint-Gaudens.

[184] *US Mint*, NARA-CP, op. cit., entry 229, box 249. Letter (excerpt) dated December 12, 1906 to Roberts from Barber. The engraver's wording suggests there is missing correspondence on this subject.

It appears that Barber created a lettered edge sample double eagle (J-1773, P-1992) from designs by himself and assistant engraver George Morgan. Its purpose was to prove to Roberts that raised lettering on the edge of a coin this large was possible.

During this time the mint also had to produce the normal complement of working dies for U. S. mints, plus new designs, hubs, and dies for new Philippine coinage, and strike a range of silver and gold coins for Cuba. Barber claimed it would take two months to complete the Philippine hubs, and he could not get to the Saint-Gaudens designs until March of 1907.[185] Even with the Janvier and Hill reducing machines working side-by-side, Barber felt he could barely keep up with the demands on his time and that of assistant engraver Morgan. His frustration was evident in a letter to superintendent John H. Landis:[186]

> In answer to the inquiry of the Director whether I cannot reduce the time in preparing dies for the Philippine coinage and also take up the new designs for the Double Eagle by the aid of the new reducing machine, I beg to state, that the new machine being new to us required some time to learn how to operate it, which we are trying to do, but being quite complicated we find it will require some time to learn how to accomplish the best results.
>
> There is no doubt that if I was in full command of the machine it would give the most efficient aid, which we so much need just at this time, and therefore, I suggest that you send for the party who was sent to explain the machine and who remained but one day and a half in both setting up the machine and giving instructions, and let him come and make the paraffin reductions of the Double Eagle design which would allow me to go on with the old machine and make the reductions for the Philippine coins, this would be very valuable assistance and of course bring the desired results in shorter time and also be much preferable to sending the models to New York as it would give us the opportunity of learning the full use of the new machine and I think be less expensive. I therefore ask authority to send for the party already mentioned at once that I may expedite the work desired.
>
> Respectfully,

Roberts approved the request for additional instruction the next day. On the 28th he wrote Saint-Gaudens to let him know about the delay, and also commented on the designs, "From an artistic standpoint the new designs are worthy of the highest praise. If only I was clear as to their practicability in actual coinage operations. We shall, however, do everything that can be done to master the problems which are involved in the use of the high relief."[187] The decision to install the Janvier machine, while thought to be a way of improving work at the mint, actually was creating additional problems. With inadequate training in use of the complicated new equipment, Barber and Morgan could not obtain results superior to the old Hill machine. Further, the expectation by Saint-Gaudens and Hering (neither of whom knew how to use the Janvier machine) that the new equipment would allow direct reductions from large models while simultaneously maintaining design detail was unrealistic.[188] Had the mint sent the models to Tiffany's, Gorham, Dietsch Brothers or another of the medal production companies in New York, and requested coin-relief hubs, it is likely that suitable hubs could have been made faster and cheaper than by mint personnel. According to a letter to Saint-Gaudens, the cost would have been $120 or less for each of

---

[185] US Mint, NARA-P, op. cit. Letter dated December 27, 1906 to Landis from Roberts.

[186] US Mint, NARA-P, op. cit. Letter dated December 28, 1906 to Landis from Barber.

[187] US Mint, NARA-CP, op. cit., entry 235, vol. 357, p.2058. Letter dated December 28, 1906 to Saint-Gaudens from Roberts.

[188] The crucial point is that Saint-Gaudens and Hering knew the Janvier reducing lathe could produce the desired results, but they did not know how it was done, and no one gave the mint engravers the in-depth training to do it.

two reductions direct from the large models to steel hubs, and would take approximately three weeks to complete.[189] The President had put forward this idea in September (see letter, above), but added that it would be an admission by the mint that it wasn't up to the task.[190] So far as we know, Saint-Gaudens did not present this suggestion to the mint, but Barber had already made his contingency plan and was about to make sure the dies were a success.

### *Eagles Standing or Eagles Flying?*

One of the turning points in the cent, eagle and double designs was the decision to abandon the standing eagle reverse for the double eagle in favor of a flying eagle. Variations on the standing eagle are the only designs Saint-Gaudens appears to have actively considered for the reverse of the largest gold coin until October or November 1906. It was similar in composition to the reverse of the 1905 special inaugural medal, and included the necessary legends and mottoes (UNITED STATES OF AMERICA, E PLURIBUS UNUM and TWENTY DOLLARS). Most of his standing eagle pencil sketches and all of the sketch models included this motto as required by law.

The sculptor sent his best model of this design to Paris in June 1906 to have reductions made by Janvier et Duval. The small bronze reductions – in several relief heights – were returned to the Aspet studio at the end of August. In late August, Homer Saint-Gaudens told President Roosevelt the coin models were finished and could be brought to Oyster Bay if desired. However, Homer suggested waiting until both obverse and reverse reductions were ready to save an extra train trip and avoid possible damage to the models.

The bronze reductions (Figure 23, above) were sent to the mint where there appears to have been little comment about the composition. A standing eagle reverse, when paired with the forward-striding Liberty with wings obverse, completed the double eagle design including all required inscriptions. This combination obviated use of edge lettering since there was no need to find a place for the mandatory motto E PLURIBUS UNUM.

---

[189] *SG*, Dartmouth, op. cit. Microfilm reel 8. Letter dated June 30, 1906 to Saint-Gaudens from Tiffany & Co. The quotation refers to making reductions for the three-inch Franklin medal dies; however, the process was similar for a coinage die.

[190] As late as 1922 engraver Morgan did not have full command of the Janvier reducing machine and was unable to make high-quality, low relief hubs from the Peace dollar models.

*Figure 26. Double eagle design as originally proposed by Saint-Gaudens. Apparently, these were abandoned by the sculptor in October-November 1906 and replaced with the now-familiar wingless Striding Liberty-Flying Eagle designs. Both obverse and reverse replacements were simpler and more forceful than the originals.* (Courtesy U. S. Department of Interior National Park Service, Saint-Gaudens National Historic Site, Cornish, NH. #1050, #1092.)

A speculative reason for the change may be that Saint-Gaudens realized his compositions were too complicated. By simplifying Liberty – removing superfluous wings and headdress, converting her into a dynamic obverse figure full of motion and life – he now needed to pair it with a reverse of similar character. His standing eagle was a medallic "still life" that had little motion or vibrancy, it was strong but static. His flying eagle, however, was all movement and dominance – characteristics consistent with the revised obverse composition. None of Roosevelt's letters mention the substitute reverse, likewise silent are Saint-Gaudens' letters and U. S. Mint documents. It was only in February 1907 that Saint-Gaudens offered an explanation mentioning that he learned the flying eagle was "illegal on the cent." But it is not clear why this was substituted for the design into which he had placed so much labor and expense.

The new designs also left no place for E PLURIBUS UNUM.

When in December the President asked to see the designs "at once," they were delivered to the White House in mid-month. The obverse was similar to that previously described only missing the angelic wings and headdress, but the reverse was new – the flying eagle originally intended for the obverse of the cent. The cent version was nearly identical to the one used on the double eagle except the legend LIBERTY was replaced by a two-line inscription: UNITED STATES OF AMERICA, and TWENTY DOLLARS.

Substitution of the flying eagle design affected both large gold coins, and indirectly affected the half- and quarter-eagle pieces issued in 1908. The cent's flying eagle composition was a very compact arrangement that had room for text only at the top rim. The single line inscription LIBERTY could be replaced with two lines of text, UNITED STATES OF AMERICA and TWENTY DOLLARS, without unbalancing the composition. More than two lines would not fit without destroying the flying eagle design's balance. Henry Hering alluded to this in his December 21, 1907 letter when he wrote:[191]

---

[191] *US Mint*, NARA-P, op. cit. Letter dated December 21, 1907 to Leach from Hering.

The inscription "Two and a half Dollars" would change the composition, making three lines of inscription, which Mr. Saint-Gaudens experimented with and discarded.

With nationality, date and denomination also required on the coin, the only alternative was to place E PLURIBUS UNUM on the obverse or the edge. The obverse was already crowded with foliage, rays, buildings, stars, a torch, the Roman numeral date and Miss Liberty. Placing the motto on the rock below the figure was tried and rejected, so that left the edge as the only available space. Having worked with lettered edge pattern coins in 1885 and on his 1906 double eagle pattern, and knowing of good results from the Royal Mint in London, Charles Barber likely had only limited objection to making a lettered edge version of the new design. After all, his view was that these were only experiments done at the President's order and not intended for circulation.

The "trickle down" effect continued when the flying eagle had to be replaced on the cent design. Here, Saint-Gaudens fell back on his idealized portrait of Hettie Anderson done for the *Sherman Memorial*, and now called *Nike Erini (Victory – Peace)*. This adaptation went to Roosevelt in February 1907, and the President liked it, but wanted an Indian headdress added. This Saint-Gaudens did, and the war-bonnet-loving President approved the change. In May, Roosevelt and Leach suggested adapting the *Nike Erini* profile for the obverse (the "Indian head") and using the standing eagle reverse for the $10 gold coin. This was quickly agreed to, and the cent largely forgotten by Roosevelt and the sculptor, as they worked to get the two gold coins in shape for eventual production. The starred edge on the $10 eagle coin appears to be nothing more than an artistic flourish done to avoid using a reeded edge.

## *I Shall Be Impeached for It*

When Roosevelt finally saw the large design models on December 15 he was hardly able to control his enthusiasm:[192]

> My dear Saint Gaudens:
> Those models are simply immense – if such a slang way of talking is permissible in reference to giving a modern nation one coinage at least which shall be as good as that of the ancient Greeks. I have instructed the Director of the Mint that these dies are to be reproduced just as quickly as possible and just as they are. It is simply splendid. I suppose I shall be impeached for it in Congress; but I shall regard that as a very cheap payment!
> With heartiest regards,

Roosevelt had been shown a reduction of the standing eagle reverse by Homer Saint-Gaudens. However, he evidently had not previously seen either the flying eagle or the wingless Striding Liberty obverse as full-size models. Director Roberts also was reminded of the President's wishes:[193]

> My dear Mr. Roberts:
> I suppose it is needless for me to write, but I do want to ask that you have special and particular care exercised in the cutting of that Saint Gaudens coin. Won't you bring the die in for me to see, even before you send it to Saint Gaudens? Of

---

[192] *SG*, Dartmouth, op. cit. Box 16, folder 37. Letter dated December 20, 1906 to Saint-Gaudens from Roosevelt.
[193] *Roosevelt*, LoC, op. cit., vol. 69, pp.282–283, microfilm reel 344. Letter dated December 26, 1906 to Roberts from Roosevelt.

course the workmanship counts as much as the design in a case like this. I feel that we have the chance with this coin to make something as beautiful as the old Greek coinage. In confidence, I am not at all sure how long I shall be permitted to have such a coin in existence; but I want for once at least to have had this nation, the great republic of the West, with its extraordinary facility of industrial, commercial and mechanical expression, do something in the way of artistic expression that shall rank with the best work of the kind that has ever been done.

Sincerely yours,

P.S. Of course keep what we are doing absolutely confidential, as I do not want anything about it to get out until the coins are actually made.

The President was trying to actively engage Roberts with his "pet baby" in hopes of bypassing Congress and avoiding publicity about the new designs. The "conspiratorial" tone of his postscript seems oddly out of place since dozens of people in the treasury department and Mint Bureau knew about the coin experiments. Roosevelt, who had already been contacted again by George Kunz – who in addition to his Tiffany's business duties was part-time curator of coins for the Metropolitan Museum of Art in New York – did not want further disclosures that might interfere with his plans.[194] (The President may not have known that Roberts had sent Frank Leach, superintendent of the San Francisco Mint, a sample of the standing eagle reverse for his comments and suggestions on producing high relief coinage.) Roberts wrote to the President the next day, commenting, "I shall be happy to have my administration of the mint service distinguished by the execution of this beautiful piece." He also provided a summary of events to the President and explained further:[195]

Acknowledging your note of the 26th, permit me to say that I fully appreciate your interest in the Saint Gaudens designs, and join you in it. I shall be happy to have my administration of the mint service distinguished by the execution of this beautiful piece. I delivered the models myself to the Engraver at Philadelphia last week, and I am assured that every man in the mint who has to do with this work will do his utmost to make the coinage a success.

I will have the dies brought to Washington for your inspection before they are sent to Saint Gaudens. I have no misgivings however about the execution of the dies; I believe that dies-cutting done at the mint is equal to any done in this country. But the high relief will present difficulties in coinage which have never yet been overcome, and when it comes to that we must ask your patience while we try to work out the problem. By the courtesy of Mr. Kunz, of Tiffany & Company, I have lately been shown through their workshop and observed their methods. They obtain high relief by use of a drop press, which works on the principle of a pile driver. No collar is used, and the metal, being unconfined on all sides, may flow or spread out under the stroke and the die sink more deeply than where a collar holds it closely. The old Greek coins were likewise made without a collar, and the collar makes our problem. Tiffany & Company finish their wares with a file, and adapt their prices to the amount of metal in the article, while the mint of course must turn out pieces uniform in weight to a nicety, and do it with great rapidity.

I mention these difficulties in some detail because I am sure you want to understand them, and we want you to make allowances for the delays which must occur.

[194] *Roosevelt*, LoC, op. cit., vol. 68, p.325, microfilm reel 343. Letter dated November 27, 1906 to George F. Kunz from Roosevelt. Kunz appears throughout the gold, minor and subsidiary silver coin redesign representing the museum, Tiffany's, the Smithsonian Institution, or the American Numismatic Society in various capacities. He seems to have been very well informed on coinage matters, and was aware of events long before other numismatists. For the Saint-Gaudens coins, this may be due to the White House having contacted Tiffany's in early September to discuss high relief designs.
[195] *US Mint*, NARA-CP, op. cit., entry 235, vol. 357, pp.2042–2044. Letter dated December 27, 1906 to Roosevelt from Roberts.

We do not think it possible to strike these coins at one blow, but are hoping to accomplish it by first giving the pieces a preliminary strike under a forming die, which will heap the metal up where it is needed to bring out the high relief on the final impression. I do not consider the extra press work on the large denominations a serious expense if we can get a beautiful coin.

Mr. Kunz has promised me any aid that Tiffany & Company may render and unless the people at the mint succeed promptly I shall draw on every available resource. The mint officials understand this. The very best that can be done will be done to give effect to these designs.

I have cautioned everybody who of necessity must know of this undertaking that it is a confidential matter.

The engravers are now at work on the dies for the new Philippine coinage, the reduction of size having compelled the making of a new master die. As the War Department is in great haste for this new coinage I have assumed that this work should be finished before taking up the Saint Gaudens design. It will require about six weeks.

I am returning the Saint Gaudens letters herewith.

"That is first-class. I am very much obliged to you," replied the President.[196]

As 1906 closed, President Theodore Roosevelt was at the peak of popularity. The Nobel Peace Prize had elevated him, and the country, from blustering backwater to an international force in the view of other nations. This had boosted his popularity with the public, and muzzled critical Democrats and the conservative wing of his own Republican Party. Many supporters urged him to quietly repudiate his hasty rejection of a second elected term and accept the desire of the citizenry.

Delivery of the new double eagle design was one of many triumphs, small and large, that came to Roosevelt. Had the first submission been less "test model" and more "production model," the President might have gotten true high relief coins produced in quantity; few in Congress or the public were prepared to oppose him. What Saint-Gaudens thought was near completion was really near its beginning. As delay and revision through the coming year would wear down artist and mint, so too would the President's power to command wane in the face of a sharp economic downturn and anticipation of William Howard Taft's presidential nomination.

## Experiments Enough to Mint a Million – 1907

Charles Edward Barber, Engraver of the United States Mint at Philadelphia, was pleased to have the new models in his workshop. Long ago he had decided no model from Saint-Gaudens' hand could be coined, but many artists were skeptical. Now he had what he needed to prove "the Saint" knew nothing of coinage. He was determined to do all he could to make coins out of the medallic designs Saint-Gaudens provided. With the information from this experiment at hand, he could finally put the sculptor in his place. He was also determined to make sure his superiors in the Bureau of the Mint knew it.

Anticipating a future assertion from Saint-Gaudens that the mint's dies or hubs were inferior, Barber turned to Dietsch Brothers for assistance. The engraver knew his skill with the Janvier lathe was limited, so he had prepared a backup plan. Unknown to anyone except the director and Philadelphia Mint superintendent, Barber arranged for Henri Weil

[196] *Roosevelt*, LoC, op. cit., vol. 69, p.328, microfilm reel 344. Letter dated January 1, 1907 to Roberts from Roosevelt.

from Dietsch Brothers to help him make the reductions and hubs.[197] Everyone at the mint remembered Roosevelt's stinging comment the previous September about it being a black mark against the service if they sent the model out. Although the work was being done at the mint, bringing in an outside expert to cut the new hubs might not agree with Roosevelt. Confidentiality was important – no one wanted the President galloping through the Philadelphia Mint issuing orders.

Weil's visit, from January 3 through 8, was officially explained as providing additional training on the new equipment, as Barber had requested in late December.[198] Part of the new training included Weil making paraffin reductions from the Saint-Gaudens models, bronze casts of the reductions, and cutting the high relief obverse hub. All this took six days during which Barber made notes so he could complete the reverse hub on his own.[199] Although pressed for time due to changes in the Philippine coins, by having George Morgan use the Hill lathe on the Philippine reductions, Barber could pay closer attention to the politically sensitive Saint-Gaudens' hubs.

Henry Hering's high relief models required multiple cuts for the reduction and hubs just as they would for a medal. Each new cut was made using progressively finer tracing and cutting tools. By using hard paraffin rather than steel under the cutting tool, a usable reduction could be accomplished fairly quickly. Paraffin was easily warped or melted but was suitable as a temporary reduction used for making a casting mold. The final bronze cast was approximately five-inches in diameter. Once he had this, Barber was in familiar territory and could work with increased confidence.[200]

With Weil's help the obverse hub was cut with little loss of detail. Apparently no attempt was made to lower the relief, this being Barber's understanding of the President's comment to use the models "just as they are," so the full design was reduced proportionally. This process was much like what Barber and Morgan had learned to do on the old Hill lathe thirty-years earlier. The part the engravers did not learn was how to reduce relief while maintaining detail in all parts of the design. This knowledge gap would haunt the mint's work until John Sinnock became engraver in 1925.

Augustus Saint-Gaudens' first models lacked much of the fine detail and finished execution of the final models. As Hering says, they were an experiment – one that Barber did not like. Hering offered his comments in a 1935 article:[201]

[197] Weil had made reductions for the 1905 special inaugural medal designed by Saint-Gaudens and Weinman. Sadly, it took the Mint Bureau a year to pay the company for their services. Weil and his brother Felix later formed the *Medallic Art Company.*

[198] *US Mint*, NARA-CP, op. cit., entry 229, box 256. Invoice dated August 2, 1907 to U. S. Mint from Dietsch Brothers, Inc.

[199] *US Mint*, NARA-CP, op. cit., entry 229, box 250. Letter dated January 3, 1907 to Roberts from Norris. This and other letters (December 28, 1907, *et supra*) also refer to the company's unpaid invoice for $65.00.

[200] The U. S. Mint had produced a large number of high relief medals over the years and had considerable experience in cutting hubs and dies for these. The difference between any ordinary medal design and Saint-Gaudens' work was that the sculptor seemed to think the coin could be made with a single blow of the press, while having relief nearly as pronounced as that on a medal. The 1906 Franklin medal, designed by Louis Saint-Gaudens, produced at the mint from hubs made by Tiffany's, was struck with little difficulty using multiple blows, yet its relief was much greater than any coin.

[201] *Adolph A. Weinman papers*, Archives of American Art, microfilm reel 414, pp.13?–13? This article accompanied a letter dated September 23, 1935 from Clyde C. Trees, president of Medallic Art Company to A. A. Weinman, forwarding a copy of Mr. Hering's "magazine story." The article was finally published in *The Numismatist*, August, 1949, pp.455–458. The accuracy of much of Hering's article is questionable. In this short quotation there are several errors including: Hering taking the model to Philadelphia, and Barber's reluctance to make a hub. The article originated in April 1933 as transcribed reminiscences by Hering to Lillian Grant, secretary to George Godard, Librarian of the Connecticut State Library. According to Godard, he and Hering had just returned from dinner and drinks when the interview was given. Go-

...I was in charge of the work and engineered the proceedings at the Philadelphia Mint. I proceeded to make a model in very high relief, knowing perfectly well they could not stamp it in one strike, my objective being to have a die made of this model and then have strikes made in order to see the various results.

I took the model to the Philadelphia Mint and was introduced by the Director to Mr. Barbour [*sic* – Charles Barber], who was the chief engraver. When he saw the plaster model of the $20 gold piece, which was about nine inches in diameter, he rejected it and said it was impossible for any mint to coin it. I told him my reasons for doing it and that we would have to experiment. After considerable discussion he finally decided to make the die.

As ordered by the President, Barber, with considerable help from Henri Weil, began cutting a hub from Hering's extremely high relief models. His experiment was to try and strike a coin from the new dies – something he knew would fail. But Barber's was not the only experiment undertaken by the bureau of the mint. Quietly, and out of reach of the pre-formed opinions of the Philadelphia Mint, director Roberts was working with Frank Leach, superintendent of the San Francisco Mint, on high relief coinage ideas. San Francisco was a logical choice for such experiments because they were currently striking the somewhat high relief Philippine and Mexican gold coins, and Leach's staff had more experience in striking large quantities of gold than the Philadelphia Mint.

Director Roberts, who had previously sent a sample of the standing eagle reverse to superintendent Leach forwarded a photo of the new design. The superintendent replied on January 4, 1907:[202]

Yours of the 29th ult., enclosing design for the new double eagle, received. I am pleased to see that it has a better appearance than I had anticipated. However, I have my doubts about the popularity of the piece – yet, there is no telling how these things may strike the public. You will remember that when you were here [in November] we had some conversation on the possibility of striking pieces with this high relief, and that I told you I thought we could put the planchets in shape by manipulation of the milling machine. Yesterday I had our pressman make an experiment and it fully confirmed my judgement in the matter. This would be easier, quicker and less expensive than using a forming die. However, it would require experiment to demonstrate to a certainty that my theory is the correct one.

I am glad to know there has been another design for the eagle submitted. This [standing] eagle is hardly a faithful representation of our national bird. The legs are altogether too long, and I think any student of natural history or of the bird family will confirm this criticism. This design inclines one to the impression of a crane in masquerade wearing pantaloons and a cutaway coat. When they decide upon the design and have the dies made I should like very much to have an opportunity of experimenting with my method of making the coins. Of course, if there is anything I can do in helping you out in this matter of the new coin, why do not be backward about calling upon me. I appreciate what you say about the confidential character of you communication, and return the design herewith....
Respectfully,

PS: I am satisfied from our little experimenting that a piece with as high relief as the sample sent can be struck on the ordinary press if the designer will manage to

dard was trying to convince Hering to donate one of his high relief MCMVII coins to the Mitchelson collection. Hering sold a fin rim version to the collection for $45 in June 1933.
[202] *US Mint*, NARA-CP, op. cit., entry 229, box 251. Letter dated January 4, 1907 to Roberts from Leach. The milling machine manipulation was used in December 1907 to make the "finless" high relief double eagles.

82

have the excessive relief within a certain radius from the center. In other words, excessive high relief cannot be carried out to the margin of the coin.

Roberts sent him some of the new Philippine coins and suggested experimenting with the milling on these designs. Leach replied, "I hardly think the relief in the Philippine coin is high enough to prove anything. If the Philadelphia Mint has any medal dies of high relief and about the size of the double eagle dies it would be much better."[203] Leach, who would become mint director in a few months, could not know that his experiments would come in handy in late 1907 as the mint struggled to improve the quality of high relief coins.

After delivery of double eagle models, Saint-Gaudens and Hering continued work on models for the cent. By February 5, 1907 the former was able to dictate a letter to President Roosevelt:[204]

Dear Mr. President:
I send you by express today the model from which the Mint may make its dies to strike the one cent piece which was included in my agreement to prepare for the United States Government, its models for coins according to the letter of Secretary Shaw under date of July 29, 1905, when he wrote: "I note that you are ready to undertake the preparation of designs for both sides of the gold coins and the one cent piece, for five thousand dollars ($5000.)" and "If you are willing to execute the designs for the gold and copper coins for $5000, you may proceed."
The illegality of an eagle on the one cent made it necessary for me to find something new for the reverse of that piece which would replace the flying or standing eagle I first submitted.
For some time I felt at a loss for a design until I fell back on this idea of using the customary female head that represents Liberty. I must own that I now feel happy about the result, for the head, at least, is out of the usual run.
Faithfully yours,

The tone of Saint-Gaudens' letter suggests the sculptor felt his work was nearly complete. Director Roberts explained about the eagle not being permitted on the cent when he sent the President's secretary a progress report on February 8:[205]

Dear Mr. Loeb:
The dies are about done. I am promised that we may have a test of them next week. I had Mr. Kunz of Tiffany and Company put on the Assay Commission, which meets next week, to get the full benefit of his advise in dealing with the problem of high-relief, and I hope to be able to make a report of progress soon. Would the President like to see the die before a test is made?
The provision of law governing designs upon the coins reads as follows:
"...but on the gold dollar piece, the dime, five, three and one cent piece the figure of the eagle shall be omitted..."

This decision, which was contrary to an earlier opinion given Saint-Gaudens by secretary Shaw, completely changed how the various designs were to be used.

[203] *US Mint*, NARA-CP, op. cit., entry 229, box 250. Letter dated January 18, 1907 to Roberts from Leach.
[204] *SG*, Dartmouth, op. cit. Box 16, folder 38. Letter dated February 5, 1907 to Roosevelt from Saint-Gaudens.
[205] *US Mint*, NARA-CP, op. cit., entry 330, box 45. Letter dated February 8, 1907 to Loeb from Roberts.

*Figure 27. First designs for the one cent piece (top) and second models for the one cent coin as delivered on February 5, 1907. Compare the reverse to the sketch, above.* (Courtesy U. S. Department of Interior National Park Service, Saint-Gaudens National Historic Site, Cornish, NH. #1098, #1138, #1153. Drawing courtesy Dartmouth College Library Special Collections.)

The head of Liberty Saint-Gaudens selected was based on the second model for the head of *Victory* in the Sherman monument.[206] The same design was later used as a three-dimensional model and a bas-relief titled NIKH EIPHNH (*Nike Erini – Victory and Peace*).[207]

Roosevelt now began to "tinker" with the designs. He had really wanted an Indian headdress on one of the coins and was disappointed when both the Striding Liberty figure and the Liberty bust lacked the presidentially requisite bit of Americana.[208]

> My dear Saint Gaudens:
> It seems dreadful to look such a gift horse in the mouth, but I feel very strongly that on at least one coin we ought to have the Indian feather headdress. It is dis-

---

[206] Hettie Anderson was the model for this portrait.

[207] In 1921 a copy of this model owned by James Fraser was loaned to Anthony de Francisci to help get the head of Liberty on the Peace dollar the way Fraser wanted it.

[208] *Roosevelt*, LoC, op. cit., vol. 70, p.401, microfilm reel 344. Letter dated February 8, 1907 to Saint-Gaudens from Roosevelt. No one seems to have thought that Miss Liberty wearing a ceremonial war bonnet was tantamount to a civilian wearing an unearned Congressional Medal of Honor.

tinctly American, and very picturesque. Couldn't you have just such a head as you have now, but with the feather headdress?

Director Roberts reports to me that the dies for the twenty-dollar gold piece are about done, and he expects to have a test of them next week.

Faithfully yours,

During the same week, Saint-Gaudens requested return of his large model of the standing eagle and the five-and-three-eighths-inch reduction. He also returned to the mint the two lead impressions loaned by director Roberts, and began working on adding the headdress to the bust of Liberty.

Barber's working dies of the first models were completed within a month, and on February 15, 1907 the first gold impressions of the new double eagle were placed in the hands of the director of the mint.[209] This first group used the Striding Liberty without headdress for the obverse and the flying eagle reverse.

*Figure 28. Extremely high relief experimental double eagle struck from the first dies. The edge collar is similar to one used on Barber's pattern double eagle of 1906.* (Photo courtesy Douglas Mudd, Smithsonian National Numismatic Collection.)

Roberts reimbursed the mint account for four coins and put them away for safe keeping. Two were of the normal diameter, although struck in extremely high relief. The other two were from the same models but struck on a thick planchet the diameter of a $10 coin. These latter two pieces were to figure in future events.

The first group included at least three complete, normal diameter coins, a plain edge piece (incompletely struck), and three partial strikes all in gold. One of the normal diameter coins, the last one struck, had a plain edge and a prominent die crack on the reverse. The others had lettered edges using a segmented collar similar to the one Barber had used on his and Morgan's experimental double eagle in late 1906.[210] The obvious intention was to strike a small quantity, but this was thwarted when the reverse die cracked. Barber had also prepared fifteen small-diameter pieces that had been struck without incident. The experimental pieces were struck during the same week the Assay Commission was meeting

---

[209] *US Mint*, NARA-P, op. cit. Receipt dated February 15, 1907 signed by George E. Roberts. The same receipt has a manuscript notation signed by Albert A. Norris stating that two double eagles were returned on August 2, 1907.

[210] Personal examination by the author in 2005.

at the Philadelphia Mint. Based on two letters by director Roberts, it is likely that Victor Brenner, George Kunz and possibly others on the Assay Commission saw or were told about the new coins. On February 18 Kunz was advised, "Please say nothing at Numismatic Society or elsewhere about our new coins."[211] To Brenner he wrote, "…it is not possible at present to give out information about the talked-of new coins."[212]

By February 18 a feather headdress had been added to the cent's Liberty head and shown to Roosevelt. He wrote to the sculptor praising the design and subtly lobbying Saint-Gaudens to add a headdress to the Striding Liberty figure:[213]

> My dear Mr. Saint Gaudens:
> I wonder if I am one of those people of low appreciation of artistic things, against whom I have been inveighing! I like that feather head-dress so much that I have accepted that design of yours. Of course all the designs are conventional, as far as head-dresses go, because Liberty herself is conventional when embodied in a woman's head; and I don't see why we should not have a conventional head-dress of purely American type for the Liberty figure.
> I am returning to you today the model of the Liberty head.
> With hearty thanks,
> Faithfully yours,

The first experimental double eagles took seven blows of the medal press to bring up the full design.[214] While making experimental gold double eagles, Barber had been asked by Henry Hering, who may have been present, to provide plaster casts of each of the intermediate blows so that he and Saint-Gaudens could study them.[215]

> … we went to the press room to see how the experimental die (the first model) would work out; so a circular disc of gold was placed in the die and by hydraulic pressure of 172 tons [*sic:* 150 tons], I think it was, we had our first stamping, and the impression showed up a little more that one half of the modeling. I had them make a cast of this for my guidance. The coin was again placed on the die for another strike and again it showed a little more of the modeling and so it went, on and on until the ninth [*sic:* seventh] strike, when the coin showed up in every detail.

Barber made the plaster casts, but discovered after they dried there were too many imperfections to show the design properly. He also tried electrotypes but these were also

[211] *US Mint*, NARA-CP, op. cit., entry 235, vol. 367. Letter dated February 18, 1907 to Kunz from Roberts.

[212] *US Mint*, NARA-CP, op. cit., entry 235, vol. 367. Letter dated February 19, 1907 to Brenner from Roberts.

[213] *SG*, Dartmouth, op. cit. Box 16, folder 38. Letter dated February 18, 1907 to Saint-Gaudens from Roosevelt.

[214] The subject of annealing the planchets between blows is mentioned by director Leach in a letter to Charles Brewster, below. It is also mentioned by director Roberts when referring to the Saint Louis medal that took thirteen blows to bring up the detail. Leach mentions annealing in his memoirs but does not state there if this was routinely done to the more than 12,000 high relief double eagles made in 1907.

[215] *Weinman*, AAA, op. cit. Microfilm reel 414, p.13?. Hering's "magazine story" does not mention annealing between blows, although both Barber and Leach confirm this was done.

unsatisfactory, although Roberts had them sent to Saint-Gaudens anyway.[216] Not having the plaster casts available, Saint-Gaudens wrote to the director on February 21:[217]

> Dear Sir:
> I find that if the Twenty Dollar gold coin required seven strikes, it will be necessary, as Mr. Hering suggested, to have a cast of each of the following strikes sent me:
>> The First.
>> The Second.
>> The Fifth.
>> The Seventh.
>> The finished strike in lead.
>> The finished strike in lead of the small coin.
> The cast of the finished steel model from which all the future dies will be made [i.e., the hub]. It will also be necessary for me to have my original plaster models, which, if you desire, I will return later.
> It is also absolutely essential that I should also have the actual gold strikings described above, as it would give me a much truer idea of the result. I can assure you that I would take the best possible care of these strikings and return them to you in a very short time.
> Very truly yours,

Evidently, Hering had told Saint-Gaudens that it took seven blows from the medal press to create a full strike of the extremely high relief double eagle dies, but had not brought back any samples.[218] Director Roberts agreed to Saint-Gaudens' request, but discovered the engraver could not supply everything requested:[219]

> Sir:
> The dies being broken I can only furnish such pieces as I have of the Double Eagle in gold, new design, namely; first, second, third strike and a finished piece, and one impression of each diameter, in lead, without the lettering on the periphery [i.e., edge].
> I have no doubt that these will answer the desired purpose.
> The finished coin is the best impression of the steel hub that can be furnished.

The gold coin and strike samples were duly sent to Saint-Gaudens and returned by him on March 13. Thinking his work complete, the sculptor sent a bill for $5,000 to the mint, but suspended the invoice on February 24 when he realized more had to be done. Director Roberts wrote urging that the modifications include a well-rounded rim, wide enough to carry the coin and withstand abrasion.[220]

The four experimental coins received by director Roberts had caused something of a stir at mint headquarters, because on March 4 Roberts authorized the production of two more samples specifically for the mint cabinet.[221] The pressure used for the first three coins

---

[216] *US Mint*, NARA-P, op. cit. Letter dated February 20, 1907 to Landis from Barber. These electrotypes survived and are now in the American Numismatic Society collection. See Chapter 7 for illustrations of the electrotypes.
[217] *US Mint*, NARA-P, op. cit. Letter dated February 21, 1907 to Roberts from Saint-Gaudens.
[218] Nine strikes are mentioned in other documents from director Leach and in Hering's 1935 article, although none of the documents is authoritative enough to settle the question. Saint-Gaudens' comment is probably the most reliable since it was made within days of the event. The actual number is probably less important than the fact that only a portion of the design could be brought up with one blow of the press.
[219] *US Mint*, NARA-P, op. cit. Internal memorandum dated February 25, 1907 to Landis from Barber.
[220] *US Mint*, NARA-CP, op. cit., entry 330, box 45. Letter dated February 26, 1907 to Saint-Gaudens from Roberts.
[221] *US Mint*, NARA-P, op. cit. Letter dated March 4, 1907 to Landis from Roberts. Superintendent Landis had requested authority to make two pieces for the mint collection on March 1.

and progress strike samples had been too much for the steel dies and resulted in the reverse die breaking.[222] To make the coins for the mint cabinet, Barber had to make a new working die from the hub. This was not completed until at least April 3, or possibly later.

Barber's experiments were quite different from Frank Leach's. He may have first tried the novel approach of making planchets the diameter of an eagle (27mm or 1.050-inch) but much thicker. Each planchet contained the same weight of gold as a normal $20 coin. He evidently felt that by using smaller diameter dies, the press would concentrate its force on the blank and produce more detail with one blow. After finding the dies from the first models too high to produce small-diameter coins with one blow of the press, he moved on to normal diameter blanks.

In the two letters quoted above, both Barber and Saint-Gaudens refer to a normal diameter $20, and a "small coin" and coins of "each diameter." This supports the idea that Barber had struck the thick, small-diameter double eagles before February 15. Further, the small-diameter coins were being treated the same as any other experimental coins.

*Figure 29. Small-diameter $20 made from the same models as the normal diameter pieces. The reverse field seems to be slightly flatter in the center than the normal diameter pieces.* (Courtesy Smithsonian NNC, photo by Douglas Mudd.)

At least 15 of these pieces were made, although each took several strikes to complete. The fact that using a small, thick planchet didn't solve the problem did not deter Barber from spending time making them. Considering that there is no mention of problems with the small-diameter dies, it is probable they were tested successfully first, followed by the larger "normal" dies. He likely recognized the merit of the design and appreciated the "collector" value of the small-diameter coins. (By 1916 Barber had eight EHR $20 pieces in his personal collection of pattern coins.)

The cent design also required changes. Roberts wrote to Saint-Gaudens on March 8:[223]

> ...I am forwarding today by express the plaster models for the one-cent piece. I suppose Mr. Herring [*sic*] has explained to you the difficulty there will be in getting a high relief from this coin having so little metal in it. I have pointed out this difficulty to the President and he told me that he did not expect the same degree of relief that he desired in the larger coin.

The sculptor replied that high relief on the cent models was intentional. He felt the mint could use the "...Janvier Machine and can reduce it to the relief you wish. I have no

---

[222] See Breen, *Encyclopedia*, p.574, #7357 for comments about die crack on a plain edge extremely high relief coin.
[223] *US Mint*, NARA-CP, op. cit., entry 330, box 45. Letter dated March 8, 1907 to Saint-Gaudens from Roberts.

objection to this."[224] Saint-Gaudens had completed his examination of the experimental coin and the progress strike samples. He had also compared the original plaster models sent to the mint with the coin, and wrote to director Roberts with his conclusions:[225]

> Dear Mr. Roberts:
> I have received the plaster models of the Double Eagle and, after careful examination, I am convinced that the die, or hub, is not as successful as it could be. This you will see by comparing the three (3) old plaster models of the Liberty side of the coin, which I am sending you today in a box by themselves. I suppose the stearining of the plaster has something to do with this, and for that reason I am now sending you much lighter and weaker plaster casts which I understand will absorb the stearine[226] better. On the back of each of the three plaster models I have written an explanation of it.
> Should Mr. Barber disapprove of these models I can send him the regulation casts.
> When you are through with the three old models, will you kindly have them returned to me?
> I am enclosing herewith a copy of a letter that I am sending to the President in this mail.
> Very truly yours,

These "weaker plaster casts" were copies from molds of a second pair of double eagle models, which Saint-Gaudens sent because he apparently thought the reducing lathe had damaged the models used by the mint. As engraver Barber predicted, Saint-Gaudens now was claiming the die or hub was not as good as it could be, implying this was part of the problem in striking coins. Although there may have been imperfections in the dies, these could not have caused it to take seven strikes to bring up the design.

On March 12, Saint-Gaudens sent a letter to the President stating that new double eagle models had been sent to the mint. It also contained additional information for director Roberts as well as Roosevelt:[227]

> Dear Mr. President:
> I send today to the mint the models of the twenty Dollar gold piece with the alterations that were indispensable if the coin was to be struck with one blow. There has been no change whatever in the design. It was simply a question of the thickness of the gold in certain places, and the weight of the pressure when the blow was struck.
> I like so much the head with the head-dress (and by the way, I am very glad you suggested doing the head in that manner) that I should like very much to see it tried not only on the one-cent piece, but also on the twenty-dollar gold piece instead of the figure of Liberty. I am probably apprehensive and have lost sight of whatever are the merits or demerits of the Liberty side of the coin as it is now. My fear is that it does not "tell" enough, in contrast with the eagle on the other side. There will be no difficulty of that kind with the head alone, of its effectiveness I am certain.

---

[224] *US Mint*, NARA-CP, op. cit., entry A1 328I, Folder "Coins, Lincoln cent." Letter dated March 11, 1907 to Roberts from Saint-Gaudens.

[225] *US Mint*, NARA-P, op. cit. Letter dated March 12, 1907 to Roberts from Saint-Gaudens.

[226] Stearine is a hardening agent used in crafts such as plaster work and candle-making. The material is brushed onto the plaster model and soaks in, making the surface much harder than the untreated plaster. If the stearine is not absorbed properly, it will harden on the surface of the work and fill fine detail. This would make it impossible for the reducing machine to properly trace the design of a plaster model.

[227] *SG*, Dartmouth, op. cit. Box 16, folder 38. Letter dated March 12, 1907 to Roosevelt from Saint-Gaudens.

Of course there is complete justification for the small figure with the large object on the other side in a great number of the Greek coins, and it is with that authority that I have proceeded.

This all means that I would like to have the mint make a die of the head for the gold coin also, and then a choice can be made between the two when completed. If this meets with your approval, may I ask you to say so to Mr. Roberts, of the Mint? I have enclosed a copy of this letter to him. The only change necessary in the event of this being carried out will be the changing of the date from the Liberty side to the Eagle side of the coin. This is a small matter.

I enclose a copy of a letter I am sending today to Mr. Roberts.

Yours faithfully,

This second pair of double eagle models were of nearly the same relief as the first. The Capitol building had been enlarged, and there were differences in Liberty's face and the flow of her gown. They also were more detailed in the olive branch, oak leaves and other parts of the design. The second reverse had than fourteen rays as on the first reverse.

***Figure 30. High relief double eagle produced from the second models. This specimen appears to be from the late December production without wire rim and with better separation between the stars and the border.*** (Photo courtesy Douglas Mudd Smithsonian National Numismatic Collection.)

It appears the sculptor and his assistant worked under the belief that sample strikes they had seen were typical of results from a production press. Although none of the samples were made on a standard press, the artists maintained that "…the alterations…were indispensable if the coin was to be struck with one blow." There was clearly a communication "disconnect" with neither mint nor artist asking the correct questions.

The Liberty head design Saint-Gaudens mentioned on the 12th was supposed to be for the one cent coin, but he liked the version with Indian headdress enough to think it might look better with the flying eagle reverse than the standing Liberty. Based on scale, the Liberty head and eagle combination was marginally better than the Striding Liberty, but Roosevelt preferred the figure of Liberty.

The President replied on March 14, letting Saint-Gaudens know he had ordered a sample double eagle coin struck according to the sculptor's wishes.[228]

[228]*SG*, Dartmouth, op. cit. Box 16, folder 38. Letter dated March 14, 1907 to Roosevelt from Saint-Gaudens.

My dear Saint Gaudens:

Many thanks for your letter of the 12th instant. Good! I have directed that done at once. I am glad you like the head of Liberty with the feather head-dress. Really, the feather head-dress can be treated as being the conventional cap of Liberty quite as much as if it was the Phrygian cap; and, after all, it is <u>our</u> Liberty --- not what the ancient Greeks and Romans miscalled by that title – and we are entitled to a typically American head-dress for the lady.

Faithfully yours,

Engraver Barber was given authority to make the hub and die of the Liberty head design necessary to strike the sample coin on March 15. Since the Liberty head design had been intended for the cent, where the date was to be on the reverse, a new reverse model also had to be made.

*Figure 31. Pattern double eagle coin with Liberty head obverse and flying eagle reverse. Date is in Roman numerals on the reverse. This coin was specifically authorized by President Roosevelt at Saint-Gaudens' request. (P-1998, be-lieved to be unique.)* (Courtesy David Akers.)

Henry Hering made a copy of one of the second models of the double eagle reverse and added the date, incuse, in Roman numerals. By March 21, the sculptor was suggesting that bronze casts be made of the models, "I think it would be well for you also to have a bronze cast made…"[229] Evidently the plaster models were too soft for use on the Janvier reducing machine so both the mint and Saint-Gaudens had bronze casts made of the second models. Barber had casts made in New York by Keller Mechanical Engraving Company, and Saint-Gaudens used a different foundry. Each man seemed to be looking for the best quality with Saint-Gaudens remarking in a letter "…and should the cast by Mr. Keller be a better one, do not hesitate to discard this one."[230]

During six weeks between the middle of February and the end of March, the mint produced the first extremely high relief experimental coins, the thick, small-diameter dou-ble eagles and the Liberty Head-Flying Eagle pattern. The President called Roberts to his office on March 23 for a conference:[231]

---

[229] *US Mint*, NARA-CP, op. cit., entry 330, box 45. Letter dated March 21, 1907 to Roberts from Saint-Gaudens.

[230] *US Mint*, NARA-P, op. cit. Letter dated April 11, 1907 to Roberts from Saint-Gaudens.

[231] *US Mint*, NARA-CP, op. cit., entry 330, box 45. Letter dated March 22, 1907 to Roberts from Loeb. The President had also asked secretary Cortelyou for information.

...[with the Director] prepared to tell him what coins we can have changed, and also to discuss the two designs for the twenty-dollar gold piece.

After discussing the situation with Roosevelt, Roberts wrote to Saint-Gaudens:[232]

I am authorizing Mr. Barber to take the plaster models to New York and have bronze casts made from them as you have suggested. I understand that both sides of the double eagle and the obverse of the one cent design are now wanting, the latter with view to the use upon a gold coin. I think we will devote ourselves at present to making a success of the gold designs.
Very truly yours,

The letter only confused things at Aspet, where Saint-Gaudens replied:[233]

Your letter of March twenty-third is at hand. I do not quite understand your meaning when you write, "I understand that both sides of the double eagle and the obverse of the one-cent design are now wanting, the latter with view to the use upon a gold coin."

The artist, possibly thinking the mint had too many models sitting around and couldn't keep them straight, requested return of all obsolete models.

Before leaving for New York, Charles Barber sent his comments to director Roberts:[234]

In compliance with your instructions I will go to New York at once and attend to the matter of the bronze casting.

In this connection I beg to state that the reductions that were made from the plaster cast sent here by Mr. Saint Gaudens were made by an expert from New York who had learned the process from Mr. Janvier, the maker of the machine we are now using, the expert above mentioned is Mr. Weil, a young Frenchman in the employ of Dietsch Brothers, the party from whom we purchased the reducing machine, this young man was sent to Paris to learn all that M. Janvier could teach in making reductions and he certainly displayed an excellent knowledge of the machine and its possibilities.

This step was taken to avoid any such complaint as is now made, as I anticipated just such an outcry....

I have started the work of making the reduction from the plaster head and will leave such instructions as to enable the work to progress while I am in New York.
Respectfully,

Keller Company charged the mint $35 to make the casts.[235] Supervision of the Liberty head reduction was left in the hands of George Morgan, who had little to do except hope the electricity did not fail and cause the job to have to be restarted from the beginning.

As letters crossed paths, the situation became somewhat confused, and Roberts wrote Saint-Gaudens on March 28 hoping to clear up any misunderstandings. In his letter he officially admits for the first time that Henri Weil, not Barber, cut the extremely high relief reductions:[236]

[232] *US Mint*, NARA-CP, op. cit., entry 330, box 45. Letter dated March 23 1907 to Saint-Gaudens from Roberts.
[233] *US Mint*, NARA-CP, op. cit., entry 330, box 45. Letter dated March 25 1907 to Roberts from Saint-Gaudens.
[234] *US Mint*, NARA-CP, op. cit., entry 229, box 251. Letter dated March 25, 1907 to Roberts from Barber.
[235] *US Mint*, NARA-CP, op. cit., entry 229, box 252. Letter dated April 1, 1907 to Roberts from Barber.
[236] *US Mint*, NARA-CP, op. cit., entry 235, vol. 367. Letter dated March 28, 1907 to Saint-Gaudens from Roberts.

92

Replying to your letter of the 25th instant I would say that we have received all the models which you report to have forwarded. My letter of the 23rd referred to the bronze castings which would be needed.

Immediately upon receiving your letter of the 25th and observing that you intended to make a set of new casts in hard plaster, I called up the Philadelphia Mint on the telephone and inquired whether Mr. Barber had already gone to New York to have the bronze casts made and found that he had done so. We are anxious to have no delay upon this work and so immediately upon receiving your former letter suggesting that we have casts made by Mr. Keller, I sent instructions to Mr. Barber to go to New York and have the work done. He tells me that the bronze cast of the standing figure has been successfully made. He tells me further that he does not think it necessary to have new [plaster] casts made as the method employed for casting is not the old one which involves considerable strain upon the model but a new and patented one which he thinks these models will stand without difficulty. Permit me to say further relative to the results obtained from the original models that inasmuch as these are the first work to be done in the mint from the Janvier machine I hesitated to have anyone inexperienced in the use of the machine do the reductions and accordingly secured, through Messrs. Dietsch Brothers, from whom we purchased the machine, the service of Mr. Weil, one of their employees whom they recommended to do the work. I was informed by Dietsch Brothers that this young man was sent to Paris to learn all that Janvier could teach about making reductions upon that machine. Mr. Weil made the reductions at the Philadelphia Mint for the original dies.

At the same time, Saint-Gaudens felt it necessary reinforce his earlier comments about the models and on March 28 sent the mint a final set of plasters.[237]

I am sending you today at the Philadelphia Mint, two (2) hard plaster casts of the Twenty Dollar Gold piece, obverse and reverse, and two (2) hard plaster casts of the One Cent piece, obverse and reverse.

I am also sending another hard plaster cast of the Eagle, with the date on the sun which will be used for the reverse, with the Indian Head, for the trial Twenty Dollar Gold piece,

I hope these will answer the propose for the bronze castings.

A few days later he sent his bill for payment of $5,000.[238] Roberts replied, "I would not like to assume that no other modifications of the design or models are required until we have made a test of the dies now being made."[239] The director wanted opinions on the new double eagle design and sent one of the first coins to Frank Leach in San Francisco, who responded:[240]

Dear Mr. Roberts:
Yours of the 12th inst., together with one of the new double eagle pieces, came duly to hand. I return the piece herewith.
I notice that the artist has changed the eagle, but with little improvement upon the design first shown me. The design is not only poor in the representation of an eagle, but it is bad for the peculiarities of the piece. This eagle is very much like

[237] *US Mint*, NARA-CP, op. cit., entry 330, box 45. Letter dated March 28, 1907 to Roberts from Saint-Gaudens. There are several other short letters on the subject of the casts. All of them – whether from Saint-Gaudens or Roberts – suggest the mint and artist were talking about different things. The mint refers to making bronze casts of the models and Saint-Gaudens refers to making plaster casts. That neither party clearly seems to understand what the other was doing is typical for much of the new design work.
[238] *US Mint*, NARA-CP, op. cit., entry 330, box 45. Letter dated April 10, 1907 to Roberts from Saint-Gaudens.
[239] *US Mint*, NARA-CP, op. cit., entry 330, box 45. Letter dated April 12 1907 to Saint-Gaudens from Roberts.
[240] *US Mint*, NARA-CP, op. cit., entry 330, box 45. Letter dated April 22, 1907 to Roberts from Leach.

the one which was designed for nickels or pennies in the early 60's and excited so much ridicule that the design was soon abandoned. The eagle is a grand bird and is worthy of a better representation than the one on this proposed new coin, which, in my estimation, will be severely criticized. If the artist is not familiar with the pose of the eagle and has not seen that bird in its attitude of dignity, resentment and defiance, I would refer him to the eagle on the presidential commission blanks which are issued to the mint officers. Not only is that the natural pose of the bird, but the figure would be well adapted to this kind of relief, bringing up the tip of each wing out to the edge of the coin where it would be shaded off into the low relief, leaving the high relief in the center of the piece.

I note what you say about the heavier rim being necessary. Of course, that is imperative. Without a good rim there is no question but that the blanks would refuse to accept the coins, and another thing in this connection is that no part of the relief of the piece must raise above the rim, otherwise the coins will not stack, and to make the coin acceptable to the bankers it must be made so as to stack properly and uniformly.

In response to your inquiry I will say that I do not think the piece could be any more easily sweated than the ordinary coin. However, that smooth edge would permit of a greater amount of rimming without detection than the reeded pieces do, and it would be more of a temptation, for when rimming our present coin the reeding has to be restored before the piece can be put [back] into circulation and this required skillful work and considerable time. I have not heard of many operations in this direction of last years. However, Chief Wilkie would be in a better position to give you information on that than I am.

I do not think the coin would gather dirt to an "offensive degree."

Your last inquiry, asking my opinion as to the probable judgement of the public upon the design, is the most difficult of all to answer. With a change made in the eagle and the adoption of a natural pose of the bird I think the piece would be very popular, at least, for a time. Perhaps when the curiosity of the public had been satisfied the popularity of the coin could end. It is my opinion that the coin should be made acceptable to the bankers before it could be expected to be put into general circulation, for if the bankers will not accept the coin I do not see how it can be got into the hands of the public. Anyway, I would not like to insure the popularity of any radical change from the present gold coin. Personally, I regard the coin as a beautiful piece of work, and those to whom I have shown it express the same opinion; but the question remains, if, while it should be so generally acknowledged, would it be accepted as a convenient article for the purpose of exchange for use as money?

Leach's judgement was that the coin was a "…beautiful piece of work…" but the eagle was poor and needed to be changed. Director Roberts also sought the views of William Macartney from the Royal Mint and M. A. Arnaune of the Paris Mint regarding high relief coinage. Both replied that it was only practical if the design could be fully struck with one blow of the press.[241]

On May 3, Charles Barber received eight double eagle planchets on which to strike samples of the second set of models.[242] The next day he wrote to superintendent Landis to report the results:[243]

---

[241] The responses were of little value to the mint director since the Paris Mint didn't reply until July and the Royal Mint delayed until December.

[242] *US Mint*, NARA-P, op. cit. Internal note dated May 3, 1907 to Landis from Barber. Accompanying this is a separate slip of paper with Henry Hering's name and address and the notation "8 -- $20."

[243] *US Mint*, NARA-P, op. cit. Letter dated May 4, 1907 to Landis from Barber.

Dear Sir:

I beg to report that I have made dies for the new designs furnished for the double eagle and have attempted to strike some pieces. I submit same for your examination.

You will notice that I have subjected the planchets to150 tons pressure each time, that being in the experience of the Mint the limit of endurance of a die of the diameter of the double eagle.

In the new designs the convexity of the die is so great as you will notice, that the area exposed to the force of the press is much less than it would be in a die of ordinary convexity for coinage, and therefore, 150 tons in this case is excessive, as it already demonstrated in the sinking, or loss of convexity in one of the dies although I have only struck these few pieces.

I feel that my obligation in this case is to demonstrate whether these designs are practicable for coinage, and not whether a few experimental pieces can be struck at the expense of a pair of dies, and therefore, I think it advisable to state that at San Francisco where the majority of double eagles are struck, they have a record of 200,000 pieces to a pair of dies of the present double eagle. I make this statement for your information only.

Respectfully,

Barber had made a progress series – striking two pieces with one blow, two with two blows, two with three blows, and two with ten blows of the press. In trying to strike complete coins, one hundred fifty tons of pressure had been too much for the second design's dies.[244] Like the dies made from the first model, these failed after only a small number of experimental coins were produced. Experimental very high relief (VHR) coins struck from the sunken dies would probably show a distorted area in the center of the obverse or reverse depending on which die collapsed. However, all eight of these coins would be of the very high relief variety – nearly the same relief as the #1 model coins made in February. Roberts sent the eight pieces to Saint-Gaudens on May 7:[245]

I am sending by express today the results of a trial of the new dies. There are two pieces given one impression; two pieces given two impressions; two pieces given three impressions; and two pieces given ten impressions.

To our great regret the results prove unsatisfactory. They go far to convince me that a radical modification of the designs is required. A single blow accomplished so much that we were misled into thinking that very slight modifications to the model would suffice. I am now inclined to think that the relief must be very much reduced. I think we ought to have a consultation and that the mint is the best place to meet. Can you come there in order that there may be a full interchange of views? It requires so much time and labor to cut and try that we ought to proceed with more certainty if it is practicable to do so. These pieces have been seen by the Secretary of the Treasury and by the President and I understand the President is to write you on the subject. I shall be pleased to have your own views as to the best course to be pursued.

The President wrote a soothing letter to Saint-Gaudens on May 8:[246]

---

[244] Relief of the second models was not significantly lower than the first model at this point in the process.

[245] *US Mint*, NARA-CP, op. cit., entry 330, box 45. Letter dated May 7, 1907 to Saint-Gaudens from Roberts.

[246] *SG*, Dartmouth, op. cit. Box 16, folder 38. Letter dated May 8, 1907 to Saint-Gaudens from Roosevelt. "Comparette" is Thomas Louis Comparette, PhD, curator of the mint's coin cabinet since May 4, 1905. He and two others, Benjamin G. Green, and George H. Russell, had applied for the civil service position. (Per letter dated May 4, 1905 to Civil Service Commission from acting secretary of the commission H. A. Taylor.) He died suddenly in 1923 at age 54, while on the Cobb Creek golf course in Philadelphia. The mint cabinet collection was transferred to the Smithsonian shortly thereafter,

My dear Mr. Saint Gaudens:

I am sorry to say I am having some real difficulties in connection with the striking of those gold coins. It has proved hitherto impossible to strike them by one blow, which is necessary under the conditions of making coins of the present day. I send you a copy of letters from the head of the Department of Coins and Medals of the British Museum, and from Comparette. I am afraid it is not practicable to have coins made if they are struck with more than one blow. Of course, I can have a few hundred of these beautiful coins made, but they will be merely souvenirs and medals, and not part of the true coinage of the country. Would it be possible for you to come on to the mint? I am sure that the mint authorities now really desire to do whatever they can and if it would be possible for you to go there I could arrange to have some of the Tiffany people there at the same time to see if here was anything practicable to be done.

With regard, believe me,

Sincerely yours,

*(Handwritten note below signature.)*

You notice what Comparette says about our country leading the way. I know our people now earnestly desire to do all they can; I believe that with a slightly altered and lowered relief (and <u>possibly</u> a profile figure of Liberty) we can yet do the trick.

Superintendent Landis was not ready to give up and wrote to Roberts requesting, "…that authority be given to reduce the relief to the present design about one-fifth." He felt this might allow the coins to be made with one or two blows of the press. New hubs were ready in time for Hering's visit to the mint on May 17. (These were to become the basis for the "high relief" coins produced later that year.) He also lamented omission of the motto IN GOD WE TRUST from the design: "It is on our present coin and was suggested by one of my predecessors, *ex* Governor Pollock, and adopted by *ex* secretary Chase. The very good reasons for adopting it then should be equally strong in retaining it now."[247]

After the latest double eagle trial strikes were made, director Roberts and secretary Shaw met with Roosevelt to show him the results. While readily admitting to the beauty of the coins, both men reinforced the practical impossibility of striking significant numbers for circulation. The fundamental problem was not the relief of the design, although that was where events had placed the emphasis, it was conformity with the double eagles already in circulation. Coinage laws were clear about the weight, fineness and diameter of United States coins, but nowhere were the coin's thickness defined. Over the previous seventy-five years the U. S. Mint had developed a *de facto* standard for coin thickness. This allowed businesses to manufacture coin counters and sorting machines that used thickness as well as diameter and weight to differentiate between various denominations.

Companies such as Brandt Cashier Company manufactured automated sorting and coin payout machines used by banks and companies to produce weekly payrolls for their workers. The machines dispensed a specified dollar amount of coin, and some models accommodated coins up to the double eagle. Since most wage earners received their pay weekly, in cash, accurate operation of these devices was very important to both the manufacturers and the users. Through years of experience with the old Longacre-design gold coins and Seated Liberty silver, equipment manufacturers had developed means to prevent over- and under-payment. Also, bank tellers and counting clerks routinely did trial sums by

---

to considerable objection from Philadelphia officials. (The Mint Bureau had decided to close all of the mints to visitors for security reasons. See NARA, RG 56, Treasury correspondence for more information.)

[247] *US Mint*, NARA-CP, op. cit., entry 330, box 45. Letter dated May 9, 1907 to Roberts from Landis.

piling coins to a specific height on counting boards, then estimating the value of each pile. Other than the legal requirements, there were two thickness-related requirements for the double eagle: 1) the rim had to be no thicker than on the old design coins, and 2) no part of the design could be higher than the rim.

Saint-Gaudens wrote back to Roosevelt:[248]

> Dear Mr. President:
> I am extremely sorry that it will be wholly impossible for me to leave Windsor at present, but I am sending to Mr. Roberts, and if you so desire, to you, my assistant Mr. Hering, who understands the mechanical requirements of the coin better than I.
> After all the question is fairly simple, and I have not the slightest doubt that making the coins in low relief will settle the matter satisfactorily. Greatly as I should like to please you, I feel that I cannot now model another design in profile for the Twenty Dollar gold piece. Indeed, as far as I am concerned, I should prefer seeing the head of Liberty in place of any figure of Liberty on the Twenty Dollar coin as well as on the One cent. If the idea appeals to you, I would refine the modeling of the head now that I have seen it struck in the small, so as to bring it in scale with the eagle. I am grieved that the striking of the dies did not bring better results. Evidently it is not [a] trifling matter to make Greek art conform to modern numismatics.
> Faithfully yours,

There was little Saint-Gaudens could do at this point but accept that the final coins were going to have to be in low relief. His illness had progressed to where he was being carried about the studio on a small "sedan chair." Many days he did not have the strength to leave his room; even dictating short letters was exhausting. Going to the mint and facing down Charles Barber – however much that might have pleased the great artist – was impossible. Roosevelt did not seem to be aware of the seriousness of the artist's illness when he wrote back on May 12:[249]

> Dear Mr. Saint-Gaudens:
> All right. Your letter really makes me feel quite cheerful. I should be glad, if it is possible for you to do so, if you would "refine" the head of Liberty; but I want to keep the figure of Liberty for at least one small issue of the coins. I look forward to seeing Mr. Hering.
> With hearty thanks, believe me,
> Sincerely yours,

The President had decided to keep the Liberty figure on the double eagle, with the Liberty/Indian head still planned for use on the cent. Arrangements were made for Henry Hering to make another trip to the mint on Friday, May 17 for consultation with Barber.[250] Roberts also asked George Kunz from Tiffany & Co. to provide a representative:[251]

> Dear Mr. Kunz:
> Since the first die was made for the Saint-Gaudens coin, he has slightly modified the design and another has been sent. A trial indicates that there must be a more radical reduction to the relief. I have been trying to get Mr. Saint Gaudens to come to the mint himself but he writes that he cannot do this and will send his as-

[248] *Roosevelt*, LoC, op. cit., vol. 70, p.401, microfilm reel 344. Letter dated May 11, 1907 to Roosevelt from Saint-Gaudens.
[249] *SG*, Dartmouth, op. cit. Box 16, folder 38. Letter dated May 12, 1907 to Saint-Gaudens from Roosevelt.
[250] *US Mint*, NARA-P, op. cit. Telegram dated May 16, 1907 to Landis from Roberts.
[251] *US Mint*, NARA-CP, op. cit., entry 330, box 45. Letter dated May 14, 1907 to Kunz from Roberts.

sistant, Mr. Hering, on Friday morning of this week. I intend to go over myself and have been wondering whether we might borrow the Superintendent of your factory, Mr. Hannweber for a day or so. I would like to have the benefit of his experience and advice in addition to that of our own people. I think perhaps it will be more satisfactory to Mr. Saint Gaudens and to the President to have the opinion of the mint officials confirmed by an outsider of experience. I want both of them to feel that everything has been done that can be done to carry out their wishes. Please let me know if Mr. Hannweber can be with us in Philadelphia Friday morning. I will see that he or you are reimbursed for the expenses of the trip.

During the meeting, the engraver told Hering the relief was too high on the most recent pair of models. These would have to be remade if the designs were to have any chance of being suitable for coinage. Barber also showed him a lower relief hub of the Striding Liberty (#2 model), of which a lead impression was requested by Saint-Gaudens on May 22.[252] Hannweber from Tiffany's confirmed Barber's comments and the little conference dispersed. Hering visited the President in Washington that afternoon.[253] Saint-Gaudens had reconsidered his opinions and now preferred the standing eagle for the reverse of the double eagle coin, as he had originally proposed:[254]

> Dear Mr. President:
> Now that this business of the coinage is coming to an end and we understand how much relief can be practically stamped, I have been looking over the other models that I have made and there is no question in my mind that the standing eagle is the best. You have seen only the large model, and probably on seeing it in the small will have a different impression. The artists all prefer it, as I do, to the flying eagle.
> Second, it eliminates the sunburst which is on both sides of the coin as it will be adopted as settled up now.
> Third, it is more dignified and less inclined toward the sensational.
> Fourth, it will occupy no more time to use this model than it will to do the other work that will be necessary, and I think it is a little more favorable for the stamping.
> The majority of the people that I show the work to evidently prefer with you the figure of Liberty to the head of Liberty and that I shall not consider any further on the Twenty Dollar gold coin.
> I write rather in haste as Mr. Hering leaves in a very little while.
> Faithfully yours,

The meeting between Hering and Barber seemed to produce more problems than solutions. Evidently each man interpreted what the other said in light of his own opinion, resulting in neither "listening" to the other.

The sculptor now wanted to combine the Striding Liberty obverse with the standing eagle reverse, a combination not previously tested. Roosevelt, however, felt the matter had to be resolved. The President and director Roberts discussed the coin design on May 25 and the latter reported the results to Saint-Gaudens:[255]

---

[252] *US Mint*, NARA-P, op. cit. Letter dated May 22, 1907 to Landis from Saint-Gaudens. He also asked for lead impressions of the double eagle with Striding Liberty and Liberty head obverses. These were received at Aspet on May 31.

[253] *SG*, Dartmouth, op. cit. Box 16, folder 38. Manuscript note, no date [May 16, 1907?], to Roosevelt from Saint-Gaudens. The appointment is not noted in the Roosevelt papers.

[254] Taxay, op. cit., p.315. Letter dated May 23 to Roosevelt from Saint-Gaudens. The original letter cannot now be found in the archives; however, a copy is in the Connecticut State Library collection.

[255] *US Mint*, NARA-CP, op. cit., entry 330, box 45. Letter dated May 25, 1907 to Saint-Gaudens from Roberts. This letter suggests that discussion about using one of the designs on the $10 coins may have occurred before May 25.

I had an interview today with the President about the designs. Your letter in which you indicated the preference for the standing eagle over the flying eagle, and for the full figure of Liberty over the Liberty head, was before us. I supported your view in both particulars but the President adhered to his own opinion except that he yielded to the extent of using the full figure of Liberty upon the Double Eagle and standing eagle for the Eagle.

It is now settled that the designs for the Double Eagle shall be the full figure of Liberty and the flying eagle, and the design for the Eagle shall be the feather head of liberty with the standing eagle.

The relief, the President agrees, shall be reduced to a degree that it will make it certainly practicable without further experiments. This is the last word on the subject. If there is anything we can do in getting ready to expedite matters, kindly let me know.

The President feels that he has compromised with us in accepting the standing eagle for the smaller coin which is the one of the most common circulation.

Very truly yours,

Roberts' letter was a clear representation of the President's mood. He was tired of delay and had made a decision – it was now up to Saint-Gaudens and Hering to complete the models in relief low enough to coin. Saint-Gaudens replied on the 28th.[256]

…I will have sent to you the necessary models in two reliefs, one in a form that Mr. Hering believes you can make practical use of, the other in the ordinary flat relief of modern coinage. I will proceed as you desire.

Based on what Hering reported to Saint-Gaudens, the mint was sent new, so-called final models for the $10 eagle but with the date in Roman numerals. This was also the first version to incorporate the "ten dollars" inscription in the standing eagle composition.[257]

On June first I sent to you my final model for the Ten-dollar gold piece [reverse] and will send the obverse of the same today.

They have been modeled to a relief which Mr. Barber gave Mr. Hering to understand could probably be struck. If they cannot be struck in that relief, there is no doubt, from what Mr. Barber also assured Mr. Hering, that they can be reduced very simply by your [Janvier] machine to whatever relief you require.

In the course of the week Mr. Hering will go to the mint to see if there is anything more which will assist me in the completion of the other model.

On receipt the letter was forwarded to the mint, where superintendent Landis showed it to Barber and had him initial the copy. Barber took exception to much of the letter and sent a blistering reply to Landis on June 7:[258]

I beg to report that I have received two models in plaster and also a copy of a letter from Mr. Saint-Gaudens to the Director, in which there are certain statements that are somewhat misleading, therefore, as I have received no instructions regarding these models and have not yet heard from Mr. Hering who I supposed would bring instruction, I think to avoid any unnecessary delay we should lay certain matters concerning both the letter of Saint Gaudens and also the models before the Director, that we may put ourselves in proper position and also have his instructions. Mr. Saint Gaudens writes that this model for the ten dollar coin is his

[256] *US Mint*, NARA-CP, op. cit., entry 330, box 45. Letter dated May 28, 1907 to Roberts from Saint-Gaudens.
[257] *US Mint*, NARA-P, op. cit. Letter dated June 3, 1907 to Roberts from Saint-Gaudens. The models arrived on June 5.
[258] *US Mint*, NARA-P, op. cit. Letter dated June 7, 1907 to Landis from Barber.

99

final model, "modeled to the relief which Mr. Barber gave Mr. Hering to understand could probably be struck."

This is a mistake, I have said from the first when consulted upon the change of design for gold coins that the relief of the design must conform to the fixed conditions and therefore, the only relief that I knew of was coin relief; the models now sent are not coin relief, though I do not say that it is impossible to make them work, as to carry the relief of a model from twelve inches [in diameter] to a trifle more than one [inch] is more than I would pretend to do, unless the model was like the first sent here by Mr. Saint Gaudens, when the relief was absurdly high.

The next statement [is] that the "models can be reduced very simply by your machine to whatever relief you require."

This is also a misleading statement, as the machine is limited, and cannot produce "whatever relief required."

The trouble is these gentlemen are not familiar with the machine, as Mr. Hering confessed, and lose sight of many features connected with the operation and result produced. – One important result of reducing the relief by the machine is loss of detail and this loss is in proportion to the extent of the reduction and therefore, before starting the work I would like to know if it is understood that I am to reduce the relief independent of the result before stated: loss of detail.

The date of the year is in Roman notation, there is no provision made for even next year, there being no place left, and as these coins have to stand for twenty-five years before another change can be made, I feel it necessary to state that in a few years it would be impossible to date the dies.

I understand the Director and yourself recommended to Mr. Hering the use of Arabic notation, and that it was so agreed, and therefore, I call your attention to this omission.

It will be necessary to have bronze castings made for use on the machine, therefore I will thank you to settle the question of the notation before any casting is made as if you decide to use Arabic notation the change must be made in the model, also whether the relief is to be mechanically reduced, even with the loss of detail.

Respectfully,

Most of Barber's letter can be distilled into one short statement: No one at the mint knew how to properly use the Janvier reducing lathe. This doomed any model that was not within the very limited experience of the mint engravers. His reference to the date being in

*Figure 32. Liberty head with headdress and Roman numeral date as first submitted for the $10 gold coin. This is a composite image intended to illustrate the likely appearance of the original model.*

Roman numerals confirms that all early models of $10 and $20 had the date in this style. Hering visited the mint again on June 11 but nothing seemed to be resolved. Director Roberts wrote Saint-Gaudens the same day to convey the difficulty with Roman numerals, and potential loss of detail if the relief were reduced. He also added a paragraph about counterfeit prevention:[259]

> … The question of the date figures is one which I overlooked in my last conference with the President. I do not know how much stress you lay upon your preference for Roman numerals. The objection to them is the practical one that the number of numerals changes from year to year. There are six for the present year, but next year seven will be required, and in 1928 nine will be required. There is scarcely any space to spare. To put in even another numeral will involve some change in the design, while if Arabic figures are used of course only four are needed at any time. I, personally, think the Arabic figures are to be preferred. I do not like the idea of leaving changes in the design to be in future years effected by the engravers. If you insist on Roman numerals I think you should prepare a model for each year. In my judgement the public will also prefer Arabic figures with which they are more familiar. They are signs of our own language, so to speak. I hesitate to dictate in the matter for I want you to have your own way so far as practicable in making the coin, but if the numerals are to stay, I think you should work out the design for each year.
>
> …Mr. Hering [is quoted] as saying that you do not regard [the loss of detail] as important. I hope you appreciate the importance of having a sharply cut coin. It is our major dependence to defeat counterfeiting. If the lines are not sharp and clear, it is comparatively easy to make a successful counterfeit by casting. We must not forget the practical features of our work.

Saint-Gaudens sent no reply and Roberts asked for a response again on June 18. The artist finally answered two days later, "The former letter was not answered because I wished to see Mr. Hering, whom I have expected would return every day. I now expect him tomorrow…I agree with you that it would be better to use figures instead of Roman numerals for the date on the coin."[260] Hering returned to Aspet as predicted and immediately changed the date on the $10 eagle to European characters. A new model – this time one that could be used – was sent to the mint on June 24.[261]

Later called the "first models" or "high relief models," the design was too high for ordinary coinage on both models, and the field curved sharply upward directly to the coin's rim. This offered little protection against wear for the central designs. Keller Mechanical Engraving Company sent a bronze cast of the Liberty head to the mint on July 8, and Barber began making the hub immediately.[262] President Roosevelt again asked secretary Cortelyou about the coins and was told "…work is proceeding as rapidly as possible…"[263]

On July 8, mint director Roberts announced he was resigning effective the end of the month. He had received a lucrative offer to become President of Commercial National

---

[259] *US Mint*, NARA-P, op. cit. Letter dated June 11, 1907 to Saint-Gaudens from Roberts. The letter was evidently removed from the director's presscopy book and inserted into the NARA file folder. The balance of the presscopy book appears to have been placed in the mint records at College Park.

[260] *US Mint*, NARA-CP, op. cit., entry 330, box 45. Letter dated June 20, 1907 to Roberts from Saint-Gaudens. This is contrary to what was discussed on May 23, 1906.

[261] *US Mint*, NARA-CP, op. cit., entry 330, box 45. Letter dated June 24, 1907 to Roberts from Saint-Gaudens.

[262] *US Mint*, NARA-P, op. cit. Telegram dated July 8, 1907 to Norris from Keller.

[263] *US Mint*, NARA-CP, op. cit., entry 330, box 45. Letter dated July 15, 1907 to Loeb from Cortelyou. George Bruce Cortelyou was appointed Secretary of the Treasury on March 4, 1907, he had previously been personal secretary to President McKinley, secretary to President Roosevelt and Postmaster General.

Bank in Chicago and had reluctantly accepted. Secretary of the Treasury Cortelyou notified President Roosevelt,[264] who expressed his dismay by letter on the 11th. Cortelyou was responsible for recommending a replacement and quickly settled on Frank A. Leach, superintendent of the San Francisco Mint, as his nominee.[265] Leach was a former newspaper reporter who had been appointed to the San Francisco Mint position in 1897. Since then he had complied an excellent record of both mint management and political activism for the Republican party. "Director Roberts informs me in response to my inquiries that he considers Mr. Leach 'far and away the best all-round man in the service.'"[266] Frank Leach was nominated in August and took office on November 1, 1907.[267] Until Leach could complete the complicated accounting necessary for replacement of a mint superintendent and move his belongings from San Francisco to Washington, Robert Preston was acting director. Absence of a permanent director was to have a significant influence on the new gold coinage.

## Gold Eagles

By July 19, Barber had made one pair of dies for the eagle and struck several experimental pieces (P-1996 – plain edge, knife rim, with "periods") for examination by director Roberts.[268] Saint-Gaudens, less than two weeks from death, was anxious to know the results. "…I am waiting to know about this in order to proceed with the other reliefs."[269] The same day, the mint sent Saint-Gaudens one of the new $10 experimental coins (#1 model) and, for reference, one of the regular issue Gobrecht-designed coins. A similar pair of coins was sent to secretary Cortelyou with a cover letter from Roberts:[270]

> I am enclosing herewith a strike from the last dies for the new eagle. I am also enclosing for comparison a new piece of the old design. I do this to call your attention to what the people at the Mint (and I agree with them) consider a serious defect in the new piece. It is the smooth finish as compared with the sharply cut details of the old design. This lack of detail in the new design is characteristic of the fine medal work with which Mr. Saint Gaudens is familiar. The objection to it for coinage is that it greatly facilitates counterfeiting. The chief obstacle which counterfeiters encounter is the difficulty in doing sharp die work with the inferior equipment which they usually possess. The simplest method of work for them is by making a plaster of paris mould from a genuine coin and casting counterfeits. This casting process gives just such a dim finish as we have in the new Saint Gaudens

[264] *Roosevelt*, LoC, op. cit. Microfilm reel 75. Letter dated July 9, 1907 to Roosevelt from George B. Cortelyou. When his bank merged with Continental National Bank, Roberts was reappointed director by President Taft in July 1910 and served until March 1914. Cortelyou, a former secretary to President McKinley, had replaced Leslie M. Shaw as treasury secretary on March 4, 1907.

[265] Frank Aleamon Leach was born in Cayiga County, New York in 1846. As a youth he went to California with his mother to join his father in the San Francisco area. He operated the Vallejo Evening Chronicle (1867–1886) and the Oakland Enquirer (1887–1894). He was an alternate delegate to the Republican national convention in 1880 and later appointed Superintendent of the San Francisco Mint as a political reward.

[266] *George B. Cortelyou papers*, LoC, box 19. Letter dated July 9, 1907 to Roosevelt from Cortelyou.

[267] Leach's appointment did not pass the Senate until February 12, 1908, although he is never referred to as "acting" from November to February. During August through October the acting director was former mint director Robert Preston (1893–1898). There is one official letter signed by Leach on October 15 and his term may also be thought to have begun on that date. However, all other documents are signed by Preston until November 1. Upon resigning as director in 1898, Preston had taken a civil service position as senior examiner with the Bureau of the Mint and was often the acting director.

[268] *US Mint*, NARA-P, op. cit. Letter dated July 20, 1907 to Landis from Robert Preston, acting director.

[269] *US Mint*, NARA-P, op. cit. Letter dated July 22, 1907 to Landis from Saint-Gaudens. Dictated to his secretary Ida Metz Reed.

[270] *US Mint*, NARA-CP, op. cit., entry 330, box 45. Letter dated July 22, 1907 to Cortelyou from Roberts.

coin. The details will not come up in a cast as they will under the pressure of the coining press where the die work is sharply cut.

I am writing to Mr. Saint Gaudens today about this matter and enclose herewith a copy of a letter I wrote him a month ago in which I cautioned him against this result. I consider it a very serious matter to weaken in the slightest degree the defense against counterfeiters. They make trouble enough when we do our best.

Again, although the relief of the new piece is now perfectly feasible for coinage I think the eagle stands a shade too high as compared to the rim. They tell me at the Mint that where two pieces are piled with the eagles against each other, they will rock which shows that they are too high to stack properly.

The lettering [i.e., stars] upon the edge of the new coin does not appear upon the enclosed piece as the collar for it was not quite ready.

I am also enclosing herewith a belated letter from the Director of the French Mint which, you will observe, supports our conclusion that the high relief originally attempted is impracticable.

Saint-Gaudens also received samples of the old and new designs:[271]

I am forwarding herewith a strike of the new eagle. I am sorry to say that the eagle [side] is still too high for the coins to stack. If you lay a straight edge across it you will see that the eagle comes clear up fully level with the edge and as there is a slight burr on the edge which will not be there in a perfect coin, the figure of the eagle will be slightly above the border. When two pieces are placed together with the eagles against each other the effect is quite apparent.

The sculptor sent the mint a check for the regular issue coin and asked if the relief on both sides of the new eagle had been reduced "as low as the machine will allow."[272] A note from Charles Barber, attached to the original letter, indicated this was the maximum the Janvier machine would allow (at least so far as Barber knew how to do). The sculptor also asked for casts of the dies used to strike the experimental coins. These were sent to Aspet on July 28 and were the last "the Saint" saw of his work.

*Figure 33. Liberty head eagle from the first models. The field curves directly up to the rim on both sides producing a sharp "knife rim"). On the reverse there are periods before and after the inscriptions.* (Courtesy Bowers & Merena.)

---

[271] *US Mint*, NARA-CP, op. cit., entry 330, box 45. Letter dated July 22, 1907 to Saint-Gaudens from Roberts.

[272] *US Mint*, NARA-P, op. cit. Letter dated July 25, 1907 to Roberts from Saint-Gaudens.

The President had made it clear to director Roberts that he wanted small quantities of the experimental coins made available to collectors. Roberts discussed this in more detail in a letter to secretary Cortelyou on July 23:[273]

> ...In connection with the new coinage I intend to also refer to the President's wish to have a number of coins struck from the high relief experimental dies. I find that there is no law against our doing this under your authority, but the Mint officials should be authorized in writing and the number of pieces specified. In considering the number to be authorized I would suggest that to strike only a few will be to give them a very high money value and very likely occasion criticism. Illustrate, an 1804 silver dollar piece, of which there are said to be only four in existence, sold in Philadelphia last week for about $3,500. It would be better, in my opinion, to strike several hundred and to at least allow the public collections of the country to obtain copies. The Superintendent of the Mint will want to be relieved of all responsibility in this distribution.
>
> I suggest moreover, that there should be no distribution of them until after the regular new issue is out. That will relieve interest to a great extent and lesson the pressure for the experimental pieces.

President Roosevelt was prepared to waive the regulations requiring destruction of all experimental pieces on July 25. This opened the door to distribution of any experimental (or pattern) pieces to collectors and museums. It also provided a way for the President to show what the designs were intended to look like, while letting the mint produce versions more suitable for circulation.

Samples of new eagle coins from the first models were sent to President Roosevelt at Oyster Bay, New York. He returned the coins on July 29 along with a letter to secretary Cortelyou:[274]

> My dear Mr. Secretary:
> I return the two coins herewith and also the correspondence you enclosed. How would it do to have a few thousand coins struck with the smooth finish, and then the rest struck with the sharply cut details of the old design? Of course if the eagle stands too high as compared to the rim, the proportion between the two must be made all right by either raising the rim or reducing the eagle, whichever you think necessary.
>
> As for the high relief coins, have several hundred struck and allow the collectors of the country to obtain specimens as you suggested, none to be issued until the new issue is out. They should be preserved as the work of a great American artist.
> Sincerely yours,

In his letter, the President accepted that high relief coins could not be issued in quantity for circulation. His solution, based on Roberts' suggestion, was to "...have several hundred..." eagles struck to Saint-Gaudens' specification for "...the collectors of the country,..." then rework the design to produce sharper details.

On the morning of July 31, secretary Cortelyou received a farewell letter from George Roberts, soon to be private banker:[275]

> My dear Mr. Secretary:
> Under its terms my resignation goes into effect today and I am leaving for Chicago this afternoon, I supposed when I fixed the date for my retirement that my

[273] *US Mint*, NARA-CP, op. cit., entry 330, box 45. Letter dated July 23, 1907 to Cortelyou from Roberts.
[274] *Roosevelt*, LoC, op. cit., vol. 74, p.144, microfilm reel 346. Letter dated July 29, 1907 to Cortelyou from Roosevelt.
[275] *US Mint*, NARA-CP, op. cit., entry 330, box 45. Letter dated July 31, 1907 to Cortelyou from Roberts.

successor would be ready to qualify by that time or very soon, but Mr. Leach will hardly be able to leave his responsibilities in the San Francisco Mint until his successor is named and has qualified. There appears to be some difficulty in finding a suitable man. He writes me that the Senators have agreed upon several parties who in turn declined it. I presume, however, that the choice will be made before long. Meantime, Mr. Robert E. Preston, who was the Director of the Mint before me and is amply capable of managing the Bureau, will be Acting Director.

There are only a few matters of importance pending to which I shall briefly refer:

The most important of these is the completion of the dies for the new gold coinage. I wrote to Mr. Saint Gaudens on the 22nd instant stating my objections to the last dies and have given the objections to you. The essential difficulty is that Mr. Saint Gaudens makes a very large model which must be mechanically reduced down to the size of a coining die. This reduction seems to inevitably take the life out of the work giving the die a smooth, dull finish instead of making the outlines sharp and clear as they should be for good coinage work. They think at the Mint that this is a fatal defect and that it can only be cured by making the original plaster smaller. Mr. Saint Gaudens' work is essentially medal work and of a very high order but the end sought in coinage work is distinctly different. I am sorry not to be able to complete this undertaking for the President. We received the first models from Mr. Saint Gaudens in December last and not an hour of time has been lost since. Our undertaking was confessedly opposed to accepted views in modern coinage for we undertook to obtain a degree of relief which had been definitely abandoned. Our work was, therefore, necessarily experimental. We had to try and fail in order to convince ourselves and in this way the work has been unavoidably delayed. I think it should still be delayed until the dies which fully meet coinage conditions are obtained. I have not yet had an opinion from Mr. Saint-Gaudens relative to the last criticism and matters are waiting on his action.

With this, Roberts took leave of Washington, his future established in banking. Yet in a few years a new President, William Howard Taft, would call Roberts back to the directorship just in time for design of the Buffalo nickel and Panama-Pacific Exposition commemoratives.

# Chapter 4 – Too Much Delay

Augustus Saint-Gaudens died August 3, 1907.

"Pray accept our profound sympathy for you and your son," wrote Theodore and Edith Roosevelt to widow Augusta Saint-Gaudens.[276]

"I count it as one of the privileges of my administration to have had him make two of our coins."[277]

Letters of condolence poured into the little post office at Windsor, Vermont. Cards and notes embellished with drawings and personal remembrances from throughout the world lined the family home called Aspet. Memorial exhibitions were planned in many cities – some elaborate, some simple, some dedicated to specific aspects of the artist's career.

It had been over two years since Saint-Gaudens actively took up the coin design commission. He had worked on the Liberty head obverse until a few days before his death without finding the combination of relief and detail that would satisfy mint officials. The double eagle was further from completion. He had seen some of the experimental and pattern pieces of both coins, but none had been minted for circulation.

Newspapers noted the sculptor's passing and added embellishment to the few facts available regarding the coinage designs on which Saint-Gaudens had been working. One correspondent to the Philadelphia Mint suggested that W. Tate Mackenzie should be hired to complete the commission. Alfred H. Landu of New York wrote to George Kunz at the ANS offices, stating, "I would like to enter a competition for an artistic coinage," and requesting information on a supposed contest.[278] Isabel Lusty of Troy, New York enclosed a

---

[276] *Roosevelt*, LoC, op. cit., vol. 74, p.229, microfilm reel 346. Letter dated August 6, 1907 to Mrs. Augustus Saint-Gaudens from Roosevelt.

[277] *Roosevelt*, LoC, op. cit., vol. 74, p.238, microfilm reel 346. Letter dated August 6, 1907 to George F. Kunz from Roosevelt.

[278] *George F. Kunz papers*, American Museum of Natural History, Library Services Department, New York, NY. "Coinage" file. Letter dated August 5, 1907 to Kunz from Alfred Landu, 142 West 14th St., NYC.

106

clipping from her local *Troy Times* and asked, "How long do we have before the designs must be sent in and can we make a design for ten coins?"[279]

Roosevelt's personal letters do not record how he felt about losing his friend, but the impact must have been deeply felt. Absence of the coins and the sculptor's death pushed Roosevelt's normal impatience to the edge:[280]

> My dear Cortelyou:
> I do not want to wait about those new coins. I would like the director of the Mint to go ahead with the dies of the coins as they now are, and then if experience shows that the clear cut finish must be obtained make the change in the original die after submitting it to me. Mr. Saint Gaudens is now dead. I do not know whether there is any man associated with him to whom we can refer. One of his assistants has been in communication with the Mint authorities about this matter. Why don't they get into touch with him again? I am sure there has been good-will upon the part of the mint authorities, but I cannot help feeling that there has been a certain cumbersomeness of mind and inability to do the speediest modern work, as shown by these delays.
> There must be no further delays. Let the two coins be finished and put into circulation at once; by September first. Then if experience shows, or even if experience does not show, that there should be a sharper cutting, let the mint authorities consult with the late Saint Gaudens' assistant and prepare dies of a sharper cutting. There has been altogether too much delay about this matter and I want it finished immediately.
> Sincerely yours,

Roosevelt was alone – without support and encouragement from the country's most honored artist. Henry Hering was a mere assistant not personally respected by the President, and certainly not capable of standing in the great artist's shoes. Secretary Cortelyou sent a note directly to acting superintendent Norris at the Philadelphia Mint:[281]

> Have this matter taken up at once and the President's instructions carried out; and everything possible must be done to expedite the work.
> Keep me advised from time to time as it progresses.

Acting mint director Preston sent a copy of the letter to superintendent Landis along with his own synopsis: "I trust every effort will be made to expedite this coinage, in obedience to the order of the president."[282]

Preston inquired about the status of the eagle and double eagle, and learned that Saint-Gaudens had not delivered final models of the double eagle (the third model). Preston asked Roberts in Chicago about the coinage, and the former director replied on August 12:[283]

> Referring to several inquiries received from Miss Kelly relative to the designs for the new gold coinage, I give you the following statement for your information: The St. Gaudens letter to me of July 25th, asking for a plaster cast of the eagle die was referred to Philadelphia, and the plaster cast was sent and full reply made to the letter. No instructions have been received from the President as to the half and quarter eagle, but I had expected that the eagle [coin] design would be used upon

---

[279] *Kunz*, AMNH, op. cit. Letter dated August 9, 1907 to Kunz from Isabel Lusty, 3 Thirteenth St., Upper Troy, NY.
[280] *US Mint*, NARA-P, op. cit. Letter dated August 7, 1907 to Cortelyou from Roosevelt.
[281] *US Mint*, NARA-CP, op. cit., entry 330, box 45. Note (manuscript) dated August 9, 1907 to Norris from Cortelyou.
[282] *US Mint*, NARA-P, op. cit. Letter dated August 12, 1907 to Landis from Preston.
[283] *US Mint*, NARA-CP, op. cit., entry 330, box 45. Letter dated August 12, 1907 to Preston from Roberts.

them. I do not recall any discussion with the President about the half and quarter eagle. The President gave me a brief memorandum in his own handwriting of the designs agreed to for the double eagle and eagle, and I gave that slip of paper to Miss Kelly to put in my private file, as I wanted it as a private memento of the coinage. It was purely informal – a memorandum made by him while we were talking about it. Have her look it up in the file but have her leave it in my file.

The President concluded to leave the One Cent piece unchanged, and there has been no discussion about any change in the Nickel piece....

...The two experimental $10 pieces which I received from the Mint at Philadelphia were sent, one to Mr. St. Gaudens and the other to Secretary Cortelyou and they were asked to return them. The two $10 pieces of present design which I got at the Philadelphia Mint I paid for, and sent one of them to Mr. St. Gaudens and the other to Secretary Cortelyou. Mr. St. Gaudens sent me a check for his, but Secretary Cortelyou has not paid for the one forwarded to him. There is $10 coming to me on that; please make a note of it.

With best regards to you personally, I am,

Telegrams sped back and forth between Homer Saint-Gaudens and Preston's office. In Philadelphia, Albert Norris telephoned Charles Barber, who was on vacation at Ocean Grove, New Jersey, and had him cut short his holiday.[284] The engraver, likely in a bad mood and resentful of having his vacation ruined, shot off a letter to superintendent Landis:[285]

I beg to state that the dies for the Eagle coin, new design, have been ready and awaiting approval since July 22nd, when some of the coins and plaster casts were submitted to the Director and also to Mr. Saint Gaudens as he requested. Since that date there has been no instruction received regarding these coins. With the instructions just received "to go ahead with the dies as they now are" I beg to state that the dies are now ready for the Eagle coin.

In regard to the Double Eagle, you will remember that dies have been made from models furnished by Mr. Saint Gaudens and coins struck as medals and submitted to the Director with a full statement of the impossibility of using dies for coinage made from the models in their present state on account of the high relief.

The last that this department heard on the subject was that Mr. Saint Gaudens had seen the impossibility of coining high relief and had determined upon reducing the relief to within the requirement of modern coinage.

I have no model for the Double Eagle that can be used, for the reason above stated namely, the relief being entirely too high.

I have been anticipating a new model that would not have this objectionable feature, but have not received such an one, therefore it is not in any sense the fault of this department that dies are not ready.

The appliances in this department for doing die work are the most improved and have been used in every possible way even to working day and night and Sundays to expedite this new coinage, and in the case of making the first reduction Mr. Saint Gaudens reported it would take six months to get it made in Paris, while I made it in one month.

I think this statement is necessary to clear up the idea that the Mint has caused any delay in the production of the new dies as from the first I have had to wait upon Mr. Saint Gaudens for models as I am now doing in the case of the Double Eagle. Mr. Saint Gaudens asked for samples of the models when reduced to the size of the Double Eagle and they were furnished, since that time I have heard nothing more of them, and do not know whether he left other models or any one to

---

[284] *US Mint*, NARA-CP, op. cit., entry 229, box 256. Letter (excerpt) dated August 14, 1907 to Preston from Norris.

[285] *US Mint*, NARA-CP, op. cit., entry 229, box 256. Letter (excerpt) dated August 14, 1907 to Landis from Barber.

take up this work, and until the new and suitable models are sent, I am powerless to produce Double Eagle dies of the Saint Gaudens model that can be used for coinage.

In the case of the Eagle Mr. Saint Gaudens reduced the model until with the aid of the new French reducing machine it was possible to make a die that would produce a coin, this has not been done with the Double Eagle models and until it is done my hands are tied.

I furnish you with this full statement of the present condition of the new designs and models and respectfully await your instructions as to who will supply the models for the Double Eagle, and also advise you that if the models were here now, it would be utterly impossible to get ready to coin the Double Eagle by September 1st.

Respectfully,

The President's order combined with the absence of a mint director put the Philadelphia Mint staff in full self-protection mode. Barber had hardly signed his tirade when acting superintendent Norris produced a more detailed version. This letter includes previously unknown information on edge collars for the eagles:[286]

My dear Mr. Preston:

Upon the receipt of your letter of the 12th, enclosing a copy of the letter from the President ordering the coinage of the new eagle and double eagle, I looked the matter up. The machine shop was working on a sectional collar for putting stars on the edge of the eagle, so I put them on overtime and we hope to have it ready for trial on Friday. This relief work on the edge of the coin is something entirely new to us. Some years ago, I think in Mr. Bosbyshell's time, a contrivance for this work was made, but only a few examples were made on it. We had expected to use this but on trial found it would not work satisfactorily for the regular coinage, so a new attachment for the coining press had to be devised. If the work on the edge of the coins was to be impressed, instead of being in relief, we would have had no trouble, as that is put on the blank in the milling machine. We wrote to Paris, France, asking for information as to how the letters were placed on the edge of French coins, but received no answer. No one here knew anything about this relief work, so we had to design this attachment ourselves. We hope to strike some of the new eagles next week. I telephoned Mr. Barber, at Ocean Grove, and he came up this morning. I was afraid to wire him for fear he would not get the telegram on account of the strike. He wrote the letter I send you today and made arrangements for the manufacture of a lot of eagle dies.

I think the President does Mr. Barber an injustice when he speaks of "a certain cumbersomeness of mind and inability to do the speediest modern work, as shown by these delays," here. The making of the models for these coins was given to Saint Gaudens, who was a sculptor and had no experience with coinage designs. When the models were received, the Bureau was notified that the dies made from them would not work in the coining press. A party in New York, in the employ of Tiffany & Company, said they could be made, but it was afterwards found out that he did not know anything about coinage [this was Hannweber – RWB]. The man in charge of the medal work there would make no such statement [this was Kunz – RWB].

Dies from the first models for the double eagle were made and it was found, as was previously stated, that they could not be used for coinage. The models were returned to Saint Gaudens, at his request, and a modified set furnished after some time. The Bureau was informed that even these would not make dies satisfactory for coinage, but the dies were made and it was found they could not be used in the

---

[286] US Mint, NARA-CP, op. cit., entry 330, box 45. Letter (excerpt) dated August 14, 1907 to Preston from Norris.

coining press. How are we going to strike coins from these for the President? These models were sent back to Saint Gaudens, at his request, and we have been waiting some time for the third set.

Mr. Barber offered to take Saint Gaudens' designs and make models from them that could be used for the manufacture of dies which would work in the coining presses, but no authority was given him to do so. The President objected to any radical modification of the relief, as he wished a relief similar to the ancient Greek coins. Such a relief has been found impractical by every nation using modern methods of coinage, where they are limited to small tolerances in weight and fineness, again to provide against counterfeiting, and have to cater to the requirements of the commercial world, as to even diameter and thickness of coins and ability to stack and to withstand abrasion. The President says he does not want "conventional" coins, but such coins are the only ones which have been found to meet the requirements of modern machinery and commercial uses.

Norris' objections continue for another two pages as he takes exception to each of the President's statements. His letter reveals that Barber had already offered to rework the designs for both coins, and that the starred edge collar for the eagles was still being prepared. The mint was currently producing incuse lettered edge pieces for Mexico. However, the use of forty-six raised stars, placed in three collar segments, meant that the distribution of stars had to be uneven – 15-15-16 – yet look even to the unaided eye.

Preston's investigation also revealed that Saint-Gaudens had been working on further modifications to the eagle design just days before his death, and that Homer Saint-Gaudens said the revised eagle models would be shipped on August 24:[287]

As Mr. Saint-Gaudens' son did not give you, in the reply to your letter, any information as to the time the double eagle models would be furnished, but simply stated that the new eagle model would be forwarded to you in a week, I wired him yesterday to inquire when the double eagle would be finished, and received the following reply: "Can finish double eagle in one month. Letter will follow."

Roosevelt was at his Oyster Bay, Long Island home pounding out another letter to secretary Cortelyou. One can imagine the President, smashing fist into hand, the large gold ring containing a lock of Abraham Lincoln's hair (a gift from the late John Hay) on his middle finger left hand glinting in the morning light as he dictated:[288]

My dear Mr. Cortelyou:
Will you find out definitely when those coins will be ready? If there is any further delay I shall ask that Mr. Kunz be put in charge to make the coins forthwith. I should like to have the information now as to exactly when those coins will be issued; and as to the number of the high relief coins that will be struck; as you know we were to strike a few thousand of those, which, however, would be issued after the regular issue of the lower relief coins has begun. There has been altogether too much delay and I do not want to wait any longer.
Faithfully yours,

The President received no response, and on August 24 Roosevelt forwarded a letter to Cortelyou, along with another threat to replace the mint staff. The enclosure was evi-

[287] *US Mint*, NARA-P, op. cit. Letter dated August 20, 1907 to Preston from Homer Saint-Gaudens.
[288] *Roosevelt*, LoC, op. cit., vol. 74, p.421, microfilm reel 346. Letter dated August 22, 1907 to Cortelyou from Roosevelt.

110

dently a letter from William D. Sohier, an old friend who had recently been talking with noted sculptor Daniel Chester French.[289]

> My dear Mr. Cortelyou:
> Perhaps the mint people ought to see the enclosed letter. Let them tell me when the new eagles and double eagles will appear. I hope a fortnight.
> If there is any further delay I shall want Kunz, French and Brenner called in and I shall have them supervise the coinage.
> Faithfully yours,

The enclosure read:[290]

> My dear Mr. President:
> Forgive an old friend for butting in with a suggestion, founded perhaps, on misinformation, but intended to help our coinage and St. Gaudens' family, who need it. It is now reported that the Treasury rejects the St. Gaudens models, asserting that they will not stack.
> I was with Daniel C. French, the sculptor, Wednesday and he said it was a pity – that there was a general impression and had been for years, among the artists, that the mint would never approve or use an outside design.
> That he thought undoubtedly the model could be adapted so that it would fill all requirements and still keep its artistic merits.
> That there was a machine that could reduce the relief proportionately, if that was necessary.
> Finally when I said I would write you, he suggested that, before the design was finally rejected, if it was submitted to the acknowledged authorities in this country, the Numismatic Society of New York, or Victor Brenner of New York of the National Sculpture Society, the "only trained medallist in the country (outside the mint)" for report and suggestion, it might solve all difficulties. Anyway, it would help remove the prevailing impression that every design submitted from outsiders would be rejected for some alleged reason by the authorities at the mint.
> I merely venture to pass along his suggestions as he is an extremely level headed and conservative expert.
> Your Provincetown speech presented the gospel of truth, statesmanship and good policy, as well, wonderfully, clearly and forcefully in the opinion of one old friend and admirer.
> Yours respectfully,

The luster of Roosevelt's presidency, so evident the previous December, had been dulled by complaints from conservative Republicans about the way that his administration was treating businesses. The decision by United States District Court judge Kenesaw Mountain Landis to fine Standard Oil Company $26 million in an antirebate case unsettled the stock market, and brought piles of letters from concerned citizens. In a normal August the President could have amused himself with relatively benign activities, but August 1907 brought only increasing pressure on the President. Economic instability would produce a short but intense financial panic in the autumn, one that ultimately led to establishment of the Federal Reserve System in 1913. The new coins were no longer a diversion, but a potential embarrassment.

---

[289] *Roosevelt*, LoC, op. cit., vol. 74, p.464, microfilm reel 346. Letter dated August 24, 1907 to Cortelyou from Roosevelt. The letter is not among Cortelyou's papers in the Library of Congress. It was forwarded to the Mint Bureau.
[290] *US Mint*, NARA-CP, op. cit., entry 330, box 45. Letter dated August 23, 1907 to Roosevelt from Sohier. Enclosed with Roosevelt's letter, above. Sohier is probably referring to a *New York Times* article of August 15 titled "Coin Design Unsuited," which states that $10 designs "…have been found unsuitable in their present shape…"

Roosevelt's frustration at further delay was evident. He knew only the mint could strike the coins, and he also knew that except for the director and superintendent, the engraver and other permanent mint employees were civil service and could not be replaced "at will."[291] He could not replace the director because officially, there wasn't one – Roberts resigned July 31 and Frank Leach had not been confirmed. The three men he threatened to bring in to supervise the coinage (based partially on William Sohier's comments) were George F. Kunz, who had been involved with the project for nearly a year; Daniel Chester French, one of America's best sculptors and contemporary of Saint-Gaudens; and Victor David Brenner, one of the country's leading sculptor-medallists.[292] It is unlikely that any of these three could have helped much, but the threat was real.

## Finishing the Eagles

To overcome problems with the sample eagles (J-1901/P-1995, J-1903/P-1996), Barber offered several suggestions to superintendent Landis along with new sample coins:[293]

> Before final adoption of the new design for the Eagle gold coin I beg to call your attention to that which in my judgement is a serious defect namely, the want of border or determinate edge to make a finish to the coin.
>
> In the present condition of the design and model, the coin when struck is without a border, consequently, when the planchet receives sufficient blow of the press to make the proper impression, there being no edge or place for the metal to flow into, it is forced up between the die and the collar making a fin or sharp edge which would not stand attrition, but would soon disappear, leaving a light weight coin that would be rejected by the Banks and custom offices and sub-treasuries.
>
> There is also another objection to the design in the present condition namely, it will not pile.
>
> There being no proper border above the relief of the design for the coins to rest upon, it is dependant upon the convexity of the die to make the concavity of the coin sufficient to clear the relief of the design when the coins are put face to face.
>
> As the convexity of the die cannot be fixed and is liable to change in the process of tempering the steel, and also in striking the pieces, it will be seen, that there is no reliable provision made to cover this requisite in these coins, and therefore, the pieces have no proper seat, but are resting in some cases upon a sharp edge and in others upon the shoulder of the Eagle.
>
> To overcome this defect I would suggest that a border be turned in the die as shown in coin exhibit No. 2, I think that you will agree with me that this change in no way detracts from any claim that may be made for artistic excellence, but on the contrary adds to the appearance of the coin and overcomes the objections mentioned above. This change will cause but little delay in the issuing of the coin and can be completed long before the models are sent us for the Double eagle.
>
> Awaiting your instructions in regard to this matter, I am
> Respectfully,

---

[291] Early in his political career Roosevelt was head of the federal Civil Service Commission. The engraver could not be replaced due to the Tenure in Office law passed by Congress in 1867. This prevented the President from removing any employee whose position had been confirmed by the Senate, unless the Senate concurred.

[292] Two years later, Brenner would scale down one of his Lincoln medal designs for use on the bronze cent. The result was artistically mediocre.

[293] *US Mint*, NARA-P, op. cit. Letter dated August 26, 1907 to Landis from Barber. Coin #1 was also from the first models.

Addition of the border was necessary to allow the coins to stack properly and to protect the design from excessive wear. As can be seen by the illustrations below, the original Eagle (J-1901/1903) has the design flowing directly to the rim of the coin. Barber's addition of the wide rim produced a raised ledge on which the coin sits. This enables coins to be stacked without the designs touching one another. Having the rim higher than the design was one of the requirements recognized by Roosevelt very early in the project.

*Figure 34. "Knife rim" eagle from the first models (top), J-1901/P-1995, and "normal rim" (border) as added by Barber, known as the second models (J-1903/P-1997).* (Courtesy Bowers and Merena; Harry W. Bass, Jr. Research Foundation.)

The letter was accompanied by two experimental pieces; #1 was the variety without border and with "periods" on the reverse (P-1995). The item referred to as "coin exhibit No. 2" in Barber's letter is the same design as the earlier piece but with a border added (P-1997, see above). Note that both coins have triangular "periods" or "stops" before and after the reverse inscriptions. It appears that Barber made a new pair of hubs from the first model, but made the reduction slightly smaller than on the #1 hub. This gave him space to cut a border (or rim) approximately two millimeters wide around the circumference of the design. He also seems to have reduced the relief somewhat more than on the #1 version, in the process loosing detail in the eagle and headdress feathers. Both coins were struck using an edge collar with irregular stars on one of the segments.

As Barber also pointed out, the fin, created by metal flowing between the face dies and edge collar, was a major problem. Aesthetically, it made the coins look rough and irregular. The greater difficulty, however, was loss of gold as the fin quickly wore off. Ten and twenty dollar coins were used primarily in large transactions and international settlements. When gold coin was exported, the cost of gold in New York was based on the face value of the coin, rather than weight. If new coins could be secured, they were nearly as satisfactory to ship as bars. (Gold coin was bought from the Treasury at face value, and credited in Europe according to weight.) However, in the case of coin that had been in circulation or was not otherwise of full weight, the banker had to receive a higher rate for his overseas drafts against the shipment than in the case of bars. Consequently, if the coins had a fin, which quickly wore off, the shipper in the United States was paying for something he didn't get. The only solution was to obtain a higher rate of exchange on drafts sold against the gold.[294] Any perception by bankers that the new-design coins were underweight could have had severe financial repercussions on international trade.

## Another Eagle in Philadelphia

Before Landis could respond to Barber's letter and issue instructions, Barber received new eagle models from Augusta Saint-Gaudens. He wrote to Landis:[295]

> Models for the ten Dollar just received, relief now reduced to coin relief and border added, dies made from these models would be a great improvement over those already made, from which samples were sent you yesterday.
> Dies from these new models would require one month for production.
> If the models for twenty dollar are made of the same relief as the models just received for ten dollar, coinage dies can be made.

For the first time, Barber displayed a small amount of optimism when he stated that not only were the latest $10 coin models satisfactory for making hubs and coinage, but the double eagle would also be acceptable if it were of the same relief. Within a month, the mint could have eagle dies ready for full-scale production. At the Aspet studio, Henry Hering and Homer Saint-Gaudens had spent nearly two weeks refining Saint-Gaudens' final Eagle models based on the sample coin and comments from the mint. Had they known of Barber's comments, almost the only positive things the engraver had to say during the entire process, they might have tipped a glass or two of good champagne.

In his letter of August 20 to acting director Preston, Homer Saint-Gaudens stated: "Mr. Hering has finally finished the eagle at a relief slightly lower than that on the French coin by Chaplin, which is the lowest relief that Mr. Hering knew my father would abide by, and which I understand Mr. Barber can mint."[296] Referred to as the "third model" this version incorporated all of Barber's suggestions and was similar, except for removal of the periods on the reverse, to the samples made from the second model that Barber had modified.

---

[294] Franklin Escher, *Foreign Exchange Explained.* The MacMillan Company, New York, 1917. pp.78–9.
[295] *US Mint*, NARA-P, op. cit. Letter dated August 27, 1907 to Landis from Barber. Augusta sent a confirming letter on the 27th.
[296] *US Mint*, NARA-P, op. cit. Letter dated August 20, 1907 to Preston from H. Saint-Gaudens.

Landis immediately wired Preston for approval to make the reductions and dies, and the work was approved the same day. He also replied to Landis about adding the border as Barber had suggested:[297]

> Your letter of the 26th instant, enclosing for approval two specimens of the new eagle, – exhibits Nos. 1 & 2, – has been received. I agree with you that by throwing up a narrow border Mr. Barber has improved the appearance of the coin as shown in exhibit #2 compared with exhibit #1. These coins will be forwarded to the Secretary of the Treasury for his inspection and his attention called to the improvement made by Mr. Barber. It is noticed that the stars on the border [i.e., edge] are not in a straight line. This, no doubt, is due to the appliance you have for making the impression of the stars. From the improved appearance of the coin, as shown in exhibit #2, I do not think there will be any objection on the part of the President or the Secretary to the modification made by Mr. Barber, especially as it does not, in any way, change the design of the coin, and certainly affords some protection from abrasion.

It is likely that all experimental coins from the #1 and #2 models had crooked stars on the edge. Pieces with straight stars were probably those later struck for circulation. Also, on August 27, Preston advised superintendent Landis:[298]

> You are authorized and requested to proceed to strike five hundred (500) experimental pieces from each of the dies, the eagle and the double eagle in high relief, in compliance with instructions given this Bureau by the Secretary of the Treasury.

Secretary Cortelyou did not want Kunz and other outsiders brought into the mint, so he approved striking a token number of eagles and double eagles before the President's September 1 deadline.[299] He could then report that coins were being produced and would soon be "issued" thus keeping Roosevelt from further meddling. The order relating to the high relief (#1 model) eagles was repeated on the 30th so there would be no mistake about which version to strike. The eagles were struck using the high relief dies from the first model ("knife rim" with "periods"), because dies of the latest eagle models had not been made (they would have taken approximately a month to make). The double eagles would have to be struck from dies of the second pair of models since the much-promised low relief version had not been delivered.

Superintendent Landis wanted to wait until Barber had made dies from the new eagle models (#3 model) to strike the five hundred eagles. He felt these would be much better coins than ones made from Barber's bordered dies, but Preston would not accept the delay: "You will please cause five hundred (500) eagles to be struck on the medal press from the high relief dies without delay."[300] This was also consistent with secretary Cortelyou's previous instructions. Preston also sent a note to Dr. Albert A. Norris at the mint, advising that he would probably receive an order from the President for one hundred of the new coins, and reminding him to have the coins on hand, "...so you can furnish them without a mo-

---

[297] *US Mint*, NARA-P, op. cit. Letter dated August 27, 1907 to Landis from Preston. Evidently the letter was sent before the telegram was received.
[298] *US Mint*, NARA-P, op. cit. Letter dated August 27, 1907 to Landis from Preston.
[299] These were from the #2 double eagle model and the #1 eagle model (with knife rim).
[300] *US Mint*, NARA-P, op. cit. Letter dated August 30, 1907 to Landis from Preston.

ment's delay."[301] The same day, Barber was sent to New York with paraffin reductions of the new eagle models to get bronze casts made by Keller Mechanical Engraving Company.[302] Assistant treasury secretary J. H. Edwards sent a report on events to Cortelyou, who was vacationing on Long Island, New York:[303]

> My dear Mr. Secretary,
> I am sending herewith correspondence regarding the new gold pieces, which in a measure explains itself. Also there are enclosed two samples of the new ten dollar pieces.
> In view of the positive instructions from the President and yourself, I have directed that the Mint immediately proceed with the coining, and this is being done. However, it seems to me the rim should at least be put on the coin, as recommended by the Superintendent. In fact, it would seem that the coinage should not be proceeded with to any extent until the relief has been reduced, as recommended in the enclosed telegram of August 27.
> You will note the stars on the rim [i.e.; edge] are rather irregular. This is proving to a very serious problem, but Mr. Barber has advised us that he feels confident a machine which he is having built will enable them to fix these stars with greater regularity.
> As above stated, the work is proceeding and will continue unless directions are received from you to cease same for the period mentioned in the Superintendent's telegram. If you take the matter up with the President, and have an opportunity to do so between now and next Tuesday, I suggest it might be better to telephone me Tuesday morning any instructions you may have...

Edwards' observation confirms that of Preston about the irregular edge stars, and also advises that Barber expected to have the problem solved soon. The samples were likely from both #1 and #2 models since Roosevelt had already approved the #1 version. The President saw the new coins on the 31st and had his secretary write to Cortelyou:[304]

> ...The President is greatly pleased with the sample coins, which I return herewith. He wishes to know if it is not practicable to go on and strike a few of the coins like these, meanwhile proceeding with the making of the dies from the new models referred to in the Superintendent Landis' telegram of the 27th ultimo.
> How are those double eagles getting along? The President asks me to inquire of you about them.

Preston followed up the initial order of five hundred eagles from the #1 models with authority to begin regular production of the coin, but specified the #2 dies with border added by the mint as preferred by the President. This was consistent with Edward's suggestion to Cortelyou the week before:[305]

> You are hereby authorized and requested to proceed with the coinage of the ten-dollar gold piece from the new design by Saint-Gaudens, with the rim as added by Mr. Barber, the engraver.

---

[301] *US Mint*, NARA-P, op. cit. Note ND [August 30, 1907] to Norris from Preston. There is no record for an order of 100 coins from the President, and available documents suggest that +/-500 of each were transferred to the Treasury in Washington in December.

[302] *US Mint*, NARA-P, op. cit. Letter dated August 30, 1907 to Landis from Preston; and telegram dated August 30, 1907 to Landis from Preston. Both initialed by Barber.

[303] *US Mint*, NARA-CP, op. cit., entry 330, box 45. Letter dated August 30, 1907 to Cortelyou from Edwards.

[304] *US Mint*, NARA-CP, op. cit., entry 330, box 45. Letter dated September 3, 1907 to Cortelyou from Loeb.

[305] *US Mint*, NARA-P, op. cit. Letter dated September 9, 1907 to Landis from Preston.

The engraving department dutifully made additional working dies from the second model with Barber's border added and delivered them to the coiner for production. $315,000 in eagles were coined from the second design (P-1997) during September and October 1907. Added to this must be the $5,000 coined in late August and early September on the medal press, for a total mintage of $320,000 (32,000) gold eagles of both varieties.[306]

On September 25, a sample eagle from the #3 model with Hering's additional border and no periods on the reverse, and an example from the second model were sent to acting director Preston:[307]

> I beg to enclose herewith for approval a specimen of the new eagle struck from the dies reduced from Saint Gaudens' last model [#3]. I also enclose for comparison a specimen taken from the $315,000 in eagles now on hand of the first Saint-Gaudens' model as modified by Mr. Barber. [#2]
>
> You will notice that the eagle from the last model [#3] is a great improvement over those of the first model [#2]. The latter are indefinite in detail and outline, not being at all sharp and look like imperfect coins or coins that have been sweated, while the former is sharp in outline, the detail shows up well, the border is broad and prominent and the coins will stack perfectly.
>
> We have on hand $315,000 of the first model [with border added], struck on the coining press, and $500 [sic – $5000] struck on the medal press. If this last model meets with your approval I would strongly urge you the expediency of immediately replacing the $315,000 now on hand, of the first model [#2] with eagles of the last models [#3]. We have $100,000 in eagle blanks ready for coinage and a larger amount in strips and unadjusted blanks and are therefore ready to proceed with this coinage at short notice.

Later, Assistant Secretary of the Treasury Edwards issued instructions to pay out the 31,500 "...eagles we had coined from the dies we had prepared from the reduction of the second design submitted." Edwards felt these coins were "...so nearly like the coins produced from the reduction of the third model that it was not necessary [to melt them]."[308] Acting director Preston, however, was confused by the production of the eagles from the second model on the coining presses. The confusion arose from Preston's September 9 order to produce the new eagles. It was unclear whether Preston meant to make them immediately, from the second model dies, or make them as soon as Barber had dies from the third model ready for use. The result was that the mint had struck 31,500 eagles from the second models, and was now ordered to strike eagles using dies of the third model (the Saint-Gaudens/Hering model with border) up to $1,000,000 using all available planchets.[309]

Director Frank Leach decided that the incorrectly minted eagles should be destroyed, and on November 9 he approved melting $315,000 (31,500) in gold eagles made from the second models (border, with periods), holding back only fifty pieces for collec-

---

[306] This does not include sample coins struck of both varieties.

[307] Taxay, op. cit., p.316. Letter dated September 25, 1907 to Preston from Landis. This letter is referenced in Taxay as being among the U. S. Mint documents in the National Archives; however, it cannot now be located. The author believes the "$500" to be a typographical error for "$5000." This amount is consistent with Preston's letters of August 27 and 30. Text in brackets has been added by the author in the interest of clarity.

[308] US Mint, NARA-P, op. cit. Letter dated October 31, 1907 to Landis from Preston.

[309] US Mint, NARA-P, op. cit. Letter dated November 2, 1907 to Landis from Leach. This duplicates an order from Preston on October 31.

tors.[310] This did not, however, include the five hundred coins from the first models made on the medal press intended to placate the President's ire.[311] It also excluded experimental pieces with irregular edge stars made at the end of August.

The borders on the #2 and #3 varieties are mentioned frequently in surviving mint documents, but the "periods" on the reverse of #1 and #2 are never mentioned. It is possible no one noticed, or paid any attention to these design elements. Since the third set of models came from Hering, and Saint-Gaudens' studio had complete discretion so far as the design went, the mint would have had no reason to question the absence of periods.[312] The 500 #1 eagles were to satisfy any possible request from Roosevelt. These were an "insurance policy" put in place by Cortelyou against additional presidential rage. When acting director Preston, who was seventy-one at the time, ordered eagle production to begin, Landis simply took the #2 dies (the only practical ones available) and had 31,500 specimens struck on the regular presses. In November, Frank Leach, on the job for a week, was still largely in the dark about what had been happening. The fact that five hundred of the #1 eagles were later transferred to the Treasurer, and that citizens could obtain an example from Leach at the Mint Bureau just by paying $10 for it, suggests that significant quantities existed through part of 1908.

A consistent theme running through the interaction between Saint-Gaudens' studio and the mint was the absence of meaningful communication. On numerous occasions neither side knew what the other was doing or what they wanted done. Face-to-face meetings produced almost as much confusion as written instructions, and presidential "commentary" often distracted everyone. In early 1912, Roberts commented to James Fraser on the Saint-Gaudens situation:[313]

> ...I should like to avoid a repetition of the misunderstanding and friction which developed between Mr. St. Gaudens and the people of the Mint, most of which I am sure was due to Mr. St. Gaudens' attitude. He started out with the determination to make the coins in an impossible relief and attributed all opposition from the Mint to jealousy and a determination to make his plans a failure. There will be no trouble with the Mint if we go about the matter in the right way.

On September 3 Augusta Saint-Gaudens sent final models for the cent to Philadelphia.[314] These consisted of the Liberty head with Indian headdress with the word LIBERTY below for the obverse, and a reverse showing a wreath surrounding the value and date. After receiving the cent models at the mint, Barber wrote to Landis asking what he should do with them. During the latter part of May, director Roberts and President Roosevelt had decided to abandon the idea of the cent and use the new designs only on the eagle and double eagle.[315] Evidently, no one had told Saint-Gaudens or Hering about the decision. Hering's time, wasted working on cent models, could have better been used to complete the double eagle models.

[310] *US Mint*, NARA-P, op. cit. Letter dated November 9, 1907 to Landis from Leach.
[311] The Treasurer should have transferred the remaining coins back to the mint for melting, but they had a more interesting fate in store.
[312] The "periods" were actually triangular text stops intended to bound the inscriptions. They were used on both eagle and double eagle designs. Poor quality reductions rendered them as round or oval pellets, or periods.
[313] *US Mint*, NARA-CP, op. cit., entry 235, vol. 395. Letter dated January 18, 1912 to Fraser from Roberts.
[314] *US Mint*, NARA-P, op. cit. Letter dated September 3, 1907 to Preston from Augusta Saint-Gaudens.
[315] *US Mint*, NARA-P, op. cit. Letter dated September 12, 1907 to Landis from Barber.

Samples of the #1 and #2 eagles and the double eagle from the #2 models (high relief, large stars and capitol) were sent to assistant secretary Edwards on September 10 and by the 12th, acting director Preston was asking how soon $200,000 in eagles would be completed. By September 18 the Treasurer determined that enough eagles had been produced and that the output of Liberty head double eagles needed to be increased. Edwards instructed Preston to suspend eagle coinage, and not to pay out any of the new coins until instructed to do so. Coinage of the old design double eagle was resumed.

On October 3, Preston said the sample eagles were shown to Roosevelt and he was able to report: "I am advised that the eagle from the last design is perfectly satisfactory to the president."[316] These were the coins (#3 model) later issued for general circulation that had a raised border similar to that on Barber's experimental samples, but no periods at the ends of the reverse legends. By November 9, director Leach had examined samples from the 31,500 eagles minted under Preston's order and advised Landis, "...you are hereby authorized to melt up the $315,000 struck from the second model of the new eagle coin."[317] Latter-day numismatists have made much of Barber's 'desecration' of Saint-Gaudens' designs, yet the eagle as issued in 1907 is largely the work of the sculptor just before his death and of his trusted assistant, Hermon Hering, acting within his understanding of the sculptor's wishes. While not of the artistic potential of the high relief version, it cannot be said that the $10 gold coin is untrue to Saint-Gaudens' vision or artistic ethic.

For the balance of the calendar year, the Philadelphia Mint struck 238,864 eagles. The design was criticized as being "fuzzy" or "blind" and lacking in sharpness due in part

*Figure 35. Final design for the 1907 eagle as prepared by Henry Hering from Saint-Gaudens' earlier models. Engraver Charles Barber may have made minor modifications, but the design is essentially as Hering and Homer Saint-Gaudens submitted it. The absence of text stops on the reverse was part of the models, and not changed by the mint.* (Courtesy Harry W. Bass, Jr. Research Foundation.)

to loss of detail during the reduction process at the mint, and in part to Hering's incomplete understanding of what was necessary to model a low relief coin.

On December 14, Assistant Secretary of the Treasury Edwards requested transfer of the five hundred double eagles and five hundred eagles ordered in August to the treasury.[318] After initial collector demand subsided, the treasurer and secretary sold most remaining coins to members of Congress and other influential persons in private transactions. In 1912 the balance was transferred to the mint cabinet where they were sold to coin

[316] *US Mint*, NARA-P, op. cit. Letter dated October 3, 1907 to Landis from Preston.
[317] *US Mint*, NARA-P, op. cit. Letter dated November 9, 1907 to Landis from Leach.
[318] *US Mint*, NARA-P, op. cit. Letter dated December 14, 1907 to Landis from Leach.

dealers (primarily Henry Chapman and Tom Elder) a market prices. Eagles brought $15 and double eagles $23 if in perfect condition. The proceeds were used to improve the mint collection. The final seventy $10 gold pieces from the #1 models were deemed too badly scratched to sell, and were melted.

According to an accounting of experimental coins provided to Cortelyou by Leach on February 5, 1908 the following gold eagles were produced:[319]

### Eagle – 1st Model

542 pieces struck

| | |
|---|---|
| 500 | Sent to Treasurer, Washington, for distribution by Asst. Secretary of the Treasury Edwards. |
| 29 | To Mint Bureau and Asst. Secretary Edwards |
| 2 | To Mint Cabinet exhibit |
| 2 | To Metropolitan Art Museum exhibit |
| 1 | Mr. Mitchelson, Conn.[320] |
| 8 | To Mint officials |

### Eagle – 2nd Model

31,500 pieces struck

| | |
|---|---|
| 31,450 | melted up[321] |
| 10 | To Mint Bureau |
| 2 | To Metropolitan Art Museum exhibit |
| 8 | To Mint officials |
| 30 | On hand |

### Eagle – 3rd Model

614,903 pieces struck    In dollars $6,149,030

Thus, the official report states that through February 5, 1908, five hundred forty-two of the #1 coins were made and subtracting the seventy #1 pieces melted between 1915 and 1918, the net mintage of #1 coins is four hundred seventy-two plus a handful of patterns. Fifty of the #2 coins survived melting, and all of the #3 coins were placed in circulation. What is not stated is the fate of experimental pieces struck for examination by officials. Because these are not specifically accounted for, it is likely that the number of #1 and #2 specimens originally available is somewhat greater than the official figures. Landis also stated that 239,406 of the #1 and #3 eagles (five hundred forty-two pieces) were minted in 1907, leaving a net production of 238,864 for general circulation.[322]

Three years after President Roosevelt told the secretary of the treasury, "…our coinage is artistically of atrocious hideousness," on December 28, 1907, the Saint-Gaudens eagle and double eagle became official designs for $10 and $20 gold coins of the United States.[323]

---

[319] *US Mint*, NARA-CP, op. cit., entry 330, box 45. Letter dated February 5, 1908 to Cortelyou from Leach. A complete transcript of the letter will be found in the chapter dealing with patterns and experimental coins.

[320] Donated to the Connecticut State Library in 1911 by Mitchelson's estate. This coin has normal edge stars.

[321] *US Mint*, NARA-CP, op. cit., entry 229, box 270. Letter dated January 21, 1908 to Leach from Landis. This letter provides much of the information Leach later quoted on February 5.

[322] *US Mint*, NARA-CP, op. cit., entry 229, box 270. Letter dated January 21, 1908 to Leach from Landis.

[323] *US Mint*, NARA-P, op. cit. Letter dated December 28, 1907 to Cortelyou from Leach. Countersigned by J. H. Edwards, acting secretary. Mint copy initialed by Barber. The order specifically applied to the eagle and double eagle, but omitted mention on the $5 and $2-1/2 coins even though they had been referred to as "adopted designs" prior to the formal acceptance order.

## *A Star for Oklahoma*

The first new gold eagles began entering circulation on November 4. For the public, the starred edge instead of conventional reeding was a novel feature. There were complaints about the eagle's appearance and absence of the religious motto. But an interesting sidelight, apparently not noticed at the time, is that the new coins actually had the wrong number of stars on the edge. Although all the coins had forty-six stars – one representing each state – Oklahoma did not become the 46th state until November 16.[324] Thus, the correct number of stars on the new coins should have been forty-five, not forty-six. This may have been partly the cause of the irregular edge stars on pattern $10 coins made in August. If instructions were given the mint mechanics (who made the first edge collars) to include one star for each state, then the logical result would have been a collar with forty-five stars, or fifteen per segment. This was the correct number of states in August 1907. Patterns with irregular stars show the stars unevenly spaced and some were larger than others. When Barber made the regular edge collars, he included forty-six evenly spaced stars presumably in anticipation of Oklahoma's statehood progressing as planned. This makes the five hundred high relief knife rim pieces, and fifty normal rim with periods pieces saved from the condemned circulation production, all the more interesting as they were "issued" with forty-six edge stars – the wrong number.

A similar situation applies to all versions of the $20 with forty-six obverse stars, although here, the number of stars is clearly in the models as far back as June 1906. Evidently, Saint-Gaudens paid close attention to newspapers because it wasn't until June 1906 that Congress approved statehood enabling legislation for the combined Oklahoma and Indian Territories.

## Double Eagles – At Last

Acting director Preston's order of August 27, for five hundred double eagles from the high relief experimental dies, meant the mint would have to use medal presses to produce the coins. They would be struck from dies of the second pair of high relief models delivered to the mint in May.[325] These models were more refined than those of the first

---

[324] Congress passed an enabling act on June 14, 1906 (known as the "Hamilton Bill" after its author Representative Edward La Rue Hamilton, chairman, Committee on Territories) which provided for the formation of one state from the Indian and Oklahoma Territories. Delegates to a state constitutional convention were elected on November 6, 1906, and prepared the appropriate documents. On November 16, 1907, President Theodore Roosevelt signed the proclamation that made Oklahoma the forty-sixth state in the Union. On the same day Charles N. Haskell took the oath of office as Governor of the State of Oklahoma. Source: Oklahoma Historical Society. *Chronicles of Oklahoma*, various volumes.

[325] Planchets for the high relief $20 had normal double eagle milling until mid-December 1907 when Barber had the milling and refining department change to a different diameter and upset angle. This information was provided by director Frank Leach who had done experiments for director Roberts in early 1907, when Leach was superintendent at the San Francisco Mint. Roberts approached Leach as something of an independent experimenter and sent him photos of the first models in December 1906. Leach had experimental "pre-shaped" planchets made, and had conducted several experiments with improving the striking of high relief coins by altering the milling. Roberts had loaned him his personal copy of the EHR $20 in April, so Leach could provide additional suggestions. Roberts used San Francisco as a "test site" because they had more experience with gold than Philadelphia. Also, they were striking Mexican and Philippine gold which had higher relief than the old U. S. $20. A final reason was that Roberts felt Leach "was the best administrator in the service." The result of using Leach's suggested milling was that the fin ("wire rim") was completely eliminated on the last third of the high relief pieces struck (generally after Dec 20, 1907). These coins are also more evenly struck and have better detail near the rim than earlier pieces.

version and included more detail in the olive branch, face, stars and Liberty's gown.[326] When the second pair of hubs was cut from these models, the mint reduced the relief as much as possible – about twenty percent according to superintendent Landis. This permitted the coins to be struck with only three blows of the press not the seven required for the initial designs in February.

*Figure 36. Models for the second version of the double eagle (top), and the high relief coins produced from them by the U. S. Mint. Note the overall loss of definition particularly in fine detail such as the olive berries (obverse) and triangular periods at ends of the inscriptions (reverse).* (Courtesy Smithsonian Institution, Peter A. Juley & Son collection. The photographs appear to date from May 1908 during the memorial exhibition in New York.)

Engraver Barber had again objected to the relief of the #2 models and Hering went back to Aspet to create yet another (the third) version of the design – this time in low relief. There had been many delays in completing this third pair of models including work on

---

[326] Hering intentionally made the first models too high to coin and that may explain the overall roughness of the finish on the plaster: they were never intended for coinage. The second models were prepared under Saint-Gaudens' supervision and it is likely they represent the artist's mature concept for this design.

the now-abandoned cent. On August 20 Homer Saint-Gaudens advised acting director Preston it would be at least a month before Hering could finish the double eagle model. Meanwhile the completed eagle models arrived and Barber, sounding rather pleased to see the low relief Liberty head, stated: "…If the models for the twenty dollar [are made to] the same relief as the models just received…coinage dies can be made."[327] Without the low relief $20 models, Barber and his staff could only fall back on the second pair of models. Dies had been made and five hundred struck at the end of August or beginning of September to comply with the President's order. A sample was shipped to Preston on September 6,[328] an additional five coins were received at mint headquarters on the 10th, which were forwarded to assistant secretary Edwards.[329] Augusta Saint-Gaudens reported to Preston, "…work on the double eagle continues to go on as it has for a month or more. It is a slow process, but we hope to have it finished within two weeks."[330]

Photos of the second pair of double eagle models and the high relief coins made from them are shown above. The high relief coins are impressive until one compares them with the models. This second pair of models is likely the most fully developed and refined version of the design produced by Saint-Gaudens and Hering. Detail and finish of the models is superior to the experimental first set (extremely high relief). If better hubs had been made, these would represent the ultimate expression of the artist's designs. As it happened, the mint's reductions were marginally better than in the past, and only the inherent strength of Saint-Gaudens' artistry assured success. The high relief hubs appear to have been made on the Janvier reducing lathe with the maximum decrease in relief possible (about one-fifth), as suggested by superintendent Landis on May 9. This would account for the noticeably lower relief of these coins versus that of the EHR pieces made in February, although they were originally described as only slightly altered.

Augusta sent the final double eagle models (third model with European date) to the mint, where they arrived on September 28, and reductions and hubbing were begun immediately. These were the models, including the date change, which Augustus had agreed to make in June. Preston asked for a report on October 8 and engraver Barber sent a long reply on the 10th:[331]

> Replying to the letter of inquiry regarding the Double Eagle, new designs, I beg to say that the models arrived at this Mint Sept. 28th.
>
> Upon examination it was found that the relief of the models was so great that it would be a waste of time to make reductions for coinage, as it would be quite impossible to coin when the dies are made. I say impossible because the relief does not conform to the mechanical requirement of modern coinage namely, that the relief shall be no more than can be made perfect with one operation of the press, and here we have an inflexible law which governs the movement of metal under pressure.
>
> The son of Mr. St. Gaudens wrote the Mint concerning the models for Eagle and Double Eagle and promised to send models of the same relief as those made by the French medallist M. Chaplin for the gold coins of France, but when the models arrived it was very evident that there was a mistake in the relief, and while it was possible to use the models for the Eagle, the models for the Double Eagle instead of being lower relief were actually higher. The relief of the design for the

[327] US Mint, NARA-P, op. cit. Letter dated August 27, 1907 to Landis from Barber.

[328] US Mint, NARA-P, op. cit. Letter dated September 10, 1907 to Landis from Preston.

[329] US Mint, NARA-P, op. cit. Letter dated September 10, 1907 to Landis from Preston.

[330] US Mint, NARA-P, op. cit. Letter dated September 11, 1907 to Preston from Augusta Saint-Gaudens.

[331] US Mint, NARA-P, op. cit. Letter dated October 10, 1907 to Landis from Barber.

Double Eagle must be lower than the Eagle, because it is larger, with greatly increased area and therefore, more difficult to make.

With the these conditions before us there was nothing to do but try to reduce the relief mechanically with the aid of the Janvier reducing lathe, but as the models were plaster and too large to be reduced [directly] to the size of the Double Eagle, I had to make paraffins, intermediate reductions, which I have done, and sent to New York on the 5th instant, to be cast in bronze from which I can make steel reductions [hubs]; you will see therefore, that out of ten days we have had but five for our work.

In answer to the question: What are the prospects that the new Double Eagle will be satisfactory, I beg to remind you of our experience with the Eagle which had to be treated in the manner already described, you will remember that it was very unsatisfactory to both yourself and the late Director, as the coin had a worn out, dull, or as we term it, blind look, no sharpness of detail; this is quite unavoidable when the relief is reduced mechanically, and not until the low relief model for the eagle was sent us was it possible to make a partially satisfactory coin.

In regard to the Double Eagle, my fear now is that before I can reduce the relief of many sudden high points of the design sufficiently to coin, the portions that are already low will be lost, and all detail will have disappeared.

That it will ever be satisfactory I cannot say, though I have very grave doubts. From the first time that this change of design in our gold coins was proposed I have tried to impress it upon the mind of Mr. St. Gaudens' representative, the absolute necessity of low relief models for coinage, and until proper suitable models are furnished, there can be no certainty that there will be any satisfactory results.

What we are now doing is in the line of experiment, as it is a departure from all well established methods of making coinage dies, which is to prepare the model for the intended purpose with a full knowledge of the process and requirements of modern coinage, this has not been done up to the present time, but on the contrary, models have been furnished, made without the least knowledge of the Minting of coins, or preparation of dies, and consequently, the result has been simply failure, and accounts for the unparalleled waste of time.

Dies enough have been made to have coined millions had the models been made with the least rudimentary knowledge of the subject of coinage, nevertheless we have done and are doing all that we can to solve, what Mr. Roberts, the late Director called the problem, to which I add, of making coinage dies from models devoid of the first requisite.

I beg to remind you that each time one of these high relief models have been sent, I have pointed out to the Director of the Mint the impossibility of making coins from such high relief models, and when the dies were made, they confirmed my statement. This condition being brought to the notice of the late Mr. Saint Gaudens, he made some slight modification and returned the models until we now have three sets of models, all of different relief for which dies have been made, or are being made, but in no case has there been sufficient change in the models to guarantee success.

A soon as I can see the effect of the reducing lathe I will report what prospect there may be of using the dies.

The Philadelphia Mint's coiner, Rhine H. Freed, added his views about the #3 double eagle models on October 22:[332]

With reference to the coinage of the new Double Eagle, I beg to state that the results produced by the Engraver in striking the piece on the hydraulic press, as well as those produced on the regular power press, indicate that for practical coinage the model of the coin should have the relief on the foot, the knee and the

---

[332] *US Mint*, NARA-P, op. cit. Letter dated October 22, 1907 to Landis from Freed.

drapery on the chest of the figure of Liberty reduced somewhat, as with the present relief a blow of the power that the dies are contemplated to withstand fails to bring out in relief the points mentioned, while the finer lines of the coin are also less sharp and clear that they should be.

With the relief on these points reduced, a lighter blow will be required to draw the metal up into the cavity of the dies, which when the cavities are filled will permit the other portions of the dies to impress themselves on the coin more sharply.

*Figure 37. Low relief double eagle obverse model (mold) by Henry Hering. The date is in European digits as agreed in June. This became the basis for the circulation coins. The corresponding mold is annotated "Final Mould Sept. 20 - 1907" along the edge. (Image has been reversed so design reads correctly.)* (Courtesy U. S. Department of Interior National Park Service, Saint-Gaudens National Historic Site, Cornish, NH. #1069-detail.)

Barber also updated his double eagle report on the 22nd, commenting on dies made from the #3 models:[333]

> ...We now find upon trial in the coining press that although the relief is very much lower than any previous models made for this coin, still it is not sufficiently low to strike a full impression with one operation of the press, as must be the case with coins.
>
> In order to obtain the proper relief from the models furnished I have reduced the relief mechanically to the full extent of the machine, and yet the relief is too high as before stated.
>
> In reducing the relief to the extent we have had to, you will notice as predicted, all detail has been lost, leaving the coin with the appearance of being old and worn.
>
> I now think I should suggest the remedy, which is to reduce the model to such an extent that the reduction could be made without extraordinary reduction of the relief, and thereby preserve the detail and modeling of both the figure and the eagle.
>
> The character of the modeling must be changed, by cutting down all sudden relief before it will be possible to coin this piece with any satisfaction.

In effect, Barber was saying the latest models were not usable, and he must remodel the design to make dies suitable for coinage.

---

[333] *US Mint*, NARA-P, op. cit. Letter dated October 22, 1907 to Landis from Barber.

Had these low relief models been delivered in a timely manner in June, it is possible the entire 1907 issue of double eagles from the new designs would have had higher relief than typical coins and would have been made from Saint-Gaudens' original work not Charles Barber's re-engraved hubs.

The next day Barber was called to Washington for a conference with assistant secretary Edwards and acting director Preston.[334] Secretary Cortelyou had shifted responsibility for getting the remainder of the new coins out to Edwards,[335] and the assistant secretary had several questions that only Barber could answer. The President wanted the coins issued and was tired of waiting. If Barber couldn't use the latest double eagle model, then the coiner would have to use the previous version. If the mint was going to use medal presses to make the double eagles as it had in September, Edwards wanted to know how quickly this could be accomplished.[336]

> The following questions are asked by Mr. J. H. Edwards, acting Secretary of the Treasury, I therefore give you the answers for transmission by special delivery as requested.
> First: How many [high relief double eagles] per day can be coined from the medal presses now in the Mint with three operations of the Press.
> Second: Cost as compared to present Coinage.
> Third: How long before additional presses can be built.
> In answer to the first question, with present medal presses now in the Mint four hundred pieces per day can be struck; second as to cost, six dollars per hundred, or six cents each, while if struck on the automatic coining press now in use the cost is one twentieth of a mill each. To recapitulate for six dollars and fifty cents you can strike 28,800 pieces with one coining press, while with medal presses you use two presses and strike but 200 pieces for six dollars [per hundred].[337]
> As it is desired by Mr. Edwards to have this letter today, I beg to state that there is not sufficient time to learn from the manufacturer the time required to furnish the presses that would, or may be required.
> As I am asked to furnish any information upon this subject, I beg to state that the only solution of this gold coinage is to have a model prepared of a relief that when dies are made coins can be struck, the same as is being done by all the civilized countries of the world namely, with automatic presses with one operation and a perfect impression of the dies.
> To show the fallacy of making coins with medal presses and with more than one operation, allow me to state that to coin the number of pieces required, that is the volume of coinage, the equipment would have to be enormous, for example: one of our coining presses with two men will strike 28,800 Double Eagles per day, to coin the same number of pieces per day on the medal press as suggested, with three operations each, would require 144 presses and 288 men.
> The cost of the presses would be about $450,000 and if they were given us we have not enough room in the Mint to store them, to say nothing about operating, nor one foot of ground upon which an enlargement of the Mint could be built and all this for no purpose, as if a proper model is furnished, the difficulty is solved, and any amount of coinage can be struck.

[334] *US Mint*, NARA-P, op. cit. Telegram dated October 23, 1907 to Barber from Preston.
[335] During most of October and November, Cortelyou was deeply involved in resolving the financial panic triggered by collapse of the Knickerbocker Trust. Working with J. P Morgan, E. H. Harriman, John D. Rockefeller, Henry Frick and other financiers, he barely avoided financial collapse of the stock market and a default by New York City.
[336] *US Mint*, NARA-P, op. cit. Letter dated October 25, 1907 to Landis from Barber.
[337] The mint had four, 300-ton medal presses in mid-1907. It appears that no more than two presses were in simultaneous operation striking high relief coins.

Barber's numbers were certainly convincing and in rough agreement with the cost of production supplied to Edwards by assistant coiner Robert Clark on September 10:[338]

> Cost of striking Double Eagle high relief new design by hydraulic press the same as medals, the only way these pieces can be made, thirteen and eight-tenths of a cent each. One hundred and five hours to make 500 pieces.
> The present [Liberty head] Double Eagle coins are struck in coining press [at] 80 per minute and cost two and a half tenths of a mill each.

Superintendent Landis also obtained a quick quote from The Waterbury Farrel Foundry & Machine Co. on October 26 and passed the information to Edwards:[339]

> ...We beg to state as a matter of information...we could duplicate the 300 ton Hydraulic Press with pump and knock-out in about four months' time for $3,000...exclusive of the two motors...furnished by you before.

The idea of adding more presses to coin the high relief design in large numbers was a practical impossibility. With it taking three strikes to produce one coin, and each press capable of producing only two hundred pieces per day, any thought of large-scale production had to be abandoned. Obviously, Roosevelt would have to ask Congress for the funds suggested by mint personnel, and Congress would likely not be pleased. There were already rumblings among some of the members about the cost of the President's new coins. The President, despite his 1904 post-election declaration not to run again and the automatic "lame-duck" status thus conferred, was immensely popular with the American public, but less so with Congress. Although firmly in Republican hands, most of the majority were "old guard" party members and not much enamored of "Teddy" Roosevelt or his "square deal." With barely six months until the Republicans would select someone else (William Howard Taft) to lead the party, Roosevelt's power was on the decline.[340]

Augusta Saint-Gaudens was also worried about the double eagle models and wrote to acting director Preston on October 25 asking what else needed to be done. Preston replied four days later:[341]

> ...The model for the double eagle has been reduced, but it is not satisfactory as the relief is still too high and it will have to be modified. The last model for the eagle is in a measure satisfactory, as it is possible to produce a coin from the dies that will stack. Nothing has as yet been done on the one cent piece. It is the desire of the Department to have the double eagle finished first. I have referred your letter of the 25th instant to the Superintendent of the Mint at Philadelphia with the request that you will be fully advised as to the difficulty in producing satisfactory coins from the dies made from the reduction of the last model for the double eagle.

This response from the mint was unsatisfactory to Augusta. She had her attorney, Charles O. Brewster, contact the mint in an attempt to resolve the situation. A meeting was held on November 14 between Brewster, Hering, Barber Landis and the new director,

---

[338] *US Mint*, NARA-P, op. cit. Memorandum dated September 10, 1907 to Edwards from assistant coiner Robert Clark. Identification based on comparison of handwriting in the telegram, and the *Proof and Medal Book* written and signed by Clark.

[339] *US Mint*, NARA-P, op. cit. Letter dated October 26, 1907 to Landis from Mr. Nickerson.

[340] The more conservative Taft was Secretary of War and Roosevelt's handpicked successor. As Roosevelt was to soon learn, handpicking your successor does not guarantee your successor will listen to you once in power.

[341] *US Mint*, NARA-CP, op. cit., entry 330, box 45. Letter dated October 29, 1907 to Augusta Saint-Gaudens from Preston.

Frank Leach, at the Philadelphia Mint.[342] During the meeting Hering was shown models and reductions and also loaned a sample double eagle (signed for by Brewster) "...struck from the third Saint-Gaudens model, this piece having been struck on a medal press."[343] Brewster wrote to the director on the 15th including several comments by Henry Hering. In his response, Leach made what could be interpreted as his "final offer" to the Saint-Gaudens' estate:[344]

>...I am not sure that I understand just what Mr. Hering wants in what he calls a "strike." I suppose he means he would like to see a piece made from the dies we have, struck on a coining press, but even then we could not tell what the maximum power is that the dies would stand. That can only be determined by experiment. The character of the dies and the different metal would determine the maximum pressure of life of the die. I have requested Mr. Barber to make a pair of dies from the last model that I may make some experiments on the press wear, and when these are obtained I shall be pleased to forward you a proof set, but I learned from Mr. Barber that this will take 2 or three weeks. I should regret very much to learn that Mr. Hering could not go ahead on the new model until that time. It seems to me if he would go ahead and produce the new models on the lines of our recent interview, bearing in mind the importance of exaggerating or preserving the detail in such a manner that it will not be lost in the reduction, that we shall have a successful issue through this last experiment.

>I have had Mr. Barber down here today and explained it to him what I wanted to do, and consulted with him in the matter of the reduction so to save the details of the models. He is going right to work along the lines of my suggestions, and with our experiments I think we will overcome some of the difficulties and be able to get out a good looking coin in our next effort.

>Mr. Barber informed me that he had already sent the models requested [back] to Windsor, Vermont.

>In the matter of obtaining further allowance from the government, I wrote you that the Secretary of the Treasury said he saw no way of increasing the compensation. He was not unfriendly to the suggestion of an increase, but I inferred that he preferred to take the matter up at some future time when there is less pressure on his office than there is now, due to the financial situation throughout the country. Certain it is that Mr. St. Gaudens and his assistants have done a great deal more work and executed different designs than the original contract contemplated, and it seems no more than justice that this fact should be acknowledged in a satisfactory way....

>After my talk today with Mr. Barber I am satisfied beyond any question that we will be able to reach results if Mr. Hering is able to carry out the ideas he expressed at the recent interview.

Obviously, Leach was going to move ahead with or without Hering's revised model. He answered to President Roosevelt and had promised to have the coins produced. The sample coin loaned to Brewster was returned to the mint on the 18th with no comment from Hering about the models. This was the Saint-Gaudens studio's final opportunity to influence the double eagle design.

[342] *US Mint*, NARA-P, op. cit. Letter dated November 11, 1907 to Landis from Leach.
[343] *US Mint*, NARA-P, op. cit. Receipt dated November 14, 1907 signed by Charles O. Brewster attorney for Augusta Saint-Gaudens, Executrix.
[344] *US Mint*, NARA-CP, op. cit., entry 235, vol. 367. Letter dated November 16, 1907 to Brewster from Leach.

The President asked about the double eagles again on November 20, and was told by Cortelyou that the mint director was checking on them.[345] Two days later, after discussions with the secretary and director and a decision to strike coins from the #2 models until the #3 dies could be thoroughly tested,[346] an order came from the President to strike high relief $20 coins:[347]

> Sir:
>
> By direction of the President you are instructed to proceed with striking the double eagles of the new design, second model, on a medal press. This is the design, which, I understand, takes nine blows or impressions to perfect. [Barber states three blows – RWB] The President is desirous of having 5,000 or 6,000 of these pieces struck by the first of December, and more if it is within a possibility to get them. You will use every facility within your control to meet the requirements of the President in this matter, working as many presses on the coins as possible, and all the overtime that can be put in to advantage. Please report to me daily the number of pieces struck, that I may keep the President advised of the progress of this undertaking.
>
> You will put these coins in bags of $5,000 each, in the usual manner of sacking your gold coin, and delivery will be made through the coiner in the usual manner, but you will not permit the cashier to pay any of these coins out until instructions are received as to their distribution. Please authorize Mr. Barber to make as many dies for this work as may be in his judgement necessary. Please inform me if these instructions will interfere with the production of the dies from the third model on which Mr. Barber has been at work during the last week. Also please inform me, if it is practicable, as to about the time Mr. Barber thinks he can have the new double eagle dies from the last model ready for test upon the regular coining press, as I wish to make plans to be present on that occasion.
>
> Respectfully,

The number of blows from the press Leach stated above was based on the extremely high relief coins made from the first model. Since the mint had already struck five hundred coins from the #2 models, they had considerable experience with them, and Barber stated that only three blows were necessary. The engraver provided the requested information to Landis the next day:[348]

> …I have made arrangement with my people to work all day and all night and Sunday, and while I cannot promise any specific number of double eagle pieces, all that is possible will be done.
>
> We are making most strenuous efforts to get another pair of dies so that I can start up another press and Mr. Hart is working up an attachment that we hope to use on the press to put the inscription on the periphery, if this works as we anticipate, it will save much time in giving the last blow, as it will save the operation of taking the collars out of the press and knocking the coin out by hand, and then placing the sectional collar back in position, which is a slow process.
>
> We want to make these coins in one thousand lots, working with a plain collar for the first blows, [then] using the inscription collar for the last blow only; we are doing this because if one die should crack before the pieces were finished it would be almost impossible to turn another die so precisely that it would follow without

---

[345] *US Mint*, NARA-CP, op. cit., entry 330, box 45. Letter dated November 20, 1907 to Cortelyou from Loeb; reply of the same date.

[346] *US Mint*, NARA-CP, op. cit., entry 330, box 45. Letter dated November 23, 1907 to Brewster from Leach.

[347] *US Mint*, NARA-P, op. cit. Letter dated November 22, 1907 to Landis from Leach.

[348] *US Mint*, NARA-P, op. cit. Letter dated November 23, 1907 to Landis from Barber.

causing a double in the impression,[349] which if it did occur would involve delay in forging it out in the press, therefore I will report as soon as the first thousand pieces are made and can then estimate how many pieces I can deliver daily.

In regard to the low relief [dies] upon which we are working, I beg to state that this new [presidential] order to make dies for the high relief coin will cause some interference with the completion of the hubs, as the high relief dies are so difficult to hub, we cannot make them in the ordinary way, but have to cut and hammer in order to get the steel to follow into all the difficult high points, therefore Mr. Morgan and myself have to do this work.

I hope to be able to report early in the coming week the day that we will be in shape to test the low relief dies for the Double Eagle, and will advise you in time to notify the Director that he may be present, as he desires.

The unusual event of working on Sunday, the only day off for employees, was confirmed by Leach, "…for some weeks prior to the close of the calendar year, work was done on Sundays…by individuals who felt that such work was necessary to enable the Bureau to keep up…This work was performed voluntarily, without orders."[350]

Brewster was unaware of the production order when he wrote Leach on November 25 asking about the condition of the models returned by the mint. The director wrote back two days later:[351]

Your letter of the 25th is at hand. I cannot understand how the model you speak of became blurred or lost its sharpness of outline. The people of the mint would not have taken the liberty of altering the models, and undoubtedly the models themselves would reveal any such alterations.

If you will send down to Mr. Landis for one of the pieces struck from the 2nd model on the medal press, he will no doubt, lend it to you for inspection. We could not exchange any for coin until the President directs the distribution to be made….

Leach kept pressure on the Philadelphia Mint to produce new double eagles, going to Philadelphia himself to support the coining staff and try the experimental dies he and Barber had discussed. By November 29 he could report considerable success:[352]

In accordance with my assurance to the President, there will be ready for shipment to-morrow afternoon over $100,000 of double eagles of the new design which have been struck on the medal presses during the past week. This will enable the Treasurer to send one to three sacks of $5,000 each to the ten several subtreasuries, thus giving a thorough and simultaneous distribution of the new coins. I will hold the delivery of the coinage to the Treasurer, however, until advised by you.

Would it not also be advisable to keep the medal presses at work for another week, unless in the meantime we secure satisfactory results in our experiments from the last models on the regular coinage presses.

---

[349] It appears that Barber is trying to say they will give two blows with a plain collar then one with the lettered collar, as was done in September, if Mr. Hart's attachment does not work. If the attachment works as hoped, all three blows will be made with the lettered collar in place. The alternative he rejects is giving every coin in a batch two blows with a plain collar, then going back and giving each coin the final lettered-collar blow. He is concerned that if a die cracks, he'll never get a new die to match the old one exactly, and all the work will be wasted. Many high relief double eagles show slight doubling due to warping of the planchets during annealing.

[350] *Treasury Department*, NARA-CP, record group 56, entry 168, box 4. Letter dated March 24, 1908 to Cortelyou from Leach. This was in reply to an inquiry of the same date from Cortelyou and the President about Sunday work. This is confirmed by the daily production list, below.

[351] *US Mint*, NARA-CP, op. cit., entry 235, vol. 367. Letter dated November 17, 1907 to Brewster from Leach.

[352] *US Mint*, NARA-CP, op. cit., entry 330, box 45. Letter dated November 29, 1907 to Cortelyou from Leach. The total was $1,063,200 or 5,316 coins.

130

In the margins of this letter are the words, "Hurrah, Hurrah, Hurrah," and "Yes, Yes!" written in Cortelyou's hand. Within a week of the President's order more than 5,000 high relief double eagles had been minted.

Roosevelt was "delighted" and proud of the new high relief double eagles; they must have seemed fine trophies. Possibly some of his pride from the American Atlantic Fleet (later known as the "Great White Fleet"), which was planning to leave Hampton Roads just before Christmas, had rubbed off on the most American of coins. He was also putting the final touches on his annual message to Congress, and had a full calendar of meetings and visitors – exactly the kind of day the President loved. During his visit with Leach, the President requested twenty more double eagles. "I would like to have you pick out twenty perfect pieces, put each one in a small individual envelope, [and] pack up in the best manner to avoid abrasion…"[353] One wonders if he intended them for Admiral Robley D. Evans, the three Rear Admirals, and sixteen Captains of the battleships preparing to set sail December 16 on a world tour.

The mint had three hydraulic medal presses capable of producing up to three hundred tons of pressure per square inch. The presses were designed to "squeeze" the planchet between the dies rather than "strike" it with a very quick blow as on the automatic production coin presses.[354] Typical tempered steel coinage dies of the era could withstand little more than one hundred fifty tons of pressure before they would collapse or crack. The coiner wanted to use the minimum pressure necessary to bring up the design since this would reduce wear on the dies and make them last longer.

High relief double eagles presented unusual problems for the mint's mechanics. The coins had high relief obverse and reverse designs, plus an edge with raised lettering instead of the normal vertical reeding. (Plain edge examples are probably production errors.) The relief took three blows of the press to bring up the obverse and reverse designs, but the edge lettering of the motto E PLURIBUS UNUM could only be imparted by an edge collar with recessed lettering. When the coin was struck, the metal flowed in the face designs as well as the raised edge lettering. Obviously, the collar had to be able to open or the newly struck coin would be locked inside the collar.

For the first five hundred high relief coins made in August and September 1907, a plain retaining collar was placed in the press and the planchet given two blows with the coin removed and annealed between blows. The plain collar was then replaced with the lettered edge collar consisting of three segments. This was surrounded by a second, solid retaining collar. The planchet was placed back on the press, aligned with the anvil die, and given one or two more blows with the edge collar in place.[355] After striking, the mechanic running the press had to lift off the retaining collar and pull the segmented collar away from the coin. This process was slow and resulted in much lower productivity than was achieved beginning in November. It was also partially responsible for a pronounced fin on many of the coins. The first batch of five hundred double eagles took 105 hours (about

---

[353] *US Mint*, NARA P, op. cit. Letter dated December 2, 1907 to Landis from Leach. The total number of coins requested exactly matches the number of flag officers in the fleet. The care in selecting and packaging the coin suggest Roosevelt had a special purpose for the coins. They would have been a relevant and completely typical memento from the commander-in-chief to his naval officers. This could also be coincidence. A notation on the same letter adds one high relief $20 and one $10 from the first models. These may have been the Roosevelt coins sold by Bowers and Ruddy Galleries, Inc. in the *Roy Hart Collection, Part III* (January 23-25, 1983), lots 639 and 641.
[354] This is analogous to squeezing the trigger on a rifle versus snapping the trigger on a shotgun.
[355] Based on Barber's description of November 23. See below for Leach's description of the process including annealing.

twelve minutes each) to make;[356] by late November the medal presses were turning out approximately four hundred eighty coins per day. Productivity continued to improve until 995 high relief double eagles were made during the day's work on December 30.[357] The improvement was due to experience gained in striking the earlier batch of coins, and from a change in the way the segmented collar was used.

Two other methods of impressing edge lettering were used on a few of the high relief coins and all low relief pieces. Most low relief coins were created using a "...Bell-crank device, designed in the Philadelphia Mint, [which] opens and closes positively in a fixed horizontal plane, taking its motion from a cam on the crank shaft [of the press] and opening and closing the segment collars by means of toggles."[358] This was called a "toggle collar,"[359] by mint mechanics. A second type of edge imprinting device was called a "cone collar" similar to one used by the Royal Mint in London. A segmented collar was again used and, "...The closing of the segments was effected by depressing them into a cone collar by means of a nut attached to and surrounding the upper die. This device was simple and was used very effectively by the engraver in striking pieces upon the hydraulic press..."[360] Both types of edge lettering collar were used in the high relief and circulation coins of 1907 and 1908. The high relief coin was removed from the press and annealed between each of the three strikes. The high relief coins with uneven bases on the letter "M" of "Unum" are possibly early strikes from the cone collar as the mint had less experience with this type of device than the toggle collar.[361]

The troublesome fin on the high relief $20 coins became an important issue for director Leach as he reported on December 6:[362]

> I was exceedingly humiliated today to have the Secretary of the Treasury call attention to the excessive burr, or fin, on one of the new double eagle pieces now being distributed.
>
> I was also surprised to find so many of these defective coins in a bag as I saw in the Treasurer's office here.
>
> I gave explicit orders when in Philadelphia that such coins should not be delivered, and directed the man who seemed to have the coins in charge to see that the same should all be gone over and the bad ones laid aside.

---

[356] *US Mint*, NARA-P, op. cit. Telegram dated September 10, 1907 to J. H. Edwards from [Robert Clark, assistant coiner].The number quoted is based on the mint's experience of making the five hundred double eagles in August and September. This is more than 12 minutes per coin! Normal production was eighty coins per minute on the automatic presses.

[357] *US Mint*, NARA-P, op. cit. Manuscript notes in Clark's handwriting accompanying letters dated mid-March 1908. Listed are dates from November 27, 1907 through January 6, 1908 with a two- or three-digit number next to each date. The time period and quantities are a good match for the Presidentially ordered production of high relief double eagles. The author believes these are a rough list of daily production for the coins. Clark's distinctive handwriting and signature are well documented in the *Proof Coin and Medals* book which contains lists of medals and proof coins struck from 1909 to 1916.

[358] *US Mint*, NARA-P, op. cit. Box 200, folder "Coinage 1908 to 1922." Excerpt from "Report on the San Francisco Mint" by P. A. Kearney, March 12, 1908. p.12. Kearney made an engineering and "best-practices" report on the San Francisco Mint for director Leach. He also visited the Philadelphia Mint and included information on that mint's operations in his report. Kearney observed use of the two edge lettering collars first-hand and also interviewed Barber and Clark. Chief Mechanic Hart developed the toggle collar.

[359] *US Mint*, NARA-P, op. cit. Manuscript memorandum dated December 14, 1907 to Norris from Robert Clark.

[360] *US Mint*, NARA-P, op. cit. Box 200, folder "Coinage 1908 to 1922." Excerpt from "Report on the San Francisco Mint." p.13. The writer is referring to low relief collectors' proof coins made from 1908 to 1915.

[361] See *Designs for the Gold Double Eagle*, below for more information. Also, see Breen, *Encyclopedia*, p.574 #7360.

[362] *US Mint*, NARA-CP, op. cit., entry 330, box 45. Letter dated December 6, 1907 to Landis from Leach.

I wish you to make [an] investigation and see why my instructions were not carried out, and if there was any negligence or carelessness, who is to blame.

Production of high relief coins on the medal presses continued with director Leach issuing a reminder:[363]

You are hereby instructed to continue striking the double eagles on the medal press from now until January 1, 1908. In the execution of this work I would suggest that the operators be instructed to work with extreme care so as to prevent the excessive burrs on the edges of the coin, and that they attempt to turn out no more work daily than can be well done. It is desired that you proceed with this work immediately, so as to get out as many of these coins as possible within the legal limit of time these designs can be used. You will receive instructions as to the distribution of these coins later, possibly through the Treasurer.

Efforts by Clark, Barber and others had resulted in almost complete elimination of the rim fin on the high relief coins and by December 20 director Leach wrote to Barber, "I am more than delighted with the results you have obtained in preventing the 'fin.'"[364] Much of the credit for improvement goes to director Leach. He had tested changes in the milling of planchets in San Francisco before he came to Washington. He had also brought several pre-shaped planchets (Roberts' "forming die" idea) to Philadelphia for testing. The pre-shaped planchets worked no better than ordinary ones, but the pieces struck from differently milled planchets produced superior results. According to Barber, "…Mr. Hart has put the mill into operation and I send you two pieces showing the result, these are not selected as all the coins now made are the same as these two, which gives me alarm, as they are so well made that I fear the President may demand the continuance of this particular coin…"[365] Leach wrote to Landis on the 23rd to tell him of President Roosevelt's reaction to the fin-less double eagles:[366]

My Dear Mr. Landis,
The President was greatly pleased with the sample of the lot now being struck off on the Medal press and not only "confiscated" these but wanted more. I am committed to secure some pieces for other parties, so please send me 40 pieces d. E. including the 10 you laid aside for me. Mr. Loeb said he would settle for the President when he gets the last lot. I have yet to collect from some few of the Cabinet Officers, but will get it all in soon.
Mr. Preston showed me one of the D.E struck on the medal press from the first model. It is a beautiful piece. If you have any more I would like three – one for the St. Gaudens people, one for the Secretary, one for myself, and if the President has not one I want another for him. I will not give these out until after the first of January or we would be bothered by all the officials and [coin] collectors in the country. The Secretary, or rather Asst. Secy Edwards, wants one of the $10 or Eagles struck on the medal press from the first model. Send one also.
Yours truly,

This was not director Leach's first look at the extremely high relief double eagles. He had seen Roberts' coin in the spring of 1907 while still San Francisco Mint superinten-

[363] *US Mint*, NARA-P, op. cit. Letter dated December 14, 1907 to Landis from Leach.
[364] *US Mint*, NARA-P, op. cit. Letter dated December 20, 1907 to Barber from Leach.
[365] *US Mint*, NARA-CP, op. cit., entry 229, box 260. Letter (excerpt) dated December 20, 1907 to Leach from Barber.
[366] *US Mint*, NARA-P, op. cit. Manuscript letter dated December 23, 1907 to Landis from Leach.

dent. As director he now may have seen the coin differently, and was impressed by the depth and beauty of the design.

By December 30, $7,233,340 in low relief double eagles had been struck and 361,667 pieces were awaiting release by the Philadelphia Mint. A total of $225,000 (11,250 coins) in high relief coins had also been struck of which $70,000 (3,500 coins) remained at the mint.[367] Another seven hundred seventy-two high relief double eagles were struck on December 31, and two hundred sixty-seven, two hundred seventy-eight and three hundred on January 2, 3 and 6 respectively. This brought the total struck for this coin to 12,867, including the five hundred struck in September.[368] The Director's Annual Report for 1908 states that the engraving department made "…111 master dies, hubs, and experimental dies for the new gold coinage."[369] The report covers the period from July 1, 1907 to June 30, 1908, and the quantity of dies and hubs made suggests as many as twenty pairs of working dies may have been made. (Each coin type would require a minimum of two hubs and two dies.)

Additional information on the experimental and pattern eagles and double eagles will be found in Chapter 6, below.

## Mr. Barber's Modified Dies

By the time the Philadelphia Mint began full-speed production of high relief double eagles on November 23, everyone at the treasury department was thoroughly frustrated at trying to deal with the Saint-Gaudens estate and Henry Hering. The President's order to mint the coins had come on the 22nd and was accompanied by the expectation of 5,000 or 6,000 coins by December 1. Hering had been promising revised models since late June, and delays in getting the #3 $20 models forced the mint to use high relief dies originally made for the August–September special issue, much to the consternation of the mint staff.

Barber had offered to rework the designs into low relief versions in August but permission was denied. On November 23 – the same day high relief double eagle production was restarted, and after his conference with director Leach a week earlier – Barber reported:[370]

> …In regard to the low relief upon which we are working, I beg to state that this new order to make dies for the high relief coin will cause some interference with the completion of the hubs, as the high relief dies are so difficult to hub, we cannot make them in the ordinary way, but have to cut and hammer in order to get the steel to follow into all the difficult and high points, therefore Mr. Morgan and myself have to do this work.

---

[367] *US Mint*, NARA-P, op. cit. Attachment to letter dated December 30, 1907 to Landis from Leach. Includes 500 pieces made in August and September and transferred to the Treasury on December 14.

[368] Total mintage was probably 12,867 plus an unknown number of experimental pieces. This is counting 500 from August/September as transferred to the Treasurer on December 14, 11,250 reported to Leach for August through December 30, plus 772 on December 31 and 845 struck in January 1908. This is close to the 12,153 reported in the 1908 Mint Director's Report, p.6.

The mintage of 11,250 usually given in catalogues is the most readily accessible number, but only includes coins struck as of December 30, 1907. The Director's Report appears to include both December and January production, although it conveniently omits mention that extra double eagles were made in 1908 and technically should have been dated "MCMVIII [1908]." By May 7, 1908 all but 51 had been distributed or were under custody of the Treasury Department in Washington.

[369] *Report of the Director of the Mint*, Treasury Department, Bureau of the Mint, Washington DC, December 9, 1908. U. S. Government Printing Office, Washington DC.

[370] *US Mint*, NARA-P, op. cit. Letter (excerpt) dated November 23, 1907 to Landis from Barber.

I hope to be able to report early in the coming week the day that we will be in shape to test the low relief dies for the Double Eagle, and will advise you in time to notify the Director that he may be present, as he desires.

*Figure 38. Low relief double eagle obverse model by Henry Hering. The date is in European digits as agreed in June. These became the basis for the circulation coins. Barber's version with re-engraved detail is shown on the right. Note differences in top of head, and flow of the gown across Liberty, particularly at the upper left leg, and next to the right leg.* (Courtesy U. S. Department of Interior National Park Service, Saint-Gaudens National Historic Site, Cornish, NH. #1068.)

On November 30, acting superintendent Albert Norris advised the director that he had delivered to the Bureau:[371]

> ...1 double eagle from Mr. Barber's modified dies, delivered to you, personally; 1 double eagle from Mr. Barber's modified dies. The last mentioned double eagle is enclosed herewith and was struck after you left the Mint. The Engraver and Assistant Coiner think it an improvement over the one you received from Mr. Clark [Assistant Coiner – RWB].

Barber had probably been working on altering the hubs from the time he returned to Philadelphia on November 16. The models had already been returned to Hering, so he had to "make do" with modifying the existing hubs and master dies. Much of his work consisted of re-engraving details lost during reduction of the #3 models.[372] Using the high relief #2 version as a guide and his own judgment as to line depth, Barber succeeded in making the changes in a manner that has proven undetectable for a century. Barber confirmed this scenario several years later when he wrote, "...third reduction, greater reduction in relief, detail lost in reducing the relief to such an extent, in trying to come to coin relief. Model changed by Saint Gaudens. *These double eagle hubs were made acceptable by the engravers restoring the detail in the hubs.*"[373] We now know that the #4 circulation design came from Hering's plaster model, with the engraver retouching the original hub to

[371] *US Mint*, NARA-CP, op. cit., entry 229, box 260. Letter (excerpt) dated November 30, 1907 to Leach from Norris.

[372] In effect the 1907 circulation coins were Saint-Gaudens' design as interpreted by Henry Hering and retouched for coinage by Charles Barber.

[373] *US Mint*, NARA-CP, op. cit., entry 229, box 290. Letter and inventory list by Barber dated May 24, 1910 to A. Piatt Andrew, director of the mint from Barber. Emphasis added.

restore detail lost when the reduction was made.[374] Visual examination of details of a normal date 1907 double eagle will reveal considerable inconsistency in sharpness between stars and the figure. This is the result of Barber's manual recutting of much of the figure detail in the hub and master die.

President Roosevelt got to see the latest experimental low relief double eagle (#4 model) made on the medal press on December 2 when director Leach paid a welcome visit to the White House:[375]

> ...I took the coin over to the President's office and showed it to him. He was greatly pleased with the appearance and immediately asked if we could have some before the holidays. I told him that we certainly could have all that was wanted before Christmas, and he again expressed his pleasure and delight over the results of our efforts.
>
> The last coin is a decided improvement over any struck while I was at the mint, and I congratulate Mr. Clarke [sic] and his assistants upon reaching such results.
>
> I wish you to have two or more collar devices made after the same pattern used by Mr. Barber on his medal press. I wish you would see that these are made immediately, so to be ready for the coinage operations of the new design of double eagles by the time the dies are ready.
>
> Before we go ahead, however, with making any more dies, or doing anything more than experimental work, I wish to submit the coins sent me to the Saint Gaudens people. I want them to pass upon the coin before we take up the coinage work on the regular scale. It would be embarrassing to have those folks make a complaint or find fault with the work after we get started. I expect to hear from them within a couple of days, and then will be able to give you directions about starting in on the coinage of the new design of double eagle.

The mint director also wrote to Augusta's attorney the same day, finally nailing the lid closed on further models by Henry Hering:[376]

> Your letter of the 29th ultimo received, but did not reach me until this morning, as I have been away on a trip to Philadelphia experimenting with the new dies from the last model [#3] of the double eagle, and I am pleased to say that I reached results that are very satisfactory to me. I showed the President, today, one of the coins struck on an ordinary press and he is delighted with the result, the more especially so for the reason he had been told it was impossible to make these coins, but I think the whole thing grew out of misunderstanding. Anyway, it can be done, and the President, consequently, is greatly pleased, and wished me to proceed with the coinage immediately, asking how many I could have struck off before the holidays. I will proceed with the work, but have enclosed [for] you herewith a specimen of the work that you may scrutinize it and see if there are any features or parts that you wish touched up, if so it can be done upon the master dies.
>
> Please let me hear from you at the earliest opportunity, for as there is so little time in which to make the dies and get to work every moment is precious.
>
> If you think the coin could be improved by making another model, and you desire in your own interests to make it, it can be done at your leisure, we [are] proceeding with the work from the dies from the last model until such time as the new model may be received...The President has requested me to make dies for the half eagles and quarter eagles from the same design now adopted for the double

[374] This is similar to the skill George Morgan exhibited in 1921 when the removed the broken sword from the reverse of the new Peace dollar hub, and created an olive branch from the remains. Until documentation was published in *Renaissance of American Coinage 1916–1921*, no one, including silver dollar variety specialists, knew this had occurred.
[375] *US Mint*, NARA-P, op. cit. Letter dated December 2, 1907 to Landis from Leach.
[376] *US Mint*, NARA-CP, op. cit., entry 235, vol. 367. Letter dated December 2, 1907 to Brewster from Leach.

eagles. I think the double eagle design will meet with a far more favorable reception than the other design. Everybody who has seen it pronounces it a handsome coin....

A sample of the low relief design (a modified version of the #3 model – which we now call #4 model) was sent to Charles Brewster on December 2. Brewster wrote back the next day indicating he was pleased with the result but wanted Augusta to examine it as well. On December 4 Leach responded:[377]

> Your letter of the 3rd inst received. I am glad to know that you are pleased with the coin-press results. I expect to get even better looking coins than the one sent you.
>
> The President is extremely pleased with what we have accomplished, and takes great pleasure in showing the coin to those interested.
>
> The last coin sent you for examination belongs to me, so when you are through with it you can return it to me here. I note what you say about forwarding it for the inspection of Mrs. Saint Gaudens at Windsor, and trust it will be satisfactory to her.
>
> You ask me what is the cause of the difference in color between the two pieces. The one produced on the medal press is struck nine [sic – three] times, and between each strike the piece is annealed, and this process of annealing has a tendency to bring the copper alloy to the surface, and the introduction, after heating, to a dilute acid solution, removed the copper, and thus by the end of the operation the entire surface of the piece is covered with a thin film of pure gold, all copper on the immediate surface having been eliminated; whereas in striking on the coin-press the piece is not subjected to heat or acid to an extent [of] removing the copper alloy.
>
> I will not be able to write you in relation to your request for consent to photograph the pieces until I can secure an interview with the Secretary of the Treasury. The opinion so far had, that of the Solicitor's office, seems to be against the power to grant the request.

The low relief, coinage press specimen was shown to Augusta and Hering, who prepared a reply for Brewster to send to the mint. Hering's suggestions were much as before – the mint wasn't trying hard enough, or he could make a new model. There was nothing to give director Leach hope that the "Saint Gaudens people" were going to be of any help. Hering wrote:[378]

> Dear Mr. Brewster:
>
> I have nothing to suggest to Mr. Leach about touching up the master die. THE thing to be done is to get a better reduction itself, and I think a great improvement could be made in that, although they say at the Mint they can make no better reduction. Perhaps if they make a very great effort as they have done with the [high relief] coinage, they might. Of course another model could be sent from here to replace the blurred one which you saw from which the other reduction was made.
>
> As you may think it advisable for Mr. Leach to see both models, they are being sent to you by express to-day. These will show him the model from which the reductions were made and that state it was in when it left here. Should Mr. Leach make another reduction and die, which I think should be done, let him make any suggestions that may occur to him without changing the relief of the figure and I will try and carry them out to facilitate the stamping. By this I mean parts of the background etc. or strengthening lines, if he will kindly state definitely where, I will do my best.

[377] *US Mint*, NARA-CP, op. cit., entry 235, vol. 367. Letter dated December 4, 1907 to Brewster from Leach.
[378] *US Mint*, NARA-CP, op. cit., entry 229, box 260. Letter (excerpt) dated December 5, 1907 to Brewster from Hering.

I am not returning the coin, as should any changes be made I must have the existing coin to refer to....

Regardless of the suggestions he made, Henry Hering could not take the place of the Saint. He had neither artistic reputation nor force of personality to cause the director to listen to him, and his comments indicate he was not prepared to follow through with Saint-Gaudens' vision. A more self-assured or publicly successful sculptor, possibly Adolph Weinman or James Fraser, might have been able to transcend the problems. But Hering was trapped in the perpetual assistant's role and could do no more. Attorney Charles Brewster did nothing to promote Hering's status and the assistant's comments were ignored. Brewster wrote to Leach on December 6:[379]

> Referring to your letter of the 4th inst., and also our telephone conversation this afternoon, I note that the impression of the double-eagle from the coinage press sent me belongs to you, and I will see that it is returned to you in due course.
> Mrs. Saint-Gaudens writes: "I am disappointed in the minted double-eagle, although the other is a beauty," that is, the one from the medal press. She appreciates, however, that you are doing all within your power to have the coins struck with as high relief as is practicable.
> I enclose herewith a copy of a letter from Mr. Hering, dated December 5th, in which he makes certain suggestions. This letter I have just read to you over the telephone, and understand from you that in view of your leaving for San Francisco tomorrow on a ten days trip – that nothing further can be done just at present. The two No. 3 models referred to by Mr. Hering are here at my office, and I will hold them until you decide later whether you wish them sent to Washington or Philadelphia for inspection...

Leach could not wait for another model – he had until the end of the calendar year to produce a significant quantity of low relief $20 coins, or scrap them entirely until 1908. Given the President's impatience, the only alternative was to move ahead with Barber's low relief recut hub. The production order for low relief double eagles came right after his conversation with Brewster on December 6:[380]

> You will proceed with the coinage of the new design double eagle on the coin presses, running at least one press while you are using the remainder of your gold coining capacity on half eagles. When sufficient number of half eagles (old design) are struck, say about one and one-half or two million dollars, you will resume coinage of double eagles, adding as many presses as possible to the coinage of the new design, dropping out the presses running on the old design as fast as you can replace them, consistent with good work.
> Keep the double eagles of different designs apart while in your hands.
> As soon as you have a half million dollars of the new design coined notify this office.
> Please acknowledge receipt of this letter and state approximately when you think the half million dollars will be ready.
> ...As these coins will be closely criticized, I trust extra care will be given the execution of the work, that no further adverse criticism shall be given our work.

[379] *US Mint*, NARA-CP, op. cit., entry 229, box 260. Letter (excerpt) dated December 6, 1907 to Leach from Brewster.
[380] *US Mint*, NARA-P, op. cit. Letter dated December 6, 1907 to Landis from Leach.

The situation in Aspet may have been chaotic, but the Philadelphia Mint was not immune to its own brand of confusion, something director Leach, in office only a month, had to confront. On December 9 Barber wrote to Landis:[381]

> In a letter from the Director of the Mint, date of December 2nd, he states that the President approves of the double eagle as modified by us and "(he) the Director has sent to Windsor to get approval from there, and as soon as he hears from there, which he expects to in a few days he will notify us to that effect."
>
> Upon inquiry I find that you have not yet received any further instructions upon this matter, and therefore I beg to ask what is the status of the modified double eagle, are we to understand that that now becomes the future double eagle coin of the United States?
>
> I ask this and the other questions that will follow, because up to the present time all that has been done, has been simply experimental and therefore no provision has been made for continuance of these designs....

Clearly, the engraver should have realized that Saint-Gaudens' design was going to be used for all future double eagles. His inquiry can be viewed either as obstinate or a natural reaction to the absence of specific orders. Upon reading Barber's comments Leach replied the next day:[382]

> Your letter of the 9th instant, calling my attention to certain matters suggested by communication received by you from the engraver of your institution, received. We have not been in a hurry in filing the formal declaration of the approval of the new designs of coin. Such steps as are necessary in this matter will be attended to at the proper time.
>
> When I wrote you on the 6th instant, directing you to proceed with the coinage of the new design double eagles on the coining presses, from the modified model, I supposed the instructions embodied, by inference at least, the necessity of making all the dies required to accommodate your press demands. However, please instruct the engraver to proceed with the making of such a number of dies of the new design of double eagle to be used in the ordinary coining press, as may be necessary for use this month and the future as usual.
>
> It is not probable that any gold coinage will take place at any mint other than yours for at least a couple of months, and then probably only at the Denver Mint. If any change in this program should be necessary notice will be given the engraver in time to prepare dies....

Barber's concern was with formalities and follow-on work, while the director was looking primarily at getting low relief double eagles out of the press room and into circulation. Leach's message must have been clear: the engraver was to concentrate on his job and leave management to the Mint Bureau.

Since the December 6 order to produce low relief gold pieces, the Philadelphia Mint had been working on dies and edge collars. Barber's recut version of the double eagle was not immune to quality problems, although they generally concerned the edge collars:[383]

> As per your telephonic request I beg to enclose herewith a specimen of the new double eagle with low relief, which the Superintendent considers imperfect on ac-

---

[381] *US Mint*, NARA-P, op. cit. Letter (excerpt) dated December 9, 1907 to Landis from Barber. This refers to the low relief double eagle; balance of letter refers to half eagle.

[382] *US Mint*, NARA-P, op. cit. Letter (excerpt) dated December 10, 1907 to Landis from Leach. Balance of letter refers to half eagle.

[383] *US Mint*, NARA-CP, op. cit., entry 229, box 260. Letter dated December 14, 1907 to Leach from Norris.

count of the stars on the edge not coming up clearly. This is about an average sample taken from a lot which is ready to put into bags.

Samuel E. Hart and his mechanics had difficulty with the English, or cone collar and did not use it extensively on the low relief coins until late in the month. Some of the first production coins were marred by a "fin" rim, and, on instructions from the director, all such low relief pieces were condemned.[384] Assistant coiner Robert Clark reported progress with the new low relief dies and edge collars on standard presses:[385]

> Dr. Norris,
> Coined $330,000 on the toggle collar press. Running fine and doing good work. On the press with the English design of collar we coined four boxes [$160,000 – RWB]. Had to condemn them. Since then, 2 am, made some changes and by Monday morning it will be doing as good work as the other. A portion of the $330,000 have been weighed and are ready for counting. The prospects are good for a large turnout on Monday. Rest easy.
> Clark

Albert Norris provided a more formal version later that day:[386]

> I have just heard over the telephone from Mr. Clark, who informs me that the press with the machine shop collar worked very satisfactorily last night up to 10 o'clock, when they stopped, having coined about $330,000, a portion of which has been weighed. They coined four boxes on the English collar but had to condemn them, because the segments of the collar had separated and made too broad a mark on the edge of the coin and there was a slight fin on the surface. Mr. Hart worked over this collar and finally has it doing as well as the machine shop collar but a set screw broke and he had to take it out of the press.

On December 13, the mint superintendent was instructed to deliver low relief double eagles to the Treasurer of the United States.[387]

> Sir:
> You are hereby instructed to accept delivery from the coiner of the new design of double eagles as rapidly as it is practicable to do so, and deliver the same to the order of the Treasurer of the United States.

This marked official release of the new low relief coins since they were now available to the treasurer for distribution to banks. Internal mint opinion of the low relief version is not mentioned in available documents; however, Augusta Saint-Gaudens made her view known to director Leach: "I am disappointed in the minted double eagle, although the other [high relief] is a beauty."[388]

On December 10 the first new design coins reserved for the mint's special assay were recorded:[389]

> I beg to enclose herewith special assay coins as follows, viz.:

---

[384] *US Mint*, NARA-P, op. cit. Telegram dated December 6, 1907 to Landis from Leach.

[385] *US Mint*, NARA-P, op. cit. Memorandum (ND; cr. December 6, 1907) to Norris from Clark.

[386] *US Mint*, NARA-CP, op. cit., entry 229, box 260. Letter (excerpt) dated December 6, 1907 to Leach from Brewster.

[387] *US Mint*, NARA-P, op. cit. Letter dated December 15, 1907 to Leach from Norris.

[388] *US Mint*, NARA-CP, op. cit., entry 229, box 260. Letter dated December 6, 1907 to Leach from Brewster. Augusta is quoted in the letter.

[389] *US Mint*, NARA-CP, op. cit., entry 229, box 260. Letter dated December 10, 1907 to Leach from Landis. The delivery also included two quarters.

Two (2) double eagles (new design) from delivery No. 100 of $25,000.
Two (2) half-eagles from delivery No. 101 of $200,000.

Thereafter special assay coins were delivered every few days although it is not always clear whether they are from the old or new designs. On December 17 the assay coins transmittal letter lists two new design (low relief) double eagles from delivery No. 107 of $500,000, and two double eagles (old style) from delivery No. 108 of $366,520.[390] Thus, it is clear both types of double eagles were coined concurrently for part of December.

A planned trip to San Francisco to testify in a Seattle Assay Office robbery case by the director was postponed, and he wrote to Charles Brewster explaining more about the low relief double eagles:[391]

> ...There is a great demand for the coins [of Mr. Saint-Gaudens' design]. So far the medal press capacity at the mint at Philadelphia has been unable to satisfy it, and I am told the coins out are all bringing a premium. I regret this, for I was in hopes that there would be sufficient struck to satisfy the wants of everybody. We shall continue running the medal presses as long as we can for this reason. We did not get the coin presses in operation on the double eagles of the new design as soon as expected. It is a very difficult piece to make. It is so different from anything of the kind the men have done in the past, they have many new things to learn and difficulties to overcome. After getting the dies in shape, we found great trouble in getting the lettering on the periphery, and it was not until Saturday evening or Monday morning that our troubles were apparently over. I learned today that they are turning them out now very rapidly. Something like $1,500,000 have been made already. We hope to get out $500,000 a day for some time. Of course, the coin from the coining press is not as fine a specimen of art as that struck on the medal press, yet, it seems to me, it is superior to anything any other country has produced. The relief is much higher than anything I have seen, and I think higher than that in existence on the gold coins of any country.
>
> When I found that I would not have to go away as I had expected, I sent for Mr. Barber and had him here discussing the matter of Hering's suggestions and the coins of the new double eagle in general pretty much all one day...I think it is useless to attempt to do anything more unless a new model should be made with lower relief...There would be no trouble about getting a better reduction if we only had to make one reduction; and with a model made on the lines suggested when I met Mr. Hering at Philadelphia I think we would get a somewhat higher relief for the coining press work...
>
> However, so far as the Department is concerned, as the President is satisfied with the coins as being struck on the coining press and has directed us to proceed with the work, I do not feel justified in making any suggestions that would cause you to incur further expense or make a bill against the Department. If...you wish...to try to improve the appearance of the piece by making another model, I shall be glad to give my efforts in assisting you to reach such result....

Leach's letter was a courtesy – something to keep Brewster informed and hold open the possibility of further changes to the low relief coins, provided it didn't cost the

---

[390] *US Mint*, NARA-CP, op. cit., entry 229, box 260. Letter dated December 17, 1907 to Leach from Landis.
[391] *US Mint*, NARA-CP, op. cit., entry 330, box 45. Letter (excerpt) dated December 17, 1907 to Brewster from Leach. Balance of letter deals with the half eagle.

mint anything. The President liked the low relief coins and if the President was happy, so was the Mint Bureau. Brewster returned the courtesy in his reply of the 18th:[392]

> ....As to making a fourth model, I think it is very doubtful whether Mrs. Saint-Gaudens would be willing to bear this expense. However, I have written her on the subject, and will advise you in a few days about her decision....
>
> Whether a fourth model is made or not, I think you are to be congratulated on the results you have attained...
>
> PS: ...Shall I have the low relief double-eagle you sent me, returned to you, or do you prefer to have me send you a cheque or money order?

Hering added his comments on December 21 but could suggest nothing more than making an enlarged cast of the #4 hub (Barber's version) and retouching it:[393]

> ....I wish you would consider a new suggestion which I am certain would give you your desired sharp model requiring but one reduction. Let Mr. Barber take the last made die and enlarge it to between ten and twelve inches, the larger the better. This will bring the model to the required relief which I can retouch with my tools in the dulled places. Then we will be certain of a result that will give a sharp stamp both in the large and small dies. I cannot emphasize too strongly my wish to have this done, first because I am sure it will save the situation, and secondly, because I am afraid that with the present reductions the $2.50 piece will blur hopelessly. I have resorted to this last measure as the only way I possibly can better the coin without changing the character of the relief which Mr. Saint-Gaudens left....

This drew a scathing rebuttal from Barber and completely closed the door on any future work with the Saint-Gaudens studio:[394]

> ...I beg to say that this is another example of dealing with parties who know nothing of the work of die making or coinage. As I have said before, had they the least rudimentary knowledge of the subject they would not make such childlike suggestions.
>
> To follow Mr. Hering's suggestion would open up the whole subject, renewing all the annoying contentions held by the Saint-Gaudens' party with which we have been laboring for more than a year, until it has become almost beyond endurance, and for no purpose as it would avail nothing.
>
> You are fully aware that so long as Mr. Hering had the double-eagle models in hand no good came out of it, and not until I was given the opportunity to make the dies in some measure suitable for coinage was there any prospect that there would be any new design double eagles made on a coining press.
>
> ....It is entirely unnecessary to trouble Mr. Hering any further, unless another year is to be wasted in vain endeavor....

By close of the calendar year, coiner Rhine R. Freed reported 239,156 new eagles, 361,667 new double eagles, and 11,250 new high relief double eagles had been produced. The high relief mintage was as of December 30 and not the final accounting for the year.

Leach and Brewster continued their cordial exchange of letters on January 2, 1908 when the director wrote:[395]

---

[392] *US Mint*, NARA-CP, op. cit., entry 229, box 260. Letter (excerpt) dated December 18, 1907 to Leach from Brewster. Balance of letter deals with the half eagle. The $20 coin referred to by Brewster was actually a pattern or pre-production trial piece.

[393] *US Mint*, NARA-CP, op. cit., entry 229, box 260. Letter (excerpt) dated December 21, 1907 to Leach from Hering via Brewster.

[394] *US Mint*, NARA-CP, op. cit., entry 229, box 260. Letter (excerpt) dated December 30, 1907 to Landis from Barber.

...As to making a fourth model, I doubt whether sufficient improvement on the coin could be made to justify the expense and trouble necessary. We are improving upon the appearance of the coin right along. Of course, it would never be possible to get the high relief that is on the coins struck on the medal press – they are beauties, as Mrs. Saint-Gaudens says – but the coinage of such a piece would be impracticable for the reason that the cost of making them would be prohibitive...

...The President is delighted with our success. He never misses an opportunity to say something nice.

## A Success of Failure

The long-term creative animosity between Charles Barber and Augustus Saint-Gaudens was the basis upon which a series of minor misunderstandings became impediments to best use of the sculptor's new coinage designs. Engraver Barber consistently stated the mint could strike medals from Saint-Gaudens' high relief designs, but that coinage in large quantities, as demanded by commerce, was not possible. Saint-Gaudens seemed to understand this from the beginning, adopting high relief only at the President's insistence, then accepting low relief as mandatory in May 1907. The technical factor that confused everyone was the mint's inability to cut coin-sized hubs from large diameter models, while retaining detail in the figures. Here, President Roosevelt made significant contribution to the confusion by his apparent misunderstanding of the importance of "design relief" and "model diameter." His consultations with George Kunz at Tiffany & Company should have cleared up any confusion, but seemed only to foster additional problems. Roosevelt appeared to be unaware of the considerable differences in production between medals and coins.

Barber admitted his initial inability to use the Janvier reducing lathe to its full potential, and it is also evident that no one in Saint-Gaudens' studio knew what to do either. Wisely, Barber brought in independent expert Henri Weil, with whom Saint-Gaudens had worked in the past, to cut the first hubs and this allowed him to refute Saint-Gaudens' initial claim of poor mint workmanship. After May 1907, with the sculptor in failing health, much of the delay in producing coins was due to the Saint-Gaudens studio's failure to deliver models on time. Ten dollar eagle models were delayed by Henry Hering's absence in June. The low relief $20 obverse was not ready for delivery until September 20, six to eight weeks later than expected. Communication between mint and artist's studio was often short circuited by Roosevelt, and frequently unclear.

Charles Barber was not the same caliber of artist as Saint-Gaudens, but he was also not the scheming obstructionist many have assumed. His long tenure as engraver was one of boring consistency enlivened by few bungled dies and "numismatic luxuries" – these grew in frequency only after his death in early 1917. Each time Barber was instructed to make hubs, dies, or to complete other parts of coinage work, he complied promptly and with no obvious sign of sabotage. Responsibility for most of the delays in producing the new coinage must fall on the Saint-Gaudens studio for failing to deliver models in a timely manner. The mint failed in its responsibility to clearly communicate to the President and artist its limitations and technical requirements for large-scale coinage. President Roosevelt, likewise, must bear responsibility for constantly confusing the project with conflicting or incomplete communication to the artist and Mint Bureau.

---

[395] *US Mint*, NARA-CP, op. cit., entry 330, box 45. Letter (excerpt) dated January 2, 1908 to Brewster from Leach.

It is notable, however, that throughout the long design, experimentation and production process, Roosevelt honored his promise to give Saint-Gaudens a free hand in making the designs. Barber had offered to remodel the double eagle in August, but permission was refused. The mint may have complained about the designs, but in only two instances did they make overt alterations: addition of a rim to the #1 model $10 coin, and re-engraving of detail on the #3 model low relief $20. Only the double eagle entered circulation, and the changes to it seem to have been done in desperation – to produce coin for circulation as the President ordered.

Coinage design events of the autumn played out against the background of a brief but severe financial panic. This caused many to question the wisdom of introducing new gold coin designs. Roosevelt faced a serious problem that was more public perception than true shortage. Hoarding of gold, precipitated by the failure of several New York trust companies, created an artificial tightening of the money supply just as additional money was needed for cyclical fall harvest settlements. The President asked ordinary citizens to help:[396]

> ...I appeal to the public to co-operate with us in restoring normal business conditions. The government will see that people do not suffer if only the people themselves will act in a normal way. Crops are good, and business conditions are sound, and we should put the money we have into circulation in order to meet the needs of our abounding prosperity.

The treasury department was under enormous pressure to produce and deliver large amounts of gold coin, as reported by many newspapers:[397]

> It is stated that within the next three months the Mint will coin $60,000,000 in double eagles. This enormous amount of gold will be distributed among the Sub-Treasuries in various parts of the country, and will be employed to relieve the money stringency.

In any assessment of the 1905–07 collaboration, recognition must also be given to the mechanics and engineers at the Philadelphia Mint. These included superintendent of machinery Matthew J. Buckley, senior machinist Samuel Hart, foreman Clifford Hewitt and George J. Schaefer who specialized in making coin collars. Largely unknown to today's numismatists, these men labored for long hours to solve practical mechanical problems associated with the new coins. They worked in a near vacuum of information on striking high relief coins, and on impressing raised lettering and stars on the edge of eagles and double eagles. Hints of possible solutions came from the Royal Mint in London and A. Loudon Snowden's 1885 experiments. Yet, if anyone knew how to perfect the coining mechanisms and adapt them to existing presses, their contribution was not recorded. We may never know the many paths of failed experiments, but we know they succeeded because we can hold coins their ingenuity made possible.

Miscommunication and confusion might seem to have had a negative impact on the gold coinage redesign project, but the result was to produce some of the nation's most interesting and creative coinage. Without the inordinate delay in delivering low relief $20 models, Roosevelt would not have ordered production of high relief coins so loved by collectors. Without delays in delivery of the low relief $10 models, Barber would not have

[396] *New York Times*, "All Records Broken in the Making of Money," November 24, 1907, p.SM2.
[397] *New York Times*, "To Coin $60,000,000," November 12, 1907, p.2.

added a rim to the original eagle design and created a new variety for collectors to enjoy. Without confusion about the bronze cent design, the gold eagle might not have been given its own design. Finally, without the peculiar edge lettering on double eagles and controversy over adding the religious motto, Bela Pratt's Indian head design might never have been considered.

A successful project would have had one obverse/reverse pair of designs in use for all gold denominations, and a different design on the cent. Measured against the coinage redesign's original goals, the project was a failure – only one of the intended designs (double eagle) was produced, one of the designs was abandoned (one cent), and a new design was substituted at the last minute (eagle). But the "failures" gave future generations a wider range of interesting designs and opened the door for other, younger artists to complete the work Saint-Gaudens and Roosevelt began.

# Chapter 5 – Trimming Loose Ends – 1908

Production of high relief double eagles evidently continued into 1908. A table written in Robert Clark's handwriting includes the following dates and quantities:[398]

| Date | Quan. | Date | Quan. |
|---|---|---|---|
| Sat. Nov. 23 | ? | Sat. Dec.14 | 114 |
| Sun. Nov. 24 | ? | Sun. Dec. 15 | 115 |
| Mon. Nov. 25 | ? | Mon. Dec. 16 | 128 |
| Tue. Nov. 26 | ? | Off | 109 |
| Off | 108 | Tue. Dec. 17 | 155 |
| Wed. Nov. 27 | 462 | Wed. Dec. 18 | 164 |
| Sat. Nov. 30 | 477 | Fri. Dec. 20 | 186 |
| Tue. Dec. 3 | 489 | Mon. Dec. 23 | 202 |
| Tue. Dec. 3 | 490 | Mon. Dec. 23 | 206 |
| ? | 109 | Tue. Dec. 24 | 207 |
| Sat. Dec. 7 | 46 | Thur. Dec. 26 | 225 |
| Mon. Dec. 9 | 59 | Fri. Dec. 27 | 232 |
| Tue. Dec. 10 | 67 | Mon. Dec. 30 | 247 |
| Tue. Dec. 10 | 68 | Mon. Dec. 30 | 748 |
| Tue. Dec. 10 | 70 | Tue. Dec. 31 | 256 |
| Wed. Dec. 11 | 78 | Tue. Dec. 31 | 257 |
| Fri. Dec. 13 | 98 | Tue. Dec. 31 | 259 |
| Fri. Dec. 13 | 102 | Thur. Jan. 2 | 267 |
| Fir. Dec. 13 | 103 | Fri. Jan. 3 | 278 |
| Sat. Dec. 14 | 107 | Mon. Jan. 6 | 300 |

Although incomplete, the table suggests work might have been done in two or three shifts per day, with one to three presses being used. It appears that high relief coins were not struck every day. Since the addenda to Leach's December 30 letter states 11,250 coins had been produced as of that day, it is plausible to assume the balance of the above table is

---

[398] *US Mint*, NARA-P, op. cit. Manuscript table on back of letter dated March 13, 1908 to Landis from Leach. The writing is in Robert Clark's hand.

a reasonably accurate record of a substantial portion of production. Knowing this, we can also estimate the quantity of coins struck during various production phases, as shown on the table below.

| Date | Quantity Struck | Running Total |
|---|---|---|
| Aug./Sept., 1907 | 500 | 500 |
| November 23-30 | 5,826 | 6,326 |
| December 1-2 | 0 | 6,326 |
| December 3-30 | 4,924 | 11,250 |
| December 31 | 772 | 12,022 |
| January 2-6, 1908 | 845 | 12,867 |

Clearly, the Philadelphia Mint put almost its entire effort behind producing nearly 6,000 high relief coins during the week from November 23 to 30. This must have entailed running the medal presses day and night at considerable extra expense.

We can also estimate the number of pieces struck without a fin rim at 3,870. This is the total production from December 20, when Frank Leach wrote to congratulate Barber on solving the fin problem, through January 6, 1908. Thus, approximately seventy percent of high relief $20 coins may have a noticeable fin and thirty percent are from improved production. This is consistent with observed auction and retail sales descriptions, although the exact quantities will be forever unknown.[399]

## *Open Sale of Experimental Pieces*

President Roosevelt had suspended the usual rule prohibiting distribution of experimental coins in July 1907. This was reinforced in August and again in December. On January 3, 1908, director Leach attempted to clean up paperwork associated with the experimental coins and internal distribution of high relief specimens to the President, cabinet and many others. He wrote to Philadelphia Mint superintendent Landis requesting official statements of the quantities of various pieces struck on the medal presses and how they were distributed. In his letter he made a very interesting offer to Landis: [400]

> ...If you wish authority to exchange some of the trial pieces for coin, please make your request and I will forward the letter, and then you can proceed to destroy the remaining pieces and be ready to execute the report when required.

[399] The quantity of high relief double eagles coined is not consistently reported in official mint documents. Director Leach reported 11,250 struck as of close of business December 30, but coiner Rhine R. Freed reported the same quantity in his calendar year close-out report of December 31. Further, the mint's annual report says that 12,153 pieces were struck. To increase the confusion, handwritten annotations on a letter dated April 22, 1910 in response to an inquiry by George Dickenson gives somewhat different quantities. "Fin edge 8,779 pieces, smooth edge pieces 3,817 pieces. 1,246 of these 12,596 pieces destroyed: 11,250 net." We don't know who added the annotation or what documents they used to support the information given Mr. Dickenson. It was not unusual for multiple mint officials to give collectors differing numbers of pieces struck, so the annotation may be someone's guess. Also, no other documents mention the destruction of 1,246, (or any other large number) of high relief $20 coins. The largest number reported is in a letter from Leach to Landis, where eighty pieces with pronounced fin were ordered recoined. (NARA-P, op. cit., box 71, folder "Gold Coin Designs," letter dated December 7, 1907.) The reader should note, however, that quantities of fin and smooth rim pieces in the annotation (30.3%) and as derived by the author (30.1%) are in very good agreement.
[400] *US Mint*, NARA-P, op. cit. Letter (personal) dated January 3, 1908 to Landis from Leach.

Thus, virtually anyone working at the mint could exchange ordinary coin for any of the experimental or trial pieces (except the small-diameter $20). This also correlates well with the order to strike six additional eagles from the #1 models on December 30, 1907, and other extra pieces reports by director Leach. Only after everyone had a chance to buy what they wanted, or could afford, would the final accounting take place and the remaining coins disposed of. This unusual procedure, when combined with public sale of most of the experimental coin types, resulted a relatively large number of pattern, experimental and limited production pieces reaching collectors. This has helped to popularize the coins and made them more available than any other gold experimental pieces.[401]

By early May the mint's stock of high relief double eagles was down to 51 pieces. Leach asked that the remaining coins be transferred to the Treasurer. This concluded the mint's immediate involvement in sale and distribution of the Saint-Gaudens' design coins.[402]

### *Double Eagle Diameter and Thickness*

Orders were issued on January 23, 1908 to prepare double eagle dies and collars for use by the Denver Mint, and on February 4 Barber sent two pairs of dies, dated 1908.[403] He noted "…they do not pile standard height…" which was one of the difficulties the Philadelphia Mint was working with, in addition to the coins having too great a diameter. Five additional pairs (No. 16 through No. 20 for both obverse and reverse) were sent on February 7.

The diameter problem occurred because Philadelphia Mint personnel had little experience with using segmented collars on automatic coinage presses. The diameter of the new coins, as measured across the edge lettering and stars was 0.012-inch larger than the 1.350-inch standard; measured between the edge lettering, the coins were still 0.007-inch too large.[404] The cause was determined to be a very slight spring in the segmented toggle collar. Barber worked with the coiner to reduce the size of the collars slightly, but did not complete this until after the first set of collars was sent to Denver. Thus, all of the no-motto Philadelphia 1907 and early 1908 coins, and the first issues from Denver were probably larger in diameter than the legal specification. There was no attempt to recall the defective coins. Such an action would probably have been very disruptive to commerce and caused considerable problems with an economy still shaky from the November panic.

Stacking height seemed to be of greater importance to the mint than other problems. Engraver Barber reported that twenty of the old design double eagles made a stack 1.937-inches high while the new coins made a stack only 1.852-inches high – a difference of 0.085-inch or almost the thickness of one coin. A similar stack of eagles differed by 0.046-inch or approximately half the thickness of a coin. To correct the thickness problem, director Leach suggested making the dies more convex and increasing the width of the rim. A letter summarizing the "official" thickness of various coins was prepared by Patrick A.

---

[401] See Chapter 7 for more information on the sale of Saint-Gaudens coins.
[402] See Chapter 9 and the section "The Treasurer's Treasure," below, for the fate of these coins.
[403] *US Mint*, NARA-P, op. cit. Letter dated February 4, 1908 to Landis from Barber. A similar letter was addressed to Mr. Hempel of the Denver Mint. The obverses were #14 and #15; the reverse dies were #11 and #12.
[404] *US Mint*, NARA-P, op. cit. Letter dated January 20, 1908 to Landis from Leach. Uses measurements taken by Norris at the director's request.

Kearney from the San Francisco Mint and submitted to the director on February 15.[405] Apparently Barber followed the suggestion and seems to have solved the problems by the end of February 1908. As a result of the internal discussions, the mint settled on specific diameters and "standard" thickness of all circulating coins. These are presented in the table below:[406]

| Denomination | Diameter (Inches) | Diameter (Millimeters) | Thickness (Inches) | Thickness (Millimeters) |
|---|---|---|---|---|
| Double Eagle | 1.350 | 34.29 | 0.0968 | 2.459 |
| Eagle | 1.060 | 26.92 | 0.0796 | 2.023 |
| Half Eagle | 0.848 | 21.54 | 0.0640 | 1.626 |
| Three dollar | 0.800 | 20.32 | Not given | Not given |
| Quarter Eagle | 0.700 | 17.78 | 0.050 | 1.270 |
| Gold dollar | 0.600 | 15.24 | Not given | Not given |
| Standard dollar | 1.500 | 38.10 | Not given | Not given |
| Half dollar | 1.205 | 30.61 | 0.0825 | 2.096 |
| Quarter dollar | 0.955 | 24.26 | 0.065 | 1.651 |
| Dime* | 0.705 | 17.91 | 0.051 | 1.295 |
| Five cent | 0.835 | 21.21 | 0.078 | 1.981 |
| One cent | 0.750 | 19.05 | 0.062 | 1.575 |

* The San Francisco Mint may have used 0.700-inch for both dimes and quarter eagles.
*Note:* Metric values were calculated using 25.40 mm per English inch. Values were rounded where necessary to maintain significant digits.

The tolerance in diameter was settled at + / - 0.0025-inch, and thickness measured at the rim of + / - 0.020-inch per pile of twenty coins ( + / - 0.001-inch per coin).

## Official Description of the Designs

Frank Leach had been superintendent of the San Francisco Mint when the Roosevelt–Saint-Gaudens collaboration began. In February 1908, secretary Cortelyou, who likewise was not in office at the project's inception, requested a summary of the project and the new designs. Director Leach replied in a memorandum dated February 18, 1908 explaining the design and discussing the high relief coins in general. The full text of Frank Leach's narrative reads:[407]

> It has been said by an eminent writer that the advance of a nation in civilization is best shown by the improvement in its coins.
> Many persons have often expressed a wish that the coins of the United States were of a more artistic character. This has been the earnest wish of President Roosevelt. To accomplish this purpose, and obtain designs of the highest artistic excellence, the late Augustus Saint-Gaudens, the eminent sculptor, was consulted.

[405] *US Mint*, NARA-P, op. cit. Letter dated February 15, 1908 to Leach from Kearney. A more detailed letter of the same date was sent to A. Leslie Lambert, assistant to the superintendent of machinery at the Philadelphia Mint. Kearney was an engineer and later appointed coiner at the San Francisco Mint.

[406] *US Mint*, NARA-P, op. cit. Letter dated February 27, 1908 to Landis from Barber, and Letter dated February 15, 1908 to A. Leslie Lambert from P. A. Kearney. Discussions about circulating coin diameter and thickness also occurred in 1906 and earlier. Dimensions for $2.50, 5-five cent and one cent pieces are from entry 229, box 298 letter dated February 4, 1913 to Roberts from Barber.

[407] *Cortelyou*, LoC, op. cit., box 19. Memorandum dated February 18, 1908 on treasury department letterhead signed by Leach.

Mr. Saint-Gaudens entered into the matter with great enthusiasm. After a number of conferences with the President, definite arrangements were made that he should model new designs for the gold coins and for the one cent piece of the United States. The double eagle and the eagle, from designs modeled by Mr. Saint-Gaudens, were issued in November last.

The obverse of the double eagle bears the standing figure of "Liberty", holding aloft in the right hand the torch of enlightenment; in the left hand the olive branch of peace. The reverse of this coin bears the flying eagle, and the periphery the words "E Pluribus Unum."

The obverse of the eagle bears the feathered head of Liberty which was originally intended for the one cent piece. The President was so pleased with this design that he decided to have it placed on the eagle. The head, the artist stated, was designed in accordance with the suggestions of the President. The reverse bears the standing eagle, and on the edge of the coins there are forty-six stars, one for each State.

The inscriptions and emblems of the coins are in conformity with Section 3517 of the Revised Statutes.

The relief of the coins of the new designs is the highest of that of coins issued by any nation, and no other country possesses coins of a higher degree of artistic merit.

The Government was limited as to the amount of money that could be expended to compensate the artist for the work of modeling the new designs. Mr. Saint-Gaudens was so much interested in this matter that he patriotically offered to execute the work for whatever sum was available, and the fact that the designing of these coins was the last effort of the great sculptor, being the crowning work of a notable career, gives additional interest to the coinage.

It was found that the relief of the model from which the dies for these double eagles was made was too high for coinage on ordinary presses, and pieces could only be struck on a medal press. Hence, that the beautiful and artistic work might be preserved and have a general distribution, as many as possible, 12,153, were struck and sent to the various parts of the United States through the offices of the assistant treasurers.

## The ANA Committee

The American Numismatic Association (ANA) was a little late out of the starting gate. Its Committee on Coin Designs for the United States, appointed in August 1907, finally got around to writing the President on December 10.[408]

To His Excellency, Theodore Roosevelt,
President of the United States

Honored Sir:
The American Numismatic Association, through its Committee, wishes to commend you for the active interest you have taken in the movement to secure a better and more artistic coinage for the United States.

We beg to express our high appreciation of your efforts resulting in the issuance of the beautiful eagle and double eagle by Saint Gaudens. These coins we regard as possessing high artistic merit, though with some faults in detail and technique – and as greatly superior to those of the old type, and as marking an advance in American numismatic art.

---

[408] *The Numismatist*, January 1908, p.12. Committee members were: S. H. Chapman; William A. Ashbrook, member of Congress; Edgar H. Adams; Dr. J. E. Waitt; A. G. Heaton; T. E. Leon; and Thomas L. Elder, chairman. Ashbrook was a Democrat and would likely have received minimal attention from Roosevelt or Loeb.

We also express the hope that you will continue to use your influence toward securing an entire new series of artistic coins for the United States.

We would venture to offer our humble services, as experienced numismatists in suggesting the names of competent artists or in criticizing their designs, and believe, with our knowledge of the coinage of the world, of every period, we could be of some service.

Very truly yours,

Thomas L. Elder, Chairman

Samuel Hudson Chapman, Secretary

As a courtesy Roosevelt's secretary, William Loeb, replied on December 12:

Your letter of the 11th inst. with enclosure has been received, and called to the attention of the President."

Not satisfied with this reply and not hearing anything more for several months, the ANA Committee wrote to Loeb on September 22, 1908 and received a reply on the 24th:[409]

My dear Mr. Elder:

Your letter of the 22nd inst. has been received. The President took the advance ground last year and did all he could but received very little support from public opinion. He does not know what more he can do, but he will of course do whatever he can.

Loeb was aware of the new half and quarter eagle designs prepared by Bela Pratt, but declined to mention anything to Elder. The ANA had no influence on the new gold coin designs and the presence of William Ashbrook, a minority member of the House Committee on Coinage, Weights, and Measures, produced no results. (Ashbrook was able to buy one of the high relief double eagles direct from the mint for his collection.)

In his ANA Committee report of August 1908, Elder presented Loeb's reply, then launched into a confused tirade about lack of interest, lack of qualified die sinkers, the need for public education, a Lincoln Centennial coin and other topics. He closed with prophetic words: "Let us appoint a Committee and get to work." The convention voted to keep the present committee.

## Memorials and Exhibitions

The Metropolitan Museum of Art in New York held a special memorial exhibition of Saint-Gaudens' work in March 1908. Featured among the displays were the original models for the new $10 and $20 coins,[410] and samples of the gold pieces, including the extremely high relief version from the first model. George F. Kunz arranged for the mint to loan the museum the models.[411] With the help of Margaret Valentine Kelly, who convinced director Leach it was *his* idea, Kunz engineered the loan of one of the mint's extremely high relief $20 pieces.[412]

---

[409] *The Numismatist*, October–November 1908. pp.315-317. Committee report delivered by Thomas Elder.

[410] *US Mint*, NARA-P, op. cit. Receipt #184 and #234 of the Metropolitan Museum of Art dated February 26, 1908. Signed by P. H. Reynolds for Edward Robinson, assistant director.

[411] *US Mint*, NARA-P, op. cit. Letter dated January 31, 1908 to Landis from Kunz.

[412] *Kunz*, AMNH, "Coins" folder. Manuscript letter on the director's letterhead dated March 12, 1908 to Kunz from Margaret Valentine Kelly.

My dear Mr. Kunz:

I spoke to Mr. Leach this morning, more particularly to get his interest in <u>lending</u> you from the Mint Cabinet the #1 (first strike) and the Experimental ("fat") coins for the lovely Saint-Gaudens Exhibit. He was so agreeable to it that I suggested sending these to you for a month or two – do you know the length of the time for the Saint-Gaudens exhibit; and he said he would write to you...I think it would give him pleasure to offer to lend them to the Exhibit....

The small-diameter coin was not loaned to the museum. When P. A. Reynolds, registrar of the Metropolitan Museum of Art, returned the extremely high relief coin, he acknowledged its value at $1,000![413]

Exhibitions and memorial services large and small dotted the country as well as Europe. Illustrated catalogues were issued and publishers vied to be the first with a biography or memorial edition about the late artist. President Theodore Roosevelt was the featured speaker at a memorial service for Augustus Saint-Gaudens held at the Corcoran Gallery of Art in Washington, DC on December 15, 1908. Amid the bright lights and pastel hues of the ladies' evening dresses, the President praised Saint-Gaudens' works and his contribution to American culture.[414] A portion of Roosevelt's remarks dealing with the coin designs began:[415]

Before touching on his larger feats, a word as to something of less, but yet of real importance. Saint-Gaudens gave us for the first time a beautiful coinage, a coinage worthy of this country, a coinage not yet properly appreciated, but up to which both the official and the popular mind will in the end grow. The first few thousands of the Saint-Gaudens gold coins are, I believe, more beautiful than any coins since the days of the Greeks, and they achieve their striking beauty because Saint-Gaudens not only possessed a perfect mastery in the physical address of this craft, but also a daring and original imagination.

His full-length figure of Liberty holding the torch is his own conception. His flying eagle and standing eagle, each in its own way equally good. His head of Liberty is not only a strikingly beautiful head, but characteristically and typically American in that for the head-dress he has used one of the few really typical, and at the same time really beautiful, pieces of wearing gear ever produced independently on this continent – the bonnet of eagle plumes. The comments so frequently made upon this eagle-feather head-dress illustrate curiously the exceedingly conventional character of much of our criticism and the frequent inability to understand originality until it has won its place.

Most of the criticism was based upon the assumption that only an Indian could wear a feather head-dress, and that the head of Liberty ought to have a Phrygian cap, a Greek helmet or some classic equivalent. Now, of course, this was nonsense. There is no more reason why a feather head-dress should always be held to denote an Indian than why a Phrygian cap should always be held to denote a Phrygian. The Indian in his own way finely symbolizes freedom and a life of liberty. It is idle conventional trappings which conventional and unoriginal minds have gradually grown to ascribe to her.

A great artist with the boldness of genius could see that the American Liberty should, if possible, have something distinctively American about her; and it was an

---

[413] *US Mint*, NARA-P, op. cit. Letter dated June 18, 1908 to Landis from Reynolds. This coin was later given to Augusta Saint-Gaudens.

[414] *Roosevelt Letters*, Harvard, op. cit., vol. 6, pp.1426–1427. Letter dated December 16, 1908 to Theodore Roosevelt, Jr. from Roosevelt.

[415] [Frank Duffield, ed.] *The Numismatist*, "New Gold Coin Designs Criticized and Defended," pp.34–35. Transcripts of all of the speakers' remarks were printed in the Washington and New York newspapers on December 16 and 17, 1908.

addition to the sum of the art of all nations that this particular figure of Liberty should not be a mere slavish copy of all other figures of Liberty. So Saint-Gaudens put the American Liberty in an American head-dress. Up to the time of this coin the most beautiful American coin was the small gold coin which carried the Indian's head with the feather head-dress, and we now again have the smaller gold coinage with the Indian's head; but Saint-Gaudens' was the head of Liberty, the head of the American Liberty, and it was eminently fitting that such a head should carry a very beautiful and a purely and characteristically American head-dress.

The President's extemporaneous remarks illustrate the personal feeling Roosevelt had for the artist and the designs on which they collaborated. He felt the need to defend particularly the Liberty head on the eagle, which had been described as "blind" and inappropriate by many. His prediction of future popularity for the new gold coins would prove true.

## Presidential Trophies

Theodore Roosevelt was justifiably proud of the new eagle and double eagle. He and the members of his cabinet purchased coins as personal mementos, as well as semi-official awards of respect and admiration for friends and government employees.

Records of mint director Frank Leach indicate that Roosevelt acquired an eagle from the first model and a high relief double eagle on about December 3, 1907; two more $20 were ordered on December 23, and an extremely high relief double eagle on about January 4, 1908.[416] He also obtained larger quantities of the high relief $20 for use as semi-official presentation pieces – ordering twenty high relief $20 pieces on December 2 and another forty on December 23, 1907. The first twenty coins may have been intended as departure gifts for the admirals and battleship captains of the Atlantic Fleet as they began a world-wide tour on December 16. The next forty were given to cabinet members, Senator Henry Cabot Lodge, Dr. William Sturgis Bigelow and other friends during the New Year period. The President also had sandblast proof $5 and $10 coins dated 1908, but we do not know when he acquired them. He may also have had an EHR $20 from the first group made in February 1907.

Reaction to the coins by the President's expansive circle of friends and political colleagues was very positive; however, the general public had little to say according to his private secretary, William Loeb. This lack of public reaction was to be expected – the $20 coin was not a circulating issue. In an era when a week's wage was less than $20, the farmer, laborer and small merchant rarely saw any gold coin larger than the half eagle. People in the Northeast states preferred paper currency to large denomination coin, and "hard money" circulated most freely in the West and South. Being absent from general circulation, the double eagle was a coin the masses hardly ever saw and almost never possessed long enough to appreciate its artistry. Further restricting public discussion was the treasury's prohibition on printing photos of coins in newspapers. Even the largest newspapers, such as the *New York World*, could do little more than describe the new coins. Only coin collectors with access to specialty numismatic publications could gaze at reproductions of Saint-Gaudens' designs.

President Roosevelt gave some of the coins to his daughter, Ethel Carow Roosevelt. Ethel married Dr. Richard Derby and the couple had four children; the eldest, Edith

---

[416] This coin is now in the Smithsonian Institution National Numismatic Collection.

Roosevelt Derby, married Andrew M. Williams. When Ethel Derby died in 1977, Edith Williams inherited the coins her grandfather had owned. Mrs. Williams consigned four of the coins to Bowers & Ruddy Galleries, Inc. and they were featured in the Roy Harte Collection – Part III on January 25–27, 1983. In the catalog, numismatist and author Q. David Bowers accompanied the auction lots with nearly four pages of commentary. The four coins whose pedigree included President Roosevelt were:

| Lot | Description | Selling Price |
| --- | --- | --- |
| 636 | $5 1908 sandblast proof | $ 5,775.00 |
| 639 | $10 1907 knife rim, periods | $14,300.00 |
| 640 | $10 1908 sandblast proof | $ 4,400.00 |
| 641 | $20 MCMVII high relief, flat rim. | $19,800.00 |

The pedigree to President Roosevelt was undoubtedly the reason for the $20 reaching over $19,000 when similar pieces could be bought from dealers for under $3,000. Representing a minor political and artistic triumph, the four coins with a face value of $45.00 realized $44,275 – nearly 1,000 times their issue price.

Augustus Saint-Gaudens treated the experimental coins he was sent as mechanical samples, nothing more. Any of the coins that happened to be in his possession at his death on August 3, 1907 were overlooked from die tests and not kept as souvenirs. Several months after the sculptor's death, his wife, Augusta, requested one of the extremely high relief double eagles made from the first models. She intended this to be part of the displays on view in the Aspet studio for visitors and potential customers of her late husband's work. Acting through her attorney, Charles Brewster, she was finally given one of the coins on June 30, 1908. Before locating a suitable coin, the mint director and President had discussed the possibility of taking one of the pieces from the mint cabinet to give to Augusta. There was even a suggestion to strike a replacement coin but from dies dated 1908.[417] After receiving the coin, Augusta had Charles Brewster keep a lookout for any others that might become available. She felt that beyond their artistic qualities, they would be worth at least $5,000 in the future and she was determined to get as many as possible for an investment.[418]

That there was a ready market for the extremely high relief coins is apparent from a letter written to George Kunz on April 11, 1915 by M. Porserger[?]:[419]

> I have seen the gentlemen who has the special $20 piece, <u>one of the eighteen</u>, of which you spoke to me in New York last week, and he is still willing to sell it. I do not know how much he wants, but he spoke of the two sales of which he knew (one at $800 and one other at $1000) and I think he would accept something in the neighborhood of the lower figure… I would not however offer him that much to start with. He says his is the best of the lot – and as it came from an unimpeachable source I think it is at least as good as the best of them. Furthermore, I have seen it

[417] US Mint, NARA-P, op. cit. Letter dated April 17, 1908 (with manuscript annotations) to Landis from Leach. A follow-up letter was dated April 20.
[418] This may account for the several extremely high relief coins supposedly pedigreed to the Saint-Gaudens estate. The artist never owned one of the coins. The coin acquired from the mint was later given to Homer Saint-Gaudens by his mother, but is untracked since then.
[419] Kunz, AMNH, op. cit. Manuscript letter dated April 11, 1915 to Kunz from M. Porserger[signature unclear]. The letterhead was handwritten: "U. S. Mint, Phila." No one with a similar name appears on either the 1912 or 1914 employee list. Was the owner John Landis who lived in Norristown, or possibly Charles Barber?

and it looks fine as any others I ever saw – though I never had one of my own. Let me hear from you and if you wish I can have it sent to you for inspection.

PS: Address me at Norristown, Pa., my home.

An undated letter to Kunz from Sidney A. Foster adds a bit of mystery to events by stating:[420]

> …I hope to reach Harrisburg [Pennsylvania] tomorrow and to hear that you have forwarded the coin to Miss Kelly.
> [I] Expect to find the bill and will notify our late associates of the amount required. All will want a share in the keepsake….

One can only speculate what mysterious coin was involved: was this before or after Charles Barber's death, was it an extremely high relief $20, or possibly the Indian Head $20, or something else? What role did Miss Kelly play?[421]

## The Great White Fleet

*(Note: Roosevelt was extremely proud of his new coins and his new Navy. The gesture of giving each captain and admiral a new double eagle was entirely consistent with his personality. However, any alleged connection between the Atlantic Fleet cruise and Roosevelt's request for 20 perfect new double eagles is highly speculative. Naval archives contain nothing that confirms this connection. The author admits to standing very far out on a thin limb.)*

On December 16, 1907 President Roosevelt observed the departure of the United States Navy's Atlantic Fleet on an around-the-world tour. The cruise, months in planning, was intended to demonstrate America's position of the stage of world events and to remind Japan that American was prepared to protect its territories in the Philippines and elsewhere. The morning of departure, Admiral Robley D. Evans, three Rear Admirals and the sixteen Captains of the fleet battleships attended a reception on board the Presidential yacht *Mayflower*. Toasts were made to the success of the mission and short speeches made by the President and Admiral Evans. The President spoke with each officer individually and might have discreetly handed each a small, square envelope, with a comment to put it in his pocket. Each of the twenty envelopes contained one of the newly minted high relief double eagles designed by Augustus Saint-Gaudens and not yet officially released by the treasury. The gift could have been a parting memento of America to each of the commanding officers. Admiral Evans could have received his envelope containing a high relief double eagle when the President took him aside to modify his sailing orders verbally. The President had ordered the coins from director Leach on December 2nd, giving specific instructions for selection and packaging of the high relief $20 pieces.[422]

> The President requested me this morning to get for him twenty (20) more pieces of the double eagles made on the medal press. I would like to have you pick out twenty perfect pieces, put each one in a small individual envelope, pack in the best manner to avoid abrasion and forward to me here by registered mail, but anyway give me your best.

[420] *Kunz*, AMNH, op. cit. Manuscript letter ND to Kunz from Sidney A. Foster.
[421] *MacVeagh*, LoC, box 16. Letter dated September 9, 1912 to MacVeagh from Kelly, and reply of September 14 to Kelly from MacVeagh. Margaret Valentine Kelly was an examiner with the mint and the highest-ranking woman in the Bureau in 1912. Her successor was Mary M. O'Reilly who later became the first woman to be officially designated "acting director."
[422] *US Mint*, NARA-P, op. cit. Letter dated December 2, 1907 to Landis from Leach.

There were sixteen battleship captains and four rear admirals with the fleet. The total of twenty commanding officers and Leach's request for twenty new double eagles might have been coincidence, as might also be the date of the request coming only two weeks before the fleet sailed. However, this is the only recorded instance of Leach specifying quantity, specimen quality and individual packaging for the new coins. His request also came the same day he had visited with Roosevelt.

At 10:00 a.m. the fleet set sail from Norfolk, ordering itself into a single line of great, white ships billowing black smoke from their funnels and stretching to the horizon. Behind, bobbing on the waves, followed the President's little yacht, *Mayflower*, as if Roosevelt was pushing them out into the world.

The battleships were arranged in two squadrons of eight ships each:

### Rear Admiral Robley D. Evans, Commanding
#### First Squadron

| First Division | Second Division |
|---|---|
| Rear Admiral Robley D. Evans, commanding | Rear Admiral William H. Emory, commanding |
| USS *Connecticut*, flagship of the Commander in Chief. Captain Hugo Osterhaus | USS *Georgia*, flagship of Divisional Commander Captain Henry McCrea |
| USS *Kansas* Captain Charles E. Vreeland | USS *New Jersey* Captain William H. H. Southerland |
| USS *Vermont* Captain William P. Potter | USS *Rhode Island* Captain Joseph B. Murdock |
| USS *Louisiana* Captain Richard Wainwright | USS *Virginia* Captain Seaton Schroeder |

#### Second Squadron

| Third Division | Fourth Division |
|---|---|
| Rear Admiral Charles M. Thomas, commanding | Rear Admiral Charles S. Sperry, commanding |
| USS *Minnesota*, flagship of Squadron Commander Captain John Hubbard | USS *Alabama*, flagship of Squadron Commander Captain Ten Eyck DeW. Veeder |
| USS *Maine* Captain Giles B. Harber | USS *Illinois* Captain John M. Bowyer |
| USS *Missouri* Captain Greenlief A. Merriam | USS *Kearsarge* Captain Hamilton Hutchins |
| USS *Ohio* Captain Charles W. Bartlett | USS *Kentucky* Captain Walter C. Cowles |

The voyage occurred at the beginning of the radio era when much communication was still done by semaphore flags and code lanterns. There were no reconnaissance aircraft, and radio was often unreliable, so when ships lost contact their only recourse was to steam to a prearranged rendezvous point. Many observers feared the ships would leave port and promptly scatter, negating the effectiveness of the massive operation. But the ships didn't lose contact, and throughout the globe circling cruise there were few major problems with ship-to-ship communication.

156

The photograph below, taken in 1908, shows most of the battleship commanders.

*Figure 39. Commanding officers of most of the fleet's battleships, photographed in 1908. Seated, left to right: Captain Hugo Osterhaus, of USS Connecticut; Captain Kossuth Niles, of USS Louisiana; Captain William P. Potter, of USS Vermont; Captain John Hubbard, of USS Minnesota; Captain Joseph B. Murdock, of USS Rhode Island; Captain Charles E. Vreeland, of USS Kansas. Standing, left to right: Captain Hamilton Hutchins, of USS Kearsarge; Captain Frank E. Beatty, of USS Wisconsin; Captain Reginald F. Nicholson, of USS Nebraska; Captain Thomas B. Howard, of USS Ohio; Captain William H.H. Southerland, of USS New Jersey; Captain Walter C. Cowles, of USS Kentucky; Captain John M. Bowyer, of USS Illinois; Captain Alexander Sharp, of USS Virginia; Lieutenant Commander Charles B. McVay, of USS Yankton (support ship).* (Courtesy U. S. Naval Historical Center Photograph, photo NH–59552. Donation of Captain Donald I. Thomas, USN [retired], 1971.)

The support ship *Yankton* was the first fleet ship to complete its voyage, docking a few days early to collect $800,000 in gold coin for crew payroll and other expenses. By the time the ships returned in February 1909, they had been made obsolete by Britain's launch of the RMS *Dreadnought*. Before the end of World War I all the "Great White Fleet" battleships had been mothballed. When the *Treaty on Limitation of Armaments* was approved in January 1922, the old ships were marked for destruction and reduced to scrap by 1927.[423]

---

[423] See *Renaissance of American Coinage 1916–1921* for the role played by the Harding administration's "Conference on Limitation of Armaments" in creation of the 1921 Peace dollar.

## Augusta's Gold

Like many artists monumental and mediocre, Augustus Saint-Gaudens was not an astute businessman. For the little Aspet homestead, it was Augusta who filled the role of business manager, accountant, paymaster and delinquent accounts collector. The Saint had agreed to design the gold coins and cent for the fixed price of $5,000. He was to deliver models acceptable to the Mint Bureau, but had no responsibility for making reductions, hubs or dies – these were to be done by the Philadelphia Mint.[424]

The agreement was simple, direct and highly subjective. Nothing specified the size of the models or how it would be decided if they were suitable for coinage. The artist had complete design freedom, and the composition was never mentioned as a point of disagreement. Other factors, only partially understood by Saint-Gaudens and Hering, affected acceptance of the models. Approximately two months after the first double eagle models were delivered to the White House, Saint-Gaudens delivered the "final" cent models and his bill. Less than a week later, he asked director Roberts not to submit the invoice for payment:[425]

> ...When I sent my bill to you a few days ago I was under the impression that my work was finished; but now, since Mr. Hering's return from Philadelphia, I find there are certain small modifications to be done so I beg you to hold the bill in abeyance until these are completed...

Through the next three months, small modifications turned into significant reworking of all the designs. On April 10 Saint-Gaudens commented, "...I have sent the final models for the coins..." and asked Roberts if he could submit his bill.[426] The director thought it was not yet time to pay for the work and responded, "...I would not like to assume that no further modifications of the design or models are required until we have made a test of the dies now being made."[427] By the end of May 1907, the President had decided which designs were to go on which coins, and instructed Saint-Gaudens to use lower relief. The double eagle needed lower relief, which it did not get for four months; the cent metamorphosed into the $10 gold, or eagle, coin; and what remained of the lowly cent was discarded as too unimportant for immediate attention. Director Roberts also convinced the artist to switch to European numbers instead of Roman numerals. New "final" models were delivered, tested – and rejected for coinage.

Saint-Gaudens received an experimental $10 coin with plain edge on July 25.[428] On seeing it, he wanted to know if the models were reduced to the maximum extent of the Janvier's capability. Barber scribbled a note: "Both sides of the coin were reduced from the models as low as the machine will allow – C. E. B."[429] Saint-Gaudens did not reply – in a week he would be dead.

[424] The original agreement indicated Saint-Gaudens would be responsible for having hubs made, but that seems to have been overlooked after it was learned the models would be sent to France for the work.
[425] *US Mint*, NARA-CP, op. cit., entry 330, box 45. Letter dated February 24, 1907 to Roberts from Saint-Gaudens.
[426] *US Mint*, NARA-CP, op. cit., entry 330, box 45. Letter dated April 10, 1907 to Roberts from Saint-Gaudens.
[427] *US Mint*, NARA-CP, op. cit., entry 330, box 45. Letter dated April 12, 1907 to Saint-Gaudens from Roberts.
[428] *US Mint*, NARA-P, op. cit. Box 71. Letter dated July 25, 1907 to Roberts from Saint-Gaudens.
[429] *US Mint*, NARA-P, op. cit. Box 71. Manuscript note attached to letter dated July 27, 1907 to Landis from Preston.

The ensuing months were spent in exchange of revised models, letters and tele-grams regarding the designs. On October 27, Augusta wrote a short note to President Roo-sevelt:[430]

> Dear Mr. President
> Your note of August third as you know came too late to bear to my husband your message of affectionate friendship. Such messages were always of so much cheer to him in his long hours of suffering and now are treasured by his wife and son.
> I should have thanked you sooner but I simply couldn't and even now must apologize for the wholly inadequate expression of what I feel.
> Very sincerely yours,
> Augusta H. Saint-Gaudens

This marked the beginning of a more active role by Augusta in the affairs of her husband's estate and in managing and promoting his legacy.

A few days later, Charles O. Brewster, Augusta's attorney, wrote to superintendent John Landis at the Philadelphia Mint asking if he and Henry Hering could visit the mint to discuss the designs. The meeting was eventually scheduled for November 14 with director Leach, assistant secretary Edwards, Barber, Landis, Hering and Brewster in attendance. Brewster left the meeting with a sample of the double eagle made from the #3 models (me-dium relief, European date) made by Hering. The experimental coin had been struck on a medal press.[431] The sample was returned on the 18th without comment from Brewster, Hering or Homer Saint-Gaudens.[432]

On November 19, Brewster wrote to Frank Leach suggesting the Saint-Gaudens estate was entitled to addition compensation for the extra work involved with the double eagles. The director replied on November 23:[433]

> I laid the matter…for additional compensation before the Secretary of the Treasury yesterday while in consultation with him in relation to getting results from the new designs for the double eagles. I told him what we were doing, and he re-ported the matter to the President, and then the President sent for me, and I went over the whole situation with him. The result is that we have ordered as many of these pieces from the No. 2 model as is possible to be struck on a medal press, and this work will go on until we have a proof [i.e., sample – RWB] from the new dies being made from model No. 3. It was the conclusion not to request another set of models made until after we got results from this second experiment on the third model.
> The fact that the plan for a new design for the copper cent was abandoned does not mean that the department would be unwilling to pay for the work. It is my understanding that Mr. Saint Gaudens fulfilled his part of the contract as to the deigns for the cent.

With the President having given orders on November 22 to begin striking coins from the #2 double eagle designs, the question of additional compensation – or any com-

[430] *Roosevelt*, LoC, op. cit. Reel 78. Letter dated October 27, 1907 to Roosevelt from Augusta Saint-Gaudens.
[431] *US Mint*, NARA-P, op. cit. Receipt dated November 14, 1907 and signed by Charles O. Brewster, attorney for Mrs. Saint Gaudens, executrix.
[432] *US Mint*, NARA-P, op. cit. Letter dated November 18, 1907 to Landis from Brewster.
[433] *US Mint*, NARA-CP, op. cit., entry 330, box 45. Letter dated November 23, 1907 to Brewster from Leach.

pensation – was delayed. Brewster wrote to the mint on November 27 asking for one of the pieces being struck on the medal press for examination:[434]

> Will you kindly send me by express one of the pieces now being struck from the second model of the double eagle on the medal press. I wish to obtain this for inspection, and as I shall have to send it to Cornish in order that Mr. Hering may see it, I would like the privilege of keeping the coin at least a week….
>
> Just as soon as the President directs the distribution of these double eagles made in the medal press, I wish you would kindly send me twelve of them, for which I will send a draft at once.

The same day, director Leach reported that "…over \$100,000 of double eagles of the new design which have been struck on the medal presses…" will be ready for shipment tomorrow.[435]

Further tests of new dies for the #4 model double eagles (Barber's retouched #3 hubs) indicated much better results than previously obtained. Leach showed the coin to the President, who approved it. Before going into production Leach wanted to be sure the Saint-Gaudens estate was aware of the modified design:[436]

> ….Before we go ahead, however, with making any more dies, or doing anything more than experimental work, I wish to submit the coins sent to me to the Saint Gaudens people. I want them to pass upon the coin before we take up the coinage work on a regular scale. It would be embarrassing to have those folks make a complaint or find fault with the work after we get started…

A sample coin of Barber's version was sent to Brewster on December 2 and he replied in part, "Mrs. Saint-Gaudens writes 'I am disappointed in the minted double-eagle, although the other is a beauty…'"[437] A few days later the attorney wrote to Landis requesting eight high relief coins and two low relief examples for Mrs. Saint-Gaudens;[438] these were paid for on the 12th. Evidently the total of ten pieces replaced Brewster's earlier request for a dozen examples.[439]

By late December it appears few people knew of the extremely high relief double eagles made from the #1 models earlier in the year. Leach got his first look (at least the first he remembered at the time) on December 23 and wrote this comment to John Landis:[440]

> Mr. Preston showed me one of the D. E. struck on the medal press from the first model. It is a beautiful piece. If you have any more I would like three – one for the St. Gaudens people, one for the Secretary, one for myself, and if the President has not one I want another for him. I will not give these out until after the first of January or we would be bothered by all the officials and collectors in the country.

Following normal procedure, acting superintendent Albert Norris reported on January 2, 1908 that "… the obverse working dies used at this mint during the calendar year

[434] *US Mint*, NARA-P, op. cit. Letter dated November 29, 1907 to Landis from Brewster. Leach had told Brewster on the 27th to write directly to Landis.
[435] *US Mint*, NARA-CP, op. cit., entry 330, box 45. Letter dated November 29, 1907 to Cortelyou from Leach.
[436] *US Mint*, NARA-P, op. cit. Letter dated December 2, 1907 to Landis from Leach.
[437] *US Mint*, NARA-CP, op. cit., entry 229, box 260. Letter dated December 6, 1907 to Leach from Brewster.
[438] *US Mint*, NARA-P, op. cit. Letter dated December 9, 1907 to Landis from Brewster.
[439] *US Mint*, NARA-P, op. cit. Letter dated December 12, 1907 to Norris from Brewster.
[440] *US Mint*, NARA-P, op. cit. Manuscript letter (excerpt) dated December 23, 1907 to Landis from Leach.

1907 were this day defaced and destroyed."[441] With that accomplished, the director wrote to Brewster regarding the smaller gold coins and public reception of the new designs. At the end of a long letter, almost as an afterthought, he added:[442]

> I have written to the Superintendent of the Philadelphia Mint to see if he has any trial pieces of the first model. It is such a beautiful thing I thought possibly Mrs. Saint Gaudens might like to have one. I suppose she has one or more of the second model.
> I think it would be well not to say anything to Mrs. Saint Gaudens about the trial pieces from the first model until I find out whether I can secure one or not.

By showing his experimental coin to Leach and probably Edwards, as well as others at the treasury, Preston evidently "let the cat out of the bag," and word spread about the extremely high relief coins. Norris had received Leach's earlier note and acted on the request by having Barber make three new pieces from the #1 model. On January 3 Norris reported to the director:[443]

> In reply to your letter of December 23rd to Mr. Landis in reference to three double eagles from the first Saint-Gaudens' die – one for the President, one for yourself, and one for the Saint Gaudens people, I would say that we had none of them on hand but Mr. Barber finished three of them on the 31st which I have forwarded [to] you today by U. S. Express charges prepaid....

For the third and final time, extremely high relief experimental pieces were struck at the Philadelphia Mint. Director Leach had requested one coin each for Saint-Gaudens' Estate, Cortelyou and himself. A fourth was requested for the President if he didn't have one, but no one at the Philadelphia Mint knew whether the President had one of these experimental coins. Landis and Norris understood the letter to request three coins and Barber made the pieces on New Year's Eve, just before the die would have to be retired and destroyed. Leach evidently thought he could get one coin for each of the four people mentioned in his letter, and that prompted him to bring the suggestion to Brewster's attention. It was only when he opened the package from Norris and realized there were three freshly struck #1 double eagles, not four, that Leach had to backtrack.

With colleagues at the treasury department now aware of the coin's existence, Leach dealt with the situation as any political officer holder would: one for President Roosevelt, one for secretary Cortelyou and one for himself. The Saint-Gaudens estate would have to wait.[444]

Charles Brewster must have thought an extremely high relief coin would be highly prized by Augusta. On January 4 he wrote to director Leach:[445]

> I hope you will be able to get one of the trial pieces from the first model for Mrs. Saint-Gaudens, and I know that she would appreciate it very much indeed. She secured a number from the second model, thanks to you and Mr. Fish the Sub-Treasurer.

[441] *US Mint*, NARA-CP, op. cit., entry 229, box 260. Letter dated January 2, 1908 to Leach from Norris.

[442] *US Mint*, NARA-CP, op. cit., entry 330, box 45. Letter dated January 2, 1908 to Brewster from Leach.

[443] *US Mint*, NARA-CP, op. cit., entry 229, box 262. Letter dated January 3, 1908 to Leach from Norris. Barber apparently acquired his eight specimens from the first and second groups struck, and was not prepared to part with any of them.

[444] More could not have been officially struck in 1908 because the working dies had been destroyed. The master hubs cut from the models dated MCMVII still existed, however.

[445] *US Mint*, NARA-CP, op. cit., entry 229, box 260. Letter dated January 4, 1908 to Leach from Brewster.

The high relief double-eagles continue to demand a premium of about $15. I suppose that fifty persons know what a double-eagle looks like now, where there was one such person a month ago. The public are being educated.

The attorney also got in a few lines about the long-delayed sculpting bill:

Am I right in thinking that the bill for designing the coins should be sent to the Secretary of the Treasury, instead of to you? I still think that the government ought to pay more than the $5,000 originally stipulated, as the amount of work has been much greater, and the expenses of changing the models has amounted to a large sum. However, I will write you about that matter later.

On the 7th Leach replied in part:[446]

I have not yet been able to secure that first model piece, for the reason I have been unable to see the Secretary, who on account of his recent illness and the bad weather has not been in his office often of late.

I enclose voucher for claim for making these designs, which will have to be signed by the executrix of the estate, and the voucher will have to be accompanied by a certified copy of the letters of administration showing her authority to sign as such.

Augusta and Brewster discussed the compensation claim. Apparently he recommended she prepare a letter to the secretary explaining the situation and officially request payment of $8,000. In a letter to director Leach he advised that Augusta would be contacting Cortelyou:[447]

As Mrs. Saint-Gaudens intends to make a formal application to the Secretary of the Treasury for additional compensation for the designs for the coins, I will delay having the blank voucher which you enclosed filled out at present....

If the mint is not going to use the design for the one cent piece, should not the plaster model which was sent you in September last be returned to Windsor?

It appears Brewster had not seen Augusta's letter when he commented about the cent models. In her missive, Augusta specifically asked for an additional $400 for these models. If the mint now accepted them as Saint-Gaudens' property, and not the mint's, her claim to the extra compensation would be weakened. Augusta's letter of January 14 established her claims on behalf of her husband's estate:[448]

The Honorable,
The Secretary of the Treasury
Sir:
In the matter of the designs for the new coinage made by Mr. Saint-Gaudens, I wish to present for your consideration the question of the propriety of an allowance by way of additional compensation for making these designs.
By referring to the correspondence on the subject you will see from Mr. Saint-Gaudens' letter to the Director of the Mint, dated July 10th, 1905, that in naming $5,000 as the price for the designs, he stated that this sum was considerably below what he received for work of like character. The letter from Secretary Shaw, dated July 29th, 1905, says:

---

[446] *US Mint*, NARA-CP, op. cit., entry 330, box 45. Letter dated January 7, 1908 to Brewster from Leach.

[447] *US Mint*, NARA-CP, op. cit., entry 229, box 261. Letter dated January 11, 1908 to Leach from Brewster.

[448] *US Mint*, NARA-CP, op. cit., entry 229, box 261. Letter dated January 14, 1908 to Cortelyou from Augusta Saint-Gaudens.

162

> *"At this time I deem it unsafe to place a contract involving the expenditure of over $5,000. If you are willing to execute these designs for the gold and copper coins for $5,000, you may proceed."*

As you know, both the President and Mr. Saint-Gaudens were anxious to have the coins in as high relief as possible, with the result that many changes had to be made in the models, at heavy expense to the sculptor. The original models were made by Mr. Saint-Gaudens, but the changes in the models to the lower relief were done by his assistant, Mr. Hering, under Mr. Saint-Gaudens' supervision. I find upon investigation that Mr. Hering has been paid over $2,200 for his work on these coins. Other expenses for modeling, making plaster casts, obtaining a reduction of the model of the standing eagle in Paris, traveling expenses, etc. bring the total amount disbursed by the sculptor and his estate to over $3,300. From this you will see that the compensation for the sculptor's own time is very small.

Included in the above expenses is the sum of $400 for work done last summer in making a third model of the one cent piece, which was forwarded to the Mint in September last. It was learned in November that the Treasury Department had decided in May last not to use Mr. Saint-Gaudens' design for the cent, and yet, through failure to notify him of that decision, he was allowed to go on and waste $400 in making a model that will not be used.

Under all the circumstances, I consider that the compensation from making the designs for the coins should be increased from $5,000 to $8,000.

Will you kindly take this matter under consideration and advise me of your decision at your early convenience.

Augusta H. Saint-Gaudens,
Executrix

On the 15th Augusta's attorney wrote to director Leach in an attempt to clear up matters of the one cent coin and push for the extra compensation. He also forwarded Augusta's letter to secretary Cortelyou:[449]

As regards the model of the <u>one cent piece</u>, I think, upon further consideration, that you are justified in retaining possession of the model, even if it should never be used by the Mint.

On the question of <u>additional compensation for the coins</u>, I enclose herewith a copy of a letter from Mrs. Saint-Gaudens which I am sending to-day to the Secretary of the Treasury. The letter is addressed to him, instead of to yourself, solely for the reason that the original contract was made by the sculptor with Mr. Shaw, the then Secretary. The statute, however, expressly gives authority to the Director of the Mint to make such contracts, with the approval of the Secretary, and I do not understand why the Secretary made the contract instead of the Director. However, you will understand that in the present instance no slight as regards yourself is intended, and I hope that when you are called upon to discuss the matter with the Secretary (and doubtless the President as well) that you will be able to put the matter in as favorable a light as possible for the sculptor's estate. Had Mr. Saint-Gaudens foreseen the amount of labor and expense that he was undertaking upon himself in making this contract, I doubt very much whether he would have allowed his enthusiasm regarding a high relief American coinage to lead him to undertake the work for such an inadequate sum as $5,000.

Whatever may be the public opinion regarding these designs, I think we are all agreed upon the point that Mr. Saint-Gaudens was by all odds the most competent American artist to undertake the task.

Mrs. Saint-Gaudens said nothing in her letter to the Secretary about laying the matter of addition compensation before the President, as I assumed that this would

[449] *US Mint*, NARA-CP, op. cit., entry 229, box 261. Letter dated January 15, 1908 to Leach from Brewster.

be done as a matter of course in view of the great interest the President has taken in the new coins.

In polite, lawyerly fashion, Brewster attempted to recruit Leach to his side of the argument – someone else made the contract; the work was much greater than expected; the compensation was too meager; Saint-Gaudens was the best artist to do the work; and finished by begging the question "...you will be able to put the matter in as favorable a light as possible." Brewster did not know that Leach had received information on the agreement from Roberts, and probably did not realize the director's many years of experience as a newspaper publisher had given him a sense of astute objectivity.

Cortelyou received Augusta's letter and asked Leach for a summary of events. This was supplied on January 21:[450]

> It would appear from the correspondence file in relation to the agreement of Mr. Saint-Gaudens to make a new design for our gold coin and one cent piece, that it was first proposed to make two designs for the gold coins, one for each side, and two designs for the penny, one for each side, and for this work he fixed a price of $5,000. This offer was accepted by Mr. L. M. Shaw, who was then Secretary of the Treasury, concluding with these words: *"If you are willing to execute the design for the gold and copper coins for $5,000 you may proceed."*
> This work upon the part of Mr. Saint-Gaudens contemplated four models, but owing to the inability of the mint operators to successfully make dies that would strike coins in the ordinary way from these models, two other efforts had to be made by Mr. Saint-Gaudens before a model of sufficiently low relief was delivered. And then the design of the reverse on the gold coin was changed, so that instead of having one design for all the gold coins there are now two designs, which was a change from the original proposition.
> There is $6,098 available in the fund from which this claim must be paid.

Although the facts are somewhat garbled, Leach was clear on the fundamental issue: Saint-Gaudens delivered more designs than originally agreed. After reading the memorandum, secretary Cortelyou asked for Leach's recommendation in the matter. The director replied on January 23:[451]

> In response to your request for a recommendation in the matter of the application of Mrs. Saint-Gaudens for an increase in the compensation to be paid for the making of the new models for the gold coin, I would say that I have some little hesitancy in the matter for the reason that I was not a party to the original contract, nor did I have any correspondence with the late Mr. Saint-Gaudens or come in contact with him in his work. From observations made since assuming the duties of the Director of the Mint, I would say that I do not think the estate is entitled to any additional compensation for the extra work required in changing the relief of the models supplied. On the other hand, Mr. Saint-Gaudens seems to have supplied an additional design beyond that embodied in his proposition of July 10, 1905, so if you ignore that possible interpretation of the reply of the Secretary of the Treasury that the $5,000 named was to cover all work for the designs, then the estate would be entitled to an additional sum of $1,250, that being the proportion of the price per model of the original sum named.
> In view of the fact that there is only $6,098.00 available in the fund from which this claim must be paid, and in view of the other facts stated and my knowledge of

---

[450] *US Mint*, NARA-CP, op. cit., entry 229, box 261. Memorandum dated January 21, 1908 to Cortelyou from Leach.
[451] *US Mint*, NARA-CP, op. cit., entry 330, box 45. Memorandum dated January 23, 1908 to Cortelyou from Leach.

the transaction, I would recommend that the estate of Mr. Saint Gaudens be paid the sum of $6,000.00

The question of the double eagle from the first model was not mentioned by Leach; however, it may have occurred to him that the coin might also be considered part of the Estate's compensation. A letter to secretary Cortelyou from the Boston Museum of Fine Arts questioned the availability of these coins and claimed that some, "…had been provisionally assigned to officials of the mint and their friends."[452] Assistant secretary Edwards investigated and was told, "Supt. Landis says there are none to be had, and none were 'provisionally assigned.'"[453]

The director's recommendation was accepted by secretary Cortelyou and he was authorized to make a settlement proposal to Augusta's attorney:[454]

> I am directed by the Honorable the Secretary of the Treasury to inform you that in response to the letter of Mrs. Saint-Gaudens, dated January 14, 1908, in relation to an increase in the compensation for work performed by the late Mr. Saint-Gaudens in making designs for certain denominations of the new coinage, it has been decided to allow the estate an additional sum of $1,000 for the extra design.
>
> It is obvious that Mr. Saint-Gaudens did a great deal more work and expended a great deal more money in carrying out his contract than he at first contemplated, but in view of the language used by Secretary Shaw in accepting the offer of Mr. Saint-Gaudens' there is a question raised as to the propriety of making any additional allowance whatever. However, in view of the subsequent order for the additional model of the eagle Secretary Cortelyou saw his way clear to approve the recommendation for the allowance of the additional $1,000. The sum of $6,000 practically exhausts all the money available for the payment of this claim and even if we were able to find justification for increasing the allowance more than $1,000, it would have to be obtained by an act of Congress.[455]
>
> Upon receipt of a bill for the sum mentioned you will receive prompt remittance. Upon making out the claim you should set forth the amount of the original contract and then make a separate charge for $1,000 for making of the extra model.

Leach's letter was polite but clear – $6,000 was all Augusta could expect without an act of Congress. The sculptor's widow thought the offer over for a few days, then had Brewster reply on February 3:[456]

> I have received yours of the 31st ult. regarding the decision of the Secretary of the Treasury of the application for increased compensation to the estate of the last Augustus Saint-Gaudens for designing the coins.
>
> While my client is disappointed that the Secretary cannot see his way clear to pay a larger sum than $6,000, she has decided to accept this amount in full settlement, and so I send herewith a voucher, made out in accordance with your instructions, as I understand them, for the sum of $6,000. I also enclose a certificate of the issuance of letters testamentary to Mrs. Saint-Gaudens.
>
> I wish to thank you on behalf of my client for the interest you have taken in regard to the coins generally, and for what you have done toward facilitating the payment of the claim.

---

[452] *US Mint*, NARA-CP, op. cit., entry 229, box 261. Letter dated January 28, 1908 to Cortelyou from Arthur Fairbanks, director of the museum.
[453] *Ibid.* Manuscript annotation signed "F. A. L."
[454] *US Mint*, NARA-CP, op. cit., entry 330, box 45. Letter dated January 31, 1908 to Brewster from Leach.
[455] He means by appropriated funds.
[456] *US Mint*, NARA-CP, op. cit., entry 229, box 261. Letter dated February 3, 1908 to Leach from Brewster.

> Have you been able to secure the first model piece referred to in your letter of January 7th?

With compensation agreed upon, the only matter remaining was the extremely high relief double eagle "promised" by Leach. He replied to Brewster on February 4 indicating that he might not be able to locate one of the coins.[457]

> I thank you very much for the kind expressions contained in your letter. I am sorry to say that so far I have been unable to get one of the first model pieces, and it now looks doubtful whether I shall succeed.
> I immediately put your bill on passage, and as soon as it goes through the Auditor's office we will be able to send you a check.

The director's official accounting of experimental coins, dated February 5, stated that thirteen of the EHR coins had been struck, with two pieces kept for the mint collection, one given to the President and ten distributed to unnamed mint officials (probably including eight pieces held by Charles Barber). Secretary Cortelyou also advised several applicants "…that there are none of the trial pieces…of the No. 1 die of the double eagle…on hand."[458]

Payment to Augustus' estate was acknowledged by Brewster on February 29:[459]

> The payment for the designs was made to Mrs. Saint-Gaudens about the 18th. Inst.
> Can you inform me whether the matter of additional compensation was referred to the President by the Secretary, or not?

Leach's reply of March 2 is particularly interesting because he offers to send samples of the half eagle made from Saint-Gaudens' designs.[460]

> ….In relation to your inquiry whether the matter of the additional compensation was referred to the President or not, I can only say I presume it was. I have no personal knowledge upon the subject, but I inferred as much from the discussion of the matter the Secretary had with me, and I think he would confer with the President for the purpose of having his approval of the increase in the compensation over the amount named in the contract.
> ….I hope soon to be able to send you some of the trial pieces of the $5.00 denomination. I think these will also be very handsome coins.

Charles Brewster apparently discussed the EHR double eagles with Augusta. She, in turn, wrote to President Roosevelt asking him for one of the pieces. Presidential secretary William Loeb sent the letter to director Leach on April 15, and Leach phoned to say that none of the coins were available. Curiously, no one in the Roosevelt administration offered to give up their coin to satisfy Augusta. On April 17 an informal "instruction" came from the White House:[461]

---

[457] *US Mint*, NARA-CP, op. cit., entry 330, box 45. Letter dated February 4, 1908 to Brewster from Leach.

[458] *US Mint*, NARA-CP, op. cit., entry 330, box 45. Letter dated February 19, 1908 to Charles M. Kurtz, Buffalo Fine Arts Academy from Cortelyou. Similar requests are scattered through the Mint Bureau correspondence files beginning in February 1908.

[459] *US Mint*, NARA-CP, op. cit., entry 229, box 262. Letter (excerpt) dated February 29, 1908 to Leach from Brewster.

[460] *US Mint*, NARA-CP, op. cit., entry 330, box 45. Letter dated March 2, 1908 to Brewster from Leach.

[461] *US Mint*, NARA-CP, op. cit., entry 229, box 264. Letter dated April 17, 1908 to Leach from Loeb.

> Mrs. Saint Gaudens has asked for a double eagle of the No. 1 model which was designed by her husband. The President thinks she is certainly entitled to it. In view of the fact that all of the trial pieces have been distributed, he asks that one be struck for her bearing this year's date.

This unorthodox request was immediately sent to the Philadelphia Mint by Leach:[462]

> Learning that Mrs. Saint Gaudens was disappointed in not receiving one of the trial pieces struck from the No. 1 model design for the double eagles, the President has directed me to have struck one piece from the dies bearing the date of the current year, 1908. If this is not practicable, you will have to withdraw one of the two pieces placed in the cabinet that it may be given to Mrs. Saint Gaudens.

Below his signature Leach wrote: "Call me up on phone." Acting superintendent Norris received the letter and made the following notes on it after his telephone conversation with Leach:[463]

> Called D/M on telephone – Wail 'till [coin from] D. E. Die 1, now in NY with Mr. Kunz is returned and send that one to D/M. If necessary can strike specimen with date 1908 for the Cabinet – Orders President U.S. – A.A.N.

The coin referred to is the one loaned to the Metropolitan Museum of Art for display during their Saint-Gaudens Memorial Exhibition. George Kunz had arranged for the Philadelphia Mint to loan one of its two examples to the museum. At the time, the Museum valued the coin at $1,000. President Roosevelt approved the suggestion of giving Augusta one of the pieces from the mint collection on April 20:[464]

> At a conference with the President in relation to supplying Mrs. Saint-Gaudens with one of the double eagles from the first model, he thought it best to take one of the two coins that are in the cabinet, and if it is necessary to have two pieces there, that the extra piece be struck with this year's date and put in the cabinet instead of being given to outside parties.
> Mr. C. O. Brewster will probably make application to you for the coin for Mrs. Saint-Gaudens, if so, deliver it to him.

As expected, Brewster sent his request to the Philadelphia Mint on April 22:[465]

> I enclose wherewith the sum of $20.12 in payment of a double eagle of the first model, which Mr. Leach advises me under date of the 20th inst. that you will send me for Mrs. Saint-Gaudens in accordance with the direction of the President. Upon Mrs. Saint-Gaudens' return from the south next month, I will ask her to send a formal receipt to you in addition to my own.
> Thanking you for your attention to the matter, I remain,

Two weeks passed and the coin did not arrive. Brewster wrote to director Leach on May 8:[466]

> I received your letter of April 20th, and on the 22nd wrote the Superintendent of the Mint enclosing $20.12 for the coin. In reply, I had a letter from Mr. Norris, the

---

[462] *US Mint*, NARA-P, op. cit. Letter dated April 17, 1908 to Landis from Leach.
[463] *US Mint*, NARA-P, op. cit. Letter dated April 17, 1908 to Landis from Leach. Manuscript annotation by Norris.
[464] *US Mint*, NARA-P, op. cit. Letter dated April 20, 1908 to Landis from Leach.
[465] *US Mint*, NARA-P, op. cit. Letter dated April 22, 1908 to Landis from Brewster.
[466] *US Mint*, NARA-CP, op. cit., entry 229, box 264. Letter dated May 8, 1908 to Leach from Brewster.

acting superintendent, dated April 23, in which he said the double-eagle would be forwarded to me in a few days, but up to the present time it has <u>not</u> been received.

Under the circumstances, I prefer not to write Mr. Norris about the matter. If one of the pieces in the mint cabinet was to be used I would have thought it could have been sent at once. If, however, they intend to strike some more pieces from the first die, I can understand the delay.

Thanking you for whatever you can do in the matter, I remain…

Leach replied on May 9 explaining that the coin was currently on display at the memorial exhibition in New York and would be sent to Augusta when the exhibition closed.[467]

Mrs. Saint-Gaudens is quite willing to wait until the exhibition closes before she receives the double eagle from the first model. I had hoped that they would keep the exhibition open all summer, but they need the space for other purposes at the Art Museum and accordingly have announced that the exhibition will close June 1st.

Augusta was very protective of her husband's work and wanted to be assured that she would receive the double eagle as promised. She wrote to director Leach on June 2:[468]

I understand from your letter to Mr. Brewster that I am to have the Twenty Dollar Gold Piece of the first strike, now in the Metropolitan Museum Exhibition. As it is labeled "Loaned by the United States Mint," unless you give instructions otherwise, the Committee would naturally return it to the Mint instead of to me. Will you kindly have this matter adjusted.

Very truly yours,
Augusta H. Saint-Gaudens

Acting director Preston reassured Augusta that the coin would be sent to her as agreed:[469]

In regard to the $20 gold piece of the first strike, now in the Metropolitan Museum, I would say that my understanding of the matter is that as soon as this coin is returned to the Mint you will have the same upon the payment of the face value of the piece, namely: twenty dollars.

Brewster received the coin on June 22 and sent it to Augusta, who then sent a formal thank you letter to superintendent John Landis on June 30:

Dear Sir:
Through the kindness of Mr. Charles O. Brewster I have received the double eagle of the first model issued in 1907 and thank you for your courtesy in the matter.

[467] *US Mint*, NARA-CP, op. cit., entry 229, box 264. Letter (excerpt) dated May 11, 1908 to Leach from Brewster. The balance of the letter concerns Brewster's objection to Congress adding the motto to the coins.

[468] *US Mint*, NARA-CP, op. cit., entry 229, box 265. Letter (excerpt) dated June 2, 1908 to Leach from Augusta Saint-Gaudens. Balance of the letter concerns an electrotype of the rejected Columbian Exhibition medal that Augusta claimed belonged to the estate.

[469] *US Mint*, NARA-CP, op. cit., entry 330, box 45. Letter dated June 8, 1908 to Augusta Saint-Gaudens from Preston. In the balance of the letter Preston rejects Augusta's ownership claim by stating that the Government paid her late husband $5,000 for the design and the electrotype was made by the mint.

Augusta's curt letter, written on Hotel Manhattan stationery, says nothing about director Leach's efforts or makes any reference to thanking the President, who personally approved taking a coin from the official government collection and selling it at face value to a private individual. Only Brewster receives her approbation. This letter marked the end of substantive communication between the Mint Bureau and Saint-Gaudens' estate.[470] The EHR double eagle eventually passed to Homer Saint-Gaudens and from there is unknown.

Later in the year, new half eagle and quarter eagle gold coins were issued based on an obverse design by Boston artist Bela Lyon Pratt, and the $10 coin standing eagle as requested by the President. The pattern half eagles of Saint-Gaudens' design Leach once mentioned to Brewster were never released.[471] No one with the mint or executive department consulted with Augusta about the change, or made any attempt to explain to her why her late husband's designs were rejected.

## Distributing New Eagles and Double Eagles

With suspension of rules against selling experimental coins, all 1907 pattern and limited production coins became fair game for collectors. Specimens could be purchased at the mint's cash window, or from the director's office for face value – provided one knew what to ask for. Notices in local newspapers mentioned the high relief double eagles with Roman numeral date. But only word of mouth and "inside" knowledge gave collectors any idea that other varieties existed. Naturally Roosevelt and Cortelyou knew about the #1 and #2 eagles, and Roosevelt seemed to prefer that his friends acquire both a #1 eagle and a #2 double eagle as their memento of the new designs.

High relief double eagles were distributed to the sub-treasuries in lots of $5,000 – two hundred fifty coins – with the pieces placed in a small canvas bag. The bag was packed in a larger box that held eight small bags for a total face value of $40,000 per box (this was normal procedure for shipping gold coin). It appears that assistant secretary Edwards tried to issue one or two bags to each sub-treasury at the same time. From comments connected with coin orders from the San Francisco Mint and some of the assay offices, it appears that most high relief $20s arrived at the sub-treasuries and were immediately purchased by employees and friends of officials. Few of the coins made it to banks and it is possible that none ever passed through a teller's cage to the general public. In such circumstances, nobody cared about stacking the coins. Not even powerful bankers, such as Frank Vanderlip, president of Continental Commercial Bank in Chicago, seemed to be able to obtain the new double eagles through conventional means. By March 1908 the coins commanded a $15 premium and were in great demand for their speculative potential.

The statement of account provided by director Frank Leach to secretary George Cortelyou on February 5, 1908 confirms that five hundred of the #1 eagles were transferred to the custody of assistant secretary John H. Edwards at the main treasury in Washington. We have very limited information about when they were distributed until after 1911. No

---

[470] Henry Hering claimed in his *Numismatist* article that the quality of reductions for the reverse of the $10 coin was an issue. Hering claimed the mint refused to pay Augusta until he proved the mint's reductions were inferior by comparing them with ones he had ordered from Paris. The original documents quoted herein say nothing about this incident, and it may have been similar to other "time-altered" events recounted by Hering.

[471] The pattern half eagles were produced in April, but evidently all were destroyed at the mint on Leach's orders.

comprehensive list of purchasers, or accounting for the coins has been located in treasury department records.[472]

It may be assumed that the director and mint sold all forty-two additional pieces claimed to have been made in addition to the regular five hundred. It is probable this number included the six #1 model eagles struck on December 30 and sold to Robert Preston. But, we cannot tell if the two plain edge patterns made just before July 22, 1907 are included – or if "42" includes any of the experimental coins. A reasonable assumption is that this group of forty-two pieces included everything with the exception of the plain edge pieces, which may have been considered too preliminary to count. How the one known plain edge piece escaped is not particularly relevant since treasury and mint employees were permitted to buy any of the experimental pieces they could afford.[473] This was less of a "pig-at-the-trough" situation than it might appear at first. For example, Samuel Hart, chief machinist at the Philadelphia Mint, earned but $2,500 per year and most employees earned much less. Some could have taken part of their pay in the new gold coins to show to the wife and kids, but then had to spend the coin for daily subsistence. The only mint employees likely to be able to afford to buy patterns and keep them for any length of time were the supervisory and professional staff such as Landis, Norris, and Barber. In Washington, the treasury department had a modest number of senior officials earning from $5,000 to $15,000 per year, and these, plus senior-level administration appointees could afford long-term indulgence of a few new gold pieces. With many coins being transferred to Washington, it is likely that most patterns entered collector circles through the offices of director Leach and assistant secretary Edwards, rather than Philadelphia coin dealers with connections at the local mint.

Two interesting observations in support of the "Washington connection" stand out when considering coin sales: first, most coins were sold to treasury officials connected with the Bureau of the Mint. Philadelphia coin dealer Henry Chapman refers to the director writing to him "...to the latter he writes me more especially than to the former..." indicating some sort of exchange of correspondence. Also, collectors appear to have routinely inflated the public display aspects of their collections to obtain favored treatment. It must be noted, however, that Leach received many inquires about the new coins, and his responses often referred to museums and public collections as having precedence over individuals. The director did much of his buying not long after the date of Chapman's letter to Robert Garrett. It is also worth mentioning that Edwards had wanted to place the #2 eagle made on normal presses into circulation, but Leach decided to have most melted. The possibility exists that Frank Leach was a conduit in 1909 for these coins to Chapman or others outside the treasury. However, as described below in "The Treasurer's Treasure," the most common source of the coins was the treasurer's office and later, the mint collection curator.

When we consider the total of all purchases versus reported mintage, the situation becomes clearer. The sales total for #1 and #2 eagles is close to the number of coins (net after melting) reported by the director. This suggests that the conduit for distribution was the director's office, or assistant secretary Edwards, and not a dealer with "connections." There is little which would have prevented Frank Leach from selling the excess pieces he

---

[472] See Burdette: *Renaissance of American Coinage 1909-1915* for additional information on disposition of these coins.
[473] One plain edge piece was last recorded in Saint-Gaudens possession at the end of July 1907. By the time his studio and its contents were transferred to the National Park Service, all the gold medals and coins had disappeared.

ordered to a dealer, likewise for assistant secretary Edwards.[474] However, the table of purchasers (see chapter 9) suggests nothing prevented collectors from acquiring coins; everyone who ordered coins received them, except for three requests for extremely high relief double eagles that came after the dies had been destroyed at the end of 1907.

Barber's #2 model eagles were first made as experimental pieces and we know that at least two survived – both are in the NNC. As to the balance – 31,500 coins – director Leach's accounting on February 5, 1908 states that all but fifty pieces were melted. This is consistent with his destruction order of November 9, 1907, except for the fifty survivors. To the fifty should be added the two known patterns with irregular edge stars. Considering the initial striking date and the "normal" production status of this design, it is likely that all circulation pieces had normal stars on the edge. Thus, an example of the fifty survivors would have normal edge stars, while one of the patterns would have irregular edge stars. As with the #1 eagles, there is not the slightest suggestion any of the coins were made as "proofs" as the term is now understood.

The #2 model eagle sold to Dr. S. E. Young on October 19, 1908 was supposed to be the last piece director Leach had available. Dr. Young's letter states:[475]

Dear Sir:
About a month ago I called at your office and you had one specimen of the Second Model 1907 10 dollars gold piece, thin rim which you said you would let me have if a party who had sometime ago applied for it did not take it in a short time. You filed my name away with the coin. If the other party has not got it, I hope you will let me have it as he has had ample time to get it if he wanted it very much.
I want it badly and no one would appreciate it more than I would and I sincerely hope you will inform me that I can get it. I will send the price immediately.
Very truly yours,
S. E. Young, MD
Baywood, Virginia

Unfortunately, the good doctor does not tell us where he learned of the #2 model eagles, but he was obviously pleased with the coin:[476]

Dear Sir:
I received the 10 dollar St. Gaudens gold pattern piece this P.M. for which I thank you very sincerely. It is a beauty and adds much to my collection.
Yours very sincerely,

David Akers' analysis of auction records indicates the #1 eagle has appeared at auction with much greater frequency than the #2 eagle, approximately an 8:1 ratio. This is roughly consistent with the record of specimens sold (549:38) and concordant with the quantities stated in Leach's report: 542 (#1) to 50 (#2) or an 11:1 ratio.

---

[474] Edwards is something of an unknown in the whole 1907 situation. He had been personal secretary to L.M. Shaw, then was then promoted to assistant treasury secretary when Cortelyou took office. Director Leach reported to him as well as directly to secretary Cortelyou. During the financial crisis in the autumn, Cortelyou was generally unavailable and instructions were given by Edwards. He initiated many of the requests for pattern coins before being forwarded to Leach or the Philadelphia Mint. He resigned on or about March 1, 1908, leaving several matters incomplete, according to a letter of March 30, 1908 from U. S. Treasurer Charles H. Treat to secretary Cortelyou. (LoC, *Cortelyou papers*, op. cit., box 19.) He was also the government representative on the Jamestown Ter-Centenary Commission from 1906–1908. His letters acting in this capacity are in NARA, record group 56.
[475] *US Mint*, NARA-CP, op. cit., entry 229, box 268. Letter dated October 19, 1908 to Leach from S. E. Young.
[476] *US Mint*, NARA-CP, op. cit., entry 229, box 268. Letter dated November 5, 1908 to Leach from S. E. Young.

## Mr. Barber's Pattern Collection

Engraver Charles Barber owned more than two hundred pattern, experimental and trial pieces.[477] The collection included coins designed by his father, William Barber, who preceded him as engraver at the Philadelphia Mint, as well as his own work and that of assistant engravers George Morgan and Anthony Paquet. An inventory prepared sometime after late 1916 catalogues coins by denomination and provides a very brief description of many. Unfortunately, where the Saint-Gaudens coins are concerned, there are no details as to date acquired or variety.

U. S. Mint documents indicate that Barber supervised the striking of all Saint-Gaudens pattern and experimental coins. It must have been soon after the coins were first prepared, that Barber purchased examples for his collection. The inventory notebook lists the following pieces along with notations:[478]

| Date | Description | Quantity |
|------|-------------|----------|
| 1907 | $20 pattern pieces. Fig Lib on Ob | 4 |
| 1907 | $10 pattern piece. Only 50 made | 1 |
| 1907 | $10 pattern piece. Only 550 made | 1 |
| 1907 | $20 pattern pieces. Fig Lib on Ob | 4 |
| 1907 | $20 pattern piece. Head lib on Ob | 1 |

From the notebook descriptions it is possible to determine most of the types which Barber owned in 1916. The note "Fig. Lib on Ob" refers to the extremely high relief $20, of which he owned eight examples. The "$10 pattern piece. Only 50 made" must refer to coins struck from the #2 models – normal rim with periods on the reverse. Likewise the next note, "$10 pattern piece. Only 550 made" probably refers to high relief eagles from the #1 models with knife rim and reverse periods (five hundred forty-two actually produced). Finally, the $20 described as, "Head lib on Ob" must be the gold Liberty head pattern made at the request of Saint-Gaudens.

Combining the notebook information with other documents indicates that Barber had invested $200 in Saint-Gaudens pattern coins, and that he held the pieces in his personal collection until at least a few months before his death in February 1917. By this time the $10 eagles were worth little more than face value – Louis Comparette having given up trying to sell the remainder from the treasurer's hoard for $15 each, and seventy were melted (see below). The EHR and Liberty head coins would have been of interest to collectors. The Liberty head/Flying Eagle $20 was sold from his estate, possibly to collector Waldo Newcomber. According to George Kunz, a "new" extremely high relief 1907 pattern became available in the New York area for $800 in 1915, suggesting that considerable demand remained for the EHR coins. These eight "new" EHR pieces may have found their way into prominent collections through Barber's estate although specific information is lacking. It is also possible that some or all of the pieces in the "Capt. North" 1907–08 gold set were supplied by Barber or his heirs.

---

[477] *Charles E. Barber papers*, American Numismatic Association Research Library; accession number SC-1999.0004.
[478] *Barber*, ANA. Folder 0003 "The Personal Notebooks of Charles E. Barber, Pt. I, Coins and Patterns," page H.

## Closing the Books

Coin collectors have long wondered what happened to experimental and pattern coins produced and sold by the Mint Bureau. The list of purchasers in Chapter 9 solves part of the mystery and additional research supplies answers for two long-standing questions:

1.  What happened to the coins transferred to the treasury department; and,
2.  Were all the dies and hubs destroyed at the beginning of 1908 as suggested by documents from the Philadelphia Mint?

Conventional speculation has been that pattern coins were sold to "insiders" in the coin business by mint employees, and that the employees somehow profited. The supposed transactions have always been thought of as somewhat "shady." As the list of purchasers indicates, many coins were sold at face value in more or less open transactions from the Mint Bureau in Washington, DC. Employees who were financially able were permitted to buy the coins for their personal use or resale, since the President had declared that ownership of the experimental pieces was legal. Answers to some of these questions can also be found by jumping four years into the future, to a small hoard of gold held by the Treasurer.

### *The Treasurer's Treasure*

On December 16, 1911, Representatives William Ashbrook (D-Ohio)[479] and Arthur W. Koop (R-Wisconsin)[480] approached Assistant Secretary of the Treasury A. Piatt Andrew (former Director of the Mint) with an unusual request.[481] Both congressmen were active coin collectors eager to find specimens for their collections. Both were members of the American Numismatic Association, and Ashbrook had also been on the Assay Commission. In 1908 Ashbrook purchased one of the high relief double eagles from director Leach. In 1911, he was a member of the House Committee with oversight of the Mint Bureau. Their joint request was "… to examine the one and three dollar gold pieces now in the hands of the treasurer with the idea of securing therefrom any such as may be of peculiarly rare date or mintage."[482]

The little hoard of gold coins was controlled by the treasurer and used at his discretion to reward favored visitors. Their existence appears to have been an "open secret" among the treasurer, secretary of the treasury, assistant secretaries and mint director.[483]

After considering the request, Andrew suggested the coins be sent to Philadelphia and melted, but mint director Roberts proposed that the coins – all of which commanded a premium when purchased from coin dealers – be transferred to the curator of the mint collection. That way they could be sold or traded for pieces needed for the mint's popular collection of coins. The premium could be used to enhance the purchasing power of the

---

[479] William A. Ashbrook (July 1, 1867 – January 1, 1940), Democrat from Ohio, was a coin collector and member of the American Numismatic Association. He was primarily responsible for the ANA receiving a national charter from Congress. He served on the Assay Commission six times, and attended many ANA conventions. He ceased active collecting in 1919 after his coins were stolen in a bank robbery.

[480] Arthur William Kopp (February 28, 1874 – June 2, 1967), was a progressive Republican member of Congress from March 4, 1909 to March 3, 1913, from Wisconsin. The was a lawyer and later circuit court judge. He was ANA member #1502 from June 1911 to his death in June 1967.

[481] *US Mint*, NARA-CP, op. cit., entry 229, box 297. Memorandum dated December 18, 1911 to Andrew from MacVeagh.

[482] *US Mint*, NARA-CP, op. cit., entry 229, box 297. Letter dated February 12, 1912 to Ashbrook from MacVeagh.

[483] See Burdette: *Renaissance of American Coinage 1909-1915* for more information on this subject.

collection's paltry $500 annual fund. Andrew, who viewed the collection as something of a national treasure, readily agreed; however, Treasurer of the United States Lee McClung felt he should be able to continue sale of the coins to members of Congress and other favored persons.

Treasury secretary MacVeagh eventually talked with McClung, insisting that the coins be transferred to the Philadelphia Mint. By April 17, 1912 the treasurer advised he was arranging for the transfer:[484]

Referring further to your letter of April 4th, I am to-day arranging for the transfer to the Philadelphia Mint of the following gold pieces:

| | | |
|---|---|---|
| $1 | 313 | $ 313 |
| $3 | 335 | $1,005 |
| $10 | 129 | $1,290 |
| $20 | 58 | $1,160 |
| Total | | $3,768 |

The number stated above constitutes all the $1 and $3 gold pieces that we have and all that we have had for sometime past.

Andrew sent the letter to director Roberts with a note stating, "…I think it would be advisable if you would prepare some sort of instructions to the superintendent of the mint in Philadelphia which will provide for a careful report to you as to the disposition made of all of these coins."[485]

As requested, Roberts prepared an advisory letter to mint superintendent Landis listing the coins he could expect to receive, and how to handle their disposition by the curator:[486]

…You are instructed to have a strict account kept of these coins all of which are to be held by you and turned over to the Curator of the numismatic Collection from time to time as the appropriation for the collection will allow and as he, with your approval, may desire to use them, either by adding them permanently to the collection or by using them for the purchase of other rare pieces.

All such purchases are to be specifically approved by you and reported to this Bureau with a statement setting forth the coins purchased, a description of the rare coins or medals purchased. Hereafter it is desired that a regular monthly statement of all coins and medals purchased shall be made to the Bureau.

The rare coins now being transformed are to be held and used for no other purpose than the one set forth in this letter, to wit: For the use of the Numismatic Collection, and your records be made to show the disposition of every coin.

Detailed monthly reports would be a nuisance, but the additional funds derived from sale of the coins represented a windfall for the mint collection. For a collection whose curator had aspirations of international recognition, the present $500 purchase fund was far too small to do more than buy a few duplicates from relatively minor collections. Treasurer McClung, in a last bit of pique at having to hand over his "personal treasure" to some academic at the mint, had the transfer order made on the standard form used for "Uncurrent and Light Weight Coin." The numismatic pieces were shipped as so much damaged goods,

[484] *US Mint*, NARA-CP, op. cit., entry 229, box 297. Letter dated April 17, 1912 to Andrew from McClung.
[485] *US Mint*, NARA-CP, op. cit., entry 229, box 297. Memorandum dated April 18, 1912 to Roberts from Andrew.
[486] *US Mint*, NARA-CP, op. cit., entry 229, box 297. Letter dated April 19, 1912 to Landis from Roberts.

174

dumped in a small bag, on April 20, 1912[487] and received by the mint on the 22nd. Albert Norris reported, "No advice of the forwarding of this coin was received from the treasurer, the tag on the bag being simply marked 'Uncurrent gold coin.'"[488]

On receipt, curator Comparette went through the hoard looking for anything that might be added to the present collection. He noted the gold dollars "...were all of one date (1889) with a single exception, and that specimen was considerably worn... The three-dollar pieces had all been in circulation and were not a little worn and nicked."[489] The $10 coins were all that remained of five hundred pieces minted in August 1907 from the #1 models. The double eagles were all of the high relief version representing the balance sent to Washington in March 1908.

With substantial purchasing power available for the first time, Comparette's initial transaction was with Philadelphia coin dealer Henry Chapman. On June 28 and 29, 1912, Chapman acquired all three hundred thirteen gold dollars at $2.00 each and thirty-six of the three dollar pieces for $4.00 each.[490] In his report of the transaction dated August 16, he felt the need to explain the prices obtained, "...Perhaps I may anticipate a natural inquiry by stating that the prices obtained... are certainly favorable to the Government and all that could be expected."[491] Coins were purchased with the proceeds of this initial expedition into the commercial coin market netted the mint collection one hundred five specimens on June 28 and an additional nineteen pieces on June 29.

The first group consisted primarily of ancient Greek and Roman coins featuring such items as a tetradrachm of Demetrius Poliorestes bought for $42.50, a gold distater of Alexander the Great for $80 and an aureus of Lucilla (C-69) for $31, along with a dozen French seventeenth century gold and silver pieces. The June 28 group included a 1912 gold proof set, several colonial pieces and a scattering of European gold. The grand total of the first Chapman purchases was $773.20 in dollars or, as Comparette preferred to figure the prices in the gold coins from the Treasurer's office, $423.81.[492]

Six months later, Comparette's report of February 12, 1913 showed considerable change in the coins held for resale:[493]

...I beg to make the following report on the special gold coins transferred to this Mint, from the Treasurer's office, to be sold and the profits used for the benefit of the Numismatic Collection:

| On hand at last report | Sold | On hand Feb 1. |
|---|---|---|
| $20's – 57 | 0 | 57 |
| $10's – 129 | 0 | 129 |
| $3's - 299 | 259 | 40 |

[487] *US Mint*, NARA-CP, op. cit., entry 229, box 297. U. S. Mint transfer form #777 dated April 20, 1912.

[488] *US Mint*, NARA-CP, op. cit., entry 229, box 297. Letter dated April 22, 1912 to Roberts from Norris.

[489] *US Mint*, NARA-CP, op. cit., entry 229, box 297. Letter dated August 16, 1912 to Landis from Comparette.

[490] *US Mint*, NARA-CP, op. cit., entry 229, box 297. Letter dated September 3, 1912 to Roberts from Norris. The receipt from Chapman was dated July 18, suggesting that either there was a delay in transferring the coins to him, or Comparette had neglected to obtain a receipt as required by Roberts.

[491] *US Mint*, NARA-CP, op. cit., entry 229, box 297. Letter dated August 16, 1912 to Landis from Comparette.

[492] *US Mint*, NARA-CP, op. cit., entry 229, box 297. Letter with inventory included dated August 29, 1912 to Landis from Comparette. The inventory is approximately four pages. Valuing purchases in the treasury coins at a discount allowed Comparette to stay under the $500 appropriation ceiling.

[493] *US Mint*, NARA-CP, op. cit., entry 229, box 297. Letter dated February 12, 1913 to Roberts from Landis.

The 259 $3.00 gold pieces were sold to Mr. Thos. L. Elder of New York City at a profit ranging from $1.00 to $1.50 apiece, the total profit received on their sale being $271.65.

His next report on March 13 indicated that most of the remaining coins had been sold, although this time he did not specify the purchaser(s):[494]

...I beg to make the following report, for February, on the special gold coins transferred to this Mint, from the Treasurer's office, to be sold and the profits used for the benefit of the Numismatic Collection:

| On hand 2/1/13 | Sold | On hand 3/1/13 | Profit |
|---|---|---|---|
| $20's – 57 | 57 | none | $171.00 |
| $10's – 129 | 24 | 105 | $120.00 |
| $3's - 40 | 39 | 1 | $43.95 |

Out of the profits, the Curator purchased and paid for during the month the following coins for the Numismatic Collection in this Mint:

| | |
|---|---|
| From Cashier, US Mint, Philadelphia. Specimen (pyx) coins from the other mints | $16.45 |
| From Royal Mint, Copenhagen. New coins of Denmark | $9.53 |
| Henry Chapman, Philadelphia. African, Italian, Roman, Syrian and other coins | $128.80 |
| Total | $154.78 |

The one $3.00 piece still on hand is mutilated and therefore unsalable – it has several initials stamped on it.

Calculating from the reported profit, the mint sold high relief double eagles for $23 each, the #1 model eagles for $15 each and the $3 pieces for an average of $3.30 apiece. These prices for the Saint-Gaudens coins suggest there was little market for either of the coins although collectors were willing to pay a higher premium for the $10 #1 coins than for their larger cousins.[495] By July 18 Comparette reported that all coins had been sold with the exception of "...about eighty (80) eagles, for which we are asking $15.00 each."

Although the project seemed to be going well and had been particularly effective at allowing the curator to purchase a wider range of coins than previously, the change of executive administration brought new questions for the mint to answer. A new assistant secretary of the treasury, John Skelton Williams, knew nothing about numismatics and had several questions about the gold coin transactions. His first inquiry was to be assured that the mint was obtaining an affidavit of authenticity for all of the coins purchased. Once this was settled, he wanted to know if there were any gold dollars at the mint, and if not, who had bought them.[496]

Acting director Dewey replied on July 26:[497]

---

[494] *US Mint*, NARA-CP, op. cit., entry 229, box 297. Letter dated March 15, 1913 to Landis from Comparette.

[495] This "market valuation" implies that Henry Chapman's comments to Robert Garrett about the coins being "...worth $400..." was likely hyperbole from a coin dealer hoping to maintain his customer's confidence.

[496] *US Mint*, NARA-CP, op. cit., entry 229, box 297. Memorandum dated July 23, 1913 to Williams from Frederick P. Dewey, acting director.

[497] *US Mint*, NARA-CP, op. cit., entry 229, box 297. Memorandum dated July 26, 1913 to Williams from Dewey.

The one dollar gold pieces which were transferred from the Office of the Treasurer of the United States to the Mint in Philadelphia in April 1912, for the benefit of the Numismatic collection of the Mint at Philadelphia have been sold. The last sale of these pieces was made to Mr. Henry Chapman of Philadelphia who paid two dollars each for them...

[*At the bottom in bold writing:*]

On what date?
Who is Chapman?
JSW

Dewey responded by providing the date the last sale was made, noting that "...Mr. Henry Chapman, a well-known coin dealer of Philadelphia...paid two dollars each for three hundred and thirteen pieces..."[498]

It appears that Williams was not entirely trusting of the Mint Bureau's explanation, and the next day he had W. U. Thompson, possibly a treasury employee, write to Henry Chapman in Philadelphia asking if he had any gold dollars for sale. Chapman replied the next day:[499]

Mr. W. U. Thompson,
Dear Sir:
Replying to your letter of 29th inst. I can supply you small gold dollars, extremely fine condition, at $2.40 each. Large size very good to fine at $2.10 each, uncirculated, $2.25 each.
Shall be glad to have your order,

At a profit of just 25¢ per coin for Chapman, this exercise must have satisfied Williams' skeptical nature for nothing more appears in mint records.

The curator was well acquainted with most of the prominent numismatists in the eastern United States and had ample opportunity to let them know of the coins the mint had for sale. With only a small number of coins remaining – a mutilated $3 piece, seventy-six 1907 eagles from the #1 dies, and one eagle from the #3 normal circulation dies – Comparette had little that was of interest to collectors or his dealer contacts. He had sold twenty-eight #1 eagles in December to bring the stock to its present level,[500] and by August 1914 he recommended sale of "...the balance of the first pattern Saint Gaudens eagles, at $15.00 each for those in perfect condition, and the unsalable pieces at face value."[501]

On October 19, the sale of another four eagles was reported bringing the total remaining to seventy-two coins. Two more were sold on November 17, 1914. With no collectors interested in the remaining coins, Comparette filed his final report on June 9, 1915 listing seventy eagles of the Saint-Gaudens design, #1 models. In response to an inquiry on June 14, 1918 from director Raymond T. Baker, Philadelphia Mint superintendent Adam Joyce commented:[502]

...I beg to inform you that the 70 eagles, which were reported as on hand at my last report, June 9, 1915, have all been melted. None has been sold since that

[498] *US Mint*, NARA-CP, op. cit., entry 229, box 297. Memorandum dated July 28, 1913 to Williams from Dewey.

[499] *US Mint*, NARA-CP, op. cit., entry 229, box 297. Letter dated July 30, 1913 to W. U. Thompson from Chapman (signed by Ella B. Wright). There is no address for Mr. Thompson.

[500] *US Mint*, NARA-CP, op. cit., entry 229, box 297. Letter dated January 8, 1914 to director of the mint from Landis.

[501] *US Mint*, NARA-CP, op. cit., entry 229, box 297. Letter dated August 25, 1914 to superintendent of the Mint from Comparette.

[502] *US Mint*, NARA-CP, op. cit., entry 229, box 297. Letter dated June 14, 1918 to Baker from Joyce.

time, and of the profits reported on hand... 24 cents, 21 cents was paid out the next day for expressage on medals which were donated to us, leaving 3 cents still on hand.

Thus, the unusual tale of the treasurer's treasure came to a quiet end. Out of a total mintage of five hundred forty-two pieces (plus patterns), the #1 model eagles had net distribution of four hundred seventy-two pieces.

## *Last of the Original Hubs and Dies*

By 1910 considerable controversy surrounded the mint's relationship with coin dealers and collectors, and the distribution of pattern and experimental pieces. Some of this was fueled by dealers Farran Zerbe and Henry Chapman, and collectors William Woodin and John Hazeltine. Significant concerns were also raised by ordinary collectors who complained bitterly about perceived preferential treatment for well-connected dealers. After a brief investigation into the situation involving pattern coins by mint director A. Piatt Andrew, he ordered the destruction of all dies and hubs of pattern, experimental and obsolete designs held at the Philadelphia Mint.[503] The work took place on May 24 and 25, 1910 under supervision of the Philadelphia Mint's four senior officers.[504]

Andrew was keenly aware of the impact of public perception, and did all he could to put the treasury department on completely fair and equitable terms. His order may have been part of an overall process of removing "temptation" from the realm of mint officials. Regrettably, it also destroyed a significant portion of America's numismatic heritage – items, which should have entered the mint's coin cabinet collection (and eventually the Smithsonian's protection), were gone forever.

Of importance to the present book is the fate of the Saint-Gaudens hubs and dies. Barber's list is clear about what was destroyed:

| Quantity | Barber's Description from List of May 25, 1910 | Author's Comment |
|:---:|---|---|
| 2 | Double eagle, obverse and reverse, first reduction from model high relief, too high to coin. | #1 model, extremely high relief |
| 2 | Same design, second reduction, obverse and reverse reduced relief, but still too high. Model changed by Saint Gaudens. | #2 model (high relief). Not clear if this is #2 or #2A as used for coinage. |
| 2 | Same design, third reduction, greater reduction in relief, detail lost in reducing the relief to such an extent, in trying to come to coin relief. Model changed by Saint Gaudens. These double eagle hubs were made acceptable by the engravers restoring the detail in the hubs. | #3 model used to cut hubs. Became #4 model after Barber re-engraved detail. |
| 1 | Liberty head design for obverse double eagle, high relief; afterward reduced in relief and used for eagle. The model was changed by Saint Gaudens | J-1905. |

---

[503] *US Mint*, NARA-CP, op. cit., entry 229, box 290. Letters dated May 24 and May 25, 1910 to Andrew from Barber. Accompanying the letters and inventory lists are affidavits signed by Barber, Landis, Eckfelt, and Freed.
[504] See Burdette: *Renaissance of American Coinage 1909–1915*, where this subject is discussed in detail.

| Quantity | Barber's Description from List of May 25, 1910 | Author's Comment |
|---|---|---|
| 3 | Saint Gaudens' design, high relief reverse for twenty dollar, standing eagle. One hub, two dies. | These were made from the reductions done in France by Janvier et Duval. |
| 2 | Double eagle, obverse and reverse. Barber and Morgan design, hubs | This is the 1906 gold $20 pattern long ascribed solely to Barber. Obverse by Barber, reverse by Morgan. (See also 1891 J-1766 half dollar pattern with Morgan's standing Liberty obverse and Barber's eagle / stars / clouds reverse) J-1773. |
| 2 | Double eagle high relief, diameter of eagle. Obverse one, reverse one | Small-diameter experimental $20. J-1917 |
| 2 | Ten dollar gold. Saint Gaudens design obverse and reverse hub from which present design is a modification. Obverse one, reverse one. | #3 $10 eagle models as prepared by Homer Saint-Gaudens and Hering. |

Barber's lists were prepared before the Adams-Woodin book on U. S. pattern coins was published. He does not appear to have consulted with the mint's curator, T. Louis Comparette, in preparing his inventory.

## Net Mintage for 1907 Eagle and Double Eagle

The following table summarizes total mintage of major varieties of 1907 $10 and $20 gold coins designed by Augustus Saint-Gaudens. Details for the sources of these quantities will be found elsewhere in this volume.

| | Plain Edge Patterns | Lettered/Starred Edge Patterns | Circulation Pieces | Other Pieces | Melted | Net Population |
|---|---|---|---|---|---|---|
| $10, Model #1. High relief, periods. | 3 | 2-3 | 500 | 42 | 70 | 472 |
| $10 Model #2. With border, periods. | 0 | 3+ | 31,500 | 0 | 31,450 | 50 |
| $10 Model #3. Border, no periods (Circulation). | 0 | 2+ | 239,156 | 0 | 0 | 239,156 |
| $20 Model #1. Extremely high relief, small Capitol.* | 1 | 13 to 20 | 0 | 0 | ? | 19 ? |
| $20 Model #1, small-diameter. Extremely high relief, small Capitol. | 0 ? | 15 | 0 | 0 | 13 | 2 |

| | Plain Edge Patterns | Lettered/Starred Edge Patterns | Circulation Pieces | Other Pieces | Melted | Net Population |
|---|---|---|---|---|---|---|
| $20 Model #2 (1st dies). Very high relief, large Capitol. | 0 | 8 | 0 | 0 | 8 ? | 0 ? |
| $20 Model #2 (2nd dies). High relief, large Capitol.[505] | 0 | ? | 11,250 (as of Dec 30) | 1,117 | [80 ?] | 12,867 |
| $20 Model #3 Low relief, poor detail. | 0 | 3+ | 0 | 0 | 2 ? | 1 ? |
| $20 Model #4 Low relief, recut detail (Circulation). | 0 | 2+ | 361,667 | 0 | ? | 361,667 |

*Note: Extremely high relief double eagles from the #1 models were made on three separate occasions, from two different pairs of face dies and two different edge collars. Several incomplete pieces are mentioned in mint documents, including the plain edge example in the above list. This is the only incomplete piece presently known to exist.*

All working dies dated 1907 for the above coins were reported destroyed in early January 1908. All remaining dies and hubs were destroyed according to the mint director's orders on May 25, 1910.

---

[505] For many years, a plain edge high relief specimen was listed in the ANS inventory and reported in various publications. When the author requested photos of this coin, it was discovered to have normal edge lettering: there was no plain edge high relief double eagle in the ANS collection.

# Chapter 6 – In God We Trust For The Other Fifty Cents

Conventional numismatic wisdom is that addition of the motto IN GOD WE TRUST to the eagle and double eagle was a straightforward affair and had little impact on other coins. But records from multiple sources suggest the effect was significant. The original plan was to use Saint-Gaudens' Striding Liberty on the obverse and the flying eagle on the reverse of the remaining gold denominations. Once Congress began considering legislation to overrule the President, the mint stopped most work on the half and quarter eagle designs. In the course of mint business, director Leach had President Roosevelt approve positions for E PLURIBUS UNUM and the style of the statement of value on December 28, 1907. Pattern coins were prepared prior to April 3, 1908. Now that motto legislation had delayed final approval, William Sturgis Bigelow had a chance to present his ideas to the President. Thus, the opportunity to use Bela Pratt's Indian head design occurred because of delay due to the motto legislation.

## History of the Motto

In November 1861 the Civil War had been underway for over six months.[506] What many Northerners thought would be a quick and easy end to the Southern insurrection, was being replaced with recognition that a long, violent conflict was ahead. Some may have realized that for the South to win, it simply had to keep the northern armies engaged until popular sentiment turned in its favor (or the British interceded). The North had to be much more aggressive if it was to be victorious – it had to defeat Southern armies, particularly the Confederate Army of Northern Virginia under General Robert E. Lee, and occupy vital Southern cities and transportation centers including the Portsmouth-Norfolk area of Virginia.

---

[506] See also Burdette, *In God We Trust – The Story of a National Motto*, for additional information.

Anxiety was manifest in the form of a rapid increase in patriotic and religious fervor among the population of both sides. Ministers called on God to smite their enemies and bring victory to their own just cause. Rhetoric of real and imagined injustices mixed with volatile brimstone on any given Sunday. Out of this caldron of faith came a letter from Reverend Mark Richards Watkinson, "supply minister" of the First Particular Baptist Church in Ridley, Pennsylvania.[507] He wrote to Secretary of the Treasury Salmon P. Chase with a patriotic suggestion for the nation's coinage. In his letter dated November 13, 1861, Rev. Watkinson said:[508]

> Hon. S. P. Chase
> U. S. Sec of Treasury
> Dear Sir:
> You are about to submit your annual report to Congress respecting the affairs of the National Finances.
> One fact touching our Currency has hitherto been seriously overlooked: I mean the recognition of the <u>Almighty God</u> in some form in our coins.
> You are probably a Christian. What if our Republic were now shattered beyond reconstruction? Would not the antiquaries of succeeding centuries rightly reason from our past that we were a heathen nation?
> What I propose is that instead of the goddess of Liberty we shall have next inside the <u>thirteen stars</u> a <u>ring</u> inscribed with the words "<u>Perpetual Union</u>"; within this ring the <u>all-seeing eye</u> crowned with a <u>halo</u>. Beneath this eye the American <u>flag,</u> bearing in its <u>field stars equal to the number of the States United;</u> in the folds of the bars the words "<u>God, liberty, law</u>."
> This would make a beautiful coin, to which no possible citizen could object. This would relieve us from the ignominy of heathenism. This would place us openly under the Divine protection we have personally claimed. From my heart I have felt our National shame in disowning God as not the least of our present national disasters.
> To you first I address a subject that must be agitated.
>
> M. R. Watkinson,
> Minister of the Gospel

Rev. Watkinson's suggestion was for a special coin design promoting the Union cause. It was to incorporate thirteen stars, an "all seeing eye" of Divine providence, an American flag with a star for each state, and two new legends: "Perpetual Union" and "God, liberty, law." (Fifty-five years later, sculptor Augustus Saint-Gaudens wanted to add the words "Justice" or "Law" to the double eagle, but was dissuaded by specifications of the coinage laws.)

---

[507] This church was renamed Prospect Hill Baptist Church on June 2, 1887, and incorporated April 3, 1888. A new building was constructed at 7th & Lincoln Avenues, Prospect Park, Pennsylvania. The unusual term "particular" in the church's name begs explanation. The Baptist churches known as "General Baptists" were Armenian in theology, which taught that all men could be saved, not just a few. The Calvinistic or "Particular Baptists" believed in limited atonement in which only the elect could be saved. This is generally followed by American "Southern Baptists" of present times. (See also, Robert G. Torbet, *A History of the Baptists*, Valley Forge Press, 1987.) Thus the term "particular" was descriptive of the Ridley church's doctrine.

[508] Report of the Committee on Coinage, Weights, and Measures accompanying House Resolution 17296, *To Restore The Motto 'In God We Trust' to The Coins of The United States*, as reported out of committee on February 27, 1908. Original document in NARA.

Although Watkinson had suggested a new coin design and inscriptions, secretary Chase concentrated on the concept of recognizing God on America's coinage. On November 21 he wrote to mint director James K. Pollock, former governor of Pennsylvania:[509]

> No nation can be strong except in the strength of God, or safe except in His defense. The trust of our people in God should be declared on our national coins.
> You will cause a device to be prepared without unnecessary delay with a motto expressing in the fewest and tersest terms possible this national recognition.

James Barton Longacre, engraver of the mint, promptly modified two reverse dies for the eagle and half dollar by adding a sample motto, GOD OUR TRUST. On December 26, 1861, the director responded with news that must have pleased Chase:[510]

> …I have caused this motto [God Our Trust] to be struck on reverse dies of the eagle and half dollar, and impressions in copper of the eagle, and in silver of the half dollar are presented herewith.

*Figure 40. Examples of pattern coins with "God Our Trust" added to the reverse die. Left, half dollar showing text on a raised ribbon, right, ten dollar (or eagle) showing text as raised letters on a plain field. These were created by the U. S. Mint in December 1861 to illustrate the possible use of the motto on circulating coins.*

It seems odd that one short letter could change the inscription on America's coinage, yet there is no record of other letters making similar suggestions. The unusual impact Rev. Watkinson's letter had may be better understood if we examine the young Baptist minister's career in more detail.

Mark Richards Watkinson was born on a farm near Burlington, New Jersey on October 24, 1824. His parents, Abel and Deborah Watkinson, had a large family to support and after Mark completed elementary school he was apprenticed to the *Mt. Holly Herald* (NJ) newspaper and commercial printer. At age fifteen he joined the Mt. Holly Baptist Church, later moving to Philadelphia in 1845 as a journeyman printer. He joined the Broad Street Baptist Church the same year and came under the influence of Rev. J. Lansing Burrows, who encouraged Watkinson to use his talents in the ministry. With assistance from the church congregation, he attended Lewinsburg University[511] for eighteen months, then entered Columbia College in Washington, DC.[512]

After serving as "evangelist" for the Baptist Church of Bristol, Pennsylvania for a short time, he moved to Ridley and joined the First Particular Baptist Church of Ridley Township on October 16, 1850. A year later he was ordained as a minister and the congre-

---

[509] *US Mint*, NARA-CP, op. cit., entry 214, vol. 3. Letter dated November 20, 1861 to Chase from Pollock.

[510] Ibid. Chase had resigned from the cabinet on December 20, but rescinded his resignation on December 22.

[511] This was a church-sponsored college that was later renamed Bucknell University.

[512] Also church-run; later renamed George Washington University.

gation agreed to pay him the sum of $400 per year as salary. As was common at the time, the young minister saw less hard money than he did vegetables, potatoes and the occasional chicken in payment for his services. He met his future wife, Sarah Isabella Griffiths, during a baptism ceremony, and the young couple stayed in Ridley until 1853. Later that year the family moved to Philadelphia, where he was minister at the Schuylkill Baptist Church until 1856. At 32, Mark Watkinson was an attractive young man, an excellent sermon writer with a reputation for being attentive to the members of his congregation. His talent for people made him a respected, well liked, and trusted member of the community.

In 1856, the Portsmouth-Norfolk area of Virginia was slowly recovering from a yellow fever epidemic of the previous summer. Approximately 18,000 people left the area out of a population of 27,000. Of those who remained, nearly 3,000 died until cold weather stopped the mosquito-borne disease.[513] Court Street Baptist Church in Portsmouth, one of the oldest Baptist congregations in Virginia, was trying to regain members and turn around its reputation for poor financial treatment of its ministers.

Rev. Watkinson learned of the Portsmouth situation and applied to Court Street church for the pastor's position. With help from church member and distinguished former pastor, Rev. Thomas Hume, Sr., the congregation examined Watkinson's credentials and unanimously elected him pastor on July 22, 1856.[514] They also agreed to a salary of $1,000 for his first year – a generous sum for the time. Watkinson used his eloquence and personal charm to bring together and enlarge the congregation. New members joined nearly every Sunday and his church prospered over the next five years.

Relations between the slave and free states had been uneasy from the beginning of the Constitutional era. Secession of the New England states[515] had been narrowly averted in 1814, and the 1850s saw continual bickering, threats, reconciliation and compromise to keep the country together. The Portsmouth-Norfolk area was home to one of the largest military ports on the East Coast including the Gosport Navy Yard. Residents were torn between close ties with northern businesses and loyalty to their home state of Virginia. As tensions rose after the election of Abraham Lincoln in November 1860, pressure mounted on the populace to choose sides. Newspapers and pulpits rang with rhetoric of states' rights and national duty. Watkinson's church, as would be expected from a large congregation, was in the thick of controversy and confusion.

On November 30, 1860, in a sermon from his pulpit,[516] Rev. Mark Watkinson let his people know where he stood. He declared himself forthrightly in favor of the course of the South, and in opposition to the views of abolitionists. The sermon created a sensation; many people were overjoyed and called for a church conference that evening to request a copy of the sermon, and ask that it be published. Other members, who sided with the Union, were critical of the sermon that they considered inflammatory or even seditious. Rev.

---

[513] Isaac W. K. Handy, *The Terrible Doings of God*. Sermon delivered in the Court Street Baptist Church, December 30, 1855. Daily Transcript Office, 1856, 24 pages. Handy was a Presbyterian minister and later a Union prisoner at Fort Delaware. See also George D. Armstrong, DD, *The Summer of the Pestilence: A History of the Ravages of the Yellow Fever in Norfolk, Virginia, A. D. 1855*. Reprint by C. W. Tazewell, 1964.

[514] Thomas Hume, Sr. (1812–1875) was one of the most distinguished Baptist ministers in Virginia during the first half of the nineteenth century. He was often called upon to give the inaugural sermon when a new church building was dedicated, or to provide advice on forming new congregations. Reverend Hume served at Court Street Baptist from 1833 to 1854. His personal papers (and those of his son) are held by the University of North Carolina.

[515] The New England secession movement gained momentum for an entire decade, but ultimately failed at the Hartford Secession Convention of 1814.

[516] Sources say November 27, however that date was a Thursday – not a likely day for important sermons.

Watkinson seemed pleased with the results of his speech and "cheerfully and promptly" consented to publication of the sermon. Copies were soon delivered to the *Daily Transcript* and other newspapers agreeing with its sentiment, and to the Baptist church's newsletter *Religious Herald.* (The sermon was never published.)

By spring, 1861 several Southern states had seceded from the Union. When the Virginia Legislature passed a secession bill in April 1861, rioting and violence threatened Portsmouth. The United States flag was torn down in Portsmouth in April 20, 1861. Ships were burnt in the Gosport Navy Yard in nearby Norfolk[517] – the region seemed in open rebellion.

*Figure 41. Burning of the U. S. ship of the line Pennsylvania, and other vessels, at the Gosport Navy Yard, Norfolk, Va. on the night of April 20th, 1861. By Currier & Ives.* (Courtesy Prints and Photographic Division, Library of Congress)

Apparently Rev. Watkinson felt responsible for some of the violence due to his sermons and his position in the community. This may have put his family in danger and he quickly sent his wife and children northward by steamer. As the last boat was about to leave for the North on April 23, 1861, he stepped aboard, leaving behind his church and congregation. There were many harsh words about his disloyalty to Virginia, and the inconsistency of his sermon versus his act of abandoning Portsmouth. Others may have understood his desire to protect his family, and defended him. Most admitted that the church and the Portsmouth citizenry had suffered the greater loss when Watkinson left. The next Sunday afternoon 19-year-old Annie M. Cox wrote in her diary:[518]

> *1861 - APRIL 28TH Sabbath afternoon.* I did not go to church this morning as it commenced raining just about church time. Pa went down but there was no preaching. Alas! We are now left without a pastor. Mr. Watkinson has taken his

---

[517] The Gosport Navy Yard is physically located in Portsmouth; however, long-standing convention identifies it with Norfolk.

[518] *Annie Matson Cox, personal diary.* Courtesy private collection of direct descendant, Mrs. Ann Benson Green, member of Court Street Baptist Church, Portsmouth, VA. Quoted by permission.

departure, gone north & sent a letter of resignation to the church. I think it would have been much more manly & better for him if he had resigned before he left. I am very sorry that he has acted thus & that is after preaching and talking so much against abolitionists to go right among them. But we cannot judge him. God alone knoweth the heart.

The turmoil in Portsmouth must have had a profound impact on the thirty-seven year-old minister. His family had been threatened, riots had broken out, the symbol of his country desecrated, and it may have felt as if the Almighty had abandoned the country. Watkinson and his family took refuge in Ridley, the small Pennsylvania community where he had first become a minister, and his wife's hometown. From this safe place he wrote to the Portsmouth church on May 10, formally resigning his position. The congregation responded by expelling him for misconduct in leaving his church. In Ridley, people welcomed back their former pastor and gave him the position of "supply minister" at $5 per week pay.[519]

By July he was in the vicinity of the Battle of Manassas, Virginia, (a.k.a. "First Bull Run") near the 27th Pennsylvania Volunteers, performing religious duties for the troops.[520] Within a few months Rev. Watkinson, troubled by the Civil War, wrote his heartfelt letter to secretary Chase.

In leaving Portsmouth, Watkinson acted for the safety of his family, but he was not alone in his concern. Those who remained in the area were still divided in their loyalties, although the majority supported the Southern cause. His many friends and acquaintances remained, and Watkinson evidently maintained contact with them through the early months of the war.

After Union forces captured Norfolk on May 10, 1862, Watkinson appears to have begun active lobbying to return to Court Street Baptist Church. He traveled to the area on August 9, 1863, probably to meet with local church members and discuss his possible return as minister. Concluding a two-week stay Rev. Watkinson wrote a detailed letter to President Lincoln:[521]

> Hon. A. Lincoln
> President of the United States
>
> Having just returned from a fortnight's visit to Norfolk and Portsmouth, Virginia;[522] in the possession of valuable news of the Rebel plans derived from men I know to be trustworthy from a protracted acquaintance, allow me to give you in detail what I have learned. Most of this information I gave to a Naval Captain before leaving Portsmouth upon the promise that it should reach you. If that Officer's report has come this will corroborate it.

---

[519] A "supply minister" was usually a seminary student supplied to a church on a temporary basis when the pastor was on leave or unable to fulfill his duties. In this instance it seems to have been a means to help support their former pastor during difficult times.

[520] The 27th Pennsylvania Volunteers were held at Centerville, Fairfax County, Virginia and did not enter into the main battle. They were caught up in the disorganized retreat (panicked flight) of Union troops and civilians back to Washington.

[521] *Abraham Lincoln Papers*, Library of Congress, Manuscript Division, Washington, DC: American Memory Project, 2000–03. http://memory.LoC.gov/ammem/alhtml/alhome.html, accessed February 2, 2003. Transcribed and annotated by the Lincoln Studies Center, Knox College, Galesburg, Illinois. Letter dated August 25, 1863 to Abraham Lincoln from Mark R. Watkinson.

[522] This may have been during Watkinson's attempt to regain the minister's position at Court Street Baptist Church.

**First.** As to Rebel resources.

Gen. Lee is trying to secure 150,000 men. His retreat from Pennsylvania left him about 60,000 reliable troops. They are near him in Culpepper, or were week before last. He has little or no force at Richmond, or Petersburg.--

That he is put to close quarters for men is known from letters to families in Portsmouth stating that the "signal corps" would perhaps have to be abolished and the men go into the ranks, -- their cavalry performing the duties of the "signal corps." I have several most intimate friends of yore in that signal corps.

Of materiel. There is abundance, no lack of food, clothing, etc--

**Second.** Their plans.

All machinery, manufacturing, Stores, etc., are removed to Fayetteville, and Charlotte, two towns in Southern North Carolina, as you will see by reference to the map. Their purpose is to retire gradually from the seaboard, burning everything behind them. They are carrying their slaves thitherward also.

To corroborate this, let me say, all the workmen from Norfolk and Portsmouth are now at those towns at work. They formerly were in Richmond, Virginia, mainly.

**Third.** Of Union feeling in North Carolina.

My information on that subject is that it is all "bosh". Only a few in the tidewater regions think yet of a return to the Federal Government,

**Fourth.** Of approaches to Richmond, Virginia.

By the James River not at all now-- For, that stream is filled with well-made torpedoes from City Point to Richmond, Then for eight (8) miles adjoining the river, below Richmond, are high hills that are regularly excavated, and case mated, with iron facings around the case mates at an angle of forty-five degrees.

Just now if Gen. Meade can hold Gen. Lee engaged in Culpepper, Gen. Hooker with some 20,000 or 30,000 men, by a *coup de main* from the head of York River might slip in and hold it; or else regular siege approaches from that point must be resorted to.

**Fifth.** Of war vessels.

Merrimac No. 2 is all ready for a raid to Norfolk and its surroundings, if the James River be not well guarded. This vessel draws only eight (8) feet of water was built at Gosport Navy Yard, and with many other vessels ran the blockade to Richmond the night before Norfolk was evacuated. She is more formidable than Merrimac No. 1 [*a.k.a.: Virginia*], except in speed, She can make but 3 miles an hour, These vessels carried a vast quantity of materiel away from the Navy Yard at that time.

**Wilmington N. C.**

I hope Gen. Foster[523] has taken, though well defended. The Alabama River is a depot for iron clads also.

It is believed in Norfolk that a vigorous fall campaign in Virginia leading to Gen. Lee's abandonment of it wholly, or in part, would lead to the reconstruction of the Old State Government, although the secessionists are thoroughly bitter at the Northern people. President Davis[524] may be a prisoner indeed in Richmond from the facts I have here given you, and because I took pains to spread it South that he had funds invested in Paris for his private behoof; and that I believed he would run the blockade thither; and might do it in six months. If I go to Portsmouth to

---

[523] Maj. Gen. John G. Foster, commanding the Department of Virginia and North Carolina.
[524] Jefferson Davis, president of the Confederate Sates of America.

188

preach for the Union men, who have desired me so to do, I may have occasion to send you letters from that point. If so, I shall sign them No. 1, 2, 3, 4, &c--[525]

**One other fact, and I close.**

You have heard a rumor of a difference of opinion between Gen. Lee and President Davis respecting the execution of Captains Sawyer and Flynn.[526] The exact truth is that two weeks ago, in Culpepper, Gen. Lee made a speech to his army in which he said, "Gentlemen, you may have heard it rumored that there was a difference [of] opinion between President Davis and myself. It is not true. We are a unit in all purposes and plans. Captains Sawyer and Flynn will be executed. I anticipate my son and Gen. Winder will be executed in retaliation.[527] But if they are, gentlemen, I never take another prisoner."

Thus the case stands.-- Our troops ought to be three to their one so malignantly will they fight.

M. R. Watkinson
Ridley, P.A.

The letter suggests a keen observer with numerous reliable contacts, and may represent only a small part of the information available to him on just one short trip to Norfolk and Portsmouth. The general tone and familiarity of this letter hint not only a commonality of cause, but previous contact between the President and Rev. Watkinson. He writes with full conviction of his cause, and expectation that his words will be read and appreciated.

According to Court Street Baptist Church records, "An effort was made to recall [Watkinson] as Court Street Baptist pastor while federal troops held our city in September, in 1863, while Brother Dobbs was pastor, but the vote was only three for him and sixty-seven against him." The sentence in Watkinson's letter to Lincoln, "If I go to Portsmouth to preach for the Union men, who have desired me so to do, I may have occasion to send you letters from that point," when read in concert with the church record, is a clear indication that Watkinson hoped to get the church appointment. If successful he planned to collect military intelligence for the Union.[528]

*Figure 42. Rev. Mark R. Watkinson (ca. 1863).* (Courtesy Baptist Encyclopedia.)

The man who signed himself simply "Minister of the Gospel" was able to travel freely to Norfolk, Portsmouth, and possibly Richmond – the political and military heart of

[525] Watkinson was rejected for the minister's post at Court Street Baptist Church on September 25, 1863, and may not have had further opportunity to collect information.

[526]Captains W. H. Sawyer and John M. Flinn had been selected by lot from among the officers confined at Libby Prison, and were sentenced to die in retaliation for the execution of Captains T. G. McGraw and William F. Corbin, who were executed by Union authorities for spying in Kentucky.

[527] Lee's son, Brig. Gen. W. H. F. "Rooney" Lee, had been captured in a federal raid on June 26, 1863 while recuperating at his wife's family home from wounds received at Brandy Station. While being held at the hospital at Ft. Monroe, he was allowed some liberty of movement on his promise not to escape. On July 15, however, he was ordered held in close confinement and threatened with execution should the Confederacy put Sawyer and Flinn to death. General Lee did not personally intervene in his son's behalf, but the Union threat worked and Sawyer and Flinn were not killed. Rooney Lee was held until March 1864. It had been mistakenly reported that a "Capt. Winder" was held hostage along with W. H. F. Lee. The second officer, in actuality, was Capt. R. H. Tyler of the 8th Virginia Infantry.

[528] He was offered the position again on August 11, 1867, but declined.

the Confederacy. He was trusted locally, and well connected in important parts of Southern society. In this capacity he kept his eyes and ears open for information that could help the Union cause. In effect, Watkinson aspired to be a part-time Union spy who might have been known to secretary Chase and possibly President Lincoln: ample reason for attention to be paid to Watkinson's earlier ideas.[529]

Through 1861 to 1863, many pattern coins were prepared utilizing current designs, and completely new compositions. Multiple permutations of the GOD OUR TRUST motto were tried and examined. Mint director Pollock, having already recommended the new motto in his 1862 mint report, repeated the appeal in his next annual report dated October 21, 1863:[530]

> I would respectfully and earnestly ask the attention of the [Treasury] Department to the proposition in my former report, to introduce a motto upon our coins expressive of a National reliance on Divine protection, and a distinct and unequivocal National recognition of the Divine Sovereignty. We claim to be a Christian Nation – why should we not vindicate our character by honoring the God of Nations in the exercise of our political Sovereignty as a Nation?
>
> Our national coinage should do this. Its legends and devices should declare our trust in God – in Him who is the "King of Kings and Lord of Lords." The motto suggested, "God our Trust," is taken from our National Hymn, the "Star-Spangled Banner." The sentiment is familiar to every citizen of our country – it has thrilled the hearts and fallen in song from the lips of millions of American Freemen. The time for the introduction of this or a similar motto, is propitious and appropriate. 'Tis an hour of National peril and danger – an hour when man's strength is weakness – when our strength and our nation's strength and salvation, must be in the God of Battles and of Nations. Let us reverently acknowledge His sovereignty, and let our coinage declare our trust in God.

In December 1863, more designs were submitted to the secretary of the treasury, who replied to the director on December 9, 1863, noting:[531]

> ...I approve of your mottoes, only suggesting that on that with the Washington obverse the motto should begin with the word, "Our," so as to read, "Our God and Our Country," and on that with the shield obverse it should be changed so as to read, "In God We Trust," or how would it do to substitute for the shield motto "God Is Our Shield?"

---

[529] Sources: histories of Prospect Hill Baptist Church, Ridley, PA; Court Street Baptist Church, 447 Court Street, Portsmouth, VA; First Baptist Church of Richmond, Twelfth and Broad Streets, Richmond, VA.

[530] Report of the Director of the Mint for the fiscal year ending June 30, 1963. Document dated October 21, 1863.

[531] *US Mint*, NARA-P, op. cit., entry 214, vol.3. Letter dated December 9, 1863 to Pollock from Chase. Balance of letter refers to two cent and three cent pieces.

190

*Figure 43. Sample mottoes on pattern two cent coins, 1863. The composition incorporating the shield was adopted in 1864 for the new denomination, but the motto was changed to IN GOD WE TRUST.*

With patriotism running high, there was considerable interest in both Union and Confederate areas in George Washington. Citizens collected many varieties of tokens, advertising cards and other ephemera, some of which featured Washington's portrait. The official seal of the Confederate States featured General Washington on horseback. The mint's patterns featuring a bust of Washington may have intended to connect with this sentiment. However, there was considerable precedent against using Washington's portrait on a coin, including his own objections.

*Figure 44. Two-cent bronze coin of 1864. This was the first circulating U. S. coin to include the motto IN GOD WE TRUST.*

Therefore the shield design with IN GOD WE TRUST engraved on a ribbon over the shield was the version of the motto selected by director Pollock for use on a new circulating coin. By its use, this became the *de facto* national religious motto. On April 22, 1864 Congress approved an amendment to the Coinage Act of 1857[532] that read in part:

> Be it enacted by the Senate and House of Representatives of the United States of America in Congress assembled, That, from and after the passage of this act, the standard weight of the cent coined at the mint of the United States shall be forty-eight grains, or one tenth of one ounce troy; and said cent shall be composed of ninety-five per centum of copper and the remaining of tin and zinc, in such proportions as shall be determined by the director of the mint; and there shall be from time to time struck and coined at the mint a two-cent piece of the same composition, the standard weight of which shall be ninety-six grains, or one fifth of one ounce troy, with no greater deviation than four grains to each piece of said cent

[532] *An Act in Amendment of an Act entitled, "An Act Relating to Foreign Coins and the Coinage of Cents at the Mint of the United States," approved February twenty-one, eighteen hundred and fifty-seven.*

and two-cent coins; and the shape, mottoes, and devices of said coins shall be fixed by the director of the mint, with the approval of the Secretary of the Treasury; and the laws now in force relating to the coinage of cents and providing for the purchase of material and prescribing the appropriate duties of the officers of the mint and the Secretary of the Treasury be, and the same are hereby, extended to the coinage provided for.

The legislation thus approved the small bronze cent and the new two cent coin, and authorized the director of the mint, with approval from the secretary of the treasury, to place whatever mottoes he felt appropriate on the two coins. Notice that the law did not extend to other denominations.

The new 1864 two cent pieces were the first to display the motto IN GOD WE TRUST on a circulating coin when nearly 20 million were produced. Legislation to enable more extensive use of the motto was approved in a bill, *An Act to authorize the Coinage of Three-Cent pieces, and for other Purposes*, passed by Congress on March 3, 1865. Section five of the act stated:

> ...And be it further enacted, That, in addition to the devices and legends upon the gold, silver, and other coins of the United States, it shall be lawful for the director of the mint, with the approval of the Secretary of the Treasury, to cause the motto "In God We Trust" to be placed upon such coins hereafter to be issued as shall admit of such legend thereon.

In authorizing specific text for the two cent coin motto, Congress followed accepted practice and used the wording on the two cent coin. The director and secretary now had authority to place the specific motto on any of the coins, provided there was sufficient room for the wording. The law did not require use of the motto, but the mint was quick to apply it to as many denominations as possible.

IN GOD WE TRUST appeared on the two cent coin from 1864 to 1873, and five nickel coins from 1866 to 1883, but was omitted from both Liberty and Indian nickel designs. On silver, the motto appeared only on the quarter, half dollar and dollar. The gold $5, $10, and $20 coins included the motto until 1908, when it was also added to the quarter eagle. It was omitted from the eagle and double eagle of Saint-Gaudens' design dated 1907, and part of the 1908 double eagles issued before May 19, 1908. It was added to the new Lincoln cent in 1909, to the Winged Liberty dime in 1916, and reintroduced on the nickel in 1938 along with Thomas Jefferson's portrait.

Rev. Mark Watkinson remained in Ridley until 1864. He then went to Second Baptist Church in Camden, New Jersey (1864–1871). On August 11, 1867, with the Civil War over and reconstruction beginning, Watkinson was again elected pastor of Court Street Baptist Church. This time, he declined the invitation. His last church was High Street Baptist Church in Baltimore, Maryland (1871–1873). He remained in Baltimore, his health rapidly declining, until his death on September 26, 1877. He was buried in the cemetery of the First Baptist Church of Pemberton, New Jersey.

It is unlikely that anyone in the treasury department or mint recognized Mark Watkinson's impact on American history. Considering the long delay between his 1861 suggestion and release of the two cent coins in 1864, it is doubtful that even Rev. Watkinson connected the new motto with his letter to secretary Chase.[533]

---

[533] Much of the credit for researching the origin of the motto and Rev. Watkinson's influence goes to Samuel H. Newsome of Middletown, PA, who was president of the Delaware County Historical Society; Harmed B. Cole, from

The religious motto was not as universally accepted as some might presume. In 1876, A. Loudoun Snowden whose family had been connected with the Philadelphia Mint for many years, commented:[534]

> [In new designs] I would omit "In God We Trust" because it is very cumbersome and doesn't please God much, I don't think – as I think he trusts more for the conversion of the world upon the faith of the people as exemplified in their lives, rather than the devices upon the coinage of the world. Indeed, it is a sign…of the degeneracy of the times, when external manipulation of piety and faith take the place of the simple, unostentatious faith and modest piety of our fathers…However, it might not be well to run contrary to the people of the country…If this message were taken from our coinage, many would conclude that Hell itself was let loose.

Snowden's remarks would be prophetic of what Roosevelt was to face in 1907.

## The Motto in 1908

President Roosevelt had been concerned about the legality of omitting the religious motto as early as April 1907, when his secretary wrote to director Roberts requesting information. Roberts replied on March 1, and included the revelation that the motto had been removed as a coinage requirement by the Revised Statutes Act of June 22, 1874:[535]

> I am sending you a copy of the report of the Director of the Mint for 1896 in which you will find on page 106 a history of the motto "In God We Trust." To this I may add some additional information, a part of which has never been published but has come to me from a reliable authority.
> The coinage acts of 1865 and 1873 as recited in the sketch I have forwarded gave authority for placing the motto on the coin. When the Revised Statutes, adopted June 22, 1874, were prepared, Secretary Boutwell referred the preparation of those relating to coinage and paper money to John Jay Knox, Comptroller of the Currency, and Dr. William [sic – Henry] R. Linderman, Director of the Mint, who eliminated the clause relative to "In God We Trust" from the statute. Their action was approved by Secretary Boutwell and adopted by Congress.
> The Revised Statutes as they appear today do not contain the authority to use the motto. However, when it became necessary to prepare a design for the new

---

Pennsville, NJ, a member of the Delaware County Coin Club; and William C. Boston from Ridley Park, PA, who was a local numismatist. The three corroborated statements made in the 1896 Mint Director's Report by collecting church and community records from the Delaware County Pennsylvania area. They coordinated the evidence and presented their findings to the public in the early 1960s. (Source: Arden Skidmore, "County Minister Fought for Motto." [Delaware County] *Daily Times*, December 26, 1964. pp.4A–5A.) Others who assisted with the project were Elsie M. Jones, Mrs. William J. Moffett, John W. Brown, and Mrs. Harry Bond, who was the last remaining direct descendant of Mark and Sarah Watkinson. In 1962 a large commemorative plaque was presented to the Prospect Hill Baptist Church by the Delaware County Coin Club in recognition of Rev. Watkinson.

The present author has confirmed the earlier material and added information from Court Street Baptist Church in Portsmouth, VA, the Baptist Historical Society, the Baptist Encyclopedia of 1881 and 1883, and the Library of Congress. Until the present research, Rev. Watkinson's letter to President Lincoln was unknown in numismatic circles.

Special appreciation goes to Mr. William Smith of Portsmouth, VA, who generously provided copies of Court Street Baptist Church histories, and located important documents owned by Portsmouth families.

[534] *US Mint*, NARA-CP, op. cit., entry 240, "Special file of H. R. Linderman." Letter dated May 23, 1876 to director Henry R. Linderman from A. Loudoun Snowden.

[535] *US Mint*, NARA-CP, op. cit., entry 235, vol. 367. Letter dated March 1, 1907 to William Loeb from Roberts. The arguments, however, are not entirely convincing. Linderman's correspondence repeatedly suggests removing the motto E PLURIBUS UNUM from the coinage. He felt this duplicated the sentiment expressed in the legend UNITED STATES. Additionally, President Hayes did not see the silver dollar patterns until December, 1877. George Morgan's design had included IN GOD WE TRUST since its inception nearly a year earlier as a proposed half dollar design.

silver dollar authorized by the Act of 1878, President Hayes insisted that the motto should go on and it has been put on everything since except the one-cent, five-cent, dime and quarter eagle. The objection made by Messrs. Knox and Linderman was that the additional lettering overcrowded the coin and marred the effect.

The authority upon which President Hayes acted is not clear but the Solicitor of the Treasury holds that the administrative branch of the government has exercised this authority so long with the acquiescence of Congress that its right to do so now can scarcely be questioned.

I am sending you the marked paragraph in the act of 1873 and marked paragraph in the Revised Statutes of 1874. There has been no later legislation.

In the midst of trying to get eagles out the mint door and into commerce, as well as strike the high relief double eagles, word began to circulate that the newly released $10 gold pieces did not have the customary motto In God We Trust on them. Newspaper writers, sensing possible embarrassment for the Roosevelt administration, prepared appropriate copy such as this article printed by New York Times on November 7: [536]

### New Eagles Lack Motto
*"In God We Trust" Does Not Appear on Saint-Gaudens Coins*

Trouble is ahead for Uncle Sam. He has failed to put upon the new ten-dollar gold coin the motto "In God We Trust."

The mint at Philadelphia has been busy the last few days turning out the beautiful yellow pieces with a new eagle on one side and an Indian head with a larger and more gorgeous pompadour on the other than has heretofore appeared on any American coin, the two designs being the work of the late Augustus Saint-Gaudens.

Within the last few days since the coins began to arrive at the Treasury Department about 5,000 of them have been sent out to different parts of the country and they are being eagerly sought everywhere.

But with all the artistic designs the new coin does not contain the motto which from the beginning has been engraved upon every coin of the Republic of a denomination larger than a dime.

The Director of the Mint, Mr. Leach, is hourly expecting protests from all over the country as soon as the church organizations have a chance to meet and formulate resolutions.

A lone comment scribbled on a postcard dated November 9 remains of those which came to the mint:[537]

Dear Sir:
The one who is responsible for omitting the motto from the new coins will have to hunt for a new job, or I am much mistaken.
W. A. Brearley

Mr. Brearley's comment was seconded by postcards and letters to the President, treasury secretary, and members of Congress about the motto. President Roosevelt dictated a form letter that was sent to several clergymen and others who had written. The letter explained his personal feeling that use of the motto on coins "…is in effect irreverence which

[536] *New York Times*, "New Eagles Lack Motto," November 7, 1907, p.8.
[537] *US Mint*, NARA-P, op. cit. Postcard dated November 7, 1907 to Superintendent of the U. S. Mint from W. A. Brearley. There is no return address on the card.

comes dangerously close to sacrilege." His reply to the Reverend Roland C. Dryer of Nunda, New York is typical:[538]

> Dear Sir:
> When the question of the new coinage came up we lookt into the law and found there was no warrant therein for putting "In God We Trust" on the coins. As the custom, altho without legal warrant, had grown up, however, I might have felt at liberty to keep the inscription had I approved of its being on the coinage. But as I did not approve of it, I did not direct that it should again be put on. Of course the matter of the law is absolutely in the hands of Congress, and any direction of Congress in the matter will be immediately obeyed. At present, as I have said, there is no warrant in law for the inscription.
> My own feeling in the matter is due to my very firm conviction that to put such a motto on coins, or to use it in any kindred manner, not only does no good but does positive harm, and is in effect irreverence which come dangerously close to sacrilege. A beautiful and solemn sentence such as the one in question should be treated and uttered only with that fine reverence which necessarily implies a certain exaltation of spirit. Any use which tends to cheapen is, and, above all, any use which tends to secure its being treated in a spirit of levity, is from every standpoint profoundly regretted. It is a motto which it is indeed well to have inscribed on our great national monuments, in our temples of justice, in our legislative halls, and in buildings such as those at West Point and Annapolis – in short, wherever it will tend to arouse and inspire a lofty emotion in those who look thereon. But it seems to me eminently unwise to cheapen such a motto by use on coins, just as it would be to cheapen it by use on postage stamps, or in advertisements. As regards its use on the coinage we have actual experience by which to go. In all my life I have never heard any human being speak reverently of this motto on the coins or show any sign of its having appealed to any high emotion in him. But I have literally hundreds of times heard it used as an occasion of, and incitement to, the sneering ridicule which it is above all things undesirable that so beautiful and exalted a phrase should excite. For example, thruout the long contest, extending over several decades, on the free coinage question, the existence of this motto on the coins was a constant source of jest and ridicule; and this was unavoidable. Everyone must remember the innumerable cartoons and articles based on phrases like "In God we trust for the other eight cents"; "In God we trust for the short weight"; "In God we trust for the thirty-seven cents we do not pay"; and so forth and so forth. Surely I am well within bounds when I say that a use of the phrase which invites constant levity of this type is most undesirable. If Congress alters the law and directs me to replace on the coins the sentence in question the direction will be immediately put into effect; but I very earnestly trust that the religious sentiment of the country, the spirit of reverence in the country, will prevent any such action being taken.
> Sincerely yours,

The same letter was sent to at least eight people on November 11.[539] Roosevelt's relations with Congress, particularly the Senate, were less than ideal, and many of the "old

[538] *Roosevelt Letters*, Harvard, op. cit. Letter dated November 11, 1907 to Roland C. Dryer from Roosevelt. The original of this letter was sold by Heritage Auctions in November 2005.
[539] *Roosevelt*, LoC, op. cit. Microfilm reel 347. Multiple letters dated November 11, 1908 to: Rev. Roland C. Dryer, Nunda, NY (pp.200–202); William H. Stanton, Scranton, PA (pp.203–205); Rev. J. W. Dunn, San Francisco, CA (pp.206–208); F. W. Edwards, Bayone, NJ (pp.209–211); Rev. A. M. Blakely, Pittsburg, PA (pp.212–214); Thomas Hensinall, Kansas City, KA (pp.215–217); Very Rev. A. P. Doyle, Washington, DC (pp.218–220); and John B. Walsh, Richmond, VA (pp.221–223), from Roosevelt. A check for letters sent to the President during the week before November 11 does not show any correspondence from the above-named men. However, the microfilm records (reel 78) do not include all correspondence sent to the White House, especially if it was originally sent to members of Congress.

guard" in his party were pleased to find a ready-made issue, guaranteed to diminish Teddy's popularity, handed them by the President. After reprinting Roosevelt's letter on November 13, a *New York Times* writer described the scene at an Episcopal Diocesan convention. After proposing a resolution to restore the motto and arguing about how long the motto had been used on coins, the members got down to debate: [540]

> Dr. Grosvenor said the proposal to take the motto from the coins aroused his deep indignation, and Dr. Gustav Carstensen of Riverdale, opposing the motion, said, "I think this effort is a mistake and misleading in the inference that we go as a nation back into apostasy. Our godliness is not shown on this, but in the way we keep our treaties. Let us avoid stultification."
>
> Dr Batten admitted that the spirit of the resolution was good. "But there are other things that are more timely for discussion and argument in our national and municipal life." The Rev. Leighton Parks declared that the passing of the resolutions would look like a rebuke to the government.
>
> "It is," shouted half a dozen of the delegates. "That's how we mean it."
>
> Other delegates urged caution before plunging into matters not within the church's province. However, "Dr. Grosvenor, red in the face, wanted to know whether there was anything more sacred than the name of God. Finally, pointing to the reporters' table, he said: " If we don't vote on this thing today, we will have the newspapers to reckon with."

A vote was eventually taken and the motions passed 131 to 81.

Newspapers also took a less serious view of the new coins. The same *New York Times* that had railed against the design, used the missing motto as the subject of its weekly "Limerick Contest." Readers were asked to provide the last line of a limerick. Nearly one hundred people submitted their creative best with the first place award of $10 (in gold?) going to T. C. O'Callaghan. Second and third place prizes of $5 each were also awarded:[541]

> The old yellow coins, it is true,
> Were handsomer far, than the new,
> Yet none has demurred,
> So far as we've heard,
> *Though Godless and Trustless, they'll do.*

When planning his composition for the cent and double eagle, Saint-Gaudens relied on his ideas for design simplification. He wanted to use only the minimum number of inscriptions necessary, and leave large open spaces to give the central figures greater force. According to his son Homer Saint-Gaudens in *The Reminiscences of Augustus Saint-Gaudens,* the sculptor considered "…the motto 'In God We Trust' as an inartistic intrusion not required by law, he wholly discarded [it] and thereby drew down upon himself the lightning of public comment." But since Augustus was dead, public ire fell on the President.[542]

Letters of complaint continued to arrive at treasury department offices. Charles D. Linskill from the *Wilkes-Barre Semi-Weekly Record* send a copy of his paper's editorial

---

[540] *New York Times*, "Denounce Motto Order," November 14, 1907, p.1.

[541] *New York Times*, "Best Efforts of Experts in Both Serious and Light Veins Called Forth by Last Week's Contests," December 1, 1907, Sunday Magazine, p.10.

[542] Not all letters received by the White House and treasury favored restoration of the motto; approximately twenty percent of surviving examples supported removal. There were also inquiries about which coins the motto had appeared on, if there were going to be sets of silver coins without the motto, and suggestions for alternative mottoes.

favoring use of the motto and tossing in references to the ten commandments, assorted scripture and Japan.[543] Jonah C. Reiff enclosed a newspaper clipping with his letter to director Leach. He closed by stating, "After all is said our people are deeply religious sentimental, the removal of the motto has greatly stirred public sentiment."[544] A petition with one hundred fifteen signatories from the *Baptist Young People's Union* arrived at the office of Representative Edwin Darby from Michigan in February 1908.[545]

Anticipating the motto would soon be required director Leach suspended all work on the half and quarter eagle until this, and the wording of the coin denominations, was settled.[546] He also moved ahead by having Barber make drawings and preliminary dies showing the position of the motto. By February 20 Leach reported:[547]

> I saw the President day before yesterday in relation to the position of the motto "in God We Trust" on the new designs. He was very much pleased with the place selected by Mr. Barber saying it was excellent. I will return the double eagle with the other coins to be melted up.
> Has Mr. Barber any suggestions for the motto on the Eagle yet?

Landis replied in a personal note:[548]

> Yours of yesterday came duly to hand. I am much pleased to know that the President is so well satisfied with the position of the motto "In God We Trust" on the new designs.
> Mr. Barber recommends the position on the ten dollar coin immediately in front of the eagle. I enclose an impression made by Mr. B. You'll see that this proposed arrangement will balance with the other motto "E Pluribus Unum." This, it seems to me, would conform to the artistic tastes of critics generally.

Evidently, Barber had struck a pattern piece for the director to show the President. By February 26, Landis could report that "...the first trial piece of the double eagle containing the inscription 'In God We Trust'....has been destroyed this day by the assistant coiner and in the presence of the assayer, the engraver and myself."[549] Samples stamped onto small pieces of thick paperboard were ready by February 27, and approved as a group by the President.[550]

Patterns of the half eagle using reduced versions of Saint-Gaudens' double eagle design had been struck by April 3, 1908 and approved, but working dies had not been made. Director Leach discussed the motto and designs with the President and Dr. William Sturgis Bigelow at lunch on April 3, and with legislation mandating the motto not yet passed, permission was given for Bigelow to work with Leach on his technical coinage ideas. By the time the motto bill passed, Roosevelt's imagination had been captured by Bela Pratt's Indian head design and the Saint-Gaudens half eagle was scrapped.

[543] *US Mint*, NARA-CP, op. cit., entry 229, box 261. Letter dated January 21, 1908 to Leach from Linskill.
[544] *US Mint*, NARA-CP, op. cit., entry 229, box 261. Letter dated January 23, 1908 to Leach from Reiff.
[545] *US Mint*, NARA-CP, op. cit., entry 229, box 262. Letter dated February 11, 1908 to Hon. Edwin Darby member of Congress from J. Manley Card, president of the Baptist Young People's Union of Detroit, Michigan.
[546] *US Mint*, NARA-P, op. cit. Letter dated January 18, 1908 to Landis from Leach.
[547] *US Mint*, NARA-CP, op. cit., entry 330, box 45. Letter dated February 20, 1908 to Landis from Leach.
[548] *US Mint*, NARA-CP, op. cit., entry 229, box 261. Letter (manuscript) dated February 21, 1908 to Leach from Landis.
[549] *US Mint*, NARA-CP, op. cit., entry 229, box 262. Letter dated February 26, 1908 to Landis from Leach.
[550] *US Mint*, NARA-P, op. cit. Letter dated February 27, 1908 to Landis from Leach.

Several similar bills were submitted to Congress with H.R. 17296 being the one finally selected for consideration by the House Committee on Coinage, Weights, and Measures. The Committee's report reads in part:

> Your subcommittee deems it unnecessary to recount in detail the history of the legislation which required the stamping of this significant motto on certain denominations of gold and silver coinage of the United States, except to say that by the act of January 1837 mottoes and devices for our coins were prescribed, and that in April 1864, in March 1865, and in February 1873, laws were enacted by Congress providing substantially that the words "In God We Trust" might be inscribed upon such coins of the United States as would admit of such inscription, and that in pursuance of such authority the Hon. Salmon P. Chase, the then Secretary of the Treasury of the United States, directed that the inscription "In God We Trust" be stamped on gold and silver coins of certain denominations. Numerous petitions have been referred to your subcommittee from various sources throughout the United States asking Congress to restore this motto on the coinage as has been done since the passage of the acts above referred to, and until the omission of the same from certain gold coins of the United States known as "The St. Gaudens." These petitions all ask for the restoration of the inscription as it existed before the issuance of the gold coins referred to. Your subcommittee has, therefore, confined itself to a compliance with these recommendations.
>
> Your subcommittee is unanimous in the belief that as a Christian nation we should restore this motto to the coinage of the United States upon which it was formerly inscribed "as an outward and visible form of the inward and spiritual grace," which should possess and inspire American citizenship, and as an evidence to all the nations of the world that the best and only reliance for the perpetuation of the republican institution is upon a Christian patriotism, which, recognizing the universal fatherhood of God, appeals to the universal brotherhood of man as the source of the authority and power of all just government...

It became clear to Roosevelt that public opinion was on the side of Congress. He spoke with Senator Thomas Carter, Republican from Montana, about the bill and the report of the committee:

> The Congressman says the House Committee wants to pass a bill restoring the motto to the coin. I tell him it is not necessary; it is rot; but the Congressman says there is a misapprehension as to the religious purport of it – it is so easy to stir up a sensation and misconstrue the President's motive – and that the Committee is agitated as to the effect of a veto. I repeat, it is rot, pure rot; but I am telling the Congressman if Congress wants to pass a bill reestablishing the motto, I shall not veto it. You may as well know it in the Senate also.

The bill was passed by the House on March 8, 1908, and by the Senate on May 13, 1908, becoming Public Law No. 120:

> An Act Providing for the restoration of the motto, "In God We Trust" on certain denominations of the gold and silver coins of the United States. Be it enacted by the Senate and House of Representatives of the United States of America in Congress assembled, That the motto "In God We Trust," heretofore inscribed on certain denominations of the gold and silver coins of the United States of America, shall hereafter be inscribed upon all such gold and silver coins of said denominations as heretofore. Sec. 2. That this Act shall take effect thirty days after its approval by the President.

President Roosevelt approved the legislation May 18, 1908 and the mint made plans to implement the will of Congress. The law decreed the motto was to be replaced on any gold and silver coins on which it had previously appeared. Since it had not been used on the dime or quarter eagle, it did not have to be added to those coins. Circumstances, however, resulted in the motto being included on the Indian head quarter eagle in 1908 and the dime in 1916. Likewise, it had not been used previously on the cent, but was introduced on the new Lincoln cent (1909) at director Leach's insistence. Shield nickels, which imitated the two cent design, were issued from 1865 to 1883, and included the motto. However, Charles Barber's Liberty design from 1883 to 1912 and Fraser's Buffalo design both omitted the motto with little public objection. It was later added to Felix Schlage's Jefferson nickel in 1938.

With the motto now required on gold coins, director Leach ordered samples of the eagle and double eagle struck on May 23:[551]

> Please have struck two double eagles from the dies with the motto, and one eagle from the dies with the motto, and also in addition please give me impressions of both sides of each denomination on cards, the same as furnished me for approval of the position of the motto. I will get these coins and cards upon my visit to your institution next week. (Tuesday)

The motto legislation became effective on June 17, 1908, thirty days after approval, and director Leach ordered IN GOD WE TRUST to appear on both of the Saint-Gaudens design coins. Later in the year, the motto would also be used on the half eagle and, for the first time, on the quarter eagle.

---

[551] *US Mint*, NARA-P, op. cit. Letter dated May 23, 1908 to Landis from Leach. William Sturgis Bigelow donated a "satin proof" of the 1908 with motto type to the Boston Museum of Fine Art of June 11, 1908 (accession number BMFA 08.300). The coin may have been one of the two patterns struck in May. The museum later disposed of this and other coins by public auction.

# Chapter 7 – Experiments and Designs

The story of Saint-Gaudens' $10 and $20 gold pieces is punctuated by the presence of several experimental or pattern coin designs of exceptional beauty. These coins attest to the artistic potential that lay within the sculptor's conception of American coinage, and to individualistic ideals of President Theodore Roosevelt. Acting alone, it is unlikely that either man would have developed the synthesis of elements the best of experimental coins reveal. In their time, these were truly experiments: of art and mechanics, of patience and exuberance, of beauty and conceit. Through over a year of making reductions, hubs and dies of Saint-Gaudens' designs, the mint consistently referred to struck sample coins as "experimental" and never as "patterns." This, they were both in composition and production, experiments.

On July 25, 1907 director Roberts sent the following letter to superintendent Landis at the Philadelphia Mint. It clearly states the President's wishes:[552]

> …The regulation requiring all experimental pieces to be destroyed will be formally waived as the President desires to have a number of these pieces struck.

President Roosevelt encouraged the sale of experimental coins to collectors. Many of his letters refer to the desirability of allowing collectors to obtain specimens of the experimental coins, and of his plan (actually secretary Cortelyou's idea) to sell them *after* the regular issues were placed in circulation. Roosevelt considered Saint-Gaudens' designs art of the most American kind, and he had little interest in hoarding art. So far as the President could command, he wanted this new art to be in the hands of the citizens – or at least to pass through the hands of bankers. A letter written to secretary Cortelyou in late July 1907 recognizes the interest of coin collectors and the secretary's ideas:[553]

---

[552] *US Mint*, NARA-P, op. cit. Letter dated July 25, 1907 to Landis from Roberts. A transcription of this letter in NARA-CP, Entry 330, box 45 incorrectly dates the letter "June 25."
[553] *Roosevelt*, LoC, op. cit., vol. 74, p.144, microfilm reel 346. Letter (personal) dated July 29, 1907 to Cortelyou from Roosevelt.

...How would it do to have a few thousand coins struck with the smooth finish, and then the rest struck with the sharply cut details of the old design?...

...As for the high relief coins, have several hundred struck and allow the collectors of the country to obtain specimens, as you suggested....

Roosevelt's overall goal was to remake the entire coinage from cent to double eagle. That was not to happen during his lifetime, but the inspiration outlasted four presidential administrations over 14 years. It would not be until 1913, when the Buffalo nickel appeared, that the common man – the man of Theodore Roosevelt's "square deal" – could regularly appreciate the best of America's new coinage art. Another three years would pass before the subsidiary silver abandoned the nineteenth century and enfolded designs rivaling Saint-Gaudens' Striding Liberty.

## Small–Diameter Double Eagles

Director Leach's most concerted efforts were made to recover and destroy the small-diameter experimental double eagles. These coins were made to determine if it was practical to mint high relief coins twice as thick as normal double eagles but of reduced diameter. A smaller–diameter planchet would allow lower striking pressures and possibly permit the high relief design to be used for circulating coins. At the time it was not realized that coin diameter was fixed by law and that small–diameter double eagles were illegal if released to commerce.[554] In response to a request from the director for replacement of two defective double eagles and $20 in currency ($60 total), Albert Norris sent him two eagles from the second model, a high relief double eagle, and a small–diameter double eagle.[555] When Leach received the coins on January 10, he expressed surprise at receiving the small-diameter coin and said, "...I...will keep it, at least until the interest in the new coinage is satisfied."[556]

The same day he received a letter from curator of the mint collection Thomas L. Comparette concerning placing one of the small-diameter coins in the collection:[557]

Among the numerous dies made from the Saint-Gaudens designs for the Double Eagle was one having the diameter of the Eagle, a very thick piece. There are several of them yet in existence and I beg leave to request that you give authority to place a specimen in the Cabinet of the Mint.

My reasons for this request are purely practical. While it is an entirely illegal "coin" and for that reason should not I believe be put into a collection of historical coins, yet it was produced by the government and for that reason the few speci-

---

[554] Mint cabinet curator T. L. Comparette in a letter to Leach mentioned the supposed illegality of the small-diameter experimental coins on January 8, 1908. Small–sized double eagles, or ones of any size except that specified by law, would have been illegal if placed in circulation. However, as experimental or pattern pieces, they were entirely consistent with many preceding variations of diameter, weight, alloy or shape accepted as being legal to own although not conforming to specification for circulating currency. The small-diameter $20 were thus legal for the mint to make and for collectors to possess. There is also some doubt about any pattern or experimental piece being legal tender. They are not formally approved and authorized as circulating coinage, and might logically be classified as scrap metal. The issue is not altogether clear. In December 1877, patterns of the new standard silver dollar were exchanged for face value in currency, yet in 1880 Goloid pattern sets were sold to members of Congress at their bullion value. At other times, pattern pieces were sold at a substantial premium over both face and bullion value.

[555] *US Mint*, NARA-P, op. cit. Letter dated January 4, 1908 to Landis from Leach. Annotation on bottom of letter initialed "AAN" for Adam A. Norris.

[556] *US Mint*, NARA-P, op. cit. Letter dated January 10, 1908 to Norris from Leach.

[557] *US Mint*, NARA-CP, op. cit., entry 229, box 260. Letter dated January 8, 1908 to Leach from Comparette.

mens will in after years command enormous prices, easily $3,000 each. Dealers are now offering large prices for them. Now it is very likely that in a few years to come the administration of the Mint and Cabinet will fall into hands that take a different view of its purpose than the one now held and in that case the purchase of one of these rare specimens at two or three thousand dollars is almost sure to follow.

To prevent such a possible waste of funds in the future is the reason for making this request. An even exchange of but $20 will render that impossible.

Very respectfully,

After receiving Comparette's letter, the director ordered "…you will have placed in the numismatic collection at your institution two each of the trial pieces from the different models made by Saint-Gaudens…and if you have any left, two of the pieces of the double eagle struck on the reduced diameter, or 'thick' pieces."[558]

Nothing more appears in documents about the thick double eagles until the treasury received letters from two museums demanding small-diameter $20 coins for their collections. Both pointedly told the director they were illegal and should be housed in museums. The letter from the Pennsylvania Academy of the Fine Arts in Philadelphia states:[559]

Hon. Geo. B. Cortelyou,
Secretary of the Treasury
Sir:

The Pennsylvania Academy of the Fine Arts makes application to you to be allowed to purchase one of the original model Double Eagle, as it came from the hand of the late Saint-Gaudens, and also a specimen of the Double Eagle produced from the same model, but having the diameter of the $10 gold piece.

There are about one dozen specimens, as I understand, still on hand from this original model, and the Pennsylvania Academy of the Fine Arts, which is the oldest art institution in America, believes that it ought to be made the custodian of one of these pieces.

The die variety which is desired, is as follows:

1. The first impression of the $20 gold piece or regular size made from the die that preceded the first, after the 11,000 were struck and distributed.
2. A specimen of those produced from the same model but having the diameter of the $10. Gold piece, yet with $20 worth of gold in them, the piece being very thick.

In making this application to you, The Pennsylvania Academy of the Fine Arts calls your attention to the fact that a specimen of each of these varieties has been given to the New York Numismatic Society, thus establishing a precedent, and that The Pennsylvania Academy of the Fine Arts, which is located in Philadelphia, is reasonably entitled to the same consideration. Besides, variety No. 2 is really an illegal coin, and ought not, therefore, get into private possession at all, but should go to art museums, and this last work of Saint-Gaudens is most fittingly placed in museums because it really belongs to the public at large.

Trusting that my application, in behalf of the Academy, may meet with your favorable consideration, I remain, your obedient servant,

Most respectfully,
John Frederick Lewis,
President

---

[558] *US Mint*, NARA-P, op. cit. Letter dated January 9, 1908 to Landis from Leach.
[559] *US Mint*, NARA-P, op. cit. Letters dated January 25 and 28, 1908 to Cortelyou from The Art Institute of Chicago and The Pennsylvania Academy of Fine Arts, respectively. Leach wrote to Landis on the 30th asking for an explanation.

Both letters contained detail that only someone in contact with officials at the Philadelphia Mint would know, and the director's interest turned to concern.[560] He sent copies of the letters to John Landis on January 30 along with a cover letter:[561]

> Your attention is called to the within letters making declaration of the existence of certain trial pieces of the Saint-Gaudens design of the double eagles. I wish you would return these letters with a statement whether or not any such trial pieces have been furnished or supplied to any museum, Art institute or collection, and whether you have any on hand or not.

Landis replied the next day:[562]

> I beg to return herewith the letters received by the Secretary of the Treasury… In reply I beg to say that Mr. Lewis is mistaken with reference to the coins furnished the New York Numismatic Society. None of the first pieces, that is of the extreme high relief, were furnished to any museum, art institute or collection, nor were any of the double-eagles of the smaller diameter allowed to go out except those sent to the Bureau, of which you have a list. We have on hand eight of the latter coins, two of which are to be placed in our Cabinet, the remainder to be destroyed in your presence when you again visit this institution. We have none of the double-eagles of the extreme high relief on hand.

The list of Mint Bureau officials having the small-diameter coins has not been located. After reading the letter, Leach was not satisfied with the explanations, and he wrote a questioning letter to Landis:[563]

> I note in your letter of the 31st ultimo that you say you have not melted up or destroyed the small or illegal sized double eagles, but that you have eight of these pieces still on hand. It is my wish that you do not wait for my presence but that you will destroy them immediately in the presence of the melter and refiner and the assayer, or representatives of those officers, and render me a statement to that effect. I note that you say you have only eight of these pieces, two of which are to be placed in the cabinet. In the memorandum you left with me you say that five of these pieces were sent to the Bureau, two placed in the mint cabinet, and eight were in your hands for mint officials. If any of these coins have been given to mint officials they must be returned, and I shall make an effort to secure the return of the five sent to this Bureau. My purpose in calling your attention to the number stated in the memorandum you left with me is that you might reconcile that statement with the number of these pieces given in your letter of the 31st ultimo. Of course, I desire to have two pieces placed in the cabinet, as you were originally instructed.
> Respectfully,
>
> *[manuscript margin comment]*
>
> "15 in all"

After investigating further Landis replied to Leach on February 3 giving a more complete accounting of the small-diameter coins:[564]

---

[560] The likely informant was Louis Comparette, who was the only mint official known to be in frequent contact with museums and coin collectors. He also seemed to be the sole determinant that the coins were illegal.

[561] *US Mint*, NARA-P, op. cit. Letter dated January 30, 1908 to Landis from Leach.

[562] *US Mint*, NARA-CP, op. cit., entry 229, box 261. Letter dated January 31, 1908 to Leach from Landis.

[563] *US Mint*, NARA-P, op. cit. Letter dated February 1, 1908 to Landis from Leach.

[564] *US Mint*, NARA-CP, op. cit., entry 229, box 261. Letter dated February 3, 1908 to Leach from Landis.

In reply to your letter of February 1<sup>st</sup>, in reference to the small double eagles, I beg to say that I have this day placed in the Cabinet two of these coins, in accordance with your instructions; eight have been defaced in the presence of the Assayer, the Engraver, the Melter and Refiner, the Assistant Coiner, and myself. One still remains in the hands of Mr. Barber, the Engraver, who states that he will return it when the other pieces are received from you for destruction. In my communication of the 31<sup>st</sup> ultimo when I stated there were eight of these coins on hand, there were two remaining in the hands of mint officials, not including the one still in the hands of Mr. Barber.

Referring further to the letters received by the Honorable Secretary of the Treasury from the President of the Pennsylvania Academy of Fine Arts, and the Director of the Art Institute of Chicago, I beg to say that I have been informed today by Mr. Comparette, our curator, that he is positive that the New York Numismatic Society has one of these small double eagles. I, of course, have no knowledge as to how they obtained this coin, but feel very certain it was not gotten from this mint.

Landis' accounting now includes: two in the mint collection, eight destroyed, one held by Barber, two held by mint officials, and one held by NY Numismatic Society for a total of fourteen pieces. Leach again found the account lacking and it only seemed to increase confusion. The director wrote back the next day:[565]

Yours of the 3<sup>rd</sup> instant, in relation to the small or thick double eagle trial pieces, received. Your statement does not seem to account for the piece I gave you to be returned, and further, I would like to know by whose authority Mr. Barber and the two mint officials hold the pieces to which you refer. I would like to have you give me the dates and the names of the persons to whom the five pieces mentioned in your statement were sent to here in the Bureau. I have written to Mr. Roberts to obtain from him the names of the persons to whom he gave these pieces, for every one must be accounted for.

Respectfully,

Reconciling the two statements, the total of small-diameter pieces was fifteen – two more than Landis originally mentioned. The art institute letters evidently prompted secretary Cortelyou to ask Leach for a full accounting of the experimental coins. The director's response, noted earlier, included Leach's best numbers as of February 5. He apparently reported only the pieces mentioned by Landis since the accounting states thirteen and not fifteen small-diameter pieces were struck.

To clear up any confusion, Landis wrote a letter on February 6 explaining the disposition of the small-diameter coins:[566]

In reply to your letter of the 4<sup>th</sup> instant, in reference to the disposition of the small diameter double eagles, I beg to say that I did not intend to convey the impression that there were still two of these coins in the hands of mint officials beside the one held by Mr. Barber. The two I referred to had been returned prior to the destruction of the eight pieces on February 3<sup>rd</sup>, and were included in the eight as was also the one returned by you.

We are reasonably sure that there were but fifteen of these small double eagles struck and they were disposed of as follows:

[565] *US Mint*, NARA-P, op. cit. Letter dated February 4, 1908 to Landis from Leach.
[566] *US Mint*, NARA-CP, op. cit., entry 229, box 261. Letter dated February 6, 1908 to Leach from Landis.

| | |
|---|---|
| The Bureau – Mr. Preston and Mr. Roberts | 4 |
| Placed in the Cabinet February 3rd | 2 |
| Destroyed February 3rd | 8 |
| Still in Mr. Barber's possession | 1 |
| *Total* | 15 |

I am unable to give you the dates that Mr. Roberts and Mr. Preston received these coins, as they were obtained by them when they visited the Mint. Mr. Barber states that he is merely holding the coin for reference and will turn it in when the others are received for destruction.

I enclose herewith a copy of a letter received from Mr. Roberts in reference to experimental pieces.

*[manuscript notation in margin signed "Frank A. Leach"]*

The coin referred to as having been given to Mr. Preston was returned to the Director some time ago.

Frank Leach also contacted former director Roberts, now working in Chicago, and Marguerite Kelly in the Washington office to learn what they knew about the coins. He wrote back to Landis on February 8:[567]

Mr. Roberts memory of the receipt of the trial pieces of the St. Gaudens design does not confirm your memorandum of the number sent to the Bureau. I wish you would look up and get the fullest details of the numbers sent here of both of the 1st Model double eagles and the "thick" piece and have that information for me when I visit your Mint this week.

I am especially desirous of locating all of the thick pieces. Your memorandum gives five as coming to the Bureau, which includes the one I returned to you personally, and I have two in my possession now, which reduces the number charged to the Bureau to two, both Mr. R. and Miss Kelly say that two of the thick ones are all they had from you, and one of these was returned to you in July last, the other I have.

This information may assist you in helping me locate the two pieces which seem to be unaccounted for if you are correct in the numbers struck and sent the Bureau.

If Comparette is correct about one of these pieces being in a collection in N. Y., that would account for one and we wish to know how it got there.

It is evident that no complete record was kept by the Philadelphia Mint or the Mint Bureau in Washington of the production and distribution of experimental coins. Two weeks after sending the secretary his final accounting, Leach was still trying to explain all of the small-diameter coins. He wrote to Landis on the 19th:[568]

Have you been able to learn anything further in relation to the report that one of the thick pieces was in the New York Association Collection? Mr. Mitchelson says so.

Congressman Ashbrook showed me a little case he says he obtained at the mint to put his $10 piece in. I suppose they could be had for double eagles as well. What is the price per case?

[567] *US Mint*, NARA-CP, op. cit., entry 235, vol.368. Letter dated February 10, 1908 to Landis from Leach.
[568] *US Mint*, NARA-CP, op. cit., entry 330, box 45. Letter dated February 19, 1908 to Landis from Leach. "Mitchelson" was J. C. Mitchelson, president of Connecticut Tobacco Corporation and a friend of agriculture secretary James Wilson. He had been introduced to secretary Cortelyou for the purpose of attempting to buy some of the pattern coins, and was also a member of the New York Numismatic Society.

As soon as Dr. Norris gets back I want you to give me the statement asked for in my letter of the 10th as to the number of Double Eagles struck from No. 1 model. The Secretary spoke to me again to-day about my report.

To a large extent, Leach may have been relying on comments from curator Louis Comparette, who was a friend of Joseph Mitchelson and Tom Elder, both of whom were members of the New York Numismatic Society,[569] which supposedly held one of the small-diameter double eagles. Landis responded by stating he thought the whole thing could be cleared up when Albert Norris returned:[570]

Referring to the small diameter double eagles I would say that I am informed by Mr. Comparette, our Curator, that he has heard from the numismatic Society of New York and they deny having one of these small pieces. Mr. Comparette says "they have all the rest," meaning, I presume, that the Society has one of the extreme high relief coins. When Dr. Norris returns I think the matter can be entirely cleared up.

Comparette provided his written comments on February 25:[571]

I beg leave to communicate the substance of a letter from Mr. Thomas L. Elder, New York, to the effect that the American Numismatic and Antiquarian Society (commonly known as the New York Numismatic Society) "…has specimens of all the dies of the new twenty except the ten-size." Those, I think, are his exact words. I did not preserve the letter after my verbal report the day following its receipt, as it was a purely personal letter and in other respects trivial.
Mr. Elder is a prominent member of that society and chairman of a committee to promote the new-design-project for our coins.

With the mint's curator on record as stating the New York Numismatic Society did not have a small-diameter double eagle, the director moved to destroy remaining examples of the coin. On March 2 Leach sent two of the small-diameter coins to the mint ordering their destruction,[572] and asked Landis to send him one high relief double eagle and two eagles from the #2 models. Evidently Leach had been forced to buy the coins back from someone (Roberts?) who had paid the mint (or someone working for the Mint Bureau) face value for them.[573] Landis sent a statement signed by himself, the assayer and the engraver stating that the two pieces had been destroyed on March 3. This left only the piece held by Barber as unaccounted for, and a week later the final "free" small-diameter double eagle was destroyed:[574]

I beg to inform you that Mr. Barber, Dr. Norris, Mr. Clark and myself today witnessed the destruction of the small diameter double eagle which had been in the

[569] In December 1907, New York dealer Tom Elder was a founder of the New York Numismatic Club, which met regularly at Keen's Old English Chop House at 36th Street and Sixth Avenue. The first regular meeting of the club was held at Keen's the following January, with the roster of attendees including William H. Woodin, Wayte Raymond, Victor D. Brenner, Joseph Mitchelson, Elliot Smith, Albert R. Frey, Frank Higgins, Edgar H. Adams, D. Macon Webster, George H. Blake and Bauman L. Belden. Nearly all of these names would become well known in the hobby, and some already had that status. (Source: Howard L. Adelson, *The American Numismatic Society 1858-1958*, photograph opposite p.157 which identifies several individuals who attended.)
[570] *US Mint*, NARA-CP, op. cit., entry 229, box 262. Letter dated February 20, 1908 to Leach from Landis.
[571] *US Mint*, NARA-P, op. cit. Letter dated February 25, 1908 to Landis from Comparette.
[572] These may have been the two coins returned by Roberts.
[573] *US Mint*, NARA-P, op. cit. Letter dated March 2, 1908 to Landis from Leach
[574] *US Mint*, NARA-CP, op. cit., entry 229, box 263. Letter dated March 18, 1908 to Leach from Landis.

possession of Mr. Barber. This, to the best of my knowledge, was the only remaining piece of the kind, excepting the two in the mint cabinet.

With the last of the experimental small-diameter pieces made between February 10 and 14, 1907 accounted for, the saga of these unusual coins came to an end.

While hunting down the "illegal" double eagle pieces, Leach had to struggle with the revelation that the new $20 coins were 0.012-inch too large in diameter and thinner than the preceding Liberty head issues. Congress was preparing to change the new coins by adding the religious motto, and morale at the Philadelphia Mint was at a low point:[575]

> ...I fully appreciate the very many difficulties attending such a radical change in the coinage operations as we have had to meet, and the only way to reach satisfactory results is for all hands to enter into the work with a harmonious spirit – each to do his part to the best of his ability.
>
> You have accomplished a great deal, and I think the worst is passed, but there are many more difficulties ahead of us to be overcome, and I trust the officers of the Philadelphia Mint will meet the issues in the proper spirit, dropping any petty differences as trifling and a source of interference to obtaining results.

The director also had to contend with requests from collectors for examples of the high relief double eagles and other experimental coins, if the collector happened to know about them. This was a huge burden on the mint staff in Washington and Philadelphia, creating bookkeeping and postal delivery headaches for employees not accustomed to the extra demands. (The normal sale of proof coins was handled by the Philadelphia Mint's cashier's office, which also managed walk-up sales of the new gold coins.) The director's office was also busy filling orders from administration officials and requesting additional specimens for the director's account. We don't know to whom Leach sold the coins he requested and it was certainly not illegal to do so. The experience probably led him to decide to prevent the problem from happening again in 1908–09 by not notifying collectors of their existence and destroying all experimental and trial pieces. In late 1908 he went so far as to refuse to place samples of the new half eagle and quarter eagle patterns in the mint's collection, thus depriving future numismatists of the pleasure of seeing some of the experiments.

## Summary of Eagle and Double Eagle Varieties

Much new information has been uncovered about the 1907 coins. It is appropriate to summarize the known variants of design for both coins, even if this duplicates part of the information presented under each variety.

### *$10 Eagle, Gold*

The gold eagle was not part of Saint-Gaudens' design work until May 1907. Originally, only the double eagle and cent designs were to be prepared. It was assumed the double eagle designs would be used on the smaller denomination gold coins. After Saint-Gaudens indicated his preference for the Liberty head with Indian headdress for the double eagle in late April, President Roosevelt decided to keep the Striding Liberty figure for the double eagle and use the Liberty head on the smaller $10 coin. He also assigned the

---

[575] *US Mint*, NARA-P, op. cit. Letter (excerpt) dated January 29, 1908 to Landis from Leach. This is one of several letters containing references to quality and morale problems at the Philadelphia Mint.

standing eagle to the $10 coin, although Saint-Gaudens had originally presented it as one of two designs for the reverse of the $20 coin. This was part of the President's compromise with Saint-Gaudens. In July 1907 Roberts suggested using the $10 designs on the $5 and $2.50 coin, and this was accomplished in part with Bela Pratt's 1908 adaptation of the Standing Eagle for the small gold denominations.

The table below provides summary descriptions of all known varieties of the new eagle coin design. All varieties are dated 1907 in European characters.

| Obverse | Reverse | Edge | Contemporary Comment | Comment |
|---|---|---|---|---|
| High relief (HR), knife rim (Judd-902) | High relief (HR), periods before & after inscriptions | Plain | One to Cortelyou, one to Saint-Gaudens July 22, 1907. | One known, auctioned 2002 by Heritage. |
| High relief (HR), knife rim (Judd-None) | High relief (HR), periods before & after inscriptions | 46 stars; irregular spacing and size | "The stars on the rim are rather irregular…" | Experimental pieces. All in SI match this description. |
| High relief (HR), knife rim (Judd-1901) | High relief (HR), periods before & after inscriptions | 46 stars; all of same size and equally spaced on edge. | "…strike 500 from the high relief dies…" | 500 struck; transferred to Treasury in Dec. plus 42 extras. |
| Normal relief, wide rim (Judd-None) | Normal relief, periods before & after inscriptions | 46 stars; irregular spacing and size | "…to which Mr. Barber has added a border…" | Experimental pieces. All in SI match this description. |
| Normal relief, wide rim (Judd-1903) | Normal relief, periods before & after inscriptions | 46 stars; all of same size and equally spaced on edge. | See Preston's order. | 31,500 struck on production presses; all except 50 melted. |
| Normal relief, wide rim (Judd-None) | Normal relief, **no** periods before & after inscriptions | 46 stars; all of same size and equally spaced on edge. | "…from the Saint-Gaudens models…" | Experimental pieces made, but cannot be distinguished from circulation strikes. |

## *$20 Double Eagle, Gold*

The gold double eagle was the basis for Saint-Gaudens' design commission. It was assumed the double eagle designs would be used on the smaller denomination gold coins. Originally, the cent was also to be designed. In May, when Saint-Gaudens indicated the his preference for the double eagle was the Liberty head with Indian headdress, as prepared for the cent, President Roosevelt decided to keep the Striding Liberty figure for the double eagle and use the Liberty head on the smaller eagle. The cent was dropped from active consideration; however, this decision by Roosevelt was not conveyed to Saint-Gaudens and Henry Hering. The result was considerable waste of time working on a cent design that would never be used.

The table below provides summary descriptions of all know varieties of the new double eagle coin designs. All varieties are dated 1907 (MCMVII) in Roman numerals except for the #3 and #4 versions, which use European characters.

**#1** – First model; submitted December 1906; first struck February 10–14, 1907; dies cracked. Seen by Saint-Gaudens. **Version #1** was called "model #1" or "first model" or "extreme high relief" by mint and Treasury officials. This is the version called "Extremely

High Relief (EHR)" in this book and some others call "Ultra High Relief (UHR)". This was an experimental medal-coin; the models had "Test Model" written on the back.

**#A** – Hybrid of cent obverse (Liberty with Indian headdress) and flying eagle reverse from #2 with date added across sun; Saint-Gaudens saw a lead impression; rejected by President for $20, but Roosevelt now decided to put on the $10.

**#2** – Slightly improved version of first design; relief barely changed (very high relief); submitted March 14, 1907; first struck April 21; eight experimental pieces made; dies collapsed; convinced Roosevelt relief was too high; all eight seen by Saint-Gaudens and Hering. Examples of this variety are unknown.

**#2B** – Same as #2 but relief mechanically lowered by about twenty percent; first struck May 15 or 16, 1907; last version seen by Saint-Gaudens. **Version #2B** was called the "second model" and later "high relief" by the mint. This was used to strike the regular issue high relief coins in September and November–January. In this book, it is called #2 model to be consistent with mint terminology. Patterns likely prepared, but cannot, at present, be distinguished from normal pieces.

**#3** – Medium relief version with European date (by Hering); submitted September 27, 1907; sample shown to Augusta Saint-Gaudens November 1907; rejected because could not be fully struck with one blow of press. **Version #3** was called the "final model" by the mint. A few lead and gold samples were struck but all appear to have been destroyed. This was supposed to have been ready in June 1907, but Hering spent his time on the eagle (which had just been added by Roosevelt in late May), and the cent (because nobody told him Roosevelt and Roberts had scrapped the cent in May).

**#4** – Low relief November–December 5, 1907; Created by mechanically reducing the relief and recutting detail in #3 hubs. Augusta Saint-Gaudens disliked it; Roosevelt approved it; Barber discovered diameter was too large; put in circulation. **Version #4** was recut from #3 hubs by Barber on Leach's orders. Barber had offered to make a low relief version in August, but the offer was rejected.

| Obverse | Reverse | Edge | Contemporary Comment | Comment |
|---|---|---|---|---|
| Extremely High Relief (EHR) | Extremely High Relief (EHR) | Sans serif font, E*P*L*U*R* etc. A-I | Director receives first two samples. | First group. |
| Extremely High Relief (EHR) (Judd-1908) | Extremely High Relief (EHR) | Plain | "dies broken" | Cracked reverse die. Would have been last of first group made. |
| Extremely High Relief (EHR) (Judd-1907) | Extremely High Relief (EHR) | E*PLURIBUS*UNUM****** B-II | "may strike two for the Mint Cabinet" | Second group. |
| Extremely High Relief (EHR) (Judd-None) | Extremely High Relief (EHR) | E*PLURIBUS*UNUM****** B-I | Requested Dec. 23, "I would like three…" | Third group. |
| High Relief (HR) | High Relief (HR) | E*PLURIBUS*UNUM******. | 20% reduction in relief. | Manual, or mechanical segmented collar. |

| Obverse | Reverse | Edge | Contemporary Comment | Comment |
|---------|---------|------|----------------------|---------|
| Low Relief | Low Relief | E*PLURIBUS*UNUM******. | | Normal lettering – toggle collar. |
| Low Relief | Low Relief | E*PLURIBUS*UNUM****** | | Normal letters spread at base – cone collar. |

## Designs for the Bronze Cent

Saint-Gaudens' original commission included a design for the bronze cent. At the time he and secretary Shaw agreed to terms, in July 1905, the $10 gold eagle was to carry the same design as the double eagle. It was not until May 1907, after Saint-Gaudens had tried to convince Roosevelt that the Liberty with headdress composition would be better on the $20 piece than the Striding Liberty, that the President directed the mint to abandon the cent and use the obverse design on the $10 coin.

The change was abrupt but typical of Roosevelt's. In this instance he seemed to be balancing his own preferences with those of the artist. Roosevelt preferred the Striding Liberty-Flying Eagle composition he already had seen as gold patterns in two slightly different versions. The artist seems to have changed his mind and now wanted to reconsider his Liberty (Indian) portrait-Flying Eagle. This ambivalence by Saint-Gaudens led to creation of the unique Liberty head (Indian)-Flying Eagle pattern in March 1907. Roosevelt complied with the artist's wishes for the pattern coin, but the request may also have increased his concern about the very slow pace of finalizing designs and producing coins. Soon after seeing the coin-sized lead pattern, Saint-Gaudens began pushing for a change in the double eagle design. By May 11, Roosevelt was prepared to give the artist a personal hearing on the final designs, but continued ill health prevented the sculptor from leaving Aspet. The ineffective Henry Hering was sent instead and seems to have created only more confusion. By May 23 Saint-Gaudens had changed his mind again and now wanted to return to the standing eagle reverse paired with the Striding Liberty obverse.

On May 25, the President decided to put an end to the vacillation. In an attempt to satisfy both himself and the artist, he followed a suggestion from director Roberts and ordered "…that the designs for the Double Eagle shall be the full figure of Liberty and the flying eagle, and the design for the Eagle shall be the feather head of liberty with the standing eagle…. It is now settled…."[576] This compromise gave Saint-Gaudens a second, large gold coin for his designs, and simultaneously eliminated the one cent piece from further consideration.

Thus, until late May 1907 there was no $10 coin design.

None of the one cent models were used to create reductions, hubs or dies (except as later used on the pattern double eagle and eagle) and no experimental coins or electrotypes are known.

---

[576] *US Mint*, NARA-CP, op. cit., entry 330, box 45. Letter dated May 25, 1907 to Saint-Gaudens from Roberts.

210

**Obverse 1**

This is the flying eagle cent obverse as inspired by Christian Gobrecht's 1836 design for the standard silver dollar and 1857 one cent piece. The date, denomination and other legends were relegated to the reverse by Saint-Gaudens.

**Description** Eagle flying left and slightly upward. Below, the rising sun with rays; above the word LIBERTY.

**Patterns** None.

(Courtesy U. S. Department of Interior National Park Service, Saint-Gaudens National Historic Site, Cornish, NH. #1098.)

This design was discarded as the one cent obverse when Saint-Gaudens was advised that use of the eagle was illegal on the bronze cent.

**Obverse 2**

**Description** Portrait bust of Liberty facing left, wearing a crown of olive. Surrounding are 13 six-pointed stars, below is the word LIBERTY.

Copied from the artist's NIKE ERINI portrait bust, which was originally the head of VICTORY on the *Sherman Monument* in New York. The model was Hettie Anderson. There is noticeably less detail in the Liberty model than in the NIKE version.

**Patterns** None.

(Courtesy U. S. Department of Interior National Park Service, Saint-Gaudens National Historic Site, Cornish, NH. #1134, #1136.)

**Obverse 3**

Same source model as #2, above, but now a direct copy but with less detail than the original.

**Description** Portrait bust of Liberty facing left, wearing an American Indian ceremonial feather headdress. Above are 13 six-pointed stars, below is the word LIBERTY.

**Patterns** None.

(Courtesy U. S. Department of Interior National Park Service, Saint-Gaudens National Historic Site, Cornish, NH. #1138.)

**Obverse 4**

From cent model #3.

This is the same profile as the third model, but adds the Indian headdress requested by President Roosevelt. Used in conjunction with the flying eagle reverse to produce a pattern double eagle at Saint-Gaudens' request. The President preferred the Striding Liberty figure for the $20 coin. This design was then used for the eagle by placing the word "Liberty" on the headband and inserting the date below the bust.

**Description** Portrait bust of Liberty facing left, wearing an American Indian ceremonial feather headdress. Above are 13 six-pointed stars, below is the word LIBERTY.

**Patterns** None for a one cent piece. Used on the obverse of the $20 pattern (P-1998; Judd-1905) requested by Saint-Gaudens on March 12, 1907 and ordered by President Roosevelt on the14th. The coin was produced in April.

(Courtesy U. S. Department of Interior National Park Service, Saint-Gaudens National Historic Site, Cornish, NH. #1107.)

212

**Reverse
1**

One of many one cent versions tried by Saint-Gaudens. This design could have been used for either obverse or reverse.

**Description**  The word Liberty surrounded by an olive wreath and thirteen stars. The wreath overlaps portions of most of the stars. The olive stems are entwined around a bundle of arrows.

**Patterns**  None.

(Courtesy U. S. Department of Interior National Park Service, Saint-Gaudens National Historic Site, Cornish, NH. #1139.)

**Reverse
2**

This appears to be one of the final two reverse designs prepared by Saint-Gaudens for the bronze cent. The plaster model lacks a rim, as required for normal coinage.

**Description**  The words ONE CENT surrounded by an olive wreath whose stems are entwined around a bundle of arrows. Encircling the wreath is the legend UNITED STATES OF AMERICA AND below the arrows is the date 1907.

**Patterns**  None.

(Courtesy U. S. Department of Interior National Park Service, Saint-Gaudens National Historic Site, Cornish, NH. #1140.)

**Reverse
3**

This version is identified as the final reverse design prepared by Saint-Gaudens for the bronze cent. The plaster model has a rim, as required for normal coinage.

**Description**   The words ONE CENT centered; above is UNITED STATES and below is OF AMERICA, both in smaller letters than the denomination. An olive wreath whose stems are entwined around a bundle of arrows encircles the central inscriptions; below the arrows is the date 1907.

**Patterns**   None.

(Courtesy U. S. Department of Interior National Park Service, Saint-Gaudens National Historic Site, Cornish, NH. #1153.)

## Designs for the Gold Eagle

Design varieties illustrated in the following tables are all derivatives of the same basic composition. Differences in relief, border and placement of details distinguish one from the other. Normally, these would be subvarieties of one obverse, or reverse; however, to avoid a confusion of subscripts, the varieties are labeled 1, 2, 3, etc., for the obverses, and A, B, C, etc., for the reverses. Where necessary, subscripts are used to designate subvarieties of the same basic design and relief. These are presented in the order in which they were created, which may not necessarily match the sequence for production of the patterns. Only those designs actually converted into usable models or from which patterns were made are included. Descriptions are used to supplement the photos accompanying each design (and also the patterns, below).

Note that there are designs for three sides of the coin: obverse, reverse and edge (edge collar).

### *Obverse Designs*

**Obverse 0**

From cent model #4.

This is the same profile as the first model, but adds the Indian headdress requested by President Roosevelt. Used in conjunction with the flying eagle reverse to produce a pattern double eagle at Saint-Gaudens' request. The President preferred the Striding Liberty figure for the $20 coin. This design was then used for the eagle by placing the word LIBERTY on the headband and inserting the date below the bust.

**Description**    Portrait bust of Liberty facing left, wearing an American Indian ceremonial feather headdress. Above are 13 six-pointed stars, below is the word LIBERTY.

**Patterns**    P-1998 (Judd-1905). Used on the obverse of a $20 pattern requested by Saint-Gaudens on March 12, 1907 and ordered by President Roosevelt on the 14th. The coin was produced in April.

(Courtesy U. S. Department of Interior National Park Service, Saint-Gaudens National Historic Site, Cornish, NH. #1107)

**Obverse 1**

From cent model #4.

This design was then proposed for the eagle by replacing the word LIBERTY with the date MCMVII in Roman numerals below the bust. Rejected by Roberts on June 11, who required that the date be in European digits.

**Description**   Portrait bust of Liberty facing left, wearing an American Indian ceremonial feather headdress. Above are 13 six-pointed stars, below is the date MCMVII.

**Patterns**   None. Existed only as a plaster model.

(Courtesy U. S. Department of Interior National Park Service, Saint-Gaudens National Historic Site, Cornish, NH. #1107 as base image, date added.)

**Obverse 2**

Referred to as the #1 model.

The first minted $10 gold coin obverse configuration as prepared in June 1907. The field curves directly to the rim, giving the coin a sharp "knife" rim. (This should not be confused with a "fin," which is a minting defect.)

**Description**   Portrait bust of Liberty facing left, wearing an American Indian ceremonial feather headdress. On the headband is the word LIBERTY. Above are 13 six- pointed stars, below is the date 1907 in European digits. Field curves directly to the rim without a border.

**Patterns**   J-1901, J-1902, plus unlisted pattern.

(Photo courtesy Smithsonian Institution, National Numismatic Collection, Douglas Mudd.)

**Obverse**
**2ₐ**

Referred to as the #2 model.

Same as the first model; however, engraver Charles Barber added a border to the hubs before the #2 coins were struck in mid-September 1907.

A small number were struck as experimental pieces on a medal press.

Later in September, 31,500 were struck on ordinary presses at the order of acting director Preston. All except 50 pieces were later melted.

At least 38 were reported sold.

**Description**  Portrait bust of Liberty facing left, wearing an American Indian ceremonial feather headdress. On the head band is the word LIBERTY. Above are 13 six- pointed stars, below is the date in European characters. Field curves to a raised border as added to the hub by Barber.

**Patterns**  J-1903, plus unlisted pattern.

(Photo courtesy Smithsonian Institution, National Numismatic Collection, Douglas Mudd.)

**Obverse**
**3**

From model #3. The final model submitted by Hering and Homer Saint-Gaudens. Completed after the sculptor's death. Lower relief than model #1 and incorporates a border similar to the one Barber added to Model #2. Approved for use on the regular issue of 1907.

Appearance is similar to the #2 coins but stars, feathers, inscription and date are sharper.

**Description**  Portrait bust of Liberty facing left, wearing an American Indian ceremonial feather headdress. On the head band is the word LIBERTY. Above are 13 six- pointed stars, below is the date in European characters. Field curves to a raised border as added to the model by Hering. Similar in appearance to the #2 version, above.

**Patterns**  Pattern pieces struck on a medal press. Quantity and whereabouts unknown.

## *Reverse Designs*

**Reverse A**

From model #1. This was first used in making reductions and lead trial pieces for the reverse of the $20. The models lacked a defined border so the design results in a knife rim at the edge of each side of the coin.

**Description** — Bald eagle standing, facing left, holding bundle of arrows and olive branch in its talons. Above, the inscription: · UNITED · STATES · OF · AMERICA · ; below, the inscription ·TEN · DOLLARS· Above the bird's back is the inscription · E· PLURIBUS · UNUM · in three lines. Text stops (periods) before and after inscriptions.

Eagle's neck and legs are disproportionately long, giving the bird an unusual appearance. Feathers are softly rendered and entire design lacks detail although it is somewhat better than on #2 model (Reverse A₁).

**Patterns** — J-1901, J-1902, plus unlisted pattern.

(Photo courtesy Smithsonian Institution, National Numismatic Collection, Douglas Mudd.)

**Reverse A₁**

From model #1. This is the same reverse as from model #1 but with a border added to the hub by Barber. Note loss of definition in the eagle's feathers when compared with reverse A (model #1), above.

**Description** — Bald eagle standing, facing left, holding bundle of arrows and olive branch in its talons. Above, the inscription: · UNITED · STATES · OF · AMERICA · ; below, the inscription ·TEN · DOLLARS· Above the bird's back is the inscription · E· PLURIBUS · UNUM · in three lines. Text stops (periods) before and after inscriptions.

Eagle's neck and legs are disproportionately long giving the bird an unusual appearance. Feathers are softly rendered and entire design lacks detail.

**Patterns** — J-1903, plus unlisted pattern.

(Photo courtesy Harry W. Bass, Jr. Research Foundation.)

218

**Reverse B**

From model #3. This was used on the eagles coined for circulation. Lettering narrower than on earlier versions, more detail in feathers and olive branch.

**Description**  Similar to previous but with wider rim, and no periods before and after inscriptions. Improved detail to feathers and inscriptions.

**Patterns**  Pattern pieces struck on a medal press. Quantity and whereabouts unknown.

(Photo courtesy Harry W. Bass, Jr. Research Foundation.)

## *Edge Collar Designs*

**Edge 1**

Used on experimental eagles made from the #1 and #2 models.

Some of the coins from model #1 (knife rim) have the stars misaligned with the rim of the coin so they appear to be crooked.

**Description**  Three-part edge collar with 46 stars arranged 15-15-16 per segment.

Stars irregularly spaced and of different sizes near the boundary of one segment.

**Patterns**  Not listed in Pollock or Judd.

(Photo courtesy Smithsonian Institution, National Numismatic Collection, Roger W. Burdette.)

**Edge 2**

Used on all versions of the eagle collectors' coins and regular issue. Combined with all three "Indian" designs.

Varieties may exist but none have been reported.

**Description**  Three-part edge collar with 46 stars; 48 stars after 1912.

Similar to above but all stars the same size and evenly spaced. Star points closest to the rim are often flattened. Pieces truck on a medal press usually show better delineation of stars than circulation strikes.

**Patterns**  Struck but not known.

## Designs for the Gold Double Eagle

Numbering of designs corresponds to the various models completed by the sculptor and likely intended for production, or used by the mint in striking experimental and circulation coins. The list is chronological, except for the Liberty head $20 experimental designs. These are placed at the end of the sequence since they had no impact on production.

### *Obverse Designs*

**Obverse
0**

This design was not used for reductions or hubs.

The relief of the figure is similar to the EHR and VHR designs; however, the wings, lettering and other features have lower relief than any final design. There is no monogram.

The anachronistic headdress give the impression or Liberty's hair in flames. The angel wings, sun's orb, Capitol and other design elements combine to produce a cluttered, confused design. A coin-sized reduction might have been disastrous.

**Description**    A figure of Liberty dressed in flowing robes climbs a rock toward the viewer as if ascending a mountain. The figure has large, angelic wings and is crowned with a small Indian headdress. In her right hand she holds an uplifted torch, emblematic of enlightenment; in her left a branch of olive, indicative of peace. At the base of the rock is a branch of oak, symbolic of military strength and glory. Below and to the figure's right is the United States Capitol building, and beyond, smoothly rippling rays of the rising sun denoting a new era of glorious freedom. Rays are short and do not extend beyond the figure. Near the upper border is the inscription LIBERTY; the date MCMVII [1907] is placed to the figure's lower left above the rock. Surrounding all is an arc of 46 small, six-pointed stars.

Design flows directly to the edge forming a knife rim.

**Patterns**    None.

(Courtesy U. S. Department of Interior National Park Service, Saint-Gaudens National Historic Site, Cornish, NH. #1052.)

This obverse composition was probably completed in May or June 1906 at about the same time as the Standing Eagle reverse. Only the reverse model was sent to Paris for reduction.

**Obverse
1**

This design was used on the #1 model experimental pieces struck between Feb 10 and 14, March–April, and on Dec 31, 1907. The same obverse die was used for all EHR pieces. Also used for the extremely high relief small-diameter $20 pieces.

Simplified version of the winged Liberty. Greatly improved composition, although Liberty's neck is a bit too long.

Completed in early December 1906.

**Description** A figure of Liberty dressed in flowing robes climbs a rock toward the viewer as if ascending a mountain. In her right hand she holds an uplifted torch, emblematic of enlightenment; in her left a branch of olive, indicative of peace. At the base of the rock is a branch of oak, symbolic of military strength and glory. Below and to the figure's right is the United States Capitol building, and beyond, rays of the rising sun denoting a new era of glorious freedom. The rays are long, sharply defined, and extend behind the figure. Near the upper border is the inscription LIBERTY; the date MCMVII [1907] is placed to the figure's lower left above the rock. Surrounding all is an arc of 46 small, six-pointed stars.

Design flows directly to the edge, forming a knife rim.

**Patterns** J-1907, J-1908, J-1909, J-1917.

**Obverse 2**

This design was used on the #2 model Very High Relief (VHR) pieces. Eight were struck using differing numbers of blows from the medal press.

This model was used to produce the high relief hubs by mechanically reducing the relief.

Completed in March 1907.

**Description** Similar to above, except the Capitol building is larger, and berries have been added to the olive branch. Stars are placed differently in relation to the legend and olive branch. Overall, the workmanship is more finished and sharper than on the #1 model.

Design has a well-defined border or rim.

**Patterns** Very high relief patterns struck. None conclusively identified. Known only from the model.

(Photo from Smithsonian Peter A. Juley & Son Collection.)

**Obverse 2A**

This design was used on the #2 model Very High Relief (VHR) patterns. Relief was mechanically lowered to produce high relief hubs.

500 were struck on a medal press in late August–early September 1907. Additional coins were struck from November 23 through January 6, 1908. Coins made after about December 20 have a flat rim and show only a slight fin (or wire rim). Earlier coins often show a pronounced wire rim that detracts from the appearance of the coin.

Coins also show varying degrees of separation between the stars and the border.

12,867 were minted including 500 made in late summer. By May 1908, all but 51 had been distributed and these were transferred to the Treasury Department.

**Description** Similar to Obverse-2. Coins were made from the same VHR models as the now-lost pattern pieces; however, the coins differ form the models due to inaccurate reductions and striking.

Design has a well-defined border or rim.

**Patterns** Pattern and trial pieces likely struck. None conclusively identified.

(Photo courtesy Harry W. Bass, Jr. Research Foundation.)

222

**Obverse
3**

This design was used on the #3 model medium relief experimental piece(s). The model was sculpted by Hering. The European numerals were used by Hering with Saint-Gaudens' reluctant approval in June 1907. Several intermediate versions were reported struck on a medal press before Leach was satisfied with the recutting. One was shown to Henry Hering and Charles O. Brewster. The coin was returned to the mint and it is unknown today.

**Description** Similar to obverse 2; however, date is in European numerals. Lacking in detail of the figure and softness of the stars due to poor hubs cut by the mint.

**Patterns** Patterns struck. Whereabouts unknown.

(Courtesy U. S. Department of Interior National Park Service, Saint-Gaudens National Historic Site, Cornish, NH. #1068.)

**Obverse
4**

This design was used on the #4 low relief coins produced on normal coining presses. It is a recutting of the hubs of Hering's #3 design with European date. The recut hub was completed by Charles Barber in late November/early December under instructions from director Leach.

Collectors should compare sharpness of figure detail with the peripheral stars. Also, compare details of gown (particularly at top of legs), shape of face, and hair with Obverse 3.

**Description** Similar to above but date in European digits. 46 stars until 1912, then 48 stars thereafter.

**Patterns** Patterns struck. Whereabouts unknown.

(Photo courtesy Harry W. Bass, Jr. Research Foundation.)

**Obverse
5**

This was originally intended for the one cent coin, but Saint-Gaudens liked it so much he felt it would look best on the double eagle paired with the flying eagle reverse.

The artist requested a sample of this combination in March 1907 and Roosevelt ordered the samples to be struck. Although the artist preferred this design in combination with the flying eagle, the President liked the Striding Liberty figure. To keep this design in the largest scale possible, it was ordered placed on the $10 eagle, and the one cent version was scrapped.

Other versions will be found in the section on cent and $10 designs.

**Description**  Portrait of Liberty facing left. She wears a Native American ceremonial headdress. Below is the word LIBERTY. Surrounding the upper potion are 13, six-pointed stars. There is a narrow rim.

**Patterns**  J-1905.

(Courtesy U. S. Department of Interior National Park Service, Saint-Gaudens National Historic Site, Cornish, NH. #1107.)

## *Reverse Designs*

**Reverse
X**

This design was adapted from the 1905 presidential inaugural medal designed by Saint-Gaudens and modeled by Adolph Weinman.

A model was shipped to Paris for reduction in June 1906, and the Philadelphia Mint made experimental dies in October of the same year. We do not know why the standing eagle reverse was abandoned for the $20. All of the artist's sketch models are consistent with use of the standing eagle. The change was made sometime in October–November 1906, after the President had seen the standing eagle reverse.

The eagle's neck and legs are too long in proportion to the body and not of the same balance as the 1905 prototype.

Adapted for use on the reverse of the $10 eagle in May–June 1907 by Henry Hering.

**Description**  Eagle standing facing left with talons holding a fasces of arrows entwined with olive. Above the eagle is the inscription: UNITED STATES OF AMERICA, and below TWENTY DOLLARS. Behind and to the right is the motto E PLURIBUS UNUM. Lettering is very close to the edge of the coin with only a slight rim.

**Patterns**  Lead impressions made from U. S. Mint dies. Whereabouts unknown.

(Courtesy U. S. Department of Interior National Park Service, Saint-Gaudens National Historic Site, Cornish, NH. #1092.)

**Reverse A**

This design was adapted from the original flying eagle obverse for the one cent coin. The change was made sometime in October–November 1906, after the President had seen the standing eagle reverse Saint-Gaudens had originally planned to use on the double eagle coin.

We do not know why the standing eagle reverse was abandoned for the $20. All of the artist's sketch models are consistent with use of the standing eagle.

**Description** Eagle flying to the left and slightly upward with talons stretched behind. Below is the rising sun with rays emanating from it. Above the eagle are the inscriptions in two lines: UNITED STATES OF AMERICA and TWENTY DOLLARS. Lettering nearly blends to the edge of the coin with little in the way of a rim.

**Patterns** J-1907, J-1908, J-1909, J-1917.

(Photo courtesy Harry W. Bass, Jr. Research Foundation.)

**Reverse B**

This is the #2 model reverse used to strike Very High Relief (VHR) patterns in April 1907.

With the addition of the date across the sun, this was used on the reverse of the Liberty head $20 pattern.

**Description** Same design as above, but lettering more sharply defined and clear. Rays sharply cut.

**Patterns** Patterns struck. None conclusively identified. Known only from the model.

(Photo from Smithsonian Peter A. Juley & Son collection.)

**Reverse B₁**

This is the #2 model reverse, with reduced relief, used to strike high relief coins in the later half of 1907.

Comparison with the original models indicate the coin is a poor realization of the artist's design.

**Description** Same design as above, but lettering less well defined and often blending into the rim. Overall has a soft, puffy look to features.

**Patterns** None known.

(Photo courtesy Harry W. Bass, Jr. Research Foundation.)

**Reverse B₂**

This is the #2 model reverse, with MCMVII added across the sun.

**Description** Same design as B above. Date in Roman numerals added to sun. Models exist with date raised and incuse.

**Patterns** J-1905.

(Courtesy U. S. Department of Interior National Park Service, Saint-Gaudens National Historic Site, Cornish, NH. #1125.)

226

**Reverse C**

Based on the #3 models by Hering. Hubs were altered by Barber, creating the #4 model.

**Description** Similar to previous versions, but in much lower relief. Sharper modeling and lettering than on high relief coins.

In mid-1908 the motto IN GOD WE TRUST was added in an arc above the sun.

**Patterns** One or two made but now unknown. May be Indistinguishable from circulation coins.

## *Edge Collar Designs*

**Edge 1**

Edge A-I as used only on the 1906 pattern and the first extremely high relief experimental coins of the Saint-Gaudens design, made from the first pair of face dies.

**Description** Collar consisting of three segments. Large, thin sans serif letters with each letter of the motto separated by a star: Characters irregularly cut.

**E\* | P\*L\*U\*R\*I\*B\*U\*S\* | U\*N\*U\*M\***

Letters irregularly spaced and mis-aligned, although not so much as on the small diameter pieces.

**Patterns** 1906 double eagle by Barber/Morgan; Saint-Gaudens EHR MCMVII first group of February 1907.

(Courtesy of Stack's Rare Coins, New York City.)

**Edge 2**

Used on the small-diameter extremely high relief experimental coins of the Saint-Gaudens design struck in February 1907. Similar to A-I but different letter punches used.

**Description** Sans serif font similar to that used on the first batch of EHR patterns. Collar consisting of three segments. Large letters with each letter of the motto separated by a star:

**E\*P\*L\*U\* | R\*I\*B\*U\*S | \*U\*N\*U\*M\***

Letters irregularly spaced and mis-aligned.

**Patterns** Small-diameter experimental $20.

(Photo by David J. Camire courtesy NGC.)

**Edge 3**

**Description** Lettering in serif (Roman) font. Collar consists of three segments. Large letters with each letter of the motto separated by a star:

******E* | PLURIBUS | *UNUM****

Edge B-II as used on extremely high relief experimental coins of the Saint-Gaudens design, except for the first group of February 1907. Edge B-I is the same collar but rotated 180 degrees (i.e.: inserted upside down) in the press.

Slightly smaller sized lettering used on the high relief circulation issues, shown at left. (However, see discussion of edge collars, below.)

Imparted to the circulation coins by using the toggle-type collar mechanism invented by the mint mechanics, or the English-design cone collar.

**Patterns** EHR MCMVII of March-April 1907, and last batch of December 31, 1907.

(Photo by David J. Camire courtesy NGC.)

**Edge 4**

**Description** Lettering in serif (Roman) font. At least two variants noted; serif (Roman) font. Collar consists of three segments. Edge alignment B-II (top image).

******E* | PLURIBUS | *UNUM*****

Used on high relief circulation coins. Variations in edge lettering may relate to high relief coin production batches or to individual collar sets used.

**Patterns** None identified.

(Courtesy American Numismatic Society, top; photo by David J. Camire courtesy NGC, bottom.)

**Edge 5**

**Description** Large lettering extends virtually full thickness of the coin. Serif (Roman) font. Collar consists of three segments. Edge alignment B-I (as shown with obverse up).

****** E* | PLURIBUS | *UNUM*****

Used on at least one low relief circulation coin (a sandblast example) of the Saint-Gaudens design from the #4 models.

May be from the same collar as used on some of the thicker, high relief coins, but reliable measurements not available. Could also be the same as the 1908 large letter edge referred to by director Leach.

**Patterns** Low relief circulation issues. Status of coin as a pattern or experimental piece cannot be determined at present.

(Courtesy of Stack's Rare Coins, New York City.)

**Edge
6**

**Description**  "Toggle collar" consisting of three segments. Mechanically different than the "cone collar," above: (See text for details.)

**\*\*\*\*\*\*E\* | PLURIBUS | \*UNUM\*\*\*\*\***

Bases of letters appear normal although individual specimens vary.

Reported by Breen (*Encyclopedia,* p.575) to be same as used on three satin-finish "proofs."

**Patterns**  Low relief circulation issues

(Photo by David J. Camire courtesy NGC.)

Used on most of the low relief coins of the Saint-Gaudens design from the #4 models. The artist did not provide edge models for the coins.

Made using the toggle-type collar mechanism invented by mint mechanics. May have been similar to the collar used in 1885 to conduct edge lettering experiments.

After refinements were made, the edge lettering made by the two collar types is indistinguishable.

**Edge
6ₐ**

[Similar to above.]

**Description**  "Cone collar" consisting of three segments. Mechanically different than the "toggle collar," below. (See text for details.)

Bases of wide letters, such as "M" may be weak or spread apart due to the collar "rolling" up the edge as the cone impressed the design.

**Patterns**  Low relief circulation issues

Used on some of the low relief coins of the Saint-Gaudens design from the #4 models. The artist did not provide edge models for the coins.

Made using the English or "cone collar" adapted by mint mechanics from a version used at the Royal Mint., London.

After refinements were made, the edge lettering is indistinguishable from the "toggle collar."

Low relief coins for 1907 and possibly 1908 were struck using both types of production edge collar mechanism. Results from the two devices appear to be indistinguishable once the mechanisms were perfected. Differences in appearance of edge lettering on some early specimens may be due to mechanical variance between cone and toggle collars. The B-II edge orientation was normal.

Several trios of collar dies were also used to strike the high relief pieces. Detailed examination of these awaits further research and possibly de-encapsulation of specimens.

The B-I edge was produced when an edge collar set was installed upside down from the intended B-II orientation (the most common), or face dies were installed opposite their normal positions (obverse in the lower, or anvil, position. Each EHR and high relief coin received multiple blows from the medal press using a plain edge collar for all but the final blow. Thus, installation of the lettered edge die was not a one-time occurrence, but had to be repeated for every coin. The opportunity for a pressman to install the edge die incorrectly – creating a B-I edge – occurred for every coin struck. Given human fallibility, it is reasonable to assume that several B-I edge specimens were accidentally produced.

# Chapter 8 – Pattern and Experimental Pieces

There is no record of any experimental or pattern $10 or $20 pieces being struck except during calendar years 1907 and 1908. All extant hubs and master dies of the Saint-Gaudens coins were destroyed on May 24–25, 1910 by order of mint director A. Piatt Andrew.

## Proof and Non-Proof Patterns

As much as collectors and coin retailers love to toss about the word "proof" in connection with rare coins, the truth is that none of the 1907 experimental or pattern coins is documented as having a generally recognized proof surface. Much as we may desire some other result, all except fifty of the eagle and double eagle coins were made from freshly cut dies, were struck on medal presses, and received no special pre- or post-production treatment.[577] The remaining pieces were struck on production presses. Available documents contain occasional requests from collectors for polished "proof" specimens. There are also occasional comments from non-collectors, such as Charles Brewster stating "…thanks for the proof double eagle…," who refer to "proof" as a pre-production sample. The mint did not have time to make special pieces for collectors other than the 12,867 high relief double eagles, and the eagles from various models. The fact that a coin is described in mint docu-

---

[577] Before putting his foot completely in his mouth, the author agrees with critics that it is possible for sandblast proof specimens of any of these coins to exist, only that no convincing example has appeared. Brilliant proofs, if made and seen by Saint-Gaudens, would have elicited howls of objection from the artist – as happened in 1916 with Weinman and MacNeil. Some may argue that the designation "proof" also depends somewhat on the circumstances under which the piece was struck, that is, on the intent of mint officials. By this reasoning, the first EHR $20 of February 1907 would be called "proofs" as would the Indian head $20, because they were specially struck experimental coins. But what do we call the EHR $20s from the second and third groups? They are not inferior to the first in appearance, yet they were made for more or less personal satisfaction of officials and not to test the design, as were the first. Are they less "proofs" due to circumstances of their production? The author leaves this to the judgment of those wise ones on the mountain peaks.

ments as "experimental" or a "pattern" or a "specimen strike" does not make it a proof.[578] These terms were simply words used to describe the circumstances of the coins' production.[579] In the few instances where the term "proof" is used in isolation by mint personnel, it is used in the sense of a "test" as one would make a currency printing proof, not as special-surface collector's coins. Only when referring to specially produced specimens made for sale to coin collectors do mint officials use the term "proof" in the accepted modern sense.

One could argue that the extremely high relief $20 medal-coins, which were annealed between blows of the press, likewise received no post-production treatment or special handling. The claim to calling these "proofs" is that their production matches that of the 1909–1910 satin gold proofs made for collectors. However, the same argument would then have to include all $10 pieces struck from the first models, and all high relief $20. These pieces were all made on medal presses, as were collector's proof coins. Mint documents contain occasional references to finishing a proof coin by sandblasting, and these are the only pieces that would qualify as "matte" proof specimens. Unfortunately, the few experimental pieces mentioned in 1907–08 correspondence as sandblast were also noted as being destroyed.

## Gold Eagle Patterns

The $10 gold coin, or "eagle," was not originally intended to have a unique design. Saint-Gaudens' commission was for a single pair of obverse and reverse designs for the four circulating gold coins, plus a separate design for the bronze cent.

As the two coins' designs evolved during discussions between the artist and President Roosevelt, the obverse of the cent – showing a flying eagle – was submitted as an alternate to the standing eagle for the reverse of the double eagle. After seeing the first large models of the double eagle with striding Liberty obverse and flying eagle reverse, the President accepted this as the $20 coin's design. The flying eagle vanished from the cent when director Roberts advised that the eagle could not appear on the one cent coin and produced a quotation from the coinage laws on February 8 to support his claim:[580]

> Dear Mr. Loeb:
> The [double eagle] dies are about done. I am promised that we may have a test of them next week. I had Mr. Kunz of Tiffany and Company put on the Assay Commission, which meets next week, to get the full benefit of his advise in dealing with then problem of high-relief, and I hope to be able to make a report of progress soon. Would the President like to see the die before a test is made?
> The provision of law governing designs upon the coins reads as follows:
> *"...but on the gold dollar piece, the dime, five, three and one cent piece the figure of the eagle shall be omitted..."*

[578] The third-party grading services have helped sort out this mess, but one still sees occasional "proof" designations for coins that were not made as proofs. The patterns of 1916–17 are in the same situation as those of 1907.
[579] One of the more interesting sources of explanation is Bureau of the Mint Circular #107 dated October 3, 1887 issued by director James P. Kimball, which describes five "technical terms" used by the mint. The list is incomplete since it omits "specimen coin" and "proof specimen" when used to refer to a trial piece. The mint has always been somewhat imprecise in its terminology and it is in numismatists' interests to be precise in their application of these terms.
[580] *US Mint*, NARA-CP, op. cit., entry 330, box 45. Letter dated February 8, 1907 to Loeb from Roberts.

This forced Saint-Gaudens to devise a new obverse for the cent, and he selected the portrait of NIKE previously prepared for the *Sherman Monument* in New York. On February 5, 1907 he dictated a letter to President Roosevelt:[581]

> Dear Mr. President:
> I send you by express today the model from which the Mint may make its dies to strike the one cent piece.... The illegality of an eagle on the one cent made it necessary for me to find something new for the reverse [i.e., portrait side – RWB] of that piece which would replace the flying or standing eagle I first submitted.
> For some time I felt at a loss for a design until I fell back on this idea of using the customary female head that represents Liberty. I must own that I now feel happy about the result, for the head, at least, is out of the usual run.
> Faithfully yours,

President Roosevelt had already lamented the absence of a feathered headdress on the Striding Liberty figure. When he saw the new Liberty (i.e., NIKE) portrait proposed for the cent, Roosevelt asked Saint-Gaudens to add an Indian headdress as being entirely American and characteristic.[582]

> .....I feel very strongly that on at least one coin we ought to have the Indian feather headdress. It is distinctly American, and very picturesque. Couldn't you have just such a head as you have now, but with the feather headdress?

This was done in a few days and by February 18 the President expressed his pleasure at the design:[583]

> My dear Mr. Saint Gaudens:
> ...I like that feather head-dress so much that I have accepted that design of yours. Of course all the designs are conventional, as far as head-dresses go, because Liberty herself is conventional when embodied in a woman's head; and I don't see why we should not have a conventional head-dress of purely American type for the Liberty figure.
> I am returning to you today the model of the Liberty head.

With this design quickly determined, Saint-Gaudens assumed work was nearly complete, and asked a favor of the President. Would it be possible for him to see the Liberty head combined with the flying eagle for the $20 gold coin design?[584]

> I like so much the head with the head-dress (and by the way, I am very glad you suggested doing the head in that manner) that I should like very much to see it tried not only on the one-cent piece, but also on the twenty-dollar gold piece instead of the figure of Liberty. I am probably apprehensive and have lost sight of whatever are the merits or demerits of the Liberty side of the coin as it is now. My fear is that it does not "tell" enough, in contrast with the eagle on the other side. There will be no difficulty of that kind with the head alone, of its effectiveness I am certain....
> This all means that I would like to have the mint make a die of the head for the gold coin also, and then a choice can be made between the two when completed.

[581] *SG*, Dartmouth, op. cit. Box 16, folder 38. Letter dated February 5, 1907 to Roosevelt from Saint-Gaudens.
[582] *Roosevelt*, LoC, op. cit., vol. 70, p.401, microfilm reel 344. Letter dated February 8, 1907 to Saint-Gaudens from Roosevelt. No one seems to have thought that Miss Liberty wearing a ceremonial war bonnet was tantamount to a civilian wearing an unearned Congressional Medal of Honor.
[583] *SG*, Dartmouth, op. cit. Box 16, folder 38. Letter dated February 18, 1907 to Saint-Gaudens from Roosevelt.
[584] *SG*, Dartmouth, op. cit. Box 16, folder 38. Letter dated March 12, 1907 to Roosevelt from Saint-Gaudens.

If this meets with your approval, may I ask you to say so to Mr. Roberts, of the Mint? I have enclosed a copy of this letter to him. The only change necessary in the event of this being carried out will be the changing of the date from the Liberty side to the Eagle side of the coin. This is a small matter.

The artist felt the scale of the portrait and eagle were in better harmony than using the full figure of Liberty. Once this sample had been made and shown to Saint-Gaudens, he felt the combination was preferable to the original pair and suggested this to Roosevelt:[585]

...as far as I am concerned, I should prefer seeing the head of Liberty in place of any figure of Liberty on the Twenty Dollar coin as well as on the One cent. If the idea appeals to you, I would refine the modeling of the head now that I have seen it struck in the small, so as to bring it in scale with the eagle.

The President discussed the coin design with director Roberts on May 25, and the latter wrote to Saint-Gaudens:[586]

I had an interview today with the President about the designs.... It is now settled that the designs for the Double Eagle shall be the full figure of Liberty and the flying eagle, and the design shall be the feather head of liberty with the standing eagle....
This is the last word on the subject....

The cent was omitted because it was felt the gold coins were more important.

The first models intended for the $10 eagle coins were delivered on June 5,[587] but the modeling was soft and inconsistent with the sharply cut edges the mint was accustomed to; the obverse also had the date in Roman numerals, which Roberts felt was impractical.[588] After a delay caused by Hering's absence from Aspet, Saint-Gaudens shipped the revised eagle models to the mint on June 24. Barber sent the models off to Keller Mechanical Engraving Company to have bronze casts made[589] and by July 19 Barber reported completion of experimental dies and the striking of "a number of experimental pieces."[590] These first coins are known as coming from the #1, or "high relief" models. The field curves upward to the edge of the coin, producing a knife rim (or "wire rim") on both sides. The reverse has irregularly shaped periods or stops before and after the legends. These were originally triangles, but the reductions rendered them more as blobs than identifiable elements.

Roberts sent one of the new-design eagles each to secretary Cortelyou and Saint-Gaudens on July 22. These pieces had plain edges. "The lettering upon the edge of the new coins does not appear upon the enclosed pieces as the collar for it was not quite ready."[591] The first pieces had a dull, smooth surface as explained by director Roberts:[592]

---

[585] *Roosevelt*, LoC, op. cit., vol. 70, p.401, microfilm reel 344. Letter dated May 11, 1907 to Roosevelt from Saint-Gaudens.
[586] *US Mint*, NARA-CP, op. cit., entry 330, box 45. Letter dated May 25, 1907 to Saint-Gaudens from Roberts.
[587] *US Mint*, NARA-CP, op. cit., entry 330, box 45. Letter dated June 5, 1907 to Roberts from Landis.
[588] *US Mint*, NARA-CP, op. cit., entry 330, box 45. Letter dated June 11, 1907 to Saint-Gaudens from Roberts.
[589] *US Mint*, NARA-P, op. cit. Telegram dated July 8, 1907, 2:02p.m. to Albert Norris from Keller & Company (a.k.a. Keller Mechanical Engraving Company).
[590] *US Mint*, NARA-CP, op. cit., entry 229, box 256. Letter dated July 19, 1907 to Roberts from Norris.
[591] *US Mint*, NARA-CP, op. cit., entry 330, box 45. Letter dated July 22, 1907 to Cortelyou from Roberts. The Saint-Gaudens letter is similar.
[592] *US Mint*, NARA-CP, op. cit., entry 330, box 45. Letter dated July 22, 1907 to Saint-Gaudens from Roberts.

> ...The smooth finish on your design is due to the several reductions which it has undergone. Instead of looking like die work, it looks like a cast piece and this is a very serious defect because it greatly simplifies counterfeiting.

This description is consistent with that of a plain edge eagle appearing in an auction in 2002. A portion of the accompanying description, later used in a hobby publication article, reads:[593]

> ...Judd-1774A [now J-1902] was produced in much the same manner that the Mint produced the Plain Edge 1907 Saint-Gaudens, Ultra High Relief and High Relief $20 double eagle patterns (Pollock 2000 and Pollock 2005, respectively). Eager to test the new Indian Head eagle dies, the Mint installed them into the press before the segmented, starred collar was completed.
> A single coin was struck in Proof format with a plain edge: Judd-1774A.
> Once the segmented collar was ready, the Mint began production of the Judd 1774 coins, but not before the dies were removed from the press and extensively polished. (Hence, examples of Judd 1774 display considerably more striations in the fields than the unique Judd 1774A specimen.)
> This sequence of events and the diagnostics that support them lead me to believe that the unique specimen of the 1907 Indian Head, Wire Rim, Plain Edge eagle is the first specimen of this classic design produced by the United States Mint.

Although portions of the information in the quote are incorrect (reference to the double eagles and "proof" finish), the conclusion that a plain edge eagle was the first of its kind appears to be correct.

The experimental plain edge coin sent to the secretary was recorded as being returned to the mint on August 20; the Saint-Gaudens piece was still at Aspet. President Roosevelt was sent the experimental coin by secretary Cortelyou and returned it on July 29 with the following comment:[594]

> .... How would it do to have a few thousand coins struck with the smooth finish, and then the rest struck with the sharply cut details of the old design?... As for the high relief coins, have several hundred struck and allow the collectors of the country to obtain specimens....

The absence of instructions from Saint-Gaudens, followed by his death on August 3, left the eagle in abeyance. However, the President was demanding that coins be issued, and acting director Preston sent explicit instructions to the Philadelphia Mint to produce the coins, to which acting superintendent Norris replied on August 14, "We are making all necessary arrangements to begin the coinage of the eagle from dies on hand...."[595]

Machinists at the mint were having trouble making the edge collar with stars.[596] Apparently spacing the stars evenly was difficult when there were forty-six stars on three segments (15-15-16). The first collar used on pattern coins had irregular stars as described both by Preston and Cortelyou.[597]

---

[593] Jeff Ambio, *Coin World*, "Unique Indian Eagle May Have Been First – Wire Rim, Plain Edge Piece Led Way," October 30, 2002. Mr. Ambio was a cataloger at Heritage Numismatic Auctions Inc., which sold the coin at auction.

[594] *US Mint*, NARA-CP, op. cit., entry 330, box 45. Letter dated July 29, 1907 to Cortelyou from Roosevelt.

[595] *US Mint*, NARA-CP, op. cit., entry 330, box 45. Letter dated August 14, 1907 to Preston from Norris.

[596] *US Mint*, NARA-CP, op. cit., entry 330, box 45. Letter dated August 14, 1907 to Preston from Norris.

[597] *US Mint*, NARA-CP, op. cit., entry 330, box 45. Letter dated August 30, 1907 to Cortelyou from Edwards. The letter written by Preston is dated August 27.

Engraver Barber had been busy since having his vacation cut short on the 14th and by August 26 he had prepared an alternate version of the eagle.[598] For this, he used the #1 models, but reduced them slightly more than had been done the first time. He then cut a rounded border or rim around the hub so that when a coin was struck, the sharp knife edge of the #1 coins was replaced with a normal rim. Since they were reduced from the same models as the previous version, the reverse retained the irregular periods at ends of the inscriptions. Samples went to the director's office in Washington.

There were now two varieties of the eagle coin at the mint: #1 with knife rim, periods and irregular edge stars, and #2 with normal rim, periods and irregular edge stars (the plain edge pieces were initial patterns and not candidates for production).

The next day, August 27, new models for the gold eagle arrived from Homer Saint-Gaudens. Barber pronounced them "...a great improvement over those already made..." and said it would take one month to produce hubs and working dies.[599] This version had a somewhat broader rim than Barber's #2 variety and the reverse lacked the blob-like periods at ends of the inscriptions. Absence of periods was part of the revised design from Hering and not something altered by the mint. Meanwhile, Preston sent the #1 and #2 samples (with irregular edge stars) to Edwards and then Cortelyou for approval. The acting director also ordered production of five hundred eagles from the high relief designs – meaning the #1 models.

Barber had the Keller Company make casts of the new #3 eagle models and proceeded to make the reductions, hubs and dies.

Things now became confused. Acting director Preston sent a letter to the Philadelphia Mint on August 27, then repeated the instruction on August 30, ordering regular coinage of the new design eagles. He explicitly stated "...from the new design by Saint-Gaudens, with the rim as added by Mr. Barber, the engraver." This was the #2 model that Barber had already said was inferior to the #3 version received two weeks earlier from Homer Saint-Gaudens. There was little logic to Preston's decision, but, the mint obeyed the order and produced 31,500 of the #2 eagles until instructed to stop on September 18.[600] Nothing appears in available documents about the edge collar used. Since continued use of the version with irregular stars would likely have been noticed, it is probable that the machinists had succeeded in their work and the stars were more or less evenly arrayed around the perimeter of the coins.

On September 25, Barber sent Preston a sample of the #3 eagle and a #2 coin for comparison. These were shown to President Roosevelt and the #3 version was approved. Presumably this coin had normal edge stars.

By the end of September there were five hundred of the #1 eagles, plus at least two plain edge patterns, plus three patterns with irregular edge stars. There were also 31,500 #2 eagles, plus at least two patterns of this design with irregular edge stars. Finally, there were patterns of the #3 eagle awaiting official approval for production.

The National Numismatic Collection includes five specimens of the #1 and #2 eagles. These were probably placed in the collection at the Philadelphia Mint and were from

[598] *US Mint*, NARA-P, op. cit. Letter dated August 26, 1907 to Landis from Barber.
[599] *US Mint*, NARA-P, op. cit. Letter dated August 27, 1907 to Landis from Barber.
[600] *US Mint*, NARA-P, op. cit. Telegram received September 18, 1907 to Landis from Preston.

among the first pattern coins struck from their respective dies. These coins are described as:[601]

> #1 Models. Three examples of the $10 (J-1774/J-1901) knife rim, with periods in the NNC were examined. All three have 46 edge stars irregularly placed on the collar segments. They are mostly small, but the last two are larger than others. All stars have 6-points and are arranged: | 15 small | 15 small | 14 small, last 2 larger. The stars appear to be more roughly cut than on the collar used on normal 1907 circulation coins. The surfaces are somewhat dull resembling a coin that has been dipped in acid too many times, or a cast counterfeit.
>
> #2 Models. Two examples of the $10 (J-1775/J-1903) rounded rim, with periods in the NNC were examined. Both have 46 edge stars irregularly placed on the collar segments. The edge is identical to that on the J-1774 pieces. These pieces have better luster than the previous.
>
> The above appear to be the examples transferred to the Smithsonian in 1923, and do not include specimens from the Eli Lilly donation or other sources.

From the above it is evident that the starred edge collar had not been perfected by the time the first of the #2 patterns was struck on or before August 26. Since production of five hundred pieces presumably began on August 30 (assuming Preston's first order was ignored), the machinists may have had time to complete the regular edge collars and it is likely these coins all had normal edge stars.[602]

The following timeline may assist in understanding how events relating to the new eagles unfolded.

| Date (1907) | Item | Reference |
|---|---|---|
| June 3 | #1 models sent to Philadelphia Mint by Hering. | 6/3/07 to Roberts from Saint-Gaudens |
| By July 19 | Sample #1 eagles made. Plain edge. | |
| July 22 | Roberts receives two #1 eagles from Cashier, pays for them. | 7/25/07 to Landis from Roberts |
| July 25 | 1 #1 eagle received by Saint-Gaudens. | 7/25/07 to Roberts from H. Saint-Gaudens |
| July 29 | TR Returns two #1 eagles to Cortelyou. | 7/29/07 to |
| Aug. 12 | TR orders new gold coins issued "as they are." | 8/12/07 to Landis from Preston |
| Aug. 20 | Preston returns one #1 eagle shown to Cortelyou. Irregular edge stars. | 8/20/07 |
| Aug. 26 | Barber encloses #1 and #2 eagles in letter. Irregular edge stars. | 8/26/02 to Landis from Barber |
| Aug. 27 | Barber advises #3 models just received. "Would be great improvement." Will take month to make dies. | 8/27/07 to Landis from Barber |
| Aug. 27 | Preston approved working on #3 models. | 8/27/07 to Landis from Preston |
| Aug. 27 | Strike five hundred experimental eagles and double eagles in high relief (#1 models). | 8/27/07 to Landis from Preston |
| Aug. 27 | "...stars not in a straight line..." (refers to #1 and #2 samples sent on 26th). | 8/27/07 to Landis from Preston |
| Aug. 30 | Repeats order to mint five hundred, but specifies use of medal press. | 8/30/07 to Landis from Preston |
| Aug. 30 | Barber authorized to take paraffin reduction to NY to have bronze cast made. | 8/30/07 to Landis from Preston |
| Sep. 6 | One eagle, one double eagle to Preston. | 9/13/07 to Landis from Preston |

---

[601] Author's revised notes from examination of the NNC coins, July 2002; confirmed December 2005.
[602] The author has examined multiple examples of knife rim and normal rim varieties. All except the Smithsonian specimens have normal edge stars.

| Date (1907) | Item | Reference |
|---|---|---|
| Sep. 9 | Preston authorizes circulation coinage from #2 models [31,500 pieces]. | 9/08/07 to Landis from Preston |
| Sep. 10 | Five #1 eagles, five #2 eagles to Asst. Sec. Edwards | 9/10/07 to Landis from Preston |
| Sep. 13 | Preston returns two #1 eagles of 8/6/07 (from TR). Pays for his Sept. 6 coins. | 9/13/07 to Landis from Preston |
| Sep. 18 | Suspend coinage of new eagles. Do not pay out. | 9/18/07 to Landis from Preston |
| Oct. 3 | Eagle #3 pattern coin received along with #2 coin for comparison. | 10/03/07 to Landis from Preston. Barber countersigns |
| Oct. 31 | Preston tells Landis to pay out #2 eagles per Edwards' order. Preston had earlier suggested melting them. Edwards thinks they are so much like #3 that it won't matter, and gold is needed in circulation due to the financial situation. | 10/31/07 to Landis from Preston |
| Nov. 9 | Leach authorizes melting $314,500 in eagles from #2 model. | 11/9/07 to Landis from Leach. |
| Dec. 14 | Five hundred eagles from #1 models ordered transferred to Treasury in Washington. | 12/14/07 to Landis from Leach per Cortelyou |

The following descriptions include only those pattern and experimental pieces struck in gold. Pieces struck in lead or white metal were trials of various sorts and not true patterns. References are to Andrew Pollock's book *United States Pattern and Related Issues,* and *United States Pattern Coins, Experimental and Trial Pieces, 8th Edition* by J. Hewitt Judd, MD edited by Q. David Bowers.

Note that only the plain edge and irregular stars edge coins are true patterns or experimental pieces. Others with normal edge stars are limited circulation production and abandoned trial strikes.

**Eagle – P-1995, 1996 (J-1901, normal stars; J-1902, plain edge). Irregular stars not listed.**
**Obverse 2, Reverse A, Plain edge, and Irregular edge stars**
Struck between July 18 and August 26, 1907 depending on variety.

Portrait of Liberty facing left, wearing a Native American Indian feather headdress. The headdress band is inscribed LIBERTY. Above are 13, six-pointed stars; below is the date "1907" in European characters. Field is strongly curved and flows directly to meet the rim. This produces a sharp "knife" rim.

Modeling and detail are soft and indistinct, with many details irregularly cut into hub as if attempts had been made to strengthen details. Thousands of minute raised die scratches throughout field, overlaid by a granular-looking surface.

Bald eagle standing, facing left, holding fasces of arrows and olive branch in its talons. Above, the inscription:
· UNITED · STATES · OF · AMERICA · ; below, the inscription ·TEN · DOLLARS· Above the bird's back is the inscription
· E· PLURIBUS · UNUM · in three lines.

As on the obverse, modeling is soft and indistinct with lettering occasionally merging with the rim.

From Model #1. High relief. Knife ("wire") rim. Periods before and after legends on reverse.

One plain edge piece sold by Heritage Coin in January 2003 (Judd 1902).

Edge: Plain or 46 small stars arranged in three segments: 15 – 15 – 16. The stars are irregularly spaced and aligned. The last two stars on the 16-star segment larger than others. This collar is specific to the pattern coins.

Specimens with normal edge stars were struck for limited circulation and as collector's pieces.

Contemporary Comments:
GBC: 7/22/07. *"The lettering upon the edge of the new coin does not appear upon the enclosed piece as the collar for it was not quite ready."*

The knife rim prevented coins from stacking easily and made small bumps and dings very noticeable. The stars and date also tend to fade into the knife rim, making the piece look unfinished.

500 Struck on a medal press during the last week in August and first week of September 1907. Six or more additional coins ordered struck by the director on December 30, 1907, plus 34 others at unknown dates.

A total of at least 49 were recorded sold by the mint, but it is not known whether all were from the 500 intended for circulation, or included some of the 42 extra pieces. A total of 542 were struck, 70 were melted in 1915–1918.

There have been suggestions that of the 500 pieces coined on the medal press, 50 were "proofs" of one sort or another. See chapter 4 for full text of the letter and discussion.

Examples in the NNC appear to have come from the small number of patterns made for examination by Saint-Gaudens and mint officials. The Smithsonian collection does not include any pieces with normal stars on the edge.

A plain edge specimen is the only 1907 pattern known to have been kept by Saint-Gaudens. All others sent to him were returned. This is also the first true pattern for proposed coinage of 1907, the others being "experimental" pieces. The Saint-Gaudens coin is not among the U. S. Department of Interior National Park Service, Saint-Gaudens National Historic Site holdings.

(Coin image courtesy American Numismatic Rarities, photo by Doug Plancencia; edge photo by Roger W. Burdette.)

There are three varieties of the first $10 gold patterns. The following will, it is hoped, eliminate any confusion.

- Judd 1902 – as pictured above; plain edge. The first of the true pattern $10 coins.

- Judd (not listed)[603] – as pictured above with forty-six small stars on edge; last two stars are larger than the others. True pattern pieces (along with J-1902); approximately 3 or 4 produced.

- Judd 1901 – From model #1 as J-1901 and J-1902. Five hundred made in late August–early September on orders from secretary Cortelyou. Edge stars are evenly placed on the collar segments and are all of the same size. Forty-two additional pieces were made later in the year; seventy were melted between 1915 and 1918. After accounting for additional pieces struck and seventy specimens melted, the net mintage is four hundred seventy-two pieces. These are not actually pattern coins.

There are no known sandblast proof examples, as that term is presently understood. All examples – patterns and five hundred forty-two circulation pieces – were struck on a medal press. Differences are due to buffing of the hubs and possible polishing and recutting of working dies. The hubs were destroyed on May 24–25, 1910.

All pieces examined with normal edge stars also have fine die tooling marks on the obverse at the third star from the right, between the outer two points of the star. They also have similar tooling marks between stars seven and eight, counting from the left.

The term "knife" rim is preferred when describing these pieces. The intersection of vertical edge and curving field produces a sharp edge similar to a knife. This is a characteristic of the die, not a defect. This term is also found in occasional mint doucments and is used in the same sense.[604] The obsolete term "wire rim" implies something resembling a

---

[603] Judd 1903 is included in the variety grid but described as the "rolled rim" (normal rim) variety, which is actually from a different hub.

[604] *US Mint*, NARA-CP, op. cit., entry 1A 328I. Letter dated March 1, 1909 to Landis from Barber who states with reference to Brenner's Lincoln cent model, "…the borders…are so narrow that by the time they are reduced ten times there will be nothing left, only a knife edge [i.e.: rim]."

thin, rounded wire. This is clearly not the appearance of this variety. Further, the term "wire rim" (or sometimes "wire edge") is also applied to a production defect known at the mint as "fin," and often encountered on double eagles and some of the eagles.

On the reverse, the irregular ovals before and after inscriptions are usually called "periods" although they were not intended to be round dots. The original models show these as triangular text stops. Their oval shape on the coins is attributable to poor reduction and hub cutting by the mint.

**Eagle – P-1997 (J-1903, normal stars). Irregular stars not listed.**
**Obverse 3$_A$, Reverse A$_1$, Irregular edge stars**
Struck between August 24 and September 18, 1907, depending on variety.

Portrait of Liberty facing left, wearing a Native American Indian feather headdress. The headdress band is inscribed Liberty. Above are 13, six-pointed stars; below is the date "1907" in European characters. Field is strongly curved, but a raised rim has been added to permit the coins to stack.

Modeling and detail is soft and indistinct, with many details irregularly cut into hub. Better definition to stars and date than previous. Thousands of minute raised die scratches throughout field but in different patterns than on previous. Surface less "granular."

Detail is inferior to the previous version possibly due to being struck on normal presses.

Bald eagle standing, facing left, holding fasces of arrows and olive branch in its talons. Above, the inscription:
· UNITED · STATES · OF · AMERICA · ; below, the inscription ·TEN · DOLLARS · Above the bird's back is the inscription
· E· PLURIBUS · UNUM · in three lines.

As on the obverse, modeling is soft and indistinct with lettering poorly separated from the rim. Noticeable die tooling marks between T and A of STATES. Periods before and after legends on reverse are supposed to be triangles. Eagle's feathers poorly defined; noticeable gap between right wing and body possibly due to insufficient striking pressure.

Slightly lower relief than on previous.

From first pair of models but called "model #2" to distinguish them from the #1 model coins. Rim as added by Barber to Saint-Gaudens' first models but the hubs were cut slightly smaller and at lower relief by Barber.

No plain edge specimens are known. 46 small stars arranged in three segments: 15 – 15 – 16. The stars are irregularly spaced and aligned. The last two stars on the 16-star segment larger than others. Segment ends are not identical resulting in the slight misalignment visible in the photo. This collar is specific to the pattern coins. This is the same "crooked stars" collar as used on the patterns from model #1.

Pieces with normal edge stars are circulation strikes from abandoned production, although they carry the J-1903 number.

Contemporary Comments:

JHL: 8/27/07. *"...by throwing up a narrow border Mr. Barber has improved the appearance of the coin as shown in exhibit #2 compared with exhibit #1. These coins will be forwarded to the Secretary of the Treasury for his inspection and his attention called to the improvement made by Mr. Barber. It is noticed that the stars on the border [sic: edge] are not in a straight line. This, no doubt, is due to the appliance you have for making the impression of the stars.*

Compare with coin from model #3, below, as used for circulation issue of 1907. Unknown number of experimental pieces struck by August 25, 1907. 31,500 struck on normal coinage presses late September by order of acting director Preston. 31,450 melted by order of director Leach after learning that Hering's third models were satisfactory. At least 38 pieces distributed in 1907-08.

Coins from the condemned circulation production had normal stars on the edge. Fifty specimens intentionally held back from melting and distributed by the Treasury Department. These would likely be less sharply defined than the pattern coins made on the medal press.

(Photo courtesy Harry W. Bass, Jr. Research Foundation.)

There are two varieties of the second $10 gold pieces. The following will, it is hoped, straighten out any confusion:

- Judd (not listed) – From model #1 with addition of rim by Barber (called model #2). Pattern strikes on a medal press made using the "irregular stars" edge collar as on the #1 patterns (the same collar segments were used). These are patterns.

- Judd 1903 – From model #1 with addition of rim by Barber (called model #2). 31,500 struck on regular coinage presses; all except fifty ordered melted. Normal stars on edge. These are not patterns and are best described as abandoned production trials.

This version was created using the same models as #1, above. The reduction to the hub was done differently so there was space to cut a rim.

These are often called "rolled" or "flat" rim; however, the engraver called this a "border." It is nothing more than a normal slightly rounded rim as commonly applied to circulating coins. The purpose was to permit stacking of the coins and protect the design from wear.

After accounting for 31,450 pieces melted, the net mintage is fifty pieces, plus patterns. There are no known sandblast proof examples, as that term is presently understood. All circulation pieces were struck on normal production presses; all patterns were struck on a medal press. No coins appear to have received special post-striking treatment. Differences are due to buffing of the hubs, possible polishing and recutting of working dies, and differences in striking pressure and speed. The surviving circulation examples should have rim and sharpness characteristics consistent with use of production presses, not medal presses. Of twelve specimens in auctions or dealers' inventory where the edge could be examined, all had normal edge stars. The original specimens in the NNC have irregular stars. The hubs were destroyed on May 24–25, 1910.

**Eagle – Regular issue (illustrated for comparison purposes).**
**Obverse 4, Reverse B**
Struck after September 25, 1907

Portrait of Liberty facing left, wearing a Native American Indian feather headdress. The headdress band is inscribed Liberty. Above are 13, six-pointed stars; below is the date "1907" in European characters. Field is curved, but a raised rim has been added to permit the coins to stack.

Modeling and detail is more distinct than on previous with many details more sharply cut into hub. Better definition to stars and date than either predecessor. Most stars are distorted on the side facing the rim. Rim is broad and well defined.

Bald eagle standing, facing left, holding fasces of arrows and olive branch in its talons. Above, the inscription:
· UNITED · STATES · OF · AMERICA · ; below, the inscription ·TEN · DOLLARS · Above the bird's back is the inscription
· E· PLURIBUS · UNUM · in three lines.

As on the obverse, modeling is greatly improved over preceding versions, and lettering is slightly separated from the rim. There are no periods (or triangles) before and after the inscriptions. This "omission" was part of the model and not the work of mint engravers.

From model #3. Broad rim as designed Hering and Homer Saint-Gaudens. Relief is similar to the #2 model coins but detail is more sharply modeled. The mint made reductions onto paraffin discs, which Barber took to Gorham, Inc. in New York to have bronze casts made. The hubs were made by reducing the bronze casts on the Janvier lathe. Documents suggest two or three patterns were struck.

There are 46 small stars on the edge arranged in three segments: 15 – 15 – 16 (16 – 16 – 16 beginning in 1912). Circulation strikes use an edge die with evenly spaced and sized stars.

Contemporary Comments:

CEB: 8/27/07. *"...relief now reduced to coin relief and border added...would be a great improvement over those already made...."*

JHL: 9/25/07. *"I...enclose for approval specimen of the new eagle from...dies from Saint Gaudens' last model."*

RP: 10/3/07. *"I am advised that the eagle from the last design is perfectly satisfactory to the President."*

Experimental strikes were made but none have been identified. Given the mint's use of a normal edge collar for the production coins from both #1 and #2 models, it is likely that the #3 patterns had normal edge stars. This would make them virtually indistinguishable from circulation coins.

The 1 or 2 known examples of sandblast proofs may have been prepared as specimens for final approval of the design, a test of the sandblasting in creating special coins for collectors, or they may have been a later invention.

(Obverse and reverse photos courtesy Harry W. Bass, Jr. Research Foundation.)

## Gold Double Eagle Patterns

The first double eagle pattern related to the 1907designs was dated 1906 (P-1992, J-1773), and prepared from models by Charles Barber and George Morgan. Little is known about creation of the coin; however, it exhibits several interesting features suggestive of production in late 1906. The first is a lettered edge made by a three-part segmented collar. Barber was familiar with the mint's previous experiments with segmented collars. A report by Philadelphia Mint superintendent James R. Snowden to the director on June 23, 1885, "… describes at length the difficulties met with in devising this collar, but declares that it worked with perfection, running the press at a speed of from 80 to 110 pieces per minute, and in conclusion states that 'valuable services were rendered by Mr. Charles E. Barber, engraver, and his assistants.'"[605] This was a version of the "toggle collar" later used on the new $10 and $20 gold coins produced for general circulation. The collar used on the extremely high relief Saint-Gaudens' medal-coins is similar to that on the 1885 pattern silver dollar with lettered edge (P-1959, J-1747) that Snowden mentions. The style of characters and their layout is nearly identical although the 1885 version is less strongly impressed on the coin. Examples of this experimental piece were in the mint collection in 1906. The edge collar on the Barber/Morgan 1906 $20 pattern is the same as that used on the February 1907 Saint-Gaudens patterns.[606]

The mint may have made this sample for director Roberts' scrutiny after learning of Saint-Gaudens' $20 design. They devised a way to produce the lettered edge based on Barber's previous experience in edge lettering, and imitated use of E PLURIBUS UNUM as proposed by either Barber or Saint-Gaudens. The gold example of this pattern is a sand-blast proof, and is the only verified sandblast proof of this series. There is no record of the President having seen this pattern or of anyone seriously considering it for use.

The first experimental, or pattern, coins of the Saint-Gaudens designs were created at the Philadelphia Mint in February 1907. These are the so-called extremely high relief[607] (EHR, or sometimes "ultra high relief") specimens made from hubs cut in January by Charles Barber and Henri Weil. Each complete coin required seven blows from the hydraulic press – six to bring up the design and a seventh to impart the edge lettering. Between each strike, the planchet was annealed to compensate for work hardening produced in the press. After heating to a deep red, the planchet was dipped into a weak nitric acid solution, which removed any oxidized copper from the surface. Repetition of this treatment left the coin's surface depleted in copper. All known mint state specimens have the color of nearly pure gold rather than .900 fine alloy color. Non-destructive tests performed by the Smithsonian in May 2004 confirm that EHR pieces have a surface of nearly pure gold.[608]

In addition to pieces of normal diameter, Barber also created dies that were the diameter of a $10 gold coin. These were used to strike fifteen experimental pieces containing $20 in gold but of the smaller diameter. Available records do not state how many blows it

[605] *US Mint*, NARA-P, op. cit. Letter dated January 31, 1908 to Landis from Leach. Quotes Snowden's 1885 report discussing tests for using lettered edges on silver dollars and other coins.
[606] Per communication from David Tripp August, 2003. Mr. Tripp discovered the sans serif EHR $20 variety and personally examined the specimens mentioned. The author has confirmed Mr. Tripp's findings.
[607] The Mint Bureau consistently used the terms "extremely high relief" and "experimental pieces" when referring to this variety.
[608] Email communication from Douglas Mudd, collection manager, Smithsonian Museum of American History, National Numismatic Collection. The tests were authorized by NNC curator Dr. Richard Doty to test the annealing theory.

took to bring up the design on these samples; however, the experiment did not produce coins that could be made with one blow of the press.

Following these initial experiments, Saint-Gaudens and Henry Hering created a more detailed model, but in relief that was only slightly lower than the first version. These are known as the Very High Relief (VHR) models. Samples were again struck from these new models using up to ten (10) blows of the press. Specimens were shown to President Roosevelt and Saint-Gaudens, but were deemed unworkable, and the artist was ordered to make a low relief model with European date.

In mid-May, at the suggestion of mint superintendent John Landis, new reductions and hubs were made from the same VHR models, this time using the maximum degree of relief reduction possible on the Janvier lathe. This created the high relief version used for limited production later in the year. Gold examples were probably struck, but there is no documentation specifying when this was done or if they differed from the subsequent high relief issue of August–September, and November–December 1907.

In between production of the extremely high relief and very high relief versions, the mint created a Liberty Head/Flying Eagle pattern at the request of Saint-Gaudens. This incorporated an obverse design intended for the one cent coin, and the flying eagle $20 reverse with date added to the disc of the sun. Lead samples were struck along with one copy in gold. President Roosevelt preferred the Striding Liberty design and nothing more was done with this pattern. It should be noted that coinage laws required the date to be on the obverse of gold coins, so this design would have required further alteration if the President had selected it.

All versions of the Saint-Gaudens $20 coins with higher than normal relief were struck on medal presses. All were given multiple blows of the press and all were annealed between strikes. To this extent the coins must be considered either all "proofs" or all "non-proofs" as the consensus of collectors may determine. Differences between specimens are attributable to die wear and post-production handling. Coin surfaces were called "bright" by the mint and were produced the same way as satin proofs (occasionally called Roman proofs) used for collector's gold coins in 1909 and 1910. No examples have been verified with an original sandblast surface as was used on a few legitimate 1907 low relief gold coins and on collectors' gold coins in 1908, 1911–15.[609]

The following tables summarize all known, or believed to exist, versions of the gold pattern and experimental double eagles of 1906–07.

---

[609] As pointed out by superintendent Landis in a 1910 letter to assistant secretary Andrew, a sandblast proof was made by lightly sandblasting a bright finish (a.k.a. "Roman" finish) coin, as it came from new dies. This could easily be done outside the mint with equipment available to almost any machinist. Any so-called matte proof high relief double eagle, or a sandblast proof from 1909–1910, must be examined with great care and skepticism before it can be declared a genuine sandblast proof created at the Philadelphia Mint

**Double Eagle – P-1992 (J-1773)**
**Obverse 1, Reverse 1**
Likely struck in December 1906.

Obverse, portrait of Liberty facing left wearing Phrygian cap crowned with olive. Thirteen fat, five-pointed stars around; date below bust.

The obverse dates from the 1890s and resembles the French Fr-20 gold coin designed by J-C Chaplain in 1898, but substituting Barbers' chubby-faced Liberty for Chaplain's lighter, Marianne. Also similar to Barber's 1916 obverse proposed for the silver subsidiary coins.

Pronounced, wire rim around most of obverse & reverse rim. Resembles a "fin" except for its uniformity.

Obverse design by Charles E. Barber, Engraver of the United States Mint.

Reverse, figure of Columbia standing, looking to her right holding Liberty pole with freedom cap. She holds a sheathed sword in her right hand. Behind is a small eagle facing left. Rays fill the upper field behind. Around the periphery are the inscriptions UNITED STATES OF AMERICA, above, and TWENTY DOLLARS, below.

The reverse is a remodeling of assistant engraver George Morgan's 1891 half dollar obverse (shown above, P-1980), with some refinements to the composition. Note the small, faint motto IN GOD WE TRUST scattered between the rays on the reverse.

Relief is very shallow with poor detail. The reduction may have been made directly from a model without retouching of the hub.

Lettered edge: A-1 edge. Sans serif font with E* | P*L*U*R*I*B*U*S* | *U*N*U*M*. on three die segments. Characters are somewhat irregularly cut and uneven as if the work had been done hastily. The same edge collar was used on the Group One extremely high relief $20 Saint-Gaudens patterns/experimentals of February 1907.[610]

Contemporary Comments:
*The only mention of this coin in available documents is Barber's hub and die inventory of May 24, 1910 where he attributes the design to himself and Morgan.*

NNC specimen is a sandblast proof. (#1985.0441.2095)

(Photos courtesy Smithsonian Institution, National Numismatic Collection, Douglas Mudd; edge photo by David J. Camire courtesy NGC.)

---

[610] See the appendix for a discussion of how the edge photographs were created and limitations on their accuracy.

Identification of the designers comes from Charles Barber's inventory of pattern dies and hubs destroyed on May 24-25, 1910. His description reads, "Double eagle, obverse and reverse. Barber and Morgan design, hubs."[611] Short, but sufficient to identify who designed which side of the coin since the obverse portrait has Barber's initial on the truncation.

The double eagle pattern dated 1906 is an anomaly. Contemporary documents from the Philadelphia Mint and the director's office do not mention the piece, and no authorization for the work has been located.

As shown in the illustration above, the obverse portrait of Liberty is by mint engraver Charles Barber and the reverse is by assistant engraver George Morgan. Both designs predate the 1906 coin. The obverse is similar to 1898 French Twenty-franc design by J-C. Chaplain; the reverse is a modification of Morgan's 1891 half dollar obverse (J-1766).

Unique among gold patterns through 1906, the coin has a raised lettered edge:

**E\* | P\*L\*U\*R\*I\*B\*U\*S\* | U\*N\*U\*M\***

The sans serif lettering style shows considerable variation in character shape, orientation and depth, giving the edge the appearance of a quick job – certainly not something expected of a serious design proposed for circulation. Barber was very strict about the technical quality of work that left the mint. The 1906 pattern is not the kind of work that the engraver was likely to want the President to see.

It is this edge that provides a link to the first Saint-Gaudens gold patterns of 1907, and that also helps to constrain the time period during which the Barber/Morgan coin was made. Research by David Tripp established that the same layout and lettering style was used for the 1906 $20 and the first 1907 $20 EHR (and small-diameter $20) Saint-Gaudens experimental pieces.

1906 edge

1907 edge

*Figure 45. Photos of the edge of Barber/Morgan pattern double eagle of 1906 (top) and edge of Saint-Gaudens' first experimental double eagle, February 1907 (bottom). Note: images are not identical due to distortions in the imaging process.* (Photos by David J. Camire courtesy NGC.)

President Roosevelt had been pushing Saint-Gaudens to submit his double eagle models to the mint since August 1906, but only reductions of the reverse had been delivered. As originally planned, Saint-Gaudens' double eagle incorporated all legally required inscriptions – IN GOD WE TRUST was optional. The original obverse showed a winged Liberty striding forward and the reverse had a standing eagle similar to the 1905 inaugural medal. The motto E PLURIBUS UNUM, later placed on the edge, was part of the reverse design. Sometime during October and November, the sculptor decided to simplify both sides of the piece. He abandoned the standing eagle reverse in favor of a large, bold flying eagle, and removed Liberty's wings and other distracting details from the obverse. In changing the reverse, the artist also eliminated E PLURIBUS UNUM. Absence of this legally required motto was quickly noticed and Saint-Gaudens tried putting the motto on the rock below

[611] *US Mint*, NARA-CP, op. cit., entry 229, box 290. Letters and inventory dated May 24 and May 25, 1910 to Andrew from Barber.

Liberty's left foot. This was artistically unsatisfactory and his final obverse and reverse models omitted E P<small>LURIBUS</small> U<small>NUM</small>.

Saint-Gaudens had evidently made no provision for the coin's edge and it was left to engraver Barber, who had been kept fully informed about the new designs, to bring up the subject on November 30, 1906. When Saint-Gaudens assistant delivered the "final" models to the White House on December 14, it is probable that director Roberts telephoned the Philadelphia Mint and described the designs. The missing inscription would have been obvious to Barber. Having worked on the 1885 lettered edge silver dollars and the Mexican fifty-pesos pieces with incuse lettered edge, Barber's solution would have been to put E P<small>LURIBUS</small> U<small>NUM</small> on the double eagle's edge die. In that, Barber was following the President's order that Saint-Gaudens have a free hand with the designs, yet the new experimental pieces would also comply with coinage law. Obviously, Roberts would have wanted to see a sample.

The large-diameter, high relief models by Saint-Gaudens did not lend themselves to quickly made reductions. Making the diameter reduction while retaining detail was beyond Barber's or Morgan's experience, thus they could not use the artist's work and make a quick sample for Roberts to approve. Rather, Barber turned to low relief, small-diameter (five to seven inches) models available at the mint. Copies of the small models could be made and retouched in a few hours. Hubs could be cut directly from the models in less than a day and working dies produced in a few more hours. The only "new" part of the "stock" design was the lettered edge. Barber's December 1906 solution was simply to hand-cut stars and lettering into a blank edge collar. This was cut into three segments so the coin could be removed from the press after striking. The resulting double eagle experimental piece was a work of expedience – a "proof-of-concept" piece – not a realistic proposal for coinage. As a sample, it served the purpose of giving Roberts something to examine and approve. In effect the 1906 double eagle pattern was an experimental piece intended to verify for the director that a lettered edge could be used on a coin of this size.

But why make the coin with raised edge lettering? The answer is that the easiest, fastest way to make edge dies is to cut lettering directly into a collar. The result is raised lettering and a coin that is slightly larger than intended when measured over the lettering. Producing incuse characters requires an edge die with raised lettering, which is much more complicated to make. With pressure from Roberts and the President to strike samples of the Saint-Gaudens designs as quickly as possible, the expedient route was to use raised edge lettering and available low relief models.

Throughout 1906 and most of 1907, engraver Barber viewed the new designs as experiments done on the President's orders – practicality was not a consideration. It is this writer's speculation the Barber/Morgan 1906 double eagle was prepared in late December of that year. It was intended as a proof-of-concept experimental piece to show that a large gold coin could have a raised inscription on the edge. The same edge die was used on the first Saint-Gaudens double eagles because Barber had no instructions to the contrary. Only after Saint-Gaudens saw the first EHR specimens was the edge changed to Roman characters, rotated one hundred eighty degrees and stars placed between words.

The hubs were destroyed on May 24–25, 1910.

250

**Double Eagle – P-2000, 2001, 2002 and 2003 (J-1907, 1908, 1909)**
**Obverse 1, Reverse A (Extremely High Relief)**
Struck February 10 – 14 (J-1907, J-1908); March 4 – April (J-1909); December 31, 1907 (J-1909).

Full length figure of Liberty striding upward on a rocky peak. She holds a torch of enlightenment in her right hand and a branch of olive in her left. Below, in front of the rock, is a bough of oak, behind her to the left is the Capitol building and rays from the rising sun. The date is in Roman numerals: M·C·M·VII. Above her is the inscription LIBERTY and surrounding are 46 stars representing the states of the union in November 1907. Stars are somewhat unevenly distributed. Notice that two stars sit above the arms of the "Y" in LIBERTY.

Some with pronounced fin rim around most of obverse and reverse rim. Does not appear to be intentional.

An eagle flying to left and slightly upward with a rising sun behind; there are 14 long rays. Above the eagle is an inscription in two lines: ·UNITED·STATES·OF·AMERICA· and ·TWENTY·DOLLARS· There are periods between each word and at the ends of each line of inscription.

Edge Die:
***Lettered edge: A-I.*** Sans serif font, **E*** | **P*L*U*R*I*B*U*S*** | **U*N*U*M***. The pattern of alternating star and letter is the same as used on Barber's 1906 pattern $20, but is from a different die set. The characters are bold and clearly cut.

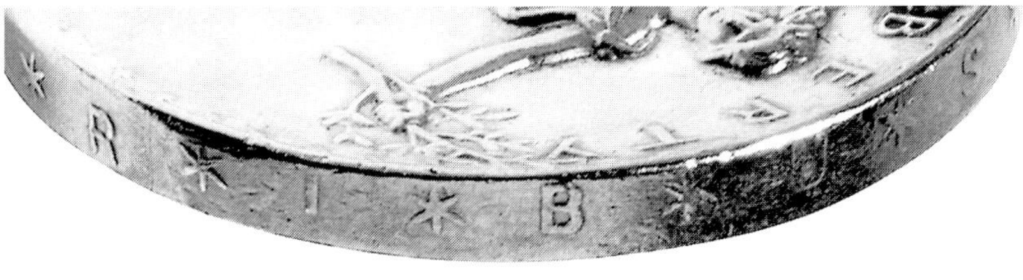

***Lettered edge: B-II.*** Serif (Roman) font *********E*** | **PLURIBUS** | ***UNUM******. On the variety with Roman characters, letters are bold and clearly cut, with exaggerated serifs. This is the normally encountered edge.

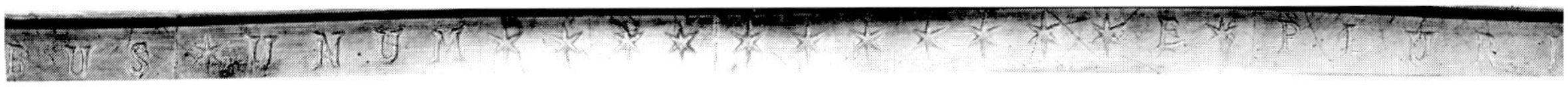

***Lettered edge: B-I.*** Same as B-II, above, but dies installed 180 degrees from normal.

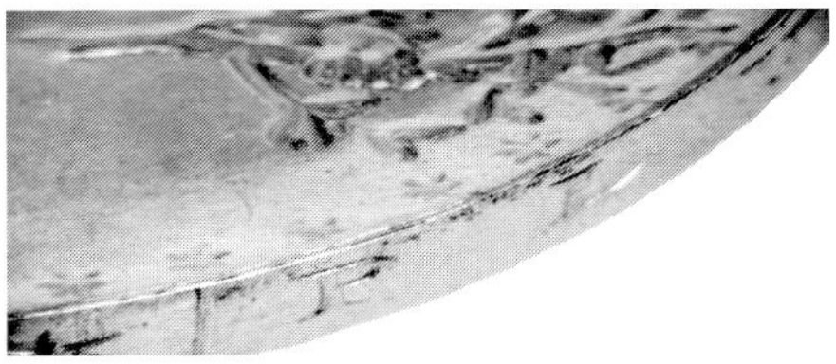

***Plain edge:*** Incompletely struck coin exhibiting slight peripheral weakness, as expected.

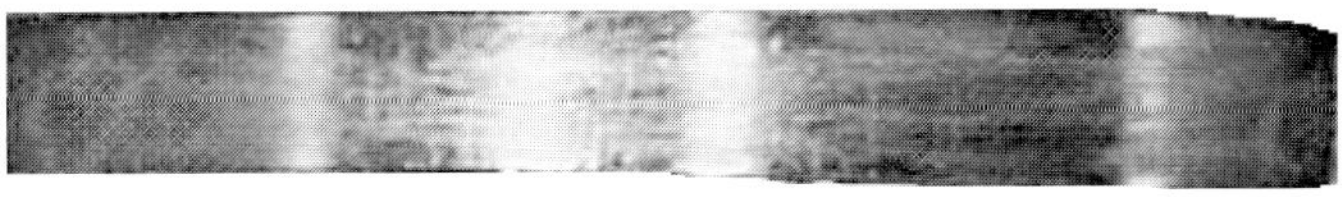

Contemporary Comments:
TR: 2/8/07. *"...dies about done... test of them next week."*
GER: 2/15/07. *"...received 4 double eagles, new design."*
*Landis states on January 3, 1908 that three additional pieces were struck by Barber, per director. Leach's orders. Intended for Cortelyou, Roosevelt, Leach and Saint-Gaudens Estate (per Leach letter December 28, 1907). Augusta Saint-Gaudens was not sent the coin until June 1908 and her example was taken from the mint collection.*

J-1908 has a plain edge; J-1907 has a sans serif-style lettered edge: **E*** | **P*L*U*R*I*B*U*S*** | **U*N*U*M***, and J-1909 has a serif lettered edge: *********E*** | **PLURIBUS** | ***UNUM****.**

Two pairs of dies were used plus two edge collars. None of the known specimens is a sandblast proof; all were produced in a similar manner.

(Top to bottom: photos courtesy Smithsonian Institution, National Numismatic Collection, Douglas Mudd; courtesy Stack's Rare Coins, New York City; ANS; NGC photo by David J. Camire; Stack's Rare Coins, New York City.)

Modeling is soft and rounded; face not well defined and it is evident that defects of the initial reduction were exaggerated when the hub was cut. Reductions made by Henri Weil, an employee of Dietsch Brothers, at the U. S. Mint. The design is impressive but does not appear to be the best artistic expression of Saint-Gaudens' intent.

When director Roberts asked for additional specimens, Barber reported the dies had broken and he had only one complete piece remaining (for a total of three complete pieces). Each medal-coin required seven blows at one hundred fifty tons pressure on a medal press. Three coins have lettered edges and a fourth, with incomplete detail and a prominent reverse crack, has a plain edge. A second pair of dies was made several weeks later and most of the known pieces are probably from these new dies, and with the Roman font edge lettering.[612]

Saint-Gaudens examined specimens from the February (Group One) coins, and changes in edge lettering likely resulted from his comments. Although we have no documentation on this point, it would be consistent with the sculptor's approach to require the edge letters to be in the same Roman style as the face lettering. Also, changing the layout of letters and their orientation in relation to the obverse converted the edge from a simple ornament to an active inscription. As used on the majority of MCMVII experimental pieces, the motto E PLURIBUS UNUM can be read as an extension of the obverse simply by tilting the coin slightly. It arches over top of the Liberty figure as if it were an encompassing philosophy. The 1906 edge dies would not have been used because they were irregular and had the wrong layout of stars and letters. Barber would not have wanted the President to see sloppy work come out of his engraving department.

## *Order of Production*

These experimental pieces were made in three groups with each group separately authorized by the mint director or President. Group One coins (at least three complete pieces plus one plain edge partial piece) were made on order from President Roosevelt between February 7 and 14, 1907. All lettered edge examples use edge dies A-I (see below). The plain edge specimen with cracked reverse die is from this group. Production was halted when the die broke. Electrotypes of gold progress strikes, shown below, were produced from samples of this group.

Group Two pieces (at least two specimens) were struck from a newly prepared reverse die authorized by director Roberts. Two pieces were ordered for the Philadelphia Mint coin collection between March 4 and April 1, 1907. Most of the other known specimens were likely made at this time since they share common face dies and the same orientation of edge dies (B-II, see below).

Group Three coins (three pieces) were struck on December 31, 1907 by Barber to the order of director Leach. Four pieces had been requested, but apparently only three were struck. All examples appear to have been made from edge dies B-I (see below), which is simply die set B-II inserted incorrectly in the press, or possibly the position of the face dies was reversed. (For later double eagles, the obverse was normally in the lower, or anvil, position.)

Edge lettering alignment and font (or lettering style) have been a source of confusion since at least 1992, when numismatist David Tripp discovered two examples with sans serif lettering. In consultation with Mr. Tripp, and with his concurrence, the author proposes the following descriptions.[613]

Two different edge die sets were used for the MCMVII EHR pattern coins:

---

[612] David Akers comments: 1907 EHR $20. In addition to lettered edge pieces, one is known with a plain edge and severely cracked reverse. "This coin was part of a set of 1907 and 1908 gold coins (which also included a lettered edge EHR coin) that was kept intact for many years until the set was sold by Stack's to New England Rare Coin Galleries in early 1980. NERCG broke up the set and the unique plain edge EHR was sold to dealer John Dannreuther, who subsequently sold the coin to a customer. The plain edge was struck from a badly cracked reverse die...."

[613] The terminology was suggested by Mr. Tripp as a replacement for the terms "inverted" and "normal," which had become confused over time.

**Edge Die Set A** has sans serif font lettering in evenly formed characters. The text is spaced **E\* | P\*L\*U\*R\*I\*B\*U\*S\* | U\*N\*U\*M\*** with a star between each letter. This version was used only on the 1906 Barber/Morgan $20 pattern and the three complete coins from Group One of February 1907.

**Edge Die Set B** has Roman font lettering in well-formed characters. The text is spaced **\*\*\*\*\*\*\*E\* | PLURIBUS | \*UNUM\*\*\*\*** with stars separating each word. This version was used on all coins from both the March (Group Two) and December (Group Three) batches.

There are also two possible alignments of each edge die set:

**Alignment I** edge letters are right side up when the coin is sitting obverse up. This alignment was used on the 1906 Barber/Morgan $20 pattern and the three complete coins from Group One of February 1907. It may also have been used on the three coins made in December 1907. (This was previously called "inverted," as in the opposite of "normal," lettering.)

**Alignment II** edge letters are upside down when the coin is sitting obverse up. This alignment was used on all coins from Group Two (March 1907).

$$\text{\*\*\*\*\textreversed{MUNU}\* | \textreversed{PLURIBUS} | \*\textreversed{E}\*\*\*\*\*\*\*}$$

Although using this alignment for most of the pattern coins might seem odd, it has a subtle elegance. If one looks at the obverse of the coin, then moves slightly to one side or the other, the edge lettering appears to be an extension of the coin's face, arching over the Liberty figure, with the text reading correctly. This counter-intuitive approach enhances the three-dimensional effect of the design, and was certainly intentional. (This was previously called "normal" lettering.)

Of the four possible combinations, three are known:

| | |
|---|---|
| **Edge Die Set A,** sans serif<br>**Alignment I,** letters right side up<br><br>3 Struck | **Edge Die Set B,** serif<br>**Alignment I,** letters right side up<br><br>3 (?) Known |
| **Edge Die Set A,** sans serif<br>**Alignment II,** letters upside down<br><br>None | **Edge Die Set B,** serif<br>**Alignment II,** letters upside down<br><br>13 Known |

These edge die set/alignment combinations appear to match known production batches:

| | | | |
|---|---|---|---|
| Edge Die Set A<br>Alignment I | A-I | February 7-14, 1907 | 3 struck* |
| Edge Die Set B<br>Alignment II | B-II | March – April 1907 | 13 (?) struck |
| Edge Die Set B<br>Alignment I | B-I | December 31, 1907 | 3 struck |

*Excluding plain-edge specimen.*

## Production Group One

Struck February 7–14, 1907, along with fifteen small-diameter versions. Lettered edge is A-I as probably prepared by Barber with little or no direction from the designer. Original owners include:

> 1 – George Roberts
> 1 – Robert Preston (via Roberts)
>> Gold examples loaned to Saint-Gaudens and returned:
>> 1 – Complete coin, lettered edge (later given to Roosevelt?)
>> 1 – First strike, plain edge
>> 1 – Second strike, plain edge
>> 1 – Third strike, plain edge
>> 1 – Complete coin in lead, plain edge
> 1 – Plain edge, defective due to die crack

Incomplete specimens were probably destroyed after the reverse die broke.

## Production Group Two

Struck during March and April 1907. Approval to strike two pieces for the mint cabinet was given by director Roberts and secretary Shaw. A total of ten to thirteen were struck with most going into Barber's personal collection. Lettered edge is B-II as probably stipulated by Saint-Gaudens.

> 2 – For Mint Collection
>> 1 – Given to Augusta Saint-Gaudens (June 1908) from mint collection by presidential order.
>> 1 – Remains in National Numismatic Collection (Smithsonian)
> Possibly eleven others – most evidently purchased by Charles Barber.

## Production Group Three

Struck December 31, 1907 on indirect orders from director Leach as interpreted by Philadelphia Mint Superintendent Landis. Three examples, probably with edge B-I, were prepared by Barber. Intended recipients were:

> 1 – Theodore Roosevelt, President of the United States
> 1 – George B. Cortelyou, Secretary of the Treasury
> 1 – Frank A. Leach, Director of the Mint

On April 22, 1907 director Roberts sent his extremely high relief $20 specimen to Frank Leach at the San Francisco Mint for his opinion. The coin was returned 2 weeks later. The February 5, 1908 accounting provided to Cortelyou by Leach says that a total of thirteen pieces were made. (Could these be only the coins made in March by Barber?) However, this is less than the number known to exist in the early twenty-first century. It is likely that the second group included more than the two pieces authorized for the mint collection, and probably accounts for most of the extant pieces.[614]

As with the #1 eagles, there are no sandblast proof specimens known. All pieces were struck on a medal press, and each piece was annealed between the seven blows it took to fully bring up the design.

Total mintage is unknown. At least three partial strikes were evidently melted. Fifteen pieces can be specifically accounted for, and others were made. Since fifteen of the small-diameter pieces were struck, it is possible Barber wanted to make the same number of normal pieces, but had to quit when the original reverse die broke. A reasonable estimate from what is known is that eighteen to twenty pieces were struck, including the lone plain edge coin but excluding other partial strikes.

The pedigrees of virtually all EHR specimens are so profoundly muddled that there seems little hope of tracking a specific coin to its original owner. Many conflicting claims about provenance have occurred over the years with several pieces attributed to Theodore Roosevelt or Saint-Gaudens. Even the NNC coin (*ex* Philadelphia Mint Collection) may have been confused with the other two pieces donated in later years. All three are from the same obverse, reverse and edge dies. From comments in Charles Barber's personal coin collection notebook, it is evident that many of the EHRs were purchased by him and later found their way to collectors.

## *Progress Strikes*

In making the first medal-coins from extremely high relief dies, Barber's experiments showed that a complete coin took seven blows from the medal press to bring up the design. Saint-Gaudens, through his assistant, Henry Hering, requested a set of plaster casts of the incomplete coins (called progress strikes) so he could determine how much of the design was brought up by each blow from the press. Barber reported the situation to superintendent Landis on February 20:[615]

> After making plaster casts of the double eagle (new design) intended to show the imperfect character of the impressions, I found the plaster not suitable for the purpose and quite unsatisfactory, and therefor have made electro deposits of the coins. These could bc better, and would be if more time can be allowed, but as I understand it, they are required at once. It would better demonstrate the result of the several blows from the press if gold pieces were sent to the Director, as any castings taken from the coins are most likely to be imperfect and perhaps misleading.
>
> The electrotypes from the hubs have imperfections, the result of taking the deposit too quickly; these imperfections are not upon the hubs.

---

[614] Many tertiary sources (auction catalogs, compilations, etc.) comment that one or more EHR pieces were "reported" melted. Incomplete strikes, being defective specimens, were likely melted and this may be the origin of such comments. The author has found no reference to the intentional destruction of any EHR $20 coins in reliable contemporary documents.

[615] *US Mint*, NARA-P, op. cit. Letter dated February 20, 1907 to Landis from Barber.

256

On February 21, Roberts sent Saint-Gaudens electrotypes of the incomplete coins, although he knew they were imperfect:[616]

> I am enclosing herewith a letter of the engraver of the Philadelphia Mint and accompanying it, electrotypes of the impressions taken from the new $20, showing successive stages of preparation. If it would be more satisfactory to you to have the original gold pieces, I will have them sent to you.

One Blow                   Two Blows

Three Blows             Seven Blows

*Figure 46. Electrotype progress strikes of the extremely high relief $20, February 1907. (top, L to R) One blow, two blows; (bottom, L to R) three blows, and seven blows at 150 tons per square inch pressure in a medal press. Differences are most evident in the upper end of the torch, which is about half-complete after the third strike. Coins were annealed between blows.* (Photos courtesy American Numismatic Society.)

In a letter of the same date, Saint-Gaudens requested samples of several intermediate state strikes, to which Barber advised:[617]

---

[616] *US Mint*, NARA-CP, op. cit., entry 235, vol. 367. Letter dated February 21, 1907 to Saint-Gaudens from Roberts. The terminology has been adopted from the medal production industry.

> The dies being broken I can only furnish such pieces as I have of the Double
> Eagle in gold, new design, namely; first, second, third strike and a finished piece…

Both coins and electrotypes were returned by Saint-Gaudens on March 13. The electrotypes, fragile as they were, somehow survived and found their way to the American Numismatic Society collection (possibly via George Kunz). Labels accompanying the items indicated how many blows the gold specimens had received.[618]

Although the electrotypes are not of very good quality, they clearly show that much of the central design was brought up by a single blow from the medal press. This is consistent with Roberts' comment in May about the effect of one blow being deceiving and may explain, in part, why his second model had nearly the same relief as the first one. The one-blow piece shows weakness in the peripheral details, such as stars, lettering and top of torch. However, central detail is good with most of Liberty's gown detail and facial features evident. After annealing the incomplete coin, a second blow at one hundred fifty tons brought up a small amount of additional detail in the center, and more of the stars and lettering; the torch is still incomplete. The difference between one and two blows is far less than that between the blank planchet and first strike. When the third blow was finished, stars and lettering were better formed, but the highest points of torch, knee, chest and similar areas remain incomplete. According to Saint-Gaudens it took three more strikes to bring up the final high-point details and a seventh blow to impart edge lettering. The electrotype of a completed coin (lower left image, below) has significantly better sharpness and overall detail than the other strikes. The gold examples would have shown better detail than these electrotypes, which Barber considered unsatisfactory. Director Roberts' comment to Saint-Gaudens summarized the situation: "A single blow accomplished so much that we were misled into thinking that very slight modifications to the model would suffice. I am now inclined to think that the relief must be very much reduced."[619]

The very limited improvement in detail produced by multiple strikes suggests that once the initial movement of metal was complete, it took considerable effort to force metal from recessed areas in the coin to the high points. Under normal conditions, the upset rim of the planchet combined with a less pronounced curvature of the die face were enough to produce full detail in central and peripheral parts of the coin. For high relief dies, the planchet was nearly flat, and the dies noticeably curved. As the dies contacted the planchet, most of the press energy was used to move metal into the central design. Little metal was left to move to peripheral areas, so lettering and stars remained ill-defined. A possible solution, as Frank Leach discovered, was to cut blanks thinner and larger than normal, then upset the rim much higher than usual. This brought the planchet into alignment with die curvature and allowed more even distribution of press energy across the coin. This would reduce the number of blows required to bring up fine detail. All of this supports director Leach's later comment that high relief coins could only be struck on ordinary presses if exaggerated relief was confined to the central part of the design.

[617] *US Mint*, NARA-P, op. cit. Internal memorandum dated February 25, 1907 to Landis from Barber.
[618] The labels are believed to be reliable although we do not know who prepared them. The electrotypes illustrated are #1949-156-2, #1949-156-5, #1949-156-6, #1949-156-8, from the ANS collection.
[619] *US Mint*, NARA-CP, op. cit., entry 330, box 45. Letter dated May 7, 1907 to Saint-Gaudens from Roberts.

**Double Eagle – P-2007 (J-1917).**
**Obverse 1, Reverse A (Extremely High Relief, Small-diameter)**
Struck between February 8 and 15, 1907.

Full length figure of Liberty striding upward on a rocky peak. She holds a torch of enlightenment in her right hand and a branch of olive in her left. Below, in front of the rock, is a bough of oak, behind her to the left is the Capitol building and rays from the rising sun. The date is in Roman numerals: M·C·M·VII. Above her is the inscription LIBERTY and surrounding are 46 stars representing the states of the union in November 1907.

This is from the same models as the extremely high relief normal diameter double eagle struck during the same week. Fourteen rays from the sun.

Pronounced fin rim around most of obverse and reverse rim. Does not appear to be intentional.

Lettered edge: **E\*P\*L\*U\*** | **R\*I\*B\*U\*S** | **\*U\*N\*U\*M\*** The sans serif characters are bold and clearly cut, but small compared to the width of the edge. This is the same arrangement, lettering style and size as on the normal diameter experimental pieces made in February 1907. The same letter punches appear to have been used.

Contemporary Comments:
AS-G: 2/20/07. *"…finished strike in lead of the small coin."*
CB: 2/25/07. *"I can…furnish… one impression of each diameter, in lead, without the lettering on the periphery."*
AAN: 1/9/08. *"Sent 1 DE, 2$^{nd}$ die; 1 DE, small die; 2 E, 2$^{nd}$ die." [to director Leach].*
FAL: 1/9/08. *"…have placed in the numismatic collection…if you have any left, two of the pieces of the double eagle design on the reduced diameter, or 'thick' planchets..."*
FAL: 1/10/08. *"I was quite surprised to receive the small double eagle, and will keep it…"*
TLC: 1/8/08. *"…it is an entirely illegal 'coin'…"*
Chicago Art Inst.: 1/25/08. *"We should like…to procure a specimen of the…diameter of the ten-dollar gold pieces….I understand these pieces to be illegal…"*
FAL: 2/1/08. *"…you have not…destroyed the small or illegal sized double eagles…" "In the memorandum… you say the five were sent to the bureau, two…in the mint cabinet, and eight were in your hands for mint officials…." "..they must be returned…"*
FAL: 2/1/08. *"…I desire to have two pieces placed in the cabinet…"*
FAL: 2/4/08. *"…your statement does not seem to include the piece I gave you to be returned…" "I have written to Mr. Roberts to obtain …the names of the persons to whom he gave these pieces…every one must be accounted for."*
JHL: 3/18/08. *"…[destroyed] the only remaining piece of the kind, except for two in the mint cabinet…"*

The obverse and reverse dies are from the same model (#1) as the extremely high relief patterns, only reduced to the diameter of the eagle. The coin is approximately twice the thickness of a normal $20 coin. There are no documents stating how many blows of the press it took to make the small-diameter coins. Fifteen struck, thirteen melted, two in the National Numismatic Collection.

(Photo courtesy Smithsonian Institution, National Numismatic Collection, Douglas Mudd; edge photo by David J. Camire courtesy NGC.)

This is the small-diameter double eagle that mint curator Comparette claimed was illegal. Director Leach went to great lengths to recover any specimens outside of the mint's collection. The coin is not illegal, since it is an experimental piece not issued for circulation. No statute restricts experimentation by the mint to those items that are in full compliance with the coinage laws. Further, President Roosevelt's order of July 25, 1907 waived mint regulations regarding experimental pieces.

These pieces do not appear to have been specifically authorized by the director. The extended discussion about them by mint officials suggests they were produced on the initiative of an officer of the Philadelphia Mint, probably engraver Charles Barber.

Based on correspondence between Leach and Landis, it appears there were fifteen pieces made with nearly all "spoken for" by mint officials. Director Roberts evidently had two (along with two of the first #1 model pieces, with one of each given to Robert Preston), but returned them on Leach's insistence. Of the fifteen pieces, two are in the National Numismatic Collection as Leach directed, and the rest were melted.

The hubs were destroyed on May 24–25, 1910.

**Double Eagle – P-1998 (J-1905).**
**Obverse 5, Reverse B₂**
Struck between March 28 and May 22, 1907. Specifically requested by Saint-Gaudens.

Obverse is of Liberty head facing left wearing an American Indian ceremonial headdress originally intended as the obverse for the cent. Thirteen six-pointed stars (although some are partially obscured) around the upper half of the portrait. The word LIBERTY below the portrait.

Relief is higher than on the version used on the $10 eagles and similar to the extremely high relief $20. This is consistent with other models of the time.

Reverse with an eagle flying to the left. Above in two lines are UNITED STATES OF AMERICA and TWENTY DOLLARS. Below eagle is a rising sun with thirteen long rays; across the face of the sun is the date in Roman numerals: ·M ·C ·M· VII· with numeral groups separated by round periods.

Reverse is the #2 model with the date in Roman numerals added, incuse, over the sun on the reverse. Models exist with the date both incuse and in relief.

Lettered edge: Serif (Roman) font ******E* | **PLURIBUS** | *UNUM**** edge die alignment B-II as on most extremely high relief coins.

Contemporary Comments:
AS-G: 3/12/07. *"…I should very much like to see it tried…on the twenty-dollar…"*
TR: 3/14/07. *"I have directed that be done at once."*
AS-G: 3/28/07. *"I am…sending…plaster with the date on the sun…for the reverse with the Indian head…"*
TR: 5/12/07. *"…I want to keep the figure of Liberty for at least one small issue of the coins."*
GR: 5/25/07. *"…This is the last word on the subject…."*
AS-G: 5/31/07. *"I acknowledge receipt…of two (2) lead impressions of the …double eagle: one with figure the other with head…"*

Saint-Gaudens specifically requested this pattern so he could see how the Liberty head would look when reduced to the size of the double eagle. Although the artist preferred this obverse, President Roosevelt liked the Striding Liberty design and ordered it used. Saint-Gaudens saw only the lead impression mentioned in correspondence on May 31. Apparently Barber kept the gold version for his personal collection. This is the only 1907 pattern with a pedigree definitively originating with engraver Barber.

(Photo courtesy David Akers.)


In 1910 Barber noted on his hub and die inventory, "Liberty head design for obverse double eagle, high relief; afterward reduced in relief and used for eagle. The model was changed by Saint Gaudens."[620]

---

[620] *US Mint*, NARA-CP, op. cit., entry 229, box 290. Letter dated May 24, 1910 to director Andrew from Barber.

Saint-Gaudens apparently did not see the gold version, which Barber kept for his own collection. (Barber also attempted to keep a small-diameter $20, and owned at least eight of the extremely high relief $20 version.) Only one example is known. The hubs were destroyed on May 24–25, 1910.

**Double Eagle – Pattern Unknown – Probable Lettered Edge.**
**Obverse 2, Reverse B - Very High Relief**
Struck May 3-4, 1907.
Illustrations are of the models, not a coin. Specimens struck but now unknown.

Similar to first EHR, above; however, the model is much more detailed than the #1 version. Prominent berries added to olive branch, Capitol building larger, stars better defined and more evenly distributed. Notice that a star sits directly above the "Y" of LIBERTY. Figure more clearly modeled and detailed. Liberty's face is less broad. 26 rays show behind the figure.

Same composition as above, with 14 long rays from sunrise.

Edge: Unknown. Presumed to be similar to: ******E* | **PLURIBUS** | *UNUM****  as used on the EHR coins in large, relatively low relief serif-style (Roman) letters with exaggerated serifs; stars nearly touch rim; portions may be weak. Alignment probably B-II as are the majority of EHR specimens.

Contemporary Comments:
CB: 5/4/07. *"I...have attempted to strike some pieces...150 tons is excessive...there is a loss of convexity...although I have only struck these few pieces ."* [Eight very high relief experimental #2 coins]
TR: 5/8/07. *"It has proved hitherto impossible to strike them with one blow..."*

This is the final medal-relief double eagle design to leave Saint-Gaudens' studio, and must be considered the sculptor's ultimate conception of the design. Obviously a more refined and perfected design than on the first models. The relief is nearly as high as on the #1 models. Eight experimental pieces made on May 3rd from Very High Relief dies. It is possible that Barber retained the two best examples for his collection, and these were later unknowingly sold as ordinary high relief coins.

The photographs were made in 1908 during the Metropolitan Museum of Art memorial exhibition.

(Photo from Smithsonian Peter A. Juley & Son Collection.)

The "missing link" in the sequence of pattern double eagles is the Very High Relief (VHR) version produced in early May 1907. We know from documentation that eight pieces were struck using varying numbers of blows of the medal press. Two pieces were struck with one blow, two with two blows, two with three blows, and the last two with ten blows of the press, all at one hundred fifty tons pressure. This sequence of test strikes approximates that of the first version seen by Saint-Gaudens in February. We also know that both Roosevelt and Saint-Gaudens saw the complete set of progress strikes before the President ordered low relief to be used.

An inventory of Barber's personal collection includes eight coins described as "patterns," separating them only into two groups of four each. The eight coins could have been any of the varieties now known, including VHR patterns. Possibly, sitting in a couple of coin collections, are two undiscovered pattern coins masquerading as normal high relief strikes. If one wanted to distinguish a very high relief pattern coin from a normal high relief there are specific points to look for. The following guidelines are based on comparison with EHR specimens and the original VHR models.

- First, the alignment B-II edge of the VHR pattern will be approximately the same thickness as the EHR pattern – or about 1.5 times that of a high relief piece, and it will have a fin rim;
- Second, a VHR pattern should exhibit significant detail on the highest points of the design including Liberty's nose, knee, toes and fingers;
- Third, the stars will be fully separated from the rim unlike any of the circulation strikes;
- Fourth, the eagle's wing will show detail across the highest points, and the tail feathers will be distinct and separated from the rim;
- Fifth, all lettering will be slightly thinner than on high relief pieces, sharper and fully separated from the rim;
- Sixth, the Capitol building will appear wider than on a high relief specimen;
- Seventh, the surface will have the color of nearly pure gold, as on the EHR;
- Finally, the overall relief will be measurably higher than on any high relief coin, and comparable to a EHR examples.

Any candidate specimen should be examined next to well-preserved examples of the EHR and high relief coins, and the illustrations of original models provided in this book.

**Double Eagle – Circulation Issue.**
**Obverse 2$_A$, Reverse B$_1$ – High Relief**
Specimen illustrated has normal lettered edge.

Produced from the same models as the VHR patterns, but hub cut at lower relief.

Produced from the same models as the VHR patterns, but hub cut at lower relief. The extreme left long ray has been lost in the reduction or intentionally removed from the hub, leaving 13 rays.

These were made from the #2 models.

Edge: B-II

******E* | **PLURIBUS** | *UNUM**** in large, relatively low relief serif-style (Roman) letters with exaggerated serifs; stars nearly touch rim; portions may be weak. Lettering style is consistent with obverse and reverse lettering of model but looks wrong on the coin. Lettering usually B-II when coin is held obverse up, however specimens are reported (but not confirmed) with B-I alignment, also. It is not known if these are trial pieces or simply mistakes in installing the collar.

Plain edge examples (P-2005; Judd-1914) are probably production errors and not intentional pattern or experimental pieces.

Contemporary Comments:

CB: 5/4/07. *"I...have attempted to strike some pieces...150 tons is excessive...there is a loss of convexity...although I have only struck these few pieces ."* [Eight very high relief experimental #2 coins]

AS-G: 5/11/07. *"...I have not the slightest doubt that...low relief will settle the matter."*

JHL: 5-9-07. Landis suggests reducing relief by 1/5 using Janvier lathe *"...as much as the machine will allow."*

ASG: 5/31/07. *"...acknowledging receipt of...the electrotype of the lowest relief of the figure of Liberty..."*

CB: 6/7/07. *"...the year is in Roman notation [with] no provision for even next year..."*

TR: 8/22/07. *"...strike a few thousand...would be issued after the regular issue of ...lower relief has begun."*

RP: 8/27/07. *" ...proceed to strike five hundred experimental pieces from... the eagle and double eagle, in high relief."*

FAL: 11/22/07. *"By direction of the President you are instructed to proceed with striking the double eagles of the new design, second model, <u>on a medal press.</u>"*

CB: 11/23/07. *"I have made arrangement with my people to work all day and all night and Sunday..."*

FAL: 12/23/07. *"The President was greatly pleased...so please send more [for him]..."*

The relief is not as high as on the #1 or #2 models. Experimental pieces made on May 3rd from very high relief dies; 500 high relief versions produced in late August–early September; 12,867 struck through January 6, 1908 for official presentation, sale to collectors and distribution to sub-treasuries. Many specimens show uneven striking at right reverse and left obverse, and/or doubling of figure outline due to warping of  the coins during annealing.

Pieces with differing edge lettering styles may or may not be patterns. High relief experimental pieces were probably struck, but there is no documentation that explains their differences from ordinary coins. Plain edge examples are probably production errors.

(Photo courtesy Harry W. Bass, Jr. Research Foundation; edge photo courtesy American Numismatic Society.)

Only pieces with non-standard edge lettering might be considered patterns. These, and plain edge specimens, could also be errors in placing the collar dies, not intentional experimental pieces.[621] Examples with B-I edge lettering could have been accidentally created by reversing the position of the dies. For the Striding Liberty design, the obverse was normally placed in the anvil, or lower, position. Coiner Freed felt this gave more energy to the obverse and brought up the design better. Inadvertent reversal of die position would produce B-I edge lettering even if the edge collar were placed correctly. The same situation applies to the EHR patterns with B-I edge.

The MCMVII high relief coins are a special circulation issue made in limited quantities for collectors and the artistically appreciative. Five hundred coins were produced in late August/early September; a second group was minted from November 23 to January 6, 1908. The total struck was 12,867 including Assay Commission[622] pieces but excluding patterns. Eighty pieces were reported melted due to excessive edge fin, leaving a net of 12,787; however, reported mintage varies with the source. These were used for official presentation, sale to collectors and distribution to sub-treasuries. Many coins, including most earlier pieces, have a fin, or "wire" rim; later coins have no fin and also show better delineation of stars and rim. Several pieces are known with obvious die cracks, suggesting that post-production inspection was somewhat superficial. (Note director Leach's complaint, discussed earlier.) The coins are pale shadows of the original models.

In May, the first attempt to produce coins from the #2 very high relief models was a failure. Superintendent Landis suggested cutting new hubs at the maximum reduction in relief the Janvier reducing lathe would allow. An electrotype sample was sent to Saint-

---

[621] The notion that plain edge high relief double eagles were patterns was put to rest by Vicken Yegparian a research cataloger for Stack's Numismatists. His examination of lots 3436 (plain edge) and 3431 (lettered edge) in Stack's *Americana Sale* of January 16-18, 2006 showed that both coins were made from the same pair of well-used dies. See pp.335, 338-339 of the catalog for a complete exposition.

[622] Assay Commission minutes do not differentiate between various designs of double eagle for 1907.

Gaudens on May 27. This evidently worked to a limited extent and later permitted satisfactory coins to be struck with three blows of the press instead of seven. No coins are known to exist from the original pair of dies, but see above for additional discussion.

As with other early examples of the Saint-Gaudens design, no sandblast proofs have been verified to exist. All pieces were struck on a medal press.[623] Each piece required 3 blows, plus annealing between the strikes. Many coins show doubling due to the planchets changing shape during heating and cooling. Coins struck in later December and early January 1908 were made from planchets that had a different upset angle and diameter than normal. This was the result of experiments done by Frank Leach at the San Francisco Mint while he was superintendent in early 1907.

It is possible the edge collar used on the first five hundred high relief double eagles had a different arrangement of stars and letters, or used a different font style than later coins. This could be determined by comparing specimens known to be from the first production with coins from the November–January production. The difficulty in verifying this theory is in locating coins that can be definitively attributed to the August-September striking.

The list of purchasers (later in this chapter) indicates at least seven (7) specimens were sold or distributed that were part of the first production. All of these specimens were distributed prior to November 23 initiation of full production. These coins are:

| 1 | Asst. Sec. John Edwards | September 10 | 5 coins |
|---|---|---|---|
| 2 | Robert Preston, Mint Bureau Acting Director | September 10 | 1 coin |
| 3 | Alexander Caldwell | November 19 | 1 coin |

The Edwards and Preston coins can only have come from the first five hundred or from experimental pieces; Caldwell's specimen also likely came from the same group since it predates the resumption of circulation production by four days. Unfortunately, these are the only coins out of the original five hundred which can be conclusively identified. After passage of a century, attribution of specimens to these three owners will be extremely difficult. To make things more confusing, Caldwell purchased a second high relief $20 on December 5, 1907 and it cannot be determined from which production group this coin originated.

While working out production problems with the Saint-Gaudens coins, the U. S. Mint made experimental coins of several different designs. In at least two instances the coins were struck by direct order of the President. In routine cases the coins were prepared so that treasury and mint officials could review the design as it would actually appear in circulation. None of these coins were prepared with any special surface other than that created when the working dies were impressed from the hubs. Any pattern or experimental coin of these designs that is called a "proof," "matte proof," "sandblast proof" or other such term implying special treatment should be viewed with caution. (Apparently, high relief $20 were handled individually after striking and did not come into contact with other

[623] David Akers comments in his 1982 book on double eagles: "High Relief, Wire Rim. There were no proofs struck for collectors, but a small number of pieces do exist that are undoubtedly proofs based on the fact that they were struck with the lettered edge collar used on the EHR coins. They are also characterized by an unusually satiny surface and myriad raised die scratches and swirls in the fields. There are other proofs with different-sized edge letters and unusual finishes, including one of the Gilhousen coins and the 'matte proof' DiBello-Auction '81 specimen. There is one piece struck with a plain edge. It appeared in a 1972 Hans Schulman sale and realized a phenomenal $43,000." (Akers: pp.280–281) *NB: The present author has not been able to examine the various pieces mentioned.*

coins until they were placed in bags of $5,000 and shipped to sub-treasuries. Pieces that had not been bagged could have left the mint in nearly perfect condition. If someone purchased a high relief $20 direct from the Philadelphia Mint, then had it sandblasted, it would be very difficult to determine whether the sandblasting were done by the mint or outside the mint.) All these coins are so infrequently seen by numismatists that third-party authentication is mandatory.[624]

Nearly all 1907 gold patterns and limited issue circulation coins have been entombed in plastic slabs that partially or completely obscure the edge. This limits differentiation of varieties because few owners ever give the edge of their coins more than a cursory examination. Thus, reliable edge die data is dubious for even the best pedigreed specimens. The hubs were destroyed on May 24–25, 1910.

[624] However, the reader is cautioned that grading services do not necessarily agree on use of the term "proof" as it relates to these pieces. In truth, none of the experimental or pattern coins issued from 1907 to 1917 appear to have been produced as deliberate brilliant or sandblast proof specimens, except the polished 1916 silver patterns of the first designs. (*Renaissance of American Coinage 1916–1921* has a more thorough discussion of this subject). A tiny number of 1907 low-relief gold pieces are known with legitimate sandblast proof surfaces, although it cannot be determined when and where they were made. Attributions by Walter Breen of various "proof" specimens are not reliable and many of these claims were allegedly repudiated by him before his death.

**Double Eagle – Not Listed – Circulation Version**
**Obverse 3 and Obverse 4 – Low Relief**
Low relief model on left; coin as struck on right.

Obverse 3. Model of Henry Hering's low relief version completed September 20, 1907. Compare with Barber's re-engraved version issued for circulation (right). Note difference in gown and rays on right, particularly.

At least three experimental pieces made from this model but none known. Due to limited previous understanding of these coins, examples may be incorrectly described as satin or "Roman" circulation version proofs.

Obverse 4. Produced from Hering's models but detail re-engraved in the hubs by Barber. Compare Liberty's gown (particularly at the top of her left leg), hair and face.

These were made from the #3 models, at left.

Slightly modified during the next five years to more closely resemble the original low relief models.

Edge: ******E* | **PLURIBUS*** | **UNUM**** in large, relatively low relief serif-style (Roman) letters.
Circulation version has edge lettering aligned B-II when coin is held obverse up, however specimens could exist (but none confirmed) with B-I alignment, also. At least three pieces reported with small edge letters, another with large edge letters and another with Gothic-style lettering, all of which may or may not be experimental pieces. In February 1908 experimental pieces with large edge lettering and stars were struck and examined by the director. However, all examples were ordered destroyed. (See the *Pattern, Experimental and Pre-Release Coins, 1907* table, below.)
Contemporary Comments:
CEB: 10/10/07. *"…the Double Eagle, new designs, I beg to say that the [low relief] models arrived at this Mint Sept. 28th."*
CEB: 10/22/07. *"In reducing the relief to the extent we have had to… all detail has been lost…"*
FAL: 11/16/07. *"I should regret very much to learn that Mr. Hering could not go ahead on the new model…It seems to me if he would… produce the new models on the lines of our recent interview…that we shall have a successful issue."*
AAN: 11/30/07. *"…1 double eagle from Mr. Barber's modified dies, delivered to you, personally…"*
FAL: 12/2/07. *"[The president]… was greatly pleased with the appearance…"*
ASG: 12/6/07. *" 'I am disappointed in the minted double-eagle, although the other is a beauty'; - that is, the one from the medal press."*
There may be multiple experimental varieties extant whose true character is obscured by plastic holders. Several pattern pieces from Hering's original models were struck on a medal press and may still exist. They will likely be satin proofs or sandblast and exhibit detail as shown on the model (above, left), although the detail will be weak.

There may also be examples of Barber's intermediate hub recutting, which do not match Hering's version yet differ from other circulation strikes. It will take considerable time and research to sort out the situation.

(Courtesy U. S. Department of Interior National Park Service, Saint-Gaudens National Historic Site, Cornish, NH. #1068.)

## Edge Collar Mechanism

The toggle and English collars used routinely for low relief circulation coins were also used for some high relief pieces. This may be the source of most lettering variations on these coins. For the EHR version, a plain circular collar was used for strikes one through six, with the coin being removed and annealed between strikes. For the seventh and final strike, a lettered collar consisting of three segments replaced the plain collar. These were held in place by a circular retaining ring. After the last strike, the lettered collar and coin were pushed out of the retaining ring. A similar process was used for most of the high relief $20 coins in August–September, and November–January, although only three blows were required to complete the coin.

Raised edge lettering did not simply appear "out of nothingness" at the Philadelphia Mint. Although often ignored by collectors, this third side of the coin may have been the most difficult side to produce for the new coins.

### *Background*

In the nineteenth century the U. S. Mint, like any other in the world, was concerned about counterfeiting and alteration of coins. In an era when gold coins contained very nearly their face value in precious metal, and were used in international trade, the mint had to do everything it could to prevent counterfeiting, or at least make the work too expensive and time consuming to be of advantage to criminals.

Since ancient times, governments have done all they could to prevent the clipping and filing of coins. Severe penalties were enacted for defacing coins by removing metal, yet the practice continued. With improvements in coining equipment mint masters had a wider range of options available to prevent filing and altering of coins. As early as 1658, the English government under Oliver Cromwell issued crown and half-crown coins with raised edge lettering, a practice that continued through the reign of George IV. Most early United States coins used sunken relief letters on the edge as a deterrent to filing and for identification of the denomination.

The U. S. Mint abandoned sunken edge lettering in 1836 with the advent of steam powered presses, and resorted to narrow vertical reeding which permitted coins to be struck and ejected from the edge collar in rapid succession.

Although sunken edge lettering and reeding made the counterfeiter's life more difficult than plain edges, the problems were quickly surmounted with the result that counterfeit, filed, split and hollowed-out gold coins had become a major problem by 1860. As early as 1857, the U. S. Mint provided research space for Dr. J. T. Barclay to experiment with making thinner coins and other anti-counterfeiting measures including the lettered edge patterns (P-317, J-269) of 1860. In 1867 A. Loudoun Snowden recommended using raised edge letters on silver and gold coins, "...but at that time found it impossible to accomplish the desired result with our present steam powered toggle joint press."

During his tenure, director Henry R. Linderman contemplated using a lettered edge on gold coins[625] in 1873 and for the new twenty-cent piece[626] in 1874. Also, an 1879 silver

[625] *US Mint*, NARA-CP, op. cit., entry 235, vol. 1, p.313. Letter dated August 14, 1873 from director Linderman to superintendent Pollock. Anthony C. Paquet squelched this idea in a letter to Linderman on October 8, 1873 by claiming that a new press would be needed for each denomination.
[626] *US Mint*, NARA-CP, op. cit., entry 229, series 2, box 1. Letter dated April 27, 1874 to Linderman from William Barber.

dollar with raised edge lettering is reported in the 1916 inventory of Charles Barber's personal pattern coin collection.[627] But circumstances were not right for more extensive experiments.

## Reasons for 1885 Edge Lettering Experiments

Late in 1884, Snowden, who was superintendent of the Philadelphia Mint, became aware of the arrest of two counterfeiters. In their possession were false dies "...prepared by a process, which if intelligently followed, would practically place the coinage of our country at the mercy of those possessing the secret....By this process, as you [director Burchard] and Secretary of the Treasury [Fairchild] are aware, I recently produced one cent pieces which...an expert, long connected with this mint, pronounced...from genuine dies."

Snowden began a series of experiments aimed at producing a mechanism for impressing raised lettering on the edge of a coin without damaging the lettering thus produced. The process is fairly simple to describe: "...a segmented collar could open to receive the blank, close when the pressure was applied, and open at the instant the lower die lifted the coin out of the collar." This was, however, a task that most of the mint mechanics thought was impossible to do on production presses.[628] After much experimentation, on June 12, 1885 Snowden and the mint staff succeeded in getting the mechanism to work at normal production speeds of eighty to one hundred ten coins per minute.

Superintendent Snowden explained the new edge collar in more detail to director Burchard.[629]

> The collar used is in three segments, with the letters, "E Pluribus Unum" sunk on the inner circle. This collar is enclosed in a steel ring fitted to the brass table of the coining press. The segments are held in place by springs underneath, which by the movement of the ring opens the collar. Through the brass table, a rod connected on each side is moved backward and forward by cams, which are worked from the main shaft of the press, closing and opening the segmented collar. The ring, through which the collar is opened and closed, has on its inside circumference, three circular widges [sic: wedges], to which the outside of the segments are fitted. The partial revolution of the ring acting on the line of the widges, forces the segments toward their common center, thereby closing the collar. The movement in opening and closing the segments, must be in exact harmony with the complex movement of the press, by which the planchets or blanks are carried forward from the tubes by the feeders, dropped on the dies, stamped, thrown up by the lower die, and carried off by the feeder in placing the succeeding blank in the collar, [all] at a speed of 80 to 110 per minute.
>
> As a mechanical appliance it is very accurate in its work, the letters can be placed even on so small and thin a coin as the gold dollar. The cost of making the attachment...will be insignificant – say one hundred and fifty dollars each.

Snowden's opinion was that coins with raised edge lettering would not only be beautiful, but more secure from counterfeiting and alteration than reeded-edge coins. But, if the mechanism worked well and was relatively inexpensive and offered greater protec-

---

[627] *Charles Edward Barber* papers, American Numismatic Association Reference Library.

[628] The earliest documented use of a segmented edge collar and lettered edge devices was that of Aubin Olivier at the Paris *Monnaie du Moulin des Étuves* (Mill Mint) sometime before 1555. The London Tower Mint struck small quantities of silver crowns for Oliver Cromwell in a similar manner. See *Hocking* in the bibliography.

[629] *US Mint*, NARA-CP, op. cit., entry 229, series 2, box. 1. Letter dated June 23, 1885 to Mint Bureau director Horatio Burchard from Philadelphia Mint superintendent A. Loudoun Snowden. pp.14-15.

tion to the coins, why was it not used? The answers may be near the end of Snowden's long letter.[630]

> As I am about retiring from the Mint, I must leave to my successor and to you the labor of obtaining such legislation from Congress as will authorize the placing of raised letters upon our precious metal coins. I enclose herewith a specimen of the coin in copper, for yourself.

Director Burchard left office within a month of receiving Snowden's letter; superintendent Snowden resigned before the end of the year. No one with the superintendent's insight, ability or willingness to experiment stepped up to complete the work. Snowden closed his report by thanking engraver Charles Barber, assistant engraver William Key and mechanic George Soley for perfecting the mechanism.

Nothing more was done with raised edge lettering in the nineteenth century. The mechanism Snowden and the others had worked so hard on was forgotten, and eventually discarded as junk. It was not until Augustus Saint-Gaudens submitted his new double eagle designs in December 1906 that the idea was resurrected. With presidential orders to use the new designs exactly as the artist submitted them, and no obvious place to put the required E Pluribus Unum motto, the artist's son, Homer, and mint engraver Barber (who had worked on the 1885 rendition) evidently agreed to use raised lettering on the coin's edge. After completing a quick experimental sample (P-1992, J-1773), probably for director Robert's approval, the mint struggled to re-invent a production-quality, three-segment edge collar for the eagle and double eagle. Without the force of President Roosevelt backing Saint-Gaudens' design concepts, conventional reeded edges might have been used on the new coins, just as they were on Bela Pratt's designs in 1908. To Saint-Gaudens, edge ornamentation – whether stars or lettering – was an artistic touch needed to complete the design. For the mint it was an engineering challenge to be met because the President demanded it. Only later did the mint revert to claiming its original purpose of edge lettering: counterfeit and alteration protection.

It was not until September 1907 that the new mechanism was completely successful on the $10 gold coins, and it was December before the double eagle version was operating reliably at Philadelphia. Denver and San Francisco mints had additional problems with the mechanism and it was August 1908 before the San Francisco Mint could strike the new coins without damaging the presses.

## Lead and Cardboard Trial Pieces, Now Unknown

Trial pieces of one or both sides of a die were routinely produced in lead for review by the engraving department and mint officials. For the Saint-Gaudens coinage these were also sent to the artist for his examination. Cardboard (actually thick paperboard) impressions were occasionally used when officials wanted to see the design, but the dies were incomplete and not hardened. The rectangular cardboard stock was dampened, struck with the dies at sufficient pressure to show the full design, then allowed to dry. (The strike squeezed most of the moisture from the paper.) The dried cardboard "coin" was reasonably durable and easily disposed of.

The table below lists all lead and cardboard trial pieces mentioned in original sources but unknown in museum or private collections. The cardboard pieces were sup-

---

[630] Ibid. p.18.

posed to have been kept by the director's office as part of the official record of acceptance of the designs, but cannot now be located.

| Description | Design Date | Strike Date | Quantity Reported |
|---|---|---|---|
| **Double Eagle** | | | |
| Lead – Standing Eagle | June 1906 | Before Nov. 28, 1906 | 1* |
| Lead – Standing Eagle | June 1906 | Before Dec. 3, 1906 | 1* |
| Lead – #1 model | November 1906 | Before Feb. 14, 1907 | 1 |
| Lead – #1 model, sm dia | November 1906 | Before Feb. 14, 1907 | 1 |
| Lead – #2 model, HR | March 1907 | Before May 17, 1907 | 1 |
| Card – motto position | Late Dec., 1907 | Before Feb. 27, 1908 | 1 |
| Card – motto position | Feb., 1908 | Before May 21, 1908 | 1 |
| **Eagle** | | | |
| Card – motto position [631] | Late Dec., 1907 | Before Feb. 27, 1908 | 1 |
| Card – motto position | Feb. 1908 | Before May 21, 1908 | 1 |

*\* Both lead trials were returned to the mint on December 12, 1906*

Lead trial pieces are usually stated as being struck without edge lettering, although there are reports of examples with lettered edges.

## Accounting for Experimental Coins

There was no formal accounting system used for the pattern and experimental pieces produced in 1907. During George Roberts' tenure as director, it appears that superintendent Landis and engraver Barber agreed on a quantity to be struck, and the superintendent distributed the samples according to the director's instructions. After Leach became director there are several comments in his letters about producing an accounting for or recovering of experimental coins (see above).

If a list was compiled other than Leach's of February 5, 1908, it has not been located. Beyond the quantities mentioned by Leach and in subsequent correspondence, we can only estimate how many of each of the pattern designs were struck and to whom they were given. Throughout much of 1908, coins were openly sold by the mint, director Leach, assistant secretary Edwards, and secretary Cortelyou in response to collector requests. In some instances there may have been only two or three samples made, in other circumstances, hundreds or thousands could have been produced to test planchet diameter and milling, or width of the rim.

Striking substantial quantities of production trial pieces was not an uncommon occurrence at the mint. In many instances the production trials were deemed satisfactory and the coins released to circulation with no public notice; these were usually identical to later issues. At other times, the trial pieces were evaluated, condemned and melted. There was increasing pressure for the mint to make production trials as a greater percentage of a new coin design work was sculpted in plaster rather than cut directly into a steel hub. The engraving and coining departments did not have any means to determine if a new design would really work correctly in production except to make a few hundred (or thousand) coins and examine the results.

In 1907, much of the work with Saint-Gaudens' designs was considered experimental. This meant there was no need to make quantities of production trial coins, since

---

[631] *US Mint*, NARA-P, op. cit. Letter dated February 27, 1908 to Landis from Leach.

the high relief designs were not intended for circulation. However, when the eagle design was modified by Barber to add a border and lower the relief (model two), acting director Preston ordered production to begin, and 31,500 coins were struck. Preston's order indicates these were intended to be coins for general circulation, but Leach's assessment in November seems to classify the pieces as unsuccessful production trials. All except fifty of these coins were condemned and melted. The five hundred high relief eagles (knife rim) and double eagles from August–September were made as a contingency to have something to show the President and for collectors, and not as fully settled designs for circulation. The double eagles eventually became part of the first design released for circulation. The eagles, however, were not released and instead were ordered transferred to the treasurer. We don't know who purchased these coins, but most were sold and others were melted.

In future years, as the mint contended with new designs, production trial coins were made of the high relief Winged Liberty ("Mercury") dime (August–September 1916), the high and medium relief experimental Peace dollars (January 1922). Both tests included striking thousands of coins, most of which were melted when they failed to meet expectations. The miniscule mintage of 1916 Standing Liberty quarters might also be considered production trials that were released to circulation. The early 1917 coins were of a different design although neither was actually Hermon MacNeil's work. Lastly, 1922 low relief Peace dollars were made by the thousands to test production characteristics several days before the design was approved. These coins were so nearly identical to the later "normal" coins that they were released to banks in February 1922.[632]

### *Pattern, Experimental and Pre-Release Coins, 1907*

| Denomina-tion | Model No. | Quan. | To (Distributed) | Date (Distributed) | Quan. (Returned) | To (Returned) | Date (Returned) |
|---|---|---|---|---|---|---|---|
| $20 | Standing Eagle | 2 | Director – lead trials | Dec. 1, 06 | 2 | Mint | Feb. 12, 07 |
| $20 | #1 | 2 | Director – EHR gold coins | Feb. 15, 07 | | | |
| $20 | #1 | 2 | Director – Sm. dia. gold coins | Feb. 15, 07 | 2 | Mint | Aug. 2, 07 |
| $20 | #1 | 4 | Director – electrotypes to S-G | Feb. 20, 07 | | | |
| $20 | #1 | 1 | SG – gold coin, LE | Feb. 25, 07 | 1 | Mint | Mar.13, 07 |
| $20 | #1 | 1 | SG – 1 strike, gold, PE | Feb. 25, 07 | 1 | Mint | Mar.13, 07 |
| $20 | #1 | 1 | SG – 2 strikes, gold, PE | Feb. 25, 07 | 1 | Mint | Mar.13, 07 |
| $20 | #1 | 1 | SG - 3 strikes, gold, PE | Feb. 25, 07 | 1 | Mint | Mar.13, 07 |
| $20 | #1 | 1 | SG – lead, large, PE | Feb. 25, 07 | 1 | Mint | Mar.13, 07 |
| $20 | #1 | 1 | SG – lead, small dia, PE | Feb. 25, 07 | 1 | Mint | Mar.13, 07 |
| $20 | #1 dies | 1 pr | Dies broken in use | Before Feb. 25 | | | |
| $20 | Thick, Small Dia. 1st model | 15 | Various | Before Feb. 25 | 13 melted | 2 – Mint Collection | By Feb. 08; Two more melted Mar. 2, 08. 1- Dir Leach (Rtd 2/4/08) |
| $20 | #1 | 2–13 | Mint Cabinet – from new dies per Sec Treas/Dir | After Mar. 4, 07 | | | |

[632] See Burdette: *Renaissance of American Coinage 1916-1921* for more information.

| Denomina-tion | Model No. | Distributed | | | Returned | | |
|---|---|---|---|---|---|---|---|
| | | Quan. | To | Date | Quan. | To | Date |
| $20‡ | #1 | 8 | Charles Barber | After March 1907 | 0 | | |
| $20 | none | 8 | Planchets to Barber | May 3, 07 | | | |
| $20 | #2 | 8 | Superintendent – Leach – President – S-G coins* | May 4, 07 | | | |
| $20 | Lib. Head | 1 | Mint – Gold | May 22 (?) | | | |
| $20 | Lib. Head | 1 | Saint-Gaudens- Lead | May 27 | | | |
| $20 | #2 | 1 | Saint-Gaudens | May 27,07 | | | |
| $20 | #2 lowest relief re-duction | 1 | Saint-Gaudens | May 27,07 | | | |
| $10 | #1 | 2 | Superintendent – Plain Edge coins | July 19, 07 | | | |
| $10 | #1 | above | Cortelyou & Saint-Gaudens – Plain Edge coins | July 22, 07 | 1 | Mint, S-G Estate | Aug. 20, 07 Jan. 11, 08 |
| $10 | #1 | 2 | Roosevelt – Plain Edge coins | July 29, 07 | 2 | Cortelyou | July 29, 07 |
| $10 | #1 | 1 | Superintendent to Dir. to Sec. Treas | Aug. 26, 07 | 1 | Mint coiner | Sep. 13, 07 |
| $10 | #2 | 1 | Superintendent to Dir to Sec. Treas. | Aug. 26, 07 | 1 | Mint coiner | Sep. 13, 07 |
| $10 | #1 | 500 | Superintendent | Aug. 27-30, 07 | 500 | To Treas. | Dec. 14, 07 |
| $20 | #2 | 500 | Superintendent | Aug. 27, 07 | 500 | To Treas. | Dec. 14, 07 |
| $10 | #2 | 2 (?) | Roosevelt | Sep. 3, 07 | | Tres. Sec | Sep. 3, 07 |
| $10** | #3 | 1 | Dir. – President | Oct. 3, 07 | | | |
| $10 | #2 | 1 | Dir. – President | Oct. 3, 07 | | | |
| $20 | #3 | 2 | Superintendent, Dir. | Oct. 22, 07 | 2 | Mint | Dec. 16, 07 |
| $20 | #3 | 1 | C. O. Brewster | Nov. 14, 07 | 1 | Mint | Nov. 18, 07 |
| $20 | #4 | 2 | Director (one to Brewster 12/4) | Nov. 30, 07 | 1 | Mint | Dec. 16, 07 |
| $20 | #2 | 1 | C. O. Brewster | Dec. 2, 07 | | | |
| $20 | #4 | 1 | Barber | Dec. 2, 07 | 1 | Mint | Dec. 9, 07 |
| $20 | #4 | 1 | C. O. Brewster | Dec. 4, 07 | | | |
| $20 | #1 | 3 | Roosevelt, Cortelyou, Leach | Dec. 31, 07 | 0 | | |
| $20 | #4 Lg. Stars | 1+ | Director † | Before Jan. 29, 08 | 1+ | Mint, de-stroyed | ? |
| $20 | #4 w/motto | 1 | Director | Feb. 19, 08 | 1 | Mint, de-stroyed | Feb. 26, 08 |
| $10 | #3 w/motto | 1 | Director[633] | Before Feb 21, 08 | 1 | | |
| $10 | #3 w/motto | 1 | Director | May 23, 08 | 1 | | |
| $20 | #4 w/motto | 2 | Director | May 23, 08 | 1 | | |

*Barber said that excess pressure caused the dies to collapse during production of these very high relief ex-perimental coins. No examples are known to have survived.*

---

[633] *US Mint*, NARA-P, op. cit. Letter dated April 7, 1908 to Landis from Leach.

*\*\*$10 design approved by Roosevelt.*

*‡ Eight EHR $20 coins are listed in the inventory of Barber's pattern collection as of 1916. There is no differentiation of variety.*

*† Director Leach stated: "It is my idea that if the size and the stars and the lettering on the periphery of the coin is to be increased, as shown on the sample coin sent me, that such change should be postponed until the question of the motto is settled; and I desire every piece struck in experimental work showing these large letters shall be melted up at once, and you will satisfy yourself that not one of these coins is permitted to go into the hands of any person, officer or employee."[634] Superintendent of Machinery Matthew J. Buckley wrote on March 19 that the large edge stars were wider than the thickness of the coin.[635]*

**Note:** *Sale of experimental coins permitted per director and President July 21 and July 31, 1907.*

*Coins returned to the mint were either melted, placed in the mint collection, or sold. It is presumed that most were available to employees (except for the gold progress strikes) unless the director gave explicit instructions to melt them (as with the small-diameter $20).*

Key:    Eagles –
- #1 = Model #1 with knife rim and "periods" on reverse (by Saint-Gaudens/Hering);
- #2 = Model #2 with border and "periods" on reverse (Saint-Gaudens/Hering, border by Barber);
- #3 = Model #3 with border, no "periods" on reverse (by Homer Saint-Gaudens/Hering)

Double eagles –
- Standing Eagle = Standing eagle reverse as originally planned for double eagle (Saint-Gaudens);
- #1 = Model #1 with extremely high relief, tiny Capitol building, small stars (by Saint-Gaudens/Hering);
- Sm. dia = Small-diameter, thick double eagle from #1 model;
- #2 = Model #2 with high relief, large Capitol building, large stars (by Saint-Gaudens/Hering);
- #2a = Reverse of model #2 with date added to sun (by Hering); Liberty head obverse from cent model;
- #3 = Model #3 with lower relief and European decimal date (by Hering);
- #4 = Model #4 with low relief, European decimal date as used for 1907 circulation (hub from Hering's #3 model with detail recut by Barber).

Experimental double eagle coins in gold were made of several low relief versions but are unknown today. These may have been destroyed (particularly during the tenure of director Frank Leach), or could be preserved in some collection masquerading as a different pattern or variety. The U. S. Mint cabinet of coins was intended to maintain samples of experimental pieces, models, drawings and related material. However, it was usually treated as an afterthought and not as the mint's primary historical archive. When the collection was transferred to the Smithsonian in 1923, only the coins and a few related items were shipped. Most of the models, drawings, dies, hubs and other materials were retained by the Philadelphia Mint. Many of the items have been inventoried but remain inaccessible to researchers and historians.

---

[634] *US Mint,* NARA-P, op. cit. Letter dated January 29, 1908 to Landis from Leach.
[635] *US Mint,* NARA-P, op. cit. Letter dated March 19, 1908 to Landis from Buckley.

# Chapter 9 – A Very Great Interest

There was considerable public and coin collector interest in the new Saint-Gaudens designs. This was to be expected when the country's best known artist and its celebrity President joined forces. As a matter of practicality, it was left to director Leach to cater to officials, coin collectors and the public at large. With a Washington staff consisting largely of accounting clerks, the director had to do much of the work himself, assisted only by Margaret Kelly. The director responded to requests, ordered specimens from Philadelphia, delivered coins in person to senior government officials or packaged them for mailing to collectors and others, collected the money, repaid the mint accounts, handled postage and registration. Although acting responsibly and efficiently in distributing the new gold coins, Leach also developed a dislike for coin collectors' demands. Ultimately, this resulted in his refusal to retain examples of the Saint-Gaudens half eagle, and to the destruction of experimental Indian head half eagles, quarter eagles and 1909 Lincoln cent pattern coins.

## The New Director

After taking office on November 1 as mint director, Frank A. Leach set about trying to put order to what he found at the Mint Bureau. His predecessor, George Roberts loved the job of director and would assume it again in 1910, but his tenure had been during one of the least innovative times in the mint's history. No changes were made to the circulating coinage and only a few commemoratives were issued, all designed by U. S. Mint engravers Charles E. Barber and George T. Morgan.[636] A political appointee, Roberts was very much one of the bureaucracy when it came to making decisions. Like any good civil servant, he did not consider risk-taking and innovation lightly and felt they were best avoided. The situation was exacerbated by Philadelphia Mint superintendent John Landis,

---

[636] The commemoratives were the Lafayette silver dollar, gold dollars honoring Thomas Jefferson and William McKinley for the Louisiana Purchase Exposition, and the Lewis and Clark Exposition gold dollar.

who showed little initiative and leadership at his facility. Roberts summarized the situation in a letter several years later:[637]

> Mr. Landis has been far from satisfactory as a Superintendent. He has no initiative and it has been necessary to go around him to subordinates in order to get any real touch with operations....No other person in the Service has tried my patience so sorely. Six or seven years ago (1906) I made a recommendation to Secretary Shaw that a change be made....Mr. Landis is an honest man, well intentioned, tractable and ready to obey explicit instructions....he conforms to the Civil Service regulations.

Where Roberts could have exercised a firm hand in guiding both mint and Saint-Gaudens to a successful design, he chose to avoid critical decisions and thus prolonged the process. In contrast, Frank Leach had been the effective "financial governor" of Northern California following the 1906 earthquake, and was often referred to as the best senior manager in the Mint Bureau. According to secretary Cortelyou:[638]

> Director Roberts informs me...he considers Mr. Leach 'far and away the best all-round man in the service...no mistake will be made if he is appointed.'

On his final day in office Roberts wrote again to Landis:[639]

> When the dies are ready for the issue of the experimental pieces from the original high relief St. Gaudens Twenty Dollar piece, please deliver two pieces to Miss Margaret Kelly of the Mint Bureau, upon payment of their face value, and in special recognition of the services she has rendered me in this connection. I understand that the original dies are unfit for further impressions, but new dies are to be made and a limited number of experimental pieces struck. From this I desire two pieces to be assigned as stated.

During the three-month hiatus between Roberts' resignation and Leach's ascendancy, the mint was under control of former director Robert Preston. On the surface this seemed to have been a good choice – a man of experience running the mint.[640] Yet beyond the résumé was the fact that Preston was ready to go along with the Philadelphia Mint staff's suggestions. Preston was a product of mint bureaucracy and possibly more wary of change than Roberts. He also held claim to being the mint director who pulled the rug out from under Saint-Gaudens in 1894 when the reverse of the Columbian Exposition medal was repeatedly rejected. (See chapter 1 for more information on the incident.) Although the artist never corresponded with acting director Preston in 1907, Augusta Saint-Gaudens certainly must have remembered events and possibly wondered what tricks fate was playing on her late husband. Preston and engraver Barber knew each other well with Barber alluding to events of 1894 in a letter to Preston: "...I think our friend is playing a game as he did when you and John G. [Carlisle] had to call him down...."[641]

---

[637] *MacVeagh papers*, LoC, box 16. Letter dated February 19, 1913 to MacVeagh from Roberts.

[638] *Cortelyou*, LoC, op. cit., box 19. Letter (excerpt) dated July 9, 1907 to Roosevelt from Cortelyou. p.2.

[639] *US Mint*, NARA-P, op. cit. Letter dated July 31, 1907 to Landis from Roberts. He is referring to the high relief version and not the extremely high relief pieces first made in February.

[640] Robert Preston joined the mint service on April 1, 1856 as a clerk in the auditor's office. He was appointed examiner in 1874 and director in 1893. Upon his resignation as director on February 14, 1898, he was immediately reappointed Examiner and remained in that position until his death on June 24, 1911. He had served as acting director under directors Burchard, Leech and Roberts. He was also in charge during much of the time when the $4 Stellas were being produced and sold.

[641] *US Mint*, NARA-CP, op. cit., entry 330, box 45. Letter dated November 26, 1906 to Preston from Barber.

Frank Leach had been superintendent at the San Francisco Mint since 1897, and led the mint and financial core of the city through the earthquake and fire of 1906.[642] He had also undertaken several experiments on coining high relief pieces in cooperation with director Roberts. Thus, he entered the director's position in Washington at full command of the technical aspects of minting coins, and with considerable practical knowledge of business management. For numismatists, one of Leach's most significant undertakings was an attempt to account for the pattern and experimental coins struck during Roberts' and Preston's tenures. With little formal accounting of the various experimental coins, no one knew exactly who had the coins, or how many had been produced. The bullion accounts, which recorded the use of gold and silver metal, only tracked the quantity of gold, not its form.

His first order in this matter was to direct the melting of 31,450 eagles minted from the second pair of models on the regular coinage presses. These were the coins to which engraver Barber had added a border to improve stacking and better protect the design. The exact quantity produced and ordered melted is clear: mintage was 31,500 made according to the acting director's order to begin production. The melted coins numbered 31,450 with fifty pieces left for sale to collectors and museums.[643] Most were delivered to director Leach (but probably for others) and assistant secretary Edwards. At least two additional pattern pieces with irregular edge stars likely came from the experimental strikes Barber made. (It is believed the circulation strikes all had normal stars on the edge rather than irregular stars of the experimental/pattern coins.)

Another task was director Leach's attempt to get the President, cabinet secretaries, assistant secretaries and others to pay for the coins they requested. This had been a continuing problem as noted by Robert Preston, who remarked, "...I would like to get this matter straightened out before we die."[644] The President's requests were particularly difficult to track since some of the coins were used as official presentation pieces, while others were "given" to officials with the expectation they would repay the government for the "gift." A very rough accounting seems to have been kept by Leach or an assistant at the Mint Bureau. A comparison of the numbers of high relief double eagles and other coins distributed, and the money received by the director, suggests that many coins were never paid for. The shortage was likely attributed to government awards paid from contingency funds.

On January 3, 1908 Leach wrote to mint superintendent Landis:[645]

> My dear Mr. Landis:
> As soon as the $70,000 [in] high relief double eagles are delivered I shall send you a formal request to make a statement of the trial pieces of the double eagle and eagle struck from each model of each denomination, showing what disposition was made of such pieces, and giving the names of the persons or associations receiving them. This letter will also show that the pieces other than those delivered on the orders of the Secretary of the Treasury or the Director of the Mint were destroyed.

[642] Frank Alemon Leach was superintendent of the San Francisco Mint from August 1, 1897 to September 18, 1907. After serving as mint director, treasury secretary MacVeagh appointed him to the same post on August 23, 1912 where he served until August 15, 1913.
[643] See Leach's letter of February 5, 1908 discussed earlier in this chapter.
[644] *US Mint*, NARA-P, op. cit. Letter dated November 25, 1907 to Norris from Preston.
[645] *US Mint*, NARA-P, op. cit. Letter dated January 3, 1908 to Landis from Leach.

You will also make a statement of the eagles and double eagles struck on the medal press at the request of the President, the number of the same delivered on transfer orders and the number exchanged for or by you, and the number destroyed. These statements will be for record in the archives of the mint bureau. If <u>you</u> wish authority to exchange some of the trial pieces for coin, please make your request and I will forward the letter, and then you can proceed to destroy the remaining pieces and be ready to execute the report when required.

Respectfully yours,

Although Landis probably had access to some of the requested information, he would have little knowledge of the recipients of various pieces unless he had been personally involved. During December, January and February (and possibly later) individuals could also purchase high relief double eagles directly from the mint at the cash window, and possibly from the sub-treasuries. Other varieties were also available to collectors who knew what to ask for, just as were prior date proof coins. It is clear that Leach wanted to straighten out the experimental coin accounts, but it is also evident that he had no objection to Landis (or others) exchanging current coin for the experimental pieces.[646] A week later, the director instructed Landis to place two experimental pieces from each of the eagle and double eagle models in the mint collection: "…and, if you have any left, two of the pieces of the double eagle design on the reduced diameter, or 'thick' pieces."[647]

At the request of the secretary of the treasury, Leach provided a written accounting of the distribution of trial pieces as of February 5, 1908.[648] No updated version has been located and the letter may have been the end of the matter as far as the secretary was concerned:[649]

In compliance with your request for a statement as to the number and manner of distribution of the various trial pieces struck in developing the Saint-Gaudens' designs for the gold coinage, I enclose such statement on a separate sheet attached hereto.

You will notice that while we have quite an accurate statement as to the number of pieces struck, the information as to the distribution is not so satisfactory. Owing to the very great interest manifested in the developing of the new designs and the great number of persons involved in the work in consultation and otherwise, quite a number of the pieces were necessarily given out and which have not been returned and there seems to be no record of the persons thus supplied.

I find in the records of the correspondence had with the Superintendent of the United States Mint at Philadelphia, a letter by the Director of the Mint in which he says:

*"The regulations requiring all experimental pieces to be destroyed will be formally waived, as the President desires to have a number of these pieces struck."*

[646] Evidently, President Roosevelt had given Roberts approval to release all experimental coins in July 1907, with Roberts referring in one of his letters to an impending Executive Order. The Executive Order was never released; however, the same effect could have been produced through an administrative order from the President, secretary Cortelyou, or directors Roberts or Leach. The fact that experimental coins of 1907 were sold to John Edwards and other treasury officials is adequate to establish legality of sale. Similar experimental coin sales occurred in 1916 when the new subsidiary silver coins were being designed. The administrative order does not appear to have been revoked by either Presidents Taft or Wilson. However, revised mint regulations were issued in July 1910 as prepared by director Andrew.
[647] *US Mint*, NARA-P, op. cit. Letter dated January 9, 1908 to Landis from Leach.
[648] Mintage figures are as of February 4, 1908.
[649] *US Mint*, NARA-CP, op. cit., entry 330, box 45. Letter dated February 5, 1908 to Cortelyou from Leach.

In the statement herewith [attached] the numbers charged to the Bureau of the Mint include the pieces for the President and other officials and individuals directly connected with the work on the new designs.

The table, below, which Leach attached to his letter, includes both experimental and circulation coins, however it does not appear to include all of the pattern versions that are known today. For this reason, Leach's accounting must be considered a starting point rather than a definitive statement of quantities.

Distribution of trial pieces Double Eagle and Eagle Saint-Gaudens designs
February 5, 1908. [650]

### Double Eagle – 1st Model

13 trial pieces struck

| | | |
|---|---|---|
| 6 | | To Mint Bureau officials and President |
| 2 | | To Mint Cabinet exhibit |
| 5 | | To Mint officials |
| | 13 | *Total* |

### Double Eagle –
Same model but small-diameter – the "thick piece."

13 Trial pieces struck

| | | |
|---|---|---|
| 2 | | To Mint cabinet exhibit |
| 11 | | Destroyed |
| | 13 | *Total* |

### Double Eagle – 2nd Model
High relief, date 1907 in Roman numerals

12,153 pieces struck — Generally distributed through the sub-treasuries, and upon orders through the Bureau of the Mint.

### Double Eagle – 3rd Model
*[this is the #4 model as recut by Barber - RWB]*

987,820 pieces struck — Or in dollars $19,756,400

### Eagle – 1st Model
542 pieces struck

| | | |
|---|---|---|
| 500 | | Sent to Treasurer, Washington, for distribution by Asst. Secretary of the Treasury Edwards. |
| 29 | | To Mint Bureau and Asst. Secretary Edwards |
| 2 | | To Mint Cabinet exhibit |
| 2 | | To Metropolitan Art Museum exhibit |
| 1 | | Mr. Mitchelson, Conn. |
| 8 | | To Mint officials |
| | 542 | *Total* |

### Eagle – 2nd Model

31,500 pieces struck

| | | |
|---|---|---|
| 31,450 | | melted up |
| 10 | | To Mint Bureau |
| 2 | | To Metropolitan Art Museum exhibit |
| 8 | | To Mint officials |
| 30 | | On hand |
| | 31,500 | *Total* |

### Eagle – 3rd Model
614,903 pieces struck — In dollars $6,149,030

---

[650] Ibid.

This list omits the names of individual recipients with the exception of Joseph C. Mitchelson.[651] It is not known why he was mentioned specifically and other purchasers were not. Quantities are cumulative through February 4, 1908.

## Coin Sales and Distribution by the Mint Bureau

The correspondence of President Theodore Roosevelt, secretary of the treasury Cortelyou, mint directors Roberts and Leach, and others indicate the sale of gold pattern and experimental coins was part of the President's overall plan for the Saint-Gaudens-designed coins. Roosevelt understood that coin collectors would be very interested in the new coins and he expected the mint to make specimens available. He also wanted to promote the new coinage art and generate enthusiasm for improved designs. At the time, these were not felt to be rarities or numismatic delicacies created for an exclusive market, but examples of America's best coinage art. The new designs might be impossible to make for general circulation, but artistic versions could be struck for collectors. Roosevelt wanted the new coins to be seen and appreciated by all, and he was particularly concerned that enough be made to satisfy the demand from coin collectors.[652]

Availability of high relief double eagles was announced by December 4, 1907, but made little impression on most coin collectors.[653] None of the major collectors' journals appear to have picked up the item. What was not stated in the tiny newspaper announcement was that more than the high relief $20 coins were available – if one knew what to ask for. After a hundred years it is difficult to determine who "leaked" information about the eagle and double eagle varieties, although it was probably several people at different times.

One source may have been George Kunz. As vice-president of Tiffany & Co. he had been in communication with Roosevelt's administration about the new coins in September 1906. His long-standing interest in numismatics and position on the "New Coinage Committee" of the American Numismatic Society gave him plenty of reasons to collect information and distribute it to friends and ANS members. He also may have seen the first EHR pieces when he served on the 1907 Assay Commission. Public announcement of the new designs was made in July 1907, but private speculation about new designs was common among the artistic community. This was followed shortly by articles about Saint-Gaudens' death, which precipitated offers to "finish the work" by several sculptors. However, it is more likely that T. Louis Comparette, curator of the mint collection, who was on friendly terms with most of the coin dealers in the eastern United States was the real conduit of information (and misinformation) to the outside world.[654]

At the end of August 1907, secretary Cortelyou ordered five hundred eagles and five hundred double eagles (from the #1 and #2 models, respectively) struck by Roose-

---

[651] Joseph C. Mitchelson purchased one of the #1 model eagles on December 23, 1907 from director Leach (who had to refund $10 because he could only locate one coin, not two as Mitchelson requested). His extremely high relief $20 was acquired after 1907 and before 1911, but available records do not give the date, seller or amount paid. He was a close friend of mint curator Louis Comparette and may have been one of the conduits for the flow of information to and from the mint. (*US Mint*, NARA-P, op. cit., entry 235, volume 367. Letter dated December 23, 1907 to Mitchelson from Leach; also *US Mint*, NARA-P, op. cit., entry 229, volume 295. Letter dated November 21, 1911 to Roberts from Emma W. Mitchelson, widow of Joseph Mitchelson.) His collection was donated to the Connecticut State Library in 1911.

[652] *Cortelyou*, LoC, op. cit., box 19. Letter dated July 29, 1907 to Cortelyou from Roosevelt.

[653] Newspaper clipping attached to Caldwell's letter of December 5, 1907. The newspaper erroneously reported that 115,000 were produced, but correctly noted they were in high relief.

[654] See Burdette: *Renaissance of American Coinage 1909–1915* for more information on Comparette's activities and relationships with coin dealers.

velt's order: "Let the two coins be finished and put into circulation at once – by September first…."[655] These were intended for "circulation" although in reality that meant something the President could hold in his hand, not coins expected to reach commercial channels. The small number of gold coin collectors, and dealers such as Henry Chapman of Philadelphia, who kept them supplied with new items for their collections, were generally wealthy and socially well connected. In a time when social status was extremely important, these connections opened many doors. The Mint Bureau's doors in Washington were locked to the average working man, but information and sometimes goods flowed more freely to higher social strata.[656]

Philadelphia coin dealer Henry Chapman sent collector Robert Garrett a high relief $20 and one of the regular issue pieces in December 1907 (after the newspaper announcement). His note states in part, "I have just succeeded in getting a superb specimen of the St. Gaudens $20 with date in Roman numerals. They are very scarce indeed and I was bid $31 for one Saturday in this city…I spent nearly all day Saturday trying to get these pieces…."[657] Apparently, somewhat later Chapman also may have acquired several experimental pieces for private sale to his clients. On February 28, 1908, he wrote to Garrett with information concerning the 1907 gold issues. The Chapman and Garrett letters to the mint are not the earliest requests for experimental coins, but they are perhaps the best documented:[658]

> I wish to give you some information. If you will act quickly upon it I think we will secure for you a couple of coins which are worth large sums. In fact, I have paid $150 cash for one of them myself. The director of the Mint, Mr. Frank A. Leach, at Washington, has in his possession, and is distributing at face value, to collectors or public museums, to the latter he writes me more especially than to the former, special $10 pieces of the Saint-Gaudens design, 1907.
>
> If you will write him and ask him to send you a specimen of the $10 gold piece, Saint-Gaudens design 1907, from die No. 1 *without any border,* and die No. 2, with

---

[655] *US Mint*, NARA-P, op. cit. Letter dated August 7, 1907 to Cortelyou from Roosevelt. Roosevelt's written instruction had the effect of administrative orders, even when contained in a letter or memorandum. The acting director wrote a follow-up letter to Landis on August 12.

[656] The total number of active coin collectors in the United States at this time was only a few thousand. Of these, possibly 200 were members of the ANS, ANA or other larger numismatic organizations. The number of people who collected gold coins was limited by the high face value of the pieces, with a score or two collectors encompassing the total. Some years later, wealthy collector William Woodin expressed amazement that the mint had sold one hundred one gold proof sets in 1908. George Kunz seems to have been the only person systematically acquiring specimens of new coins for the ANS or any other "museum-type" organization. Kunz's numismatic activities continued through the 1916–17 silver coin redesign.

[657] Bowers, *The History of United States Coinage As Illustrated by the Garrett Collection*, appendix II, p.476. Letter dated December 23, 1907 to Garrett from Chapman. The letter's date is just after Chapman bought the same two pieces from the Philadelphia Mint. Was Chapman "aiding" his business by adding a good "tale" to the coins he sent Garrett?

[658] Bowers, op. cit., p.475, p.477. Letter dated February 28, 1908 to Robert Garrett from Henry Chapman. The Philadelphia dealer wrote a follow-up letter to Garrett on or about March 14, 1908 suggesting Garrett try to locate specimens of the #1 model double eagle in both normal, and small-diameter versions; however, Chapman then states "…Of this [small-diameter] gold piece the mint has lately rolled out ten pieces and I am told that the two in the cabinet are the only ones saved…" [Bowers, p.447.] This, and other information from Henry Chapman, is generally accurate, indicating that his source was either someone in a senior position at the mint or the director in Washington. Considering Chapman's earlier claim that Leach wrote to him, it is probable his source was the director; however, he and T. Louis Comparette knew one another and Comparette also had "insider" information. (Later, Comparette sold quantities of gold dollars, three-dollar pieces and #1 eagles to Chapman, while purchasing several thousand dollars worth of U. S. and foreign coins from him.) A Philadelphia Mint source could have easily acquired quantities of the high relief pieces for Chapman. Among early requests from collectors, five came from New York City, twelve from San Francisco, two from Kansas, and one from Philadelphia. The unexpected number of requests from California is likely due to director Leach having formerly been superintendent at the San Francisco Mint. His son, Edwin, was employed there as cashier in 1907-08.

a wire or thin edge, you might say to him that you have been informed that he has a few of these for distribution to collections which are exhibited to the public. I would tell him that your collection is on exhibition at Princeton College and that you would like to have him send you them. Send him $20 in gold notes and 12¢ in postage stamps, and I think you will succeed. Do not mention my name or your source of information.

Of the coin without the border, 500 were made, of number 2 only 50 were kept out of several thousand that were minted. The rest were melted. As he has but a few of the wire edge, which he refuses to let me have a specimen of, I would suggest that you write immediately upon receipt of this. If you can bring to bear any influence of your senator or congressman, it might be well to do so, but I think that it is possible you will get them without bringing anyone else into the matter, which might cause delay. If you succeed in getting them, you are going to get two coins worth $400....

Garrett wrote two separate letters to director Leach and was rewarded with specimens of the eagle from the #1 and #2 models. To obtain the #2 eagle, Leach had Garrett write directly to Landis in Philadelphia, implying that the director's office in Washington had none of the coins.[659] It is interesting to note that Chapman quoted net mintage figures similar to those in Frank Leach's accounting of February 5.

Given the circumstances, there is little reason why employees of the mint would have hesitated in giving details of the new coins to persons outside the mint. Nothing was done internally to restrict private ownership of experimental coins, and Roosevelt explicitly encouraged this in his conversations with director Roberts.[660] In January 1908 director Leach offered to let the Philadelphia Mint staff buy whatever experimental coins they wanted (except the small-diameter double eagles), so long as they accounted for the bullion. This offer could not have come without the consent of secretary Cortelyou and encouragement from the President.

The first documented sale of an experimental coin was authorized by Roberts to Margaret Valentine Kelly, an examiner and assistant to the director, in appreciation of her service to the director. She was permitted to buy two high relief double eagles for face value of $40 (but she didn't receive the coins for nearly six months).[661] By September, with experimental coins now "officially" in circulation (meaning available on Roosevelt's whim), mint correspondence files contain many letters from collectors requesting gold coins. The names of some, such as Alexander Caldwell, John Story Jenks, William Woodin, Joseph Mitchelson and Robert Garrett have come down in numismatic lore; others are unknown to today's coin collectors. As one collector obtained an experimental coin from the mint, he likely passed word to friends and by word of mouth (actually letters) the information spread to the small number of gold collectors and dealers. One of the last recorded sales was approved by secretary Cortelyou on October 2, 1908 to William Woodin, who would one day become secretary of the treasury.[662]

In parallel with sales to coin collectors, the Roosevelt administration provided new coins to members of the cabinet and others willing to pay the face value of the coins. Cabinet and secretary-level administration members seemed to have usually purchased a #1 ea-

---

[659] *US Mint*, NARA-P, op. cit. Letter dated March 4, 1908 to Robert Garrett from Leach. Garrett sent his request to Philadelphia on March 6 and acknowledged receipt of the coin on March 9.

[660] Letter of July 25, 1907 where Roberts says the President will waive mint regulations.

[661] The first "sale" might also be considered the one to Roberts for two extremely high relief $20 and two high relief $10 coins on July 25.

[662] *Cortelyou*, LoC, op. cit., box 19. Letter dated October 2, 1908 to Cortelyou from Woodin.

gle and a #2 double eagle as mementos of their service. Director Leach was a major conduit for these government purchasers, but we don't know all of the buyers or even the extent of transactions. If one assumes that as much as half of relevant mint correspondence has been lost, the quantities given in the accompanying table could be understated by fifty percent or more for some varieties. Specifically, we do not know how many pieces were sold at the Philadelphia Mint or Treasury cash windows. We also do not know how many coins were exchanged by Philadelphia Mint staff at director Leach's suggestion. (Senior Philadelphia Mint employees also could have struck additional specimens for sale to themselves. However, Albert Norris sent a statement to the director on January 2, 1908 declaring that all 1907-dated obverse dies were destroyed. "There were 753 obverse and 791 reverse dies destroyed",[663] however, he may have been referring to circulation coin dies, only.

The following table consolidates purchase records from several sources. It lists 109 separate purchases of the new coins by collectors and government officials. It is assumed these records are incomplete and the actual number of specimens sold or distributed was greater than on this list. Further, sales through the mint's cash window are known to have occurred (including several high relief double eagles returned as defective) but there is no record of these sales. Dates refer to when the order was approved, and may differ from the shipment or receipt date. For each entry there is at least one written document attesting to the transaction. If there is no document confirming a transaction, then it is omitted from the table even if the transaction might reasonably have taken place. For example, coin dealer Farran Zerbe sent a letter to director Leach on December 2, 1907 asking to purchase two high relief double eagles for "...my educational money exhibit...."[664] Although Zerbe likely received the coins, there is no receipt, shipping order or other document stating that he paid for the coins and they were sent to him. Thus, this possible transaction is not included in the table.

| Purchasers | Date | Eagle #1 | Eagle #2 | [8] Eagle #3 | Double Eagle #1 | Double Eagle #2 | Double Eagle #3 | [8] Double Eagle #4 |
|---|---|---|---|---|---|---|---|---|
| [1] Alexander Caldwell | 9/21/07 | 1 | | | | | | |
| Alexander Caldwell | 11/19/07 | | | | | 1 | | |
| Alexander Caldwell | 12/5/07 | | | | | 1 | | |
| Charles O. Brewster (for Augusta S-G) | 12/2/07 | | | | | 1 | | |
| Charles O. Brewster (for Augusta S-G) | 12/9/07 | | | | | 8 | | 2 |
| O. C. Bosbyshell | 12/10/07 | | | | | 3 | | |
| Henry Chapman | 12/20/07? | | | | | 1 | | 1 |
| Edward Brush | 12/23/07 | | | | | 5 | | |
| Joseph C. Mitchelson | 12/23/07 | 1 | | | | | | |
| George Kunz (for ANS) | 1/2/08 | 2 | 2 | 2 | | 1 | | 1 |
| E. B. Stevens | 1/7/08 | | | | | 2 | | |
| E. W. Hardin | 1/26/08 | | 1 | | | | | |
| Frank Vanderlip | 1/26/08 | | | | | 1 | | |

[663] US Mint, NARA-CP, op. cit., entry 229, box 260. Letter dated January 2, 1908 to Leach from Norris. The hubs were not destroyed until May 1910.
[664] US Mint, NARA-CP, op. cit., entry 229, box 260. Letter dated December 9, 1907 to Leach from Zerbe. The letterhead notes he is "President – American Numismatic Association."

286

| Purchasers | Date | Eagle #1 | Eagle #2 | [8]Eagle #3 | Double Eagle #1 | Double Eagle #2 | Double Eagle #3 | [8]Double Eagle #4 |
|---|---|---|---|---|---|---|---|---|
| Harry J. Maxwell | 1/29/08 | | | | | 1 | | |
| M. A. Edwards | 1/28/08 | | | | | 1 | | |
| William H. Woodin | 2/8/08 | 1 | | | | 1 | | |
| James W. Ellsworth | 2/17/08 | | 1 | | | 1 | | |
| R. P. Tarr | 2/17/08 | ? | ? | | | ? | | |
| John Story Jenks | 2/20/08 | 1 | | | | | | |
| S. Phillips | 2/21/08 | | | | | 1 | | |
| Henry C. Chesebrough | 2/24/08 | | | | | 1 | | |
| Art Institute of Chicago (William H. R. French) | 2/24/08 | 1 | 1 | | | | | |
| [2]Thomas L. Elder | 2/25/08 | | | | Req. sm. dia. $20 | | | |
| Buffalo Fine Arts Academy | 2/25/08 | 1 | 1 | | | 1 | | |
| E. B. Stevens | 2/28/08 | | | | | 1 | | |
| Robert Garrett | 3/4/08 | 1 | | | | | | |
| Robert Garrett | 3/6/08 | | 1 | | | | | |
| S. Phillips | 3/9/08 | | | | | 1 | | |
| L. L. Chase | 3/21/08 | | | | | 1 | | |
| Charles Hendricks | 4/22/08 | | | | | 1 | | |
| T. B. Miller | 4/22/08 | | | | | 1 | | |
| Mr. Pinkham | 4/22/08 | | | | | 1 | | |
| George E. Roberts | 4/25/08 | | | | | 1 | | |
| Frank M. Dixon | 4/27/08 | | | | | 4 | | |
| [3]Augusta Saint-Gaudens | 6/30/08 | | | | 1 | | | |
| William H. Woodin | 10/2/08 | | 1 | | | | | |
| Dr. S. E. Young | 10/19/08 | | 1 | | | | | |
| **Sub-total** | | **9** | **9** | **2** | **0** | **42** | **0** | **4** |

### Government Officials

| Purchasers | Date | Eagle #1 | Eagle #2 | [8]Eagle #3 | Double Eagle #1 | Double Eagle #2 | Double Eagle #3 | [8]Double Eagle #4 |
|---|---|---|---|---|---|---|---|---|
| [4]George Roberts | 2/18/07 | | | | 1 | | | |
| Robert Preston | 2/18/07 | | | | 1 | | | |
| George Roberts | 7/25/07 | 2 | | | | | | |
| Margaret Valentine Kelly (delivered 1/3/08) | 7/31/07 | | | | | 2 | | |
| Asst. Treas. Secretary John H. Edwards | 9/10/07 | 5 | 5 | | | 5 | | |
| Robert Preston | 9/10/07 | 1 | | | | 1 | | |
| Justice O. W. Holmes | 11/30/07 | | 1 | | | 1 | | |
| Frank A. Leach | 11/30/07 | 9 | | | | 15 | | |
| Theodore Roosevelt | 12/2/07 | 1 | | | | 21 | | |
| Frank A. Leach | 12/2/07 | | 1 | | | 1 | | |
| Sec. George Cortelyou | 12/3/07 ? | 1 | | | | 1 | | |
| Theodore Roosevelt | 12/3/07 | 1 | | | | 1 | | |
| Sec. Victor Metcalf | 12/4/07 | 1 | | | | 1 | | |
| Postmaster Gen. Meyer | 12/4/07 | 1 | | | | 1 | | |
| Sec. James Wilson | 12/4/07 | 1 | | | | 1 | | |
| Sec. Oscar S. Straus | 12/4/07 | 1 | | | | 1 | | |
| Sec. James R. Garfield | 12/4/07? | 1 | | | | 1 | | |

| Purchasers | Date | Eagle #1 | Eagle #2 | [8] Eagle #3 | Double Eagle #1 | Double Eagle #2 | Double Eagle #3 | [8] Double Eagle #4 |
|---|---|---|---|---|---|---|---|---|
| Sec. Charles J. Bonapart | 12/4/07? | 1 | | | | 1 | | |
| Sen. H. C. Lodge | 12/4/07? | | | | | 2 | | |
| Sec. Elihu Root | 12/6/07 | 1 | | | | 7 | | |
| Treasurer of U. S. (per Edwards custody) | 12/14/07 | 500 | | | | 500 | | |
| Frank A. Leach | 12/20/07 | | | | | 10 | | |
| Frank A. Leach | 12/21/07 | | | | | 3 | | |
| Theodore Roosevelt | 12/23/07 | | | | | 2 | | |
| Leach, *for TR, others* | 12/23/07 | | | | | 40 | | |
| Frank A. Leach | 12/23/07 | 1 | | | | | | |
| Frank A. Leach | 12/23/07 | | | | | 8 | | |
| John H. Edwards | 12/23/07 | 1 | | | | | | |
| San Francisco Mint | 12/23/07 | | | | | 3 | | |
| Frank A. Leach | 12/26/07 | | | | | 48 | | |
| [5] Robert Preston | 12/30/07 | 6 | | | | | | |
| Robert Preston | 1/3/08 | 1 | | | | | | |
| Frank A. Leach | 1/3/08 | | | | 1 | | | |
| Leach *for Cortelyou* | 1/3/08 | | | | 1 | | | |
| Leach *for Roosevelt* | 1/3/08 | | | | 1 | | | |
| John H. Edwards | 1/3/08 | 1 | | | | | | |
| Frank A. Leach | 1/4/08 | | 2 | | | 1 | | |
| [6] Frank A. Leach | 1/4/08 | | | | 1, sm. dia. $20 melted | | | |
| J. F. Wilder (NY Assay Office) | 1/7/08 | | | | | 4 | | |
| Mint collection | 1/9/08 | 2 | | | 2, sm. dia. $20 | | | |
| [7] Mint collection | 1/9/08 | | 2 | 2 | 1 | 2 | | 2 |
| Judge Sweeney (SF Mint) | 1/16/08 | | | | | 2 | | |
| Ben W. Day (SF Mint) | 1/16/08 | | | | | 1 | | |
| Ed Leach (director's son - SF Mint) | 1/16/08 | | | | | 2 | | |
| J. Fitzpatrick (SF Mint) | 1/16/08 | | | | | 2 | | |
| Frank A. Pedlow (SF Mint) | 1/16/08 | | | | | 1 | | |
| C. H. McCartney (SF Mint) | 1/16/08 | | | | | 1 | | |
| T. B. Burns (Cashier, SF Sub-Treasury) | 1/16/08 | | | | | 1 | | |
| Dan T. Cole (SF Mint) | 1/16/08 | | | | | 1 | | |
| William M. Cutter (SF Mint Coiner) | 1/16/08 | | | | | 1 | | |
| W. W. Ward (SF Mint) | 1/16/08 | | | | | 1 | | |
| Dr. J. H. Barr (SF Mint) | 1/16/08 | | | | | 1 | | |
| Frank Healy (SF Mint) | 1/16/08 | | | | | 1 | | |
| George R. Comings (NY Assay Office) | 2/3/08 | | | | | 1 | | |
| William M. Cutter (Coiner SF Mint) | 2/7/08 | | | | | 15 | | |
| W. F. Bowen (Denver Mint) | 2/10/08 | | | | | 2 | | |
| William E. Curtis (NY Assay Office) | 2/17/08 | | 1 | | | 1 | | |

| Purchasers | Date | Eagle #1 | Eagle #2 | [8]Eagle #3 | Double Eagle #1 | Double Eagle #2 | Double Eagle #3 | [8]Double Eagle #4 |
|---|---|---|---|---|---|---|---|---|
| William H. Taft | 2/26/08 | 1 | | | | 1 | | |
| Frank A. Leach | 3/2/08 | | 2 | | | 1 | | |
| Leach (for other parties) | 3/4/08 | | 2 | | | 4 | | |
| Frank A. Leach | 3/16/08 | | 1 | | | 2 | | |
| Frank A. Leach | 3/21/08 | | | | | 5 | | |
| [9]Rep. William A. Ashbrook | 3/20/08 | | | | | 1 | | |
| Frank A. Leach | 3/25/08 | | 4 | | | | | |
| Frank A. Leach | 4/7/08 | | 8 | | | 5 | | |
| Frank A. Leach | 4/18/08 | | | | | 5 | | |
| R. S. Colcord (Carson City Assay Office) | 4/22/08 | | | | | 1 | | |
| Frank M. Downer (Sptd. Denver Mint) | 4/27/08 | | | | | 4 | | |
| C. E. Vilas (Seattle Assay Office) | 4/28/08 | | | | | 3 | | |
| D. J. Pope (Charlotte Assay Office) | 4/30/08 | | | | | 1 | | |
| Major Liddell (Boise Assay Office) | 5/1/08 | | | | | 1 | | |
| H.W. Furniss (Ambassador to Haiti) | 6/13/08 | | | | | | | 1 |
| **TOTALS** | | 540 | 29 | 2 | 6 | 752 | 0 | 3 |
| | | | | | | + 2 sm. dia. | | |
| **TOTAL– ALL** | | 549 | 38 | 4 | 7 | 794 | 0 | 7 |

Key:  Eagles –

- #1 = Model #1 with knife rim and "periods" on reverse (by Saint-Gaudens/Hering);
- #2 = Model #2 with border and "periods" on reverse (Saint-Gaudens/Hering, border by Barber);
- #3 = Model #3 with border, no "periods" on reverse (by Homer Saint-Gaudens/Hering)

Double eagles –

- Stg. Eagle = Standing eagle reverse as originally planned for double eagle (Saint-Gaudens);
- #1 = Model #1 with extremely high relief, tiny Capitol building, small stars (by Saint-Gaudens/Hering);
- Sm.dia. = Small-diameter, thick double eagle from #1 model;
- #2 = Model #2 with high relief, large Capitol building, large stars (by Saint-Gaudens/Hering);
- #2a = Reverse of model #2 with date added to sun (by Hering); Liberty head obverse from cent model.
- #3 = Model #3 with lower relief and European decimal date (by Hering);
- #4 = Model #4 with low relief, European decimal date as used for 1907 circulation (hub from Hering's #3 model with detail recut by Barber).

## Notes to the Coin Distribution Table:

[1] Caldwell was told about the new coins in a letter dated September 13, 1907 from Treasurer of the United States, Charles H. Treat. This was in response to an inquiry from Caldwell on the previous day. We don't know how Caldwell learned of the coins only days after they had been struck, but his location in New York would suggest a "heads up" from someone at the Treasury Department. He was later a member of the 1909 Assay Commission.

[2] Thomas Elder had contacted mint curator Louis Comparette in hopes of getting one of the double eagles struck on small, double thick planchets. Elder called his organization the *American Numismatic and Antiquarian Society*, which was "…commonly known as the *New York Numismatic Society*." The date of his request came after the director ordered the coins melted and while the director was trying to recall and melt all the specimens. It is unlikely he received an example.

[3] The extremely high relief double eagle sold to Augusta Saint-Gaudens was transferred on orders from President Roosevelt, who directed that she be given one of the two coins from the mint collection. The President also approved striking a mint collection replacement piece dated MCMVIII [1908] if director Leach felt it necessary to have two of the #1 model $20 coins in the collection. At the time, these coins were valued at $800–$1,000, and Augusta issued standing orders to buy all that could be found – she felt they were good investments. See also note 7, below.

[4] Roberts bought two extremely high relief $20 and two small-diameter $20 from the first group made on or before February 15, 1907. One of each were given to Robert Preston. Both small-diameter coins were returned on the demand of director Leach and melted.

[5] On December 30, Albert A. Norris, chief clerk of the U. S. Mint, was authorized to strike six additional high relief coins from the first eagle model. These were probably the coins former director Preston purchased. This suggests that no more were available at the mint bureau in Washington, or the Philadelphia Mint; however, we know that more than one hundred pieces were still in the Treasurer's Cash Room in 1912. There may have been internal reasons why Preston couldn't buy the pieces direct from assistant secretary Edwards' office, or treasurer Treat.

[6] Fifteen (15) small-diameter double eagles appear to have been produced with thirteen accounted for as melted. Two are in the Smithsonian National Numismatic Collection.

[7] The mint collection originally had two double eagles struck from the #1 models. These were authorized to be struck from new dies made after March 4, 1907. According to Charles Barber the original pair had broken sometime between February 14 and 25 (a plain-edge, incompletely struck coin with cracked reverse is known). One coin from the cabinet was given to Augusta Saint-Gaudens in June 1908. (A second coin from the #1 models was donated to the National Numismatic Collection in 1968 by the Josiah K. Lilly estate. See also note 7, above. A third was donated by Theodore Roosevelt's grandson and was claimed to be a coin owned by the President.)

[8] Eagle #3 and double eagle #4 are the regular-issue coins dated 1907.

[9] Ashbrook was an ANA member and responsible for Congress granting the organization a Federal charter. His coin collection was stolen in December 1919. Presumably the high relief double eagle, housed in a small case bought from the Philadelphia Mint, was among the purloined property.

[10] Some of the cabinet purchases are listed in a memorandum from secretary Cortelyou to director Leach dated December 4, 1907. These do not appear to duplicate other purchases. Attorney General Bonapart also purchased an eagle and a double eagle, but the date is not known.

Lists such as the one above make interesting reading. They can also lead to unexpected insights for collectors of pattern and experimental coins. Careful investigation of "new" 1907 experimental pieces coming on the market may reveal their origin as the estate of one of the persons listed. Then, by knowing the date of purchase and variety, it may be possible to build a better understanding of the varieties (particularly the first five hundred $10 and $20 coins, and the fifty coins remaining from model #2). One obvious opportunity for investigation concerns the six eagles from model #1 sold to former director Preston on December 30, 1907. The same quantity was ordered struck by Norris on that date, making it very likely that these coins were intended for Preston. Because this occurred after the December 14 order to deliver the original five hundred eagles from model #1 to the treasury, it suggests that Preston did not have access to the coins at the treasury, although he worked one floor below assistant secretary Edwards. This situation is further confused because it is the same time period during which director Leach was passing out #1 eagles to the President's associates. It is probable the edge die was the same one used for the five hundred coins of August–September rather than the irregular die used on the patterns.

The most obvious outcome of listing all the mint's coin sales is that it establishes a minimum number of specimens for each variety. We now know that at least thirty-eight #2 eagles and forty-nine #1 eagles were distributed. We can also verify that at least five hundred #1 eagles were made, although we don't know (from the list alone) if that includes patterns, or if there is a difference between patterns and the five hundred made to improve "Roosevelt's circulation."[665] Most recorded sales of #1 eagle specimens occurred after sample production, so we cannot establish whether a particular specimen came from the patterns or five hundred collectors' coins. The only certain exceptions are the plain edge eagles mentioned in correspondence of July 22, and the pieces with irregular edge stars.

| | Eagle #1 | Eagle #2 | Eagle #3 | Double Eagle #1 | Double Eagle #2 | Double Eagle #3 | Double Eagle #4 |
|---|---|---|---|---|---|---|---|
| Director 2/5/08 | 542 | 50 | N/A | 13 | N/A | 0 | N/A |
| Total Sold (above) | 549* | 38 | 4 | 7 | 794 | 0 | 7 |
| Known Melted | 70 | 0 | 0 | 0 | 0 | ? | N/A |

*This includes seven pieces from the original five hundred which are duplicated in the count of coins sent to the Treasury Department. The total mintage is five hundred forty-two pieces.

## Low Relief Proof Coins

Several specimens of low relief circulation designs are reported in sandblast or satin proof versions. These may have been made to show the new designs to their best advantage, or to test changes in edge lettering on the double eagle, and could technically be called experimental pieces. These were not officially distributed to collectors, and several were supposed to have been melted.[666] However, the order permitting sale of experiential coins of the new designs could be interpreted as applying to any new design for the gold $10 and $20 pieces, including the low relief versions. Although it would be a "stretch" to keep a copy of a coin the director had ordered melted, it might not have been technically illegal.

---

[665] Coiner Rhine Freed stated in 1908 that production figures included "proof" coins made for collectors, and the $20 extremely high relief patterns, but was unclear about other varieties.

[666] In 1982 David Akers noted: 1907 Arabic – Proof: "Several proofs of this issue are known including the Jerome Kern specimen… that appeared in the 1982 Miami Beach Auction. Another proof, struck with the lettered edge collar of the High Relief, was in the 1907–08 set, sold by Stack's to NERGC in early 1980. A third, and in my opinion the most interesting, is the specimen from Stack's December 1979 sale (at $70,000) and, later, from NASCA's December 1981 sale. This particular coin, now in a private collection in California, has a lettered edge with 'Gothic' style lettering that is unlike any other edge lettering I have ever seen. One or two other proofs are reported and all of them seem to be experimental pieces of some sort, testing new finishes or edge devices." [p.287] If Mr. Akers is correct, the logical source for these singular experimental pieces would have been the mint director's office or Charles Barber.

### *Sandblast and Satin Proofs*

Coin collectors have long admired the sandblast (matte) and satin (Roman) proof coins issued by the Philadelphia Mint from 1908 to 1915.[667] Many have wondered why the traditional brilliant or polished proofs were abandoned and how the mint produced the matte-surface coins. In a letter written on November 14, 1908 acting superintendent Albert Norris explained availability of collector's proof coins for the current year:[668]

> In reply to your letter of the 13th instant, relative to the manufacture of proof sets for this year, I beg to inform you that proof sets of the silver and minor coins have been supplied during the year. The Engraver has on hand ready for delivery five hundred sets of gold proofs, but the Superintendent thought they should not be issued until we had coined some eagles and double eagles, with motto, of the regular issue for circulation, which we expect to do next week. The designs of the new gold coins are such that the dies cannot be polished, therefore we could not make proofs, similar to those heretofore supplied, with a polished surface, so the Engraver has finished these proofs similar to medals with a dull surface.

Five hundred sets of gold proofs is considerably more than reported in standard catalogues. It is likely that quantities reported at the end of 1908 – one hundred one sets – were the quantity sold, with the balance melted.

Part of the answer can also be found in correspondence between Assistant Secretary of the Treasury Abram Piatt Andrew and numismatist William Woodin in 1910. Andrew was previously director of the mint from November 1909 to June 1910, and retained considerable interest in the Mint Bureau and its products: coins. Woodin was one of the country's best known numismatists with particular expertise in pattern and experimental coins. On August 4, 1910, Woodin wrote to Andrew complaining about the quality of gold proof coins sold to collectors:[669] He received a reply from superintendent Landis and mentions some of Landis' comments in a letter on August 19:[670]

> Dear Doctor Andrew:
> I am surprised at the statement that the dull finish of the gold proof coins was objected to by many collectors. If any collectors objected to this finish it was because they did not understand that the St. Gaudens designs are not adapted to the production of polished proofs. The present proofs of the St. Gaudens designs and of the Pratt designs are simply <u>rotten</u>. I know of no other word to express it, and I would personally very much appreciate it if you could see your way clear to instruct Mr. Landis to make a few proof sets with the dull finish for collectors who may desire them.

Before 1907, all proof coins    gold, silver, copper-nickel and bronze    were made with polished fields and sometimes a dull, unpolished portrait and lettering. In 1907, the Saint-Gaudens designs were adopted for the eagle and double eagle. Due to die curvature and texture of the field (or "ground" as mint engravers called it), polishing the dies to make brilliant proofs was not practical. A similar situation occurred in 1908 with the Pratt-designed half and quarter eagle. To provide special coins for collectors, the Philadelphia

---

[667] The terminology used in this book is consistent with that in *The Official Red Book of U. S. Gold Double Eagles*, by Q. David Bowers, published by Whitman Publishing Company, 2004. The present writer contributed to the discussion on this issue and believes that both "sandblast" and "satin" are appropriate descriptive terms.
[668] *US Mint*, NARA-CP, op. cit., entry 229, box 268. Letter dated November 14, 1908 to Leach from Norris.
[669] *US Mint*, NARA-CP, op. cit., entry 229, box 295. Letter dated August 4, 1910 to Andrew from Woodin.
[670] *US Mint*, NARA-CP, op. cit., entry 229, box 295. Letter dated August 19, 1910 to Andrew from Woodin.

Mint produced sandblast (also called "dull" by mint staff) proof coins for all four gold denominations in 1908.

To help understand the differences between each version of collectors' "proof" coin, the following table illustrates each, along with a short description of how the pieces were manufactured.

| Name | Photo | Description & Manufacture Method* |
|---|---|---|
| **Brilliant Proof, Gold** | | Polished mirror like surfaces on field and devices. Struck on a hydraulic press from new, carefully impressed dies. Dies and planchets usually polished. Standard minor "proof coin" sold to collectors from 1858 to 1909/1913; silver from 1858 to 1915; gold from 1858 to 1907. Standard for collectors' proof sets when modern series was begun in 1936. Very easily hairlined due to cleaning or rubbing with a cloth. |
| **Cameo Proof, Gold** | | Polished mirror like fields with frosted devices (lettering and portrait). Struck on a hydraulic press from new, carefully impressed dies. Only field of dies polished; planchets usually polished. Seen on proof coins sold to collectors from 1858 to 1915 as consequence of incomplete die polishing. Highly prized today because of the visual contrast between portrait and field. Often encountered on modern proof coins made after 1936. |
| **Sandblast Proof, Gold** | | Dull, non-reflective surfaces. Struck on a hydraulic press from new, carefully impressed dies. Dies and planchets not polished although planchets selected for smooth surfaces. After striking, the coins were lightly sandblasted in a manner similar to medals. Standard gold proof coins sold to collectors 1908 and 1911–15. Correctly called sandblast proof since this describes how the pieces were made. Surface very delicate and easily marred.<br><br>Sandblasting tends to exaggerate the color of the gold, particularly the greenish specimens (caused by excess silver in the alloy). |
| **Satin Proof, Gold** | | So-called Roman proof of 1909–1910. Lustrous non-mirror surfaces. Lacking mint frost commonly seen on normal circulation strikes. Produced on a hydraulic press from new, carefully impressed dies. Hubs were lightly buffed before annealing to remove stray burrs left from cutting the metal on the reducing lathe. Planchets not polished although planchets were selected for smooth surfaces. No post-strike treatment. Easily confused with early circulation strikes that were made the same way but on normal coining presses. Standard gold "proof coin" sold to collectors 1909 and 1910. Surface easily marred. Minimal visual distinction between these and ordinary circulation strikes. Analogous to satin proofs of later years. |

| Name | Photo | Description & Manufacture Method* |
|------|-------|-----------------------------------|
| **Sandblast Proof, Silver** | | Dull, non-reflective surfaces. Struck on a hydraulic press from new, carefully impressed dies. Dies and planchets not polished although planchets selected for smooth surfaces. After striking, the coins were lightly sandblasted in a manner similar to medals. Used on 1921 and 1922 Peace dollar proofs and some commemorative halves. Correctly called sandblast proof since this describes how the pieces were made. Surface very delicate and easily marred.<br><br>Sandblasting tends to give silver a gray, pewter-like color. |
| **Satin Proof, Silver** | | Smooth, fine-grained, non-reflective surfaces with little "mint bloom" and only slight luster. Struck on a hydraulic press from new, carefully impressed dies. Hubs not buffed, resulting in very fine texture. Dies were not treated; planchets not polished although planchets were usually selected for smooth surfaces. No post-strike treatment. Analogous process to "Roman" proofs as seen on gold coins 1909–1910.<br><br>Seen on 1921–1922 Peace dollars and occasional later Saint-Gaudens gold coins. Also on some commemorative half dollars from the 1920s and '30s. This surface was called "bright" in contrast to "sandblast" by mint personnel in 1922.[671] Easily confused with "first strikes" from new dies, since this is essentially what a satin proof is, except for the greater detail and square rims imparted by the hydraulic press. Not a standard mint "proof" surface until late 1980s when US. Mint started calling them "matte proof." Surface easily marred. |

*Before hydraulic medal presses were available, the Philadelphia Mint used a large screw press to strike medals and proof coins. Some early proof specimens may have been struck more than once. After hydraulic equipment was introduced, proof coins normally received one blow from the press.*

Results of sandblasting and other techniques often varied from coin to coin and year to year, depending on which assistant did the work and whether procedures were followed carefully. The so-called Roman proofs typically look like perfect first strikes from new dies – which they were – and are similar to the 1907 Saint-Gaudens patterns which were not produced as deliberate proofs. As John Landis implied (see Andrew's letter of September 22, 1910, below) a dull proof could be made by sandblasting a satin proof piece. Except for sandblast proofs, excess pieces were usually put into circulation.

Assistant secretary Andrew wrote to Woodin on August 24:[672]

> I have just written to Mr. Landis to try to secure from him some information with regard to the objection to the dull finish proof gold coins. I should be very glad to accede to your request to have a few proof sets made with the dull finish, except for the objection, which I think you will understand, that I do not want any peculiar issues to be made for any particular people from the Mint in Philadelphia which are not available for purchase by all. If collectors will agree in favoring the dull proof coins I shall be only too glad to order that all proofs hereafter of gold coins be

[671] *US Mint*, NARA-CP, op. cit., entry A1-328N, box 4. Letter dated January 24, 1922 to director Baker from superintendent Styer. "The bright and sand-blasted pieces were of the first strike…" Evidently sandblast and satin proofs of the medium relief version were also sent to the director.

[672] *US Mint*, NARA-CP, op. cit., entry 229, box 295. Letter dated August 24, 1910 to Woodin from Andrew.

made in dull finish, but I do not think that we ought to make a few sets of an exceptional kind for any particular individuals. In that way lies great opportunity for abuse, as the past has shown, and as you very well know.

On becoming mint director, Andrew had campaigned for consistency of operation and removal of any form of special treatment for those doing business with the U. S. Mint. Only a few months before his correspondence with Woodin, Andrew had ordered the destruction of all remaining nineteenth and early twentieth century pattern and experimental coin dies.

Woodin replied the next day:[673]

Your letter of August 24th has just been received. Thank you very much for your letter to Mr. Landis. I certainly understand your position in regard to proof coin matters, but it seems to me that the difference between the dull proofs and the proofs that are now issued is so great and so obviously in favor of the dull proof coins, that I should think the Mint Dept. would be justified in making them, as certainly the most artistic results are desired for coins of this class that go into the hands of collectors. I can get quite a number of letters favoring dull proof coins from collectors, but I could not get all collectors to agree on anything. They are a very peculiar class of people as a rule, and you would be amused if you could hear some of their ideas.

Woodin's complaint was about the gold proofs issued in 1909 and 1910. Unlike the dull, or sandblast proofs made in 1908, the mint tried making the collectors' coins by striking the pieces on a medal press as was usually done for proofs, but with no post-striking treatment.[674] Modern collectors sometimes call this a "Roman" finish proof although it has noting to do with Rome or the Roman empire. All the proofs had sharper details and rims than normal-circulation coins, but to Woodin, the 1909 and 1910 gold proofs were little more than imitations. Andrew sent a little more information on the afternoon of August 26:[675]

Dear Mr. Woodin:
I have just received word from Mr. Landis in reply to my letter in reference to the gold proof coins. I enclose [for] you a copy of the portion of his letter referring to that subject. I think his suggestion is well taken that if a change is to be made it should be made at the beginning of a calendar year so that we would not have two kinds of proof coins bearing the same date. If you can secure anything like a consensus of opinion, say at the meeting of the Numismatic Association, in regard to this question, I will order the proof coins for the coming year to be made in the dull finish, which you suggest. Please let me know your wishes in this matter and whether it would be feasible to get a resolution of the Numismatic Association or of some committee of that association in regard to this matter.
Yours sincerely,

The American Numismatic Association's annual convention was coming up and Andrew felt that a resolution from them would give him the support necessary to change the way the gold proofs were prepared. Woodin expressed no interest in the silver or minor coin proofs. All were still made in traditional brilliant versions with exception of the new

---

[673] *US Mint*, NARA-CP, op. cit., entry 229, box 295. Letter dated August 25 1910 to Andrew from Woodin.
[674] The hubs were routinely buffed to remove stray particles during the pre-1917 era. This is the only difference in production between Roman and later satin proofs.
[675] *US Mint*, NARA-CP, op. cit., entry 229, box 295. Letter dated August 26, 1910 to Woodin from Andrew.

Lincoln cent, which was being made with a semi-matte surface. Although all proofs were made on medal presses, and thus much sharper than ordinary coins, only the polished examples were obviously different to all but the most discerning viewer.[676]

Andrew wrote back to Landis on August 26:

> I am grateful for your letter of August 25th. I have communicated your statements with regard to the dull finish coins to Mr. Woodin, with the request that he try and secure some consensus of opinion among numismatists with regard to the way these coins should be produced. I have suggested that at the annual meeting of the Numismatic Association, which takes place in New York in the course of next week, the subject might be discussed and a resolution secured.

Woodin wrote back on August 29, having decided that a resolution was probably the best way to go, but not giving up on convincing Andrew to make a few sandblast-finish sets in 1910:[677]

> Many thanks for your letter of August 26th, enclosing letter from Mr. Landis, in reference to the finish of the gold proof coins. I think it might be feasible to get a resolution of the Numismatic Association in regard to this matter, and I think I shall exhibit the two proof sets showing the difference in the finish, and I am sure any man who can use his eyes properly would most certainly prefer the dull finish. Of course there will be some objectors to this. Collectors are a peculiar class of people and it does not make any difference what kind of a proposition you put up to them as a body, most strenuous objections are raised by certain members. If I can secure a resolution of this sort I wish you would consider making up some additional proof sets this year with the dull finish. The present gold proof coins are not worth keeping.
>
> I note Mr. Landis' complaint of the few proof sets sold during the year 1908. I do not know how many gold proof sets the Mint is in the habit of disposing of each year, but the number strikes me as pretty large, larger than I had any idea, especially the eagles and double eagles. I do not believe there are twenty-five collectors of double eagles in this country, and the sale of 101 pieces looks to me pretty good.
>
> I also note that Mr. Landis has no definite data in regard to the criticisms of the dull proof finish. There were over one hundred full sets sold, and if five or six of the people would have objected to them it would have seemed a great many in comparison with the ones who said nothing. I also do not think that the objectors realized how the bright proof coins would look with the St. Gaudens designs.
>
> I am afraid I am making you a lot of trouble about a very little thing
> With kind regards,

The "two proof sets" referred to are sets for 1908 in sandblast and 1909 with satin finish. Displayed side by side, the differences are obvious, with the sandblast finish being more medal-like than the satin.

Andrew had evidently been convinced by Woodin's pleas for "dull finish" proof sets for 1910:[678]

> I have you letter of August 29th and am glad you are going to undertake to secure a resolution of the Numismatic Association [with] regard to the finish of the

[676] A hundred years later, collectors and dealers still have difficulty determining if an early Lincoln cent is a proof or very sharp circulation strike. Given the mint's habit of tossing defective proofs into circulation, a "super strike Lincoln" offered for sale may have originally been a rejected proof coin.
[677] *US Mint*, NARA-CP, op. cit., entry 229, box 295. Letter dated August 29, 1910 to Andrew from Woodin.
[678] *US Mint*, NARA-CP, op. cit., entry 229, box 295. Letter dated August 31, 1910 to Woodin from Andrew.

proof coins. If you can get any definitive opinion on this matter I will be quite willing to consider having additional proof sets of this year made with the dull finish....

Woodin followed up with a resolution for the ANA meeting, then wrote to Andrew on September 8:[679]

> Referring again to the question of the gold proof coins, a resolution was passed yesterday by the convention of the American Numismatic Association, requesting that all gold proof coins hereafter be struck in dull finish. I trust in view of this, that you will ask the Mint in Philadelphia to place sets on sale of this year in the dull proof finish, as some of us are very anxious to procure them.
>
> I received a list from Mr. Preston, Acting Director of the Mint, showing the gold proof coins delivered since 1876, and I note that the deliveries in the year 1908, in the dull proof coins, was greater than any year since 1903, and much greater than the following year, 1909. I am sure they will be found to be a very popular coin.
>
> PS: You will receive in due course the suggestion from the Ass'n.

By September 22, Andrew had not received the promised ANA resolution and he wrote again to Woodin:[680]

> ...I have not yet received the resolution, however, but I have explained to the new Director of the Mint, Mr. George H. [sic] Roberts, that I had arranged with you to have such proof coins sold in the mint hereafter if the American Numismatic Association as a body requested it. It appears that the ordinary proof coins are given this dull finish by means of a sandblast, and that anybody could make such proof from the ordinary proofs by this simple process.
>
> I have referred your correspondence with regard to the matter to the Director, and I have little doubt that he will agree with the desires of the American Numismatic Association.

The ANA resolution eventually arrived on Roberts' desk; however, Andrew and Landis objected to striking a few special pieces, and it appears the Philadelphia Mint did not strike 1910 gold sandblast proofs for Woodin and other collectors. From 1911 to 1915 the gold proofs were all of the sandblast variety although occasional specimens may have escaped sandblasting.

## *Proof Coins Discontinued*

When the new silver coin designs were introduced in 1916, they had field curvature and texture similar to the Saint-Gaudens gold coins. Brilliant proof specimens, as had been made for silver coins in previous years, were not an option. On October 17, Philadelphia Mint superintendent Adam Joyce wrote to mint director von Engelken about proof coins for 1916:[681]

> The issue of the silver coins of the new designs will complete the series of changes in the coin designs. The ground of all these designs is uneven, which makes it impossible to produce proof coins which are distinctive from the regular coins made on the coining presses from new dies, the only difference between the proofs and the regular coins being the sharper edge and design.

---

[679] *US Mint*, NARA-CP, op. cit., entry 229, box 295. Letter dated September 8, 1910 to Andrew from Woodin.

[680] *US Mint*, NARA-CP, op. cit., entry 229, box 295. Letter dated September 22, 1910 to Woodin from Andrew.

[681] *US Mint*, NARA-CP, op. cit., entry 229, box 305. Letter dated October 17, 1916 to mint director von Engelken from Joyce.

> Formerly the full set of proofs was made in January or February and orders filled when received, but since the manner of manufacture and issuing the proofs has been changed so that some of the denominations may not be issued until late in the year (we are only allowed to make each denomination after the regular coins for circulation have been issued) great dissatisfaction has been shown by persons desiring these proofs and a seemingly unnecessary amount of correspondence entailed on this office, returning orders and answering complaints.
>
> In order to distinguish gold proofs from the regular issue, it has been necessary to give them a sandblast finish, which changes the appearance of the coins to such an extent that it is almost impossible to put them in circulation. This is something I am not sure we have a right to do.
>
> The extra charge for the silver and minor proof coins, 5¢, does not cover the cost of manufacture.
>
> I would, therefore, suggest for your consideration the advisability of ceasing the manufacture of proof coins.

It didn't take mint director von Engelken long to make a decision – the mint was losing money on each proof coin made, collectors were complaining, and paperwork had become a nuisance. Rather than look for ways to correct the problems, the director decided to eliminate all proof coins. A decade earlier the mint had actively supported coin collectors. Now, his terse order of October 18 ended fifty-seven years of continuous issuance of proofs for purchase by ordinary collectors.[682]

> I am in receipt of your letter of October 17<sup>th</sup>.
> Effective at once, you will please discontinue the manufacture of proof coins.

Across the spectrum of coin collectors, from Robert Garrett's almost unlimited budget, to Giles Anderson's modest annual expense of 25¢ for two minor proof sets,[683] the special collector's coins were no more. It would be twenty years before they returned.

---

[682] *US Mint*, NARA-CP, op. cit., entry 229, box 305. Letter dated October 18, 1916 to Joyce from von Engelken.

[683] See above for Garrett's gold purchases in 1907, and Burdette: *Renaissance of American Coinage 1909–1915* for Giles Anderson's letters about discrimination in distribution of Lincoln cent proofs.

# Chapter 10 – Design and Commentary

All four Saint-Gaudens coin designs were derived from either the sculptor's own work or previous United States coins. The double eagle obverse is based on the artist's

*Figure 47. Gold double eagle and eagle designs by Augustus Saint-Gaudens as initially issued for circulation.*

statue of *Victory* as used in the Sherman Monument in New York City. The forward-striding figure of Liberty mimics the sense of movement of the golden *Victory* figure. At Roosevelt's insistence, Saint-Gaudens' initial double eagle obverse composition featured a forward-striding Liberty adorned with expansive wings and an Indian headdress. This arrangement was consistently used from 1905 through September 1906. Over that time,

Saint-Gaudens added a shield with various inscriptions – LIBERTY, LAW, JUSTICE (in Latin lettering as IVSTICE) – to his sketch models, but eventually replaced it with a simple olive branch.

*Figure 48. Evolution of the Winged Liberty design (top left to bottom right) from 1905 to mid-1906. Although the shield and wings eventually disappear, the basic figure of Liberty remains largely unchanged. The sketch at upper right includes directions for Hering: "Head higher; shield lower. Arm, more extention; more of right fo[ot]." The small head at right center shows Liberty wearing a cap instead of headdress.* (Courtesy Dartmouth College Library Special Collections; U. S. Department of Interior National Park Service, Saint-Gaudens National Historic Site, Cornish, NH. #0947, #1048, #1050.)

In the version at lower left, Figure 48, the words LIBERTY and IVSTICE are above the figure and MCMVI [1906] is below at the bottom rim. There are many differences between *Victory* and Liberty, which make each a unique creation. Saint-Gaudens' sketches and models with wings on the figure represent steps toward expressing the artist's ideas and, eventually, reducing complexity. As used on the coin, Liberty is wingless possibly in recognition of the small size of the coin. The statue's palm frond and the shield from various sketches have been replaced with an olive branch and the right hand now thrusts forward a flaming torch representing justice.

Simplification also enabled the artist to more strongly suggest the wind blowing from Liberty's left to right. In earlier versions the Indian headdress does not respond to the wind while Liberty's hair and the partially obscured flame are blown rightward. The final version shows gown, hair and flame all carried rightward as Liberty strides forward and upward toward the summit.

*Figure 49. Double eagle obverse very high relief (#2 model) and Victory from the Sherman Monument.* (Courtesy Smithsonian Institution, Peter A Juley & Son Collection; courtesy U. S. Department of Interior National Park Service, Saint-Gaudens National Historic Site, Cornish, NH.)

In simplifying his designs, Saint-Gaudens also recognized that E PLURIBUS UNUM had to be included on the coin. The motto had been incorporated in the original standing eagle reverse design. However, the new flying eagle reverse had no obvious space for the motto except possibly across the sun. The sculptor experimented with placing it on the

*Figure 50. Left: Striding Liberty design with E PLURIBUS UNUM added to the rock beneath the figure. This version may date from October–November 1906 during transition to the "final" obverse compositions. Right, detail showing motto just below Liberty's foot. Note the artist's monogram hidden among the oak leaves.* (Courtesy U. S. Department of Interior National Park Service, Saint-Gaudens National Historic Site, Cornish, NH. #1061.)

obverse, but may have been dissuaded by the obvious faux pas of having goddess Liberty stepping on the motto of national unity. It was eventually decided to use the edge of the coin for this inscription. The artist does not appear to have specified lettering style or arrangement until after he saw the first experimental pieces in February 1907.

The same model, Harriet (Hettie) Eugenia Anderson, a young woman reportedly of mixed racial heritage from South Carolina, posed for the figure of *Victory* and the portrait. It was the Victory head that eventually was proposed of the obverse of the cent and then used on the eagle coin.

*Figure 51. Portrait bust of Hettie Anderson (left), design for the one cent coin (center), design for the $10 gold coin with addition of Indian headdress as requested by President Roosevelt.* (Left-Center: Courtesy U. S. Department of Interior National Park Service, Saint-Gaudens National Historic Site, Cornish, NH #1138; right: Harry W. Bass, Jr. Research Foundation.)

Ms. Anderson's involvement in the Sherman monument project was largely unknown until research by William E. Hagans revealed her presence at the sculptor's New York studio in 1897 and Cornish in early 1906.[684]

Reverse of the double eagle is derived from the Flying Eagle one cent coin obverse design by Christian Gobrecht. Saint-Gaudens specifically mentions his admiration for the flying eagle as used on the cent from 1857 to 1858, and states his intention to update the

*Figure 52. Saint-Gaudens updated version of the 1857 flying eagle (left). The 1906 version intended for the one cent coin obverse (center), and the high relief 1907 minted version are much more powerful and graceful than their predecessor of fifty years.* (Center: Courtesy U. S. Department of Interior National Park Service, Saint-Gaudens National Historic Site, Cornish, NH. #1098)

bird "...on the 'Liberty' side of the cent I am using a flying eagle, a modification of the device which was used on the cent of 1857. I had not seen that coin for many years, and

---

[684] William E. Hagans, *American Art*, "Saint-Gaudens, Zorn, and the Goddesslike Miss Anderson," Smithsonian American Art Museum publication, volume 16, No. 2 (Summer, 2002). Research by Mr. Hagans, supported by Saint-Gaudens expert John Dreyfhout, established Miss Anderson's role as model for the eagle and double eagle obverse designs.

was so impressed by it, that I thought if carried out with some modifications, nothing better could be done."[685]

The flying eagle, as originally proposed, was rejected by either secretary Shaw or Saint-Gaudens as being illegal on the cent. The decision to use it on the double eagle, must have taken place sometime in the late summer of 1906 because the first pair of double eagle models was delivered in December 1906, and included the flying eagle reverse. "The illegality of an eagle on the one cent made it necessary for me to find something new for the reverse of that piece which would replace the flying or standing eagle I first submitted."[686] The one cent coin version showed an eagle flying left with the rising sun below and the inscription LIBERTY, above. When the decision was made to use it on the reverse of the $20 coin, the eagle and sun were placed slightly lower in the field.

Initially, the inscriptions UNITED STATES OF AMERICA and TWENTY DOLLARS were in two lines of small letters above the eagle. This left sufficient space for a third line of text, possibly intended for E PLURIBUS UNUM. Visually, this arrangement was crowded, with small letters weighing down the eagle and confusing the composition. The next and final version adopted a two-line inscription in large letters, omitting space for any other text. The sun and eagle were shifted slightly lower in the circle. In 1908, Charles Barber used the last fragment of reverse real estate to add the religious motto IN GOD WE TRUST just above and parallel to the curve of the sun.

*Figure 53 Evolution of the Flying Eagle design as adapted for the double eagle coin October-November 1906. Left: eagle only , sun outlined, no rays or inscription; center: inscription outlined in small letters; right: final version with two lines of text in larger letters, eagle and sun slightly lower.* (Courtesy U. S. Department of Interior National Park Service, Saint-Gaudens National Historic Site, Cornish, NH. #1127, #1100, #1102.)

The original standing eagle reverse of the double eagle was an adaptation of the reverse of the 1905 inaugural medal designed by Saint-Gaudens and sculpted by Adolph A. Weinman. This, in turn, was supposedly based on an illustration on Plate 28 of *A Guide to the Principal Gold and Silver Coins of the Ancients* by English numismatist Barclay V. Head, a copy of which was owned by Saint-Gaudens and had been loaned to Roosevelt. However, it is more likely that the eagle was simply one of the many variations available in the artist's repertoire, and not inspired by a specific illustration.

---

[685] *Roosevelt*, LoC, op. cit. Microfilm reel 65. Letter dated June 28, 1906 to Roosevelt from Saint-Gaudens.
[686] *SG*, Dartmouth, op. cit. Box 16, folder 38. Letter dated February 5, 1907 to Roosevelt from Saint-Gaudens.

*Figure 54. Presidential inaugural medal reverse of 1905 (left) and $20 gold coin reverse of 1906. Both images are of bronze reductions. The $20 is one of three reductions made in Paris by Janvier et Duval. Note changes in proportion of the bird, particularly head and neck, also differences in feather detail, motto placement and base on which the eagle stands. Weinman's 1905 eagle is clearly a more powerful and decisive emblem than the scrawny-necked 1906 effigy.* (Courtesy U. S. Department of Interior National Park Service, Saint-Gaudens National Historic Site, Cornish, NH. #1161, #1091)

In adapting the bird, Saint-Gaudens simplified the feathers so they would reproduce better on a small coin. He also placed the eagle on a fasces entwined with olive to symbolize strength and peace. A final touch was to move the motto to the upper right, behind the bird. This produced a large open space in front of the eagle, adding to the leftward motion of the figure. Multiple sketches and sketch models indicate that Saint-Gaudens did not simply copy his previous design. He started from the beginning in exploring various configurations of lettering and eagle until he settled on one similar to that on the medal.

*Figure 55. Sample standing eagle sketches by Saint-Gaudens, ca. late 1905.* (Courtesy Dartmouth College Library.)

Most concepts used in the pencil sketches, except for the legends completely surrounding the eagle, are repeated on sketch models. The sketch models, below, are a sample of the artist's continuing search for an ideal composition. More that seventy of these small plaster sketches were made from late 1905 to spring 1906. They were sometimes placed in the studio where assistants could examine them and "vote" for their preferred compositions.

*Figure 56. Sketch models in plaster prepared for the standing eagle reverse originally intended for the double eagle. The motto E PLURIBUS UNUM was included on nearly all of the sketch models, suggesting the artist understood it had to be on the coin.* (Courtesy U. S. Department of Interior National Park Service, Saint-Gaudens National Historic Site, Cornish, NH.)

Saint-Gaudens was intent on simplifying his compositions by eliminating as much inscription as possible and reverting to classic forms of lettering. He followed this approach on the inaugural medal and applied it again to the coin designs. In large part, the inaugural medal reverse was the work of Adolph Weinman, and it is possible Saint-Gaudens felt the need to artistically explore the standing eagle design to his own satisfaction. Legally mandated mottoes complicated the issue because the words/phrases LIBERTY, E PLURIBUS UNUM, UNITED STATES OF AMERICA, along with the date and denomination, were all required on the coin. Add to the list the semi-optional IN GOD WE TRUST and small coin spaces could quickly become crowded with lettering.

*Figure 57. Final design (center) for the reverse of the $10 gold coin by Saint-Gaudens as modified by Henry Hering and Homer Saint-Gaudens; submitted August 27, 1907. Compare to the model (left) and earlier $20 version (right), June 1906, particularly proportions of head, neck and wings.* (Left and right: Courtesy U. S. Department of Interior National Park Service, Saint-Gaudens National Historic Site, Cornish, NH #1120, #1091; center: courtesy Harry W. Bass, Jr. Research Foundation.)

Saint-Gaudens used a medallic approach to details including triangular text stops between words and at ends of inscriptions. His June 1907 model has all the requisite orna-

306

ments; however, the final standing eagle design by Hering and Homer Saint-Gaudens (above, center) avoids most ornamentation including removal of the small triangles at the ends of legends. The standing eagle design is extensively documented in remaining drawings, sketch models, full-scale models, reductions and coins. As the eagle evolved from inaugural medal to $10 coin, the bird's proportions changed. This is particularly noticeable in the neck, where it becomes overly long on the coin and loses scale with the eagle's head and body. If this "snapshot" of the sculptor's work is reliable, he seems to have spent a disproportionate amount of effort on the one composition most closely resembling previous work. Possibly the required legends interfered with artistic vision, or the full-length Liberty figure simply coalesced in the sculptor's imagination better than the eagle. We will likely never know and can only marvel at the results conveyed in so small a space.

Saint-Gaudens and his legacy of creative assistants were heavily influenced by French art. The techniques and subject treatment for coin designs often began with variations on French prototypes. This was as true with Saint-Gaudens in 1905–07 as it was later with Adolph Weinman in 1916. The most obvious instance of artistic reverence occurred in 1909 when Victor Brenner churlishly attempted to "swipe" designs from current French coins for use on the new one cent coin he was designing.[687] Much less obvious was Weinman's homage to Louis-Oscar Roty. The medallic and bas-relief portions of Saint-Gaudens' career paralleled that of two of France's greatest artists and medallists: Louis-Oscar Roty (1846–1911) and Jules-Clement Chaplain (1839–1909). Both were beneficiaries of a golden age of medallic sculpture during the final decades of the nineteenth century. Roty's full-length sculpture *Sower*, also known as *Marianne,* was transferred to the obverse of the 1-Franc silver coin and became the female personification of France and French liberty. The image was so loved by the French that it remains in use on the nation's coinage.

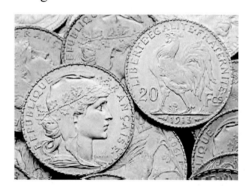

*Figure 58. Obverse and reverse of the French 20-franc gold coin issued from 1899-1916 designed by Jules-Clement Chaplain. In the center is a sketch for the cent (?) by Saint-Gaudens. Henry Hering attempted to emulate the relief of the French coin in modeling the final version of the gold eagle. Note the similarity also with Barber's 1906 double eagle pattern obverse (right).* (Center: Courtesy Dartmouth College Library; right: Smithsonian National Numismatic Collection, Douglas Mudd.)

As noted in a letter from Homer Saint-Gaudens to the mint on August 20, 1907, the sculptor had instructed Hering to model the eagle in a relief comparable with that used on the current French gold coin by Chaplain. This was the lowest relief which Hering felt Saint-Gaudens had indicated was acceptable. French sculptor Jules-Clement Chaplain was a winner of the *Prix de Rome* in 1863, and found almost immediate success in the salon exhibitions of Paris. In 1877, Chaplain was named the official medallist of the French gov-

[687] See Burdette. *Renaissance of American Coinage 1909–1915,* or Taxay's *U. S. Mint and Coinage,* pp.330–339.

ernment. Unlike the United States Mint, the French Mint (*Monnaie de Paris*) used outside artists to produce coin and medal designs of the highest artistic caliber. When the models were completed, the mint's engravers were charged with cutting dies that captured the look and feel of the original as closely as possible, while still being suitable for mass production.

Chaplain received the commission to design the gold coinage of France in 1898 at the urging of medallic art patron, connoisseur and critic Claude Roger-Marx. In creating his effigy for the Third Republic's new Fr-20 gold coin, Chaplain breathed new life into French monetary aesthetics that had remained largely unchanged since 1791. His portrait of "Marianne" used on the obverse of the Fr-20 gold coin contrasted her smooth features with the flowing locks that escape from her Phrygian cap. The reverse, illustrating a proud Gallic cockerel, gave the coin it's English nickname of "Rooster." Chaplain was also responsible for official portraits of every President of the French Republic from Patrice Mac-Mahon in 1877 to Émile Loubet in 1899.[688]

Chaplain's minted design is more detailed and "sharper" than Saint-Gaudens' yet the relief is lower than on the American $10 coin. This is due in part to the cooperative approach of the French Mint and the designer, who worked together to achieve the most effective modeling within a very small circle. Also, the skill of the French engravers in using the Janvier reducing lathe to control both diameter and relief resulted in reductions of the highest quality and detail. It is apparent that Saint-Gaudens and Hering had access to the French coin, which is how they could decide the relief was acceptable. However, it is very unlikely either man had seen Chaplain's original models for the coin, or were aware of how the Janvier lathe was used to modify the relief while simultaneously cutting a reduced size steel hub.

When he ordered reductions of the standing eagle design from Janvier et Duval in June 1906, Saint-Gaudens requested three versions in different relief heights. The two remaining examples show similar detail while clearly of different relief. It is unlikely U. S. Mint engravers could have obtained this level of quality and engraving control.

## Later Design Adjustments

The Roosevelt-Saint-Gaudens collaboration broke new ground for coinage designs by non-mint artists. It also established precedent for subsequent adjustment to the artist's original work.

As soon as the 1907 eagle and double eagle coins were in production, engraver Barber began work on new hubs for 1908. For most other denominations this was handled by assistant engraver Morgan, but Barber took a very personal interest in the new gold pieces and did this work himself. Director Leach and Barber both felt the original designs were too "soft" and "impressionistic," which might encourage counterfeiting. To correct this, Barber re-engraved much of the detail on both sides of the coins for 1907 and created completely new hubs for 1908.[689] Director Leach notes this in offhand comments to Charles Brewster: "As to making a fourth model, I doubt whether sufficient improvement on the coin could be made to justify the expense and trouble necessary. We are improving upon the appearance of the coin right along…I think we have a beautiful coin in the one

---

[688] David and Constance Yates, *The Renaissance of the Cast Medal in Nineteenth Century France,* New York, 1997. Source of the information on Chaplain.
[689] There are three obverse hubs for 1908 and two reverse hubs.

we are now turning out."[690] A side by side examination of circulation pieces dated 1907 and later reveal altered legends, stars and portraits. These changes were consistent with the mint's understanding of the coinage laws that implicitly permitted minor alterations to improve mechanical performance or correct problems. In later years, this concept would be stretched to include removal of designer's initials (1909), noticeable change in the reverse composition (1913), and complete modification of design details and composition (1917).

The photos below illustrate a 1907 (model #3) eagle with the 1910 version. Note

*Figure 59. Obverse of $10 gold eagle design of 1907 and the "evolved" version of 1910. Barber began making changes for calendar year 1908 and continued through 1916. Additional modifications were later made by engraver George Morgan and his successor John Sinnock.*

differences in stars, legend and date, and also the sharper delineation of feather outlines and interior detail. This is particularly noticeable above the forehead and to the right of the date. Compare, also, hair details at the neck and changes to the flow of the hair just below "Y." The reverse design was similarly modified to produce a sharper-looking coin. Comparable modifications were made to the double eagle, although much had already been done in December 1907 in preparation for production. The most evident changes were to the obverse stars olive branch, which were sharpened. (The engraver made similar changes to Pratt's half eagle, but the work was done before the coins were issued for circulation, and most of the original pattern pieces were destroyed. The result was a cluttered, overly busy detailing of feathers and headdress that gave the coins a shoddy appearance.)

Through late 1916 (1917-dated coins) Barber continued to sharpen and refine the independent artists' designs in his attempts to improve appearance and increase die life. Although some modern collectors complain about the engraver ruining the original designs, the truth is that most collectors recognize that Barber's adjustments resulted in more attractive coins. Direct comparison of 1916-dated minor coins with the first year of issue show significant differences in sharpness and detail.[691] Those who collect by first year of the type, are among the few who have pieces that are closest to the designer's original intention.

[690] *US Mint*, NARA-CP, op. cit., entry 330, box 45. Letter dated January 2, 1908 to Brewster from Leach.
[691] See Burdette, *Renaissance of American Coinage 1909–1915* and *Renaissance of American Coinage 1916–1921* for comparison photos and additional information.

## 1908 Mint Report

The United States Mint Bureau had this to say about the Saint-Gaudens coins in the Director's Report ending June 30, 1908:[692]

### New Designs for the Gold Coinage

In response to a popular demand for an improvement in the designs used on our coin, the President took steps early in the year 1905 to accomplish this result. It was decided to make the first change to the gold coins, and the eminent sculptor, Mr. Augustus Saint-Gaudens, was employed at the request of the President to prepare models for all denominations of the gold coins, and with the purpose in view of securing a much higher relief in design than was ordinarily used in modern coinage. Several models were made of the same design but with different heights of relief. But it was found to be impossible to work any of the designs upon an ordinary coining press until a third model was made with a greatly reduced relief. This was somewhat disappointing to those urging a high relief, and therefore some 12,153 pieces of double eagle from the second model were struck on a medal press and sent to such places in the United States where a general distribution of them could be made. Of the new Saint-Gaudens double eagle perfected for coinage in the regular way, $105,939,360 were struck by the close of the fiscal year.

The new designs for the eagle were also prepared by Mr. Saint-Gaudens, and are regarded by competent critics as artistic. The standing eagle is true to nature, while the feathered head of Liberty is a radical departure from the head heretofore appearing on any of our coins of either gold or silver.

There were coined in eagles during the fiscal year $4,829,060 in the new design.

The dollar value given above translates into 5,296,928 double eagles struck from July 1, 1907 through June 30, 1908. Director Leach may be excused the omissions and limited detail of his report – there had been much confusion in preparing the coins, and there was little value in a lengthy discussion. The report of 12,153 high relief double eagles is interesting in that it is approximately midway between the total of 12,867 pieces (714 more than the mint's report) indicated by Albert Norris' notes, and the 11,250 (903 less than the mint's number) traditionally reported.

## Opinion – Informed and Uninformed

The new gold coin design generated considerable newspaper interest, if only because of Saint-Gaudens' reputation and untimely death. Much of the initial comment was, at best, poorly informed. The treasury department refused to permit publication of coin photos in the newspapers, and it was not until the pieces were released into circulation that "ordinary" citizens got to see the work. By that time, sides had been taken for and against the designs based on hearsay and neither reality nor reason were permitted to intrude.

The nation's artists were unanimous in praise of Saint-Gaudens, particularly on creating artistic designs for the small coin modules. Commercial publications such as the Wall Street Journal complained bitterly about change and how foreign governments would reject the new pieces. As it turned out, gold was still gold and the bankers didn't care as long as weight and purity were correct.

---

[692] *Report of the Director of the Mint*, Treasury Department, Bureau of the Mint, Washington DC, December 9, 1908. U. S. Government Printing Office, Washington DC. pp.5–6.

From *The International Studio*, a publication of art and design, came this comment:[693]

> Both [coins] are too high for the working of modern machinery. Neither appeals to those schooled to our flat coins. To those trained by earlier models, the designs of Saint-Gaudens are the only ones in our day above the mere draughtsman's level. Little more depressing has occurred in our day than the baiting these coins have had from newspaper and sciolist. No application of art to familiar objects is possible where men are wedded to their preconceptions and are ignorant of the succession of art. These coins had precisely the reception which a great portrait would receive in a land where no man had ever looked on aught but a village photograph.

From the American Numismatic Association, whose leaders thought they should have been part of the review process:[694]

> To His Excellency, Theodore Roosevelt,
> President of the United States
>
> Honored Sir:
> The American Numismatic Association, through its Committee, wishes to commend you for the active interest you have taken in the movement to secure a better and more artistic coinage of the United States.
> We beg to express our high appreciation of your efforts resulting in the issuance of the beautiful eagle and double eagle by Saint Gaudens. These coins we regard as possessing high artistic merit though with some faults in detail and technique – and as greatly superior to those of the old type, and as marking an advance in American numismatic art.
> We also express the hope that you will continue to use your influence toward securing an entire new series of artistic coins for the United States.
> We would venture to offer our humble services, as experienced numismatists in suggesting the names of competent artists or in criticizing their designs, and believe, with our knowledge of the coinage of the world, of every period, we could be of some service.
>
> Thomas L. Elder, Chairman of the Committee
> Samuel Hudson Chapman, Secretary of the Committee

An undated letter from Ebenezer Gilbert printed in *Elder Monthly*, Volume 2, October–November 1907 indicates Elder had been able to acquire some of the new coins for his customers:[695]

> My dear Mr. Elder:
> I have examined the new Saint-Gaudens ten dollar gold coin which you so kindly obtained for me and will briefly give you my opinion of it.
> Upon the obverse, the head and appurtenances and date are too large for the size of the piece, and the stars too small. The face of Liberty is an anomaly. The prominent nose and chin indicate determination and strength of character, but the

---

[693] Talcott Williams, LL.D., *The International Studio,* "Augustus Saint-Gaudens." February 1908. Page CXXIII to CXXXVIII [pp.123-138] (John Lane Company, 110-114 West Thirty Second St, New York, NY). Courtesy library of Fred Weinberg.
[694] *The Numismatist*, January 1908. p.12.
[695] Q. David Bowers, as quoted on USPatterns.com "Wire-Rim $10 Story." Gilbert was from New York City, a close friend of Elder's, a frequent consignor to his auctions, and years later in 1916, the author of *The United States Half Cents. From the First Year of Issue, 1793, to the Year When Discontinued, 1857*, published by Elder.

effect of over hanging 'upper jaw' and lip with open mouth is idiotic. While the face is not that of an Indian, the headgear is.

On the reverse, we find a turkey buzzard in pantalets. The words of the legend above and value below the effigy are not sufficiently spaced, and are too close to the outer rim of the coin. There should be a marginal space between the top of these letters and the rim. 'E Pluribus Unum' is added as a postscript.

The style of letters used on both obverse and reverse and the figures of date show very poor judgment viewed from a typographical standpoint.

In one respect the piece may be called a "howling success." It is entirely different from anything ever before issued by the United States Mint, and no patent is needed to protect the designer from infringements.

The coin, both obverse and reverse, is a humiliating disappointment, without one redeeming feature, and is a 'foozle.'

Yours very truly,
E. Gilbert [Ebenezer Gilbert]

Gilbert's comment is similar to that of Frank Leach when he saw the standing eagle design on January 4, 1907. "I am glad to know there has been another design [the flying eagle – RWB] for the eagle submitted. This [standing] eagle is hardly a faithful representation of our national bird. The legs are altogether too long…This design inclines one to the impression of an crane in masquerade wearing pantaloons and a cutaway coat…[696] In contrast to Leach and Gilbert was numismatist Howland Wood's letter in the same issue of Elder's journal:[697]

My dear Mr. Elder–
I am enclosing a couple of rubbings of Bryan dollars, and descriptions of another one that has parodies of 'In God We Trust.' A search in the bar rooms will reveal a lot more parodies for at one time these places were especially rich in such mottoes. I trust that you will speak well of the new eagle. I have just sent off to Editor Heath [Dr. George Heath, Monroe, Michigan, editor of *The Numismatist*] a word of praise about the piece.

In justification of the Greek type of the new $10, the placing of the head as it is and the feathers going to the edge, almost identical types can be found among many Greek coins. I can only think of a few offhand, including the Athenian pieces, and those of Thurium, Pharsalos, and Velia.

In justification of the 'pants' of the eagle, a glance at our own coins of the seated liberty type will show that trousers were worn long in those days, as well as in the time of the Ptolemies, and good examples can be found on those Ptolemaic coins with one and two eagles on the reverse. I think the design of the obverse and reverse are grand conceptions, but the technical execution or die work I do not consider good.

Yours very truly,
Howland Wood, Secretary [corresponding secretary of the ANA]

General circulation newspapers were often uncomplimentary about the new designs, particularly the eagle. Negative criticism of the new $10 coin designs was not long in coming. By November 16, in addition to objections to omission of the religious motto,

---

[696] *US Mint*, NARA-CP, op. cit., entry 229, box 251. Letter dated January 4, 1907 to Roberts from Leach. The milling machine manipulation was used in December 1907 to make the "finless" high relief double eagles.

[697] Q. David Bowers, "Notes on the 1907 Saint-Gaudens $10 With-Periods, Wire Rim." Letter dated November 13, 1907 printed in the Elder Monthly, Volume 2, October–November 1907. Source: http://www.bowersandmerena.com/articles/article 3001.chtml.

there were complaints about the eagle, mirroring those mentioned by Gilbert and Wood, as reported in the *New York Times*:[698]

> Those…who are interested in the Government's coinage found something to talk about yesterday when some of the new $10 gold pieces began to circulate in the financial district. It may be said at once that there seemed to be no dissenting voice in the chorus of disapproval. There was general unanimity also in character-izing the eagle on the coin as a "bird" – that is, whenever it was not referred to as a turkey buzzard. Modest persons found something to gratify them in the disposal of the eagle's feathers, which carefully concealed his limbs, and prevented, undoubt-edly, any Comstockian comment on the National bird. Naturally enough, there was little expert opinion, but popular comment was heard on the ability of the Indian lady on the coin to carry such a fine head-dress of feathers. One practical com-ment was that the substitution of stars on the edge of the coin for the old milling, would result in a great deal of abrasion which might bring the coins below the limit of legal tolerance quicker than in the old coins.

The *Philadelphia Inquirer* had these caustic comments about the new $10 piece, particularly the eagle:[699]

### The New Gold Coin
Take a gold coin of the old style and compare it with the atrocity now being turned out by the Mint and then figure out, if you can, why, in the name of good taste or anything else, the change was made.

There was dignity about the old coin. It was a production worthy of any nation. It was pleasing to the eye. It was a work of art. But this new contrivance is a thing to laugh at.

On one side of this remarkable production is the head of Liberty – with a head dress of chicken feathers or something like them. On the other is a fowl of some sort. We are asked to believe that it is an eagle, but we are accustomed to seeing our eagles, when drawn upon a coin, in a posture that denotes strength. In this lat-est pose, it is difficult to tell whether the bird is a rooster in pantalettes, a hen dry-ing herself after a hard experience in a rain storm, or a pouting pigeon. It might be some other creature just as well – a partridge or a guinea chick.

We predict a short life for the pouting-pigeon-in-war-paint piece.

The *Wall Street Journal* of December 11, 1907 added its complaint about the "omitted" religious motto:[700]

### The New Coins
The new gold coins of the United States are not only defective in that the words "In God We Trust," which were first put upon them in Lincoln's time and which rep-resent the reverence of a majority of our citizens have been left off, but also be-cause they are utterly lacking in artistic attractiveness.

Mint headquarters in Washington received a number of complaints about the new coins. Many of these apparently were concerned with the workmanship of production rather than design. Director Leach forwarded a copy of one letter to Philadelphia "…simply [to] let you see a sample of the most recent criticism of the new coinage, and to impress upon your people the fact I shall expect there will be no cause for such or even

---

[698] *New York Times*, "Discussing the New Coins," November 16, 1907, p.13.
[699] *Philadelphia Inquirer*, "The New Gold Coin," November 23, 1907. Also reprinted in the *Wall Street Journal*, November 25, 1907.
[700] *Wall Street Journal*, "The New Coins," December 11, 1907, p.1.

milder complaints."[701] The letter was from F. H. Watriss from the law firm of Bartlett, Frazier and Carrington in New York:[702]

> Gentlemen:
>
> As an American citizen I take some pride in seeing our Government do its best in everything it undertakes. I have just seen the new $10 & $20 gold coins and although the design may be open to discussion the workmanship cannot be; the latter would be a disgrace to any mechanic. Both issues should be called in. Why the Department should permit such work is beyond comprehension.
>
> Very Respectfully Yours,

The workmanship complaints seem to have concentrated on the fin rim common to these coins, as well as the worn look of the $10 piece. After receiving the letter from Watriss, Leach wired the mint with instructions "…condemning all pieces with 'fin' edge be sure no more such defective coins get out."[703]

The next day he had $1,600 in high relief double eagles (eighty pieces) sent back to the mint for "recoinage."[704] A follow-up letter on December 12 indicates that Leach was not pleased with the response from Landis:

> …I fully understand the unavoidability [sic] of some imperfect work in all coinage operations, and that the striking of the new design double eagle on the medal press was not an exception. The information I sought to have you obtain, and still desire, is to be informed if my directions to have all of the pieces gone over and examined with the purpose of rejecting the defective pieces, or those with excessive burrs, was carried out; and if that work was done, who was responsible for its being executed in such a careless manner….The first time it was brought to my attention was when one of the employees of the coiner's department approached me with one of the double eagles in his hands, and asked me if such pieces like those should not be rejected. I replied that it should, by all means,…
>
> I enclose herewith a coin that was given to a party applying at the cashier's office in the Treasury Department here this morning, which seems to indicate that the work of examination of these pieces has not been carried on with proper care and judgement….

But coiner Rhine Freed reminded Leach that *all* the high relief coins had a fin and in normal circumstances *all* would have been condemned. The adjusters' job was to pick out the worst for recoinage while allowing most pieces to be distributed. The director's order was suspended and eventually forgotten.

By December 20 the fin (or burr) problem seems to have been solved on the high relief coins. Leach wrote to Barber: "I am more than delighted with the results you have obtained in preventing the 'fin.' I know the President will be pleased too. I have an appointment to see him Monday A.M."[705]

[701] *US Mint*, NARA-P, op. cit. Letter dated December 7, 1907 to Landis from Leach.
[702] *US Mint*, NARA-P, op. cit. Letter dated December 6, 1907 to U. S. Treasury Department from F. H. Watriss. The low relief $20 had not been released as of the date of Watriss' letter.
[703] *US Mint*, NARA-P, op. cit. Telegram dated December 6, 1907, 2:22 p.m. to Landis from Leach.
[704] *US Mint*, NARA-P, op. cit. Letter dated December 7, 1907 to Landis from Leach.
[705] *US Mint*, NARA-P, op. cit. Letter dated December 20, 1907 to Barber from Leach.

The general opinion of sculptors and other artists might well have been embodied in comments from Charles Moore, chairman of the Commission of Fine Arts in January 1932 as he reviewed designs for the proposed Washington quarter.[706]

> The Commission also considered a suggestion that the Saint-Gaudens eagle on the twenty-dollar gold coin be used for the reverse. They considered that to use a design that had been used on another coin would be unfortunate...Moreover, the eagle as it now appears on the coin has lost that essential quality which Saint-Gaudens gave to it. In reducing the relief vigor has been lost. Now the eagle has the quality of an engraving; it has become a picture instead of an emblem.

Public complaints soon vanished as Congress responded to the missing motto, and newspapers found other things to deplore. The eagles found their greatest use in interbank exchanges and holiday gifts. The large double eagle served a minor role in international trade, although gold bars were preferred for payments. Both designs lasted until 1933, when the United States suspended all gold coin production. Many $20 pieces that had been exported to Europe remained there until after World War II, when their slow repatriation became the source of many coins now actively collected by Americans.

---

[706] *US Mint*, NARA-CP, op. cit. Entry 1A 328I #104-83-0042, box 2, folder: *Coins – Geo. Washington Quarter Dollar Act Approved March 4, 1931.*

# Half Eagle and Quarter Eagle
# 1908

# Chapter 11 – The Boys From Boston

The five dollar and two-and-a-half dollar gold coins have often been treated as the "poor stepdaughters" of their larger siblings, the eagle and double eagle.[707] The large coins were in daily use by banks as reserves and for cash transfers between institutions. Many international transactions required payment in gold bullion or gold coin, and the $10 and $20 pieces were convenient for these purposes. Domestic circulation was limited in part because wage earners preferred smaller-denomination coins in their weekly pay envelopes. With average annual worker income of approximately $800, weekly pay was generally under $20 so small denomination silver coins were commonly used.[708] Daily cash requirements for average families was about $2.50 – an amount easily accommodated with quarters, dimes and nickels. People with large incomes normally used checks rather than cash for most payments. Then, as now, many objected to carrying weighty coin in their pockets or purses.

Saint-Gaudens' original commission was to design all four of the circulating gold coins and the bronze cent. From the beginning it was assumed that whatever design was selected for the double eagle would be scaled down for use on the eagle, half eagle, and

---

[707] The conventional story of Bela Lyon Pratt's $5 and $2.50 coin designs can be traced to a small number of early articles in *The Numismatist* and the *American Journal of Numismatics*, plus Don Taxay's excellent 1966 book *The U. S. Mint and Coinage*. Due to a general lack of contemporary research on the design process in 1908, and the untimely death of sculptor Pratt in 1917, even Taxay found little substantive information on the coins. He devotes only four pages to the topic and suggests, "…The issue must have gone without a hitch…" (p.326).The late numismatic research genius Walter Breen, who collaborated with Taxay on many publications, adds very little to the story in his massive *Encyclopedia*. A contributing factor is the absence of many U. S. Mint documents for the period, and the unavailability of Pratt's personal papers. This author's approach has been to widen the search for relevant documents (which has uncovered additional information) and incorporate published material by author Cynthia Sam. These have been synthesized into a meaningful and more accurate story of how these unusual coins were created. The story may change radically when the Pratt papers are available to researchers.

[708] The treasury department preferred to strike subsidiary silver and minor coins because their production produced large profits for the government. Gold coins contained their full face value in gold and were produced at a slight loss to the government.

quarter eagle.[709] Nearly two years into the project, in May 1907, President Roosevelt decided to use the Striding Liberty figure on the double eagle and a bust of Liberty, now with an Indian ceremonial headdress, on the eagle; the cent was eliminated. No work was done by the sculptor or mint on half and quarter eagles, and evidently little thought had been given to either denomination. An offhand remark by director Roberts in May 1907, that he assumed the small coins would use the design from the $10 piece, is the first admission that these denominations were part of the plan. A handwritten notation by secretary Cortelyou on a letter of November 29, 1907 is the earliest indication that anyone wanted action taken on the small gold pieces:[710]

> Director Leach advise accordingly. Design for double-Eagle to be used on the smaller coins. Want on all to [be] prepared at once.

In December 1907, with eagle and double eagle designs finally under control, attention was turned to the smaller gold coins. On December 2 mint director Frank Leach instructed the Philadelphia Mint to make dies for the half and quarter eagles:[711]

> You will proceed with the making of the dies for the half eagles and the quarter eagles, using the same design as that adopted for the double eagle.

A week later, after reworking the low relief double eagle design and seeing to its initial production, engraver Barber got around to replying to director Leach's instructions. He was already exasperated about the indefinite status of the eagle and double eagle, neither of which had been officially adopted as regular issue coins:[712]

> …if as hinted by the Director the design for the Double Eagle may be used for the five and two and a half dollar we should have instructions to that effect at the earliest moment, as it will take many weeks to prepare master dies and hubs for reproducing working dies.
>
> The question of design must also be considered, for instance, the design now is on reverse, 'United States of America' and in second line 'twenty dollars,' this can be altered to read 'five dollars,' but what shall be done in the case of the two and a half dollar coin, and again, I think it will be quite a difficult task to put the inscription 'E Pluribus Unum' upon the periphery [edge] of so small a coin as the two and a half dollar and yet the act of 1873, sec. 18 calls for this inscription to be placed upon the coins; these questions must all be settled before any steps can be taken to prepare the master dies and hubs. As before stated, considerable time will be required before we can be in a position to go on with gold coinage of the new designs, and therefore we should know at once what is required that we may make such preparation as will be necessary and at the same time keep up a supply of dies to satisfy the extraordinary demand that is now being made upon us, otherwise there will be a demand for gold coinage and no dies to coin with.

Superintendent Landis sent Barber's letter to the director who, in replying the next day, indicated his own uncertainty about the two small gold denominations:[713]

[709] For visual analogy, compare the U. S. Mint's 1986 gold bullion tokens, which use a bastardized version of Saint-Gaudens' Striding Liberty on the obverse. These tokens are issued in 1, ½, ¼, and 1/10 ounce weights, roughly equivalent to the old $20, $10, $5, and $2.50 coins.

[710] US Mint, NARA-CP, op. cit., entry 330, box 45. Letter dated November 29, 1907 to Cortelyou from Leach.

[711] US Mint, NARA-P, op. cit. Letter dated December 2, 1907 to Landis from Leach. The new design had not been officially adopted by December 2.

[712] US Mint, NARA-P, op. cit. Letter dated December 9, 1907 to Landis from Barber.

[713] US Mint, NARA-P, op. cit. Letter dated December 10, 1907 to Landis from Leach.

> ...The question asked, "how will the finer parts of the double eagle design appear when reduced to the size of the quarter eagle," can probably be better answered by Mr. Barber. I understand him to say, when asked that question some weeks ago, that we could get better results on the smaller coin. However, he may not have had in mind at that time the making of the quarter eagle.
>
> In relation to the selection of words or figures to indicate the denomination of the quarter eagle, I suppose we would have to use the figures, "2-½ Dol." But inasmuch as Mr. Barber has raised the question, I will submit it to the Secretary of the Treasury for his decision. It is possible we might want to use the words, "Two and a half D," or "Quarter Eagle," or the figures "2-½ D." I would suggest that Mr. Barber make drawings of these three or four methods of expressing the denomination and submit them to me.
>
> I know it will be difficult to put the inscription, "E Pluribus Unum" on the periphery of a quarter eagle, but I do not see where else it can [go] and we must try to do it.

It was left to the irascible Barber to raise the questions, and then be assigned the task of finding a solution. This was not what Barber wanted and his letters suggest an extraordinary reluctance to do anything unless specifically instructed. The mint director, for his part, seemed to be expecting more initiative from the superintendent and engraver. Director Leach wrote to Charles O. Brewster, Augusta's attorney, commenting on the design problems they were facing with the half and quarter eagle coins:[714]

> ...I have been directed by the Secretary of the Treasury to proceed with the preparation of dies for the $5.00 and $2.50 pieces, the President desiring that the design for the double eagle should be used on these two pieces. In as much as these pieces are so much smaller, Mr. Barber thinks we can use the number two model for them. But there is one thing which Mr. Barber calls attention to, which is a matter that will have to be soon decided, and before laying the matter before the President I thought to consult you, and that is in the matter of stating the denomination on the coin. Of course, in the $5.00 piece it will be easy to substitute the words "Five Dollars" in place of the "Twenty Dollars," but the $2.50 piece is far more difficult. If the three coins had been designated as "Double Eagle," "Eagle," and "Half Eagle," of course we might have very appropriately used the term "Quarter Eagle," but in as much as we did not use that term, it would seem somewhat inconsistent with the rest of the work to introduce it on the $2.50 piece. Of course, to use the words, "Two and a half dollars," as shown on the sketch enclosed herewith, would be out of the question; and to use figures and signs, would, I fear, seem inconsistent with the design of the coin. I would like to hear from Mr. Hering on the subject. Please have him return the card with his remarks.

Brewster wrote back asking if the mint wanted Hering to do the lettering and offering, "...I think it probable that Mrs. Saint-Gaudens would provide the new lettering at actual cost." The letter from Leach was given to Henry Hering, who wrote to Leach on December 21:[715]

> In answer to your letter of December 17 to Mr. C. O. Brewster, in which you wish my opinion regarding the smaller coins, I would frankly advocate using the words "Half Eagle" and "Quarter Eagle" on the $5.00 and $2.50 pieces. The inscription "Two and a half Dollars" would change the composition making three lines of inscription, which Mr. Saint-Gaudens experimented with and discarded.

---

[714] *US Mint*, NARA-CP, op. cit., entry 330, box 45. Letter dated December 17, 1907 to Brewster from Leach.

[715] *US Mint*, NARA-CP, op. cit., entry 229, box 260. Letter dated December 21, 1907 to Leach from Hering.

Therefore, as there are two distinct designs for the gold, I think the use of the words "Quarter Eagle," would be feasible.

You will notice the freedom of the use of such inscriptions on the gold issue of 1905-06 where the Quarter Eagle bears "2 ½ D." and the Half Eagle exhibits "FIVE D." and on the present ten cent piece which is called "One Dime." The other alternative, that of putting on numerals would change the character of the coin. You will remember that Mr. Saint-Gaudens avoided all numerals, and only altered the date after much persuasion. It seems to me that some sacrifice should be made in order to keep within the lines of composition, and the words "Quarter Eagle" would accomplish the result.

I notice in your letter that Mr. Barber thinks of using model Number Two for making the smaller coin dies. Why he proposes this I do not understand, for as Model Number Three, which I call the last models, is much lower in relief and sharper in detail, I should think he would get better results from it than from Number Two.

However, before you proceed with the small dies of $2.50 and $5.00, I wish you would consider a new suggestion which I am certain would give you your desired sharp model, requiring but one reduction. Let Mr. Barber take the last made die and enlarge it to between ten and twelve inches, the larger the better. This will bring the model to the required relief which I can retouch with my tools in the dulled places. Then we will be certain of a result that will give a sharp stamp both in the large and small dies. I cannot emphasize too strongly my wish to have this done, first because I am sure it will save the situation, and secondly, because I am afraid that with the present reductions, the $2.50 piece will blur hopelessly. I have resorted to this last measure as the only way I possibly can better the coin without changing the character of the relief which Mr. Saint-Gaudens left. I hope it will meet with your approval, as I feel certain if Mr. Barber gives me a fairly good enlargement, I can retouch it to the satisfaction of all.

Hering began his letter by discussing the issue of how to express the denomination, as had Barber although Hering came to the conclusion that "quarter eagle" was the best inscription to use, where Barber had been instructed to make drawings. Hering had already seen a sample of the circulation strike $20 that the mint had sent Brewster, and should have been aware that the figure and eagle had been re-engraved by Barber. Yet in the second paragraph he again pushes for use of the third model even though in its original form it was never used by the mint except to strike a pattern coin. But it was his last idea – enlarging the $20 die – that must have convinced the director that dealing with Hering was a waste of everyone's time. The situation had already been "saved" by Barber, and Hering's suggestions were of no importance. Leach passed the letter on to Landis on the 24th along with two "…cards showing the designs adopted for designating the denomination of the $5.00 and $2.50 gold pieces." He also stated he would write to Hering telling him the mint was going to proceed with its plan, but that if the results were not satisfactory, Hering would be brought in to help.[716] This was nothing more than the final removal of Hering from any further work on the coins. Director Leach showed the cards to secretary Cortelyou and President Roosevelt, who approved them on December 28.

As one might have anticipated, engraver Barber thought Hering's suggestion for an enlarged scale model was a travesty:[717]

Replying to the letter to the Director in relation to the suggestion made by Mr. Hering, namely, that I make enlarged models from the last made die enlarged to

---

[716] *US Mint*, NARA-P, op. cit. Letter dated December 24, 1907 to Landis from Leach.
[717] *US Mint*, NARA-P, op. cit. Letter dated December 30, 1907 to Landis from Barber.

ten or twelve inches, the larger the better, and send them to him, I beg to say that this is another example of dealing with parties who know nothing of the work of die making or coinage. As I have said before, had they the least rudimentary knowledge of the subject they would not make such child like suggestions.

After this bombastic introduction, Barber again hit his long-winded stride:

> To follow Mr. Hering's suggestion would be to open up the whole subject, renewing all the annoying contentions held by the Saint-Gaudens' party [and by the Mint bureaucracy – RWB] with which we have been laboring for more than a year, until it has become almost beyond endurance, and for no purpose as to avail nothing.
>
> You are fully aware that so long as Mr. Hering had the double eagle models in hand no good came out of it, and not until I was given the opportunity to make the dies in some measure suitable for coinage was there any prospect that there would be any new design double eagles made on a coining press.
>
> What I now propose doing is this – to make my reductions for the five, and two and a half dollar coins from the last and third models furnished, the same as was used for the double eagle, and [then make] any and all alterations needed to make dies that can be possibly used for coinage we will make, as we have done in the case of the double eagle.
>
> It is entirely unnecessary to trouble Mr. Hering any further, unless another year is to be wasted in vain endeavor.
>
> The designs showing the arrangement of letters designating the denomination for the five and two and a half dollar coins are approved by the President and Director. I therefore need nothing further and shall proceed at once with the work, trusting that the same degree of success obtained in the double eagle case may attend our efforts with these last two coins.
>
> Respectfully,

Barber's plan was to re-engrave the $5 and $2.50 hubs just as he had done on the double eagle, plus make necessary changes to the design to incorporate all mottoes and legends required by law. He would use Hering's #3 model as a guide but also do considerable sharpening of details. Director Leach sent Brewster a letter on January 2, 1908 updating events regarding the small gold coins:[718]

> ...I have not had time to devote to the new coinage matter further than to see the President in relation to designation for the $2.50 piece. Mr. Hering recommended the designating of "Quarter Eagle" which was approved by the President. It will not be necessary for Mr. Hering to do the lettering. That can be done by the Engravers at the Mint following the style and form of letter adopted by Mr. Saint Gaudens.

The director also wrote to Henry Hering letting him know of Barber's decision about the enlarged cast. He also gave Hering credit for acceptance of "quarter eagle" as the inscription on the coin:[719]

> In reply to your letter of December 21st in relation to the coinage of the smaller denominations of gold, I am pleased to state that upon submitting the matter of designation of the $2.50 pieces to the President, he readily endorsed your suggestion of the term "Quarter Eagle."

[718] *US Mint*, NARA-CP, op. cit., entry 330, box 45. Letter dated January 2, 1908 to Brewster from Leach.
[719] *US Mint*, NARA-CP, op. cit., entry 330, box 45. Letter dated January 3, 1908 to Hering from Leach.

I find that I made a mistake in informing you that Mr. Barber intended to use model No. 2 in making the dies for the smaller coins; he proposed to use the last model as suggested by you. However, your suggestion as to making a model by making an enlargement from the dies, Mr. Barber says is impracticable and cannot be done; but he thinks, from the progress he has made, that he is going to be able to get out very satisfactory dies for the smaller coins. I shall make an effort to make the dies from the same model as used on the double eagles, and when we strike some trial pieces from these dies then and only then can we determine what we will have to do. I expressed the opinion to Mr. Barber that it would be making an extremely small reduction of the design, and was afraid of its being too small. He, however, was quite sanguine of getting a good result. Of course, the smaller the coin the less trouble we have in getting relief, within certain limits.

Hering thanked the director for letting him know about the value designation on the $2.50 coin and asked for a sample when they were released to circulation.[720]

The engraving staff began making the necessary models and reductions for the Saint-Gaudens-designed half and quarter eagle gold coins. After successfully working with edge lettering for the eagle and double eagle, the mint mechanics were working on segmented collars for the half eagle. The lettering of E PLURIBUS UNUM would be tiny but it could be done. There was considerable demand for gold coins and the Treasurer of the United States was pressuring the mint to produce them. In the middle of the work, director Leach received word that Congress was going to insist the motto IN GOD WE TRUST be restored to the eagle and double eagle.[721]

In view of the fact that Congress is about to take action on the matter of replacing the motto "In God We Trust" on certain of the gold coins, you are directed to suspend work on the new dies being made for the $5.00 piece.

While work on the $5 (and $2.50) coin was suspended, the Philadelphia Mint provided design models and samples of the 1907 Saint-Gaudens coins to the Metropolitan Museum of Art for a memorial exhibition. In addition, they had the normal work of production, Cuban and Philippine coins to strike, plus the director was concerned about irregularities in diameter of the lettered edge $20 and thickness.

From a practical viewpoint, the standing Liberty design was too complicated to be effective on the smaller diameter coins. The Liberty head with Indian headdress would have worked, but there was still the problem of getting all the required mottoes and legends in such small circles. Had omission of the religious motto not become an issue, the small gold might also have carried Saint-Gaudens' designs. With no one actively supporting their use on the two smaller coins, they became orphans subject to chance and President Roosevelt's whim. In characteristic style, the President fell back on the advice of one of his oldest friends.

[720] *US Mint*, NARA-CP, op. cit., entry 229, box 261. Manuscript note dated January 14, 1908 to Leach from Hering.
[721] *US Mint*, NARA-P, op. cit. Letter dated December 24, 1907 to Landis from Leach.

## Boston Aristocracy

William Sturgis Bigelow, MD was of one of the finest Boston families.[722] He was nominally a physician but his real interest was oriental art and culture. He was primarily responsible for development of the Japanese collection of the Boston Museum of Fine Art. After Charles Freer and Ernest Francisco Fenellosa he was probably the most outstanding connoisseur of Japanese and oriental art in America. A close friend of Senator Henry Cabot Lodge, Bigelow became part of Roosevelt's far flung empire of cultural and scientific interests in 1887:[723]

> Dear Cabot:
> In Paris we dined at the Jays, and there, to our great delight met Bigelow; and the following evening (our last before coming home) dined with him at a restaurant. He was most charming; but Cabot, why did you not tell me he was an esoteric Buddhist? I would then have been spared some frantic floundering when the subject of religion happened to be broached...

He also knew Saint-Gaudens and in January 1905 had asked the sculptor to solicit letters of support for Edward Robinson, director of the Boston Museum of Fine Art, whom several of the Trustees were trying to force to resign. Bigelow threatened to leave the Museum's Board and, "...take my duds with me."[724] But in 1907 Bigelow was still a trustee of the Museum.

Bigelow seems to have had Roosevelt's ear for many years and his opinions on subjects far afield from medicine were given careful consideration by the President. In 1897, when Roosevelt was Assistant Secretary of the Navy, Dr. Bigelow wrote with some suggestions regarding the aiming of naval artillery. Roosevelt's reply is interesting in the degree of confidence expressed in Bigelow's ideas:[725]

> ...Now the whole thrust is exactly as you say, that it is a matter of that kind of skill which we call "knack." In each ship's crew there is a limited number of men who can become first-class gun pointers, and only a limited number. We have tried the experiment of making the petty officers captains of the guns, and it does not work well; and now we are trying to develop gun pointers pure and simple.
> ...I am going to use your letter as a basis for trying to get some reforms in our target practice, so you can see you have done good work by writing.

*Figure 60. Sketch of William Sturgis Bigelow (ca. 1917) by John Singer Sargent (based on a photograph).* (Photo ©2006 Museum of Fine Arts, Boston.)

---

[722] He was related to most of the finest families in Boston including the Lowell and Sturgis clans. His cousin was astronomer Percival Lowell, who claimed to have discovered numerous water-filled "canals" on Mars in the late nineteenth century.
[723] *Roosevelt Letters*, Harvard, op. cit., vol. 1, p.125. Letter dated March 7, 1887 to Henry Cabot Lodge from Roosevelt.
[724] SG, Dartmouth, op. cit. Box 2, folder 30. Letter dated January 12, 1905 to Saint-Gaudens from Bigelow. He means he will take back the artwork he has loaned the museum.
[725] *Roosevelt Letters*, Harvard, op. cit., vol. 1, pp.702-703. Letter dated October 29, 1897 to William Sturgis Bigelow from Roosevelt.

324

Bigelow had been in Japan for most of 1907, and on his return heard about the Saint-Gaudens coins from Henry Cabot Lodge. In his typical relaxed style, Bigelow wrote to the President:[726]

> Dear Mr. President:
> I was very much obliged indeed for the proof $20.00 – a fact you will have gleaned already from the promptness of my answer (of this, more anon).
> When it reached me it could still be identified, though nearly unrecognizable in consequence of your giving two at once to Cabot, who – Wm. Endicott tells me – came into the room holding them aloft in triumph – and – listen and shudder! – _jingling them together!_ Can sacrilege go further?
> It is the best coin that has been struck for 2000 years. An "epochmachender bahnbrechender büster."[727] It ought to set the gait for the next 2000. Of course the folks whose first and last idea of a coin is something that will stack do not like the sharp edge, but that will be got 'round – both the edge and the difficulty – eventually, and in the meantime this is a model for the coin-makers of the world. You have done some great things, but nothing more monumental than this!
> The reason I did not write sooner is because I have got an idea, and have had two die-cutters and the Art Museum experts wrestling with it. I think it may be possible to make a stacking coin with high relief.
> The plan may be bad, but it is new, and nobody yet has been able to say why it is not good. I have been waiting to get models to suit me, and will send them to you as soon as they do. In the mean time I hammer the floor with my head, moré Japonico, in contrite apology for the delay.
> Gratefully yours,
> Wm S B[igelow]
>
> PS: I enclose an Assyrian lioness (?) that I ran across at the Museum – nothing to do with coins, but rather in your line.

Roosevelt was basking in artistic success of the Saint-Gaudens double eagles and an auspicious beginning to the Atlantic Fleet's "training cruise" around the world. He wrote back to Bigelow on January 10:[728]

> Dear Sturgis:
> I am very much pleased that you like that coin. I shall have all kinds of trouble over it, but I so feel what you say is true, that is, that it is the best coin that has been struck for two thousand years, and that no matter what is its temporary fate it will serve as a model for future coin makers, and that eventually the difficulties in connection with striking such coins will be surmounted. I had a hundred thousand of them struck before Congress could get at me, which they did on the score of expense, and the subsequent coins are not as good as the first issue. I am extremely interested in the experiments you are making and I am obliged for the Assyrian lioness. I have been familiar with the figure for a long time. It is very fine, altho of course painful. I have had no photographs of it.
> Ever yours,

Sturgis Bigelow had begun working through his coinage idea before he wrote the President on January 8. He had gone so far as to employ Bela Pratt to make a sample model of such a coin for the sum of $300. His idea and Pratt's own interests combined to

---

[726] *Roosevelt*, LoC, op. cit. Microfilm reel 80. Letter dated January 8, 1908 to Roosevelt from Bigelow. "Proof" is used in the sense of a sample, not "proof coin" as a specially made piece for coin collectors.
[727] The phrase can be translated as "epoch–making change of direction," or "epoch–making trendsetter."
[728] *Roosevelt*, LoC, op. cit., vol. 77, p.340. Microfilm reel 347. Letter dated January 10, 1908 to Bigelow from Roosevelt.

produce results quickly and of a subject guaranteed to appeal to Roosevelt's concept of American heritage: an Indian in ceremonial headdress.

Bela Lyon Pratt (1867–1917) was born in Norwitch, Connecticut. His father was a successful lawyer and his mother, Sarah Victoria Whittlesey, was from one of New England's most creative bloodlines. At nineteen Pratt entered the Art Student's League in New York, where Augustus Saint-Gaudens was an instructor. Saint-Gaudens encouraged Pratt to go to Paris to study at the *École des Beaux-Arts* with Falquiere and Chapu among others. Upon his return in 1892, he worked on two of the colossal figure groups for the Columbian Exposition in Chicago. Recommendation from Saint-Gaudens lead to Pratt's appointment as Professor of Sculpture at the Boston Museum School of Fine Arts in 1894.[729]

The Saint-Gaudens designs for the eagle and double eagle were of considerable interest to many American sculptors, particularly those who had worked with the artist at the Art Student's League or the Aspet studio. Although very few had seen the original models, and would not until the Metropolitan Museum of Art's exhibition opened on March 2, 1908, there seems to have been considerable speculation on what the original designs were like before the mint got hold of them.[730] Others, such as Adolph Weinman, wondered how to make really effective designs for coins while retaining the most important characteristics of fine art.[731] According to Pratt's biographer, Cynthia Kennedy Sam, the sculptor and an assistant had discussed how they might have handled the design problems of double eagle and eagle. They had been considering making the relief *intaglio*, or recessed below the field of the coin, but felt the idea was too extreme to be considered by mint officials. Not long after this discussion (but several days before January 8), Dr. Bigelow stopped by Pratt's St. Botolph studios and asked if there was anyone who could turn a coinage idea of his into a sample model.[732] Considering Bigelow's familiarity with Roosevelt's interests and his knowledge of artists in the Boston area, it is likely that the Indian head design was "recommended" to Pratt by Bigelow with awareness that it would appeal to the President.[733]

> ...His idea was even more radical and startling than mine, for while I had thought of a ground sloping more or less gradually to the relief, his idea was to sink the [outer edge of the] relief at right angles to the coin after the manner of the old Egyptian reliefs. I at once began work on the models, and they looked so well and promised so much that I could hardly keep away from them long enough to make a bluff at doing my regular work....

By January 17, 1908 Bela Pratt was busy with a sample design embodying Bigelow's concepts for the President to examine. Bigelow wrote the President a long letter dealing primarily with an exchange of professors between the United States and Japan, and how to get "... some considerable quantity of books and paintings of very high grade that

[729] Bela Pratt was not one of Augustus' assistants, and may have considered The Saint more of a competitor than mentor.
[730] The exhibition was organized by the assistant director, Edward Robinson, and George Kunz, who arranged for the loan of models and coins from the mint. It ran from March 2 through May 30, 1908.
[731] As the *de facto* designer of the 1905 inaugural medal, Weinman had modeled the standing eagle based on Saint-Gaudens' sketches. This was similar to the reverse design of the $10 gold coin.
[732] Sam, op. cit., p.165. Letter dated [?], 1908 to Sarah Pratt from Pratt. Sarah Pratt was the sculptor's mother to whom he wrote weekly letters.
[733] Sam, op. cit., p.165. Unspecified document apparently dating from early January 1908.

Anthony Comstock will not let me bring into this country…" past the Japanese and U. S. Customs authorities. [734]

> …The coin is progressing finely. Will send you something soon to beat the one-hoss-shay both for style and wear.
> Is it true that you are going to meet the criticisms on taking – "In God We Trust" – off the coins by putting "I know that my Redeemer livith" on the Treasury notes?

The President replied with a comment based on contract bridge: "I should like to copper the ace with such an inscription. But alas, I am afraid it is a counsel of perfection!"[735]

One of Pratt's personal interests was in American Indian artifacts. He was an avid collector, amateur archeologist and ethnographer. Among the materials in his collection were many photographs of Native Americans, and he used one of these as the prototype for the Indian in his new design. Wearing a full ceremonial war bonnet, the head and headdress, like Saint-Gaudens' Liberty with headdress, fit well within the confines of the small circular coin. The design was efficient at using the limited space available and uniquely American following in the tradition of Chief Ta-to-ka-in-yan-ka ("Running Antelope") depicted on the $5 silver certificate of 1896 designed by G. F. C. Smillie. By February 2, Pratt wrote:[736]

> I've got the coin model very well along and it has worked out very nicely. I can't believe that those in authority can possibly fail to see that it is just what we have all been looking for! It really looks handsome to me and everybody to whom I have shown it says that it is the best ever. I wish you could see it just to help out in the general excitement and give me the courage to see the thing through. Do you suppose that I will really take it to Washington to show it to Teddy? I don't think there any use in just sending it. There are too many ways that it would get sidetracked, which is just what is most likely to happen to it anyhow.…

Sturgis Bigelow had been ill for some days and Pratt, seemingly running on pure adrenaline, continued to work on the Indian head model:[737]

> The coin continues to be the admiration of all to whom I show it, but Dr. Bigelow has been sick abed with the grip and so things are rather at a standstill. I need not tell you that I am feeling very happy and cheerful. I always do when there is plenty of work promised and I am feeling well enough to tackle it. The fact is I'm feeling very aggressive just now. There seems to be something in the atmosphere of Boston not unlike that found in Paris, among the artists, and I am right in the midst

---

[734] *Roosevelt*, LoC, op. cit. Microfilm reel 80. Letter dated January 17, 1908 to Roosevelt from Bigelow. Roosevelt replied on the 20th suggesting the Boston Museum of Fine Arts take the initiative in requesting a permit to import the pictures. The materials Bigelow referred to were erotic books and paintings occasionally encountered in "eastern" art. They were also of the type the prudish Comstock abhorred. Interestingly, President Roosevelt's father had been a financial supporter of Comstock. He also thought the professorial exchange would be an "admirable thing." Bigelow must have thought well of his comment about the motto, since he repeated it in a note to Roosevelt on March 17.

[735] *Roosevelt*, LoC, op. cit. Microfilm reel 80, p.280. Letter dated March 18, 1908 to Bigelow from Roosevelt.

[736] Sam, op. cit., p.165. Letter dated February 2, 1908 to Sarah Pratt from Pratt.

[737] Sam, op. cit., p.165. Letter dated February [9 ??], 1908 to Sarah Pratt from Pratt.

of it. I think and believe it is what we have all been looking for, for so long, the beginning of a real American School of Art. I wonder if I am right!...

Bela Pratt had good reason to be excited about his coin design. Dr. Bigelow was a friend to both the President and Senator Lodge and had easy access to executive and legislative authorities.[738] On February 19, Pratt sent the completed model to Bigelow for his examination and presentation to the President whenever the opportunity might arise.[739]

> Dear Dr. Bigelow:
> I am sending you the medal in plaster, of the coin on which we have been working for the past fortnight. It seems to me that your idea of having a sunken relief is going to work out perfectly. This arrangement protects the design from wear as well as possessing the advantage of presenting a level surface which will not interfere with the coins being stacked satisfactorily. Owing to the fact that the surface exposed is broad and flat, the wear on the coin will obviously be less than the wear on the irregular surface of the ordinary coins; thus reducing the loss of metal and rendering the coin of considerable economic value.
> Aside from these practical considerations, the sunken relief has a distinct and original decorative quality. The Indian head seems particularly appropriate for use on a United States coin, being essentially American in character. The Indian is a decorative type, and the headdress adapts itself admirably to artistic treatment. The backward sloping arrangement of the feathers allows space for a head of generous proportions, while the contour of the profile and the shape of the headdress are in sympathy with the circular shape of the coin...
> One set of the casts is gilded and the other set has a dark finish. The relief of these coins may be strengthened or diminished to any extent necessary in the minting.
> All the artists and others who have seen these designs have been enthusiastic in their admiration of it and I feel sure that if the project could be carried through that it will be found entirely satisfactory.
> Very truly yours,

The sculptor's comments mirror those of Saint-Gaudens and Hering as far as the presumed ability of the mint to modify relief and retain detail. As had been amply demonstrated in the frustrating process of getting the $10 and $20 designs into coinable shape, no one at the mint really knew how to use the Janvier reducing machine. Pratt, like Saint-Gaudens, Weinman, Hering and others before him, assumed the mint was at least as capable in making reductions to hubs as were Tiffany, Gorham or Roman Bronze in the world of fine art medals. The practicalities that completely enveloped mint engraver Charles Barber eluded Pratt and Dr. Bigelow. Unfortunately, both Sturgis Bigelow and Bela Pratt were more out of contact with the mint artisans than Saint-Gaudens or Henry Hering had been. Pratt never got the chance to receive "instruction" from Barber or to ask questions. There appear to be virtually no letters or memoranda between the sculptor and mint staff. Bigelow's contacts were limited to director Leach and the President, and these concentrated on political and legal aspects rather than artistic ones.

During the next weeks, visitors to Pratt's studio could see the ten-inch-diameter model when they stopped by on business, or simply to visit. Praise flowed from nearly every visitor: "...they all felt they had been most fortunate in getting me to do it instead of

---

[738] Through his friendship with Lodge, Bigelow had access to the United States Senate chambers and occasional letters to Roosevelt originated from Senate desks.
[739] Sam, op. cit., pp.166-167. Letter (excerpt) dated February 19, 1908 to Bigelow from Pratt.

328

St. Gaudens! Also, they all thought my coins much superior to St. G's. Of course they are quite right in both cases!..."[740]

Dr. Bigelow had lunch with the President on April 3 and reported to Pratt that the meeting went well, with Roosevelt approving both the concept and Indian head design. Roosevelt was particularly pleased with the feather headdress, which was in complete agreement with his ideas of the "purely American type" he had pressed on Saint-Gaudens almost two years earlier. [741] Mint director Leach also was present for lunch that day and commented on the event in his biography:[742]

> Originally it was the intention to give the $5 and $2.50 pieces the same design as that used on the double eagle or $20 piece, but before final action to that end was taken President Roosevelt invited me to lunch with him at the White House. His purpose was to have me meet Doctor William Sturgis Bigelow of Boston, a lover of art and friend of the President, who was showing great interest in the undertaking for improving the appearance of American coins, and who had a new design for the smaller gold coins. It was his idea that the commercial needs of the country required coins that would "stack" evenly, and that the preservation of as much as possible of the flat plane of the piece was desirable. A coin, therefore, with the lines of the design, figures, and letters depressed or incuse, instead of being raised or in relief, would meet the wishes of the bankers and business men, and at the same time introduce a novelty in coinage that was artistic as well as adaptable to the needs of business. The President adhered to the idea the high relief afforded greater possibilities of artistic results, and referred to the beauties of ancient gold coins. Unquestionably he was correct in this opinion, but I called his attention to the fact that he and the other promoters of the new coinage were trying to do more than the ancient Greek artists and coiners had found possible, and that the Greeks had only been able to produce a high relief on one side of their coins, while we were endeavoring to give a high relief on both sides. We had in a way succeeded, for by the use of a medal press we had outdone the Greeks. But the uncompromising demands of trade would not tolerate even the one-sided coins of ancient Greece. The President expressed surprise at my statement, and at once sent a messenger to his room for a beautiful example of Grecian work in the shape of a gold coin of the days of Alexander the Great. Of course, he found one side quite flat, while the other was in high relief.
>
> ...It was after the lunch, and we had excused ourselves from the others, that the question as to the new design for the half and quarter eagles took place. The discussion ended by the President authorizing Doctor Bigelow and me to go ahead and produce some trial pieces after the suggestions of the doctor. Bela L. Pratt, an artist of high repute in Boston, was selected to make the models for the designs, which were to be a faithful copy of an Indian head and the eagle with shortened legs. The models and dies were not finished until some time in September. When the trial pieces were produced I was pleased with their appearance, for the nationality was so plainly stamped on the coin that it needed no lettering to tell anybody in any part of the world that it has been issued by the United Stated of America. It pleased the President, and he at once gave the official approval necessary for the adoption of the new design.

---

[740] Sam, op. cit., p.167. Letter (excerpt) dated February 23, 1908 to Sarah Pratt from Pratt. The "they" was Mrs. Tyson, head of the committee charged with getting Pratt to make a portrait bust of Henry L. Higgenson, founder of the Boston Symphony.
[741] *SG*, Dartmouth, op. cit. Box 16, folder 38. Letter dated February 18, 1907 to Saint-Gaudens from Roosevelt.
[742] Leach, Frank A., *Recollections of a Newspaper Man – A Record of Life and Events in California*, Samuel Levinson Co., San Francisco, California, 1917. Reprinted by Bowers and Merena Galleries, Inc., 1985. Director Leach's sometimes accurate, sometimes confused recollections.

Although Leach's comments contain minor mistakes, it is evident from his account the President had determined to follow Bigelow's suggestion and was using the luncheon to "facilitate" action. Sturgis Bigelow's letter to Pratt about the meeting was written from the United States Senate Chamber:[743]

> The President likes the coin – both the idea of a countersunk relief and your Indian head. I saw Mr. Leech [sic] (Director of the Mint) at the White House yesterday and again at the Freeman this morning. He seems well disposed. The laws limiting the changes in design to once in fifteen or twenty years (I forget exactly) make it doubtful when either process or design can be adopted, but he is going to look it up and see what coins will be available for new designs within a reasonable time. I told him to go ahead with the sunken relief idea on anything, as far as I am concerned but that I could *not* give him authority to use *your design* without consulting you, and moreover that I thought you would want to retouch it if it were adopted.
>
> He asked me to write to you about it. Of course, you are insured against loss in any case since it stands as a private commission from me even if the gov't does not take it. But suppose they do. Shall I refer Mr. Leech directly to you for terms, or can I give him any message?
>
> Of course the suggestion of the gov't paying out money will set a different set of wheels turning, and the creaking may wake up some watch-dog of the Treasury from Illinois or S. Dakota who is trying to make his constituents think him a financier, and it might be an obstacle to getting this thing judged on its merits, and it is conceivably possible that the best may be for me to say to Mr. Leech: "This idea of a sunken relief I give to the gov't outright – the design of the Indian Head has cost me so & so. If there is no appropriation available I will pay the bill & give the Gov't the design too for the sake of seeing the experiment tried." That would eliminate the idea of a job, which every department official shies at like a colt at a pile-driver.

Naturally, director Leach could be expected to be "well disposed" since the President liked the idea and Leach was not going to do anything to displease his boss.

Not giving Pratt a chance to contact director Leach on his own, Bigelow called Leach just after writing to Pratt. He told the mint director that he was paying Bela Pratt the miserly sum of $300 for the Indian design. The director figured he could pay this from the Philadelphia Mint's contingency fund, so offered to pay the bill.[744]

> I told Mr. Leech [sic] about the $300 and offered to foot the bill myself. He said he had been looking for available funds, and that the U. S. will pay the bill... Now the only question he knows of is what [gold] coin it can be got on to, and he is going to Phila. to the mint to see. The President wants the St. Gaudens eagle on the reverse, also in "recessed relief," but there is a technical question whether "recessing" it would be "changing the design" within the meaning of the [Mint] act [of 1890]. There is hope of getting it on a $5.00 piece anyway. Everything is ready for a new issue, but only the specimen pieces have been struck and none have gone out. There is a chance that this whole issue can be stopped and our coin substituted. But keep all this to yourself 'till further notice.
>
> Yours sincerely,
>
> PS: I am much pleased with the outlook.

---

[743] Sam, op. cit., pp.167–168. Letter (excerpt) dated April 4, 1908 to Pratt from Bigelow. Leach and Bigelow saw the President at lunch before he left for Fort Meyer, Virginia in the afternoon. The Army base is across the Potomac River from Washington, DC, adjacent to Arlington National Cemetery.

[744] Sam, op. cit., pp.168-169. Letter (excerpt) dated April 4, 1908 to Pratt from Bigelow.

Bigelow had good reason to be pleased with the outlook. The mint engravers had been working on reducing the Saint-Gaudens designs to $5 and $2.50 size since December 1907. Once the question of wording the denomination had been settled, they still had to contend with the motto E PLURIBUS UNUM, and based on pending Congressional action, would have to incorporate IN GOD WE TRUST also. Had Congress not been rumbling about the omitted motto, the reduced-size Saint-Gaudens designs could have been issued for circulation in late January. According to Bigelow's letter, the "specimen pieces" of the Saint-Gaudens $5 had been struck sometime before April 3. Evidently the President had not given final approval for the new designs, possibly because he was waiting to see what Bigelow would come up with.

Mint director Leach, now in office for six months, had learned a few things from his experience with the Saint-Gaudens $10 and $20 coins. The first was that his "customer," one Theodore Roosevelt, President of the United States, was always right, most particularly when he was "wrong." Second, the Philadelphia Mint's engravers and bureaucracy were adept at nitpicking a situation to the point of frustrating all except the most hardy of politicians. After the eagle and double eagle were released to circulation, the director had extensive discussions about coin diameters and stacking heights, with statistics and specifications flying about. Charles Barber's engraving department generally argued they were doing as they were told and the fault was entirely that of "outside" designers. The director may also have known how poorly Barber and Morgan understood the Janvier reducing machine's operation – a fault which severely degraded the quality of reductions. Lastly, Leach had learned that coin collectors were pests who would bother him, the Treasury Department and the mint staff incessantly for copies of experimental and trial coins; consequently Leach determined that all trial coins would be melted – none saved even for the mint's cabinet of coins.[745]

Bela Pratt wrote to the director on April 27 confirming that he would make the coin models and incorporating some changes Leach had suggested:[746]

> Yours of April 25th received. I will proceed at once with the model and alter same as directed. I think I can have the model finished within a few weeks.
> Yours very respectfully,

On May 1, Dr. Bigelow reported further progress on government acceptance of the Indian head design:[747]

> Dear Mr. Pratt,
> Mr. Leach has got back from Phila. and reports everything favorable there. He had started one of the men there on the reverse, but when I told him what you said about doing it, he said he saw no objection to your going ahead, and that he – or we – could see which came out the best. Do you want to try on that basis? Why don't you? I will stand in the gap as before. The President wants the *standing* St. Gaudens eagle of the $10.00 piece reproduced in "sunken relief..." Mr. Leach said unofficially that he did not think it necessary for you to reproduce "every feather." I got the idea that he would not object if you should improve it in any way. But I would not, if I were you, get *too* far from the original, as the President likes it. Perhaps you can make him like it better.

[745] This last may or may not be strictly true. Although no trial pieces of the Saint-Gaudens or original Pratt $5 coins are known, the available Mint records do not account for all pieces that were produced.
[746] *US Mint*, NARA-CP, op. cit., entry 229, box 264. Letter dated April 27, 1908 to Leach from Pratt.
[747] Sam, op. cit., p.169. Letter (excerpt) dated May 1, 1908 to Pratt from Bigelow

Yours sincerely,

PS: They thought highly of your Indian at the mint, Mr. Leach says. How are you getting on with him? Don't be too careful or you may spoil him. *Le mieux est l'ennemie du bien…*[748]

Two weeks later, Bigelow had again spoken with director Leach. He revealed that the new half eagle of the Saint-Gaudens design was ready and the dies had been made, but production had not begun. Director Leach was prepared to use Pratt's Indian head design instead of the Saint-Gaudens standing Liberty, provided a satisfactory legal opinion was rendered relating to changing the design.[749]

The coin it goes on depends on whether it is possible to get it on the $5.00. Everything is prepared for a new issue, and the dies are made. But the coins are not yet struck. If they were, nothing more could be done for twenty-five years. Mr. Leach takes the ground that the law refers to the date of issue of the coins, and not the date of the cutting of the die – this is the point we are now wrestling with.
Yours sincerely,

PS: I hope you are getting on well with injuns and eagles. Don't get the slope from surface to outline too gradual, or you may lose the character the outline gives….

Less than a week after Bigelow's letter, President Roosevelt approved use of Pratt's design for the obverse of the half eagle, instead of the Saint-Gaudens standing Liberty.

Although Pratt had finished the obverse design, the mint didn't have an official contract with the sculptor for the work. As agreed between Pratt and Bigelow, the cost would be $300 for the obverse design, with the mint engravers cutting the reverse based on Saint-Gaudens' standing eagle as used on the $10 gold coins. On May 22, 1908, director Leach informed superintendent Landis of the design contract:[750]

I have to inform you that, by direction of the President, I made a contract with Bela L. Pratt to make [a] design for the half eagle for the sum of $300.00 which will be paid from your contingent fund upon the approval of the bill by me.

Some revisions were necessary to the obverse design and Pratt had to rework the model. The mint director decided that it would be best to have the reverse also made by Pratt, in competition with the mint, who agreed to make his version of the standing eagle, then let the best one be selected for use. This avoided differences in lettering style and also gave Pratt claim to being the sole designer of the coin. Pratt wrote to the Mint Bureau again on May 29 about the position of the mandated motto IN GOD WE TRUST:[751]

I have yours of May 27th. I am making good progress on the designs for the coin and expect to have both sides finished within a few days. I saw Senator Lodge a few days ago and he spoke about the inscription, "In God We Trust," which has been voted back on the coin. Am I to put this on the coin, and if so where should it be placed? It would balance the "E Pluribus Unum" on the eagle side of the coin and in that position would look very well.
Kindly let me know about this.

---

[748] "Best is the enemy of good," or meaning "attempting perfection may ruin something which is good."
[749] Sam, op. cit., pp.169–170. Letter (excerpt) dated May 13, 1908 to Pratt from Bigelow.
[750] *US Mint*, NARA-P, op. cit. Letter dated May 22, 1908 to Landis from Leach.
[751] *US Mint*, NARA-CP, op. cit., entry 229, box 265. Letter dated May 29, 1908 to Leach from Pratt.

The model and casts went to Philadelphia on June 29. The intersection of design and field had been made steeper, and the required motto added behind the eagle:[752]

> As directed by Mr. Frank A. Leach, Director of the Mint, I am sending you today the models, obverse and reverse, of the half-eagle. I trust that in having the dies made from these designs, you can carry them out literally, advising me of any necessary change.
> Very truly yours,
>
> [*Handwritten postscript, below*]
>
> I notice that in casting, the models have been discolored, also the obverse and reverse are not quite the same size. I trust that this will not bother you.
> B.L.P.

Pratt also sent a letter to director Leach, who was in San Francisco, advising him that the models had been sent to Philadelphia:[753]

> I am sending to the mint in Philadelphia, the models of the coin which I have prepared and I hope same will prove satisfactory. I wish that those in charge of making the die would follow the models absolutely or at least would make no changes without consulting me.
> I shall be exceedingly interested in seeing the finished coin. Will you kindly let me know when we may hope to see the coins?
> Yours truly,

In using Saint-Gaudens' standing eagle design as a prototype for the reverse, as the President requested, Pratt remodeled the eagle changing the bird's proportions. He shortened the legs and neck, and modified the feathers to produce a more natural appearing eagle. He also moved the motto E PLURIBUS UNUM from behind the bird's shoulder to the field in front of the breast. He added IN GOD WE TRUST to the space behind the eagle, but low and somewhat cramped between wings and the legend.

*Figure 61. Reverse of the $10 gold coin (left) and the $5 gold coin (right). Note the change in position of the motto "E Pluribus Unum," addition of "In God We Trust" and altered proportions of the eagle.*

The result was an improved eagle with more realistic proportions, but a bottom heavy and awkward composition. The sunken relief technique compounds the problem due to extra lines necessary to outline the figure. This adds multiple reflections further confus-

[752] *US Mint*, NARA-P, op. cit. Letter dated June 29, 1908 to Landis from Pratt, countersigned by Leach.
[753] *US Mint*, NARA-CP, op. cit., entry 229, box 267. Letter dated June 29 1908 to Leach from Pratt. Transcription in Taxay, *US Mint*, p.326. Contains minor errors.

ing visual impact of the design. No explanation has been made for why Pratt made the change in motto positions. However the mottoes are larger in relation to the bird than on Saint-Gaudens' coin, and it may have been felt the longest word, "pluribus," needed to be in the largest space in front of the eagle.

## Preparation for Production

The sultry summer months of July and August were, as now, relatively inactive in Washington and Philadelphia. In the era before air conditioning, heat and humidity conspired to drive all but the lowest government functionaries from their stuffy offices. Many took extended vacations. Senior officials, often accompanied by a small working staff, went to their summer cottages in the mountains or by the ocean. Frank Leach was away from Washington during June and July on vacation and business at the western mints and assay offices, and Robert Preston served as acting director. At Philadelphia, engraver Barber spent his month-long August vacation in Ocean Grove, New Jersey. Upon his return on September 1,[754] it appears the Philadelphia Mint made reductions and hubs from Pratt's models without incident.[755] (It is possible Barber cut the hubs directly from the models and let the design produce whatever results it naturally made in the reducing lathe.)

Experimental strikes of the new designs were shipped to director Leach on September 21. The total value of the shipment was $75, and if equal numbers of half and quarter eagles were included, then the package contained ten coins of each denomination.[756] The samples were shown to President Roosevelt on September 26 and approved. "The President is very much pleased," reported the mint director to Landis.[757] Leach then wrote to Landis letting him know dies could be made after Barber completed a few "improvements:"[758]

> I have to inform you that the President is very much pleased with the appearance of the trial pieces of the Dr. Bigelow design of half eagle and quarter eagle, and requests us to adopt the design. I will send you formal notice of its acceptance and directions for coinage in a few days, but in the meantime I wish you would request Mr. Barber, the engraver, to go ahead with the work of making a new die [i.e., hub] of the Indian head, as talked over with me. He knows what is needed to perfect the piece. I desire that this shall be accomplished as soon as possible as I am under obligation to the President to have several thousand pieces coined by the first of November next, and I want enough half eagle dies made so that a couple of pairs at least can be supplied Denver and San Francisco. The quarter eagle will be coined only at your institution.
>
> I shall return the trial pieces I have, with the exception of the one given to the President, with directions that they shall be melted up immediately so as not to be bothered with demands for any of these pieces. Do not give out anything yet to the press in relation to this coinage, for I want to see the President first and get some facts from him in relation to the origin of the design, etc.

---

[754] *US Mint*, NARA-CP, op. cit., entry 229, box 266. Letter dated September 1, 1908 to Leach from Norris.

[755] See correspondence files in *US Mint*, NARA-CP, op. cit., entry 239, vol. 368–372.

[756] *US Mint*, NARA-P, op. cit. Memorandum of Bill of Lading #38 dated September 21, 1908 to Leach from Philadelphia Mint.

[757] *US Mint*, NARA-CP, op. cit., entry 235 Volume 368, page 818. Letter dated September 26, 1908 to Landis from Leach.

[758] *US Mint*, NARA-P, op. cit. Letter dated September 26, 1908 to Landis from Leach.

Clearly, Leach and Barber had discussed the new design before showing the pattern coins to Roosevelt, and they had already agreed on certain changes: "...he knows what is needed to perfect the piece." Leach says that the President kept one of the coins – probably a half eagle. He also specifically states that the trial pieces are to be melted so that the mint will not be bothered by requests for the coins from collectors. Unfortunately, none of the pattern pieces were saved for the mint's collection. Two days later Roosevelt wrote to Dr. Bigelow with obvious pleasure:[759]

> Dear Sturgis:
> I enclose [for] you the visible proof of a great service you have rendered the country – and I am speaking with scientific accuracy. Here you will see the five dollar gold piece, the copy of the models you had prepared, and a month hence our five dollar gold pieces that are issued from the mint will all be of this type. This one I send you is the first one struck. It therefore has a peculiar historic interest and I feel you are peculiarly entitled to have it; so please accept it with the compliments of Director Leach and myself.
> Ever yours,

Seeing the new coins, replete with the Rooseveltian-preferred Indian war headdress, must have been a fine diversion from writing press statements supporting Taft's presidential campaign for Roosevelt. When the coin had not been acknowledged by October 10, Roosevelt spoke to Bigelow by telephone, then sent him the registration receipt for the letter. Before he could receive the President's second letter, Bigelow and Cabot Lodge located the "lost" envelope:[760]

> Dear Mr. President,
> At last I have received your kind letter and its precious enclosure.
> It had been waiting at the Boston P. O. while I was at Nantucket. The envelope shows that they sent me three notices, but there has been some confusion in my household about forwarding my mail this summer, and I do not think they got [all the mail] to me. I cannot make them. Cabot and I got the letter out of pawn yesterday.
> I am very glad you like the coin. It looks well to me. The design is handsome and I believe the principle is sound. It is a great pleasure and privilege to have the first one struck – the _only_ one, as it turns out, of the first lot – and a still greater to have your letter. To "have rendered a great service to the Country" is a thing I never dreamed of aspiring to. I am going to have that cut on a tombstone forthwith and keep it in the storage warehouse 'till I need it.
> One thing is sure – I should never have rendered the service if it had not been for you. If the thing turns out well it is your doing!
> Thanks!
> Sincerely yours,

Roosevelt's gift was a half eagle he had kept from the group of trial (or pattern) coins shown him by Leach. Had Roosevelt mentioned his purpose in keeping the coin, it is unlikely that the mint director would have refused the President the coin. When he spoke to Bigelow about the "lost" coin, the President must have known this was not a regular strike, but one of the trial coins made before Barber altered the hubs. Bigelow's letter acknowledges he understands this to be the only one of the pattern coins in existence. How-

---

[759] *Roosevelt*, LoC, op. cit., vol. 85, p.307. Microfilm reel 351. Letter dated September 28, 1908 to Bigelow from Roosevelt.
[760] *Roosevelt*, LoC, op. cit. Microfilm reel 85. Letter dated October 11, 1908 to Roosevelt from Bigelow.

ever, the director's letter to Landis on the same day accounts for the full $75 worth of trial coins, probably by adding one of the old design half eagles plucked from circulation:[761]

> I send you by express today $55.00 on account of special gold coins sent here. I also return $75.00 in half eagles and quarter eagles of the last proposed design, and one $5.00 piece of the Saint-Gaudens design. Please see that these pieces, and all others not needed by the engraver, are melted up without delay. In this connection I have to say that the new design for the half eagle and quarter eagle will not be finally adopted until after the engraver has made new dies and submitted sample pieces.
> Respectfully,

We don't know what pieces the $55.00 is to be applied to since there is no mention of previous trial pieces of Pratt's designs. Also, the odd amount cannot be solely for $10 and $20 coins. Normally, the director would have been reimbursing the mint for the cost of the "special gold coins," which may have included one or more trial strikes of the Satin-Gaudens $5. Given that director Leach specifically ordered melting of the Saint-Gaudens design $5 coin, it is possible the group consisted of additional coins of the Striding Liberty design as originally planned for the small gold coins.[762]

Further evidence that Roosevelt's half eagle made it into Bigelow's pocket comes from Bela Pratt, who reports seeing the trial piece on October 10:[763]

> *Remember, the coin is a secret!*
> We went to the Symphony concert last night, the first night of the season with the new conductor, Max Fiedler. He's all right! The program was fine and he kept the orchestra together in a very masterful style; but that is not what I want to write about....
> Well, Helen thought it would be nice to walk in the corridor to see if we could find our friends. We found Woods, one and all, waiting for us and I had only just shaken hands when Dr. Sturgis Bigelow pounced on me and with a most mysterious manner, hustled me off under a light, away from the crowd and produced the first of the coins from his pocket! He says the President and mint people are most enthusiastic and it is their plan to get the coin all distributed for circulation and in fact into circulation before there is a chance to raise a row. Bigelow says there is sure to be a big fuss. I suppose he will get all the glory if there is any. There is always somebody ready to snatch every bit of credit for things of this kind, but it is a fact that Bigelow has engineered this thing through and it is sure that without him it never would have gotten through. I shall feel badly to have it called the "Bigelow coin" when it is really the "Pratt coin...."

It is odd, and very unfortunate, that the President did not extend the same courtesy to Bela Pratt as he did to Sturgis Bigelow. Roosevelt kept only one coin from the twenty patterns Leach showed him, and made no attempt to request another for presentation to

---

[761] *US Mint*, NARA-P, op. cit. Letter dated September 28, 1908 to Landis from Leach.

[762] An interesting conjecture is that someplace, an heir to Frank Leach has a little box of "junk" containing the long-lost Saint-Gaudens half eagle patterns – and doesn't know it.

[763] Sam, op. cit., pp.170–171. Letter dated October 11, 1908 to Sarah Pratt from Pratt. Helen was Bela Pratt's wife. Bigelow received the coin on October 9. The concert was by the Boston Symphony Orchestra conducted by Max Fiedler (conductor from 1908 to1912). The performance was given in Symphony Hall, which had been designed by Saint-Gaudens' friend Charles McKim of McKim, Mead & White. McKim also designed the Boston Public Library that opened in 1892. The library included sculptures by Saint-Gaudens and relief panels at the entrance by Bela Pratt. Saint-Gaudens' original sculpture designs (ca. 1892–94) included nude figures which the Library Trustees felt were too *avant guard* for their building. Pratt's initial designs were judged by Saint-Gaudens to be "...not interesting...and should be more imaginative, and treated with greater freedom." (Letter to Pratt dated April 27, 1894.)

Pratt. After examination of the September trial strikes director Leach, superintendent Landis, and engraver Barber decided that changes had to be made to "sharpen" the coins. Just as with Saint-Gaudens' double eagle, Barber reworked the master hub of the Indian Head. This time he removed the border, and changed the modeling of the feathered headdress. This placed the stars so close to the edge of the coin that portions occasionally "drop off the edge" unless the planchet is perfectly centered on the die. It also altered the rounded layering of the original feathers and headband into scratches looking more like hash-marks than feathers. A reeded edge topped off the mutilation.

As would become increasingly prevalent for non-mint artists, Bela Pratt was kept in the dark about all that was occurring. On September 30, a week after Leach had proudly shown the samples to the President and the lone $5 pattern had been mailed to Bigelow, the artist wrote to the mint director:[764]

> Dear Sir:
> Not having heard from the coin designs which were exhibited by you last spring, I am interested to know what is to be done in the matter and when the sample coins are apt to appear.
> Kindly let me hear from you, and greatly oblige,
> Yours respectfully,

Apparently, not even the amiable Dr. Bigelow had told the artist anything about the fate of his coin designs.

Coin collectors were aware that new designs would soon be issued and were anticipating being able to buy some of the experimental coins as they had in 1907. Collectors were also interested in purchasing proof surface examples of the coins and had been disappointed that by late 1908, no gold proofs had been issued. Prominent numismatist (later, secretary of the treasury) William H. Woodin wrote Cortelyou asking about proof coins:[765]

> ...I want to call your attention to the fact that the United States Mint at Philadelphia have issued no proof gold coins for the year 1908. They tell me that they are subject to the orders of the Director of the Mint, at Washington.
> This is the first year since 1858 that the Mint has not issued proof gold coins, and as several collectors, including myself, have practically complete proof sets from the above date, it almost breaks our hearts to see a year passed by....

He was told they would be made after the new quarter and half eagle designs were officially adopted, before the end of the year. Director Leach was also involved and wrote to Landis on November 13 regarding striking proof coins for the current year:[766]

> I think it is imperative that you should endeavor to have proof sets made for supplying to coin collectors for this year. The word has got out that no proof sets are to be had, therefore a regular storm is brewing, and appeals are being made to the Secretary.

In his response to secretary Cortelyou's information about the proofs being available, Woodin mentioned experimental coins:[767]

---

[764] *US Mint*, NARA-CP, op. cit., entry 229, box 267. Letter dated September 30, 1908 to Leach from Pratt. A similar situation was to occur in 1916 when the Mint completely shut off contact with sculptor Hermon MacNeil for four months, then issued quarters with a mint-contrived design on them.

[765] *Cortelyou*, LoC, op. cit., box 20. Letter dated September 16, 1908 to Cortelyou from Woodin.

[766] *US Mint*, NARA-CP op. cit., entry 235, vol. 368, p.956. Letter dated November 13, 1908 to Landis from Leach.

[767] *Cortelyou*, LoC, op. cit., box 20. Letter dated September 25, 1908 to Cortelyou from Woodin.

> ...If it is entirely consistent to give me an opportunity to secure any of the varieties of the new designs for the Quarter Eagle and Half Eagle, it would be most highly appreciated. I am most happy to hear that proof coins will be struck before the end of the year.

The treasury secretary checked with director Leach and was informed:[768]

> It has been decided that there will be no experimental pieces struck of the half eagle and the quarter eagle of the new designs. No coins will be struck in these denominations until the new designs have been finally adopted and the new dies made.

Secretary Cortelyou wrote back to Woodin on October 1, advising him that there were no experimental versions of the new coins.[769] Woodin, always the interested collector, wrote again "...At the risk of being considered a nuisance..." asking for one of the Saint-Gaudens eagles from the second model. Cortelyou sent him the coin.[770]

Demand for subsidiary silver coins was very strong during the latter half of 1908, and the Philadelphia mint had difficulty striking enough coins to satisfy customers. In part, the difficulty was due to the time and manpower needed to prepare for production of the small gold denominations and continue heavy production of the new eagles and double eagles. The director advised the superintendent to be prepared for requests for the new coins:[771]

> ...I cannot say at this time how many $5.00 pieces will be wanted, but by having dies prepared for Denver and San Francisco where the coinage can be made, it will relieve the pressure upon your institution. I think it very probable that the coins will be much sought after. I do not wish any struck this month. I will see the President and see how long he will consent to putting off the coinage that we may get out as much subsidiary [silver] as possible.

On October 9, engraver Barber wrote to Landis letting him know two sample coins of each denomination had been struck. Barber, now showing far more initiative than he had with the Saint-Gaudens designs, also stated he had already made working dies from the hubs:[772]

> The following coins, two half eagles and two quarter eagles are struck from the new dies.
> I beg to state that I have carried out the wish of the Director as far as possible, namely in working out the detail and also to give the design the appearance of bold relief.
> As I can see no reason or benefit in further change, I have dies now prepared that can be sent to any of the Mints if it is determined to adopt this design and considered desirable, that any of the Mints should at once coin some of these pieces.

With his "improvements" to Pratt's design complete, satisfied with his own work, and not bothering to call in the original artist for consultation or assistance, Barber made

[768] *Cortelyou*, LoC, op. cit., box 19. Memorandum dated September 28, 1908 to Cortelyou from Leach.
[769] Unlike in 1907, Roosevelt apparently had little substantive interest in the small gold coins and did nothing to encourage the mint to support collectors' interests. See also letter dated September 24, 1908 to the ANA from William Loeb.
[770] *Cortelyou*, LoC, op. cit., box 20. Letter dated October 2, 1908 to Woodin from Cortelyou.
[771] *US Mint*, NARA-P, op. cit. Letter dated October 7, 1908 to Landis from Leach.
[772] *US Mint*, NARA-P, op. cit. Letter dated October 9, 1908 to Landis from Barber.

338

working dies for all three mints. Landis wrote to director Leach on October 9, enclosing the four trial coins from Barber's new dies "…having worked up the detail and given the design the appearance of bold relief."[773]

Frank Leach saw the latest trial pieces on October 10 and thought Barber's changes resulted in "…about as fine a specimen of work as could possibly be made:"[774]

> I am in receipt of your letter of the 9th instant, together with two half eagles and two quarter eagles of the proposed new design. This work is very satisfactory indeed, and I desire you to express my congratulations and approval to Mr. Barber for the excellent result he has given us in the new die. It is about as fine a specimen of work as could possibly be made. I will submit the coins to the President for his inspection some time next week when I can secure an audience with him.
>
> I do not desire to have the dies for the half eagles sent to San Francisco or Denver until the design is officially adopted, and I will advise you as to the time of shipment.

To avoid further delay and save money, the mint used Pratt's half eagle design on the quarter eagle. As usual, this was done without either consultation or payment. This had been the original plan for the Saint-Gaudens design, but it had also been the President's intention that the artist prepare (or at least supervise) the models for each coin.

On October 15, 1908 the director of the mint, with approval of Secretary of the Treasury Cortelyou, issued an instruction in two parts: 1) his order of December 2, 1907 to make dies for the half and quarter eagle coins using the standing Liberty design of Augustus Saint-Gaudens was revoked; and, 2) designs by "Bigelow and Pratt" for the same denominations were approved by the President and adopted as of October 14, 1908.[775] The director also was careful to let Landis know the plan for producing the new coins:[776]

> I send you herewith formal notice of the adoption of the new design for the half eagle and the quarter eagle.
>
> I wish you to have the dies and collars made to be ready to commence operations in coining the half eagles on Monday, November 2d. I also wish to have five pairs of half eagle dies, with collars, made and sent to each of the mints at Denver and San Francisco. In the meantime, let nothing be given out about this new design until you have some pieces struck and ready for distribution. I am preparing for the press, if wanted, a statement as to the origin of the coins. The coins will probably be known as the Bigelow-Pratt design, as distinguished from the Saint-Gaudens pieces, for the reason that Dr. Wm. S. Bigelow of Boston introduced the idea to the President, and Mr. Bela L. Pratt, of the same city, made the models for the engraver. In any statement given out, I think attention should be called to the extraordinarily fine work of the engraver, Mr. Barber, shown in the fineness and sharpness of detail reached in making the new coins.

In other circumstances Leach's praise for Barber might have been humorous; however, the mint had adopted a final design that did not have approval of the original artist.[777]

---

[773] *US Mint*, NARA-P, op. cit. Letter dated October 9, 1908 to Leach from Landis.

[774] *US Mint*, NARA-P, op. cit. Letter dated October 10, 1908 to Landis from Leach. The trial pieces were made with dies aligned medal-turn so Barber could identify them if Leach or the President rejected the samples. See text.

[775] *US Mint*, NARA-P, op. cit. Letter dated October 15, 1908 to Landis from Leach, countersigned by Cortelyou.

[776] *US Mint*, NARA-P, op. cit. Letter dated October 16, 1908 to Landis from Leach.

[777] This theme is repeated throughout the 1907–1922 era and continues well after Barber and George Morgan were dead. A low point occurred in January 1917, just before Barber's death, when the mint released new quarter designs featuring an obsolete obverse and a mint-concocted reverse, then claimed the design was by Hermon MacNeil. (See *Renaissance of American Coinage 1916–1921*.)

This obviated much of the work put into the design by Pratt, and reinforced the insularity of the Mint Bureau.

*Figure 62. Half eagle design completed by Bela Lyon Pratt in June 1908, as modified by mint engraver Charles E. Barber in October.*

A sample half eagle and quarter eagle were sent to Dr. Bigelow, who showed them to Bela Pratt around October 21:[778]

> .....After the first of November you can [get] all you want of my coins at any bank, but that is still a secret. They have "knocked spots" out of my design at the mint. They let their die cutter spoil it, which he did most thoroughly, so try not to be too disappointed when you see the coins. The little $2-½ coins don't look so badly but the $5 is a sight! I could not sleep for a night or two after I saw it. The first impression, which Dr. Bigelow showed me at the Symphony two weeks ago, looked quite well. But they tried to retouch it and gee! They made a mess of it! With a few deft touches the butcher or blacksmith,[779] who is at the head of things there, changed it from a thing that I was proud of to one [of which] I am ashamed! Still it is the best coin the U. S. has ever had…

The disappointment felt by Pratt is clear from his letter, and it was more poignant because only two weeks earlier he had seen the first trial strike and thought the work was fine. How could the mint have been so "right" and then turn it all around to make "a mess of it?" The answer is that mint engravers were mechanical artisans who followed certain rules to produce coinage. The proliferation of tiny dots, lines and feathers was consistent with their concepts of coinage requirements. The staff were also subject to the whims of political appointees, and lacked training in the latest equipment and techniques for doing their jobs. Barber and Morgan were nineteenth century artisans as much out of date as the old Hill reducing lathe they still depended upon.

---

[778] Sam, op. cit., p.171. Letter (excerpt) dated October 25, 1908 to Sarah Pratt from Pratt.
[779] The same terminology was used twelve years later by Charles Moore, chairman of the Commission of Fine Arts, when referring to a plan to have the Maine Centennial half dollar commemorative modeled by the U. S. Mint from drawings by Harry Cochrane. In 1920, the "blacksmith" was George Morgan, whose engraving skill would later save the government considerable embarrassment with the 1921 Peace dollar.

Oblivious to the artist's objections, director Leach ordered five pairs of half eagle dies sent to Denver and San Francisco on October 23.[780] A week later, October 30, Leach wrote to Landis to settle up his account for "special sample coins." The total due was $55.00 and he sent $47.50 in currency leaving a balance of $7.50. He also enclosed checks from Sturgis Bigelow for $450.00 from which $7.50 was to be deducted, probably to pay for the two sample coins sent in late October, and applied to clear director Leach's account. The remaining $442.50 was to be sent to Dr. Bigelow at 56 Beacon Street, Boston, in fifty-nine half eagles and fifty-nine quarter eagles.[781] Production was expected to begin on November 2, but release would be delayed until a sufficient quantity were available to satisfy immediate demand. The coins were shipped on November 6 and Dr. Bigelow acknowledged receiving them on the 9th.

Public demand for the two new gold coins was averaging $250,000 per day in early December 1908. Much of this was due to the novelty of the designs and the approaching Christmas season. Gold coins were popular holiday gifts and the new designs further increased interest in the coins.

On November 2, Pratt sent a voucher to the mint for his work. He also apologized "…that you have been caused this extra trouble and I hope that Dr. Bigelow has explained the misunderstanding to your satisfaction."[782] Two days later, director Leach notified Landis that the compensation paid to Bela Pratt was being corrected from $300 to $600 because Pratt had prepared models for both sides of the new half eagle. Surprisingly, the suggestion had come from Charles Barber: "On conference with Mr. Barber it was thought best that Mr. Pratt should model the reverse side."[783] (Compare with $6,000 Saint-Gaudens' estate was paid; $1,100 to Brenner for his second-hand Lincoln; or $2,500 that would be paid to Fraser in 1913.) The check was issued on November 7, and immediately mailed to the sculptor at his Boston studio. Pratt wrote to his mother again on November 8:[784]

> There have been several newspaper notices of the "New coin designed by W. S. Bigelow." They usually mention that Dr. Bigelow got me to "make the models." There seems to be no excitement about it at all and I suppose that is because they have not yet appeared.[785] Anyhow, I shall have very little of either the credit or discredit. I had not thought it possible that they would play such a trick on me and it really looks much as if Dr. Bigelow was to blame. If a person gave a painter an order for a picture and told him in a general way what sort of a picture he wanted, he would never think of claiming that he "designed" the picture, and then proceed to take all the credit for it. As near as I can make out that is what Dr. Bigelow has done…. This seems to me the meanest kind of robbery….

The artist's frustration is understandable. Bigelow had come in the studio door with an idea. Pratt turned it into reality – a physical model incorporating Bigelow's technical

---

[780] *US Mint*, NARA-CP, op. cit., entry 229, box 268. Letter dated October 22, 1908 to Leach from Landis. Five pairs of dies were sent to each mint (NARA-CP, op. cit., entry 235, vol. 368, p.889).

[781] *US Mint*, NARA-P, op. cit. Letter dated October 30, 1908 to Landis from Leach.

[782] *US Mint*, NARA-CP, op. cit., entry 229, box 269. Letter dated November 2, 1908 to Leach from Pratt. Was the misunderstanding about the reverse design?

[783] *US Mint*, NARA-P, op. cit. Letter dated November 4, 1908 to Landis from Leach.

[784] Sam, op. cit., p.171. Letter (excerpt) dated November 8, 1908 to Sarah Pratt from Pratt.

[785] During this era newspapers were prohibited from printing photos or drawings of United States coins – new or current designs. Only numismatic specialty publications could reproduce coin images on their pages. The general public had little concept of what the new coins might look like, so they generally ignored the "event."

idea with Pratt's artistic skill and creativity. There had been little recognition or reward for the sculptor; no visits to the White House, not even a "thank you" letter from the President. His design had been altered without his knowledge or consent by one of the mint's artistic "butchers," so that now he felt there was little of which to be proud. Bigelow and his friend Senator Lodge had been hobnobbing about Washington, visiting the mint director and President seemingly at will.

Sturgis Bigelow must have been aware of the emphasis on his involvement with the new coin and wrote to Pratt on November 17 in an attempt to soothe the situation:[786]

> Dear Mr. Pratt:
> I have a quantity of clippings taken from papers all over the country about the new coins. Would you like to see them? There is only one comment that is otherwise than favorable and that is a short paragraph from the *New York Herald*. There is also one from the [Boston] *Transcript* which said point blank that I designed the coins. If I had seen this when it came out I should have written to correct it.
> I am sorry that they do not put you more in the foreground as a general thing. I have in my hand a copy of a memorandum I sent Mr. Leach who asked if I had anything to say about the designs for publication, as he expected an invasion of inquiring reporters. It ends with these words: "The credit for this particular design is wholly Mr. Pratt's." In a private letter to him enclosing this memorandum I said: "If we could be sure that the thing was going to be a success I should be inclined to withdraw entirely and have the thing known as the Pratt design. As it may turn out a popular failure, however, I think it may be safer to couple the names and call it either the 'Pratt-Bigelow' or the 'Bigelow-Pratt' design."
> Of course you and I, who have thought more about it than anybody else, can now see points where the thing could be done better if it were done over. Some of these the Mint is responsible for, others not. But on the whole the thing seems to be a success and I think we may well congratulate ourselves. At any rate nothing but an act of Congress can withdraw these coins from circulation for twenty years [*sic*], at the end of which time I hope they will come to you for another design. If they do, remember and get the relief completely below the level of the surrounding surface at all points....

We don't know Pratt's reaction to the letter, although his hometown newspaper's failure to credit him with the design must have hurt deeply. Dr. Bigelow seems unable to openly praise the sculptor for his work without promoting his own contribution to the project. To Bigelow, who had hired "...two die cutters..." to work on his idea, the difficulty of creating the designs and models may have been greater than he realized. Likewise, in his letter he seems to minimize the effects of Barber's changes and never discusses the critical point: no one asked Pratt, the creator, to change his design.

Pratt commented publicly on the new designs at a lecture presented to the *Thursday Evening Club* in Boston, in January 1909:[787]

> ...When we had the models well along, Dr. Bigelow proposed we ship them to Washington...It was not long before things began to happen. I got letters written on Congressional paper, Cabot Lodge paper, and paper stamped with the stamp of the White House. We soon knew that we had a very good design: Mr. Roosevelt said so. The models were sent to the Mint and there slaughtered after the manner in which the Mint always treats designs. They milled the edge, chopped off the margin, re-modeled the feathers and did other things....

[786] Sam, op. cit., p.172. Letter (excerpt) dated November 17, 1908 to Pratt from Bigelow.
[787] Sam, op. cit., pp.172–173. Manuscript (ND) January 1909 prepared by Pratt.

> One of the principal advantages of this coin is that it is nearly friction proof, as nearly so as a coin can be made; the background being slightly above the level of the relief, the broad surfaces of the background taking all the wear and being perfectly smooth, the friction loss is very slight....

Pratt's available papers suggest that he never fully accepted Dr. Bigelow's explanation. He might have been further disappointed to learn that the mint director was following Bigelow's suggestions by calling them the "Bigelow design" or the "Bigelow-Pratt" coins in his correspondence.[788] In all respects Bela Pratt was treated shabbily by the President, the mint and his collaborator. He received less compensation for his coin design work than any sculptor from 1907 to 1921; the President showed limited interest in Pratt's work and concentrated on Bigelow's contribution; the mint insisted on hyphenating the coin's name thus lessening his contribution; and Bigelow did little to promote the artist, not even attempting the courtesy of obtaining a specimen of the original pattern coin for the sculptor.

Bela Lyon Pratt was New England's finest sculptor of the era and one of America's best and most prolific at the close of the gilded age. He was expected to have a long and distinguished career, but died suddenly on May 18, 1917.

William Sturgis Bigelow, physician, Harvard lecturer on Buddhism, oriental art connoisseur, friend of President Roosevelt, died in 1926, leaving most of his art collection to the Boston Museum of Fine Arts. His unique pattern half eagle has not been located.[789]

Frank A. Leach left the director's position in July 1909. He was succeeded by A. Piatt Andrew of Massachusetts, who served only from November 1909 to June 1910. Leach's memoirs, *Reminiscences of A Newspaper Man*, published in 1917, are one of the few first-hand accounts of what it was like to be director of the mint.[790] Although not scrupulously accurate in detail and occasionally placing events out of order, his numismatic account in Chapter XVI, *Official Life in Washington*, is interesting and adds a human side to the dry correspondence of mint and Treasury officials.

## Loose Ends

Although the pattern half eagle sent to Bigelow by the President is the only pattern piece of the new designs known to have escaped the Bureau of the mint, it was not the only trial coin struck. On November 2, Philadelphia Mint Acting Superintendent Albert Norris wrote to director Leach:[791]

> In reply to your letter of the 31st ultimo I beg to inform you that the Engraver reports that he has no perfect specimens of the half eagle and quarter eagle of the new design. On account of your instructions in regard to secrecy only a sufficient number of these coins were struck to satisfy us that the dies would work perfectly. We would like very much to have the two quarter eagles, sent to you as specimens, returned, as they were struck as medals, not as coins, the bases of the de-

[788] Herein, the author refers to the coins as the "Pratt design" since he is the one who designed the coin; Dr. Bigelow providing technical and political influence.

[789] The original letter from President Roosevelt turned up in the possession of coin dealer James Ruddy in the 1970s. He later sold the letter to a collector who added an ordinary 1908 half eagle to the document for display purposes. We don't know how the letter escaped from Bigelow's estate. (Source: e-mail to the writer, May 2003, from Q. David Bowers, former business partner of Mr. Ruddy.)

[790] Director Robert W. Woolley's autobiography *Politics is Hell* exists only in rough draft and typescript. Woolley's comments about his term as director (Chapter 25) are less detailed than Leach's.

[791] *US Mint*, NARA-CP, op. cit., entry 229, box 268. Letter dated November 2, 1908 to Leach from Norris.

signs on opposite sides being together instead of reversed as on coins. If these two coins are not returned, they will be unique. I will send you ten pieces of each design as soon as they are struck by the Coiner.

As stated in my letter of October 31st, we expect to make a delivery of $50,000 in half eagles on Thursday of this week, and $25,000 in quarter eagles on the following day.

Leach returned one of the medal-turn coins on January 25, 1909:[792]

Enclosed herewith please find an envelope containing $75.00 in currency and return coin, being in settlement for $75.00 in sample coins of the Bigelow-Pratt design sent to me....

In the envelope first mentioned you will find the imperfect quarter eagle which you recently called my attention to. Please have the same destroyed in the presence of the proper officers so that the fact of its destruction can be attested, if necessary. As verbally stated to you, the other imperfect quarter eagle had passed out of my possession before my attention was called to its imperfection, and I was unable to secure its return. However, I understand it will be presented to one of the museum collections of coin in Boston.

Thus, the only remaining trial piece may be sitting in a Boston museum drawer, masquerading as a normal, quite ordinary 1908 quarter eagle.

The new design was not as simple to strike as Dr. Bigelow had supposed and comments came from branch mints as soon as they began using the new dies. Director Leach began hearing about stacking and other problems with the new coins almost from the moment production began. Superintendent Frank Downer of the Denver Mint telegraphed the director's office:[793]

In re: new half eagle can not make them stack with coins of old design. Please advise whether I shall strike coins for delivery with new dies we have. In twenty pieces they stack two and one half pieces low. Should there be change in punches for cutting these blanks?

On November 7 he wrote to Dr. Bigelow about the overall reception of the new designs. Bigelow wrote back on the 9th:[794]

I am very glad to hear that all is well with the new coins and that the verdict in general is favorable. Also that Mr. Pratt's mind has recovered its wonted tranquility. I received the coins Saturday afternoon and was delighted with their appearance. What took me a little aback, however, and what I telephoned you that evening about is the unexpected fact that they do not seem to stack as accurately as there appeared to be every reason to expect they would. Apparently the flat surface of the original disc buckles a little in the process of stamping the design so that it is no longer accurately flat. The distortion is infinitesimal but it is enough to be perceptible when two coins are held in contact and pinched together alternately at opposite edges. If ten or a dozen are stacked, the pile becomes distinctly "wobbly."

The phenomenon is curious and if it is due simply to the process of striking the design it shows that coin gold has an amount of elasticity which it does not generally get credit for. Is there any point in the manufacture of the coin which is exposed to the heat? That would account for an amount of warping or buckling.

[792] *US Mint*, NARA-P, op. cit. Letter dated January 25, 1909 to Landis from Leach. Inquiries made in 2003 of several Boston Museums have not uncovered the medal-turn quarter eagle.

[793] *US Mint*, NARA-CP, op. cit., entry 229, box 269. Telegram dated November 4, 1908 to Leach from Downer.

[794] *US Mint*, NARA-CP, op. cit., entry 229, box 268. Letter dated November 9, 1908 to Leach from Bigelow.

Would it not be practical, as well as interesting, to strike two or three dozen half eagles in lead so as to make sure whether the inequality is due to the warping of the coin itself or to the warping of the die in the process of tempering it? It seems hard to believe that metallic gold of coin fineness should have enough elasticity to spring out of shape after being exposed to pressure. Is such a thing as a warped die recognized as a possibility in the experience of the mint?

With kind regards,

The San Francisco mint joined Denver's objections on November 12 with a letter from William M. Cutter, coiner, to Edward Sweeny, superintendent:[795]

Before commencing the coinage of the Bigelow-Pratt design half eagles, in accordance with instructions, it was thought best to make an experimental test, as it was something entirely new. So one ingot was rolled and cut and the blanks annealed and whitened and pressed. As the memoranda sent from the Bureau made no reference to milling we were obliged to use our own judgement, and some of the blanks were put through the half eagle mill. As a result a slight mark showed in the center of the stars when pressed. We then put other blanks through the eagle mill and found a slight improvement. We think if the blanks were milled on a compromise between the eagle and double eagle milling probably the best results would be attained. We would like, however, to receive advice from the Bureau on this regard and as to the standard mill tool to use.

A more serious objection is as to the piling of the new coin. The standard thickness of the half eagle is .065. The thickness of the new coins as pressed by us is but .0585. The standard height for a pile of twenty half eagles is 1.300. The actual height of a pile of twenty of the new half eagles as pressed by us is 1.170, or two pieces lower than standard.

In view of the uncertainty with reference to the proper method of milling, and the great discrepancy between the actual and the standard milling height, I would suggest that coinage of the new half eagles of the Bigelow-Pratt design be deferred until the Bureau is advised of the result of our experimental test and sends further instructions.

Leach contacted the Philadelphia mint and received a reply on November 17:

Referring to the information you desired from the Assistant Coiner over the phone today I beg to say in confirmation that we cut the half eagle the size of the collar and mill 5/1000 smaller, just rounding off the blank enough to prevent a "Fin" or "Burr." The height of twenty pieces of half eagles is 1.170. Thickness of one piece = .0585. Finished diameter = .848. Diameter of cut blank = .834. Diameter of milled blank = .829.

Respectfully,

John Landis, Superintendent

Assistant coiner Robert Clark's numbers for dimensions of the finished coins were in agreement with those from the San Francisco mint. The large expanse of raised field made the coins thinner than expected. When combined with the slightly curved surfaces identified by Dr. Bigelow, the coins could not be reliably used in automatic coin counters when mixed with old design pieces.

The last recorded exchange between Bela Pratt and the U. S. Mint occurred in February 1909. Pratt had placed models of one of the early versions of his Indian head coin

---

[795] *US Mint*, NARA-CP, op. cit., entry 229, box 268. Letter dated November 12, 1908 to Sweeny from Cutter.

design in an exhibition at the Academy of Fine Art in Philadelphia. Someone from the mint learned of this and alerted director Leach, who wrote to Pratt on February 24:[796]

> My attention has been called to the fact that there is on exhibition at the Academy of Fine Art in Philadelphia some models made by you of the new half eagle and quarter eagle. This fact has caused some little uneasiness in the department, as it is argued that it would be a very easy matter for some one to remove these models, with little risk of being discovered, and use them for counterfeiting purposes.
>
> In making arrangement with you for the production of the models, I think I overlooked calling your attention to the fact that it has always been required that all such models, or other models used in producing the coin, either must be destroyed or be turned over to the government when the finished model is produced. It has been the practice for the government to loan models for exhibition purposes when requested, but such loans have always been made with assurances of protection against loss.
>
> In relation to the models on exhibition in Philadelphia, I will have to request that you impress upon the exhibitors the necessity of protection, and that when the exhibition is closed you will see that these models are turned over to the Superintendent of the mint at Philadelphia.

Pratt's reply has not been located, but it is evident from Leach's subsequent remarks that the artist felt he was being unfairly criticized:[797]

> Your letter of the 25th instant received. I assure you that it was not my purpose to criticize your action in loaning the models for exhibition purposes, inasmuch as I had neglected to inform you of the requirements of the government.
>
> I note what you say about having the models on exhibition at Philadelphia turned over to the mint authorities there.
>
> With many thanks, I remain.

With this brief note, it appears Pratt sent the half eagle models to the Philadelphia mint, and correspondence between the mint and the sculptor ended.

---

[796] *US Mint*, NARA-CP, op. cit., entry 235 vol. 380, p.369. Letter dated February 24, 1909 to Pratt from Leach.
[797] *US Mint*, NARA-CP, op. cit., entry 235 vol. 380, p.397. Letter dated February 27, 1909 to Leach from Pratt.

# Chapter 12 – Designs, Images, Acceptance

Pratt's half eagle design resulted from the confluence of three events: controversy over use of the religious motto, William Sturgis Bigelow's idea for getting high relief coins with normal striking pressure, and Roosevelt's interest in an American Indian design. Bigelow's suggestion of "sunken relief" (also called "sunk relief," or sometimes "outline relief") was primarily a mechanical one, although it was evidently inspired by Egyptian or Assyrian reliefs he had seen in thc Boston Museum of Fine Arts and on his travels. He felt that by sinking the outline of the design below the field of the coin, they could be struck in high relief using normal coinage presses. He also decided this would reduce abrasion on the central portrait, thereby improving the stacking qualities of the coins.

Bigelow commissioned Pratt to make a sculpted sample in plaster, and adroitly suggested a subject. But, he evidently conducted no experiments to confirm his initial or later assumptions. He had little knowledge of the coining process and could not speak with technical authority on the subject. He does not seem to have contacted Tiffany and Co., Gorham, or others experienced in striking medals for either expertise or samples. Strangely, there is also nothing in available documents suggesting that engraver Barber had anything to say on the subject. This left the doctor's good intentions unsupported by practical experience. Nevertheless, he convinced President Roosevelt of the benefits of using sunken relief for coinage, and the mint director and engraver, already gun-shy of the President, followed Roosevelt's orders to produce the coins as Bigelow specified.

Bela Pratt had been thinking along the same lines as Bigelow, but instead of an abrupt boundary between portrait and field, he envisioned gradually sloping the field from rim to outline of the portrait. This was closer to the normal process, although the field would have been much more curved.[798] The Indian motif closely follows the sculptor's personal interest in the American Indian and in native American artifacts.[799] The acquisi-

---

[798] This would likely have resembled curvature of the extremely high relief experimental double eagles of 1907.

[799] A possible influence on Pratt was *The North American Indian* by Edward S. Curtis of Boston. Beginning in the late 1880s and backed by grants from J. P. Morgan, Curtis photographed every major Native American tribe in North Amer-

348

tion and collection of such artifacts was popular among middle-class citizens – partially as a minimal, highly romanticized, indulgent realization of the suffering their forbears had caused the first Americans – partially as a way of "preserving" the few strands of native American culture still to be found in the eastern states. It was not unusual for popular journalists to compare the bison with the American Indian, although the metaphor was hardly of any blessing to either. Pratt was of the upper end of collectors and had a genuine and deeply felt sympathy for the sad history and ignominious present of 1908. In contrast, there were many more "collectors" who were little more than grave robbers, with interest only in the money to be made from selling their finds.

Sunken relief, as used by the Egyptians, Assyrians and other ancient cultures 4,000 years ago, had several advantages over conventional bas-relief. First, it was faster to complete a sculpture because stone cutting was limited to the subject – the ground (or field) surrounding the subject was left in its original condition, or minimally smoothed. Second, there was no need to have the cut exactly the same depth all around the subject; the sharp edge effectively masked small differences. Third, the visual appearance was similar to painted subjects where a strong outline was made to the figure before the details were painted in. Finally, the work was easy to repair if a major mistake was made. All the artist had to do was fill the old work with plaster, let it dry and recut the correct design. A quick coat of paint, as was usually applied anyway, hid the mistake until the patron was long dead and only his mummy could see the work in the afterlife.

*Figure 63. Examples of Egyptian relief carving. Left, bas-relief of the god Hapi showing figures carved above the surrounding field. Right, a sunken relief carving of the sun god Ra and Pharaoh Sety-II, where the figures are outlined and only the subject is carved in relief; the field remains at its original height. Note the use of hollow outlines in the three small cartouches in the center.* (Courtesy Cairo Museum/Luxor Project.)

Egyptian artists made a cut at nearly right angles to the surface of the stone (or plaster). This gave a strong, sharp outline to the work. Pratt could not use so steep an angle because a die made from such a model would invariably stick to the coin by mechanical

ica. Published a limited edition from 1907 to 1930, the volumes still exert a major influence on the image of Indians in popular culture. Curtis said he wanted to document "the vanishing race…the old time Indian, his dress, his ceremonies, his life and manners," as they were prior to the loss of their homelands.

pressure during the strike. Bela Pratt used a shallower angle, approximately sixty degrees instead of ninety degrees, so the coin would release properly.[800] He also had to be sure the highest point of his design was level with or below the field of the coin to ensure the portrait was fully struck during minting. The sunken relief style also had one significant artistic drawback: small design elements, such as stars, lost much of their distinctive internal detail; they became little more than outlines.

*Figure 64. The use of sunken relief for the stars and lettering gave these elements an incomplete appearance. Compare with stars on the previous $5 issue (right) designed in normal bas-relief style.*

Examination of the Indian head $5 and $2.50 coins shows that stars and lettering are outlines with little detail in their raised central portion. This makes lettering look incomplete. Stars on the Indian $5 are nearly twenty percent larger than those on the previous design (1.9mm vs. 1.5mm), yet they look small and ineffective. Ancient Egyptian sculptors avoided this when preparing sunken relief hieroglyphs by cutting away the interior of the symbol, leaving a "hollow" outline.

Most defects of the half eagle were the result of Bigelow's incomplete understanding of the mechanical aspects of coinage. The mint had access to a lengthy report on the technical aspects of minting and metal flow prepared in early 1908, but we do not know if it was given to Bigelow, and the results suggest not.[801] Bigelow's initial commission to Pratt was for a sample of what a coin might look like. When the President indicated his pleasure with the Indian head model, Bigelow moved ahead without making tests. It is particularly interesting that available records show virtually no controversy within the mint about sunken relief, nor any debate about striking quantities of trial pieces until after they were placed in circulation. Considering the many pages of grumbling from Barber, Landis, Roberts, Leach and others about the Saint-Gaudens designs, one would expect to find similar complaints. It is possible that after the experience of the previous autumn, director Leach simply ordered mint personnel to do whatever the President wanted and not raise objections.

---

[800] It's possible this was altered by Barber as one of his "improvements."
[801] *US Mint*, NARA-P, op. cit. Technical report on metal flow under pressure found in Box 200. [Writer unknown.]

Bigelow and Pratt both stated that creating the design in sunken relief would reduce wear on the coins, and aid in stacking the pieces. Neither proved to be the case when the coins were issued. Sunken relief made the blank field the highest area of the coin. This meant that almost all contact with other coins took place along a wide expanse of gold rather than on the narrow rim and design high points as on previous coins. The result was

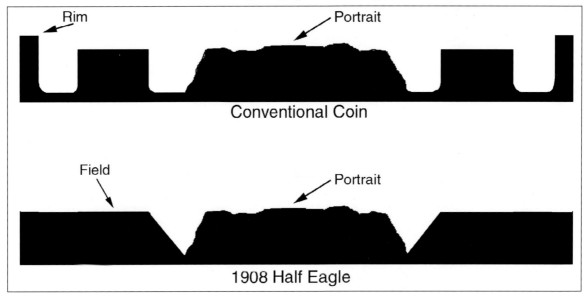

*Figure 65. The illustration above shows a cross section of a conventional coin and of Dr. Bigelow's concept for the half eagle. Bela Pratt executed the relief within a sharply angled outline. The field was not sunken as was normal for coins, so the coins had the appearance of being without a rim. This subjected a large portion of the coin to abrasion resulting in excessive wear and surface damage.*

that half and quarter eagles were quickly marred by nicks, scrapes and abrasion. The broad fields also did not receive enough pressure during striking to fully erase marks on the planchets left from blanking and upsetting operations. The central Indian design maintained most of its integrity, but the overall appearance of the coin could best be described as scruffy. Barber's modifications probably also contributed to degradation of the coins' appearance as suggested by Pratt in his January 1909 lecture.

In later years the Mint Bureau recognized problems with the quarter eagles. Director Roberts commented to W. Howard Gibson, Assistant Treasurer of the United States:[802]

> I am disposed to doubt the wisdom of melting the quarter eagles. They count in the reserve against gold certificates just as well as any other coin, and on general principles the melting of our coins is objectionable because it always costs something. I should think the best thing to do with the quarter eagles was to pile them away in a back corner of a vault where they would be out of the way, and would simply count in the gold reserve. I am interested in what you say about the coins going to the melting pot.

In 1922 director Baker commented on excessive wear and why the small gold pieces were not being struck by the mint: "…the $2.50 is not being struck due to the relatively large amount of abrasion involved in their circulation."[803]

[802] *US Mint*, NARA-CP, op. cit., entry 235, vol. 405. Letter dated June 16, 1914 to Gibson from Roberts.
[803] *US Mint*, NARA-CP, op. cit., entry 235, vol. 446. Letter dated February 10, 1922 to Senator William M. Calder from Baker.

Stacking problems were exacerbated by the nearly flat fields that tended to slide easily over one another when the coins were piled. Had the field actually been flat, the coins would have stacked properly; however, the mint was rarely able to produce dies of the correct curvature after hardening, which was required to produce consistently flat coins. Many pieces exhibited uneven field curvature that caused the coins to wobble even when laid on a smooth surface.

Bigelow's original claim, that his idea would allow high relief designs to be used on coins made with ordinary minting presses, failed to materialize, and vanished from his letters after the first few weeks. As produced by the U. S. Mint, the fields were the thickest portion of the coin and contained most of the metal. With little pressure from the dies to squeeze metal into the central design, getting a fully struck coin from normal dies was a challenge, and high relief dies might have perforated the planchet before the design was complete.[804] Finally, the absence of sufficient metal flow caused the diameter of the coins to expand in a somewhat irregular fashion. This produced coins with stars cut off, lettering seemingly ready to fall off the edge and shallow reeding. Compared with earlier versions of the same denomination, the new pieces were noticeably inferior in technical execution. It would be reasonable to presume that these defects made the new gold pieces attractive to counterfeiters, but available documents do not discuss the potential problem.

## Obverse

While the sunken relief format of the half eagle was innovative, the obverse and reverse designs were conventional in style and execution. Pratt's obverse composition features the portrait of a Native American wearing a ceremonial feather headdress. According to Bigelow's letter to S. H. Chapman, Pratt worked from a photograph rather than using a live model.[805] Comparing the quarter eagle and half eagle coins, it is evident that the mint did considerable retouching of the hubs. Examination of details of the feather headdress indicates extensive hand cutting within each feather. Since the exact placement of re-engraved detail differs between the two coin denominations, it is apparent that mint engravers did not make new models and reductions, but simply recut the master hub and master die much as had been done to Henry Hering's low relief model of the Saint-Gaudens $20. Rework also extended to tiny beading on the headdress that was enhanced and multiplied by Charles Barber's steady hand. Microscopic examination of high quality 1908 specimens shows sharp lines and dots from engraving tools, as well as remnants of softer lines produced by the reducing lathe. As with the 1907 low relief double eagle, only the artist seems to have noticed.

---

[804] This did not happen with the Saint-Gaudens design because the field was lower than the design and pushed metal into recesses of the die better.

[805] *The Numismatist*, "New U. S. Gold Series Criticized and Defended." February, 1909. Letter dated December 10, 1908 to S. H. Chapman from Bigelow.

*Figure 66 . "Indian head" designs on circulating United States coins during the early twientieth century. L-R: Saint-Gaudens $10, Pratt $5, and Fraser five-cents.The half eagle and five-cent coins are approximately the same diameter.* (Photo on right by Bill Fivaz.)

The three "Indian" portraits used on coins during the 1907-1921 period represent a clear, although not necessarily conscious, evolution from classical to realistic. Saint-Gaudens' 1907 version is adapted from his *Nike Erini* portrait bust and was given a Native American headdress at President Roosevelt's insistence. The artist never intended it to represent an Indian but the coin was given the "Indian Head" moniker as soon as it was released. Her features are classical European and the headdress is sufficiently stylized to fit within the required coin format. In this case, the Liberty portrait is simply a vehicle for carrying out the President's orders. It is an elegant costume for the lady but not a reasonable American Indian visage. Pratt's conception of a Native American is, to his credit, far closer to reality than that of his early mentor. Unfortunately, we do not know what his original Indian portrait looks like. The residue from Barber and Leach's re-engraving and "improvements" is uncomfortable and oddly proportioned at the chin and cheek. It also lacks the depth usually associated with sculpture, having more the look of a flat drawing or photo than bas-relief. This detracts from the potential strength of the subject resulting in a neutral, characterless picture. As with Saint-Gaudens, the headdress has been altered to better fit the frame although detailing is better portrayed in Pratt's version. Chapman's comment that Pratt worked from a photograph leads to speculation that the Indian on the half eagle may be a portrait of an individual. If so, this would be the first instance of a specific person appearing on America's circulating coin. In comparison, James Fraser's 1912 Native American is very close to an accurate and idealized composite portrait. Photographs confirm that at least one of the artist's models wore hair and headdress feathers much as Fraser depicts them. There is a depth and careful use of the visual space that reinforces the character of the subject. It is possible Fraser's extensive use of coin-size electrotypes helped the artist adapt to the small diameter coin. The result is an exceptionally strong portrait successfully adapted to the small diameter and low relief of coinage.[806]

As issued for circulation, the half eagle portrait has a "drawn" and "emaciated" look with very high, pronounced cheekbones and deeply inset cheeks. Use of a photograph rather than live model may account for part of the problem. However, based on Pratt's comments after the coins were issued, it is evident the mint made significant changes to the portrait without consulting with the sculptor: "They made a mess of it!"[807] Changes were made to the face and feather work of the headdress, according to Pratt. Unfortunately, no

[806] See Burdette, *Renaissance of American Coinage 1909-1915*, for details on Fraser's nickel designs and the models.
[807] Sam, op. cit., p.171. Letter (excerpt) dated October 25, 1908 to Sarah Pratt from Pratt.

photos of the original models are known, and we cannot compare Pratt's artistic conception with the mint's product.

## Reverse

President Roosevelt decided to use Saint-Gaudens' standing eagle design for the reverse. He must have been very fond of the composition; it was used three times during his presidency. Bigelow told Pratt he could make minor changes but not to go too far in altering the eagle since the President liked the design. Pratt made relatively small modifications to the eagle by changing the bird's features. He shortened the legs and neck to give the bird natural proportions, and slightly modified the feathers to improve definition. Saint-Gaudens' eagle for the 1905 inaugural medal, as modeled by Adolph Weinman, has the same long legs as on the coin, however the neck and head are much better proportioned on the medal. Pratt's modifications suggest he adopted the coin's approach to feathers rather than that used on the 1905 medal because his feather work has little resemblance to the medal. These were substantial improvements over the prototype eagle on the $10 coin.

*Figure 67. Reverse of the 1905 Inaugural medal (left), $10 gold coin (center), and $5 gold coin (right). Note change in position of the motto "E Pluribus Unum," addition of "In God We Trust" and altered proportions of the eagle.*

Pratt also changed position of the motto E PLURIBUS UNUM on the $10 coin from behind the bird's shoulder to in front of the eagle's breast. He added IN GOD WE TRUST to the space behind the eagle, but low and somewhat cramped between wings and the legend. This was evidently an attempt to provide open space around the upper portion of the eagle and emphasize the bird. Given legally required inscriptions, small-diameter of the coins and the extra lines required by sunken relief, there was little the artist could do to avoid crowding.

The result was an improved eagle, but a bottom heavy and awkward composition. Sunken relief compounds the problems due to extra lines necessary to outline the figure and lettering. This adds multiple reflections, further confusing the design's visual impact. A large raised "lump" between the eagle's legs and the arrows, also distracts the viewer. No explanation has been made for why Pratt made the change in motto positions. His composition may have been more effective as a normal bas-relief.

Within the overall context of the American coinage renaissance from 1907 to 1921, Bela Pratt's half eagle designs fall next to the bottom of the scale, just above Victor Brenner's anemic Lincoln portrait. The artist succeeded in correcting many of the faults of Saint-Gaudens' standing eagle, yet simultaneously introduced others. His Native American portrait, as reproduced by the Mint Bureau, is a static, characterless exposition. A significant part of the design problems come from Pratt's acceptance of the sunken relief concept as being appropriate for a small coin. This approach to bas-relief was contrary to how the ancients used it and to how the technique best enhanced the subject. That the work was completed with no recorded complaint from engraver Barber is testament to President Roosevelt's trust in Dr. Bigelow, and to the narrowness of vision imparted by the President's orders.

## Patterns and Proofs

No pattern or experimental coins of Pratt's design are presently known to numismatists. However, available mint records and correspondence confirm that one $5 piece of the #2 design was owned by William Sturgis Bigelow and was in his possession on October 9, 1908. The coin was a gift from President Roosevelt and acknowledged by Bigelow as being the only example from the pattern (or experimental) dies. The coin was also seen by Senator Henry Cabot Lodge on October 9, and by Bela Pratt on October 10.[808]

Later, a trial piece, this time a quarter eagle was given to Leach. This coin was one of several half eagles and quarter eagles intentionally prepared by Charles Barber with "medal turn" dies. Two of each denomination were sent to Leach as samples of the revised dies. The quarter eagle with inverted reverse is of the normal design for circulation, but was intentionally prepared by Barber so he could identify pre-production coins sent to director Leach. The director didn't realize this and accidentally gave one of the pieces to someone (Bigelow or Senator Lodge, possibly) who later promised to donate it to a Boston museum.[809] Other pieces may have "leaked" out of the mint, but there have been no rumors of any existing.

*Figure 68. Recreation of the first 1908 pattern half eagle based on descriptions by Bela Lyon Pratt. This is a conceptual illustration and not a known coin.*

Alleged half eagle patterns (see illustration above) would be distinguishable from normal coins in the following ways:

1. Stars, legend and date well removed from edge of coin;
2. May be struck medal turn;

---

[808] This is the coin that Taxay and Breen claim was lost in the mail before Bigelow received it. The letter was sent by registered mail and claimed unopened by Bigelow and Cabot Lodge. The pattern coin was shown to Lodge, Pratt and possibly others. It may have been in possession of the person who obtained the coin's cover letter from the Bigelow Estate, then sold as a common coin. Its whereabouts is presently unknown.
[809] *US Mint*, NARA-P, op. cit. Box 71, "Gold Coin Designs." Letter dated January 25, 1909 to Joyce from Leach.

3. May have a slight border (or flat rim) intended to prevent a fin from occurring;
4. Feathers rounded and more softly defined than on circulation coins;
5. Absence of fine dots on headband and elsewhere;
6. Indian's cheekbone less prominent and the entire face less hollow looking (more closely resembling James Fraser's composite Indian on the nickel);
7. Possibly has a plain edge rather than reeding;
8. Designer's initials might be omitted.

Pratt's original models, and possibly intermediate reductions, might be sequestered in a Philadelphia Mint vault. Requests to examine the vault's contents have been consistently denied by mint officials, who explain that security restrictions and cost make it impossible to examine the contents, or release the inventory.

The table below lists all pattern and experimental pieces mentioned in available correspondence.

| Denomination | Design No. | Quan. | Distributed To | Date | Returned Quan. | To | Date |
|---|---|---|---|---|---|---|---|
| $5 | S-G | ? | Director-Roosevelt | Before 4/3/08 | ? | Mint | ? |
| $2.50 | #2 | 10 | Director | 9/21/08 | 10 | Mint | 9/28/08 |
| $5 | #2 | 9 | Director | 9/21/08 | 9 | Mint | 9/28/08 |
| $5 | #2 | 1 | Director-Roosevelt-Bigelow | 9/26/08 to 10/09/08 | ? | ? | ? |
| $5 | S-G | 1 | Director | ? | 1 | Mint | 9/28/08 |
| $2.50 | Circ (#3) | 1 | Director-Roosevelt | 10/9/08 | 1 | Mint | |
| $5 | Circ (#3) | 1 | Director- Roosevelt | 10/9/08 | 1 | Mint | |
| $2.50 | Circ (#3) | 2 | Director (medal turn) | ? | 1 | Mint | 1/25/09 |
| $5 | Circ (#3) | 2 | Director (medal turn) | ? | 2 | Mint | 1/25/09 |
| $5 | Circ (#3) | 1 | Director-Roosevelt-Bigelow | ? | ? | ? | ? |
| $2.50 | Circ (#3) | 59 | Bigelow | 11/6/08 | ? | ? | ? |
| $5 | Circ (#3) | 59 | Bigelow | 11/6/08 | ? | ? | ? |
| $2.50 | Circ (#3) | 10 | Director | Before 1/25/09 | ? | ? | ? |
| $5 | Circ (#3) | 10 | Director | ? | ? | ? | ? |

*Note:*

Design #1 was sent to the Mint in May 1908, but was not used to strike experimental coins.
Design #2 was Pratt's revision of #1 sent to the mint in June. Patterns struck.
Design #3 was Barber's adaptation of Pratt's #2 design as finally used for circulation. Medal-turn trial pieces struck.

## Lead and Cardboard Trial Pieces, Now Unknown

Trial pieces of one or both sides of a die were routinely produced in lead for review by the engraving department and mint officials. For the Saint-Gaudens coinage these were intended for internal mint use in verifying the position of the motto E PLURIBUS UNUM on the half and quarter eagle designs. No one from Saint-Gaudens' studio was consulted on this except for a single letter to Henry Hering. Cardboard (actually thick paperboard) impressions were occasionally used when officials wanted to see the design, but the dies were incomplete and not hardened. The rectangular cardboard stock was dampened, struck with the dies at sufficient pressure to show the full design, then allowed to dry. (Striking squeezed most of the moisture from the paper.) The dried cardboard "coin" was reasonably durable and easily disposed of.

356

The table below lists all lead and cardboard trial pieces mentioned in the original sources but unknown in museum or private collections. The cardboard pieces were supposed to have been kept by the director's office as part of the official record of acceptance of the designs, but cannot now be located.

| Description | Design Date | Strike Date | Quantity |
|---|---|---|---|
| **Half Eagle** | | | |
| Card – denomination position | Before 12/24/07 | Before 12/24/07 | 1 |
| **Quarter Eagle** | | | |
| Card – denomination position | Before 12/24/07 | Before 12/24/07 | 1 |

*All of the above are of the Saint-Gaudens design with flying eagle reverse.*

## Proof Coins

Proof coins were issued for collectors from 1908 through 1915. The special coins were made with a sandblast finish (1908 and 1911–15), which gave the coins a dull look and was not as popular with collectors as brilliant proofs. Small nicks and marks were very apparent on the sandblast proof coins as shiny spots. An alternative surface, nicknamed "Roman proof" and more accurately called a "satin proof" (used 1909–10) was even less popular.[810]

In a letter written on November 14, Albert Norris explained availability of collector's proof coins for 1908:[811]

> In reply to your letter of the 13th instant, relative to the manufacture of proof sets for this year, I beg to inform you that proof sets of the silver and minor coins have been supplied during the year. The Engraver has on hand ready for delivery five hundred sets of gold proofs, but the Superintendent thought they should not be issued until we had coined some eagles and double eagles, with motto, of the regular issue for circulation, which we expect to do next week. The designs of the new gold coins are such that the dies cannot be polished, therefore we could not make proofs, similar to those heretofore supplied, with a polished surface, so the Engraver has finished these proofs similar to medals with a dull surface.

Five hundred sets of gold proofs are considerably more than reported in standard catalogues. Figures reported at the end of 1908, one hundred and one gold sets, were the quantity sold, with the balance melted. This high destruction rate may have contributed to the mint's decision to make satin proofs (struck the same way, but not sandblasted) in 1909–10. Sandblast proofs were too unusual-looking to permit the mint to place excess pieces in circulation, as was usually done.

## Comments on Half and Quarter Eagles

President Roosevelt showed little public enthusiasm for the new gold coins. His personal tribute to Bigelow and defense of the attack on the design by Samuel Hudson Chapman are the only written comments the President made on the coins. Unlike the high relief double eagle design of 1907, Roosevelt didn't order any for personal distribution,

---

[810] See the extended discussion on proof coins in Part I of this book for more information.
[811] *US Mint*, NARA-CP, op. cit., entry 229, box 268. Letter dated November 14, 1908 to Leach from Norris.

and there is no record of them being given to the cabinet or other administration officials. In a sense, this was to be expected. The President had no particular connection to Bela Pratt and may have considered him little more than a local Boston artist hired by Bigelow. The coins were not artistically special in any way except for the new design, and they could be obtained by anyone at banks across the country. Lastly, contrary to the collaboration with Saint-Gaudens, Roosevelt gained nothing by associating himself with Bela Pratt.

Philadelphia numismatist Samuel Hudson Chapman did not like the new small gold coins. Within a month of their release by the treasury department, Chapman had put his opinions in a personal letter to the President:[812]

It was the hope of every one that when our new coinage appeared we would have one of great beauty and artistic merit. But the new $5 and $2.50 gold pieces just issued totally lack these qualities, and not only those of beauty, but actually miss the practicability to which every effect of beauty in relief has been sacrificed.

The idea of Dr. William S. Bigelow, of Boston, to sink the whole relief below the flat surface of the coin causes it to appear like a design merely incised in the blank, and precludes entirely the effect of miniature bas-relief.

The head of the Indian is without artistic merit and portrays an Indian who is emaciated, totally unlike the big, strong chiefs as seen in real life. The treatment of the head is quite crude and hard, with sharp, abrupt outlines, as if carved by a mere metal chaser; and on the reverse is a reproduction of the Saint-Gaudens' eagle, which represents not our national bird (the white-headed eagle – commonly but erroneously called the bald eagle – which has no feathers on its feet), but resembles more closely the golden eagle, which is also indigenous to Europe.

The placing of the design below the surface of the flan, with deeply incised outlines, gives the effect of having been engraved into the metal, and can, therefore, be closely imitated by any metal chaser with the graver, without dies or moulds. And I am certain that if this had been suggested to the secret service officials it would never have been issued by the Treasury Department, and the issuance ought to be immediately stopped and the coins recalled, for every one will be in danger of the imitations.

The sunken design, especially the deeply sunken portion of the neck of the Indian, will be a great receptacle for dirt and conveyor of disease, and the coin will be the most unhygienic ever issued.

The principal claim put forth for this coin, and which, according to the claim, would appear to be the most important any design can have, is that it will stack. But, alas! even this is not obtained by this means, for I have before me a stack of twenty pieces – $100 – the stack used by cashiers, and it is the most tottering stack of modern coins, rocking to a great degree, and when the table is jarred about four times the upper coins slide off.

They will fall when carried on a bank tray. It is well known that you cannot strike a lot of flat blanks and get them perfectly true. As a connoisseur remarked to me: "Coins should be like a table, which we do not make with a flat bottom, but with feet to stand upon, and this result in coins can and has always been obtained by a flat rim."

And then the new coins, being thinner, as the metal is taken up by the full field, they do not make stacks equal in height to the old, and when mixed with the other issue cause piles to be of unequal height, and the cashier cannot use the height of a stack as a test count, but must sort this issue out [from earlier coins].

The criticism from the bankers that the first model of the $20 and $10 pieces did not stack firmly should not cause mint officials to throw all other considerations to

[812] *The Numismatist*, "New U. S. Gold Series Criticized and Defended." February 1909. Letter dated December 7, 1908 to Roosevelt from S. H. Chapman. He was Henry Chapman's brother and former business partner.

the winds, for the firmness in stacking a coin, as stated above, could be obtained by the use of a sufficiently wide and high rim.

These coins are a disgrace to our country as a monument of our present ideas of art as applied to coinage.

As compared to those of recent issues of European countries, not to mention the beautiful works of the ancient Greek coin engravers, it is an utterly miserable, hideous production, and let us hope that its issue will not be continued and that it will be recalled and remelted.

I would summarize the above objections as follows:

First – Lack of beauty. The coinage of our country should be an example of beauty and art to all its citizens.

Second – ease with which it may be counterfeited.

Third – unhygienic. Its filth-bearing capacities.

Fourth – not forming stacks of equal height.

I would suggest as a means of obtaining a competent committee to pass upon designs for coinage, that in future all designs for coinage be submitted to the American numismatic societies. For instance: The American Numismatic Society of New York, President Archer M. Huntington, and the American Numismatic Association, President Farran Zerbe.

The matter would then be weighed by men who have devoted their lives or leisure to the study of the art of coinage from the earliest period to the present time, and thus, having a complete purview of the subject, they would be able to judge of the merits of designs offered, and if such course were adopted we would be save the mortification of seeing generally the worst designs accepted and the taste of our people degraded, instead of elevated, by the coinage passing through their hands.

Chapman's letter caused some consternation at the White House and the President prepared a reply, which he sent to Sturgis Bigelow for his comments. Bigelow convinced the President not the send his letter, but to substitute one that Bigelow had written:[813]

Dear Sturgis:

...If you will return Mr. Chapman's letter to me so that I may have his address, I shall send him the letter that you designed to have sent him; and oh, how I would have liked to send him the other letter, which you did not design to have sent him!

Roosevelt had his secretary send a note to Bigelow, who then sent his reply directly to Chapman on December 12. As finally crafted, the reply was reasoned and moderate, unlike the version Roosevelt would have preferred to send:[814]

Dear Mr. President:

I have a line from [your personal secretary] Mr. Loeb dated December 8th enclosing an interesting letter from Mr. Samuel Hudson Chapman concerning the new gold coins. Some of Mr. Chapman's criticisms are well founded, others less so. He says that "sinking the relief below the surface makes it look like an incised design and precludes the effect of bas-relief." This is hardly correct, as Mr. Chapman can readily see for himself in photographs of the Egyptian sculptures. There my be at the Museum at Philadelphia some casts or originals of Egyptian wall-carvings which will illustrate the principle. The bas-relief effect is accentuated and not diminished by the shadow of the sharp outline.

---

[813] *Roosevelt*, LoC, op. cit., vol. 88, p.494. Microfilm reel 353. Letter dated December 12, 1908 to Bigelow from Roosevelt.

[814] *The Numismatist*, "New U. S. Gold Series Criticized and Defended." February, 1909. Letter dated December 10, 1908 to S. H. Chapman from Bigelow.

He says the head of the Indian is "without artistic merit and portrays an Indian who is emaciated, totally unlike the big, strong chiefs as seen in real life." The answer to this is that the head was taken from a recent photograph of an Indian whose health was excellent. Perhaps Mr. Chapman has in mind the fatter but less characteristic type of Indian sometimes seen on the reservations.

"The treatment of the head is quite crude and hard, with sharp, abrupt outlines, as if carved by a mere metal chaser." This doubtless refers to the feathers of the head-dress which were retouched in the die, the modeling of Mr. Pratt's design having been a little too delicate to hold its own in the reducing machine. I enclose a photograph from a plaster cast of Mr. Pratt's clay [model], which illustrates this point.

The matter of the eagle was thoroughly threshed out at the time of the issue of the Saint-Gaudens' coin. That design proved to be an absolutely correct representation of the white-headed American eagle, except that the head was, perhaps intentionally, a little small and the leg feathers a little heavy. Both these criticisms Mr. Pratt has met in the present design. Mr. Chapman says that the American eagle has not feathers in its feet. This statement is true, but not exactly new.

"The placing of the design below the surface of the flan, with deeply incised outlines, gives the effect of having been engraved into the medal [sic], and can, therefore, be closely imitated by any metal chaser with the graver, without dies or moulds." This criticism can hardly be take seriously. If a forger were going to engrave anything he would not waste his labor on a single coin. It would be as easy to engrave a die as a coin of any issue.

"The sunken design, especially the deeply sunken portion of the neck of the Indian, will be a great receptacle for dirt and conveyor of disease, and the coin will be the most unhygienic ever issued." This remains to be seen. The question of hygiene has more relation to silver coins than gold, as they find their way into dirtier pockets. A dirty gold coin would be an anomaly. I have never happened to see one.

What Mr. Chapman says in regard to the fact of the coins not stacking is perfectly true. I noticed it as soon as they were issued and called Mr. Leach's attention to it. It proved to be due to an accidental warping of the steel die in hardening. Mr. Leach tells me that it can and will be avoided in the future.

"Coins should be like a table, which we do not make with a flat bottom, but with feet to stand upon, and this result in coins can and has always been obtained by a flat rim." This is true, and it is exactly the principle on which the present issue is made. The flat rim extends from the edge of the coin to the edge of the design.

The thickness of the coins after striking depends on the amount of metal displaced by the die. A stronger relief would give greater thickness. I agree with Mr. Chapman that it would be well if all the coins in circulation were of the same thickness....

Chapman wrote again to Roosevelt. *The Numismatist* dutifully printed all three letters, but nobody at the mint or White House bothered to reply. The new coins were issued and would remain as they were for twenty-five years, or until Congress ordered them changed.[815]

I am in receipt of your letter of December 16th, enclosing copy of a letter from Dr. Bigelow, date December 10th, in which he reviews the criticisms I expressed in regard to the new half and quarter eagles.

Dr. Bigelow practically admits the principle points of my letter.

---

[815] *The Numismatist*, "New U. S. Gold Series Criticized and Defended." February, 1909. Letter dated December 18, 1908 to Roosevelt from S. H. Chapman.

I cannot agree with him that the bas-relief effect is accentuated by the shade of the sharp outline, as it is really the shadow of the surrounding blank plane left standing at level with it or above the design proper, and which prevents top high light.

The Egyptian wall-reliefs, from which, of course, I recognized Dr. Bigelow obtained his idea, do not equal in effect bas-reliefs where the surrounding surface is cut away to the level of the lowest part of the design. The first or general effect of the Egyptian wall-reliefs is simply that they are wall-paintings with incised lines and slight modeling to help out or accentuate, and give the effect of shade on mural paintings; and when viewed at an oblique angle are invisible.

Egyptian art, unlike the Greek, remained frozen in conventionalism and did not progress to the full free rendering of the round.

I am glad to hear from Dr. Bigelow on one phase of the subject, on which he has expert knowledge, that the health of the Indian is excellent. But, to me his shrunken mouth and nostrils indicate a man below par in his physical condition.

He admits crude treatment in regard to head and eagle.

He thinks that the coin could not be easily imitated by incision, as a "man would make a die instead of a single piece." With this, I would beg to differ on account of actual experience as I have met with several incised counterfeits. Recently I saw as small a denomination as a dime, which had been made by engraving on the piece of metal. The effect was that of a very much worn example. To make dies requires more time, mechanical appliances to use them, or, if moulds be used, furnaces to melt the metal, whereas a skillful engraver can make a copy rapidly on inferior alloy and without having the evidence against him of dies or moulds in his possession.

Anyone can see that these coins will be more dirt-bearing than previous types, on account of the extreme depressions.

When Dr. Bigelow says "a dirty gold coin would be an anomaly," he is evidently thinking only of the gold coins he sees in the East, which are from reserves in the backs, as gold is not used in circulation here; but I have seen many filthy gold coins and am advised that in the West poor and dirty people, when their little hoards amount to enough to convert them into gold, usually do so, and the gold coins in the filthiest condition are often seen in California.

He fully admits the coins do not stack, but he misunderstands the quotation I made, "that coins be like a table…with a rim." That means a rim or foot near the circumference, but these coins are a plane, lacking only the surface around the design.

Frank Leach offered his support to Bigelow in a note written January 2, 1909:[816]

…I was somewhat amused by their savage attack, and should have liked to have been in a position to reply to this unjust criticism.

However, I am pleased to say that adverse criticism of the coins is an exception. I feel very well pleased with the result.

As circumstances worked out, by the time twenty-five years passed and the designs could be changed, it was 1933. The country was in the middle of a great economic depression and a new President Roosevelt, Theodore's cousin, Franklin, withdrew all gold coins from circulation.

---

[816] *US Mint*, NARA-CP, op. cit., entry 235 vol. 380. Letter (excerpt) dated January 2, 1909 to Bigelow from Leach.

# Appendix

## Biographies

**Bela Lyon Pratt** (December 11, 1867 – May 18, 1917)

Bela Lyon Pratt was born in Norwich, Connecticut, to a family that prized education. His father, George Pratt, was a Yale-educated lawyer, and his maternal grandfather was the founder of an early music conservatory in Connecticut. His mother was Sarah Whittlesey Pratt. At age sixteen, Pratt began studying at the Yale University School of Fine Arts, where his teachers included John Henry Niemeyer (1839–1932) and John Ferguson Weir (1841–1926). Four years later, he entered the Art Students League in New York. There he took classes with William Merritt Chase (1849–1916), Kenyon Cox (1859–1919), Francis Edwin Elwell (1858–1922) and Augustus Saint-Gaudens (1848–1907), who became a crucial mentor and model for his career. After working in Saint-Gaudens' private studio for a short time, Pratt went to Paris, where he trained with sculptors Henri-Michel-Antoine Chapu (1833–1891) and Alexandre Falguière (1831–1900) and won several medals and prizes at the École des Beaux-Arts. At Saint-Gaudens' invitation, he returned to the United States in 1892 in time to create two colossal sculptural groups representing *The Genius of Navigation* for the 1893 World's Columbian Exposition, thus becoming one of the new generation of sculptors whose careers were launched at the Chicago fair. At this time, he also began a twenty-five-year career as an influential teacher of modeling in the school of the Museum of Fine Arts, Boston, and an advocate for the role of sculpture in public and private life.

Described as a mild-mannered, modest, congenial man who loved music and the outdoors, Pratt married Helen Pray (1870–1965), a sculpture student. By 1897 the couple had four children, whom they raised in comfortable circumstances. Over the next two decades, Pratt created a wide range of work, from small portrait busts, reliefs and memorial tablets to ideal nudes, fountain figures and public monuments of heroic size. A number of his students became his assistants, helping to turn out this prolific array of sculpture. His work was characterized by a combination of technical skill, naturalism and simple restraint that his contemporaries often described as quintessentially American.

Pratt created a gallery of sculpted portraits of Boston's intellectual community, some of which were featured at the first major exhibition of his works at the Saint Botolph Club in Boston in December 1902. His best-known portraits include busts of Episcopal minister Phillips Brooks (1899, Brooks House, Harvard University), Colonel Henry Lee (1902, Memorial Hall, Harvard University) and Boston Symphony Orchestra founder Henry L. Higginson (1909, Symphony Hall, Boston). His medals and coins included an early medal of Harvard University president Charles William Eliot (1894) and highly unusual sunken relief designs for five and two and a half dollar gold coins.

In 1895–96, Pratt won the prized commission for six female allegorical spandrel figures carved in granite above the bronze doors at the main entrance of the Library of Congress in Washington, D.C. He also designed *Philosophy*, one of eight figures in the library's rotunda, and medallions of the four seasons for the library pavilion.

During a year abroad after his marriage, Pratt exhibited works at the salon in Paris, including a recumbent neo-Renaissance figure of Dr. Henry Augustus Coit for Saint Paul's School, Concord, New Hampshire, which won honorable mention in 1897, and in 1898 a life-sized *Orpheus Mourning Eurydice*, a nude that fit within French academic traditions. He also created *Floral Wreath* for the esplanade of the Pan-American Exposition in Buffalo in 1901, as well as other architectural sculpture for that fair, at which he was awarded a silver medal for his marble statuette of a nude girl. In 1909, his terracotta reliefs of *Music*, *Drama*, and *The Dance* executed for the façade of the Boston Opera House received considerable attention. His large-scale permanent public sculpture included: a figure of a young soldier at Saint Paul's School in Concord, New Hampshire, in memory of one hundred twenty of the school's alumni who served in the Spanish-American War (dedicated 1906); *The Andersonville Prison Boy* in the National Cemetery, Andersonville, Georgia (1907), a memorial to Civil War soldiers who died in Southern prisons; the *Butler Memorial* for Lowell, Massachusetts (1909), a Beaux-Arts high relief of personifications of Peace and War reminiscent of the work of Daniel Chester French (1850–1931); and the *Soldiers' and Sailors' Monument* in Malden, Massachusetts (dedicated 1910). His *Whaleman's Monument* in New Bedford, Massachusetts (1913) features a man, a boat and a decorative wave in bronze against a granite background on which sculpted gulls fly above an inscription from Herman Melville's *Moby Dick*.

Large-scale portrait statues included a standing figure of Connecticut Revolutionary War martyr Nathan Hale, dressed in homespun with hands tied behind his back, for Yale University (1908–1914); a seated Nathaniel Hawthorne in Salem, Massachusetts; and a bearded Edward Everett Hale (1913), with hat in hand, cane and heavy overcoat, placed on a low pedestal in Boston's Public Garden. Pratt's long career intertwined with Saint-Gaudens' even after the older sculptor's death in 1907. Saint-Gaudens had begun work on, but never completed, designs for two groups of allegorical figures for the piazza of the Boston Public Library designed by McKim, Mead, and White. Pratt later was awarded a commission for personifications of Art and Science to stand in front of the library. Also, a controversy had developed over the suitability of a sculpture honoring minister Phillips Brooks, left incomplete at Saint-Gaudens' death but finished by his former studio assistants and installed on the lawn of Trinity Church, Boston, in 1910. Pratt was commissioned by an opposition group to make a replacement statue of Brooks in 1916, but a legal battle prevented its placement and it did not gain a permanent home until 1925 (North Andover common, Massachusetts). Pratt was active until his death of heart disease on May 18, 1917, when he was working on a statue of Alexander Hamilton for Chicago's Grant Park. A retrospective exhibition of 125 of his sculptures was held at the Museum of Fine Arts Boston in the spring of 1918. [This is an edited version of the artist's biography published, or to be published, in the National Gallery of Art Systematic Catalogue. Used by permission.]

**Bibliographic References**

Downes, William Howe. "The Work of Bela L. Pratt, Sculptor." *New England Magazine* 27 (February 1903): pp.760–771.

Downes, William Howe. "The Work of Bela L. Pratt, Sculptor." *International Studio* 38, no. 149 (July 1909): III-X.

Coburn, Frederick W. "Americanism in Sculpture. As Represented in the Works of Bela Lyon Pratt." *Palette and Bench* 2, nos. 5 and 6 (February-March 1910): pp.95–97, pp.127–131.

Caffin, Charles H. *American Masters of Sculpture*. Garden City, New York, 1913: pp.181–183.

Dorr, Charles Henry. "Bela L. Pratt: An Eminent New England Sculptor." *Architectural Record* 35, no. 6 (June 1914): 508–518.

Cornish, F. Ogden. "Bela Pratt–Citizen and Sculptor." *Boston Evening Transcript* (19 May 1917): 4.

Downes, William Howe. "Mr. Pratt's Sculpture: Memorial Exhibition Opened Yesterday by Guild of Boston Artists..." *Boston Transcript* (30 October 1917): p.13.

Obituary, *Boston Evening Transcript* (18 May 1917): p.2.

Obituary, *Boston Herald* (19 May 1917): p.14.

Obituary, *The New York Times* (19 May 1917).

Gilman, Benjamin Ives. "Memorial Exhibition of the Work of Bela Lyon Pratt." *Museum of Fine Arts Bulletin* 16 (April 1918): pp.28–29.

Taft, Lorado. *The History of American Sculpture*. New York, 1924: pp.491–496.

DAB, 8: pp.166–168.

Armstrong, Tom, et al. *200 Years of American Sculpture*. New York, 1976: pp.298–299.

Craven, Wayne. *Sculpture in America*. Rev. ed. Newark and New York, 1984: pp.495–497.

Kozol, Paula M. "Bela Lyon Pratt (1867–1917)." In Kathryn Greenthal, Paula M. Kozol, and Jan Seidler Ramirez, *American Figurative Sculpture in the Museum of Fine Arts Boston*. Boston, 1986: pp.309–322.

Butler, Ruth, and Suzanne Glover Lindsay, with Alison Luchs, Douglas Lewis, Cynthia J. Mills, and Jeffrey Weidman. *European Sculpture of the Nineteenth Century*. The Collections of the National Gallery of Art Systematic Catalogue. Washington, D.C., 2000: pp.434-435.

**Henry Hering** (February 15, 1874 – January 15, 1949)

Hering studied at the Art Students League and Cooper Union in New York, the worked with Philip Martiny for six years before relocating to Paris for study at the École des Beaux-Arts and Académie Colarossi. He was hired as a studio assistant by Saint-Gaudens in 1900 and worked at the Cornish studio until early 1908.

His primary contribution to American art was as the modeler of Saint-Gaudens' concepts for revised coinage designs of 1907. Due to Saint-Gaudens' illness nearly all of the modeling work fell to Hering, who also assumed a major role as the great artist's surrogate in meetings with mint officials and President Roosevelt. His portrait reliefs and sculpture show clearly delineated forms, illustrating the strong idealistic tendency in Hering's independent work compared with the more naturalistic representation of other Saint-Gaudens students.

An article by Hering explaining how the 1907 gold coins designs were created appeared in *The Numismatist* in 1949. This has confused generations of numismatists about events and Hering's role in the project. The article originated in April 1933 as transcribed reminiscences by Hering to Lillian Grant, secretary to George Godard, Librarian of the Connecticut State Library, and curator of the Mitchelson coin collection owned by the library. The article was originally published in the Hartford Connecticut *Curant* newspaper and later revised. Much of Hering's article is refuted by contemporary documents by the persons directly involved.

Sources:
Barbara A. Baxter. *The Beaux –Arts Medal in America*. American Numismatic Society. 1987.
Roger W. Burdette. Research in NARA, Library of Congress, Connecticut State archives and other archives.

## William Sturgis Bigelow (April 4, 1850 – October 6, 1926)

William Sturgis Bigelow was the only son of Henry Jacob Bigelow and Mary Scollay. William was a physician/surgeon as were his father and grandfather.

Bigelow was profoundly affected by the death of his mother when he was three. His father, a renowned surgeon, was something of a martinet, and young William was evidently something of a rebel: his report card from the Private Latin School in 1865 rated him twenty-second academically in a class of 55, but fifty-fourth in "conduct."

After graduating from Harvard Medical School in 1874, Bigelow went to Europe. He stayed five years, studying in Vienna, Strasbourg and finally in Paris under Louis Pasteur. He brought back to Boston the new research on bacteria, and established privately one of this country's first laboratories in that field. This displeased his father, who wanted the line of distinguished Bigelow surgeons at Harvard and Massachusetts General Hospital to continue. William was duly appointed surgeon to outpatients at the MGH. "Few men," wrote medical historian John F. Fulton, "could have less taste for surgery than the sensitive Bigelow, and it was not long before he gave up all thoughts of practice."

In 1881, believing that the world was moving too fast and that much of life in Boston was ugly, he went to Japan, following Edward S. Morse and Ernest Fenollosa, who were among the first Americans to study Japanese culture. He later called the cruise to Japan the turning point of his life. During his prolonged stay he studied, traveled and collected the treasures that Japanese were discarding in their rush to become Westernized. After returning to Boston in 1889, Bigelow devoted much of his time to the study of art and Asian religions. He was an authority on and a collector of Japanese and Chinese art. He amassed a tremendous collection and in 1911 presented Boston Museum of Fine Arts with 25,000 items of painting, sculpture, porcelain, etc.

He also entertained lavishly in his home at 56 Beacon Street, often welcoming such college friends as George and Henry Cabot Lodge, Brooks and Henry Adams, and Theodore Roosevelt, who regularly made Bigelow's home his Boston headquarters. He became an active trustee of the Museum of Fine Arts and continued to collect paintings, often consulting with Isabella Stewart Gardner. Reportedly somewhat reserved in his dealings with the opposite sex, he once wrote to her coyly, in the third person: "She is very attractive." At his favorite spot in America, however, a summer house on tiny Tuckernuck Island, off the shores of Nantucket, he entertained men only, and his guests wore pajamas, or nothing at all, until dinnertime, when formal dress was required. A staff of servants provided food and fine wines; the library contained 3,000 volumes "spiced with racy French and German magazines," one chronicler reported. Henry Adams described Bigelow's retreat as "a scene of medieval splendor;" George Santayana may have modeled Dr. Peter Alden, the father of the protagonist in *The Last Puritan*, after Bigelow.

The *Boston Evening Transcript*, the unofficial gazette of Boston's Brahmins, ran two bold headlines on October 6, 1926. One told of Babe Ruth's feat of hitting three home runs in a World Series game, but the larger headline reported the death of William Sturgis Bigelow. His funeral, at Boston's Trinity Church, was conducted by his Harvard classmate William Lawrence, former Episcopal bishop of Massachusetts. His ashes were divided, with half interred in Mount Auburn Cemetery, which had been envisioned by his grandfather Jacob as a spiritually uplifting as well as "hygienic" burial site. The rest were buried by a Buddhist temple, overlooking Bigelow's favorite lake in Japan.

**Frank Alemon Leach** (August 19, 1846 – June 19, 1929)

Frank and his mother emigrated to California in 1851 to join his father, who had settled in Sacramento. Frank Leach's newspaper career began when he obtained employment as a compositor for the Napa *Echo*, just before the outbreak of the Civil War. He had been there only a short while when his editor demanded he typeset inflammatory anti-federal government copy. A heated disagreement followed and young Frank found himself unemployed.

He founded and was editor/publisher of the Napa *Reporter*, Vallejo *Chronicle*, the Benicia *New Era*, and the Oakland *Enquirer*. In 1879 he was induced to accept the Republican nomination for the State legislature. He was elected and served two terms in the assembly. From 1882 to 1884 he was postmaster of Vallejo.

He was appointed superintendent of the San Francisco mint in 1897 shortly after selling the Oakland *Enquirer* and retiring from the newspaper business. He was appointed director of the mint in July 1907 on the recommendation of George Roberts, the outgoing director. He resigned in 1909 to become President and manager of the Peoples Water Company of Oakland. In 1917 his autobiographical book, *Recollections of a Newspaper Man – A Record of Life and Events in California*, was published by Samuel Levinson, Inc. in San Francisco. The book is considered one of the best first-hand accounts of ordinary life in California at the close of the nineteenth century. Although his chapter on life in Washington, DC as mint director reveals the personal side of the job, it also includes several inaccuracies which have crept into numismatic lore.

His personal interests extended to natural history and astronomy, and he wrote a series of articles for the Oakland *Tribune* titled "California Nature Studies." His son, Edwin R. Leach, worked at the San Francisco mint as cashier for part of 1907–08. Edwin later became a noted entomologist and expert on certain species of beetles. Another son, Harry E., worked in the weighing department in 1906.

Sources:
California Historical Society
Roger W. Burdette. Research in NARA, Library of Congress.

**George Evan Roberts** (August 19, 1857 – June 6, 1948)

George Roberts was born in Colesburg, Iowa. His family moved to Fort Dodge, Indiana in 1873. He left high school at sixteen to become an apprentice printer for the Fort Dodge *Times*. In early 1877 he purchased the Jessup, Iowa *Vindicator* newspaper, which he sold the following year after taking the job of city editor of the Sioux City *Journal.* When the owner of the Fort Dodge *Messenger* died in late 1878, Roberts returned to Fort Dodge and purchased the newspaper from the owner's estate. He was editor/publisher of the *Messenger* until appointed director of the mint in 1898 by President McKinley. During his newspaper career he had developed a deep interest in money and economic problems, and in the fallacies of popular thinking about money. In 1895 he wrote a famous refutation of bi-metalism titled *Coin At School in Finance*. The booklet parodied the economic writings of William Jennings Bryan and other "free silver" proponents.

In looking for publication support for his booklet, Roberts met Lyman J. Gage, president of the First National Bank of Chicago. Gage supported the printing and distribution of Roberts' parody. When McKinley was elected President in 1896, Lyman Gage was appointed secretary of the treasury, and took a Chicago financial writer named Frank A. Vanderlip to Washington with him. Vanderlip recommended Roberts join the treasury department as director of the mint. Roberts resigned the directorship in July 1907 and was president of Commercial National Bank in Chicago from 1907–10. In June 1910 he was nominated to a second term as mint director, replacing A. Piatt Andrew, and served until November 1914.

He joined The National City Bank of New York in 1914 as assistant to president Frank A. Vanderlip. In 1919 he was appointed vice-president (succeeded as vice-president by his son, George Bassett Roberts; another son, Henry Akison Roberts, was manager of the Varick Street branch office; a daughter was Mrs. Leslie Springet), and in 1932 became economic advisor, a position he held until his retirement on January 14, 1941.

Sources:
National City Bank. *In Memory of George E. Roberts.* 1947.
Fort Dodge, Indiana Historical Foundation
Roger W. Burdette. Research in NARA, Library of Congress and other archives.

## Edge Photographs – Creation and Limitations

Key factors in identifying edge varieties of the 1907 gold coins are the layout and character font used by the mint. Until a few years ago, the differences were largely limited to presence or absence of lettering with little attention paid to the shape of characters or how they were used. The normal edge of the $10 eagle coin consists of forty-six (later forty-eight) stars evenly spaced around the circumference of the coin. This is an attractive substitute for conventional vertical reeding, but offers only limited opportunity for significant variation. The double eagle, however, is a different matter.

Beginning in December 1906, the large gold coin was intended to have an edge inscription consisting of the motto E PLURIBUS UNUM and thirteen stars. The Barber/Morgan experimental coin of 1906 and the first Saint-Gaudens experimental pieces placed the motto around the entire circumference with a star between each letter. The edge text thus formed an endless inscription to which there was no specific beginning or end. This was consistent with the approach used in 1885 tests in which engraver Charles Barber participated. After Saint-Gaudens saw the first experimental pieces in February 1907, he appears to have ordered a change in the edge design. This resulted in the motto being placed upside-down (as viewed with the coin obverse up) beginning approximately at Liberty's torch and arcing over her head to end near the olive branch. A star was placed between each word, and the gap between ends of the inscription was filed with the remaining stars.

As the project progressed, the edge font and layout of letters and stars was altered, producing varieties that were from the same face dies, but had differing edge dies. Documenting these edge varieties can be difficult and frustrating. In this book three methods have been used to photograph the edge of coins: 1) direct photography of a portion of the edge; 2) oblique angle photography of a portion of the edge and one face of the coin, and; 3) annular photography using a concave mirror to show the edge and one face of the coin. Examples of these are shown in the following illustration:

***Figure 69. Examples of edge photographs of 1907 gold pattern coins. Left, direct image of a portion of the edge, center, oblique image of part of the edge and face, right, annular image made using a concave mirror.*** (Left and right photographs by David J. Camire courtesy NGC; center photograph courtesy of Stack's Rare Coins, New York City.)

The direct image (left, above) can show only a small portion of the design and does not tell us anything about the relationship of edge devices to face design. An oblique image (center, above) shows only part of the edge, but indicates orientation of edge devices to the coin's face. An annular, or ring, image (right, above) shows the relation between face and edge designs, but has the drawback of portraying edge lettering reversed due to the use of a concave mirror.

A fourth option is to electronically alter the annular photo to straighten the curved image and correct for the mirror image. The result, shown below, is similar to a "rollout" image often used by archeologists to document ancient bowls and storage jars.

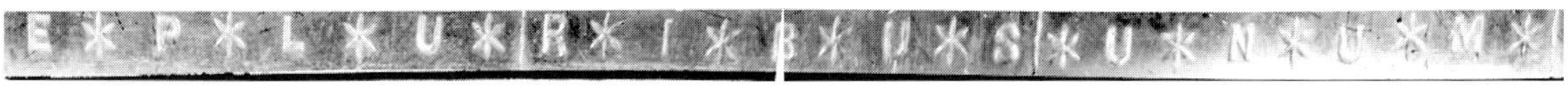

***Figure 70. Electronically-generated rollout image of the edge of small diameter EHR doble eagle of 1907 (on right in figure 67). Note slight distortion of letters. The white gap in the center is an artifact of the process.*** (Image by the author based on an original photograph by David J. Camire courtesy NGC.)

While this method produces a more readable image of the coin's edge, it introduces several distortions. First, unless the coin was perfectly centered in the concave mirror for the original image, the rollout version will show slight curvature. Second, differences in distance between the mirror and the top and bottom of edge characters, makes the characters appear slightly elongated. Third, the rollout process may warp the characters slightly. On the direct image, above, compare the characters **M * E * P** with the corresponding portion of the rollout image. True rollout images, created with a special camera and stand to hold the coin, can produce very accurate edge images. Unfortunately, the specialized technology is only available within large academic institutions.

For the reasons stated above, the rollout photos shown in this book should not be used to definitively identify varieties. Only direct, expert examination, supplemented by direct photographic evidence will give reliable results.

## Hidden Patterns

The present research has identified two previously unrecognized pattern $10 gold coins. These are documented and discussed in Chapters 4 and 8. However, they are not the only pattern and experimental pieces for 1907-08 that remain to be discovered. "Hidden patterns" are experimental, pattern and trial strike coins that are generally unknown to most collectors. Official records indicate the coins were struck, but none are known today. In most cases descriptions of these coins will not be found in standard references such as the Judd and Pollock books on U. S. pattern and experimental coins.

The table below describes hidden patterns from the Saint-Gaudens and Pratt issues. None of these pieces are known today, but one or more of them could be lying in someone's collection or inventory. Each item is documented as having been produced by the Philadelphia mint as a pattern, experimental or trial coin. Letters and memoranda supporting their existence will be found in the main text of this book. Some pieces may no longer exist, having been melted during the 1933 gold coin recall, or shipped to Europe as commercial payment, or returned to the mint as defective coin.

Former holdings of major Boston and New York museums might have included one or more of these hidden patterns among the duplicates sold at auction several decades ago. Absence of historical documentation and limited professional numismatic resources could have easily led to an experimental piece being described as an ordinary circulation strike.

| Item | Description & Comment |
|---|---|
| MCMVII $20 | **Very high relief** experimental double eagle made from the #2 pair of dies. These were the same models later used to make the high relief dies used for limited circulation production. Eight examples were made as a progress series and the pieces were shown to President Roosevelt and Saint-Gaudens, then returned to the Philadelphia Mint. Mint documents reveal nothing more about these experimental coins. It seems reasonable that Barber or another mint official would have kept one or two of the best examples. |
| | VHR $20 will show detail similar to the high relief coins although the 14th ray on the reverse will be more prominent. Relief will be nearly as high as the EHR pieces. The edge will probably have the same collar as on the EHR coins from Group 2. VHR coins will be nearly as thick as the EHR coins and much thicker than either high relief or low relief pieces. The surface will be nearly pure gold in color with the same satin finish as on the EHR coins. |
| 1907 $20 | **Low relief pattern** coin as made from Hering's #3 models. Compare with the images on page 267, particularly the flow of Liberty's gown across her thigh. These will probably have either normal edge lettering or lettering the size of that used on high relief examples (which will look too wide for the coin). Detail will be indistinct and the coins may more closely resemble poor strikes than legitimate patterns. The surface could be like other 1907 patterns with a smooth satin finish (called "bright" by the mint) or they may have been sandblasted. Easily confused with normal 1907 double eagles. |
| | Several examples were struck on a medal press and distributed outside of the Philadelphia |

| Item | Description & Comment |
|---|---|
| | Mint. It is unclear if all were returned and destroyed. |
| 1908 $2.50 | **Identical to the 1908** Indian head design issued for circulation, however the reverse is rotated 180-degrees. This makes the obverse/reverse die alignment "medal turn" rather than the normal "coin turn." |
| | This was one of several thousand trial pieces struck at the Philadelphia mint in late October 1908 to test production characteristics of the new design by Bela Pratt. Engraver Charles Barber intentionally used medal turn so he could differentiate the trial pieces from normal coins. Two specimens were sent to Mint Director Leach, who accidentally gave one to an unnamed person from the Boston area who later promised to put it in one of the local museums. |
| | The coin is presently unlocated. |
| 1908 $5.00 | **Superficially like the 1908** Indian head design issued for circulation, however there are many differences in detail of the feathers, portrait and stars. In general, the design will be farther from the edge of the coin (there is no defined rim). Feather detail will resemble the Saint-Gaudens $10 with fewer fine lines. The headband will have less ornamentation and largely free of the tiny dots that Barber added to the hub. The Indian will likely look less "starved" with the cheekbone less prominent and the portrait smoother (see Fraser's Indian portrait on the nickel for guidance.) |
| | The obverse/reverse die alignment *may* also be "medal turn" rather than the normal "coin turn." |
| | This was one of 10 pattern half eagles struck at the Philadelphia mint in late September 1908. All were shown to President Roosevelt, who picked out one half eagle and sent it to Dr. William Sturgis Bigelow in Boston. The gift of the unique coin was in recognition of Bigelow's contribution to the new Indian head design. (The sculptor, Bela Pratt, got nothing.) Bigelow knew of the importance of the coin, but it has not been traced since his death in 1926. |
| | The coin is presently unlocated. |

Are more hidden patterns possible? Yes, there are several more experimental or trial designs that may still exist from the 1907-1922 period and later.

# Bibliography

Akers, David. *United States Gold Coins, An Analysis of Auction Records, Volume VI: Double Eagles 1850-1932*. Paramount Coin Corp. Englewood, Ohio. 1982.

American Numismatic Association. ANA Research Library, 818 N Cascade Ave., Colorado Springs, CO 80903.
Various extracts from *The Numismatist* and *American Journal of Numismatics*.

American Numismatic Society. New York, NY.
ANS was the preeminent numismatic organization of the period active in supporting the artistic aspects of numismatics as well as research and publications. Many medallists and coin designers of the era loaned or donated their works to the ANS.

Anonymous. *A History of Court Street Baptist Church – Sesqui-Centennial Edition*. Internally published [Portsmouth, VA] 1939.
Commemorating the 150th anniversary of Court Street Baptist Church, Portsmouth, VA.

Armstrong, George D. DD. *The Summer of the Pestilence: A History of the Ravages of the Yellow Fever in Norfolk, Virginia, A. D. 1855*. Reprint by C. W. Tazewell. 1964.

Bancroft, Hubert Howe. *The Book of the Fair*. The Bancroft Company, Chicago. 1893.

*Barber, Charles Edward; papers*. American Numismatic Association Research Library, 818 N Cascade Ave., Colorado Springs, CO 80903; accession No. SC1999.0004. Photocopies. [Barber: ANA.]
Consists of 21 notebooks including an index #1-4; 19 deal with U. S. coins including Barber's personal collection. Balance concerns foreign coins struck, or proposed for production by the Bureau of the Mint. Approximately 400 pages total. These are photocopies of originals donated to the Smithsonian in 1991 by Stacks' Inc., a prominent New York coin retailer. The Smithsonian originals are presently unlocated.

372

*Baptist Encyclopedia – 1881, The.* Virginia Baptist Historical Society. Richmond, VA

Baxter, Barbara A. *The Beaux-Arts Medal in America.* American Numismatic Society. New York: 1987.

Bernstein, Iver. *The New York City Draft Riots: Their Significance for American Society and Politics in the Age of the Civil War.* Oxford University Press. January 1990.

*Bigelow, William Sturgis, papers.* Houghton Library of the Harvard College Library, Cambridge, Massachusetts. bMS AM 1785 (851).

Bowers, Q. David. *The History of United States Coinage As Illustrated by the Garrett Collection*, Bowers and Ruddy Galleries, Inc., Los Angeles, California. 1979.

_____ *The Official Red Book of U. S. Gold Double Eagles*, Whitman Publishing Company. 2004.
Certain material from the present volume was provided to Mr. Bowers for use in his double eagle book.

Breen, Walter H. *Walter Breen's Complete Encyclopedia of U. S. and Colonial Coins.* F.C.I. Press/Doubleday, New York, 1988.

Burdette, Roger W. *In God We Trust – The Story of A National Motto.* Court Street Baptist Church, Portsmouth, VA. 2004 (special printing); Seneca Mill Press, Great Falls, VA. 2005.

_____ *Renaissance of American Coinage 1909–1915.* Manuscript. Projected publication in 2007.

_____ *Renaissance of American Coinage 1916–1921.* Seneca Mill Press, Great Falls, VA. 2005.

*Commission of Fine Arts.* National Archives and Records Administration (NARA), Washington, DC. Record Group 66. [*CFA;* NARA]

*Cortelyou, George Bruce; papers.* Library of Congress Manuscript Division. Washington, DC. [LoC]

Cortissoz, Royal. *Augustus Saint-Gaudens.* Houghton, Mifflin & Co. Boston. 1907.

Dalton, Kathleen. *Theodore Roosevelt: A Strenuous Life.* Alfred Knopf, New York. 2002.

Department of the Treasury, United States Mint, 809 Ninth Street, NW Washington, DC. Ms. Maria Goodwin, historian.

Dryfhout, John H. *The 1907 United States Gold Coinage.* Northlight Studio Press, Barre, VT. 1986.

_____ *The Work of Augustus Saint-Gaudens.* University Press of New England. 1982.
The definitive resource for the works of Saint-Gaudens.

Escher, Franklin. *Foreign Exchange Explained.* The McMillan Company, New York. 1917.

Evans, George G. *History of the United States Mint and American Coinage Ancient and Modern.* George G. Evans, Co., Philadelphia. 1886.

Failor, Michael M. and Eleonora Hayden, *Medals of the United States Mint Issued for Public Sale.* Department of the Treasury, U. S. Government Printing Office. Revised edition. Washington, DC. 1972.

Fort Dodge Historical Foundation, P. O. Box 1798, Fort Dodge, Iowa 50501.
Newspaper clippings relating to George E. Roberts.

Hart, Robert A. *The Great White Fleet: Its Voyage Around the World, 1907-1909.* Little, Brown & Company, New York. 1965.

Heckscher, August. *Woodrow Wilson.* Charles Scribner's Sons, New York, 1991.

Hocking, William J. "Simon's Dies in the Royal Mint Museum, with Some Notes on the early History of Coinage by Machinery." *Numismatic Chronicle*, 4th series, vol. 9, pp.56-118. 1909.

*In Memory of George E. Roberts. Excerpts from the writings of George E. Roberts in the Monthly Letter of the National City Bank of New York.* The National City Bank of New York, 1948. Iowa State Historical Society HC-103.I5-R6 #129517.
A collection of excerpts from Roberts' articles in the bank's monthly newsletter issued in honor of his memory in 1948.

Jones, Robert D. *With the American Fleet from the Atlantic to the Pacific.* Seattle, WA, Harrison Publishing Co. 1908.
Includes complete lists of officers and men for each vessel of the fleet.

Judd, J. Hewitt. *United States Pattern, Experimental and Trial Pieces.* 3rd Edition. Whitman Publishing Company. 1965.

Judd, J. Hewitt, ed. by Q. David Bowers, Saul Teichman. *United States Pattern, Experimental and Trial Pieces.* 8th Edition. Whitman Publishing LLC. 2003.
The present writer was a contributor to this edition. Certain material from the present volume was provided to Mr. Bowers for use in this update of the Judd pattern book.

Kohler, Sue A. *The Commission of Fine Arts: A Brief History 1910–1995.* The Commission of Fine Arts, The National Building Museum, Suite 312, 441 F Street, NW, Washington, DC 20001. 1995.

*Kunz, George H.; papers.* American Museum of Natural History, New York, NY.

*Leach, Frank Alemon; papers.* California Historical Society manuscript collection (MS 1267), 678 Mission Street, San Francisco, CA 94105.
The CHS has two small boxes of Frank Leach's personal papers in its collection. These include a few letters to and from the Bureau of the Mint.

Leach, Frank A. *Recollections of a Newspaper Man – A Record of Life and Events in California.* Samuel Levinson pub., San Francisco, California. 1917. Reprinted by Beekman Publishers, New York, 1974. Reprinted by Bowers and Merena Galleries, Inc., 1982.
Interesting if somewhat inaccurate account of life in California in the late 19th century. The final chapter reviews the author's work as mint director. A useful resource although it includes many errors and personal distortions.

\_\_\_\_\_ *The Seattle Assay Office Robbery.* Unpublished manuscript, circa 1906. California Historical Society, *Frank Alemon Leach papers*, box 1.

Lumpkin, William Latane. *A History of Court Street Baptist Church.* Internally published [Portsmouth, VA] 1989. A bicentennial edition commemorating the 200th anniversary of Court Street Baptist Church.

Matthews, Franklin. *With the Battle Fleet: Cruise of the Sixteen Battleships of the United States Atlantic Fleet from Hampton Roads to the Golden Gate, December 1907–May 1908.* B.W. Huebsch, Co., New York. 1908.

McSherry, Jack L., CQM, USN. *Things We Remember.* Printed privately, 1966.
McSherry was a crewmember on baord the Minnesota serving in the Great White Fleet under the command of Admiral Robley D. "Gimpy" Evans.

*Francis Millet Rogers, papers*; Archives of American Art, Smithsonian Institution, 7500 9th Street, NW, Suite 2200, Washington, DC 20560. Microfilm reel 1095, pp.1208–1213.

*Mitchelson, Joseph, papers*; Connecticut State Library, Record Group 12, *Correspondence Relating to the Joseph Mitchelson Coin Collection.* Letter file boxes 76 through 79. Miscellaneous documents: cartons 1 through 4.
Miscellaneous correspondence primarily from the 1911 to 1933 period. Letters to/from George S. Godard State Librarian regarding acquiring newly issued coins for the collection. Many letters to/from T. Louis Comparette, Curator of the Mint collection. Many letters refer to Comparette obtaining specimens from the "pyx" coins. Coins were also sent to CSL prior to their official release, particularly commemoratives. Some were specially handled (i.e.: removed from the press by hand) to provide the best specimens possible. From 1912 to 1921 most coins were obtained in pairs, and the same order was duplicated for State Senator Hall (d. Feb., 1922). Seven pocket-sized coin check lists apparently used by Mitchelson in forming and tracking his collection are included. There are only occasional references to origins of a coin.

*Moore, Charles; papers.* Archives of American Art, Smithsonian Institution, 7500 9th Street, NW, Suite 2200, Washington, DC 20560. Microfilm reels 1887 - 1889.

*Moore, Charles; papers* (1901–1940). University of Michigan Bentley Library. Ann Arbor Michigan.

Morison, Etling E. ed., John H. Blum, Alfred D. Chandler. *The Letters of Theodore Roosevelt.* Harvard University Press, Cambridge, Massachusetts. 1952.
Authoritative collection of many of the letters of Theodore Roosevelt.

Morris, Edmund. *The Rise of Theodore Roosevelt.* Coward, McCann & Geoghegan, New York. 1979.

_____ *Theodore Rex.* Random House, Inc., New York. 2001.

*Murphy, James; collection.* Georgetown University Library, Special Collections Division, Washington, DC.
A collection of autographed photos of famous persons from the 1920s to 1950s assembled by James Murphy and donated to Georgetown University.

National Archives and Records Administration [NARA-P], Philadelphia, PA. Record Group 104: records of *The United States Mint, Philadelphia*

National Archives and Records Administration [NARA-CP], College Park, MD. Record Groups 56 and 104: records of *The United States Mint, Director's Office.*

Pepys, Samuel. *The Diary of Samuel Pepys.* Ed. Robert Latham and Williams Matthews. University of California Press. Berkeley, CA. 1983

Pollock, Andrew W. III. *United States Patterns and Related Issues.* Bowers and Merena Galleries, Inc, Wolfeboro, NH. 1994.

*Pratt, Bela Lyon; papers.* Houghton Library of the Harvard College Library, Cambridge, Massachusetts.

Reckner, James R. *Teddy Roosevelt's Great White Fleet: The World Cruise of the American Battle Fleet, 1907–1909.* Naval Institute Press, Annapolis. 1988.
The definitive history of the "Great White Fleet." Winner of the 1989 Roosevelt Naval History Prize.

Roosevelt, Theodore. *Roosevelt and Our Coin Designs: Letters Between Theodore Roosevelt and Augustus Saint-Gaudens.* Collected by Homer Saint-Gaudens; photographs by DeWitt C. Ward. New York, Century Co. 1920.

*Roosevelt, Theodore; papers.* Library of Congress, Manuscript Division. Washington, DC. [LoC]

*Roosevelt, Theodore; papers.* Harvard University Library, Manuscript Collection. Boston, MA.

*Saint-Gaudens, Augustus; papers.* Dartmouth College, Rauner Special Collections, manuscript.
Letters and personal papers of Augustus Saint-Gaudens and members of this family. Portions missing due to destruction in 1904 studio fire. Many letters to and from Theodore Roosevelt are duplicated in the Theodore Roosevelt papers in the Library of Congress collection. Includes original drawings of coin designs.

*Saint-Gaudens, Augustus; papers.* Library of Congress, Manuscript Division. Washington, DC.
Microfilm copy of the Dartmouth collection.

Sam, Cynthia (Pratt) Kennedy. *Bela Lyon Pratt (1867–1917): Medals, Medallions and Coins.* Coinage of the Americas Conference. American Numismatic Society; New York. 1988.
Excellent article reviewing the sculptor's medallic work. The author is the granddaughter of the artist and maintains exclusive access to the artist's personal papers. Ms. Sam is preparing a definitive biography of the artist.

Sargent, John Singer. *Portrait of Dr. William Sturgis Bigelow, 1917* [based on a photograph]. Charcoal and white chalk on paper, Museum of Fine Arts, Boston. Gift of the Committee on the Museum. 17.3174.

Sargent, Thomas J. and Francois R. Velde. *The Big Problem of Small Change.* Princeton University Press, Princeton, NJ 2002. ISBN0-691-11635-0

Smithsonian Institution, Museum of American History, National Numismatic Collection [NNC], Washington, DC. Richard Doty, PhD, Curator of Numismatics; Douglas Mudd, Collection Manager.
Examination of pattern coins, models and related materials 1905–1913. Photos of the coins provided by David Mudd, National Numismatic Collection.

Stewart, William H. (Colonel). *A History of Norfolk County, Virginia and Representative Citizens.* Biographical Publishing Company, Chicago. 1902. Chapter XIV, p. 231.
Covers the period from 1637 to 1900.

Taxay, Don. *The U. S. Mint and Coinage.* Arco Publishing Co. Inc., New York, 1966.

Tharp, Louise Hall. *Saint-Gaudens and the Gilded Era.* Little, Brown & Company. Boston, 1969. Biography of Saint-Gaudens based on original sources from Dartmouth College and elsewhere.

Torbet, Robert G. *A History of the Baptists.* Valley Forge Press, 1987.

United States Navy Department. *Information Relative to the Voyage of the United States Atlantic Fleet Around the World, December 16, 1907 to February 22, 1909.* Government Printing Office. Washington, D.C. 1910. Includes detailed itinerary for each vessel.

Tolles, Thayer. "A Bit of Artistic Idealism: Augustus Saint-Gaudens's World's Columbian Exposition Commemorative Presentation Medal." *Coinage of the Americas Conference.* American Numismatic Society; New York. 1997.
Excellent article reviewing the sculptor's struggle to complete the Exposition Award medal.

Vanderlip, Frank A. *From Farm Boy to Financier.* D. Appleton-Century Company Inc., New York & London. 1935.

Vermeule, Cornelius C. *Numismatic Art in America – Aesthetics of the United States Coinage.* Belknap Press of Harvard University Press, Cambridge, MA. January 1971; ISBN 0-674-62840-3. 278 pages.

*Weinman, Adolph A.; papers.* Smithsonian Institution Archives of American Art. Washington, DC.
Microfilm plus ten boxes of manuscript and photos from Weinman's albums.

Williams, Talcott, LL.D. *Augustus Saint-Gaudens,* pre-exhibition article in The International Studio, February 1908. Pages CXXIII to CXXXVIII [123–138] (John Lane Company, 110-114 West Thirty Second St, New York, NY.)
Original article provided courtesy of Fred Weinberg, Fred Weinberg & Co., Encino, CA.

Wimmel, Kenneth. *Theodore Roosevelt and the Great White Fleet: American Sea Power Comes of Age.* London; Washington, D.C. Brassey's. 1998.

# Index

382